EVALUATION OF
HUMAN SERVICE
PROGRAMS

CONTRIBUTORS

C. CLIFFORD ATTKISSON

ALLAN BEIGEL

ROGER A. BELL

ANTHONY BROSKOWSKI

TIMOTHY R. BROWN

JOANNE M. BUHL

LINDA G. CARSON

ROBERT L. CHAPMAN

HAROLD W. DEMONE, JR.

JEAN DRISCOLL

J. RICHARD ELPERS

HUGH D. GROVE

WILLIAM A. HARGREAVES

MARDI J. HOROWITZ

THOMAS J. KIRESUK

ALAN I. LEVENSON

DONALD A. LUND

SANDER H. LUND

TUAN D. NGUYEN

HERBERT C. SCHULBERG

LARRY M. SIEGEL

JAMES E. SORENSEN

ELAINE N. TAYLOR

ROBERT VINEBERG

GEORGE J. WARHEIT

J. RICHARD WOY

EVALUATION OF HUMAN SERVICE PROGRAMS

EDITED BY

C. Clifford Attkisson
William A. Hargreaves
Mardi J. Horowitz

Langley Porter Institute
University of California, San Francisco
San Francisco, California

James E. Sorensen

University of Denver
Denver, Colorado

ACADEMIC PRESS
New York   San Francisco   London   1978
A Subsidiary of Harcourt Brace Jovanovich, Publishers

ACADEMIC PRESS, INC.
111 Fifth Avenue, New York, New York 10003

United Kingdom Edition published by
ACADEMIC PRESS, INC. (LONDON) LTD.
24/28 Oval Road, London NW1 7DX

Library of Congress Cataloging in Publication Data

Main entry under title:

Evaluation of human service programs.

Includes bibliographical references.
1. Social service—Evaluation.   2. Community
mental health services—Evaluation.   3. Evaluation
research (Social action programs)   I.   Attkisson,
C. Clifford.   II.   Hargreaves, William Alfred, Date
III.   Horowitz, Mardi Jon, Date   [DNLM: 1. Com-
munity mental health services.   2.   Evaluation studies.
WM30 E924]
HV41.E96   658.4'01   77-6585
ISBN 0-12-066350-3

CONTENTS

v

10 Service Utilization, Social Indicator, and Citizen Survey Approaches to Human Service Need Assessment   253

Roger A. Bell, Tuan D. Nguyen, George J. Warheit, and
Joanne M. Buhl

IV MEASUREMENT AND EVALUATION OF PROGRAM EFFECTIVENESS

11 Evaluating Program Outcomes   303

William A. Hargreaves and C. Clifford Attkisson

12 Goal Attainment Scaling   341

Thomas J. Kiresuk and Sander H. Lund

13 Using Cost–Outcome and Cost–Effectiveness Analyses for Improved Program Management and Accountability   371

James E. Sorensen and Hugh D. Grove

14 Quality Assurance in Human Service Program Evaluation   411

J. Richard Woy, Donald A. Lund, and C. Clifford Attkisson

15 Evaluation of Indirect Services to Schools   445

Elaine N. Taylor and Robert Vineberg

V RETROSPECT AND PROSPECT

16 Evaluation: Current Strengths and Future Directions   465

C. Clifford Attkisson, William A. Hargreaves, Mardi J. Horowitz, and James E. Sorensen

17 The Education of Evaluators   479

William A. Hargreaves, C. Clifford Attkisson, Mardi J. Horowitz, and James E. Sorensen

LIST OF CONTRIBUTORS

Numbers in parentheses indicate pages on which the authors' contributions begin.

C. *Clifford Attkisson* (3, 59, 215, 303, 411, 465, 479), Langley Porter
    Institute, and the Department of Psychiatry, University of California,
    San Francisco; and Program Evaluation Service, District V Mental
    Health Center, San Francisco, California

Allan Beigel (97), Southern Arizona Mental Health Center, and Depart-
    ment of Psychiatry, College of Medicine, University of Arizona,
    Tucson, Arizona

Roger A. Bell (253), School of Medicine, University of Louisville, Health
    Sciences Center, Louisville, Kentucky

Anthony Broskowski (3, 27, 43, 189), Northside Community Mental
    Health Center, Tampa, Florida

Timothy R. Brown (59), Office of Research, Department of Social and
    Health Services, State of Washington, Olympia, Washington

Joanne M. Buhl (253), Department of Psychiatry, School of Medicine,
    University of Florida, Gainesville, Florida

Linda G. Carson (215), Napa State Hospital, Napa, California

Robert L. Chapman (173), Systems Consultant, Organizational
    Psychologist, Irvine, California

Harold W. Demone, Jr. (27), Graduate School of Social Work, Rutgers—
    The State University of New Jersey, New Brunswick, New Jersey

Jean Driscoll (43, 189), Boston College, School of Law, Newton Centre,
    Massachusetts

xi

J. Richard Elpers (127, 173), Orange County Department of Mental
Health, and Department of Psychiatry and Human Behavior, University of California, Irvine, Santa Ana, California

Hugh D. Grove (371), School of Accountancy, College of Business Administration, University of Denver, Denver, Colorado

William A. Hargreaves (59, 303, 465, 479), Langley Porter Institute, and
the Department of Psychiatry, University of California, San Francisco, San Francisco, California

Mardi J. Horowitz (465, 479), Psychotherapy Evaluation and Study
Center, Langley Porter Institute, and the Department of Psychiatry,
University of California, San Francisco, San Francisco, California

Thomas J. Kiresuk (341), Hennepin County Medical Center, and Program
Evaluation Resource Center, and University of Minnesota Medical
School, Minneapolis, Minnesota

Alan I. Levenson (97), Department of Psychiatry, College of Medicine,
University of Arizona, Tucson, Arizona

Donald A. Lund (411), Bureau of Program Evaluation, Office of Evaluation and Inspection, Department of Mental Hygiene, State of New
York, Albany, New York

Sander H. Lund (341), Program Evaluation Resource Center, Minneapolis, Minnesota

Tuan D. Nguyen (253), Department of Psychiatry, School of Medicine,
University of California, San Francisco, and Program Evaluation
Service, District V Mental Health Center, San Francisco, California

Herbert C. Schulberg (27, 189), University of Pittsburgh, School of
Medicine, and Office of Education and Regional Programming,
Western Psychiatric Institute and Clinic, Pittsburgh, Pennsylvania

Larry M. Siegel (215), Institute for Social Rehabilitation, National Center
for the Transcendental Meditation Program, Pacific Palisades,
California

James E. Sorensen (127, 371, 465, 479), School of Accountancy, College
of Business Administration, University of Denver, Denver, Colorado

Elaine N. Taylor (445), Human Resources Research Organization, Western Division, Carmel, California

Robert Vineberg (445), Human Resources Research Organization, Western Division, Carmel, California

George J. Warheit (253), Department of Psychiatry, School of Medicine,
University of Florida, Gainesville, Florida

J. Richard Woy (411), Program Analysis and Evaluation Branch, Office
of Program Development and Analysis, National Institute of Mental
Health, Rockville, Maryland

PREFACE

Many circumstances account for the present urgency to identify practical evaluation methods and to implement these methods productively in applied settings. Economic depression combined with inflation, political crises, competing governmental priorities, and overburdened local tax bases are several of the most salient factors that have resulted in a demand for closer scrutiny of the efficiency and effectiveness of human service organizations. Concurrently, there is increased governmental and popular conviction that human and material resources are not being optimally deployed. As a result of these pressures, more efficient, effective, and relevant programs must emerge if headway is to be achieved in the effort to ameliorate human and social problems.

This volume was written and edited during a time of uncertainty and ferment in the human service evaluation field. While the need for program evaluation is almost universally acknowledged, our experiences indicate that many fundamental steps must be taken before evaluation can become a dependable feature of program management. Progress will require

- Development of program administrators who are informed about the deployment and utility of evaluative methods
- Fiscal support for development and/or implementation of evaluative methods within community programs

- Systematic training of program evaluators
- Continuing commitment to the evolution of evaluative technology

While these are long-range objectives, the urgency to accomplish them as rapidly as possible is reflected in a variety of current realities—the mandates of recent legislation, the rapidly increasing costs of human services, and the entropy produced by an increasingly complex mosaic of overlapping but uncoordinated human service programs.

This volume presents *program evaluation* as a feedback process within ongoing program management—a support system essential to decision making at each administrative level of the care system. Continued development of program evaluation methods must be coordinated with parallel efforts to increase the managerial skills of program leaders. A primary conviction guiding our writing is that effective program administration depends on appropriate evaluative capacity at each stratum of policymaking *and* at the locus of service delivery. Integration of the evaluative function within all levels of program administration is, then, a focal emphasis throughout this book.

From our perspective, building program evaluation capacity is a critical component of current efforts to strengthen program management. Training in program evaluation will likely become a standard core segment of educational curricula for those who will enter professional practice and management roles in the human services. These developments in formal professional education must also be supplemented by continuing education programs for those already working in human service organizations.

This book is designed to provide an introduction to program evaluation at the advanced undergraduate level and in graduate schools of public and business administration, public health, health sciences, and the behavioral sciences. The volume is also designed for the practitioner—the manager, evaluator, or service provider—and for government personnel at all levels who direct, assist, and guide the administration of social programs.

Our choice of major topics within the program evaluation field reflects the content of recent legislation, educational curricula, and frequently expressed educational and consultative needs of program administrators and evaluation practitioners. To address the areas of interest suggested by these various sources, the volume includes coverage of several major issues in human service evaluation

- The historical context of and contemporary trends in the delivery of human services
- Analysis of the programmatic roles and multiple functions of evaluation
- Information system concepts and methodology
- Assessment of community needs for services
- Evaluation of program quality and effectiveness in relation to costs
- Current trends and future directions within the program evaluation field

These major issues are presented in five sections within the text. Each section is self-contained and can be used separately as text material for classroom or seminar purposes. Although the chapters within each section are designed to be read sequentially, we have attempted to provide enough useful redundancy across major themes and sufficient cross-referencing to allow readers with specific interests to move directly to individual content areas. Cross references within chapters will alert the reader to additional material elsewhere in the text that we consider prerequisite background for a given topic. For those readers seeking an initial introduction to program evaluation, we strongly recommend a sequential reading of the text since the contextual overview provided in the initial sections is essential as an orientation to the evaluation concepts and methods presented in later sections.

Several persons worked energetically toward the completion of this volume. Jessica Gaynor, Daniel L. Larsen, and Tuan D. Nguyen gave very helpful editorial assistance and critiques of portions of the final manuscript. Bettie M. Bowen, Patricia J. Duff, Sally A. Mason, and Kathleen L. Poole provided assistance in manuscript preparation and typing. Marilynn J. Bottino provided valuable editorial assistance and volunteered support tirelessly and creatively to difficult tasks and to a wide variety of more mundane chores. Special appreciation is extended to these persons.

Timothy R. Marvin coordinated manuscript preparation. His work was consistently accurate and timely. A very special note of thanks is also extended to him.

Finally, Ian R. Tuller developed the automated process through which the computer-stored manuscript was prepared for direct composition by the typesetter. His unique creativity in matters technical and interpersonal provided an enduring and crucial contribution to our work.

I

INTRODUCTION TO THE FIELD

The effectiveness of human service systems during the next decade will depend upon skillful completion of several difficult organizational tasks. These tasks include

- Reorganization of the human service network to achieve coordination, efficiency, and integration among specialized services
- Preservation and further enhancement of the unique contributions and expertise of specialized programs that currently function with relative autonomy in a categorical approach to service delivery
- Increasing the administrative skills of program leaders and fostering the application of more effective organizational designs
- Linkage of professional, paraprofessional, and generalist training to the goals, objectives, and realities of a re-structured human service network
- Use of program evaluation capacity as an internal management tool within *every* level of program organization and *especially* at the local community level, where services are actually delivered to citizens.

These tasks stand both as barriers and opportunities. Reorganization will be difficult, time consuming, and costly, but it seems to us to be an essential step if we are to construct a network of human services that is (*a*) understandable to citizens, (*b*) accessible to those who need services, (*c*) comprehensive for the range of service needs, (*d*) cost–effective, and (*e*) capable of being improved through action based on evaluative information and changing values.

Part I reviews the historical roots of our human service system and analyzes the current trends in the organization and delivery of these services. Within this context, we describe program evaluation methods for improving internal program management and external accountability.

Within the administrative context, we present evaluation as an evolutionary process—one that begins with analysis of program resources and their use in meeting human needs and shifts progressively toward measurement of program performance, efficiency, adequacy, and community impact. This model of evaluation requires preparation, expertise, and motivation, as well as an adequate budget. There are many steps that community-based programs can take to initiate the development of evaluation capacity. These initial steps, as described in Part I, can simultaneously provide information that is useful for management, planning, and accountability purposes.

1

EVALUATION AND THE EMERGING HUMAN SERVICE CONCEPT

C. Clifford Attkisson and Anthony Broskowski

Despite the current national focus on evaluation, human service providers and administrators are not wildly enthusiastic about the program evaluation process. Historically, community-based human service personnel and administrators have held a persistently negative view of evaluation. Evaluation is generally perceived as a critical, subjective, and externally imposed requirement for which there has been neither adequate preparation nor sufficient funding. Human service personnel frequently argue that evaluation is a manipulative device used by governmental authority to terminate unwanted programs or as a rationale for justifying prior administrative decisions. Moreover, human service personnel have felt that the evaluation process, couched in "scientific and objective" methods, is insensitive to the complexities, ambiguities, goals, and work demands that characterize their activities and programs.

However, as the 1970s began, a quest for more constructive and useful program evaluation emerged. Profound economic crises and declining funds for service programs stimulated a new investment in program evaluation as a primary method to strengthen and preserve the integrity of the human service system that was inaugurated in the 1960s. This shifting investment of resources into program evaluation activities is due primarily to the urgent need to control and contain costs and to the increasingly obvious managerial crisis in human service programs. Costs of services remain unchecked, and program administrators have few adequate sources of information about program pro-

3

cesses or impacts to guide their decisions. In addition, most program managers can claim only sparse training in public administration and have very limited experience in the basics of economics, general systems concepts, organizational theory, and political science.

This book presents basic concepts and methods for the evaluation of human service programs. It reviews incentives for *self-evaluation* in community programs, and documents the current state of the art of the evaluation process. As an introductory overview, this first chapter outlines the multiple perspectives that must be considered when approaching the evaluation of service programs. We then review some of the shortcomings of earlier approaches to evaluation that were too dependent upon a more limited range of viewpoints, and then present a brief history of the growth of multiple but fragmented service programs in America. Such a history is vital to a comprehensive understanding of program evaluation and its most appropriate functions within the broader context of integrated program planning, administration, and service delivery. The major blueprint of this larger context is provided through a review of current concepts and working models of integrated human service systems. These concepts and models emphasize the recognition of multiple functions of evaluation, and attempt to integrate these functions in a cohesive and viable service system. Finally, having presented our views on the proper context for evaluation, we end this chapter with a definition of program evaluation, which forms the basis for subsequent chapters.

SUCHMAN'S EVALUATIVE CRITERIA

Suchman (1967) discussed evaluation criteria in terms of program *effort, performance, adequacy, efficiency,* and *process.* His presentation of these levels of criteria was a seminal contribution to the program evaluation field. Paraphrasing Suchman, these levels have clearly differentiated characteristics:

1. *Effort*

This level focuses on the quantity and quality of programmatic *inputs,* including information on the number and type of clients, type and efforts of staff, money and other resources being expended, and programmatic sanctions and/or expectations as mandated by law, regulations, and standards. Suchman also emphasized that *capacity* for effort is a key feature of level of effort criteria.

2. *Performance*

This level reflects on programmatic *outputs,* including information on the number and types of changes in clients and in the nature of the system being evaluated. Suchman described this level as the measurement of the consequences of effort. In Suchman's view, performance evaluations therefore require clarity of immediate and future goals specific to clients, programs, and service delivery systems.

3. Adequacy

Adequacy focuses on the relationship of program effort and performance to the level of need for the program within its larger environment. "This criterion of success refers to the degree to which effective performance is adequate to the total amount of need . . . [and] is obviously a relative measure, depending upon how high one sets one's goals [Suchman, 1967, p. 63]." Adequacy, then, can be conceptualized as the rate of program effectiveness multiplied times the number of persons exposed to the program relative to the number of persons in need of the program.

4. Efficiency

Efficiency refers to the relationships among effort, performance, and adequacy, and is measured by examining strategies for minimizing effort while maximizing program performance and adequacy. "Efficiency is concerned with the evaluation of alternative paths or methods in terms of costs—in money, time, personnel, and public convenience. In a sense, it represents a ratio between effort and performance—output divided by input [Suchman, 1967, p. 64]."

5. Process

This level focuses on the mechanisms by which effort is translated into outcome—including the application of research methodologies to isolate causality and to foster the discovery of new knowledge. Suchman viewed process as the study of the means whereby a program produces its results. While Suchman did not view process research as having as high a priority as the first four levels of criteria, he did feel that process studies can have both administrative and scientific significance. Suchman further indicated that measurement of process should include four major areas of investigation: (a) specification of salient program attributes that determine its effectiveness; (b) analysis of differential effectiveness among target populations served by the program; (c) specification of contextual conditions associated with optimal program functioning; and (d) specification of the range and potency of effects associated with the program.*

Subsequent to Suchman's work, other contributors to the evaluation field have developed criterion measures and methodological tools applicable to each of these domains. Many of these contributions are described or cited in the present volume. Expanding on Suchman's approach to evaluation, Table 1.1 summarizes, at a conceptual level, typically recommended criterion measures and illustrative methodological tools.

*Material in this section was adapted by permission from: E. A. Suchman, *Evaluative research: Principles and practice in public service and social action programs.* Copyright 1967, Russell Sage Foundation, New York.

TABLE 1.1

Evaluative Domains: Typical Criteria and Measurement Tools

Evaluative domains (cf. Suchman, 1967)	Typical criteria and informational requirements	Typical methodological tools, procedures, and indices
I. Effort Measurement Input	Information about the amount and distribution of resources put into the program: • Sources of income and expenditures • Allocation of staff time • Numbers and types of clients • How dollars, staff, and clients are interrelated	• Management information systems • Explicit structural and process standards mandated by law, regulations, and accreditation bodies • Quality assurance procedures such as utilization review and peer review • Capacity for effort as reflected by indices of service availability, accessibility, comprehensiveness, and integration
II. Performance Measurement Output	Information about the outcomes and effectiveness of program effort: • Clients' acceptance of services offered • Improvement in clients' status • Changes in incidence or prevalence of problems addressed by programs • Acceptability of services to clients • Effective linkage of clients to other necessary and appropriate service resources • Level of service availability and accessibility achieved over time	• Scales measuring client functioning and status • Scales assessing client satisfaction • Goal-oriented idiosyncratic scales developed for specific clients • Rates of successful referrals for multiproblem clients • Range of services available that are known to be necessary for specific communities • Enumeration of cultural, linguistic, psychological, geographic, and organizational barriers to service accessibility. Measurement of reduction in barriers to accessibility over time.

III. Adequacy Measurement $\dfrac{\text{Output}}{\text{Need}}$	Information about effort and performance relative to measures of community need or demand: • Match between efforts and needs • Adequacy of performance effectiveness relative to level of need • Appropriateness of clients being served relative to high risk groups or mandated target populations • Awareness of services among citizenry	• Review and analysis of mandated services or documented needs • Undertake needs–resources assessment methods • Review and analyze management information system and outcome assessment data to assess client utilization rates relative to known service needs, mandated target populations, and high risk groups • Survey citizens' awareness of available services
IV. Efficiency Measurement $\dfrac{\text{Output}}{\text{Input}}$	Information about how effort is organized so as to get greatest *performance* and *adequacy*: • Cost of providing effective services • Comparisons of the efficiency and efficacy of different programs or methods of service	• Calculation of costs per unit of service • Cost- outcome and cost–effectiveness comparisons using management information system data and outcome assessment data • Cost–effort–outcome–effectiveness comparisons for different target groups • Efficiency studies to compare different organizational methods in costs and effectiveness
V. Process Measurement Outcome = f(Effort)	Information about the underlying processes by which effort is translated into outcome: • Specification of salient attributes, recipient characteristics, contextual conditions, and the potency and range of effects associated with the program • Identification of causal relations between effort and outcome • Establish maximal generalizability of effects to other environments • Control or explain other factors, independent of program effort, that could possibly account for program outcomes	• Descriptive, correlational, and experimental methodologies that vary type or amount of independent variables and measures immediate and long range dependent variables • Alternative quasi-experimental research designs • Replication of studies demonstrating causal relationships • Studies designed to establish and enhance data reliability and validity • Decision-theoretic approaches to maximizing the quality of administrative decisions and thereby program efforts and outcomes • Operations research methodologies • Multisite, collaborative randomized clinical trials

7

MULTIPLE PERSPECTIVES ON PROGRAM EVALUATION

The primary goal of program evaluation is to improve the impact of ongoing programs. This simple statement implies a wide range of evaluative activities and functions, because program impact can be viewed from many perspectives. The most common perspectives in the literature of evaluation are those of the service providers, administrators, legislators, regulators, and funders. Program impact criteria, therefore, will usually include measures of program efforts by staff, service outcomes for individuals or groups, efficiency in terms of costs, and effectiveness and adequacy in meeting the estimated levels of problem severity and community needs for the service.

Viewed from the perspective of the individual client, however, a good program is one that does more than simply reduce a single problem or increase some restricted level of positive functioning. A good service must also be readily available when needed, and operate in a fashion that does not create undue burdens or expenses for the consumer. An additional impact criterion, therefore, becomes one of accessibility—geographical, temporal, and financial.

A research model for the study and analysis of "service-seeking transactions" has been formulated by Kahn, Katz, and Gutek (1976) who, using their own research model, studied a representative national sample of adults and analyzed the delivery of government services as experienced from the citizens' perspective. Their research indicated that accessibility of services is strongly related to citizens' satisfaction with the outcome of services.

Service accessibility, however, is frequently very poor under our current methods of service delivery. An interim report on Services Integration Projects of the Department of Health, Education, and Welfare (*1*) noted: "Data from three independent studies (one in Los Angeles, one in rural Macon County, Illinois, one in Boston) indicate that the mere intake probability for any social service chosen at random is only .4—that is, the average client who seeks service has only 4 chances in 10 of ever being admitted [p. 3]."

In the case of persons with a single common problem (e.g., alcoholism), a good program could therefore be judged by the extent to which it was accessible and effective in reducing the negative effects of the problem. Yet, it is frequently observed that many persons seeking service have multiple problems. In other words, problems tend to cluster and may therefore require simultaneous or well-integrated sequential treatments. Although a highly specialized treatment may be judged "effective" by the provider, it may be judged relatively inadequate by the client if there is no system of related treatments or services to help with the interrelated cluster of problems. For example, Spencer (1974) points out that a "disadvantaged teen-age girl" who becomes pregnant may need as many as 10 specific services, such as prenatal medical care, prenatal education, obstetrical care, vocational education, job placement, day care, and even transportation. "If she fails to get more than two or three of these services she is likely to become a typical AFDC mother, with tragic consequences for her own and her child's life chances [Spencer, 1974, p. 8]."

Therefore, the program impact criteria listed above must be expanded to include a measure of systemic comprehensiveness. That is, evaluation must address the issues implicit in *the single-input fallacy*—the belief that a single service or treatment, in isolation of others, will be sufficient to restore a multiproblemed individual to an effective level of overall functioning. The importance of comprehensiveness criteria are clear when we recognize the prevalence of the multiproblemed client: "Studies indicate that between 86 percent (HEW study) and 95 percent (Lancaster study) of all HEW clients have multiple problems, and that single services provided independently of one another do not result in changes in client's dependency status or life chances [*1*, p. 3]."

Finally, if a client's multiple problems are to be treated in a simultaneous or sequential fashion, the client's perspective of good services must include the degree to which one service is coordinated with another, or at least the degree to which the client can be referred from one program to another. Evaluation criteria must also include, therefore, a measure of program continuity. Presently, it appears to many observers that the rate of effective referrals between separate programs is very low and that consequently the impact of single programs for multiproblemed clients is being severely limited:

> Frequently, the failure to receive referred services prevents clients from benefitting from a service already provided. There is mounting evidence that more programs actually reduce the probability that clients' needs will be met, that complex eligibility criteria serve more to select clients out of than into programs. Further, the probability of effective referral ranges from a low of .07 to a high of .22, that is if a client is turned away from one HEW service and told to go to another, the odds are less than 1 in 5 that he will ever get there and be served [*1*, p. 3].

Kirk and Greenley (1974) studied a range of social agencies and reported that an average of one-third (37.6%) of all persons applying for a service did not receive it from the agency they approached, nor were they referred elsewhere. Of those applicants referred elsewhere, only two out of three (63%) ever completed the referral and became applicants at the agencies to which they were sent. Therefore, from the perspective of the individual service recipient, evaluation must assess not just the effectiveness of each separate and specific service program in the community—it must also assess the degree to which multiple and diverse services are effectively integrated into a network of resources for many different *combinations* of personal and social problems.

WIDE-SCALE NATIONAL PROGRAMS: LIMITATIONS OF EVALUATIVE STUDIES TO DATE

Most of the early literature on program evaluation has stressed the degree to which single but wide-scale national programs have been effective in achieving legislative intent, including the goals as envisioned by specialized service providers and program administrators (Rivlin, 1971; Ullman & Huber, 1973; Weiss, 1972; Wholey, Scanlon, Duffy, Fukumoto, & Vogt, 1970). Most of these large-scale studies neglected to take into account the systemic interconnection of human problems because the evaluators and their funding sources were committed to looking at limited service programs. While aware of systemic connections, many evaluators have been forced to neglect them because of the pressures to adopt "scientific" designs that are oriented to discovering cause–effect relationships between single or limited treatments and single or limited outcomes.

Furthermore, many of these national evalution efforts neglected to place evaluation into a broader context of program planning and administration. For example, measures of service costs were generally very crude, and seldom related to the actual cost of delivering a single unit of service or an episode of care for one or more related problems in a single client. The design and timing of these national evaluations limited their influence on the highest levels of program planning and management, since they were conducted at the most local level of service delivery. Advocates and defenders of local projects were able to argue that the local variations made any negative national evaluation finding irrelevant at best, and destructive at worst. In brief, the national evaluations of service programs were captured and limited by the same conceptual traps that have historically limited the planning, funding, and administration of services (Wholey, 1972).

We do not wish to imply that wide-scale national evaluations of programs are without value. Federal legislators and administrators will continue to seek broad-based information as to how effectively national programs are being implemented, and how effectively they are reaching some more-or-less measurable objectives (Horst, Nay, Scanlon, & Wholey, 1974). There will also be a continual need to pilot-test the effects of new concepts and methods inherent in new national policies and programs. We strongly urge, however, that program evaluation not be confused with policy research (Riecken & Boruch, 1974). We view the former as committed to the improvement of ongoing programs, whereas the latter remains devoted to pilot research on the potential effects of implementing new policies and programs.

THE GROWTH OF AMERICA'S HUMAN SERVICE PROGRAMS

To appreciate further the distinctive importance and potentials of evaluation, as well as its difficulties and limitations, one must understand the history of human services in America and the larger environment of our present service programs. As suggested earlier, it is our contention that the current methods of service delivery, program planning, funding, and administration have placed upper limits on the degree of effectiveness that can be achieved by any single service program. Therefore, the serious student of program evaluation must come to see evaluation within the context of contemporary struggles throughout many quarters to reform and rationalize the confusing and complex nonsystem of service planning, management, and delivery.

To understand these struggles, it is necessary to recount the historical process that has brought us to this opportune time for the reorganization and integration of human services. This historical review will also help us to assess how the emerging concept of human services is relevant to the multiple perspectives of clients, providers, administrators, legislators, regulators, funders, and, hence, of utmost concern to program evaluators.

Until the end of the nineteenth century, organized human service programs were extremely limited, local in character, and based solely on the needs of special groups. Although as early as 1798, the federal government had established the Marine Hospital Service to provide some limited health benefits for neglected merchant seamen, these services were considered as exceptions, on behalf of the national interest. What became known under President Theodore Roosevelt as the Public Health Service had its beginnings in South Boston at Fort Independence—the first great bastion of defense in the War of Independence. On July 16, 1798, President John Adams signed legislation that officially put the United States into the health business. Fort Independence was the first location of publicly funded hospital services. The establishment of this facility was prompted principally by the threat of a smallpox epidemic set off by merchant seamen who were infected in foreign ports and spread the disease on return to the United States.

Beyond the immediate smallpox threat, the Marine Hospital Service was established to solve the social and health problems created by the practice of leaving at the nearest port any seaman unfit for duty. Ships had no sick bays, and ordinary seamen were bunked in extremely crowded quarters. The average seaman had few financial resources beyond the clothes he wore. Thus, these sick and destitute men were often set ashore in cities where they had no resources or relatives. The cities, with their limited services, did not welcome these aliens. Yet it was unconscionable to have sick seamen with no recourse but the streets. The problem became so conspicuous and inhumane that the federal government established the Marine Hospital Service.

The legislation signed by John Adams set up a payroll deduction plan and thereby created a prepayment mechanism for merchant seaman medical care. American shipmasters were required to deduct 20¢ per month from the pay of each sailor aboard ship (Snow, 1971). Within a year, the program was extended to cover every officer and sailor in the U. S. Navy, and, over the next century, expanded to include a network of hospitals and facilities—the Public Health Service.

Although the government made an early start in health care, it was not until 1867 that it created within the Department of the Interior an Office of Education. This agency's responsibilities, however, were limited to gathering and disseminating facts about public education and rates of literacy.

By the turn of the century, the recognition of the need for national social welfare programs slowly took hold. Until 1930, however, the primary motivation was still basically one of charity. In fact, the initial impetus for nationally organized programs was provided by such private organizations as the National Child Labor Committee and the National Consumers League. Child welfare legislation was a major trendsetter in the establishment of a philosophy of government role in service provision. By 1912, the federal government had established a Children's Bureau, and the Public Health Service was established in the Treasury Department, and by 1923 President Harding had proposed a Department of Education and Welfare.

By the early 1930s the ideology of organized services began to change. Until then, our society had been dominated by "rugged individualism" and a view that poverty was caused by vice or idleness. The philosophy and policy of direct intervention by the federal government in the planning, financing, and *delivery* of human services arose as a result of the Great Depression. This massive failure of the economy stimulated a different public understanding of the conditions of poverty. The increased need for services was beyond the capacity of the charitable private sector and state and local government solutions also proved to be inadequate. At this time President Hoover maintained the older ideology of private solutions to personal problems but did allow some federal loans to States through the Emergency Relief Act of 1932. President Hoover's federal reorganization proposal of 1932 also called for a merger of federal health, education, and recreation activities into a single executive department. Following his election in 1932, President Roosevelt signed the Emergency Relief Act of 1933 and sanctioned a radical shift in ideology to the point of assuming that the federal government was responsible for the citizens' general human welfare. The Social Security Act of 1935 laid the foundation for the federal government's role in citizens' income maintenance. By 1937, a Presidential Committee on Administrative Management recommended that health, education, and social security programs be placed in a Department of Social Welfare. By 1939, all these previous ideas were partially implemented when Congress created the Federal Security Agency (FSA). The FSA consisted of an office for the administrator, the Public Health Service, the Civilian Conservation Corps, the Office of Education, and the Social Security Board.

The policy of the federal government's direct intervention into personal social problems continued throughout President Roosevelt's administration and was further influenced by public attitudes and the growth and mobility of the population in the period prior to World War II. Although the government did become heavily involved in problems of human welfare prior to World War II, there generally remained a clear division between the roles of federal and state governments and the private sector as represented by nonprofit charitable agencies. Throughout the 1930s a rising population mobility and the resultant dissolution of the extended family created a pressure for state governments to absorb the responsibilities for those most costly categories of problems formerly cared for by extended families; namely, hospitals for the mentally ill, homes for the poor and sick elderly, and "training schools for wayward children." Prior to the 1930s the private sector, motivated by a sense of charity, had provided a variety of personal services to the "needy" and also for those wealthier persons who were able to pay. These latter services were generally less expensive and provided through local community agencies. They ranged from personal counseling for family and child welfare to recreational services. Thus, state governments became heavily committed to custodial programs, whereas those remaining services that were no longer available through the extended family were developed independently by the private sector. At no point was there a consistent policy that these diverse programs be coordinated in terms of (a) interorganizational relations within and between the public and private sector; (b) funding priorities; (c) clientele to be served; (d) methods of interagency referral; or (e) criteria for effectiveness.

Following World War II, there was another acceleration in social mobility and an increase in the problems created by rapid change and community transitions. Returning veterans increased the demand for a wide variety of social, educational, and health-related services. The magnitude of these demands led to a major commitment by the federal government in the actual operation of human services through the Veterans Administration. Through the process of collective bargaining, labor unions further promoted a variety of social and health services by adding human service benefits to their collective bargaining demands. New demands were also matched by new technologies and a further growth of professional training programs. In brief, the formally organized and specialized service programs began to develop in sufficient number to supplant the informal, family-based, and generic helping modalities of an earlier period. For a more extensive review of the period, including changes in the models of service delivery financing, the reader should see Rosenthal (1975).

The Federal Security Agency created by the federal reorganization of 1939 grew rapidly in size until 1953, when President Eisenhower submitted a reorganization plan calling for the dissolution of the Federal Security Agency and the creation of a cabinet level department that would include health, education, and welfare programs. This proposal became effective in April of 1953, giving birth to the Department of Health, Education, and Welfare (Department of Health, Education, and Welfare, 1970).

By the late 1950s, the rationale for federal involvement in service delivery drew further sustenance from the civil rights movement and the conviction that equitable local services for all citizens could only be assured by national control and direction. During the 1960s the growth in the number and costs of federal programs was further accelerated. The administration and Congress attempted to meet every emergent problem of our turbulent society with a new program, each requiring separate funds and administrative staff. It was also during the decade of the 1960s that the community mental health ideology reached its fruition. For example, Hersch (1972) related the community mental health movement to certain social and historical changes in the United States. It was his hypothesis that the 1960s were characterized by a spirit of sociopolitical reform with an emphasis on a "revitalized humanistic concern for the disadvantaged, the oppressed and the powerless [Hersch, 1972, p. 751]."

The proliferation of these new programs during the 1960s was keyed to the identification of highly specialized categories of problems or narrowly defined categories of clients (e.g., the *blind,* the *veteran,* the *unemployed,* the *drug abuser*), ignoring the overlap among these similar services and common recipients. Thus the term "categorical approach" is commonly used to characterize this piecemeal strategy of planning and delivering human services.

THE RATIONALE AND PROBLEMS OF CATEGORICAL PROGRAMS

The strategy of creating separate categorical programs for highly interrelated problems was preferred by the architects of the government's service system, because it had several specific advantages. The individual senator or representative could appear to constituents as addressing major social problems. The categorical program administrators sensed a greater degree of control over funds and program implementation when these ran in direct, or nearly direct, lines from Washington to the community level. Separate categorical funding for alcohol and drug abuse programs was established, for example, because mental health program administrators remained opposed to large increases for such services within mental health facilities, whereas other areas of mental health remained static. In contrast, advocates of separate programs for alcohol and drug problems felt that adequate services would not emerge out of the existing mental health bureaucracy. Finally, professional organizations and citizen groups supported the categorical approach, because it was an effective vehicle for their special interests.

Although it is true that each new program was sincerely intended to meet the special needs of a particular category of citizens, the creation of separate agencies and funding sources unnecessarily created additional costs and inefficiencies among potentially related service programs. In its beginning, the budget of the Department of Health, Education, and Welfare (HEW) in fiscal year 1954 was slightly more than $7 billion, which included over $5 billion of trust funds that were beyond the discretionary control of HEW administrators. By 1970, the total budget had grown to over $58 billion, of which $40 billion were in trust funds devoted to social security payments and other uncontrollable accounts. In another 5 years, the HEW budget nearly doubled, to over $110 billion in 1975, of which $77.4 billion was for uncontrollable accounts. Looking at budget growth in terms of per capita expenditures, HEW spent an average of $33 per person in 1954 and almost $400 in 1972. Paid employees in 1953 numbered over 25,000; there were almost 78,000 HEW personnel by 1970, and 123,000 by 1975. In 1955, HEW estimated that it operated approximately 80 separate programs. In 1970 the estimate had grown to over 260 (Department of Health, Education, and Welfare, 1970; 7). By January 1973, outgoing HEW Secretary Richardson (6) pointed out that the HEW categorical programs exceeded 300 in number. In his February 1975 budget for HEW, Secretary Caspar Weinberger (7) noted: "In the context of the total Federal budget, HEW is the largest single agency accounting for one-third of all

Federal outlays—five years previously HEW accounted for 29% of Federal outlays and ten years previously HEW's share of the budget was less than 20% of the total [p. 1]."

Competition for limited governmental funds and jealous administrative turf control has gradually replaced an integrated approach to the multiple and overlapping problems of individuals and families. The 300-plus categorical programs in HEW alone are frequently judged to be fragmented, duplicatory, inefficient, at times contradictory, and generally unmanageable from either the office of the secretary of HEW or from other agencies or levels of government, state and local, through which these programs operate. A particularly interesting review of the problems of fragmentation, inefficiency, duplication, and managerial slippage in the health field is provided by Strickland (1972).

Furthermore, many HEW programs are redundant with those in other federal administrative departments such as Labor, or Housing and Urban Development. We have reached the point where legislators, administrators, providers, and clients, are incapable of determining what is being done, by whom, for whom, and at what costs.

Falkson (1976), writing about the politics of "New Federalism," summarizes the impact of the categorical program strategy and describes emerging alternative proposals:

> As the federal bureaucracies and domestic budget have expanded, programs have become more functionally specific and categorical. Over time the inevitable result has been a duplication of effort and an overlapping of administrative responsibilities at the state and local program levels (as well as at the federal level).
>
> New Federalism asserts that the categorical grants-in-aid system, the principal vehicle for federal domestic resource allocation, has proved inefficient and ineffective in accomplishing national objectives through the use of federal dollars. Whatever the intent of grants-in-aid programs, their impact has been to (a) maldistribute federal resources among states and communities; (b) establish often impenetrable and irrational regulations and standards for the disposition of federal grants; (c) make it exceedingly difficult for states and localities to establish coherent and comprehensive plans for interrelated functional problem areas; and (d) create complex systems of program management and administration that often ignore elected officials at state and local levels, giving appointed bureaucrats in Washington the authority to make resource-allocation decisions at the community level which are executed by local bureaucrats virtually independent of general-purpose state and local governments.
>
> To redress these asserted failures of the existing domestic policy system, New Federalism proposes a fourfold change. First, it would return the power to act to local elected officials by reducing federal control of resources. Second, it would decentralize those functions that remain federal to federal agency regional offices, away from Washington-based offices. Third, it would help improve the capacities of states and localities to devise programs that meet their particular needs

through improved programs of technical assistance. And finally, it
would utilize federal dollars less as permanent subsidies for dependent
state and local programs and more as "investment capital" to stimulate
state, local, and private-sector investment in particular programs [pp.
97–98].*

The difficulties in comprehending, much less funding and managing myriad categorical programs, have led some policymakers to seek their commonalities, to consolidate specialized terminology, and to bring about some
manageable order in the present chaos. By the 1970s the policy pendulum
began to swing away from the categorical program approach as analysts began
to stress the systemic properties of the citizens' problems and the "crisis of
performance and accountability" brought about by the proliferation of
categorical solutions (6). The capstone of these efforts at redefinition and
policy shift from categorical to integrated programs was the concept of human
services.

THE EMERGING CONCEPT OF HUMAN SERVICES

The growth of the human services concept has been stimulated by at least
three converging factors: (a) the recognition of systemic connectedness among
the problems of living in our society; (b) the recognition of similarities in the
specific techniques and activities of help providers; and (c) the recognition of
the inefficiency, fragmentation, barriers to accessibility, gaps in service, and
discontinuities characteristic of the present categorical system of funds and
service delivery. Increased recognition of these converging factors has provided a basis for the growth of human service ideology (Gage, 1976).
    As early as 1968, March characterized the human service movement as
heading toward:

> comprehensiveness of services, toward decentralization of services. . .,
> toward concerting of resources from different programs, toward
> collocation of service components, and toward operational integration
> of services so that they can be geared together in a continuum ordered
> in a proper sequence and effectively administered without the present
> duplication and time-wasting that goes on for clients and for employees
> [March, 1968, p. 99].*

Baker (1974) describes the human services ideology as consisting of five basic
themes: (a) systemic integration of services; (b) comprehensiveness and access-

*Reproduced by permission from: J. L. Falkson, Minor skirmish in a monumental struggle:
HEW's analysis of mental health services. Policy Analysis, 1976, 2, 93–119. (Copyright 1976,
University of California Press, Berkeley.)

    *Reproduced by permission from: M. March, The neighborhood center concept. Public
Welfare, 1968, 26, 97–111. (Copyright 1968, American Public Welfare Association, Washington,
D. C.)

ibility; (c) client troubles defined as problems in living; (d) generic characteristics of helping activities; and (e) accountability of service providers to clients. In Baker's framework, human service ideology implies planned interorganizational relationships at the level of agency administration and client services, a careful analysis of the generic and unique tasks to be performed by various helping professions, and a redefinition of client problems that does not necessarily reinforce any single categorical modality of treatment services by a given profession.

Klein (1975) provides a very broad definition of human services when he speaks about them within the context of developing new communities:

> It should be emphasized at the outset that I am defining human services in such a way as to go well beyond the traditional limits of health, education, and welfare. The more involved I became in thinking about new towns, the more convinced I was that *planning for human services must take into account all those physical and social arrangements which affect significantly the physical safety, personal security, problem-solving capabilities, and social significance of the community's residents.* By this definition, an effectively functioning, human police force and law enforcement system is a crucial human service [p. 251].*

Further discussion of the human service field is presented in Chapter 2, where Demone, Schulberg, and Broskowski analyze five major developmental trends: (a) evolving ideologies and social values, (b) emerging technologies, (c) changing administrative practices, (d) modified program structures, and (e) altered manpower utilization patterns.

MODELS OF INTEGRATED HUMAN SERVICES

While possessing some consensual validity, it is more difficult to provide a precise and standardized operational definition of the human services concept. In fact, the concept of human services is currently more a term of convenience and a reflection of policy innovations than a referent to a specific and limited domain of services. Government administrators, legislators, service providers, consumers, and the general public will conceive of various definitions or highlight different aspects based upon their relationship to the delivery of services. The operational definition of what constitutes human services will vary from one state, county, or town, to another depending more on the organization of governmental agencies and funding patterns than upon any professional consensus as to what specific activities provide a human service (Council of State Governments, 1974). For example, in most states, human services will include health, mental health, rehabilitation, and a variety of social service programs such as day care, adoption, and homemaker services. In some states the term may or may not include corrections, and in many

---

*Reproduced by permission from: D. C. Klein, Developing human services in new communities. In H. C. Schulberg & F. Baker (Eds.), *Developments in human services* (Vol. II). Copyright 1975, Behavioral Publications, New York.

states education is talked about as a human service but may be administratively autonomous in the state's governance structure. O'Donnell (2) noted that by 1969 approximately 20 states had already combined several services and many other states were seriously considering similar reorganizations. In Massachusetts, for example, the Executive Office of Human Services was created to coordinate the traditionally separate public health, mental health, rehabilitation and social welfare programs of the state (Baker & Broskowski, 1974). A survey in 1972–73 by the Council of State Governments (1974) indicated that 26 states had by then reorganized their own agencies to create comprehensive human resource departments which administer both public assistance and social service programs and at least three other major types of human service programs. Minnesota and Utah are two states which have moved strongly in the direction of integrating services at local levels (4).

Besides integrating these categorical programs within and between administrative levels of government, it is essential to create viable linkages between the actual service providers and their clients at the most immediate level of service delivery.

Lyle Spencer (1974) has provided a general framework for integrated local service networks by building upon the distinction between *core services* and *support services.* Core services refer to the various specialized activities of professional service providers (e.g., surgery, blood tests, teaching, counseling). Support services are those administrative activities necessary to maintain the provision of core services (e.g., management, information systems, purchasing, payroll, accounting). Spencer notes that we frequently find in a community needs/resources assessment a wasteful duplication of expensive support services and a shortage of necessary core services. In a totally fragmented system, each core service provider must absorb the costs of maintaining each of the necessary support services. As an integrated system develops, more and more of the similar support services of multiple service providers are taken over by a special unit, which Spencer calls the *integrator*. Integrators may be general management systems operated by local government, or private nonprofit consortiums, specifically created by a network of core service providers to function on their behalf.

In an ideally designed integrated network, the integrator provides a variety of linkage mechanisms to assure service continuity to clients, relate the local service providers to one another, and to link the total system to higher levels of government administration and funding. In terms of linkages operating among local core service providers, Spencer (1974) noted that some 40 different linkage mechanisms have been identified. These range from the obvious mechanisms of joint planning and budgeting to the use of integrated information systems. Linkage mechanisms also include coordination in client diagnosis and treatment procedures.

Chattanooga, as an example of a service integration system, has coordinated 600 human service agencies, public and private. Any client, regardless of the referring problem(s), is asked for the same 12 items of information.

Accountability data are collected by independent system auditors and clients are followed up 30 days after service:

> Chattanooga will soon be able to associate the cost data in its consolidated accounting system with its casework data on client progress, thus permitting precise estimates of the average costs, number of services, and time taken to elevate clients with a given set of problem characteristics from one dependence category to the next [Spencer, 1974, pp. 10–11].*

Another model for client-centered services integration is based on the prototype of services offered by the American Automobile Association to its members. Using this approach, a local human services organization would provide a comprehensive package of services to its members through several mechanisms: (a) direct provision of information, education, assessment, and referral services; (b) indirect provision of specialized core services and related benefits through contracts it writes with diverse primary service providers; and, (c) evaluation of the quality of services being provided to its members through followup with providers and serviced clients. Incentives for quality and efficiency would be built into such an organization through its client fee schedules and the provision of its contracts with service providers (Long, 1974).

Within the local community, therefore, working models of integrated services may range from the simple notion of a connective information and referral system, through such devices as single-point-comprehensive-problem-diagnosis-centers, neighborhood multiservice centers, and contractual networks among separate agencies with or without consumer organized third-party groups. Among agencies within a community, linkages may vary from consolidated top-level policy making and management, through levels of exchange among staff of different agencies, co-location of service facilities, to client-centered coordination by case managers, cross-agency case conferences, and shared transportation resources to move shared clients.

Gans and Kaplan (Department of Health, Education, and Welfare, 1972) surveyed and visited integrated services demonstration projects throughout the United States and identified some of the major facilitators and inhibitors of various linkage mechanisms and the impact of each linkage on such criteria as service accessibility, continuity, and comprehensiveness. Spencer (1974) summarized the work of Gans and Kaplan and others when he wrote:

> As might be expected, the three most important variables in predicting an integrator's success in integrating-service-provider activities are: (1) the integrator's degree of control over service-provider funds . . .; (2) the leadership—charisma—of the integrator's director and the system-planning competence of his staff; and (3) the existence and quality of

---

*Reproduced by permission from: L. Spencer, The federal approach to services integration. *The Urban and Social Change Review*, 1974, 7, 7–13. (Copyright 1974, Graduate School of Social Work Alumni Association, Boston College, Chestnut Hill, Massachusetts.)

the integrator–service-provider information systems. Where these pre-
conditions exist, political and legal obstacles to services integration are
rapidly solved; where they do not, projects have trouble [p. 11].*

Additional useful descriptions of integrated service projects throughout the
United States are available through publications of The Human Ecology Institute (1975) and Project Share—a national clearinghouse of information for
improving management of human services, operated under contract with
HEW (3). Other specific service integration projects also have developed written materials describing their objectives, methods, and accomplishments (8).

THE UTILITY OF THE HUMAN SERVICES
CONCEPT

In the concept of human services, the common and integrative elements
of services are emphasized as opposed to the specific and distinctive elements
of different services (e.g., psychotherapy, homemaker services). The human
service concept highlights the breadth of services rather than the depth of any
one of them. The human services concept recognizes the problems inherent in
the overlaps and duplication of service activities as well as those related to the
gaps and missing elements. Consequently, the utility of the concept will be
greatest to those who must maintain an integrated and systemic view of all
services. This perspective is particularly critical for the generalist—the gover-
nor, the mayor, the legislators, administrators, and program planners (Yessian
& Broskowski, 1977). At the level of the direct service provider, concerned
foremost with a particular and specialized service, the concept may have less
value. Other personnel, such as information and referral specialists, case advocates, and service ombudsmen will find the concept to be useful to the extent
that it emphasizes the importance of connective linkages among the multiple
specialized services needed by the typical multiproblem client. Most importantly for purposes of this chapter and book, the concept has utility for
program evaluators because it highlights and integrates the multiple perspectives on program impact; including service effort, accessibility, comprehensiveness, continuity, effectiveness, adequacy, and efficiency.

It is important to understand that human services, as a concept of utility
for evaluation purposes, *does not imply* that specific and categorical services
are unnecessary. A human services ideology does not imply the elimination of
specialization in favor of all-purpose generalists at the most direct level of
client contact and service transactions. Rather, the concept of human services
implies a better set of linkages and connections between specific and specialized programs and a consolidation of unnecessary duplication in administrative support systems that are created to maintain separate services. As a
concept, human services places primary emphasis on the administrative inte-

*Reproduced by permission from: L. Spencer, The federal approach to services integration.
The Urban and Social Change Review, 1974, 7, 7–13. (Copyright 1974, Graduate School of Social
Work Alumni Association, Boston College, Chestnut Hill, Massachusetts.)

gration of specialized services and widens the perspective of evaluation from the narrow criteria of the categorical service provider to include criteria of interest to the multiproblem client, the cost-conscious funder (i.e., taxpayer), and the systemwide policy planner.

An excellent summary definition of integrated services that places it within a proper context of existing specialized services was provided by HEW Secretary Elliot Richardson in a memorandum dated June 1971:

> Services Integration refers primarily to ways of organizing the delivery of services to people at the local level. Services integration is not a new program to be superimposed over existing programs; rather, it is a work within which ongoing programs can be rationalized and enriched to do a better job of making services available within existing commitments and resources. Its objectives must include such things as (a) the coordinated delivery of services for the greatest benefit to the people; (b) a wholistic approach to the individual and the family unit; (c) the provision of a comprehensive range of services locally; and (d) the rational allocation of resources at the local level so as to be responsive to local needs [5].

THE PROPER CONTEXT FOR PROGRAM EVALUATION

So far, we have developed and related several major themes that will point toward a general understanding of the proper context in which to define, plan, and implement the program evaluation process. In summary, six basic themes were emphasized:

1. The goal of evaluation is to improve program impact.

2. There are multiple perspectives on what constitutes "impact," not the least of which is the frequently neglected perspective of clients.

3. The development of our social service program has been largely unplanned, highly categorical, specialized, fragmented, discontinuous, costly, and inefficient.

4. The concept of human services has been introduced to focus on service program commonalities, and the potential linkages to overcome inefficiencies and discontinuities for the multiproblem client.

5. The concept of human services has been demonstrated to be technically and organizationally feasible in action at levels of state administration, local service networks, and client-centered service linkages. The full impact of integrated service models on the quality and costs of care must undergo continued evaluation.

6. While of limited use to specialized service providers, the *concept* of human services will have primary utility to policymakers, planners, administrators, program evaluators, and others who must maintain a generic and systemic perspective on service funding, delivery, and impact.

Based on these themes, three basic conclusions about the evaluation of human service programs have been formulated:

1. Single categorical program approaches to human service delivery restrict the effectiveness and efficiency of services;

2. Program evaluation must be viewed as an integral aspect of organizational design and organizational development;

3. Program evaluation is primarily a process that must occur within
ongoing organizational management, decision making, and planning.

These conclusions will now be briefly reviewed in more detail.

LIMITATIONS OF CATEGORICAL SERVICE PROGRAMS

*It is concluded that the present low level of systemic integration will limit
the impact of any single categorical service program.* Assessing the effectiveness of a single categorical program is but one principal building block in
determining overall systemic effectiveness of an entire human service network.
One of the major goals of program evaluation efforts must be to assess systemic
integration and then help to increase and maintain it.

Embedded in the questions of systemic effectiveness and individual program effectiveness are the issues of resource management efficiency, quality
assurance, utilization review, continuity of care within and across categorical
boundaries, comprehensiveness of care, accessibility of care, and the effectiveness of the referral process. In addition, primary prevention and the evaluation
of preventive efforts must emerge as major targets of evaluation in the next
decade (Broskowski & Baker, 1974).

THE ORGANIZATIONAL FUNCTION
OF PROGRAM EVALUATION

*It is concluded that program evaluation must be viewed as an integral
aspect of organization design and organizational development.* In other words,
program evaluation is a function that takes place *within an organizational
context.* Although individual private practice remains as an important service
modality within the larger service delivery system, the greatest bulk of service
—whether measured by client problem episodes or dollar value—is currently
being delivered within the structure of formal organizations. As a complex and
expensive enterprise, the evaluation of these organized public or third-party
supported services must necessarily involve an understanding and analysis of
their organizational context. Evaluators must, therefore, understand the dynamics of organizational structures and interactions, including the multiple
types of transactions within and between organizations that must be carried
out in the process of service delivery. Chapter 3 is devoted to such issues.
Furthermore, the conduct of program evaluation activities per se will require
a wide range of organizational resources and management skills.

PROGRAM EVALUATION AND
ORGANIZATIONAL DECISION MAKING

*It is concluded that evaluation is primarily a process within ongoing
organizational management, decision making, and planning; and is only sec-
ondarily a research enterprise for the purpose of new scientific discoveries.* In
brief, we must build toward a greater conceptual distinction between program

evaluation and evaluative research (Suchman, 1967; Weiss, 1972). Successful program evaluation does indeed require scientific research skills, as well as organizational sophistication and some substantive knowledge of the specialized services being evaluated. Nevertheless, while dependent on organizational, scientific, and substantive service knowledge, program evaluation is foremost a practical matter, of use to others primarily to the extent that it informs their current decision making, fulfills environmental demands for accountability, and points to future program improvement and efficiency. Program evaluation, therefore, is part of the essential but basic process of internal planning and controlling of human services operation; in brief, it is an integral part of the managerial process and must be linked to both long- and short-range planning efforts, as well as to varying control systems that seek adherence to, and signal deviations from, plans.

GENERAL CONCLUSIONS

Three basic conclusions were drawn in the preceding section of this chapter:

1. The categorical approach to the delivery of human services results in fragmented and poorly integrated programs for citizens. Furthermore the categorical strategy, with its currently inadequate systemic integration, restricts the effectiveness and efficiency of services to citizens, especially those with multiple service needs.

2. Program evaluation must be viewed as an integral aspect of organizational design and development that promotes external accountability to citizens, consumers, and funders. Evaluation also must function as a linkage mechanism for the systemic integration of human services.

3. Program evaluation is primarily a process that must occur within ongoing organizational management, decision making, and planning.

These conclusions indicate that the products of the evaluation enterprise must meet *external* as well as *internal* management and planning needs. That is, program evaluation functions must address the organization's responsibility to be accountable to its external environments. This external accountability demand requires that evaluative information be available, when useful and appropriate, to meet the administrative needs of other government or private sector agencies. The external agencies to which an organization may be accountable will vary along many dimensions, including level of government, public or private auspice, category of program service, and degree of interdependence by way of funds or regulatory responsibilities. Despite the complexities, and in some cases the conflictual requirements for external reporting that are placed on a given program, the evaluation subsystem must be able to produce information in a timely, reliable, and efficient manner.

However, one important caveat must be emphasized. Evaluators internal to a program or systemic level cannot supply all of the evaluative information needed by its own external environment. Evaluation at a given level of program can provide information for that program's internal management and planning purposes, can comply with external reporting requirements, can collaborate with other organizational levels, can receive and provide consultation—but cannot satisfy the full range of information needs of an external program level. Furthermore, external agencies will always have to supplement the information received from other program levels with additional information obtained through their own independent efforts.

If the foregoing assertions are taken seriously, program evaluation capability must include knowledge and skills in management information systems, cost-accounting, and program outcome measurement. These tool skills are covered specifically in Chapters 5–8, and 11–13. Chapters 4, 14, and 15 also relate to the interface of management information and outcome evaluation. In addition, Chapters 16 and 17 assess the current status of the evaluation field and discuss implications for the education of evaluators.

Not only must evaluation provide information to the organization's environmental constituents, program evaluation must be capable of assisting management by monitoring the organization's changing societal environment. These contextual demands require skills in need assessment methodologies and other long-range planning strategies. Some of these issues are covered in Chapters 9 and 10.

Finally, because of its placement in the context of complex organizations and their shifting environments, program evaluation must depend on multiple sources of data, varying in level of detail, source, cost and ease of collection, validity of interpretation, and scientific merit. The methods by which these data are collected, processed, and blended into useful information will vary considerably, but should, in all cases, be systematic. The evaluator must accept tradeoffs between precision and timeliness (Roos, 1973). In the balance, one can only expect reasonable judgments and not scientifically verified facts.

PROGRAM EVALUATION DEFINED

Based on this chapter's analysis of the proper context for program evaluation activities, a working definition for program evaluation is proposed. Program evaluation is:

1. A process of making reasonable judgments about program effort, effectiveness, efficiency and adequacy
2. Based on systematic data collection and analysis
3. Designed for use in program management, external accountability, and future planning
4. Focuses especially on accessibility, acceptability, awareness, availability, comprehensiveness, continuity, integration, and cost of services.

This working definition is summarized in Table 1.2 and has been used as the guiding orientation to program evaluation used in the editing of the remaining chapters of this volume. The definition emphasizes the systemic role of evaluation in that it focuses on the utility and efficiency of the human service network both in terms of specific client need(s) and the range of human service needs within our communities.

TABLE 1.2
Program Evaluation: A Working Definition

Program Evaluation
A process of making reasonable judgments about program:
 • Effort
 • Effectiveness
 • Efficiency
 • Adequacy
Based on systematic data collection and analysis
Designed for use in
 • Program management
 • External accountability
 • Future planning
Includes special focus on:
 • Accessibility
 • Acceptability
 • Comprehensiveness
 • Integration of services
 • Awareness
 • Availability
 • Continuity
 • Cost of services

REFERENCE NOTES

1. Department of Health, Education, and Welfare. *Interim report of the FY 1973, DHEW Services Integration R & D Task Force,* 1973.
2. O'Donnell, E. *Organization for state administered resource programs in Rhode Island.* Report to the General Assembly by the Special Legislative Commission to Study Social Services, Rhode Island, June 1969.
3. Project Share, P.O. Box 2309, Rockville, Maryland 20852.
4. Purvis, T. *Toward integrated human services.* Proceedings of the Services Integration Capacity Building Conference. San Francisco, November 1974.
5. Richardson, E. L. *A proposed strategy for HEW services reform.* Memorandum of the Secretary of Health, Education, and Welfare, December 23, 1971.
6. Richardson, E. L. *Responsibility and responsiveness (II): A report on the HEW potential for the seventies.* Memorandum of the Secretary of Health, Education, and Welfare, January 18, 1973.
7. Weinberger, C. W. *Fiscal year 1976 budget.* Statement of the Secretary of Health, Education, and Welfare to Congress, February 1975.
8. While such additional unpublished literature is not plentiful, the reader may find interesting the materials from the Human Services Coordination Alliance, 916 Brown Education Center, 675 River City Mall, Louisville, Kentucky 40202.

REFERENCES

Baker, F. From community mental health to human service ideology, *American Journal of Public Health,* 1974, *64,* 576–581.
Baker, F., & Broskowski, A. The search for integrality: New organizational forms for human services. In D. Harshbarger & R. F. Maley (Eds.), *Behavior analysis and systems analysis: An integrative approach to mental health programs.* Kalamazoo, Michigan: Behaviordelia, 1974.
Broskowski, A., & Baker, F. Professional, organizational and social barriers to primary prevention. *American Journal of Orthopsychiatry,* 1974, *44,* 707–719.

Council of State Governments. *Human services integration: State functions in implementation.* Lexington, Kentucky: Council of State Governments, 1974.

Department of Health, Education, and Welfare. *A common thread of service: An historical guide to HEW.* Washington, D. C.: Office of the Secretary, Office of Public Information, U. S. Department of Health, Education, and Welfare, 1970.

Department of Health, Education, and Welfare. *Integration of human services in HEW: An evaluation of services integration projects* (Vol. I). (DHEW Publication No. SRS 73-02012.) Washington, D. C.: U. S. Government Printing Office, 1972.

Falkson, J. L. Minor skirmish in a monumental struggle: HEW's analysis of mental health services. *Policy Analysis,* 1976, *2,* 93–119.

Gage, R. W. Integration of human service delivery systems. *Public Welfare,* 1976, *34*(1), 27–33.

Hersch, C. Social history, mental health, and community control. *American Psychologist,* 1972, *27,* 749–754.

Horst, P., Nay, J., Scanlon, J. W., & Wholey, J. S. Program management and the federal evaluator. *Public Administration Review,* 1974, *34,* 300–308.

Kahn, R. L., Katz, D., & Gutek, B. Bureaucratic encounters—An evaluation of government services. *Applied Behavioral Science,* 1976, *12*(2), 178–198.

Kirk, S. A., & Greenley, J. R. Denying or delivering services? *Social Work,* 1974, *19,* 439–447.

Klein, D. C. Developing human services in new communities. In H. C. Schulberg & F. Baker (Eds.), *Developments in human services* (Vol. II). New York: Behavioral Publications, 1975.

Long, N. A model for coordinating human services. *Administration in Mental Health,* 1974, Summer, 21–27.

March, M. The neighborhood center concept. *Public Welfare,* 1968, *26,* 97–111.

Riecken, H. W., & Boruch, R. F. (Eds.). *Social experimentation: A method for planning and evaluating social intervention.* New York: Academic Press, 1974.

Rivlin, A. *Systematic thinking for social action.* Washington, D. C.: The Brookings Institution, 1971.

Roos, N. P. Evaluation, quasi-experimentation, and public policy. In J. A. Caporaso & L. L. Roos, Jr. (Eds.), *Quasi-experimental approaches: Testing theory and evaluating policy.* Evanston, Illinois: Northwestern University Press, 1973.

Rosenthal, G. The economics of human services. In H. C. Schulberg & F. Baker (Eds.), *Developments in human services* (Vol. II). New York: Behavioral Publications, 1975.

Snow, E. R. *The islands of Boston harbor.* New York: Dodd, Meade, 1971.

Spencer, L. The federal approach to services integration. *The Urban and Social Change Review* (Boston College Graduate School of Social Work), 1974, *7,* 7–13.

Strickland, S. *Politics, science, and dread disease: A short history of United States medical research policy.* Cambridge, Massachusetts: Harvard University Press, 1972.

Suchman, E. A. *Evaluative research: Principles and practice in public service and social action programs.* New York: Russell Sage Foundation, 1967.

The Human Ecology Institute. *The design of human service systems: An overview.* Boston: The Human Ecology Institute, 1975.

Ullman, J. C., & Huber, G. P. *The local job bank program: Performance, structure, and direction.* Lexington, Massachusetts: Lexington Books, 1973.

Weiss, C. H. (Ed.). *Evaluating action programs.* Boston: Allyn & Bacon, 1972.

Wholey, J. S. What can we actually get from program evaluation? *Policy Sciences,* 1972, *3,* 361–369.

Wholey, J. S., Scanlon, J. W., Duffy, H. G., Fukumoto, J. S., & Vogt, L. M. *Federal evaluation policy: Analyzing the effects of public programs.* Washington, D. C.: The Urban Institute, 1970.

Yessian, M., & Broskowski, A. Generalists in human service systems: Their problems and prospects. *Social Service Review,* 1977, *51,* 265–288.

2

EVALUATION IN THE CONTEXT
OF DEVELOPMENTS
IN HUMAN SERVICES

Harold W. Demone, Jr., Herbert C. Schulberg, and Anthony Broskowski

The current emphasis upon human services evaluation seems timely and promising to some but naive and misguided to others. The merits of these differing perspectives on program accountability and assessment can best be determined by relating pressures for evaluation to the broader array of ideologies and trends affecting service delivery. Through such an analysis it becomes clear that evaluation's impact is inexorably linked to the multiple forces simultaneously reshaping conceptual definitions and program priorities for persons in need. The purpose of this chapter, therefore, is to review contemporary trends in human services, since these developments provide the framework within which program evaluation seeks to grow and flourish.

WHAT ARE HUMAN SERVICE PROGRAMS?

Most private and public organizations are designed to satisfy the demands of our society yet only some are considered part of the human services system. Generally, human services are defined as those public and private programs, profit and nonprofit, specifically designed and formally organized to alleviate individual or family problems, or to fulfill human needs in the areas of personal growth and development (Demone & Harshbarger, 1974; Schulberg, Baker, & Roen, 1973). Although we would classify education as a human service, we would exclude school construction from this category. Similarly, specific transportation services for the elderly would be considered a human service, but general transportation services and highway construction would be excluded

Even within these definitional constraints, human services are a major industry when measured by any of the usual business yardsticks. In size of all American industries, recreation is the largest, education second, health third, and defense only fourth. In fact, over the past several years, the health field has been the fastest growing of the nation's major economic forces. Thus, the delivery of organized human services now consumes billions of dollars, and involves millions of consumers and only somewhat fewer providers. It likely consumes 40% of the gross national product.

Industrialization has created social and geographic mobility patterns that severely hamper the extended family's ability to meet the basic human needs. If social intervention is to occur, it becomes increasingly necessary for many of these functions to be assumed by nonfamilial, formally organized, and specialized agencies. As society has expanded its sanction for the range of human conditions requiring and deserving collective rather than personal solutions, it has traditionally established categorical programs to meet discrete needs. Each program, with its particular special interest and/or technology, identified its clientele on the basis of such varying criteria as geographic residence, economic condition, nature of the focal problem, common group membership, etc. The more narrowly a caregiving agency defined its services and clientele, the more specialized the staffing pattern it developed. Thousands of publicly and voluntarily supported agencies are providers of expert help, and by the early 1970s most communities were liberally dotted with a multitude of categoric but unconnected health, education, and social welfare resources. These categorical organizations, with few exceptions, have been sponsored and financed by varying combinations of federal, state and local governments, and private associations. For example, public welfare systems arose around the needs of low-income children and aged, and were principally oriented toward providing financial support.

The problems resulting from the myriad contemporary categorical programs can be illustrated by an analysis of how well child guidance clinics have met children's mental health needs. For many decades, the programs of these clinics were shaped by psychoanalytic concepts that narrowly defined professional practice, encouraging little deviation in clinical technique to suit individual children. On a policy basis, these clinics focused on school-age children and utilized intake practices that excluded adolescents beyond the age of 16. Staff and treatment orientation, in general, were such that they most effectively served the children of well-motivated, middle- and upper-class families possessing strong internal resources. The children of lower-class families with unstable community relationships and meager psychological and material resources fared far less well, even if they managed to get inside this limited treatment system. Furthermore, child guidance clinic staffs were often ineffective in collaborating with the other community caregivers needed to resolve the multiple family problems that were frequently observed in connection with the child's emotional difficulties.

In general, the proliferation of categorically delimited programs has resulted in tremendous complexity, rigidity, inefficiency, ineffectiveness, and incalculable red tape. In addition to the duplicative overhead costs of managing separate programs delivering similar services to overlapping clientele, a great many persons with multiple problems find it difficult, if not impossible, to wend their way through the maze of different agencies (Spencer, 1974). Interorganizational relationships among agencies are absent or neutral at best, and competitive for limited resources at worst. Like agencies seldom refer clients to each other.

Despite these problems, we continue to witness continual pressures to create additional specialized and categorical service programs. Such proliferation persists, probably because of our greater capacity to react to special interest group demands than to determine proactively overall priorities for the allocation of limited resources (Lynn & Salasin, 1974). Furthermore, in order for human service organizations to be established and survive, it is necessary for legislative bodies or other formally organized community groups to appropriate monies for their support. Therefore, funds have been most readily appropriated for those problem areas that could be empirically verified, societally sanctioned, and that possess the potential for reaching some clearly identified constituency. This reactive orientation toward social welfare problems and the need to maintain a consumer constituency have been major factors in the development of categorical human service nonsystems that are remedially rather than preventively oriented (Broskowski & Baker, 1974; Demone & Harshbarger, 1974). Recent debates about social welfare and national health insurance amply illustrate these dynamic principles at work.

As a consequence of the fragmentation, inefficiency, and discontinuity of the categorical approaches, a countertrend has taken root during the past decade. Now there is an increasing tendency to designate the wide variety of educational, health, and social welfare interventions as general human services. This tendency reflects both a discontent with categorical programming, as well as a recognition of the many common elements underlying both the presented problems and the helping actions of diverse professional and non-professional caregivers. As a result, the long-adhered-to distinctions between the problems germane to a psychiatric clinic and a family services agency, or the traditional distinctions between the functions of different mental health professionals have become increasingly artificial. "Developmental disabilities" subsumes a number of handicaps. Many agencies have drastically revised their intake policies and clinical practices accordingly. Neighboring child guidance clinics and adult psychiatric clinics are being reorganized as combined family-oriented facilities, and agencies that previously excluded alcoholics, drug addicts, juvenile delinquents, and other special problem cases now routinely accept such individuals. In general, there has been an attempt to make all organized human services more accessible, continuous, and comprehensive (Department of Health, Education, and Welfare, 1972).

WHERE IS THE HUMAN SERVICES INDUSTRY GOING?

The types and levels of human services provided to the residents of a community stem from the complex interaction of many factors, which have been categorized by Demone and Schulberg (1975) as (*a*) evolving ideologies and social values, (*b*) emerging technologies, (*c*) changing administrative practices, (*d*) modified program structures, and (*e*) altered manpower utilization patterns. The remainder of this chapter reviews the trends associated with each of these interrelated categories so that the concerned program evaluator can maintain a sensitivity and appreciation for the many factors significant to local human services.

IDEOLOGIES AND SOCIAL VALUES

The fundamental characteristics of any society are evident in the values and assumptions through which it determines what is right and important for helping its citizens. Specific social values differ with regard to stability and degree of popular acceptance. Despite the homogenizing effects of increased mobility and improved means of communication and transportation, this country is still composed of heterogeneous populations retaining widely diverse values, interests, and life-styles. It is not unusual for the preferences and assumptions of one segment of society to be in direct conflict with those of other segments. For example, high- and low-income groups view governmental spending for human services very differently. The former may oppose public welfare programs and guaranteed annual incomes; the latter are often in favor of such interventions. Consequently, human services program planning must seek to satisfy the value assumptions of one group while recognizing that such activities may contradict the fundamental premises guiding the desires of other community groups. The design of human services is further complicated by the fact that the values of various segments of the population often are not conscious or explicit. In addition, the value assumptions guiding decision making are likely to change over time in relation to the shifting dominance exercised by various societal subgroups. Ideologies also come into vogue to rationalize or make comprehensible a complex set of activities that are already taking place for many reasons (Baker, 1974; Schulberg & Baker, 1969).

Recognizing that ideologies and social values are neither universal nor eternal, we can identify six contemporary belief trends that are helping to mold our current and future human services delivery systems. Most of these trends have their genesis at the community and state levels, since it is there that people express their personal concerns and responsive actions must be taken. Some belief trends are quickly promoted to the national level and adopted throughout the country as well, so that they become even more powerful influences upon local programs.

The following belief trends are deemed as the currently significant ones for human services:

1. *Equity of Care*

Debates over whether people should be provided human services as a right or privilege have generally subsided; even the American Medical Association has abandoned its traditional precept that health care is a privilege rather than a right. Most politicians and citizens now agree that equity of care in terms of availability, accessibility, and quality is fundamental in a democratic society, and various efforts are being made to eliminate a "two track" caregiving system. For example, the national health insurance proposals now being considered by Congress are intended to provide low-income persons with fiscal equity as they seek necessary health care.

2. *Personal Choice*

Closely related to the growing national belief in the equity of care is the wide support now evident for a person's right to participate in the choice of a clinically and psychologically relevant treatment plan. No longer are professional judgments sacrosanct; on the contrary, the judicial and legislative systems increasingly are supporting the client's right to be informed about the nature of his or her problems and to participate in the choice of suggested remediations. A pregnant woman's decision of whether or not to have an abortion, and a terminally ill person's selecting an earlier rather than later death are examples of personal choice more commonly exercised today than a decade ago.

3. *Citizen Participation*

Not only are we accepting the contemporary value system that permits personal choice of human services, but we are also accepting the merits of lay determination of program policy. Traditional distinctions between professional expertise and lay contributions are becoming increasingly blurred, and citizen participation in the establishment and operation of human services is now widespread. Indeed, citizen control is more the rule than the exception in contemporary human services agencies.

4. *Deinstitutionalization*

Socially deviant and chronically ill persons were, for decades, managed or cared for in large and impersonal facilities, designed and located as to minimize community responsibility and involvement. A more compassionate set of contemporary values has modified society's impulse to extrude such individuals as the tuberculous, chronically and mentally ill, developmentally disabled, juvenile and adult offender. More personalized, "human scale" alternative caregiving arrangements are now available in many communities. As a consequence, the viability of such large and remote institutions as mental hospitals is waning.

5. *Decriminalization*

Closely associated with society's diminished belief in the value of extruding deviant persons is its greater willingness to acknowledge that therapeutic rather than punitive measures may be more beneficial for both society and the offending person. Thus, in recent years, an increasing number of objectionable behavior patterns are coming within the purview of a community's human services network for remediation rather than being handled within its criminal justice system. More than 20 states eliminated the crime of public intoxication between 1970 and 1975, and their alcoholic citizens are being treated in human service facilities rather than in jails. The personal possession or use of minor drugs has been similarly decriminalized in many jurisdictions, and the responsibility for treatment of drug addiction in these areas has shifted to human services agencies.

6. *Profit-Making*

The human services field traditionally has been viewed as primarily the realm of socially conscious academicians, social workers, physicians, and others whose fundamental value system revolved around the alleviation of human suffering rather than the achievement of personal fiscal gain. However, with the geometric growth rate experienced by the human services field in recent years, its operations increasingly have come to resemble that of a "socioindustrial complex." An inevitable correlate of such growth is that profit-making has been legitimized by local and national policysetters. Proprietary organizations such as nursing homes, day care centers, and homemaker services are mushrooming in many communities, and they are providing formidable competition to well-established nonprofit public and voluntary human services organizations.

When taken in composite fashion, these contemporary ideologies and social values may certainly be judged as increasingly liberal, democratic, and universal in character. As a result, the scope and quality of human services have been moved in various new and sometimes uncharted directions. Although pressures from society's more conservative factions restrain implementation of some of the more radical program proposals, liberal ideologies nevertheless are significantly altering the manner in which society responds to human distress.

TECHNOLOGICAL INNOVATIONS

The second major set of forces affecting contemporary human services is society's level of technological sophistication in dealing with given problems. When scientific knowledge exists about the etiology and treatment of distressing conditions, remedial or even preventive interventions may be undertaken. When such knowledge is lacking and interventions are not possible, custodialism often is the result. It is fair to assert that all of the human services, and particularly health care, have benefited tremendously in recent years from scientific and technological advances (Lanyon, 1974). Some of these innovations are relatively inexpensive and can be widely utilized; others are highly expensive and can be applied only in selective instances. Nevertheless, new standards of human services care become established on the basis of even rarified technological advances, and they inevitably become the yardstick against which all relevant programs are assessed (Collen, 1974).

Technological innovations generally are applauded for the more effective care which they make possible and for their alleviation of human distress. When widely applicable, they enhance such social values as equity of care. There are instances, however, when technological advances conflict with contemporary ideologies and values, creating difficult situations requiring complex, even controversial, solutions. For example, recent refinements of behavioral therapy techniques and psychopharmacological agents have made it possible to rehabilitate many persons previously deemed chronically maladjusted. These efforts occasionally, however, violate the previously described social value of "personal choice," as when negative reinforcement procedures and tranquilizing drugs are utilized with inmates of correctional facilities. Thus, psychiatric projects supported with Federal Law Enforcement Assistance Administration funds to reduce violent behavior among prison inmates have provoked the wrath of civil libertarians. Under these circumstances, the conflicting needs of the caregiver and the client must be resolved. In contrast to earlier times when the client's needs would have been bypassed in favor of the caregiver's, the balance increasingly is being altered in the client's direction.

Finally, even though we most often associate human service technological advances with new intricate equipment, refined drugs, and even novel interpersonal therapies, we should be aware that long-available legal procedures are having an increasingly potent impact upon the nature of services being provided to clients. Troubled groups or their representatives are turning to such legal technologies as class action suits demanding due process and equal protection. Many state and federal courts are ruling in favor of the plaintiffs. For example, publicly oriented psychiatric facilities have been ordered to provide treatment to court-committed patients who otherwise must be discharged. The mentally retarded residing in state schools have benefited from similar rulings about the right to treatment, with the result that censuses in mental hospitals and schools for the retarded have been reduced even further in recent years. Class action suits in the correctional field pose similar threats to the maintenance of punitively oriented penal institutions. These legal actions already are influencing administrative and programmatic patterns away from custodialism in the direction of greater efforts to rehabilitate inmates within community-based facilities.

ADMINISTRATIVE PRACTICES

The third set of forces affecting present and future human services are the new administrative practices developing within, or being imposed upon, the organizations providing these services. Except for the unusually sophisticated human services agency, administrative considerations have generally been secondary to clinical predilections in determining program directions and practices. Even though clinicians may deny their power in determining organizational priorities, the wishes and priorities of service personnel have held greater sway than those of managers and the latter often resort to negativism and recalcitrance in order to make their influence felt.

While such management–treatment tensions continue to prevail in many human services organizations for reasons both national in origin and uniquely local in rationale, fresh administrative practices are nevertheless emerging with significant implications for human services delivery. Among this trend's several key elements are accountability and evaluation techniques, management controls, planning procedures, and personnel practices. What are the key features of each element as they impinge upon human services?

1. *Accountability and Evaluation Techniques*

Most human services traditionally have failed to formulate goals and objectives lending themselves to subsequent evaluation of achievement. The intangible nature of most human services certainly contributes to this situation, but the lack of goal clarity and evaluation has been maintained through society's deference to professionals in areas wherein most laypersons are ignorant. Furthermore, most national programs created by federal legislation are notoriously lacking in measurable goal attainment criteria, because the legislative process frequently requires ambiguity and generalities to achieve the necessary congressional consensus (Mogulof, 1973). Program interventions are usually vaguely defined, not linked to measurable outcomes or ultimate impact by testable assumptions, and then operated by "pseudomanagers" who lack power or incentives to control resources or implement evaluation findings (Horst, Nay, Scanlon, & Wholey, 1974). Thus, for many years, the human services operated beyond the pale of public scrutiny. In the past decade, however, the public's blind acceptance of professional assurances and government sponsorship has changed to a chary wariness, even suspiciousness, and evaluation schemata are being imposed upon human services endeavors. For some years now, federally funded contracts and grants have required that evaluative procedures be incorporated as integral elements of the total program; at the operational level, this mandate is increasingly moving from the stage of lip service to actual practice. Clinicians and administrators are engaging in creative dialogues concerning the concepts and techniques of program evaluation, and they are forging new alliances if for no other reason than that of mutual support against external threats. The subsequent chapters of this book are devoted to a more complete explication of these complicated issues.

2. *Management Controls*

The willingness of human services administrators and clinicians to function within the principle of accountability has necessitated the growing use of other relevant management controls. Thus, human services agencies have moved in recent years from simple cost-accounting procedures and line item budgets to more sophisticated program budgets and management information systems. Human services practitioners are identifying the discrete caregiving elements comprising their total effort and are generating appropriate data about the clients, personnel, and costs associated with each component. On this basis, operations research, systems analysis, and other sophisticated managerial control mechanisms long used by business and industry can now be applied to the human services as well. Finally, management controls are also being exercised through reorganizations intended to place proper responsibility in the hands of executives at various operating levels. This process is reflected in recurrent cycles of program centralization and decentralization. Since different time periods require different administrative models, the reorganization of human services must be accepted as an ongoing process if managerial effectiveness is to be enhanced.

3. *Planning Procedures*

Short- and long-term planning procedures are assuming a new legitimacy within the human services as client, program, and fiscal projections become more firmly rooted in hard information rather than resting primarily upon theoretical predictions. Through ever more complex computer programs, innumerable variables can be manipulated and huge clusters of data meaningfully analyzed. Along with the expanded use of technological decision-making apparatus, the planning of human services at all program levels must also utilize the inputs of key citizens reflecting their communities' humanistic concerns. Planners and administrators are challenged to maintain a balance between these impersonal and personalized contributions; an overreliance upon either can produce misleading projections.

4. *Personnel Practices*

As primarily nonprofit corporations, the human services developed personnel systems which by and large avoided the adversary relationship intrinsic to management–labor interaction in much of the business world. This pattern of pseudoamicability was sanctioned by human services personnel who thought that their personal and guild interests could best be served through national or local professional-type organizations rather than by organized labor. However, unions are now becoming increasingly successful in rallying to their banners nonprofessional and even professional human services workers, and the entire character of personnel–management relations has undergone dramatic changes in the past decade. Local chapters of the AFL–CIO State, County, and Municipal Employees Union are now the recognized representatives for many nonprofessional employees in publicly operated agencies; and union recruiting has become a major administrative dilemma in such voluntarily operated facilities as general hospitals. Grossly underpaid lower level employees are demanding dramatically improved salary schedules. The fact that human services agencies are usually nonprofit in nature is deemed by them to be irrelevant.

It is also of interest to note that the unionizing of publicly employed personnel is emerging at the same time that program administrators are attempting to reduce the near-stranglehold exercised over public human services by civil service and merit system controls. Since these two trends are in many ways antithetical, heightened management–union friction can be expected. Such tensions are already evident in those instances where the phasedown of large custodial facilities such as mental hospitals and training schools for delinquents has or will eliminate thousands of existing jobs. The continued reduction of institutionally-based human services and the expansion of community-centered ones may well depend upon a successful resolution of this knotty personnel problem. Desperately needed are feasible personnel incentive systems based upon performance appraisal criteria.

PROGRAM STRUCTURES

Local human services agencies have long shared common service goals and clients. Nevertheless, interactions and cooperative ventures to ensure comprehensive care are minimal when organizational concerns rather than client benefits are paramount. One of the most pressing problems facing planners, clinicians, and administrators, therefore, is that of linking the many caregiving elements comprising the human services field. Since no single agency can provide the total array of help required to meet the diverse problems troubling people, organizational and administrative barriers to care must be minimized.

If the previously described trend toward accountability is to be accelerated, how should human services be organized so that client needs will be met more fully and efficiently? An ideal service model must be consistent with the ideologies and social values dominating the contemporary scene, and it must build upon the technologies and administrative practices now being injected into human services practices. More specifically, the service model should create integrative mechanisms to ease the flow of clients, resources, and information among various service subsystems. What strategies are emerging to meet this goal?

1. *Purchase of Service*

The distressed person's lack of personal resources with which to purchase human services in the private sector produced during the Roosevelt era of the 1930s a geometric expansion of publicly supported and *operated* programs. New Deal philosophy, as expounded by Harry Hopkins and others, viewed direct governmental involvement and administration as necessary and appropriate, and these precepts guided the funding and delivery of human services during the subsequent three decades. In more recent years, there has been a significant departure from this long-standing philosophy. Increasingly, federal, state, and local governments are removing themselves from the direct delivery of personal services, and concentrating on the functions of planning, funding, standard-setting, regulating, monitoring, and evaluating. Governments are now subsidizing human services in the voluntary and private sectors through grants-in-aid and purchase-of-service contracts. In some instances, clients are provided vouchers that permit them to negotiate arrangements directly with personally selected caregivers. Under the well-established Medicare and Medicaid programs, public welfare clients and the medically indigent are no longer forced to use municipal health services, and they can turn instead to private practitioners and voluntary hospitals. The trend toward purchase-of-services can also be expected to affect dental care and legal assistance as prepayment and third-party fiscal arrangements become more common in these areas as well.

If the trend toward limiting governmental involvement to that of fiscal agent rather than service provider continues, the present nature of human services will be dramatically altered. The nonprofit sector of service agencies will experience new growth as it assumes responsibilities in areas where previous involvement was either limited or constrained. For example, the "Donated Funds" program authorized by the 1967 Amendments to the Social Security Act has significantly expanded such voluntary agency programs as day care, children's protective services, and camping, as Departments of Public Welfare write purchase-of-service contracts for low income clients unable to afford these benefits. An obvious benefit of this trend will be a reduction of government's inherent conflict of interest when operating and regulating its own human services (Broskowski, Demone, & Kaplan, 1973). By purchasing rather than operating services, public agencies will be in a better position to play a standard-setting and regulatory role. The government's ability to demand evaluation data will also increase through this transition.

2. Decentralization and Devolution

The optimal geographic and governmental level for service delivery and administrative responsibility is often a matter of controversy. Demone and Schulberg (1971) have reviewed the factors upon which such decisions should be made, and have suggested guidelines relevant to the human services. Regardless of the differing possibilities, the clearcut trend in recent years has been toward geographical decentralization and governmental devolution (i.e., shifting decision responsibility to lower echelons of government); in some program areas, such as mental health, these trends have assumed groundswell proportions. The federal government under former President Nixon strongly supported the shift of responsibility for human services to local government, and general revenue sharing was one of the Nixon administration's most notable achievements in domestic policy. Many federally supported categorical grant programs are being eliminated, and state and local governments must themselves accept and assign priorities for human services. Executive actions by President Nixon furthered this process even when congressional support was lacking. For example, President Nixon established 10 federal regional councils, and, as an experiment in local devolution, mayors in selected cities are encouraged to review and comment on *all* federal grants.

Thus, considerable momentum has been generated (a) for decreasing the power and influence of Washington-based federal agencies, (b) for elevating the influence of regional federal offices and governors, and (c) for substantially increasing the power of general purpose local government. With this shift, the many "special interest" constituencies that traditionally have exerted a potent influence upon national human services policy—for example, the handicapped and aged—will find their leverage significantly attenuated. Rather than lobbying a single federal government, or even 50 state agencies, special interest groups will be required to direct their messages to thousands of general purpose local governments for a continuing share of public funds.

The movement toward more localized decision making addresses problems of citizen and client alienation but, like most solutions in a complex field, it also generates new problems. First, very few human needs can be met within

the limited confines of local geographic bases; the causative factors and reme-
dies for many, perhaps most, human problems are regional if not national in
character. Second, local governments generally are essentially conservative in
nature since their principle constituency is concerned about low tax rates.
Thus, they resist rather than encourage necessary social change, and they limit
rather than increase services to "undesirables." Although on the one hand,
more appropriate decisions may be made about diversified local needs, bureaucratic problems may not necessarily be reduced as the locus of power is moved
closer to the client. Although the personal element can be reasserted and
impersonal administrative vagaries minimized, local petty politics and traditional community prejudices against many of those persons needing human
services assume renewed viability. A recognition of this danger is evident in
the federal government's decision to *centralize* welfare payments to the aged,
blind, and disabled under the Supplemental Security Income Program that
became effective January 1, 1974. Thus income transfer is being centralized
and service management decentralized.

The pressure on organized human service constituencies and agencies will
be to support efforts to use existing funds more effectively. The "guns and
butter" principle, i.e., continued high spending for human services as well as
other domestic and military programs, will find little support. Increased tension, concomitant with pressures to increase "productivity," will trouble the
many professional groups dominating the human services. The net result will
likely be further substantial changes in the current organizational and personnel patterns and practices discussed earlier.

3. *Caregiving Networks*

During the late 1960s and even more so in recent years, human services
administrators have focused on building linkages between existing and newly
planned organizations, rather than seeking to incorporate all relevant services
within a single corporate entity. This approach recognizes that in most communities it will not be fiscally nor practically feasible for an individual facility
to provide by itself all elements of a comprehensive human services program.
In fact, usually most of the services will be already available elsewhere. For
example, the network approach is presently evident in meeting the needs of
such diverse groups as runaway youths and the elderly. After determining the
basic needs of these groups and the essential services for meeting them, a
consortium of agencies divides responsibilities according to their particular
expertise. The use of "interface teams," that include the staff of several agencies to review specific cases, has been particularly helpful in resolving out-
standing problems and in fostering cooperative activities. Since the network
model of human services implicitly accepts the pluralistic nature of American
society, it will become increasingly common as it attempts to maximize our
assets and minimize the deficits of contemporary community patterns.

4. *Self-Help Groups*

A final influence upon the delivery of human services is the rapidly
growing self-help movement (Caplan, 1974; Dumont, 1974). Countless small,
aggressive, nonprofit groups have been spawned in recent years by persons

distressed with a variety of problems. Their efforts are predicated upon the principle that persons with similar needs can help each other as much or more than professionals. The public has been made dramatically aware, for example, of the fiercely independent services initiated and operated by former drug users, and has exhibited unusual largesse in funding these ventures.

Since self-help groups are now an alternative support system to the professionally dominated one, we must devise ways for linking with them when necessary. Despite the self-help movement's general hostility toward, and suspicion of human services professionals and agencies, many persons nevertheless use a variety of helping systems and we must ensure their movement across organizational boundaries in their quest for proper care. Another crucial aspect of the self-help movement's development is that of continued funding, a factor which varies in severity with its programming format. For example, Alcoholics Anonymous services, based upon the program design and strategies of its founders, are fiscally viable. If AA members extend their efforts, however, to incorporate the operation of detoxification centers and halfway houses, they must compete for rather limited funds and subsequently risk the same fiscal crises plaguing professionalized human services agencies.

MANPOWER UTILIZATION PATTERNS

The preceding analysis of evolving human service programs has implicitly considered the manpower requirements associated with varying organizational structures and technological advances. Since optimal manpower utilization is such a key determinant of program success, it is appropriate that we conclude our review of human services developments with a discussion of this issue.

A basic impetus for developing generalized, comprehensive human services systems was growing consumer dissatisfaction with specialized agencies focusing on segmented problems rather than the total person. Service fragmentation and the lack of continuity of care stem from many factors, but surely a key one in any community is the ever-expanding array of highly specialized professionals supported by powerful universities and administrative bureaucracies, guild-oriented licensing regulations, and expensive technologies. Elite professional training programs annually produce new cadres of workers committed to this categorical approach, which is easily maintained in the absence of skilled generalists possessing a broader perspective on client needs. Moreover, strong citizen lobbyists have insisted that separate systems be established for clientele against whom human services caregivers discriminate.

Various solutions to this dilemma have been proposed. Among the most promising are efforts in several states such as Utah and Maine to define far more precisely the objectives for which clients seek assistance and the job tasks required to fulfill these objectives. In reviewing this development, Broskowski and Smith (1974) recognize that the ambiguity of many human service functions makes it difficult to develop a coherent classification scheme that would then permit the aggregating of meaningful job roles. Thus, most jobs currently are based upon professional requirements or idiosyncratic frameworks. However, Broskowski and Smith suggest that if the total number of tasks performed by human services agencies are accurately categorized and computerized, a comprehensive system can be redesigned with specific types of service provided by the most relevant personnel. For example, the "functional job analysis" conducted within Utah's social services agencies identified staff as performing over 600 discrete tasks. Having this information, experts in resource allocation and planning could determine whether to design new jobs by recombining tasks, or whether existing roles should be modified only as new service tasks are identified.

What are the implications of functional job analyses for optimal utilization of specialists and generalists? This question must be considered from many perspectives, including those of administrative accountability, specific client needs, service personnel training opportunities, technological requirements, and funding mechanisms. We suggest that functional job analyses be related to a systemic perspective that maintains a proper balance of specialists and generalists, lest improper overloads strain the total network. Difficulties in achieving this balance are exacerbated, however, by antiquated fiscal policies. Thus, a community mental health center supported by third-party payments may enjoy a surplus of highly trained specialist inpatient staff for whose services insurance reimbursements can be collected, while suffering from a dearth of generalist outreach workers whose services are ineligible for such payments.

SUMMARY

This review of the factors associated with the present and future nature of the human services industry has suggested that administrative and evaluative decision making can be enhanced through an understanding of evolving ideologies and social values, emerging technologies, changing administrative practices, modified program structures, and altered manpower-utilization patterns. Our analysis of these interwoven factors leads us to conclude that after several decades of geometric growth and expansion, the human services are stabilizing, even contracting, in the face of adverse economic conditions. Societal measures to remedy people's problems will be directed at individual vulnerability rather than at the broader array of causative factors residing within society itself. In contrast to wide-ranging "wars on poverty" during the 1960s, the more focused human services interventions of the future will seem palliative in nature. Although our ideologies may thus become less grandiose and ambitious, on the other hand, we may find it easier in the future to evaluate the effectiveness and efficiency of the diverse caregiving interventions we have come to call the human services system.

REFERENCES

Baker, F. From community mental health to human service ideology. *American Journal of Public Health,* 1974, *64,* 576–581.
Broskowski, A., & Baker, F. Professional, social, and organizational barriers to primary prevention. *American Journal of Orthopsychiatry,* 1974, *44,* 707–719.

Broskowski, A., Demone, H., Kaplan, H. The influence of state regulatory processes on mental health programs. *Health Services Report,* 1973, *88,* 562–568.

Broskowski, A., & Smith, T. Manpower development for human service systems. In D. Harshbarger & R. Maley (Eds.), *Behavior analysis and systems analysis: An integrative approach to mental health programs.* Kalamazoo, Michigan: Behaviordelia, 1974.

Caplan, G. *Support systems and community mental health: Lectures on concept development.* New York: Behavioral Science Publications, 1974.

Collen, M. F. *Technology and the health care systems in the 1980's.* (DHEW Publication No. HSM-73-3016.) Washington, D. C.: U. S. Department of Health, Education, and Welfare, 1974.

Demone, H. W., Jr., & Harshbarger, D. *Issues in the management and planning of human services.* In H. W. Demone, Jr. & D. Harshbarger (Eds.), *A handbook of human service organizations.* New York: Behavioral Publications, 1974.

Demone, H. W., Jr., & Schulberg, H. Human services trends in the mid-1970's. *Social Casework,* 1975, *56,* 268–279.

Demone, H. W., Jr., & Schulberg, H. Regionalization of health and welfare services. In R. Morris (Ed.), *Encyclopedia of social work* (Sixteenth Issue). New York: National Association of Social Workers, 1971.

Department of Health, Education, and Welfare. *Integration of human services in HEW* (Vol. I). Washington, D. C.: U. S. Government Printing Office, 1972.

Dumont, M. Self-help treatment programs. *American Journal of Psychiatry,* 1974, *131,* 631–635.

Horst, P., Nay, J., Scanlon, J. W., & Wholey, J. S. Program management and the federal evaluator. *Public Administration Review,* 1974, *34,* 300–308.

Lanyon, R. I. *The new technology of mental health care.* (Final Report of Grant No. MH20233.) Rockville, Maryland: National Institute of Mental Health, February 1974.

Lynn, L. E., & Salasin, S. Human services: Should we, can we make them available to everyone. *Evaluation,* 1974, Special Issue (Spring), 4–5.

Mogulof, M. Elements of a special-revenue-sharing proposal for the social services. Goal setting, decategorization, planning, and evaluation. *The Social Service Review,* 1973, *47,* 593–604.

Schulberg, H., & Baker, F. Community mental health: The belief system of the 1960's. *Psychiatric Opinion,* 1969, *6,* 14–26.

Schulberg, H., Baker, F., & Roen, S. (Eds.). *Developments in human services* (Vol. I). New York: Behavioral Publications, 1973.

Spencer, L. The federal approach to service integration. *The Urban and Social Change Review,* 1974, *7,* 7–13.

3

THE ORGANIZATIONAL CONTEXT
OF PROGRAM EVALUATION

Anthony Broskowski and Jean Driscoll

During the past 20 years the rapid growth of government funded programs has made the organization and delivery of human services a major sector of the American economy (Quie, 1974). At the same time, the rate and diversity of this growth has spurred enormous organizational complexity and stimulated confusion and doubts about the value and effectiveness of the services. More recently, inflation and increased diversification in program funding sources have created pressures for better cost control, service efficiency, and improved fiscal accountability.

During this same period there has been an increase in the extent to which services have been delivered within the context of formal organizations. Yet it is alarming to note that the management of most human service organizations has remained at a level of sophistication analogous to that of the neighborhood small business. Most frequently the organizational leaders of human service agencies emerged from the ranks of direct service professions. In this tradition the most capable service providers were promoted to administrative positions for which they had little or no formal preparation. When pressures for evaluation and accountability initially materialized, managers of organized services turned to social scientists to provide models and technologies for program evaluation. In response, social scientists tended to restrict their interests to the outcomes of specific services delivered to individual clients. Consequently, administrators and social scientists alike generally ignored program management and methods of organization as those factors relate to the effectiveness and efficiency of services.

In more recent years, managers, funders, and evaluators have come to recognize the important effects that organizational variables can have on the effectiveness and costs of human services. Because program evaluation is now urgently needed within the context of organized service-delivery systems or institutions, program evaluators must have reasonable models of how organizational systems function, or, more simply, some useful ways to think about organizations.

The need to understand principles of organizational structure and process emerges from several considerations. The evaluator must be able to comprehend organizational realities in order to be responsive to managerial and organizational issues. Conducting complex program evaluations requires organizational and management skills. Also, the multiple methodologies and processes of evaluation will frequently be used within an organization for reasons that go beyond the more obvious concerns for program effectiveness or efficiency. For example, the evaluation process may be implemented within an organization for purposes of internal conflict resolution, integration of fragmented structure, or as a contribution to long-range planning. For these reasons the program evaluator, working to evaluate programs delivered by organizations, must understand something about the intricate dynamics of organizational life.

This chapter addresses principles of organizational structure and process with particular focus on the evaluation of program productivity and efficiency. The chapter begins with a brief review of some historical models of organizational design in order to provide a basis for understanding their inadequacies when applied to current management problems. Older models of organization and management that were sufficient for small agencies within stable communities can no longer carry the burdens of navigating contemporary human service agencies through their turbulent environments. Following a review of selected principles from classical organizational theory, we present (a) alternative organizational design models, and (b) concepts taken from general open systems theory applied to organizational settings. It is concluded that an open systems model of organizational life is particularly compatible with the specific concerns and multiple methodologies of the program evaluator.

An overriding theme in the approach of this chapter is that human service agencies must be managed more effectively so as to make their services more *productive, efficient,* and *effective.* Furthermore, it is argued that greater productivity and efficiency are likely to emerge from management systems that are built upon principles of flexible and nonhierarchical structures, where information flow and evaluation results provide much of the basis for organizational control and decision making. This argument is based upon our observation that too many human service agencies have become more enthralled with processes than with products or services, and that too few agencies are sufficiently accountable to the purposes they were designed to serve. It is stressed that management systems within large and complex agencies must promote task accomplishment, production efficiency, and program accountability. At the same time, management systems must avoid the rigid and hierarchical control procedures that lead to costly morale deterioration and decreased responsiveness to constantly changing client and community needs and demands. The major thesis is that program evaluation must be planned and implemented within the broader context of these organizational structures and management processes.

CLASSICAL ORGANIZATIONAL THEORY

Classical theories of management place a heavy emphasis on formal and hierarchical structures to design and manage organizations. Clearly delineated lines of authority and functional responsibility are viewed as essential ingredients of sound management. The classical approach highlights such variables as the manager's span of control (i.e., the number of persons the manager controls) and the design of a table of organization to specify all of the necessary internal connections.

The emphasis on structural variables brings with it a keen awareness of the alternative ways to differentiate a complex organization. Large and complex organizations, for example, could conceptually and operationally differentiate themselves into smaller operating units on the basis of such dimensions as time (e.g., the assembly line), technology (e.g., production, marketing, sales, and purchasing), or territory (e.g., the east coast branch, the west coast branch). Regardless of the dimension used, the classical solution to problems of large size is reduction to smaller subunits. The answer to complexity is simplification through differentiated structures and processes, using a variety of classification schemes (Miller, 1959).

Recognizing the need to coordinate these differentiated units, classical management theories provide a variety of mechanisms for holding the pieces together. Overlapping committees, companywide policies, and superordinate goals and ideologies are frequently recommended as integrative mechanisms. The most trusted and frequently used mechanism, however, is the hierarchical table of organization with well-defined lines of communication and control.

These integrative mechanisms are not without problems, but the values inherent in centralized control are judged to outweigh such disadvantages as delays in decision making, blockage of clear communications, diversion of top executives' attention to trivia, low morale, and a shortened and limited time–space perspective at lower levels of the hierarchy. Although authority is to be delegated in centralized systems, there is typically a mismatch between operational responsibilities and necessary authority. Frequently, decision making occurs at levels in the organization that are remote from the sources of most valid information. Such errors and mismatches, however, can usually be corrected in time if speed and flexibility are not critical because the organization exists in a relatively stable environment.

FUTURE SHOCK AND ENVIRONMENTAL AWARENESS

The increasing rate of societal change has been dramatically described in the popular literature as "future shock." A great deal of this accelerated change phenomena has arisen directly out of our rapid growth in population, resources, and new technologies. The human services sector of the economy has not escaped the consequences of future shock. This exponential rate of change has increased our awareness of the complex and turbulent environments in which human service agencies must operate.

Environmental instability can be seen as a product of at least three factors: (a) the rate of change in the external organizations and groups with which an agency interacts, (b) the degree of interdependence the organization has with diverse constituencies, and (c) the nature of its interorganizational commitments (Osborn & Hunt, 1974). Using a variety of measures of these three factors we are likely to find that most human service agencies are operating within increasingly turbulent environments.

Osborn and Hunt (1974) point out that "while an organization's environment is composed of an infinite set of elements outside the boundaries of the organization, other organizations, associations of individuals, and broad forces represent important segments of the organization's environment [p. 231]." Osborn and Hunt group these elements into three broad categories: (a) macro-environment, (b) aggregation environment, and (c) task environment. The *macro-environment* is the broad and general "cultural context" of the organization's geographical area that will influence its character. The *aggregation environment* is defined as those associations, professional groups, and other interest groups operating throughout the general environment. "This environmental segment is perhaps the most difficult to define and analyze operationally, since associations, interest groups, and constituencies not only overlap, but form and reform in attempts to alter and/or adjust to macro-environment conditions [p. 232]." Osborn and Hunt go on to state that the *task environment* ". . . of a given organization consists of those organizations with which it must interact to grow and survive [p. 233]."

Useful typologies for describing organizational environments have been developed by Emery and Trist (1965), Lawrence and Lorsch (1969), Terreberry (1968), and Thompson (1967). Such dimensions as environmental stability, diversity, and predictive reactivity were combined with other dimensions by Jurkovich (1974) to yield a typology for the classification of organizational environments that yields 64 "types" of environments.

The environment of an organization will influence to some extent such factors as managerial autonomy, priority setting, and its internal flexibility or rigidity. For example, the research of Lawrence and Lorsch (1969) indicates that organizational effectiveness is contingent upon the degree to which internal structures and processes are differentiated and integrated to accommodate multiple and rapidly shifting external demands from the task environment.

The increased awareness of the impact of a shifting environment on organizational effectiveness has stimulated the current emphasis on such methodologies as need assessment or other general strategies to monitor an organization's environment. Furthermore, the increased awareness of the importance of organizational environments has led to a reexamination of classical theories of organizational design in light of the realities of modern institutions.

CONTEMPORARY ORGANIZATIONAL THEORIES

Classical organization theory is inadequate in several ways, particularly for contemporary organizations, such as those in the fields of technology and communication, where rapid changes are common (Learned & Sproat, 1966). In developing alternative models, Drucker (1974) identified two earlier models of classical theory: the "functional" design approach that dates back to 1910 and the theories of Henri Fayol (e.g., purchasing, production, sales); and the "federated decentralization" design, which Alfred Sloan used to organize General Motors. Drucker states that both designs are inadequate under many of today's circumstances, which demand new organizing principles. Older designs were suited for single-market firms, whereas many organizations today are multiproduct/service, multitechnology, and multimarket. In these latter types of firms, one will find diverse language and/or logic systems existing within the organization. For example, in a multidisciplinary and multipurpose community mental health center, not all staff will "speak the same language," or use the same theories or treatment methods.

Drucker (1974) suggests three alternative models for contemporary organizational design: team organization, simulated decentralization, and systems structure. *Team organization* is contrasted with the older "functional" model in that the latter assumed that the skills and people were in static departments (production, sales, etc.) and the "work" or "product" flowed through these subunits. In the team approach, one assumes the "product" or "project" is static and skills from various parts of the organization are brought together to work on the project at times and places where it is deemed necessary. *Simulated decentralization* sets up each phase or function of the organization as if it were a single and distinct business with genuine profit and loss responsibilities. With this approach one uses such accounting fictions as transfer prices and cost-based overhead allocations among program-budgets as if these were real exchanges between separate businesses. This latter type of design may make most sense in organizations that are too complex to be functionally organized and too integrated to be truly decentralized, as in the federated decentralization model (e.g., the General Motors model). Simulated decentralization, for example, could work in universities, large hospitals, and government agencies. Finally, Drucker's *systems structure* approach is a combination of the team organization and simulated decentralization models. This approach is based on the National Aeronautics and Space Administration's (NASA) project management model. The NASA model was a prototypical case whereby government, private-profit, and nonprofit organizations collaborated to produce a complex product that depended on more than a single logic or language system.

Forrester (1965; 1975) has also provided a thought-provoking forecast of corporate designs for the future. It is not possible in this brief space to review extensively the stimulating concepts of Forrester's model. However, we will list Forrester's major points. We recommend that the serious student of organizational theory read the original. Forrester prefaces his basic design principles with four "new ideas" that have emerged within organizational theory during the past two decades:

1. Decreasing authoritarian control can increase motivation, innovation, and personal growth and satisfaction.

2. The emphasis on a superior–subordinate basis for control should be replaced by constitutional and democratic forms.

3. Analysis of systems dynamics permits the design of broad policy structures for an organization to enhance both growth and stability.

4. Modern computer and communication technology can stimulate concepts of corporate organization that allow greater flexibility, efficiency, and individual freedom of action.

From these "new ideas" Forrester extrapolates eleven principles that he thinks will characterize profit-making organizations of the future:

1. *Elimination of the Superior–Subordinate Relationship*

Superior control would be replaced by individual self-discipline arising from self-interests created by internal incentives and market mechanisms.

2. *Individual Profit Centers*

Each person or small team is a profit center and a decision point responsible for the success of activities in which the center chooses to engage. A profit center is different from a budget center in that a budget center compares actual costs of activities against promised costs, whereas a profit center compares costs and accomplishments. "In contrast to a budget center, a profit center values activity and resources in terms of the difference (profit) between input costs and a sale price . . . . The incentive is to maximize the difference between cost and value . . . and to reduce expenditure of time and resources where this can be done without a more than corresponding reduction in the value of the product . . . . Rewards [for staff] . . . must depend on profit and not on expenditure rate [Forrester, 1965, p. 7]" which usually forms the basis of rewards for budget centers.

3. *Objective Determination of Compensation*

With individuals or small groups as profit centers it is possible to base compensation and bonuses on more objective measures of performance. In brief, objectivity is attained from the value set on a person's contribution by peers who negotiate for the services of the profit center. For this process to work effectively, there must be sufficient internal flexibility for the person or profit center team to move away or toward alternative internal projects or alignments with other profit centers.

4. *Policy Making Separated from Decision Making*

Policies and decisions are not the same. Policy addresses the general case and provides rules for specific decisions. Four criteria of the policy structure will have important impact on initiative and innovation: (a) freedom from constraining rules, (b) accessibility to the decision maker, (c) source of policy as self or others, and (d) consistency. Policy making should guide decision making, but should be removed from the short-term pressures of operational decisions.

5. *Restructuring through Electronic Data Processing*

The typical mesh network (i.e., numerous repositories and connecting linkages) of information flow within a firm is unreliable, biased through multiple filtering, wasteful of internal energies, and prone to draw attention to internal channels and away from external relationships with the environment. Modern technology allows newer designs of information flow that enhance data accuracy, increase accessibility to decision points, give freedom from rigid internal structuring, and turn attention to the importance of evolving environmental information.

6. *Freedom of Access to Information*

The way an organization internally extends or withholds information reflects its views of staff competency and initiative. Use of information monopolies to maintain power or secure organizational status will decrease rationality and morale. "Secrecy is a poor foundation for success compared with competence, and to maintain secrecy reduces competence [Forrester, 1965, p. 11]."

7. *Elimination of Internal Monopolies*

The efficiencies and incentives of a competitive system are enhanced when, within the organization, every type of activity and service exists in multiple so that there is no single source to satisfy any one person's need, and no one is dependent on a single consumer for one's output. This seventh characteristic is related to the second, whereby each person or team is an internal profit center that develops a level of exchange with other internal profit centers.

8. *Balancing Reward and Risk*

Individuals can move from self-managers, to team managers, to entrepreneurial developers of new projects that match client needs to organizational goals only if the organization helps to collectivize individual or team risks and provide for a balance of rewards and penalties so as to dissuade repeated failures among aspiring managers, yet encourage, attract, and maintain competent ones.

9. *Mobility of the Individual*

Unlike the usual case, new organizations should provide greater freedom for internal movement and exit and put more restraint on initial entry. Internal competitive mechanisms will stimulate internal skill diversification and learning. Delayed incentive systems such as retirement plans that are used to reduce personnel turnover usually help to promote mediocrity and to hide negative internal conditions while still failing to retain competent people whose security lies in marketable ability rather than seniority.

10. Enhanced Rights of the Individual

There must be a reduction in the exercise of capricious and arbitrary authority, particularly over technical and management personnel who may lack unionized protection. A constitutional-based sense of direction and policy making must be developed.

11. Education within the Corporation

Members must understand the dynamics of growth and stability in order to participate in the policy structure design that will govern them. Time for education can be realized from savings in the "25 percent or more of their potential effectiveness [Forrester, 1965, p. 15]" that is unnecessarily consumed by organizations in the coordination of internal activities. Organizationally sponsored education is economically feasible as a result of greater long-term effectiveness and adaptability. Education must also link organizational goals to individual personal growth goals.

Forrester argues that these characteristics of new organizations are "particularly suited to those industries which feel the impact of rapid change in science and technology and in which conventional management approaches have often been wanting [Forrester, 1965, p.17]." We would suggest that they are also applicable to human service agencies with the admitted difficulty of developing a concept or unit that would be equivalent to "profit," as used by Forrester.*

Drawing upon the theme that service provision is surpassing goods production as the central activity of our postindustrial society, Simon (1973) has suggested that information processing and decision making should become the new bases upon which we design and structure organizations, replacing principles of design based on differentiated production or service functions. The division of labor and the integration of organizational subsystems should be structured so as to optimize "attention management." Simon argues that our contemporary world is swimming in a "rich soup of information" and that the scarce resource is not information, but the "processing capacity to attend to information."

Not only are the time and resources for attention to information limited, the important sources of information for top levels of any organization are usually outside the organization's own boundary, that is to say, coming from its environment. Information, then, may come in forms or quantities outside the control of the organization's management. Simon (1973) suggests the implications of these notions when he writes:

*Material from J. W. Forrester in this section was adapted by permission from: J. W. Forrester, A new corporate design. *Industrial Management Review,* 1965, 7(1), 5–17. (Copyright 1965, Sloan Management Review Association, Cambridge, Massachusetts.)

In summary, the inherent capacity limits of information-processing systems impose two requirements on organizational design: that the totality of decision problems be factored in such a way as to minimize the interdependence of the components; and that the entire system be so structured as to conserve the scarce resource, attention. The organizational design must provide for interfaces to handle information that originates outside the organization, and special provision must be made for decisions that have particular time limits associated with them [p. 271].*

Drucker, Forrester, and Simon are suggesting that a new era of organizational life is close upon us. These authors have cast their ideas, however, in a framework more compatible to new profit-making organizations and have not attempted to relate them to the human services area, which is frequently government operated or government subsidized, and generally nonprofit in corporate character. To integrate more fully these newer approaches with the management and evaluation of human service programs, we have used general systems theory as an alternate model for human service organization, administration, and evaluation. Evaluators must be particularly sensitive to the systemic functions of evaluation, particularly the ways that evaluation is used by managers as a mechanism for (a) internal integration, (b) conflict resolution, (c) feedback and adaptation, and (d) environmental boundary control. The final sections of this chapter describe these uses of evaluation in human service organizations conceptualized as open systems.

ORGANIZATIONS AS OPEN SYSTEMS

Management principles must begin with the premise that viable organizations are ever-changing internally because they are, by necessity, open systems with permeable boundaries. As open systems, organizations are continually in transaction with their surrounding environments—that collection of all persons and other organizations that influence or can be influenced by the organization. When surrounded by a stable environment, with a slow rate of change, management can afford to be less sensitive to the organization's permeable boundary because there will be little noticeable change on a daily or monthly basis. A manager of an agency within such a stable environment will find it possible to direct and control organizational resources using such mechanisms as a well-defined table of organization where tasks and lines of communication are clearly defined. It follows, therefore, that organizations within stable environments can more readily allow themselves to be highly differentiated inter-

*Reproduced by permission from: H. A. Simon, Applying information technology to organization design. *Public Administration Review,* 1973, *33,* 268–278. (Copyright 1973, American Society for Public Administration, Washington, D. C.)

nally while remaining sufficiently integrated to respond and adapt to their environment.

THE IMPORTANCE OF INTEGRATION

Although managers of contemporary human service agencies must continue to concern themselves with techniques for the internal differentiation of their agencies, the increase in environmental turbulence has made the process of integration relatively more problematic (Lawrence & Lorsch, 1969). Highly differentiated subunits of an organization tend to develop and highlight their own subgoals and these can come to replace the superordinate goals of the total organization. This phenomenon is particularly present in human service organizations where superordinate goals tend to be vague, nonoperational, and overly ambitious. Goal ambiguity is used or becomes necessary to achieve consensus, and goal ambitiousness helps to motivate workers in the absence of real incentives for performance. Unfortunately, the overuse of superordinate goals as integrative mechanisms also tends to inhibit measurable goal setting and accountability. The program evaluator and manager may find it difficult or impossible to capture sufficiently reliable feedback regarding program performance and degree of goal attainment if superordinate organizational goals are overused as integrative mechanisms.

In highly differentiated but poorly integrated organizations it is also possible for the subgoals of different subsystems to come into direct conflict. For example, the subgoal of a highly specialized treatment unit to achieve a homogeneous and manageable caseload may come into conflict with a specialized client-advocacy unit whose subgoal is to increase community accessibility and maximize comprehensive service delivery to a wide diversity of client subgroups.

Highly differentiated subsystems also tend to become closely identified with *limited* and *specialized* sectors of the environment, losing sight or awareness of the organization's total task environment. For example, if a hospital is emphatically differentiated on the basis of different professional groups (e.g., the nursing department or the social work department) the departmental members may come to be more concerned with those specific services or outputs that satisfy the specialized standards or opinions of their own colleagues and professional associations than with those outputs that satisfy the interdependent needs of the other hospital departments or, more importantly, the patients. This phenomenon forms the basis for the frequently noted "cosmopolitan" orientation of some service professionals.

Other factors that tend further to reinforce differentiation at the expense of overall organizational performance are internal communication patterns promoting subsystem saliency, selective recruiting and retention of personnel suited to unique subsystem needs, use of organizational slack to enhance subsystem distinctiveness, and internal competition for any additional but limited resources or power. In brief, if a system becomes too highly differentiated and insufficiently integrated, subsystems can build strong internal boundaries among themselves, weakening internal linkages, management control, and overall accountability.

Management can integrate subsystems through a variety of mechanisms. These mechanisms include policy structures, formal hierarchies, committees of overlapping membership, staff support to line positions, integrated information and evaluation systems, and intermittent reorganizations that break up rigid subunits and build new intraorganizational arrangements. To date, human service managers have *underutilized* the potential of information and evaluation systems and have *overutilized* most of these other mechanisms. The Department of Health, Education, and Welfare, for example, has undergone a major reorganization almost every year for the past two decades. Continual pressure for internal reorganization is not just a sign of future shock, but a symptom of management's inattention to, or difficulty with, alternative mechanisms for organizational integration and flexibility.

Integrative structures, such as committees, or integrative mechanisms, such as information systems, can usually be observed at work when the organization engages in such activities as program planning, policy formulation, priority setting, conflict resolution, and *evaluation.* Program evaluators, therefore, must look for these integrative features of organizational life when planning and conducting their own evaluation efforts. Evaluators must also remember that they are most likely to be judged useful as primary integrative servomechanisms for other organizational units, particularly top management. That is, evaluation is not an end unto itself, but a systemic process with integrative potential.

FEEDBACK AND ADAPTATION

Another general principle of systems is that they will strive to maintain *equilibrium,* or a quasi-steady state, because such a condition is more conducive to efficient production. Efficient systems devote the largest share of their available energy to productive outputs or services, using only minimal energy for the necessary maintenance and internal coordination activities. However, in view of the ever-changing environment, an ideal steady state is not possible. The adaptive system, therefore, must process *feedback* to remain on a relatively stable course vis-à-vis its total environment. Nevertheless, some subsystems within a system may try to *shut out feedback* from other subsystems or the environment because the feedback will call for change, or a shift from their preferred stability. Since change requires additional energy expenditure, a reallocation of energies, and new behaviors, change is usually viewed as problematic, rather than adaptive.

Whereas some subsystems may resist change, others may wish to stimulate change to enhance their specific goals, to achieve more supremacy and influence, or as an appropriately adaptive response to feedback from their subenvironment. Thus, within the total system, we are likely to find simultaneous resistance to, and pressure for, change. Management's responsibility is to integrate these differences, orchestrating the tensions for adaptation and change while keeping the system sufficiently stable for continuing productive outputs (Broskowski, Mermis, & Khajavi, 1975).

The feedback and adaptation mechanisms for service organizations are usually embodied in special structures or subsystems such as research and development units, evaluation and planning units, and training/retraining (e.g., continuing education) units. Special intelligence-gathering methods will be used to monitor the environment in the sense so strongly urged by Simon (1973). *Environmental monitoring* may include such activities as the employment of systematic needs assessment methodologies, staffs' intermittent attendance at professional conventions or public meetings, and the routine reading of newsletters, journals, and other externally generated documents. Thus, these feedback and adaptation mechanisms overlap with those integration mechanisms reviewed earlier in this chapter. The evaluation process is one of the most critical integrative and adaptive mechanisms used by an organization. Personnel within the evaluation component, however, will be subjected to considerable tensions and buffeting because total organizations or specific internal subsystems will have conflictual and ambivalent reactions to evaluative feedback (Wildavsky, 1972).

SYSTEMIC REACTIONS TO FEEDBACK

Because program evaluators are frequently the providers of adverse feedback, they must come to anticipate some common systemic reactions. When confronted with feedback that demands major change and disequilibrium, systems may try to ignore the information and build stronger, less permeable boundaries as a defense against further feedback. The history of institutionalization of mental hospitals in the United States is an example of this mode of reaction to criticisms and adverse feedback (Caplan, 1969). Other systemic reactions to feedback from specific environmental sectors may include (a) attempts to co-opt the outside forces by bringing them into the organization; (b) merger with the intrusive environmental sector; (c) destruction of the sector; (d) increased efforts at market control or monopolization of the environment; or (e) splitting off one or more subsystems (functions) that are under attack in order to save the remaining parts.

Chronic use of these maladaptive reactions to adverse feedback can reduce a system's overall boundary permeability and adaptability to the point that its management and control functions begin to concentrate solely on internal issues at the expense of environmental awareness. Reduced boundary permeability, in turn, will lead to the common phenomenon we observe in the human services arena: a preference to avoid rather than to develop interorganizational relationships and interactions. It is critical that the evaluator learns to provide feedback in ways that increase the chances for the system to react in an open and nondefensive manner, to continue to monitor its efforts and effectiveness, and to use feedback for the difficult task of reallocating its resources.

MAINTAINING OPTIMAL BOUNDARY PERMEABILITY

There are several reasons why a system may judge that its own best interests are served by avoiding environmental interactions and intersystem linkages. Such linkages may consume a large amount of energy with no immediate or obvious payoff. For example, the linkage may demand allocation of that limited resource, attention, to process even more new information.

There may be real or potential loss of autonomy and control. The system may begin to receive feedback that it would rather ignore.

Despite their tendencies to avoid interorganizational relationships, all agencies find it necessary to maintain a minimum level of transaction with other agencies or groups for purposes of gaining the necessary inputs for survival (e.g., money, sanction, and personnel). In fact, most systems develop specialized substructures or processes to carry out these environmental transactions. These special units are the system's *boundary-spanning* subsystems. In manufacturing firms these units typically are the purchasing, personnel, or sales units that negotiate with the firm's outside suppliers or buyers. In human service agencies the boundary-spanning subsystems include such units as intake, consultation, and discharge teams. Management is always a key boundary-spanning subsystem. Program evaluators employed by an agency are clearly boundary spanners to the extent that they must cross internal or external boundaries to collect the feedback necessary to evaluate program efforts, effectiveness, or efficiency.

Boundary-spanning units are also critical to the organizational change process because they are in a position to bring in or filter out environmental information, including feedback on past performance. Boundary spanners may thus come to be feared or mistrusted by those inside the system because, as units in touch with the outside environment, they have the potential to divulge secrets, distort information, or in other ways be co-opted by other environmental sectors. The problem of internal mistrust is common to most program evaluators. Evaluators frequently are viewed by committed insiders with tremendous hostility at worst and with ambivalence at best.

The management of an agency's limited resources will require delicate control of the degree of boundary permeability. If a system is too open, it may become excessively reactive, committed beyond its resources, or overly fragmented without clear goals and priorities. If a system is too closed to its task environment, it may become rigid, inefficient (i.e., entropic), and nonproductive. Optimal boundary permeability is easier to adjust and maintain if management devotes sufficient attention to the system's shifting boundary and turbulent environment rather than focusing exclusively on internal subsystems. This systemic principle creates a pervasive dilemma for managers of contemporary human service organizations. As organizational size or complexity increases, or as environmental turbulence increases, or both, greater *integration* efforts are essential. But integration consumes energy that is not directly translated into production. Excessive emphasis on integration for the purpose of systemic maintenance diverts attention away from *production goals* —(e.g., "what we're here to provide") and the organization begins to behave *as if* the integration *process* was *the* major goal. The means become the ends. *In this way, the maintenance of process may come to displace the production of services.* By providing information on shifting environmental needs and on the organization's efforts, costs, and effectiveness, the evaluator can help management to maintain an appropriate balance among the necessary tasks of environmental monitoring, internal integration, maintenance, and productivity.

BOUNDARY PERMEABILITY AND THE CONCEPT OF CORE TECHNOLOGY

Underlying all of the integrative, boundary-spanning, and adaptive sub-systems, one can identify the *core technology* subsystems—those primary processes that an organization performs in order to produce its major outputs (i.e., goods or services). For an organization to survive, the products of core technology subsystems must be exchanged for new income, credit, sanction, and reward. Management and other boundary-spanning subsystems are important only because they help the organization to *seal off* and protect the organization's core technology. With its core technology protected from environmental intrusions, a system can simultaneously maintain equilibrium, increase resource control, increase productivity and efficiency, and develop improvements in future products and services. Thompson (1967) has identified four mechanisms that organizations prefer and sequentially employ to protect their core technologies:

1. *Buffer* the core with input/output boundary-spanning subsystems to seal out the highly variable environmental influences.

2. *Level-out* any variability in the input and output transactions that cannot be buffered.

3. *Anticipate* or *forecast* environmental changes that cannot be buffered or leveled.

4. When buffering, leveling, and forecasting fail, protect the core technology from environmental disruption through *rationing*—the allocation of scarce input resources on a priority basis.

For example, a human service agency such as a community mental health center may *buffer* its core technology of mental health treatment services (e.g., psychotherapy and hospitalization) by a pre-intake screening mechanism to ease the information-gathering demands on clinicians. *Leveling* is achieved by trying to maintain a steady staff–client caseload ratio or by screening out "inappropriate referrals." *Forecasting* is illustrated by planning new programs or reorganizing existing programs based on anticipated changes in demand for services based on need assessment studies. *Rationing* is employed when fringe programs are cut back in the face of funding shortages. Other examples of these mechanisms include (*a*) *buffering* on the input side through "stockpiling" needed resources (e.g., client waiting lists, drug or plasma inventories, financial endowments); (*b*) *buffering* on the output side by manipulating demands for particular types of core services with pricing incentives or disincentives (e.g., charging above costs for inpatient services and/or offering bargain rates for less demanded services such as education); (*c*) *leveling* fluctuating demand through *scheduling* appointments or using low-cost but early interventions with high-risk groups to reduce later overutilization of more expensive services; (*d*) *forecasting* peak periods or points of high demand that cannot be leveled (e.g., planning for seasonal holiday crises or assigning special units to high-risk neighborhoods); and (*e*) *rationing* such system development activities as in-service training, research, and travel when income fails to rise with expenses.

A human service organization has as its primary goal the efficient and reliable delivery of high quality services. At the same time, the organization must continually adapt to those environmental demands and pressures that it cannot buffer, level, or forecast. Therefore, management must continually seek a balance between the stability needed for efficient production and the change needed for growth or survival. In the language of general systems theory, effective evaluation is critical for meeting the organization's need for stability as well as its need for change. The evaluation process, therefore, must help management to buffer, level, and forecast at least as much as it provides the feedback that calls for change. That is, evaluators must at times promote stability as well as change (Broskowski, Mermis, & Khajavi, 1975).

SUMMARY

Viewing an organization as an open system helps us to place it within the context of its environment and to bring about a better balance of management's interest in both its external and internal affairs. Whereas classical management theory is extensively devoted to internal organizational *structures,* general systems theory emphasizes that a key task of management is to promote stabilized productivity while remaining responsive to constantly changing external pressures and demands (cf. Baker, 1973, for a more detailed review of systems theory). While promoting stability in the interest of productivity, however, management must also negotiate the opposing tensions for continual change. Program evaluation must be understood within this broader set of organizational considerations.

Although general systems theory remains a highly abstract set of concepts and principles by which to guide the evaluation process, we have found general systems theory useful for the practical purposes of reorganizing our agency and in designing an information system that has been instrumental in agency planning, management, and evaluation. This system is called the Management Information and Planning System (MIPS) and is fully described in Chapter 8. General systems theory has also proven to be a practical framework for the analysis of other organizations and for the planning and design of alternative management and evaluation processes.

In closing, it is stressed again that the key concepts emphasized in this chapter are *productivity, efficiency,* and *effectiveness* (i.e., Buckminster Fuller's axiom of "doing more with less"), while the processes of management, information systems, accounting, and evaluation are simply the means to achieve these critical systemic conditions.

REFERENCES

Baker, F. Organizations as open systems. In F. Baker (Ed.), *Organizational systems: General systems approaches to complex organizations.* Homewood, Illinois: Richard D. Irwin, 1973.
Broskowski, A., Mermis, W., & Khajavi, F. Managing the dynamics of change and stability. In

J. E. Jones & J. W. Pfeiffer (Eds.), *1975 annual handbook for group facilitators.* La Jolla, California: University Associates Publishers, 1975.

Caplan, R. *Psychiatry and the community in nineteenth century America.* New York: Basic Books, 1969.

Drucker, P. New templates for today's organizations. *Harvard Business Review,* 1974, *52,* 45–53.

Emery, F., & Trist, E. The causal texture of organizational environments. *Human Relations,* 1965, *18,* 21–32.

Forrester, J. W. A new corporate design. *Industrial Management Review,* 1965, *7*(1), 5–17.

Forrester, J. W. A new corporate design. *Collected papers of Jay W. Forrester.* Cambridge, Massachusetts: Wright-Allen Press, 1975.

Jurkovich, R. A core typology of organizational environments. *Administrative Science Quarterly,* 1974, *19,* 380–394.

Lawrence, P. R., & Lorsh, J. W. *Organization and environment: Managing differentiation and integration.* Homewood, Illinois: Richard D. Irwin, 1969.

Learned, E. P., & Sproat, A. T. *Organization theory and policy.* Homewood, Illinois: Richard D. Irwin, 1966.

Miller, E. Technology, territory and time: The internal differentiation of complex production systems. *Human Relations,* 1959, *12,* 243–272.

Osborn, R. N., & Hunt, J. G. Environment and organizational effectiveness. *Administrative Science Quarterly,* 1974, *19,* 231–246.

Quie, A. H. Reply to Lynn and Salasin's "Human services: Should we, can we make them available to everyone?" *Evaluation,* 1974, Special Issue (Spring), 21–24.

Simon, H. A. Applying information technology to organization design. *Public Administration Review,* 1973, *33,* 268–278.

Terreberry, S. The evolution of organizational environments. *Administrative Science Quarterly,* 1968, *12,* 590–613.

Thompson, J. D. *Organizations in action.* New York: McGraw-Hill, 1967.

Wildavsky, A. The self-evaluating organization. *Public Administration Review,* 1972, *32,* 509–520.

4

ROLES AND FUNCTIONS
OF EVALUATION
IN HUMAN SERVICE PROGRAMS

C. Clifford Attkisson, Timothy R. Brown,
and William A. Hargreaves

A flexible capacity for *internal* self-evaluation is fundamental to the management and ongoing improvement of community-based human service programs. In performing this function, program evaluators provide staff support and information for two basic management tasks: (*a*) communicating effectively with the organization's external environment, and (*b*) maintaining effective service delivery and administrative accountability within the organization. Organizational management and accounting procedures are the traditional methods employed by administrators to achieve external accountability and to maintain internal planning and monitoring functions. We view emerging internal program evaluation activities as extensions of the more traditional management and accounting procedures. As the preceding chapters have emphasized, more powerful evaluative activities are currently necessary because political realities and resource limitations now require human service programs to be far more efficiently operated, increasingly productive, more accessible, and more responsive to community needs (*1*).

As a consequence of political pressures and resource constraints, human service programs are seeking diversified sources of revenue to augment declining categorical funding. In addition—as health and human service planning shifts gradually from the federal level to regional, state, and county levels— community-based programs are moving to bolster political relations with their local governments and their citizen constituents. These shifts toward broadening the fiscal support base and increasing community control of human services are also stimulating an increased need for evaluative and management information, closer scrutiny of resource utilization, and the first steps toward regionally integrated planning and service delivery. All these developments have engendered considerable ambiguity about program funding, budgetary stability, and lines of authority.

This fluid and stress-laden context has mixed implications for a developing, applied activity like program evaluation. We must seriously question if the evaluation field is ready for what is currently asked of it. Many factors preclude rapid growth of adequate evaluative capacity:

- Excessive expectations for evaluative information by its consumers
- Sparse funding for evaluative activities and for development of evaluative methods
- A dearth of adequately trained evaluators
- Impoverished information systems within community-based organizations
- Ambiguity about the most useful organizational roles for evaluators.

On the positive side, it can be argued that the persistent need for relevant information *may* serve as the consistent and meaningful stimulus that all new applied disciplines require for continuous maturation and productivity. As an applied discipline, program evaluation requires enduring external stimulation from program leaders—stimulation that will shape evaluative functions, mold careers of individuals involved in these functions, and eliminate esoteric and irrelevant activities that may characterize the initial work of many in this new field.

The principal issue we must address, however, is whether the evaluation field is currently mature enough to respond to the hefty expectations being placed upon it by law, by administrators, and by evaluators. Is the self-evaluating organization a potential reality in the near future? Do we have sufficient methodological clarity and technology for the tasks at hand? How can the human service organization integrate evaluation as a functional aspect of its management process? This chapter addresses these important questions. Our views are rooted in two basic assumptions: (*a*) that human services—as we know them—are useful, and (*b*) that program evaluation *can* further enhance this usefulness.

THE SELF-EVALUATING ORGANIZATION

The concepts of the self-evaluating organization proposed by Wildavsky (1972) furnish a useful beginning point for our response to the principal issue posed in the introduction to this chapter: Is the evaluation field ready for what is currently asked of it? Wildavsky holds that the ideal organization would be self-evaluating. That is, it would engage in continuous monitoring of its own activities, assessing whether goals were met and examining the relevance of those goals. Evaluative data suggesting insufficiencies would be taken seriously by administrative decision makers and evaluative data would become the basis of program development and change. The self-evaluating organization would be a paragon of efficiency and effectiveness.

Wildavsky candidly confesses that the pure self-evaluating organization is probably an unattainable ideal. The obstacles before it are enormous. Wildavsky envisions major practical problems associated with these unresolved questions: Who is to evaluate? What is the role of evaluation vis-à-vis administration? How are the costs of evaluation to be borne? How is evaluation to be administered within the organization? How does evaluation's knowledge become matched with power? As evaluation requires the trust of others, how is trust to be obtained and maintained? Human service organizations are currently grappling with these problems as they attempt to plan for and use program evaluation. The self-evaluating human service organization, then, remains the ideal—something to aim toward—and is a promising concept around which to develop and restructure community-based agencies.

Weiss (1973) stated that program evaluation itself, with its fundamental tenet of improvement based on assessment, is a political movement within the field of human services. Most human service programs were originally conceived as providers of specific types of services having some assumed value. Frequent negative evaluation findings and the failure to utilize evaluative research over the last few decades, however, have cast doubt on the inherent merit of many programs. Yet, the original human service problems and needs still require solutions. As a consequence, human service organizations must shift from being static providers of predetermined types of services toward becoming organizations whose goals are (a) to meet human needs with what seems to be the best service methods available, (b) to monitor the effectiveness of service methods, and (c) to improve or change services in light of new information. Without such an internal change process, human service organizations will continue to lose credibility and face the loss of public and fiscal support. Human service agencies must become more like Wildavsky's self-evaluating organization. How can they become so?

PROBLEMS IN MAKING EVALUATION USEFUL

An examination of the current literature on human services evaluation reveals two paradoxical conclusions. The first view is that community-based agencies should do more and better evaluation. The second is that evaluative findings do not have much impact on the agencies in which they are undertaken. What accounts for this lack of fulfillment of the promise of evaluation? Why are evaluative findings disregarded by administrators of human service programs?

VALIDITY

Limited validity of evaluative findings is a frequent problem. The complexities and difficulties of doing evaluation in applied settings are so great that the results of many such efforts have reduced credibility. Caro (1971) and

Weiss and Rein (1970) described several factors that emerged as barriers to useful external evaluation within broad-aim programs initiated by the federal government in the late 1960s. They call attention to problems such as (*a*) the difficulty in translating broadly-stated goals into measurable objectives, (*b*) the essentially uncontrolled operations of these programs, (*c*) the discovery that services provided are not standard across organizational elements, (*d*) the conflict between evaluators and administrators over program development, and (*e*) the influence of community groups on program operations combined with citizen hostility toward external evaluation. Unfortunately, these problems are not unique to broad-aim programs, but apply to many other community-based human services. Sometimes the problems are so overwhelming that evaluations are not completed and results are never reported or arc reported ineffectively. More frequently, the validity of results is so questionable that the study is likely to be disregarded by administrative decision makers. As Weiss (*4*) stated, "Much evaluation is poor, more is mediocre. Evaluation in action settings is a difficult, demanding enterprise, and calls for a high order of imagination and tenacity as well as research ability." This challenge is not met frequently enough.

UTILITY

Irrelevance is perhaps a more important reason than low validity for failure of many evaluative studies to have an impact on agencies. The academic training of evaluative researchers orients them to validity. They are taught how to design experiments that protect against competing internal and external explanations, how to collect accurate and thorough information, how to analyze results using sophisticated statistical techniques if necessary, and how to interpret the results with care, not going beyond clearly justified conclusions. These research procedures are undertaken to ensure that evaluative efforts are scientifically credible. Unfortunately, none of these strategies helps to ensure that study results will have maximal usefulness to the settings in which data are collected. Social scientists are rarely trained to plan research for immediate program relevance, and when hired as evaluators, they continue to design studies that attempt to maximize validity at the expense of relevance. Even when such studies are successfully executed, they frequently have little utility, and are disregarded for a number of reasons. For example, the questions addressed by the investigator may not be issues of concern to the administrator. Although the outcome measures selected by the investigator are standard ones of known validity, the measures may not adequately tap content that concerns administrators. The data analysis may be too complex to be interpreted by someone not specifically trained in research. The carefully limited conclusions may leave the decision maker to determine the most important implications of the evaluation. Finally, it could be that when the highly valid data are finally available, decisions have already been made. Data or no data, decisions must be made within some time interval, and untimely information, regardless of its validity, is useless if the decision has already been made.

Roos (1973) has argued that evaluative information must be both valid and useful to decision makers. Roos points out that these are often conflicting requirements, necessitating compromises. While retaining as much scientific credibility as possible, evaluative studies should be planned to support decision making. The questions under study and the evaluative design should be pertinent to the management and policy issues faced by the administrator. The timing and precision of the study must be determined by management and policy schedules and the results should be communicated in a form that can be readily understood by administrative decision makers. Although these practices should be standard, Brown and Harris (2) and Nelson (3) report that many evaluative studies have not been developed or conducted with *utility* in mind, and as a consequence, have had reduced or negligible impact.

NEGATIVE RESULTS, PROGRAM JUSTIFICATION, AND THE STATUS QUO

Even when evaluative studies result in valid and potentially useful findings, they often have limited influence on management and policy issues. Rossi (1971) provides two illustrations in which conclusive evaluative results were rejected by policymakers, and, in one case, were repeatedly rejected over a number of years, because their negative findings conflicted with cherished beliefs. R. K. Carter (1971) catalogs a host of such instances across virtually the entire range of human services and at all levels of program management. He concludes that most administrators equate program evaluation with *program justification*. And administrators do not seriously entertain the idea that their programs do not work, so when negative results occur, the findings are rejected. For example, Ullman and Huber (1973) described the repeated disregard of negative findings by lower-level administrators within the federal Job Bank Program. Ullman and Huber further documented that negative results were rarely transmitted from lower to higher administrative levels. Clearly, negative results run a high risk of being ignored.

PROGRAM MANAGEMENT DEFICIENCY

Wholey, Scanlon, Duffy, Fukumoto, and Vogt (1970) analyzed the state of evaluation within programs of five federal agencies. They found few examples where evaluations later had impact on the operations of these programs. One of the major reasons they cited for this lack of impact was the poor organizational responsiveness to evaluative results. Subsequently, these investigators concluded that deficiencies in human service program management is a basic underlying factor that explains why evaluations do not have significant impact (Horst, Nay, Scanlon, & Wholey, 1974). Horst *et al.* argued that human service programs tend to (*a*) lack clear definitions of the problems to be addressed, the interventions to be made, and the outcome or impact expected; (*b*) lack a clear logic that links assumptions to expenditure of resources, the implementation of the program intervention, or the outcome; and (*c*) lack management skill due to low motivation, understanding, ability, or authority to act on evaluative results. For Horst *et al.*, all other reasons for the low utilization of evaluative findings are symptoms of the underlying causal defect of inadequate program definition and management.

It is true that there are relatively few formally trained management personnel involved in the development or operation of human service programs, except in hospitals. Most human service program managers have received little, if any, formal training in administration. Typically they are human service professionals who previously functioned as service providers and were subsequently promoted to administrative positions. Their training in management comes from experience on the job and from observing the methods of their predecessors. The effect of this specific educational deficit is that human service programs generally are not well managed. Moreover, human service administrators trained through their own job experience tend to rely on their own observations as the information base for decision making. They tend not to be familiar with other sources of information, and therefore to underutilize them. Program evaluation data, when not seen as negative input, may be viewed by administrators as an interesting novelty, but not something to utilize in decision making.

COMPLEXITY IN DECISION MAKING

Finally, evaluation has not been an influential force in management and policymaking because it has not dealt with the complexity of the administrative decision-making process. To some extent, program evaluation has been victimized by its own limited concept of organizational functioning. The developmental schema discussed in evaluation texts and articles describes human service programs as evolving in phases from planning, to development, and finally to operations—with evaluation occurring potentially at each stage, but primarily the last—serving the function of a simple servo-mechanism feeding back results of effort. Obviously, this is an oversimplification, but until recently, these generalizations comprised virtually the sole conceptual framework for evaluators and administrators in human service programs. This inadequate concept of evaluation blinds evaluators and administrators to more functional roles for program evaluation within organizational life.

Weiss (1973) argues that evaluation takes place within a political process and, therefore, should be viewed as an intricate part of that process. Discussing both private-sector and government-initiated activities, she points out that human service programs typically are proposed, debated, enacted, and funded through political processes, and remain susceptible to these pressures. Because evaluation is undertaken to support decision making about these programs, it enters the political arena. In this adversary domain, evaluative findings must compete with a number of other perspectives, values, and influences. The more limited concept of evaluation as the sole source of feedback ignores these other influences on administrative decisions. As a consequence, evaluative results may not make a substantial impact on decisions if evaluative information does not compete successfully with other types of information. Evaluators must recognize that their findings are one of many internal and external sources of information that administrative decision makers will utilize. If evaluative results are not used by administrators, we must ask why other sources of information and values are preferred.

The simple servo-mechanism concept of evaluation also does not adequately account for the systemic complexity of organizations. Theories of organizational decision making as proposed by E. E. Carter (1971), Cyert and March (1963), Ference (1970), Mintzberg (1973), and Vroom and Yetton (1973) suggest that our approach to evaluation must recognize the complex effects of administrative levels, varying types of organizational goals, outside influences, leadership styles, communication networks, and other influences. Each influence could enhance or reduce the impact of program evaluation, depending on the systemic configuration of a specific organization. These influences are rarely addressed in the development and design of evaluation or in the feedback of results. This, too, partially accounts for why evaluation is not influential with administrators. In addition, as discussed in Chapter 3, program evaluators must become knowledgeable about organizational influences or continue to expect a low utilization of their findings.

In summary, there are five explanations why program evaluation is so frequently disregarded by administrators of human service agencies. The *first* is the frequent low validity of program evaluation because of the difficulty of doing careful research in applied settings. The *second* is the lack of usefulness of evaluation for administrative decision makers, because so many evaluations are not designed to have managerial utility. The *third* reason is that evaluative results are frequently negative and therefore flatly rejected. The *fourth* is that many human service agencies are not organized well enough with management staff able or willing to incorporate the evaluative input. And *fifth,* that the complexity of administrative decision making—along with competing sources of internal input and a variety of other external influences—attenuates the impact of evaluative findings.

TWO EXAMPLES OF UTILIZED EVALUATIONS

After describing the array of factors that can reduce the effectiveness of human service evaluation, illustrated by example after example of findings being disregarded, a further and basic question emerges: *Why do evaluation at all?* It might seem to be a pointless and useless endeavor. However, by becoming aware of the historical reasons why evaluation has not been utilized, we should not conclude that it can have no impact at all. Indeed, there are instances where it has had remarkable influence on programs.

Although the tenor of the foregoing discussion has been negative, and it is probably true that program evaluation, as currently practiced, is not dependably useful, there are steps that can be taken to enhance the utility of program evaluation. In many instances, program evaluation can have constructive value for human service programs. In the past, successful evaluations rarely have been reported. It would seem that such success is rather naively viewed as the normal and expected course, not meriting comment. Publications on the effect of program evaluation tend to dwell on what went wrong and not on what went right. In what follows we give two examples of program evaluations that were useful in constructively changing an existing human service program.

Several years ago, a systematic investigation of the client screening and intake process in a community mental health center was conducted by Timothy R. Brown. Descriptive information was collected on all clients who applied for service during a fixed time interval and each was followed until the client either was referred to alternative services or was formally accepted for treatment. Staff were interviewed about their understanding of and compliance with established procedures. The data were evaluated in terms of continuity of care goals and accessibility of services to clients. Results indicated that the screening and intake process was, on the whole, inadequate. One of the most important deficiencies was a low rate of accepted clients per number of initial contacts. The evaluation report sparked controversy and conflict within the agency, culminating, 7 months after its release, in a decision to set up a new central intake unit. Five months were required to determine the scope of the new unit, train staff, and create new procedures. Data were collected to monitor the intake process beginning a month before the new unit began to function. It was found that during the first month, there was a 50% increase in the rate of accepted clients. On this and other indices, the new central intake unit was seen as a marked improvement. After 3 years, monitoring data indicated that this unit was still functioning at the improved level.

The second example involves a state corrections program. A study was undertaken (*a*) to estimate the numbers of newly sentenced prisoners who could be considered for confinement within the various state correction programs, and (*b*) to assess the suitability of these programs for the range of sentenced offenders. Program evaluation staff, in collaboration with high-level corrections administrators, developed a three-dimensional schema by which offenders could be classified. The three dimensions included type of offense/ pattern of criminal behavior, offender personality pattern, and predicted responsiveness to rehabilitation programs. The records of a sample of recently admitted prisoners were examined and each was classified on the three dimensions. Additionally, a panel of experts, without knowledge of the actual distribution of offenders, rated which type of prisoners could be reasonably placed into the four correctional programs currently available. These ratings were then used to estimate the maximum number of offenders that could be accommodated within each available placement alternative. The findings of this study became the basis for allocating resources to the various programs and placement of prisoners. Moreover, examination of the data was partially responsible for convincing administrators that there were no appropriate programs available for some types of offenders. In response, an additional program alternative was specifically developed for those who did not fit existing programs. This new corrections program recently has been funded on a pilot basis by the state legislature.

Neither of these examples was published. Each was seen by the investigators as program evaluation meant for internal use only. Both studies have serious methodological limitations. Yet, the circumstances combined in such a way that evaluative data were utilized to an extent that they were partially responsible for new program development and for an acknowledgment that existing programs and procedures were inadequate to meet the range of needs and demands for services. What is it that accounts for the success of these two examples as opposed to the failures discussed in current evaluation writings?

We think that the success of these two examples was due to the capacity of administrators and evaluators to work in syncrony with commonly shared goals, and to focus on evaluative issues that had great saliency for the organizations. Effective internal program evaluation in these organizations, therefore, was due to existing evaluative capacity and the integration of evaluation and management. This self-evaluative capacity, mirrored in many other similar situations we have observed, is rooted in a conceptual model for evaluation that is described in the following four sections of this chapter. The final major section of this chapter presents basic principles by which evaluation and management can be integrated.

EVALUATION CAPABILITY: A THREE-DIMENSIONAL MODEL

Many human service organizations that have been in continuous operation for years, some for decades or more, now find themselves faced with the task of planning for self-evaluation. Despite the enormous pressures to move rapidly, an organization's program evaluation capability must be developed thoughtfully over time. If growth in evaluative capacity is to be continuous to a point of realistic strength, and if the cost of program evaluation is to be repaid by its usefulness to management, executives and evaluators must proceed realistically. Growth in evaluative capacity must proceed in harmony with the organization's present level of systemic maturity, the kinds of information tools needed for current and future tasks, and the multiple functions evaluation must perform in relation to program leadership and other staff.

Program evaluation, as defined in Chapter 1, can be applied to any level of program organization. The particular configuration of evaluative activities for a given program or organizational level must be designed to meet the unique information needs of that level. Regardless of organizational level— whether in a rural community, in a complex urban district, at the state level, or in a federal bureau or department—four central issues tend to structure the configuration of evaluative activities and the productivity of evaluative work. These issues can be formulated as four fundamental questions:

1. What information does the organization require for internal management and external accountability purposes?
2. What are the basic evaluative tasks?
3. What information collection and processing capacity is required by the organization's informational needs and the related evaluative tasks?

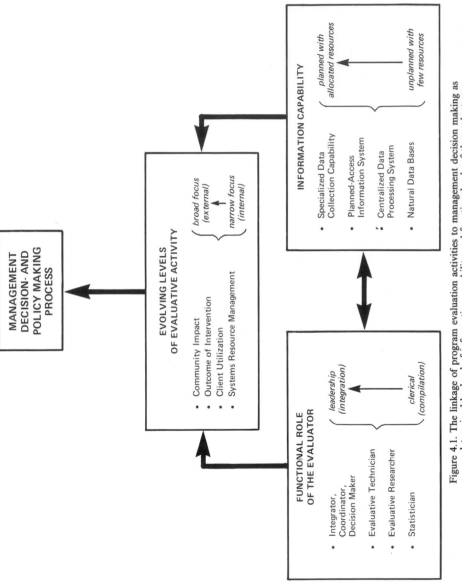

Figure 4.1. The linkage of program evaluation activities to management decision making as determined by level of information capability and functional role of the evaluator.

4. What functional and organizational role must evaluators assume to ensure that evaluative information is available and utilized?

While each human service organization and every level of program organization must separately address itself to these key questions, there is some general agreement about how to plan and structure useful evaluative activities. Our conceptual model responds to these questions by articulating three essential dimensions of internal evaluation. As illustrated in Figure 4.1, these dimensions are (a) *Evolving levels of evaluative activity,* (b) *Information capability,* and (c) *Functional roles of the evaluator.* While these dimensions do not include every relevant aspect of evaluation, they do describe the minimal framework necessary to produce the kind of information that can make evaluation an effective support system for program administration at all organizational levels.

The central dimension in Figure 4.1 outlines *evolving levels of evaluative activity* that range from systems resource management to community impact. These evaluative activities are presented as "levels" because we view them as being naturally ordered on a developmental hierarchy. Effective evaluation at a given level depends, at least to some extent, upon adequate initial mastery of the lower levels. The other two dimensions, the *information capability* of the service setting and the *functional roles of the evaluator,* determine the quality and utility of evaluation activity within a human service organization. The model expresses our conviction that the effectiveness of evaluative activities depends on appropriate evaluator roles and adequate informational capacity within the organization (Attkisson, McIntyre, Hargreaves, Harris, & Ochberg, 1974). We will now examine each of the three dimensions delineated in Figure 4.1.

EVOLVING LEVELS OF EVALUATIVE ACTIVITY

Each level of evaluative activity represents a domain of management responsibility and the evaluation functions relevant to it. For example, at the dimension's *systems resource management* level, the focus is on the internal operations of a human service program; at the extreme end of the dimension, the *community impact* level, the focus is on the program's impact on the ecology of social systems within a particular community. Therefore, these evaluative levels shift from a narrow focus, oriented toward internal administrative systems and resource management, to the broader perspective of a program's community impact. Typical management tasks and evaluation activities at each level are presented in Table 4.1 (Attkisson & Hargreaves, 1977). A newly formed evaluation unit often must focus entirely on the first level, whereas well-developed evaluation units will progressively address all four levels as conditions become optimal.

TABLE 4.1

Typical Management Tasks and Evaluation Activities at Four Progressively Evolving Levels of Evaluation Activity

Level of evaluation activity	Typical management tasks	Typical evaluation activities
I. Systems resource management	• Clarify organizational objectives • Develop program plan and budget • Establish lines of management responsibility • Obtain and maintain financial support • Allocate fiscal resources and staff effort • Coordinate personnel supervision • Establish new services and phase out existing services • Relate to community advisory groups • Meet external reporting requirements and program standards • Monitor income and expenditures • Establish fees and billing rates	• Review objectives and formulate indicators of attainment • Meet external reporting requirements • Clarify roles of evaluator and integrate with management tasks • Develop improved information capability and integrate data collection systems • Review mandated services or documented needs • Establish evaluation liaison with community advisory groups and evaluators from other organizational levels • Monitor staff effort and deployment of human, fiscal, and physical resources • Collaborate in establishment of a cost-finding system and determine unit costs of services • Provide effort feedback to management and service staff
II. Client utilization	• Make workload projections • Maintain efficiency of service delivery • Assure equity of service access • Assure appropriate client screening and treatment assignment • Assure adequate treatment planning • Assure appropriate service utilization and integration with other community services at the individual client level • Assure continuity of care • Establish quality assurance program	• Monitor unduplicated counts of clients served • Analyze caseloads and client flow • Compare client demographics to census data and high risk-need populations • Analyze reasons for premature dropout and under-utilization of services • Assist in installation of problem oriented client record and monitor service needs of clients • Provide technical support for utilization review and other quality assurance activities • Analyze continuity of care • Analyze costs per episode of care within specific client groups or service settings

III: Outcome of intervention	• Provide services acceptable to clients and referral sources • Detect and correct grossly ineffective service activities • Assure that services are generally effective • Improve cost-effectiveness of services • Reallocate resources to support and enhance most cost-effective services • Communicate service effectiveness to funding sources and advisory groups	• Routinely monitor client status • Study client and referral source satisfaction • Study posttreatment outcomes • Compare program outcomes to outcome norms • Undertake comparative outcome experiments • Do systems simulation and optimization studies • Compare cost-outcomes of different approaches to service needs and establish cost-effectiveness of services • Find cost-outcome per duration of problem or illness within specific client groups and/or service settings
IV. Community impact	• Participate in regional health planning • Develop joint interagency services and administrative support systems • Provide effective primary prevention and indirect services • Collaborate in integration of services for multiproblem clients and stimulate effective interagency referral system	• Assess community needs • Undertake incidence and prevalence studies • Test primary prevention strategies • Evaluate consultation and education services • Participate in systematic regional need assessment • Facilitate and provide technical assistance to citizen and consumer input to need assessment, program planning, and evaluation

SYSTEMS RESOURCE MANAGEMENT (LEVEL I)

The function of evaluation at the level of systems resource management includes several activities critical to the program planning and management process: (a) assisting the organization to meet minimum standards for human service settings; (b) assisting in the formulation of program goals that are based on mandated services or documented needs; (c) framing the information needed to set program priorities; (d) identifying and allocating resources; and (e) translating program priorities into measurable intervention strategies, based on identified or legally mandated needs.

As suggested by Table 4.1, Level I evaluative activities deal with decision-making concerns that focus on internal regulation and control and the organization's ability to meet minimum standards for contractual compliance and organizational survival. The evaluator must, therefore, understand the organization's commitments and agreements regarding its core operations. These are evidenced by such documents as grant applications (or other funding agreements and procedures), the budget, fiscal management and audit procedures, state and municipal reimbursement requirements, staff employment contracts, job descriptions, third-party billing regulations, accreditation certificates, and other contractual as well as quasi-contractual records. Such documents comprise the basic operational commitments of the organization. The management and evaluation goal at this stage is to develop routine monitoring procedures to flag errors and deficiencies that threaten smooth operations and to detect deviations from established standards.

Another set of evaluative functions at the level of systems resource management is to define in operational terms an agency's abstract and often vague statements about purpose, organization, procedures, and program components. This would include such activities as examining goal and objective statements, reviewing legal or formal agreements such as grants or contracts, studying budget agreements, tracking informal agreements between the agency and the community, and reviewing staff responsibilities and organizational procedures. The initial purpose of these evaluation activities is to explore the organization's existing range of commitments, nonnegotiable contracts, available resources, and core responsibilities. Analysis of these commitments and available resources then provides the framework to explore the aspirations of staff and administration for improving the scope, efficiency, and quality of organizational services. Additional evaluative activities must then be designed to monitor attainment of commitments and aspirations.

The final set of evaluative functions at Level I is to monitor and assess the adequacy of resource allocation and the relevance of intervention procedures in light of established goals and objectives. Problem solving and analytic techniques borrowed from business management and labor research have been applied to such tasks. Task analysis, performance analysis, critical incidence analysis, PERT diagramming, and network analysis are techniques often used to identify performance standards and correct deficiencies (Mager, 1972; Mockler, 1972). Systems methodology provides guidelines for designing more efficient procedures and improving the organization of management activities (Mintzberg, 1973). An evaluator familiar with these techniques can offer valuable assistance to administrators in operations management. It is not universally agreed, however, that these decision-making concerns come within the usual boundaries of evaluative responsibility.

CLIENT UTILIZATION (LEVEL II)

The organization's service-delivery processes must also be adequately monitored (hence the common term "process evaluation" for tasks within the first two levels of evaluative activity in our model). Without an adequate monitoring system, even in organizations with few staff, it quickly becomes impossible to understand the organization's activities. Consequently, statistical summaries are needed to keep all organizational activities *visible,* and thereby more governable. As suggested by Table 4.1, evaluative studies at this level examine client entry requirements, referral patterns, units of service rendered, and factors that influence service delivery and channel client demand. These surveys can ascertain the degree to which target populations are being served.

Findings from client studies are often submitted to funders to meet accountability requirements. Information about utilization patterns may also suggest ways that administrators can improve the relevance of services to needs of the clientele. In addition, each stage in the process of providing services can be monitored in order to review (a) the appropriateness of client screening criteria and initial assignment to a service setting, (b) the adequacy of service planning for clients (e.g., by using a problem-oriented client record), (c) the safeguards against inappropriate utilization (e.g., by applying utilization review procedures), and (d) the level of continuity of care achieved with multiproblem, chronic, or relapsing clients.

Implicit in any organization's operating agreements is the expectation that it will provide services to specific populations in need. Federal statutes and regulations place explicit emphasis on evaluating the adequacy and accessibility of services for specific populations in need. No standardized method exists, however, for identifying appropriate target populations, and this programmatic expectation has generated acrimonious controversy. To what age groups, what social and ethnic populations, and/or what types of client problems should the human service organization differentially address itself? Does the leadership for deciding these questions reside with funding agencies, legislative bodies, regional health planning administrations, or community advisory groups? Agency utilization statistics per se do not define priority target populations or provide evidence about the relevance of service to overall community needs. Advisory board deliberations, community surveys of expressed health and human service needs, and census data analyses are all relevant to forming reasonable judgments about the programmatic implications of utilization data (cf. Chapters 9 and 10). Discussions between the human service organization and its constituents to clarify expectations for, and limitations of, service programs is a primary (but often avoided) technique for identifying service needs. When service needs have been defined, utilization data allow the evaluator to examine the organization's relevance and responsiveness to these needs.

In addition to client or patient utilization surveys, quality assurance activities are also important aspects of the *client utilization* level of program evaluation. Service settings are expected to provide "high quality" services to recipients; but without refined processes for evaluating treatment effectiveness, the actual quality of services cannot be known. Several indirect approaches can be used at this more rudimentary level. While quality of care standards are defined traditionally by professional or governmental organizations that establish training and licensure requirements, the assessment of quality and appropriateness of intervention has until recently been reserved for the practitioner's (or the organization's) self-scrutiny. Quality of care assessment is now receiving increased attention, however, through peer and utilization review methods.

In the health and mental health fields there are three basic and complementary quality assurance techniques: admissions (or entry) certification within concurrent review, medical care evaluation studies, and profile analyses. In the health field, all are the responsibility of a regional professional standards review organization (PSRO) (Decker & Bonner, 1973). In most cases, however, the PSRO delegates the review responsibility to the specific health organization, unless the PSRO determines that the local organization cannot or will not carry out effective review procedures. Under PSRO sanctions, utilization review aims to eliminate overutilization of hospital-based care in order to contain health care costs. Utilization review includes (*a*) *concurrent* review of care provided by health professionals that focuses primarily on process criteria and (*b*) *continued stay review* that assesses appropriateness of continued hospitalization and quality of such care. Medical care evaluation studies are conducted to study in depth the quality and administration of health care services. Medical care evaluation studies include *retrospective* and *concurrent* review of aggregate *provider performance,* as judged against both process and short-range patient *outcome* criteria. Profile analysis is a form of retrospective review using aggregated patient care data displayed in formats that portray patterns of health care over a selected period of time. Such studies are used to focus concurrent review efforts, to develop local hospital utilization norms, and to assess the effectiveness of hospital quality assurance review activities (Goran, Roberts, Kellogg, Fielding, & Jessee, 1975). Quality assurance activities and their integration with program evaluation activities are covered more extensively in Chapter 14, where additional source documents are cited.

OUTCOME OF INTERVENTION (LEVEL III)

The most common motivation for studying outcome is to aid management and service providers in a specific major decision about program change. Such studies deal with policy decisions about service delivery methods and are generally time-limited rather than ongoing monitoring activities (see Table 4.1). For example, a comparative study of two different approaches to providing posthospitalization care to cardiac patients could have the objective of selecting a treatment approach that maximizes the cost–effectiveness. The utility of a comparative outcome study is most obvious when it is unclear whether a new method will be a significant improvement over existing procedures.

A second approach to outcome analysis, more closely linked to day-to-day management, is routine monitoring to detect specific program strengths, weaknesses, or trouble spots. Only easily collected and inexpensive outcome indicators are practical for these purposes. In many health programs, survival rates and symptom ratings at various stages of treatment are the most obvious indices; global ratings of functional impairment before and after receipt of services as well as measures of client satisfaction might also be used. Normative data from the professional literature, or from funding and accreditation agencies may be available for interpreting such measures. At the least, time trends within the same program and types of clients can be examined.

A third contribution of outcome evaluation to program management is to demonstrate whether each component of the program is functioning with reasonable effectiveness. It is difficult, however, given current technology and resources, to demonstrate overall program effectiveness. Untreated comparison groups are generally unavailable, and, therefore, estimating program efficacy requires normative studies among subsets of similar programs. The methods and resources for such studies are frequently lacking.

These three potential contributions of outcome evaluation—as well as many other issues relevant to instrumentation, design, and utilization of outcome data—are discussed in Chapters 11 and 12. Chapter 13 integrates costs of services with service outcomes and presents methods for cost–outcome and cost–effectiveness analyses.

Difficulty in applying standardized outcome measures to assess quality and appropriateness of treatment arises in part from the diversity of the service system's vested interests. Satisfactory outcomes of human service interventions may be defined in various different ways by clients, private clinicians, training institutions, professional organizations, professional peer groups, legislators, fiscal intermediaries, consumer advocates, and community advisory groups. Since the search for realistic expectations and outcome norms is in its infancy, usable data are very uneven. For example, death rates and posttreatment survival expectancies have been extensively monitored for many forms of cancer, but usable normative outcome data are rarely available in conditions producing chronic disability.

In the health care field, normative data are being gathered on some process and outcome variables by the Professional Activity Study operated by the Commission on Professional and Hospital Activities in Ann Arbor, Michigan (Holloway, Wiczai, & Carlson, 1975). The Joint Commission on Accreditation of Hospitals, as well as many PSROs, are also collecting patient care criteria developed in local patient care audits. These criteria often include outcome standards and norms. Establishing normative standards on long-range functioning in conditions for which death is not a major risk is particularly crucial.

There is sometimes confusion between definitions of client outcome and program outcome. Good client outcome is always, of course, a prominent human service organization goal. Yet program objectives may also include such other outcomes as community awareness of the availability of services, or community acceptance of service programs, or good staff morale. Regarding client outcome, it is useful to distinguish short-range outcomes that can be assessed easily during the course of providing services from long-range outcomes that may require data collection at some point following client exit from the service setting. Short-range outcomes represent a sensible starting place for examining many policy issues. The monitoring of these measures might be integrated into utilization review and client care audit procedures.

COMMUNITY IMPACT (LEVEL IV)

Level IV evaluation is the least technically developed but the most relevant to the preventive goals of health and other human service programs (see Table 4.1). At this level, evaluators assess the broad community effects of preventive efforts, aid in coordinating comprehensive regional health and human service networks, contribute to regional needs assessment and health planning, and facilitate broad community input into program planning whenever possible. Level IV activities require that evaluators shift away from their intra-organizational focus and create external linkages with evaluators, planners, and administrators at other program levels, at other governmental levels, and across categorical program boundaries.

Broskowski and Baker (1974) argue that evaluation of preventive efforts must emerge as a major priority during the 1980s. Yet, to determine the effects of primary prevention programs, it generally is necessary to introduce them experimentally in large-scale, multicommunity undertakings. Thus, collaborative networks of program evaluators supported by university and government researchers may be required to evaluate different methods of organizing prevention efforts. The support and leadership of evaluators in fostering the development of this interorganizational capability will be important. More importantly, within the present chapter's focus, internal evaluators must carry out feasible evaluations of prevention-oriented units *within* their own organization. These may include consultation services to other agencies, health education, and the like. Approaches to evaluating such "indirect services" have been discussed by Bloom (1968), Canfield and Kliewer (1977), and Mannino and Shore (1975). Chapters 8 and 15 in the present volume also describe approaches to the evaluation of consultative, planning, educational, and administrative services.

The second emphasis at this level is the development of regional strategies for comprehensive need assessment. Several approaches to community need assessment are available, including direct citizen participation, analysis of public data, social area demographic analysis, surveys of related human service agencies, and epidemiologic surveys (Siegel, Attkisson, & Cohn, 1977). Community need assessment is best accomplished as part of a comprehensive, continuing program evaluation. Costs may be contained through collaborative approaches to regional need assessment and planning activities. At the more rudimentary levels, need assessment utilizes impressionistic methods to identify populations at risk or to estimate the type and locus of various community problems.

Current health planning strategies for determining need remain poorly integrated and fragmentary. In the future, regional need identification and health planning should proceed with clear sanctions and sufficient resources. Collaborative networks must be organized, probably at the multicounty level, to act as regional systems. Such networks could perform or sponsor intensive field surveys and serve as a conduit through which the implications of regional data can be conveyed to individual communities and organizations. Improved regional planning can help to suppress the typical governmental response to pressing or newly emerging health and human service problems—adding new categorical programs. This tendency encourages redundancy, promotes needless expenditure of limited resources, and maintains institutional separatism, which ultimately results in programs that are out of phase with social forces and health needs. Instead, organizational structures and interrelationships must change in response to altered community needs, rather than simply adding new programs (Demone & Harshbarger, 1974). These issues and methods in community need assessment are discussed more extensively in Chapters 9 and 10.

The third aim of evaluation at Level IV is to promote the integration of human service programs within a regional delivery system. As argued in Chapter 1, the current low level of integration among diverse community service programs will limit the potential effectiveness and impact of any single categorical service program. Assessing the effectiveness of a single categorical program is but one building block in determining overall effectiveness of the entire human service network. Consequently, one of the major goals of program evaluation must be to assess and then help increase systemic integration. Since human services are increasingly provided within service delivery organizations, rather than by individual practitioners, the analysis and evaluation of human service networks requires that evaluators understand and monitor the transactions between, as well as within, service delivery organizations. Because program evaluators attend to many tasks that extend beyond the boundaries of their own organizations, as well as to the gaps and limitations in service programs, they become natural advocates for service network integration.

The community impact level is the most advanced of the levels of program evaluation activity, starting with the level of systems resource management, and moving up through the client utilization and outcome evaluation levels. The ability of program evaluation capacity to develop through these levels, and the effectiveness of evaluation activities at all levels, depends in turn on the other two aspects of evaluation capacity: information capability of the organization and the functional roles of the evaluator.

INFORMATION CAPABILITY

An organization's *information capability,* as outlined in Figure 4.1, can be conceptualized as ranging from poorly planned and uncoordinated *natural data sources* to a level of *planned-access information systems* supported by allocated resources. In today's typical human service organization, several data sources are maintained internally and function semi-autonomously. Examples are the informal grapevine, patient care records, budgets, financial accounting documents, personnel records, statistical monitoring systems, logs, and other types of informal records. For evaluation purposes, it is difficult and expensive to obtain meaningful, reliable information from these independent, nonstandardized, and uncoordinated data sources. It is important for most human service programs to have some type of internal information system that encompasses and gradually supplants the redundant natural data sources, and yet allows collected data to be used for multiple purposes. Reporting stipulations, needs for improved administrative efficiency, cost-finding and rate-setting requirements, monitoring staff productivity—as well as the general need for evaluation—dictate this shift toward integrated data processing.

An integrated information system does not necessarily imply computerization. Where a computerized system becomes necessary because of organizational size or complexity, it is important to keep in mind that there is no royal road for introducing automated information systems to a human service organization. The applicability of computer technology to human service systems has, for the most part, been impeded by several major problem areas: (a) computer software (i.e., programming) has failed to match the excellence of available computer hardware (i.e., the computer itself); (b) programmers rarely are familiar with the communication styles or data needs of human service providers; (c) the data that flow into automated systems typically are seriously lacking in reliability and validity; and (d) automated data system developers have frequently placed such excessive, overlapping reporting requirements on service providers that the systems intrude on the provision of services. These problem areas, although not insurmountable, remain serious obstacles to creative use of the computer as a tool for management decision making within human services. Sterling (1975) presents useful guidelines that can be used to "humanize" information systems and to make such systems more acceptable within organizations.

In addition, effective management information capability is dependent upon identifying which elements of program, staff, and client information are sufficiently meaningful for routine monitoring, ensuring the availability of essential data, capturing reliable data at its source while minimizing the degree of reliance on professional staff for data collection, reducing overlapping or redundant activity reporting, providing direct return of usable data to the service provider, translating abstract data summaries into decision-making material, and performing specialized studies for immediate and long-term planning.

As noted in Figure 4.1, information capability is best viewed as a continuum. On one end of the continuum, the unprocessed data are least certain, least available, or least relevant to decision-making needs. Moving up the continuum, the data are collected and analyzed more systematically so that decision making can acquire precision and sophistication. Toward the top of the continuum, the data have been transformed into relevant information and can be integrated into the decision-making process where they have the most impact on program operations and development. At the highest level, it is possible to integrate qualitative as well as quantitative measures into the decision-making process, implement specialized time-limited studies, and analyze program strategies that are related to overall organizational policies.

THE NATURAL DATA BASE LEVEL

This initial level of information capability exists when no effort has been made to coordinate or centralize the data generated by the respective functional and support units of a human service organization. Examples of such data include accounting and auditing records, budgets, client records, service utilization records, hospital procedure manuals, contractual documents, staffing grant applications, and personnel records. Each operational unit may collect a wealth of potentially useful information, but it exists in a disconnected, fragmentary, and idiosyncratic form that greatly reduces its relevance to decision making and planning.

Idiosyncratic data collection practices, ambiguous statistical summaries, and unreliable or biased information about system activities greatly complicate the evaluator's tasks when information capability remains at the level of the natural data base. Ideally, the evaluator and the administrator should have reason to believe that the information collected represents what it purports to represent. For example, if a mental health outpatient department reports admitting 25 new patients during a given month, the evaluator needs to know that this statistic accurately reflects a specific departmental activity and has consistent meaning for those collecting and reviewing this information.

CENTRALIZED INFORMATION PROCESSING SYSTEM

At the second level of information capability, data flow is coordinated and channeled from the various functional units of the care system through a centralized information bank, although data coverage and format may still be idiosyncratic within each unit. The efficiency of evaluation is greatly improved when comparable information about program activities can be summarized across the entire organization. Standardized data collection requires uniformity in definitions of organizational events, uniform accounting procedures, uniform client and personnel records, and the merging of diverse data within centralized though not necessarily computerized files. Tables displaying the service activities of an organizational unit cross-tabulated with that unit's various classes of service providers are examples of information system products at this level of information capability. A centralized information processing system must be constructed so that separate organizational units retain their own source files for unit-level informational needs, and submit for higher-level processing only that information required for total organizational use.

The ability to compile program statistics flexibly makes it possible to describe some quantitative characteristics of program activities; but mere tabulations are inadequate for many administrative tasks. This level of information capability lacks the planning, coordination, and sanction necessary for use in the decision-making process. Executives concerned with program accomplishment remain dependent for information upon a variety of idiosyncratic data forms and collection processes, as well as upon gross summary statistics. Nevertheless, this information processing level can be distinguished from the previous one in that some organizational effort has been made to centralize and process information.

PLANNED-ACCESS INFORMATION SYSTEM

The first two levels of the information capability dimension allow for filing, merging, and tabulating the separate data systems indigenous to the organization's functional and support units. However, such file systems are inaccessible, cumbersome, and expensive when used for evaluation purposes. At the planned-access information system level, the evaluator *creates* data collection and file systems that can be easily accessed, merged, and analyzed. The key distinction here is planned, achievable access to a wide range of organizational data. At this level reliable data are collected routinely so that they are readily available to ongoing decision making, the principal transactions (events such as client contacts or consultation meetings) are systematically recorded and stored, the overall data bank of stored information is available for prompt retrieval, and the data system is flexible so that it can inexpensively and quickly adapt to changing needs. When combined with fiscal accounts, budgets, staff time allocation data, and personnel information, this level of information capability provides the evaluator and administrator with a very powerful resource.

If information is to be relevant for management decision making, it must be based upon reliable and valid data. The planned-access information system level assumes that adequate error control procedures are indeed functioning so that the evaluator can devote greater effort to analyzing operational difficulties, identifying their causes, and posing solutions. The higher up the information capability dimension, the more standardized, dependable, and reliable is the data gathering process. The more confidence one can have in the accuracy of the data, the more credible are evaluative analyses.

It is clearly advantageous to have the data collection and analysis process centralized and available for planned access. A more subtle advantage, however, is that centralized responsibility and accountability for meaningful, decision-oriented analyses are supported by appropriate executives. Furthermore, centralized control over the operations and staff associated with the evaluation process helps maintain identifiable, clear-cut boundaries between the responsibilities of evaluation and other program functions (Elpers & Chapman, 1973). Achieving this information processing level is a highly technical undertaking that requires careful planning and implementation (Chapman, 1976).

As information capability improves, there is a subtler risk of distortion that cannot be met with error control procedures and staff training in using common definitions. There is always the risk of misinterpreting abstract statistical summaries of service processes. There is no corrective for this other than first-hand knowledge of the service process. Previous evaluator or administrator experience as a service provider can be some help, but is not sufficient in itself. When the evaluator is trying to draw implications for program improvement from abstract program data, it will usually be essential to review these implications with those actually engaged in the service delivery process. This is not to deny that front line service staff may have their own defensive or myopic distortions of the true state of affairs. However, service providers often raise issues that can help the evaluator avoid unjustified overinterpretations and erroneous inferences.

At the lowest two levels of the information capability dimension, evaluators systematically collect "naturally" generated data, analyze these data, and attempt to assemble an organizational overview. Using such uncoordinated data as a basis for secondary analysis is problematic, however, since the information is usually based on nonstandardized definitions, and is unreliable, particularistic, fragmented, and difficult to interpret. At the third level of information capability, the evaluator can integrate varied types of uniformly collected information to accomplish meaningful program analyses (Cooper, 1973; Sorensen & Phipps, 1975). More detail about the theory and process of designing integrated, planned-access information systems is presented in Chapters 6 and 7.

SPECIALIZED DATA COLLECTION CAPABILITY

This final level assumes the existence of a planned-access information system, and is the next logical investment for a human service organization wishing to augment its information processing capability through specialized evaluations and investigatory projects. Such projects are best construed as time-limited studies of special problems or management policy issues related to program improvement and innovation strategies. These studies might, for example, examine the cost–outcome and cost–effectiveness performance of alternative program strategies. Specialized data collection capability also allows for the linking of internal data with externally relevant information such as need assessment or normative data.

At the level of specialized data collection capability, the task is to integrate both quantitative and qualitative information and independently to analyze program strategies with an appreciation for management's critical policy questions. Policy analysis might involve such questions and studies as the effectiveness or efficiency of alternative program strategies in meeting community demands or assessed needs for service. Specialized data collection capability may exist with or without an integrated management information system (Broskowski, 1977). However, when this capability exists *without* a planned-access information system, results of time-limited studies have less than optimal impact and relevance for systemic planning since results cannot be compared with an ongoing organizational baseline. Time-limited studies at any of the four levels of evaluative activity can be expected to be more useful when presented in the context of baseline information about personnel, program effort, cost, and service utilization.

FUNCTIONAL ROLES OF THE EVALUATOR

This third dimension of program evaluation is as important as an organization's information capability in determining the utility of evaluative activities. As depicted in Figure 4.1, functional roles of evaluators vary from the *statistician* level, where data compilation is the basic task, to the *decisionmaker* level where analysis, coordination, and policy implementation are the principal tasks. To be optimally effective, the evaluator's role should be embedded in the organization's decision-making process at both the operational and the long-range policy planning levels.

In order to ensure that evaluation can function usefully in relation to program management, first, talented evaluators should be recruited, and, second, their role should be assigned sufficient authority and sanctions. Creative evaluation depends, however, not only on the evaluator's training, experience, and mandate, but also on the evaluator's participation in, and understanding of, management concerns. Thus, evaluative capability is enhanced when the evaluator has access to the decision-making process. In this way, the evaluator can ask relevant questions, propose appropriate studies, suggest planning strategies, and have an advocacy role in implementing changes that are decided upon as the result of an evaluative activity. This linkage of evaluative activities to management tasks is the essential element in the role of the evaluator.

THE STATISTICIAN AND EVALUATIVE RESEARCHER ROLES

Unfortunately, it is the atypical human service organization where evaluation staff—regardless of talent—can have easy access to, and participate in the decision-making and planning process. In most human service organizations evaluators currently function either at the basic *statistical* level, compiling facts from natural data sources for funder-report purposes, or at the *evaluative research* level where problems of applied research interest are investigated. In the latter case, data reports often lag years behind the data collection process, and the objectives of the research are, at best, only peripherally related to management decisions (Hargreaves, Attkisson, McIntyre, & Siegel, 1975).

THE EVALUATIVE TECHNICIAN ROLE

Similar difficulties plague the *evaluative technician* role, where the evaluation effort principally involves reporting to management, but does not include direct participation in the decision-making process. In this case, the evaluator may generate valuable and relevant information for administrators, but the reporting process does not allow continuing input from an evaluator who has first-hand knowledge of the organizational information and understands evaluative activities as they relate to management and policy issues.

THE EVALUATOR AS INTEGRATOR, COORDINATOR, AND DECISION MAKER

Evaluators need access to the decision process if evaluative information is to receive direct, reasonable, and participative advocacy in relation to other influential factors such as community politics, service provider allegations, administrative predilections, and financial constraints. This is especially important when, as is often the case, program managers lack skill in relating program information to decision options.

When management uses evaluation effectively, a common sequence of events is evident: (a) a specific problem area is identified as requiring evaluation support; (b) relevant information is gathered and analyzed; (c) reports are generated and presented in a form compatible with the management decision process; (d) alternative solutions or actions are posed and reviewed by evaluators and administrators in the light of both evaluation data and other factors; and (e) a decision is implemented, often with continued monitoring of the effect of the decision on the attainment of program objectives. This process can be seen even at the most rudimentary level of evaluation activity, and in the most limited state of information capability or evaluator role in the organization. As the organization progresses along the three dimensions of evaluation capability, this process can be applied to a wider range of problems with results that are increasingly timely and focused on crucial management issues.

THE INTEGRATION OF EVALUATION AND ADMINISTRATION

Earlier in this chapter we raised two questions: How do we account for the fact that some evaluations are influential and others are not? How can human service agencies become more like self-evaluating organizations? These questions have been our main focus to this point, and now a third may be added: How can we ensure that an agency's evaluation capability is used effectively? The answers to all three questions involve the same concept: the integration of program evaluation with administrative decision making. The nature of the solution is easy to state. However, practical solutions are more difficult to implement. Integration will require changes in the typical roles of both program evaluators and administrators. We shall continue to see poorly administered programs and disregarded evaluative findings *until* the self-evaluating organization becomes a reality and there is a day-to-day working integration of administration and evaluation fully using the organization's evaluative capability.

By integration, we do not mean that either administration or evaluation should be so controlled by the other that the capacity of administrators and evaluators to carry out their responsibilities is impaired. There needs to be a system of mutual collaboration with appropriate checks and balances. Program evaluators, being new to human service environments, have stressed the need for their autonomy. Yet both evaluators and administrators are bound by their responsibility to the goals and objectives of the agency. The task of the administrator is to manage the programs guided by these goals and objectives, whereas the task of the evaluator is to assess in detail the ongoing match between program activities and the attainment of program commitments and aspirations. Although program goals may change, this does not mean that either the administrator or the evaluator is free to operate independently. Both remain accountable to the goals of the organization.

What principles should guide integration of evaluation and management? Articles about the relationship between evaluators and administrators (e.g., Argyris, 1958; Rodman & Kolodny, 1965), in general, focus on how persons in these roles can better understand and get along with one another. The literature, however, has not adequately examined how these two functions should be integrated. Nevertheless, several excellent reviews of research dissemination and utilization do provide clear implications for the process of integrating administration and evaluation of programs (Department of Health, Education, and Welfare, 1972a,b,c; Havelock, 1975; Rogers & Shoemaker, 1971). Although these latter studies have focused on the utilization, or lack thereof, of formal research results, we can translate the basic concepts and apply them to ongoing organizational self-evaluation.

Ronald Havelock's model of research dissemination and utilization is especially promising as a framework within which to discuss the integration of program evaluation with administrative decision making. Havelock (1975) sees dissemination and utilization as an act of communication between a research *resource system* and a *user system*. A resource system includes the body of knowledge of some area of research plus the persons informed of this knowledge and any other resources that could be used to impart this information—for our discussion, the organization's program evaluation capacity. A user system is some applied area in which this knowledge, if adopted in the form of innovation, might result in improved performance—for our purpose, program management and service operations. Integration is created through a two-way interaction process that connects the resource and user systems. Both systems function more successfully when there is ample dialogue between each system—a communication pattern that continuously stimulates mutual problem solving behavior. Havelock outlines seven factors that describe how the resource and user systems can be optimally interconnected: linkage methods, program structure, openness, capacity, reward, proximity, and synergy.

LINKAGE METHODS

"Linkage" between resource and user systems can be measured by the number, variety, and mutuality of contacts, and by the degree to which the two systems or functions collaborate. The more linkages there are, the stronger the interconnectedness, the more effective any specific contact will be, and the greater will be the overall impact each system will have on the other. Information will be exchanged more easily and will be more influential. Research or evaluation that is "highly linked" to a user system will develop in the direction of more closely meeting user needs and will be more readily accepted.

Linkage is seen as the key concept by Havelock because he and other reviewers have found that an enormous gap exists between research activity and user practice. Each arises from a system independent of the other. Researchers tend to write for other researchers and are read only by them.

Practitioners are not knowledgeable about research and modify their programs based on conversations with other practitioners. As a result, researchers tend to do research of little interest to practitioners and practitioners continue to operate service programs with methods that have little or no basis in research. Linkage between researchers and practitioners, however, has been shown to improve the relevance of research and to result in programs that incorporate methods of proven merit.

All too often we see a similar lack of linkage as evaluation and administration go their independent ways, not interacting with one another. What is missing is the formal link, the persons who overlap in responsibility for evaluation and administration and understand both. This is more than merely an assignment of responsibility as shown in an organizational chart. The critical element is the real and knowledgeable participation in both processes.

Linkage is often real in appearance only. To illustrate this, consider an example of pseudolinkage in the situation where the *evaluative researcher* or the *evaluator technician* reports to an administrator. The administrator, who has had no training in evaluation or research, is initially uneasy about the prospect of supervising the evaluator, fearing that the evaluator may expose managerial ignorance. The evaluator, coming from a research background, is equally concerned with reporting to an administrator who does not understand research and may be unsympathetic. Each is unfamiliar with the organizational role of the other. A weak relationship based on mutual anxiety and lack of understanding develops between them. The evaluator is typically left to do evaluative research of personal choosing, rarely meeting with the administrator, and communicating through formal written reports. The administrator may see the reports as tangible evidence of the productivity of the evaluator as well as the administrator's own "successful" supervision—but only limited and sporadic use of evaluative findings occurs, if any occurs at all. Mutual discussion about administrative decision making and the related information the evaluator might supply rarely if ever occurs. The relationship, therefore, does not evolve to a point where the administrator clearly defines the agency's decision-making and information needs. Consequently, administration and evaluation are left as separate processes.

Conceptually, there are two models of effective formal linkage: (a) the *administrator–evaluator;* and (b) the *evaluator–administrator.* The administrator–evaluator is an administrator who has management responsibility for evaluation among other responsibilities. Although typically not a formally trained or professional evaluator, the administrator–evaluator either has obtained a working knowledge of evaluation through experience—understanding the general evaluative methods with a seasoned perspective on their strengths and limitations. Within an administrative position, the administrator–evaluator conducts or participates in decision making. Consequently, this executive possesses an understanding of the agency's ongoing information needs. The administrator–evaluator views evaluation as a management tool established to supply the needed administrative information. The administrator–evaluator's function is to translate these information needs to an *evaluative technician,* to monitor the degree of success with which the technician meets these needs, and to integrate the information into administrative decision making.

The second model of effective linkage is the evaluator–administrator. This individual is a formally research-trained evaluator who directs and conducts the agency's evaluation activities. In addition, the evaluator–administrator regularly participates in the agency's high-level decision making. He or she attends administrative meetings where management concerns are discussed and is free to communicate information. The evaluator–administrator frequently uses such occasions as an opportunity to convey both written and oral evaluative information. This person also takes an active part in deliberations, is seen as sharing in the fundamental decisions, and generally participates in both evaluation and administration. By being directly involved in the decision-making process, the evaluator–administrator knows the agency's administrative information needs. Such knowledge permits both short- and long-range planning of evaluative activity so that useful information will be available for all types of decisions and policy issues. The evaluator–administrator is responsible for the full range of evaluation activities—planning studies, data collection, synthesizing information, and reporting information to other administrators.

There is a third possible linkage model: the "change-agent" linkage. A great deal of emphasis in the research dissemination and utilization literature has been placed on the role of persons who are knowledgeable about empirically validated practices and who can actively communicate this body of information to practitioners. The change-agent would be neither a researcher nor an administrator, but would serve as the link between the two. Although this function is certainly appropriate for evaluators, the change-agent role is also a potential barrier to communication between evaluators and administrators within an organization.

The administrator–evaluator and evaluator–administrator appear to be the most promising formal linking roles. The former is probably closer to typical current practice. The training of administrators in program evaluation is a necessary step in making this model effective. The training process need not transform the administrator into an evaluator, but should educate program executives to administer and utilize evaluation. The evaluator–administrator role is more controversial and in some settings will necessitate a major change in the perception of the evaluator's function. The active participation in administration as a stated part of evaluator responsibilities, runs counter to traditional research training and requires the evaluator to be knowledgable about service delivery and management. There is an inevitable pull on evaluators to become involved in administration. Rather than reject such activism, we feel it is better to structure this action orientation—both in the organizational role of the evaluator and in the training of evaluators—so that they can be knowledgable in service administration.

Linkage should not be viewed as occurring only at the top of the agency structure. Evaluation and administration must be formally linked at the various administrative levels. At lower levels of a large organization, specific evaluation staff should have formal consultative and information providing roles with unit managers. This pattern facilitates closer linkage of evaluation to all important levels of program administration, but must be weighed against the problems in supplying technical consultation and support for these decentralized evaluation staff. These issues in organizing evaluative effort bring us to the second of Havelock's factors that facilitate integration of evaluation and administration: the factor of *structure*.

PROGRAM STRUCTURE

"Structure" involves the degree of systematic organization and coordination of programmatic elements. In order for evaluative information to be successfully incorporated into administrative decision making, service programs must have an effectively organized structural framework. This step requires an organizational structure with a rational sequence of functional elements, and a compartmentalized and coordinated division of labor within the agency. There must be organizational structure for the agency as a whole, within administrative and evaluative functions, and between the administrative and evaluative components of the organization.

There are four ways that structure is directly important for evaluation. First, evaluation needs to have its own division of labor and coordination of effort. Whether conducted by one person or a large staff, evaluative activities should be organized into a functional system. Second, evaluation should have a structured and coherent view of the rest of the agency. It should be able to understand the various levels and subcomponents and how they are interrelated. It should know the needs of the clients and be familiar with the organization's goals. It should have a good view and understanding of the agency's decision-making process. Third, evaluation should be able to plan how information will be communicated in a structured sequence into the decision-making process. Like the development and operation of evaluative studies, data utilization should be a planned and structured activity, not a hit-or-miss afterthought. Fourth, evaluation must be structured within the agency so that it is not administratively accountable to the management of the program element being evaluated.

The formal linkage point between evaluation and administration should be at a high organizational level. Although evaluation must be integrated into the agency, it needs to maintain as much internal autonomy as possible. This will enable evaluation staff to work closely with the most relevant program and administrative personnel, but maintain adequate independence from them. Evaluation staff should have a commitment to the agency's goals, but not to the methods chosen to reach them. This is the major difference between those who are responsible for the evaluative function and others within a human service organization.

A basic structural principle for community-based program evaluation is that *two* levels of organizational bonds are required for optimal utilization: the direct tie with the operational level being evaluated, and connection to a higher administrative level that provides sanction for the evaluator's autonomy and that also provides policy direction in planned change processes. If evaluation is sanctioned by the highest administrative level of an organization, this sanction may enable the evaluator to function effectively at any lower operational level. Discussions of "internal" versus "external" evaluation tend to ignore this need for a dual-level connection. The evaluator must be "internal" enough to have adequate ties to the program functions being evaluated, but be "external" enough for autonomous advocacy at the administrative level that provides policy guidance in the process of planned change. Therefore we recommend that the evaluator, or the director of the evaluation unit, report directly to the top organizational executive. This administrative sanction can provide a broad umbrella for evaluation across several lower administrative levels.

In large organizations, it is usually necessary to decentralize evaluative functions across administrative levels. More than one level of decentralization may be needed in very large organizations. The resulting tiers of evaluative responsibility would then extend from the level of direct service delivery to the highest executive and legislative level that has responsibility for human services. At present, vast areas of this evaluative structure remain to be established. However, program planners need to attend both to gaps in the evaluation structure, and to the inevitable redundancies where overlapping evaluation responsibilities may waste resources and confuse lines of accountability.

OPENNESS

Havelock's third factor, "openness," refers to the readiness to give and receive information. It requires a willingness and readiness for the user system to accept help, as well as the willingness and readiness of the evaluator to listen to user needs and to give help. Openness is based upon organizational acceptance of a guiding ethic of the self-evaluating organization: that change is desirable and possible.

So long as a human service agency sees as its purpose to deliver *fixed types* of services that are assumed already to be optimal, openness will not occur. For such an agency, program evaluation will be viewed as an irrelevant or destructive threat to its existence. Human service agencies that take this defensive position may continue to deliver services of unproven or disproven usefulness until a higher administrative level forces a process of planned change. This external force may paradoxically create internal openness to evaluation. Agency leaders come to see the higher administrative level as the primary threat, accept the reality that change is necessary if the agency is to survive, and form an alliance with the evaluator in an attempt to regain some control over the change process.

For evaluators, openness means being willing to collect information that will be of use to administrators. This in turn requires the evaluator to listen to administrative needs and develop responses tailored to meet them. A primary evaluation objective, then, is to obtain and communicate information with utility for administrative decision making. As a consequence, the validity of findings may be lessened; to a point, evaluators must be willing to run this risk. Obviously, if validity is too greatly reduced, the information will be meaningless. A part of the professional skill of the evaluator is to maximize utility by judging the optimal balance between the need for validity and the need for economy and timeliness.

For administrators, openness means being willing to expose areas where they are uncertain or believe there are deficiencies. It should be an active process of requesting and seeking out information rather than passively waiting to be asked and served. As part of a self-evaluating agency, administrators are not held accountable to operate perfect programs, but to be actively seeking to improve the efficiency and effectiveness of programs and to initiate new services when existing services are found to be inadequate.

CAPACITY

Within human service agencies both evaluation and administration must have the "capacity" to do their jobs in order for evaluation findings to be utilized. Capacity involves having the resources and competence to perform satisfactorily. The concept of information capability was discussed earlier. Evaluation must have sufficient resources to collect valid and useful information, and must have sufficient skill and influence to impart the data to administration in ways that heighten acceptability.

Evaluation capacity should be geared to the size of the agency. As we have noted, the type of persons who have the functional role of the *evaluator* in different agencies range from statistical clerks to professionally trained researchers who participate in high-level administrative decision making. These types of persons reflect the capacity of such organizations to conduct and utilize evaluation. For small agencies, a clerk may be sufficient; larger and more complex organizations require a greater capacity. Even in the small agency, an administrator will need to direct and supervise the clerk, in effect, assuming part of the evaluation function; hence, even in small agencies there must be a significant commitment for meaningful evaluation. The overall resources and competence of the agency should be matched by a comparable evaluative capacity.

Management capacity is also essential for evaluation effectiveness. Without good management, even the most capable evaluation will not change or improve agencies. Agencies must have the capacity to operate and modify programs before they can incorporate evaluative information. Like evaluators, administrators must have the ability to assemble and invest program resources wisely. Moreover, they need self-confidence as well as administrative skill and sophistication. Adequate administrative capacity is the basis for both good programs and effective evaluation.

REWARD

By "reward" Havelock refers to the availability, frequency, and amount of positive reinforcement for the evaluation and user systems. In order for evaluation to be influential in human service agencies, a system must be created in which evaluators are rewarded for good evaluation, and administrators are reinforced for incorporating evaluative findings into their decision making. Currently, neither evaluators nor administrators are regularly or frequently rewarded for the quality or use of evaluative information. All too often, the evaluator becomes a target of attack, even if only part of evaluative findings are critical of current organizational functioning. The evaluation design with its inherent methodological limitations may be compared to narrow research standards and then judged scientifically inadequate. The evaluator's professional ability may be challenged and motivations questioned. Even though evaluative effort may eventually effect program changes and improvements, the evaluation process may be a negative experience for the evaluator. For the administrator, evaluation can be equally unpleasant and unsatisfactory. Although administrators typically expect that a program's worth will be confirmed, evaluation frequently fails to provide this confirmation, at least for some major part of program operation. Such findings may jeopardize the program's funding. The administrator may feel that his or her professional ability is under attack. Indeed, the program staff or others may blame the administrator for the poor results rather than accepting more appropriate shared responsibility for program shortcomings, and working to correct them.

Lack of appropriate incentives for participation in evaluation has a stifling effect. Campbell (1969) argues that new human service programs should be conceptualized as social experiments and not proposed as final solutions. They should be viewed as attempts to meet certain social problems. It is true that, if evaluation were viewed in this light, adverse effects would be diminished. In the context of negative evaluative findings, administrators of human service agencies may begin to hold a more modest opinion about their program's degree of success, stating them conditionally. On the other hand, evaluators too often take the preevaluation rhetoric about "assessing program effectiveness" literally, and design studies aimed to assess lofty objectives, assuming that more modest achievement should be assessed as failures. Although formal program goals have to be taken literally in *summative* evaluation, most evaluation should be *formative,* intended for program improvement—determining relative success to be that which improves on the effects of current standard practice. With adjustment in administrative expectations *and* commensurate modification in evaluation strategy, meaningful and useful assessment of human service programs can be achieved that is rewarding to both evaluators and administrators.

PROXIMITY

The closer the "proximity" between evaluators and administrators, the more likely the effective linkage between them and in turn the greater utilization of evaluative information. Evaluators should not be distant figures within an "ivory tower" in the agency. They should be located close to administrators and practitioners, seeing them frequently, formally and informally. The evaluator should be able to speak in the terms and slang of the agency as an insider and be seen as "one of us," although with a different function.

There is also another, more psychological, meaning to proximity: the proximity of evaluative information to the administrative decision-making process. Evaluative information should be timely, and produced in relation to the pace of administrative decision making. If evaluative data are communicated long before a decision or after a decision, they will have limited or no usefulness. Time and place are critical to administrative decision makers. Evaluators often must modify evaluation designs, at the cost of validity, in order for some information to be available when the decision is to be made. Administrators must also be willing to delay certain decisions for which evaluative results will be crucial.

SYNERGY

"Synergy" includes the variety, frequency, and persistence of forces that are used to communicate evaluative findings. Havelock reports that successful research utilization requires redundancy in communication. Evaluative information, like other information, must be repeated until it is received and absorbed. Moreover, this redundancy should be organized in a coherent fashion in which findings are presented in a variety of formats.

The concept of synergy also requires the evaluator to modify some lessons of social research training. Researchers are educated to believe that the end of a successful study is a written report, hopefully published in a journal. Evaluators, too, typically see the end of the evaluation as a final written report. However, if the evaluator is serious about having an impact on the agency, then the evaluation report is only one of the ways by which evaluative information must be communicated. The evaluator should fully utilize the existing linkage with administration, presenting information in both formal and informal meetings, using summary abstracts as well as complete written reports, giving talks, and making pictorial presentations. Much evaluative information continues to be relevant long after the data collection and initial description of results. Like aging wine, historical information should be brought up from the written report cellar and served from time to time. Administrators will come to see the evaluator as a repository of useful information and will actually seek out evaluative information for their decision making. Thus, synergy will become an active process both for evaluators and administrators.

CONCLUSION

Can we conclude after all this discussion that there is a meaningful role for evaluation in human service programs? If this question implies that there is a needed role for evaluation, the answer is undoubtedly "yes." The need for program improvement based on feedback about organizational functioning is clear. If the question asks more specifically whether there is currently a viable, effective role for evaluation in human service programs, the answer is less certain. Based on the literature it would appear that a negative answer might be best. Our personal experience with a number of influential evaluations suggests that the better response is "maybe." Finally, if our conclusion applies only to organizations having adequate evaluation capability integrated with administration, the answer is "yes." Whether the prevalence of effectively utilized evaluation will increase in the near future as much as needed, is yet to be seen.

SUMMARY

Evaluation as a component of human service organization management requires several fundamental characteristics if it is to be useful. Capacity for internal program evaluation must be developed over time in syncrony with the organization's management style, the availability of information processing tools, and establishment of specific administrative and evaluator role relationships.

A three-dimensional model of internal program evaluation capability can be used to portray these developmental factors. *Levels of evaluative activity,* the first dimension, describes the progression from the narrow concerns of resource management to the broad issues of program impact on the community. *Information capability,* the second dimension, specifies the technical tools needed to move along the continuum from unplanned and uncoordinated natural data bases to planned-access information systems supported by allocated resources. *Functional roles of the evaluator,* the third dimension, contrasts three self-limiting roles with an alternative organizational stance that effectively integrates the evaluator into the management process. The three-dimensional model can help managers and evaluators plan a flexible and effective approach to evaluation within human service organizations.

Following Havelock (1975), seven principles for use in integrating evaluation with administrative decision making were discussed: linkage methods, program structure, openness, capacity, reward, proximity, and synergy. Additional resource materials are available that will aid in creating organizational readiness for program evaluation (Attkisson, Hargreaves, Tuller, Temoshok, McIntyre, & Siegel, 1977; Broskowski, Attkisson, Tuller, & Berk, 1975; Hargreaves, Attkisson, & Sorensen, 1977). Using our model and these other resource materials, program managers and evaluators can assess their organization's current evaluation status, compare it with similar programs, and plan for future development.

REFERENCE NOTES

1. Our focus on internal program evaluation does not imply that external evaluative input has no value. Tripodi, Fellin, and Epstein (1971) discuss the circumstances in which a manager will prefer external help. For example, specific technical skills may be needed that are not practical to maintain internally, or observers with an outsider's perspective may be required. Despite particular advantages, Bernstein and Freeman (1975) and Mitchell (1973) have emphasized the limitations of relying solely on external or contracted evaluation. The constant need for relevant and timely information in the management of human service programs generally requires that internal program evaluation have first priority. The internal–external issue is often confused with the issue of organizing evaluation at different levels of program administration. Evaluation units within community-based programs will not meet the *total* information needs of funding and regulatory agencies at county, state, and federal levels. A governmental echelon responsible solely for funding and/or regulating an array of decentralized service delivery settings must have its own program evaluation capability. This capability may be maintained internally or contracted, but it must be organized to serve the decision processes at that specific governmental or program level. Evaluation activity at higher echel-

ons depends on service delivery agencies to supply information or to have that information available for audit on-site. If these reporting requirements and other governmental evaluation activities are designed in collaboration with executives and evaluators in community-based service organizations, the superordinant evaluation requirements may sometimes also enhance local evaluation capability. At the least, competition for scarce evaluation resources should be minimized. Therefore, although internal evaluation at the service delivery level is the focus of this chapter, we emphasize that such assessment cannot substitute for, or be replaced by, careful evaluation at other management levels (Chadwin, 1975; Heighton & McPheeters, 1976).

2. Brown, T. R., & Harris, D. E. *Integrating a research and evaluation unit into the decision making structure of a community mental health center.* Paper presented at the National Conference on Evaluation in Alcohol, Drug Abuse, and Mental Health Administration, Washington, D.C., April 1974.

3. Nelson, R. N. *Accountants 1, Psychologists 0.* Paper presented at the National Conference on Evaluation in Alcohol, Drug Abuse, and Mental Health Programs, Washington, D.C., April 1974.

4. Weiss, C. H. *Utilization of evaluation: Toward comparative study.* Paper presented at the American Sociological Association Meeting, Miami Beach, September 1966.

REFERENCES

Argyris, C. Creating effective relationships in organizations. *Human Organization,* 1958, *17,* 34–40.

Attkisson, C. C., & Hargreaves, W. A. A conceptual model for program evaluation in health organizations. In H. C. Schulberg & F. Baker (Eds.), *Program evaluation in the health fields* (Vol. II). New York: Behavioral Publications, 1977, in press.

Attkisson, C. C., Hargreaves, W. A., Tuller, I. R., Temoshok, L., McIntyre, M. H., & Siegel, L. M. A workingpeople's guide to the community mental health program evaluation literature. In W. A. Hargreaves *et al.* (Eds.), *Resource materials for community mental health program evaluation* (2nd ed.). (DHEW Publication No. ADM 77-328.) Washington, D. C.: U. S. Government Printing Office, 1977.

Attkisson, C. C., McIntyre, M. H., Hargreaves, W. A., Harris, M. R., & Ochberg, F. M. A working model for mental health program evaluation. *American Journal of Orthopsychiatry,* 1974, *44,* 741–753.

Bernstein, I. N., & Freeman, H. E. *Academic and entrepreneurial research: The consequences of diversity in Federal evaluation studies.* New York: Russel Sage Foundation, 1975.

Bloom, B. The evaluation of primary prevention programs. In L. Roberts, N. Greenfield, & M. Miller (Eds.), *Comprehensive mental health: The challenge of evaluation.* Madison: University of Wisconsin Press, 1968.

Broskowski, A. Management information systems for planning and evaluation. In H. C. Schulberg & F. Baker (Eds.), *Program evaluation in the health fields* (Vol. II). New York: Behavioral Publications, 1977, in press.

Broskowski, A., Attkisson, C. C., Tuller, I. R., & Berk, J. H. *Human services program evaluation: An edited bibliography of key references.* Milwaukee, Wisconsin: V-U Publishing Company, 1975.

Broskowski, A., & Baker, F. Professional, organizational, and social barriers to primary prevention. *American Journal of Orthopsychiatry,* 1974, *44,* 707–719.

Campbell, D. T. Reforms as experiments. *American Psychologist,* 1969, *24,* 409–429.

Canfield, M., & Kliewer, D. *Conference evaluation manual.* In W. A. Hargreaves, C. C. Attkisson, & J. E. Sorensen (Eds.), *Resource materials for community mental health program evaluation* (2nd ed.). (DHEW Publication No. ADM 77-328.) Washington, D. C.: U. S. Government Printing Office, 1977.

Caro, F. G. Evaluation in comprehensive urban antipoverty programs: A case study of an attempt to establish the evaluative research role in a Model City Program. In F. G. Caro (Ed.), *Readings in evaluative research.* New York: Russell Sage Foundation, 1971.

Carter, E. E. Behavioral theory and top level corporate decisions. *Administrative Science Quarterly,* 1971, *16,* 413–428.

Carter, R. K. Clients' resistance to negative findings and the latent conservative function of evaluation studies. *The American Sociologist,* 1971, *6,* 118–124.

Chadwin, M. L. The nature of legislative program evaluation. *Evaluation,* 1975, *2*(2), 45–49.

Chapman, R. L. *The design of management information systems for mental health organizations: A primer.* (DHEW Publication No. ADM 76-333.) Washington, D. C.: U. S. Government Printing Office, 1976.

Cooper, M. *Guidelines for a minimum statistical and accounting system for community mental health centers: A working handbook with illustrative end-product tables, document forms, and procedures.* (DHEW Publication No. ADM 74-14.) Washington, D. C.: U. S. Government Printing Office, 1973.

Cyert, R. M., & March, J. C. *A behavioral theory of the firm.* Englewood Cliffs, New Jersey: Prentice-Hall, 1963.

Decker, B., & Bonner, P. (Eds.). *PSRO: Organization for regional peer review.* Cambridge, Massachusetts: Ballinger, 1973.

Demone, H. W., Jr., & Harshbarger, D. (Eds.). *A handbook of human service organizations.* New York: Behavioral Publications, 1974.

Department of Health, Education, and Welfare. *Planning for creative change in mental health services: A manual on research utilization.* (DHEW Publication No. HSM 71-9059.) Washington, D. C.: U. S. Government Printing Office, 1972. (a)

Department of Health, Education, and Welfare. *Planning for creative change in mental health services: A distillation of principles on research utilization* (Vol. I). (DHEW Publication No. HSM 71-9060.) Washington, D. C.: U. S. Government Printing Office, 1972. (b)

Department of Health, Education, and Welfare. *Planning for creative change in mental health services: A distillation of principles on research utilization* (Vol. II). (DHEW Publication No. HSM 71-9061.) Washington, D. C.: U. S. Government Printing Office, 1972. (c)

Elpers, J. R., & Chapman, R. L. Management information for mental health services. *Administration in Mental Health,* 1973, Fall, 12–25.

Ference, T. P. Organizational communications systems and decision process. *Management Science,* 1970, *17,* 83–96.

Goran, M. J., Roberts, J. S., Kellogg, M. A., Fielding, J., & Jessee, W. The PSRO hospital review system. *Medical Care,* 1975, *13,* 1–33.

Hargreaves, W. A., Attkisson, C. C., McIntyre, M. H., & Siegel, L. M. Current applications of evaluation. In J. Zusman & C. Wurster (Eds.), *Program evaluation: Alcohol, drug abuse and mental health services.* Lexington, Massachusetts: Lexington Books, 1975.

Hargreaves, W. A., Attkisson, C. C., & Sorensen, J. E. (Eds.). *Resource materials for community mental health program evaluation* (2nd ed.). (DHEW Publication No. ADM 77-328.) Washington, D. C.: U. S. Government Printing Office, 1977.

Havelock, R. G. *Planning for innovation through dissemination and utilization of knowledge.* Ann Arbor, Michigan: Center for Research on Utilization of Scientific Knowledge, Institute for Social Research, The University of Michigan, 1975.

Heighton, R. H., & McPheeters, H. L. *Program evaluation in the state mental health agency: Activities, functions, and management uses.* (DHEW Publication No. ADM 76-310.) Washington, D. C.: U. S. Government Printing Office, 1976.

Holloway, D. C., Wiczai, L. J., & Carlson, E. T. Evaluating an information system for medical care evaluation studies. *Medical Care,* 1975, *13,* 329–340.

Horst, P., Nay, J. N., Scanlon, J. W., & Wholey, J. S. Program management and the federal evaluator. *Public Administration Review,* 1974, *34,* 300–308.

Mager, R. F. *Goal analysis.* Belmont, California: Lear Siegler, 1972.

Mannino, F. V., & Shore, M. F. Effecting change through consultation. In F. V. Mannino, B. W. MacLennan, & M. F. Shore (Eds.), *The practice of mental health consultation.* (DHEW Publication No. ADM 74-1120.) Washington, D. C.: U. S. Government Printing Office, 1975.

Mintzberg, H. *The nature of managerial work.* New York: Harper & Row, 1973.

Mitchell, T. An interview study points out the problem with "contract" evaluations. *Evaluation,* 1973, *1*(2), 21–23.

Mockler, R. J. *The management control process.* New York: Appleton, 1972.

Rodman, H., & Kolodny, R. L. Organizational strains in the researcher–practitioner relationship. In A. Gouldner & S. M. Miller (Eds.), *Applied sociology: Opportunities and problems.* New York: Free Press, 1965.

Rogers, E. M., & Shoemaker, F. F. *Communication of innovations.* New York: Free Press, 1971.

Roos, N. P. Evaluation, quasi-experimentation, and public policy. In J. A. Caporaso & L. L. Roos, Jr. (Eds.), *Quasi-experimental approaches: Testing theory and evaluating policy.* Evanston, Illinois: Northwestern University Press, 1973.

Rossi, P. H. Evaluating social action programs. In F. G. Caro (Ed.), *Readings in evaluation research.* New York: Russell Sage Foundation, 1971.

Siegel, L. M., Attkisson, C. C., & Cohn, A. H. Mental health needs assessment: Strategies and techniques. In W. A. Hargreaves, C. C. Attkisson, & J. E. Sorensen (Eds.), *Resource materials for community mental health program evaluation* (2nd ed.). (DHEW Publication No. ADM 77-328.) Washington, D. C.: U. S. Government Printing Office, 1977.

Sorensen, J. E., & Phipps, D. W. *Cost-finding and rate-setting for community mental health centers.* (DHEW Publication No. ADM 76-291.) Washington, D. C.: U. S. Government Printing Office, 1975.

Sterling, T. D. Humanizing computerized information systems. *Science,* 1975, *190,* 1168–1172.

Tripodi, T., Fellin, P., & Epstein, I. *Social program evaluation: Guidelines for health, education, and welfare administrators.* Itasca, New York: F. E. Peacock, 1971.

Ullman, J. C., & Huber, G. P. *The local job bank program: Performance, structure, and direction.* Lexington, Massachusetts: Lexington Books, 1973.

Vroom, V. H., & Yetton, P. W. *Leadership and decision making.* Pittsburgh: University of Pittsburgh Press, 1973.

Weiss, C. H. Where politics and evaluation research meet. *Evaluation,* 1973, *1*(3), 37–45.

Weiss, R. S., & Rein, M. The evaluation of broad-aim programs: Experimental design, its difficulties, and an alternative. *Administrative Science Quarterly,* 1970, *15,* 97–109.

Wholey, J. S., Scanlon, J. W., Duffy, H. G., Fukumoto, J. S., & Vogt, L. M. *Federal evaluation policy: Analyzing the effects of public programs.* Washington, D.C.: The Urban Institute, 1970.

Wildavsky, A. The self-evaluating organization. *Public Administration Review,* 1972, *32,* 509–520.

5

PROGRAM EVALUATION ON
A SHOESTRING BUDGET

Allan Beigel and Alan I. Levenson

During the past 20 years, tremendous growth has taken place in the development and implementation of human services. During the latter part of the 1950s, triggered largely by the onset of the civil rights movement, government and its partners began to recognize a need for a variety of human services. These services were designed to enhance the quality of life of individuals who did not have access to needed services because their social, economic, and cultural status left them outside traditional and available care systems.

By the early 1960s, efforts to correct this situation had led to the beginning of the community mental health center program, and the launching of the "War on Poverty" through the implementation of the Model Cities Program and the opening of the Office of Economic Opportunity. These programs and others led to an expenditure of billions of dollars in an attempt to improve the quality of life of neglected and underpriviledged Americans.

More recently, a new theme has emerged to influence these efforts. As Baker (1974) points out, "It is often the case that change occurs first and then is followed by conceptual efforts which attempt to rationalize the activity [pp. 577–578]." These conceptual efforts have included an emphasis on the theme of *comprehensiveness*. This has become a major theoretical base justifying not only the growth of community mental health centers but also multiservice centers, neighborhood service centers, youth opportunity centers, neighborhood health centers, and health maintenance organizations (Demone, 1973).

However, this trend resulted in tremendous coordination problems for programs. At the federal level, coordination has been attempted most recently among a variety of "behavioral" services through a merger of the National

97

Institute of Mental Health, the National Institute of Alcohol Abuse and Alcoholism, and the National Institute on Drug Abuse into the Alcohol, Drug Abuse, and Mental Health Administration. The need for coordination and comprehensiveness also has been emphasized by many states which have made vigorous efforts designed to reorganize a variety of public health, mental health, mental retardation, social welfare, and corrections programs under one of several types of superadministrative umbrellas.

In addition, as Baker (1974) further points out:

> Changes are occurring not only in the ways that services are organized, but also in the way they are thought about. There is an increasing tendency to conceptualize the variety of health and social welfare services in a new way which emphasizes an assumption of the generic quality of the helping actions of professional and nonprofessional caregivers despite a diversity of training and titles. There is also a growing professional as well as societal recognition of the common denominator inherent in the very problems presented by clients of helping agencies. There is an increasing tendency to designate a community's variety of health, mental health, and social welfare programs as "human services" [p. 578].*

Parallel to the development of this thrust toward a concept of "human services," a demand for accountability has also emerged. Perhaps in response to the often massive programmatic and administrative disorganization which many of these programs for the culturally and emotionally disadvantaged have demonstrated, those who are responsible for the amount of funds being spent have come to the fore with their call for accountability. This requirement has manifested itself in a number of ways during the past 10 years, and has led to the use of a variety of mechanisms designed to meet its mandates.

Although some human service program administrators have been able to respond to the demand for accountability through their access to sophisticated computer-based evaluation systems, most have not had sufficient economic or staffing resources to utilize such evaluative support systems. Nevertheless, this does not negate the importance of evaluation. Instead, it places these administrators in the midst of a profound dilemma—how to meet the demand for accountability without adequate fiscal or staffing resources? Some have responded to this question by ignoring it, whereas others have rapidly attempted to develop strategies that have not been soundly thought out.

This chapter will first attempt to delineate more clearly some of the principal ideological and pragmatic problems faced by the human service program administrator who does not *immediately* have access to specialized evaluation staff and adequate budgetary resources. Evaluation strategies that are useful and easily deployed will be described. These will enable the administrator with few readily available budgetary supports to begin some aspects of a comprehensive evaluation strategy and will result in the development of information that is useful for policy decisions.

*Reproduced by permission from: F. Baker, From community mental health to human service ideology. *American Journal of Public Health,* 1974, *64,* 576–581. (Copyright 1974, American Public Health Association, Washington, D. C.)

The problems that many program administrators face and how they may employ evaluation strategies without access to adequate fiscal and staffing resources will be illustrated through several case examples derived from our experiences in the Southern Arizona Mental Health Center. Following a description of the center, both historic and programmatic, several aspects of evaluation on a shoestring budget will be presented to illustrate how it can be carried out. With an appropriate definition of objectives, even though limited by inadequate fiscal and staffing support, shoestring evaluation can be of great value in the planning and implementation of services. Finally, the potential impact of shoestring evaluation strategies will be discussed.

IDEOLOGICAL AND PRAGMATIC PROBLEMS

Before presenting specific shoestring evaluation strategies, it is useful to understand the often overwhelming problems that the administrator may face in beginning and maintaining a commitment to evaluation in a human service program.

MAKING A COMMITMENT TO UNDERTAKE EVALUATION

Very few human service program directors have received specific or adequate preparation for the various tasks inherent in administration, including evaluation. Nevertheless, it is often upon this same administrator that the burden of performing these evaluation tasks falls. This situation can provide a challenge or a threat. Unfortunately, the tendency among many administrators is to view it as a threat. Documentation for this conclusion is provided through a review of the literature. For example, the majority of articles authored recently on the subject of evaluation in mental health, health, and social welfare service delivery systems have been prepared by individuals whose interest and expertise is in the area of research. Very few have been authored by individuals whose primary responsibility has encompassed human service program administration. When this situation is more closely examined, two factors can be viewed as playing an important role.

First, most human service program administrators have had little or no training in evaluation. However, this lack of training is a relatively easy situation to correct, particularly since more and more training opportunities in program evaluation are being offered and are available to interested administrators. Persistence of this problem, despite the increasing availability of training programs, suggests that other factors may be at work which should be examined more closely. In this latter regard, many administrators fear that evaluation will place the administrator in a "double bind." A failure to conduct an evaluation may be viewed by some as an abrogation of responsibility to the demand for accountability. On the other hand, if the administrator follows through with this responsibility, there is the "risk" of losing credibility or one's position if evaluation results are negative (Murphy, 1971)—as well as the possibility of false negatives because of insensitive or inappropriate measures. Therefore, it is understandable that many administrators try to avoid this double bind by busying themselves with other tasks, of which there are many, and hoping that the "problem" of evaluation will go away.

Second, many human service administrators come to their managerial positions with a background in which both prior training and work experiences have been primarily clinical or service oriented. They often resent allocating a significant portion of their attention to the preparation of methodologies, issues in data collection, and analyses of data—essentially nonclinical activities. Therefore, these "service-oriented" administrators may have a tendency to view evaluation as a "nonprofessional" task, leading to its rejection. If possible, the administrator would often prefer to turn this task over to another person; more often, finding no one available, the matter is dropped. In addition, administrators often assume that statisticians have evaluation design expertise that frequently computer programmers and statisticians do not have —an assumption that frequently leads to inappropriate choices of design or evaluation technology.

The solution to these conflicts is not easy, readily available, or tangible. In fact, the only solution is often transcendental. The human service program administrator must often take a "great leap forward" by making a more realistic commitment to the importance of evaluation. If the administrator is unwilling to respond and make a commitment, it is unlikely that effective evaluation will take place in that human service program even though he or she may pay lip service to it through a superficial verbal recognition of its importance to staff, funding sources, and the community.

MAKING A SUCCESSFUL APPROACH TO THE PROBLEMS OF EVALUATION

As McMahon and his colleagues have pointed out, significant evaluation of any program cannot go forward until the administrator and those assigned to help with the problem of evaluation have been able to determine what type of evaluation is required through an adequate definition of the program, the population to be served, and the programmatic effects desired (McMahon, Pugh, & Hutchinson, 1961).

Consequently, the human service program administrator must avoid following previously held allegations and convictions about the program's effectiveness and design evaluation mechanisms that will allow for objective and clearly defined approaches to the issues to be studied. Only in this way will an administrator be able to obtain information which is truly useful for future policy decisions (Fox, 1972).

RECORD KEEPING

Even if the human service program administrator is able to make a commitment to the implementation of ongoing program evaluation and to identify evaluation strategies that will allow review of specific programs designed to serve specific populations or target problems, he or she still faces realistic problems associated with establishing a useful data base.

To solve this problem, the administrator must often set aside the "biases" of the service provider, and recognize that the purpose of records is not only to "tell a story," but also to provide a data base that can yield useful planning information and that can be handled statistically. Some administrators may see these two requirements as being in conflict and many staff members may be resistant to completing records in a manner that meets these two requirements. Consequently, it is the responsibility of the administrator to review the record-keeping system being utilized in the human service program and to ensure that it provides an adequate statistical base for basic evaluation purposes as well as adequate descriptive material for clinical or other professional purposes. Later illustrations will identify specific aspects of a record-keeping system that could be used for the development of an adequate evaluation strategy.

CONTINUITY OF CARE

On behalf of a single client, help may require not only the involvement of numerous services within a single human service agency, but also the services of numerous agencies within a single human service system. Therefore, the ability to "track" a client through the various services of an agency or the various agencies within a system becomes a paramount consideration in the development of adequate evaluation strategies.

Often, the human service program may find itself not having a sophisticated data collection system that allows it to have computerized "tracking" of the clients it services. Such a situation, when achieved, emphasizes the importance of cooperative working relationships not only among members of different service teams in a single human service program, but also between the administrators of all agencies involved in the human service delivery system of a community. If it is recognized that this interagency cooperation may have potential benefits for all agencies, it is often possible initially to introduce noncomputerized, more simplistic strategies that will effectively create a more immediate possibility of "tracking" clients through the human service system.

STAFF RESISTANCE

The resistance of service delivery staff to data collection often significantly hampers the ability of a human service program administrator to implement effective evaluation. However, it must also be recognized that, although the involvement of service delivery staff in evaluation is important, they are not necessarily the sole personnel resources for data collection available to the innovative program administrator. Most human service programs have a support staff, consisting primarily of secretaries and clerks, whose availability for data collection is often unrecognized or underutilized. Consequently, a potential route for overcoming staff resistance may be found through the placement of significant responsibility for data collection upon staff members other than service delivery personnel. This "end-around" may not eliminate staff resistance, but will certainly enable an administrator to reduce it. However, further "lowering" of resistance will occur only if the administrator routes the data (collected by personnel who do not provide services) and the results back to service delivery personnel. This formal feedback is more likely to enhance service providers' recognition of the usefulness of evaluation strategies and to encourage service providers' willingness to participate more actively in the collection of information.

CONTINUOUS VERSUS EPISODIC MONITORING

The publicity given during the recent years to complex computer-based evaluation systems has led to the creation of overwhelming expectations, which, if accepted uncritically by the human service program administrator, may undermine his or her ability to initiate an effective beginning evaluation effort. The important objective in introducing evaluation is not to see how much can be undertaken, but how much of what is done is relevant. Consequently, the human service program administrator must guard carefully against unrealistic evaluative expectations as well as prevent "information overload." Certain information may have great interest for evaluators, but to those without specialized training or a singular interest, too much data may be overwhelming. Furthermore, an approach that generates "information overload" may be contrary to the philosophy underlying effective evaluation in which the problem to be defined and the data to be collected are clearly delineated at the outset.

The human service program administrator who faces the problem of developing innovative evaluation strategies should recognize that useful strategies may not require a continuous information input about all aspects of the entire program. Effective evaluation can be carried out by carefully selecting information to be gathered. The adoption of an "episodic" system in which several specifically defined evaluation strategies are employed at different times may not only yield the most effective evaluation protocol for the program which the administrator is attempting to supervise, but may also help the administrator to overcome the feeling that there is too much to be done in too short a time.

SELECTION OF AREAS TO BE EVALUATED

Closely related to the problem of episodic versus continuous monitoring is a myth that has often been detrimental to the development of program directors' interest in evaluation. This myth is that effective evaluation requires the availability of information about everything. Although it is true that resources such as computers exist that can effectively analyze all information collected and provided to them, it does not follow necessarily that all of this information is of equal importance to the program or to its administrator. Consequently, the creative program administrator can play an important role in designating those program areas that require evaluation and those that do not.

However, a word of caution is warranted since it would be foolish for an administrator to assume that only he or she possesses the ability to designate and select those areas which require evaluation. In this regard, it is particularly important for the administrator to take advantage of those available human resources—such as staff members, advisory boards, and the community at large—who can participate in identifying specific areas relevant to policymaking and planning activities of the program, and therefore requiring priority for evaluation. Much of the negativism that human services programs encounter within a community is a result of inadequate communication between the human service program and the community regarding those evaluation strategies the program wishes to undertake. Insufficient input by the community will hinder the development of proper priorities for an evaluation strategy as well as possibly create negative reactions to the overall efforts of the program (Mercer, Dingman, & Tarjan, 1964).

Before proceeding to describe specific evaluation strategies, using several case examples derived from our experiences, we will sketch the environment in which these strategies were developed.

A MENTAL HEALTH PROGRAM

The Southern Arizona Mental Health Center in Tucson, Arizona (Pima County) was established in 1962 as an outpatient branch of the Arizona State Hospital, located in Phoenix, 100 miles away. It was created initially to function as a followup clinic for discharged patients, with the primary purpose of preventing their return to the Arizona State Hospital. It failed miserably in this approach during its first 7 years of existence, principally because it operated without an inpatient service. The major psychiatric inpatient service in the community, the Pima County General Hospital, was not tied to the Southern Arizona Mental Health Center through any formal agreement—and informal cooperation was minimal.

Consequently, while the Southern Arizona Mental Health Center had been charged by the legislature with the responsibility of preventing the return of patients to the Arizona State Hospital, the actual responsibility for commitment of patients from Pima County to the State Hospital resided almost entirely at the Pima County Hospital. Subsequently, over the years it became apparent that a comprehensive and effective community mental health service system was lacking in Pima County.

This emerging awareness led, in 1969, to the formation of a task force that included representatives from the Southern Arizona Mental Health Center (and its parent, the Arizona State Hospital), the Pima County Hospital (and its parent, the Pima County Board of Supervisors), and the Department of Psychiatry at the newly formed University of Arizona College of Medicine. From these discussions, a tightly organized agreement was developed and signed by the three groups, which resulted in the pooling of a variety of mental health services and their placement into a unified community mental health service network. This network was administered through a single table of organization, while continuing to derive support from several funding sources.

This "Combined Mental Health Care Program" was designed to provide all services of a comprehensive community mental health center including emergency services; inpatient services including short-term hospitalization at the local level (Pima County Hospital) as well as long-term hospitalization at the state level (Arizona State Hospital); partial hospital services including day care and halfway house services located at the Southern Arizona Mental Health Center; outpatient services, both adult and child; and consultation and education services.

Since 1970, it has been headed by a coordinator who functions both as chief of psychiatry at Pima County Hospital and director of the Southern Arizona Mental Health Center. A conference committee was organized, and consisted of representatives from the three organizations that signed the agreement. This conference committee and a community advisory board acted in a policymaking and advisory capacity to the community mental health service system (Beigel, Bower, & Levenson, 1973).

Since the inception of the Combined Mental Health Care Program in 1970, two federally funded community mental health centers have opened in Pima County, servicing smaller target populations than the Southern Arizona Mental Health Center which has responsibility for all of Pima County. To avoid a potential duplication of services, the Inter-Agency Mental Health Conference was formed in 1971. Its major purpose is to encourage all mental health centers and other related human service agencies to develop and use more informal and formal communication mechanisms with the goal of developing better service coordination.

Although the Southern Arizona Mental Health Center continues to have a legislative mandate to provide services to all of Pima County, it works cooperatively with the other community mental health centers to ensure that clients will have access to services closest to their residence. For example, all three mental health centers maintain separate and complete adult and child outpatient services directed toward different target populations in Pima County, but utilize together the halfway house services of the Southern Arizona Mental Health Center.

EVALUATION STRATEGIES

In the context of this complex mental health services delivery system, related to and coordinated with other mental health and human services through the Inter-Agency Mental Health Conference, the demand for accountability from state legislative funding sources, county budgetary committees and the community as a whole led the director to consider what evaluation strategies would answer their past and future questions. The initial absence of adequate fiscal and staffing support mandated a narrow focus for the evaluation process and led to the development of evaluation strategies that would specifically assess the nature and impact of services on clients and which would generate information that could provide important feedback for use in future policy decisions.

DATA CAPTURE CONSIDERATIONS AND THE
EVALUATION PROCESS

In determining the availability of staff to assist in the development of evaluation strategies, the resistance of many clinical staff to participating in evaluation and especially staff resistance to the necessary data collection was encountered. It became apparent that other resources would have to be utilized if evaluation was going to be pursued successfully.

As a result, one of the principal resources for this mental health center's evaluation program has been the utilization of support staff. In the illustrations that follow, most of the data have been collected by clerks at the time a client appears for service. Therefore, not only does the number of staff hours involved in the completion of an evaluation task remain small, but the cost is also minimized since higher salaried clinical personnel are not significantly involved and no additional staff are hired.

Because of the absence of a computerized data gathering network, simple forms that could be handled easily by the clerical staff were needed. Figure 5.1 illustrates a "ticket" that is the basic form utilized by the Southern Arizona Mental Health Center to collect data about all direct services to clients. It is completed by the clerks in each treatment unit from their own observations and from information received from clinical staff members at the time the client is seen. This information serves as the principal resource for the evaluation of services rendered as well as for the assessment of staff efficiency in their service delivery activities. The use of this basic form not only makes it simpler for clerks to collect data, but also enhances the ease of codification and analysis by the business office, which then forwards reports to the director.

As will be illustrated later, the use of volunteers can also be an important facet of initiating successful evaluation strategies without adequate fiscal and staffing support. Volunteers may be utilized both in providing direct services to clients as well as in assisting clerks in data collection.

These resources, easily available at minimal cost, can assist the director of a human service program in implementing specific evaluation strategies when there is no specialized staffing or adequate financial backing. The several examples that follow are designed to illustrate some of the important principles associated with the performance of "evaluation on a shoestring" by a human service program administrator.

The provision of direct services to clients of the Southern Arizona Mental Health Center constitutes only a portion of the total services provided. Therefore, evaluation strategies could not be limited to an analysis of direct services since the large amount of time spent by staff in a variety of indirect services would otherwise go unrecognized and unevaluated.

In Figure 5.2 an indirect services data collection form is illustrated. This form is designed to record all consultation, education, and service coordination activities not involving direct client services and, therefore, not recorded on the direct service "ticket" described previously (Figure 5.1). The indirect services form is designed to monitor the activities of staff members who participate in service relationships with other human service agencies, community groups and organizations, institutions, or individuals who indirectly effect the services delivered by the Southern Arizona Mental Health Center and the Combined Mental Health Care Program.

The form (Figure 5.2) is completed on a weekly basis and filed by a service clerk on Monday following a completed work week. A variety of indirect service methodologies are listed on the form (Caplan, 1964):

SOUTHERN ARIZONA MENTAL HEALTH CENTER
DIRECT PATIENT SERVICES TICKET

1. PATIENT NAME _____

2. TREATMENT CENTER ☐☐

3. PATIENT NUMBER ☐☐☐☐☐

4. DATE OF SERVICE

MO. ☐☐   DAY ☐☐   YR. ☐☐

5. ENVIRONMENT ☐

6. ELEMENT OF SERVICE ☐

7. SERVICE TYPE ☐☐

- 1 - INDIVIDUAL INTERVIEW
- 2 - MEDICATION REVIEW
- 3 - GROUP THERAPY
- 4 - DIAGNOSIS / EVALUATION
- 5 - PSYCHOLOGICAL TESTING
- 6 - FAMILY THERAPY
- 7 - SPECIAL EDUCATION
- 8 - COLLATERAL INTERVIEW
- 9 - VOCATIONAL REHABILITATION
- 10 - HEARING THERAPY
- 11 - SPEECH THERAPY
- 12 - OCCUPATIONAL THERAPY
- 13 - OTHER REHABILITATION
- 14 - EMERGENCY
- 15 - PROLIXIN INJECTION
- 16 - THERAPEUTIC TELEPHONE CALL
- 17 - PATIENT DAY
- 18 - OTHER
- 19 - PRE-PETITION SCREENING

8. STAFF DISCIPLINE ☐☐

9. PRESCRIPTION ORDERED ☐

1 - YES
2 - NO

10. TIME INVOLVED

HOURS ☐   MIN. ☐☐

11. GROUP SIZE ☐☐

12. SPECIAL RESEARCH ☐☐☐☐

Figure 5.1. Southern Arizona Mental Health Center transaction document for direct services.

106

NAME _____   STAFF DISCIPLINE _____

MONTH _____ YEAR _____   UNIT _____

Con-tact	Date	Hours	Method	Organization	No.

CONTACT

01 Personal (SAMHC)
02 Personal (Field)
03 Telephone

METHOD

01 Client-Centered Case Consultation
02 Consultee-Centered Case Consultation
03 Program-Centered Admin. Consultation
04 Consultee-Centered Admin. Consultation
05 Staff Training/Education
06 Workshop
07 Demonstration
08 Lecture
09 Discussion
10 Program collaboration
11 Negotiation for Consultation & Education
12 Community Organization
13 Other (specify)

DATE

In the date space, place the day (by number) on which the service was provided.

HOURS

In the hour space, place the time (including travel) that elapsed during the C&E contact—to the closest half-hour.

ORGANIZATION

In the organization space, place the specific organizational title of the agency, group, or institution contacted.

NUMBER

In the number space, place the total number of people to whom consultation and/or educational activities were extended.

Figure 5.2. Southern Arizona Mental Health Center indirect services report form.

1. *Client-Centered Case Consultation*

In this situation, the human service professional is asked to consult on a specific case. The primary focus of both the consultant and the consultee is finding the most effective care for a specific client. A secondary goal is to assist the consultee so that he or she may later help this class of clients more effectively and unaided.

2. *Consultee-Centered Case Consultation*

This designation is used for those situations in which cases are presented to the consultant and discussed. Primary effort is aimed at analyzing the difficulties experienced by the consultees in providing services to their own clients and to help consultees overcome those difficulties. This is in contrast to client-centered case consultation in which the emphasis is on assessing problems of clients served by the consultees' human service program.

3. *Program-Centered Administrative Consultation*

This code describes situations in which human service program personnel are requested by another agency, group, or institution to assist in handling problems of administration. The problems may relate to design, planning, or implementation of programs or the use of program personnel.

4. *Consultee-Centered Administrative Consultation*

This code describes situations in which human service program personnel are asked to consult with regard to the overall functioning of an agency by its administrator or a group of administrators. The consultant may help the consultee to deal more effectively with a variety of administrative problems such as interpersonal conflicts. These services may be delivered individually or in a group.

5. *Staff Training/Education*

This code is used for those situations in which a staff member provides individual or group training or education to a specific outside agency regarding a specific subject. Cases are not the direct focus, but may be used as examples. The purpose of this consultation is to upgrade that individual's or group's skills.

6. *Workshop*

This denotes the attendance at and participation in a meeting of individuals interested in a given human service problem. These people come together with the intention of bringing about some resolution to the problem.

7. *Demonstration*

This describes the demonstration of skill by a human service program staff member to other professionals or nonprofessionals on a one-time or ongoing basis.

8. *Lecture*

Included in this category are speeches to other organizations and agencies providing an explanation of specific topics related to the human services field.

Courses offered to other professionals and nonprofessionals may be sponsored by the human service program through universities or other agencies.

Through the utilization of this data collection mechanism (Figure 5.2), the program's administrator is able to gather significant information regarding the types of indirect services provided by the program and the amount of time being spent by staff members in these indirect service activities. These data will assist the administrator in making a further determination of the extent to which outreach activities performed by the program are consistent with management objectives in the direct service area. Finally, the availability of these data will allow the administrator to assess accurately the cost of these services. By having this information available, an important data base is added to the administrator's knowledge when planning allocation of staff time.

COST-FINDING ANALYSES

In any service system, an analysis of services delivered is vital to the implementation of future policy planning and decision making. An effective analysis depends on the availability of data that can be collected through mechanisms that are within the financial capability of the program and that yield information about the types of services delivered and the individuals providing them. Tables 5.1 and 5.2 contain an example of direct and indirect services cost analysis using the data collected through the "ticket" described previously (Figure 5.1) and the indirect services form (Figure 5.2).

Both the "ticket" (Figure 5.1) and indirect services form (Figure 5.2) capture the raw data about hours of service delivered by staff members. These effort data are summarized for a selected month in Table 5.1. In Table 5.2, a method is illustrated for determining the unit cost for each service component of the mental health center. Since the actual cost of mental health personnel services is known for each component of the mental health center, the percentage of the total cost of mental health care personnel services for each unit can be calculated. The monthly cost of all administrative support staff and other operating expenses (Table 5.2) are also known. These administrative expenses are allocated to each service unit based upon the proportion of the total mental health care personnel costs expended by the unit; combining direct personnel and the allocated administrative cost results in a total monthly operating cost for each service setting (Table 5.2). For example, in the month selected, the total operating cost of the outpatient unit was $24,201 in contrast to a total operating cost for the walk-in clinic of $14,823. With the availability of the total operating cost of each treatment unit and the total hours of direct and indirect services delivered by each, the administrator can compute the cost per hour of those direct and indirect services delivered by each unit (Table 5.2).

In some situations, indirect services may not be billable to the recipients and, in order to recover these costs, the costs of consultation and education may be "reallocated" to the direct services. In Table 5.2, for example, the $3520 would be spread over the direct service hours (4688) and each hour of direct service would be increased by $.75 ($3520 divided by 4688). While the approach may be useful for establishing reimbursement rates (when such a practice is allowable) it has more limited usefulness for "monitoring" purposes

TABLE 5.1

Hours of Direct and Indirect Services Delivered for a Selected Month

Service settings	Hours of service delivered within weekly intervals of a selected month					
	1st–2nd	5th–9th	12th–16th	19th–23rd	26th–30th	Totals
Direct services						
Outpatient	71	265	261	294	266	1157
Walk-in	66	101	109	126	110	512
Day program	176	462	469	465	382	1954
Children's	34	102	70	103	92	401
Halfway house	86	138	161	161	118	664
Indirect services						
Consultation and education	30	30	25	25	30	140
Totals	463	1098	1095	1174	998	4828

TABLE 5.2
Operational Cost Analysis of Center Services for a Selected Month

Program components	Service personnel costs	Percentage of total service personnel costs	Apportioned share[a] of ancillary operational costs	Total operational costs	Units of service provided	Cost per unit of service
I. Service programs						
1. Outpatient	$12,972	33	$11,229	1. $24,201	1,157	$20.92
2. Walk-in	8,018	20	6,805	2. 14,823	512	28.95
3. Day program	5,560	14	4,764	3. 10,324	1,954	5.28
4. Children's	6,968	17	5,784	4. 12,752	401	31.80
5. Halfway house	4,498	11	3,743	5. 8,241	664	12.41
6. Consultation and education	1,819	5	1,701	6. 3,520	140	25.14
Totals	$39,835	100%	$34,026	$73,861	4,828	$15.30
II. Ancillary operations costs						
1. Support service staff salary	$12,542					
2. Operating expenses	21,484					
Total	$34,026					

[a] Based on Proportionate Share of Direct Personnel Costs (e.g., Outpatient = .33 × $34,026 = $11,229).

111

since changes in the mix of direct and indirect services will be masked through aggregation. This masking can potentially lead to ineffective decision making since actual unit costs and actual distribution of staff effort may be distorted. These issues and more detailed coverage of cost-finding methodology are extensively covered in Chapter 13 of this volume.

Cost analysis can be a very powerful administrative tool. Significant variations in hourly costs will alert an administrator to the need to examine service strategies for the underlying causes. If the cost per service hour in a service setting should drop significantly, it might suggest a more effective utilization of the program in response to a prior service strategy change or an overutilization of the program requiring additional staff. Conversely, if the cost per service hour in a specific treatment setting should rise markedly, it might suggest an underutilization of that program, requiring a service strategy change or a need to transfer staff to another setting where service needs are greater.

USING COST ANALYSIS IN BUDGET JUSTIFICATION

In facing the demand for accountability, many human service program administrators must demonstrate clearly how the services they provide are essential to the community in which they are based. In this regard, it may become important for the human service administrator to analyze how the program is "saving" money because it has reduced fiscal needs in other areas that may not even be under his or her direct control. An example of this kind of evaluation strategy for direct services is offered through the following experience of the Combined Mental Health Care Program.

By creating the Southern Arizona Mental Health Center in 1962, the Arizona State Hospital hoped to justify the additional expenditure for personnel in Tucson by decreasing the rate of hospitalization at the Arizona State Hospital from Pima County. When this did not occur, despite increasing the expenditures, creation of the Combined Mental Health Care Program took place as a "last-ditch" attempt to justify the continued existence of the Southern Arizona Mental Health Center.

Therefore, it became important to the administrator to develop a method for performing a cost analysis of the effectiveness of the center's services as they related to the Arizona State Hospital. In pursuing this evaluation strategy, the method utilized was an analysis based on the "fair share" of the Arizona State Hospital budget for Pima County, computed solely on the basis of population distribution, with Pima County being entitled to 20.3%—this proportion being equal to the percentage of people in the state residing within Pima County.

Tables 5.3 to 5.5 illustrate the impact of the Combined Mental Health Care Program on expenditures for the care of patients from Pima County at the Southern Arizona Mental Health Center and the Arizona State Hospital. As noted in Table 5.3, prior to the initiation of the Combined Mental Health Care Program the service programs for Pima County residents at the Southern Arizona Mental Health Center and the Arizona State Hospital were operating at an annual deficit of $439,857. In other words, the combined cost of caring for patients from Pima County at the Arizona State Hospital and the Southern Arizona Mental Health Center was $439,857 more than was allotted for Pima County ($1,406,342) as its "fair share" of the total Arizona State Hospital budget.

By March 1971, 6 months after the initiation of the Combined Mental Health Care Program, this "deficit" had been reduced to $25,727 (Table 5.4). In December 1971, 9 months later, a "surplus" of $108,534 (Table 5.5) had been generated. It had been jointly agreed that any surplus in the "fair share" would be reallocated into additional positions for the Southern Arizona Mental Health Center and expended to deliver additional community-based services. Conversely, any deficit would be taken out of the budget of the Southern Arizona Mental Health Center and assigned to the care of patients from Pima County at the Arizona State Hospital.

An added benefit of this cost analysis which focused on the program's fiscal savings was the value of the method in approaching the Arizona Legislature. It provided both the fiscal and service data necessary to substantiate a request for additional services in Pima County. At that time (1971), the most specific need was a halfway house program; and, as a result of a presentation of the cost-savings data, the legislature appropriated $178,000 to purchase land and buildings. The funds for the additional staff needed to operate a halfway house program were generated from the surplus that had been accumulated as a result of the impact of the Combined Mental Health Care Program.

TABLE 5.3

Cost Analysis and "Fair Share" Calculation for Pima County Residents, June, 1970

Treatment modality	Daily charge per patient (June, 1970)	Pima County census at Arizona State Hospital (ASH)	Total daily cost
Adult psychiatry	$15.46	132	$2,040.72
Physically infirm	26.41	5	132.05
Geriatrics	16.75	26	435.50
Mental retardation	15.76	36	567.36
Child psychiatry	30.61	6	183.66
Maximum security	18.92	10	189.20
Total		*215*	$3,548.49
			×365
Annual cost of Pima County residents at ASH			$1,295,199.00
Southern Arizona Mental Health Center budget			+551,000.00
Total expenditures for Pima County			$1,846,199.00
Pima County "fair share" of total ASH 1969–1970 budget[a]			−1,406,342.00
"Deficit" from "fair share"			$439,857.00

[a] 20.3% of $6,927,795.00

TABLE 5.4

Cost Analysis and "Fair Share" Calculation for Pima County Residents, March, 1971

Treatment modality	Daily charge per patient (March, 1971)	Pima County census at Arizona State Hospital (ASH)	Total daily cost
Adult psychiatry	$16.54	75	$1,240.50
Physically infirm	31.40	6	188.40
Geriatrics	18.74	20	374.80
Mental retardation	17.49	30	524.70
Child psychiatry	38.40	6	230.40
Maximum security	27.50	12	330.00
Early discharge	30.59	1	30.59
"Flamenco II" program	16.54	10	165.40
Total		*160*	$3,084.79
			×365

Annual cost of Pima County residents at ASH	$1,125,948.00
Southern Arizona Mental Health Center budget	+637,582.00
Total expenditures for Pima County	$1,763,530.00
Pima County "fair share" of total ASH 1970–1971 budget[a]	−1,737,803.00
"Deficit" from "fair share"	$25,727.00

[a] 20.3% of $8,560,605.00

TABLE 5.5

Cost Analysis and "Fair Share" Calculation for Pima County Residents, December, 1971

Treatment modality	Daily charge per patient (December, 1971)	Pima County census at Arizona State Hospital (ASH)	Total daily cost
Adult psychiatry	$24.80	35	$868.00
Physically infirm	39.11	4	156.44
Geriatrics	22.11	16	353.76
Mental retardation	21.93	31	679.83
Child psychiatry	51.84	3	155.52
Maximum security	29.71	13	386.23
Social learning	37.50	3	112.50
"Kachina II" program	24.80	7	173.60
Total		*112*	$2,885.88
			×365

Annual cost of Pima County residents at ASH	$1,053,346.00
Southern Arizona Mental Health Center budget	+763,970.00
Total expenditures for Pima County	$1,817,316.00
Pima County "fair share" of total ASH 1971–1972 budget[a]	−1,925,850.00
"Surplus" over "fair share"	$108,534.00

[a] 20.3% of $9,486,946.00

SOURCES OF REFERRAL AND DISPOSITION

In any human service program, it is important to analyze and follow client flow into the service programs, as defined by those clients who seek help and the other service providers from which they are referred. Although this analysis can include an evaluation of the demographic characteristics of the clients, we will focus more on how knowledge of the sources of referral can become an important factor in making policy decisions. Even though the examples presented in this section of our chapter are derived from the mental health program described previously, it is important for every human service program director to recognize that studies of client flow into service programs are valuable whether the specific program is a neighborhood health center, a multiservice center, or a YMCA. Without the availability of this client flow data, the human service program administrator will be unable to plan appropriate service delivery strategies designed to meet the needs of the target populations.

Table 5.6 illustrates the referral pattern both into and out of the comprehensive emergency services network within our mental health service system. This services network is available 24 hours a day, 7 days a week. As noted in Table 5.6, these services are available during the day, Monday through Friday from 8:00 a.m. to 4:00 p.m., at the main community mental health facility, the Southern Arizona Mental Health Center; and 24 hours a day in the emergency room of the Pima County Hospital where the short-term inpatient services are also located.

Prior to the implementation of the Combined Mental Health Care Program in 1970, and because of the lack of coordination between the Pima County Hospital and the Southern Arizona Mental Health Center, there was no true "emergency services system," and an overwhelming majority of patients (79% in 1969) in crisis situations presented themselves between the hours of 4:00 p.m. and 8:00 a.m.

Consequently, the initial program protocol for the Combined Mental Health Care Program set up a "management objective" to develop a preventive strategy that would encourage clients to come for help not only in an emergency, but also earlier, and preferably during "normal" daytime working hours (Beigel, 1971). Therefore, the walk-in clinic was opened.

The data in Table 5.6 are useful in analyzing the impact of this strategy. During the month used as an example, 464 clients were seen for an initial evaluation either at the Southern Arizona Mental Health Center or the Pima County Hospital. The data further reveal that 186 (40%) were seen during the 40 hours of the week (24% of total available time during the week) between the hours of 8:00 a.m. and 4:00 p.m., Monday through Friday. This is almost twice the percentage of clients served during these hours prior to the implementation of the Combined Mental Health Care Program, and the initiation of the walk-in clinic. Therefore, these data would suggest to the planners that the strategy of implementing a daytime walk-in clinic with a staff team devoted only to emergency services has been successful in diverting a significant number of people from waiting to seek help until the last moment either in the evening or at night when the situation has become "emergent."

TABLE 5.6

Comprehensive Emergency Services Network: Client Flow, Referral, and Disposition Patterns, March, 1973

NEW PATIENTS SEEN IN SERVICE SETTINGS

Time of day	Walk-in clinic of the Southern Arizona Mental Health Center (SAMHC)	Pima County Hospital	Totals
8:00 a.m. to 4:00 p.m.	147	39	186 (40%)
4:00 p.m. to 12:00 p.m.	NOT OPEN FOR SERVICE	167	167 (36%)
12:00 p.m. to 8:00 a.m.	NOT OPEN FOR SERVICE	111	111 (24%)
Totals	147	317	464 (100%)

New patients: source of referral	Walk-in Clinic (SAMHC)		Pima County Hospital
	Number	Percentage	
Self	33	22	
Friends/relatives	44	30	
Pima County Hospital emergency room	13	9	

	Number	Percentage
Other health agency or physician	28	19
Other mental health agency	8	6
Other community agency	10	7
Law enforcement and courts	11	7
Totals	147	100

New patients: dispositions	Walk-in clinic (SAMHC)	
	Number	Percentage
No referral	29	20
Pima County unit	6	4
SAMHC outpatient programs	44	30
SAMHC day program	3	2
Tucson South MHC	7	5
Tucson East MHC	10	7
Still being seen in walk-in clinic	37	25
Other agencies	11	7
Failed to return	0	—
Totals	147	100

Pima County Hospital	Number	Percentage
Pima County Unit	73	23
SAMHC walk-in clinic	51	16
Other programs of SAMHC	5	2
No referral needed or requested	137	43
Other agencies	17	5
Pima County Medical Service	8	3
Pima County Drug and Alcohol Program	26	8
Totals	317	100

Other aspects of the data in Table 5.6 require comment. Fifty-two percent of the patients seen in the walk-in clinic at the Southern Arizona Mental Health Center during its open hours (8:00 a.m. to 4:00 p.m.) were either self-referred or referred by friends or relatives. This can be viewed as an indirect indicator of the program's ability to achieve another management objective—increased visibility and acceptance within the general population. Following this statistic over time will give the program administrator an indirect measure of any change in the program's community acceptance. When individuals present themselves (self-referral and family-referral), without having been referred by a community agency or professional, we can assume a greater degree of community acceptance of the concept of seeking help for an emotional problem at an earlier stage and directly from a mental health resource.

Furthermore, the relatively few patients ($N = 39$) seen in the emergency room at the Pima County Hospital during daytime hours, Monday through Friday, in comparison to the number of new clients at the walk-in clinic at the Southern Arizona Mental Health Center (approximately 4 miles apart) offers an additional indication of the program's success in achieving another management objective—programmatic identification separate from that of the hospital. The creation of this separate identification is critical to the success of any community mental health program, since one of its established roles is to provide easily accessible services and to encourage individuals to come for help prior to perceiving their situation as being so serious that they must be admitted to the hospital.

Analysis of other referral sources to the walk-in clinic also provides the administrator with help in assessing the relationships this program has with other service resources in the human services network. Any significant decrease over time in this referral percentage might suggest that a problem, perhaps an interagency conflict, may be present. On the other hand, an increase in referrals from a specific resource in the human service system might suggest a need for further consultation to determine the underlying reason for such increased referrals or might reflect the result of previous consultation efforts.

Disposition data can also be helpful to the program director. For example, another management objective of the walk-in clinic is to serve as a crisis-intervention clinic as well as a resource for the screening and referral of clients for further treatment. Therefore, the percentage of individuals for whom no further referral is made can be an indication of the effectiveness of this crisis-intervention strategy. As shown in Table 5.6, 20% of the clients seen in the walk-in clinic did not require further referral. Furthermore, if the anticipated proportion of the 25% who were still being seen in the walk-in clinic at the end of the month (probably 20%) also did not require further referral, this total would increase to 25%. Significant downward or upward shifts in the number of clients who do not require further referral will help the administrator to assess the clinic's ability to maintain its management objective of being the primary locus for crisis-intervention services.

Since the walk-in clinic is open only 8 hours a day, 5 days a week and the rest of the emergency services are delivered at Pima County Hospital, continuity of care between the two organizations is critical to the creation of an effective emergency service delivery system. Referral and disposition data can also provide a measure for assessing the effectiveness of continuity of care. As noted in Table 5.6, 51 patients were referred during the specified month from the Pima County Hospital Emergency Room to the walk-in clinic at the Southern Arizona Mental Health Center; but in a subsequent analysis, only 13 of these patients (26%) appeared for further evaluation. These data suggested to the program administrator that it was necessary to look further into mechanisms for improving continuity of care between the two agencies. Upon investigation, it was discovered that two possible causes for the low followup percentage were that patients who lived within the immediate vicinity of the Pima County Hospital and those referred to the walk-in clinic during nighttime hours (midnight to 8:00 a.m.) were less likely to followup.

These data suggested a need to utilize more adequately other mental health resources for some patients, such as other community mental health centers mentioned previously, which are based closer to the hospital. Consequently, instructions were forwarded to the emergency room that, despite the Combined Mental Health Care Program agreement, referral to the Southern Arizona Mental Health Center or any other mental health center should be made primarily on the basis of residence and accessibility of services. Followup after the implementation of this order revealed a marked increase in the percentage of successful referrals to the Southern Arizona Mental Health Center (26% to 58% 2 months later), and also an increase in the rate (90%) of successful followup to the mental health center which is closest to Pima County Hospital.

Next it was speculated that the low followup that was occurring after nighttime visits to the emergency room might be related to the lack of availability of services at those times from a trained mental health professional who could provide on-the-spot evaluation. Consequently, these data were given to the hospital administrator to support a request for funding of a mental health professional in the emergency room during these hours. This position has not yet been funded, and the low rate of followup after referral continues during these hours.

In summary, this small area of data analysis has been chosen to illustrate how significant data, that are easy to collect, can have an important impact on many policy and decision-making areas that confront the human service administrator. Furthermore, these analyses indicate that data can be obtained without optimal fiscal and staffing support and in the absence of a computerized data collection network.

EVALUATION STRATEGIES FOR FOLLOWUP

The importance of followup and outcome studies for any human services program has been well described (Department of Health, Education, and Welfare, 1955; Greenberg & Brandon, 1964). However, it is equally clear that a program facing this component of comprehensive evaluation without adequate fiscal and staffing support has a very difficult problem because the objective assessment of outcome is virtually impossible without substantive fiscal support. However, subjective analysis is possible, and should be implemented even if objective analysis cannot be immediately undertaken.

Outcome evaluation implies an assessment of the progress that a client has made as a result of services received. However, it is often not possible to measure realistically a client's progress until services have been completed, because the dependency engendered by the service-giving relationship may influence "outcome" assessment. Consequently, a human service program interested in completing useful outcome evaluation should focus on the period following the client's discharge from care.

With limited fiscal and staffing support, the program should recognize the potential importance of volunteers in assisting the outcome evaluation process. Utilizing home visits and phone calls, a trained volunteer can make a competent subjective assessment of a client's status. This subjective analysis can provide not only evaluation data, but also can have important ramifications for the client, since it provides a means of continuing contact not dependent upon the client's initiative.

Another important aspect of this often-ignored type of outcome evaluation occurs at the time when a client may return for further service. Many individuals seen in a human service program have been clients of that program or others in the past and the opportunity to assess progress or lack of it at the time that a client returns for further help should not be ignored. Consequently, it is important to emphasize to staff personnel the importance of taking an adequate intake history which includes not only those problems that have precipitated the return for further service, but also a description of how the client has functioned since last receiving service.

A strategy that makes evaluation a part of ongoing service may also help to reduce staff resistance. Since it is unlikely that the staff person who does the outcome evaluation at a followup point will be the same person who was involved in the original service delivery, the independent perspective will help to "objectify" the data collected. Utilization of this subjective evaluation methodology also offers an opportunity for "episodic" rather than "continuous" monitoring. For program policy planning, "continuous" monitoring is not necessary if care is taken to randomize those clients who will be "followed" in the manner described.

Finally, in conducting outcome evaluation studies, attention should also be paid to other aspects of former clients' environments, particularly the family. A brief questionnaire given to the family and completed at the same time that followup of the client is done by a volunteer can be a further control against subjective biases that may be introduced by the evaluator or the former client.

Although none of the strategies suggested are purely objective, or pertain to actual symptom or behavioral analysis; they can be valuable to the innovative administrator, because they provide critical "feedback." The use of "volunteers" as well as the intake worker when a "former" client returns for care does not represent significant additional cost to the human service program, and, therefore, keeps to a minimum the cost of these limited and admittedly subjective outcome evaluation strategies.

IMPACT OF EVALUATION STRATEGIES

This section describes four important areas—the staff, the administration, funding sources, and the community—upon which the performance of evaluation can have a profound impact. It is important to recognize that the limited evaluation strategies, such as have been described in this chapter, can have an important impact on each of these four areas. Several examples will help to demonstrate this impact.

IMPACT ON STAFF

The impact of evaluation on the staff of human service programs can be clearly demonstrated. It may range from a simple recognition of its importance by the staff to an actual lowering of staff resistance toward participating in the evaluation process. A positive recognition of its value also may lead to a better understanding of the purposes for which services are being delivered and a better conceptualization of their relative value in the program hierarchy. Evaluation may also provide useful feedback to staff members, which will enable them to participate as change agents in future program planning and reorganization.

In the examples cited previously, the walk-in clinic staff's awareness of the poor followup of patients from the Pima County Hospital Emergency Room after referral to the walk-in clinic led to the staff's recommendation of a new continuity of care system to improve client followup. This helped to increase the staff's recognition of how data could be helpful to them in their own jobs, and thereby decreased their resistance to participating in data collection.

IMPACT ON ADMINISTRATION

The availability of evaluation data can also have a profound impact on the administrator of a human service program. Not only can it help program leaders to have useful insights into the nature and scope of the services that are administered, but evaluative data can also allow the executive to present the staff with recommendations for program change which are based on "hard" data rather than on theoretical constructs or selective biases.

The availability of data regarding the high cost of service delivery in the outpatient unit led to an examination for underlying causes, which revealed that excessive costs were partly determined by the low availability of group services. This discovery led to an administrative decision to recruit personnel for that treatment team who had special skills in group therapy. After this was accomplished, the volume of group services being delivered increased and the cost per service hour in the outpatient unit decreased.

Another example of the impact on administration of these limited evaluation strategies was a change in the orientation of the state hospital. With the
decrease in clients being treated at the state hospital, because of the increased
assumption of responsibility by local mental health programs, the state hospital was able to develop specific therapeutic programs that better met the needs
of those specific patient groups that remained within the hospital, such as the
chronic mentally ill and the geriatric patient (Caplan, 1964).

IMPACT ON LEGISLATURES AND OTHER FUNDING SOURCES

While it can be demonstrated clearly that the impact of evaluation mechanisms on both the staff and the administration of human service programs
is profound, an even more critical relevance of the development of evaluation
mechanisms is in the area of program funding.

Clearly, an important reaction to the large-scale introduction of human
service programs during the past decade has been the questioning of many in
responsible funding positions as to "what works?" The early overwhelming
faith that poverty could be cured by the simple influx of a large amount of
dollars has been replaced by a later skepticism that is not only healthy in that
it can lead to a much needed reexamination of the value of certain programs,
but also is dangerous in that it can lead to a "backlash" that will undermine
even the effective human service programs by "throwing out the baby with the
bath water."

Consequently, the responsible human service program administrator will
engage in evaluation not only to preserve funding sources and to justify continued existence of the programs, but also to fulfill properly a moral and ethical
obligation to utilize those limited dollars available in the most effective manner
possible. An example of how limited evaluation strategies can have a tremendous impact on legislatures and other funding sources occurred when the
distribution of remaining clients at the Arizona State Hospital revealed a
disproportionately high number in the geriatric category. Further study indicated that this was due in part to the lack of available nursing homes and
other extended care resources in the community. Discussion with nursing
home personnel revealed that, although they were willing to render service to
the emotionally disturbed geriatric patient, nursing home administrators had
been reluctant to do so without professional mental health consultation.

This suggested to the administrator the necessity of employing a consultant to these groups. Justification for funding this consultant was based upon
the potential impact that the consultant might have upon the geriatric patient
hospitalization rate. Funds were then made available on a trial basis. The
subsequent reduction of the census of geriatric patients at the Arizona State
Hospital led to the continued availability of funding for this consultation
activity.

IMPACT ON THE COMMUNITY

Finally, the use of effective evaluation strategies can have a great impact
upon the community that the human service program is targeted to serve. For

example, the availability of evaluation data coupled with an effective public relations campaign can not only increase the visibility of a human service program, but can also add to its credibility among those people who often resist seeking services at the early stage of a particular problem.

However, it must also be pointed out that credibility with the community is also dependent upon allowing the community to plan an active role in the development of evaluation strategies through seeking its input into determining those parts of the program that require critical evaluation (Mercer et al., 1964). Without doing so, the program and its administrator may fall victim to increasing community militancy and the forces of consumerism. The utilization of volunteers, while occasioned by the lack of adequate fiscal and staff support for evaluation strategies, had a tremendous secondary benefit upon the relationship of the community mental health center with the community. For example, the involvement of volunteers in the evaluation process not only assisted the center in helping the community to understand better the necessity for evaluation, but also made the evaluation more acceptable to those in the community who were asked to participate.

SUMMARY

In this chapter, we have noted the evolving transition toward a human service ideology that has marked the development and implementation of programs designed to meet the needs of the culturally and socioeconomically disadvantaged.

During the past decade, almost in parallel to the development of this human service ideology, a demand for accountability has been more loudly voiced. In response to it, human service programs have been attempting, with varied success, to implement evaluation strategies.

The importance of evaluation is underscored by the broad range of target groups that are both concerned and affected by evaluation—namely the administrator and staff of a program, the funding sources, and the community.

However, recognizing the importance of evaluation in today's human service marketplace is not sufficient to guarantee that effective evaluation strategies will be implemented. The problems of making a personal commitment, defining the scope and target of evaluation, record keeping, continuity of care, staff resistance, the development of a monitoring plan, and the process of selecting those areas to be evaluated are all critical and must be addressed by the human service program administrator prior to the implementation of any specific strategy for program evaluation.

The administrator who does not feel immediately competent to undertake sophisticated evaluation strategies should not be discouraged since more limited evaluation techniques are available. Several low-cost strategies for evaluation have been described in this chapter that can be used to gather critical information for effective program planning and policy making. These techniques are simple, effective and not excessively costly; but their overall implementation and success depend on the willingness of the human service program administrator to make a commitment to the importance of evaluation.

Without evaluative data, program administrators not only will be unable to have important information available to assist in decision making, but administrators also will fail to meet the demand for accountability and consequently suffer a loss of credibility and funding.

REFERENCES

Baker, F. From community mental health to human service ideology. *American Journal of Public Health,* 1974, *64,* 576–581.

Beigel, A. Alternatives to psychiatric hospitalization. *Medical Insight,* 1971, *3,* 34–44.

Beigel, A., Bower, W. H., & Levenson, A. I. A unified system of care: Blueprint for the future. *American Journal of Psychiatry,* 1973, *130,* 554–558.

Caplan, G. *Principles of preventive psychiatry.* New York: Basic Books, 1964.

Demone, H. W., Jr. Human services at state and local levels and the integration of mental health. In G. Caplan (Ed.), *American handbook of psychiatry* (Vol. 2). Basic Books: New York, 1973.

Department of Health, Education, and Welfare. *Evaluation in mental health: A review of the problem of evaluating mental health activities.* (Public Health Service Publication No. 413.) Rockville, Maryland: National Institute of Mental Health, 1955.

Fox, P. D. Some approaches to evaluating community mental health services. *Archives of General Psychiatry,* 1972, *26,* 172–178.

Greenberg, E. M., & Brandon, S. Evaluating community treatment programs. *Mental Hospital,* 1964, *15,* 617–619.

McMahon, B., Pugh, T. F., & Hutchinson, G. B. Principles in the evaluation of community mental health programs. *American Journal of Public Health,* 1961, *51,* 963–968.

Mercer, J. R., Dingman, H. F., & Tarjan, G. Involvement, feedback, and mutuality: Principles for conducting mental health research in the community. *American Journal of Psychiatry,* 1964, *121,* 228–237.

Murphy, H. B. M. Methods of evaluating community mental health programs. *Canadian Psychiatric Association Journal,* 1971, *16,* 525–532.

II

INTEGRATED MANAGEMENT INFORMATION SYSTEMS

The management information system is an essential cornerstone of effective program evaluation within human service organizations. Program evaluation is an integral part of the administrative process—a process requiring *planning information* about what services the organization will render and what resources will be used to provide these services, as well as *performance information* about how effectively the organization did its job and how efficiently resources were used. Both planning and performance information flow from well designed and effectively implemented information systems. But learning how to build an information system is not easy. The literature about management information systems is rapidly expanding with contributors emerging from a broad array of administrative and social science disciplines. Integration of this literature for application in human service programs, however, remains an important contemporary task.

The chapters in Part II address this task and provide an overview of the theory of information systems, principles and strategies of information system design and implementation, the basic technology of information systems, and illustrative examples of information systems in human service organizations. These chapters represent a synthesis of methods used in successful human service field applications and contain the distilled experiences of knowledgeable human service information system consultants. Readers should gain new skills in guiding and evaluating the development and implementation of an information system. We hope that Part II will also provide essential background for understanding the complexities of subsequent chapters, especially those chapters that link fiscal data with client and program outcomes.

6

DEVELOPING INFORMATION SYSTEMS FOR HUMAN SERVICE ORGANIZATIONS

James E. Sorensen and J. Richard Elpers

From the earliest civilizations, human beings have required information for survival and social progress. For a primitive tribe stalking animals for food and clothing, survival depended on simple communications, such as hand signals, about the direction of the wind. In stark contrast to more primitive times, the survival of today's organization serving human needs depends on a management control system that enables human service managers

1. To make better *plans*—plans that relate to organizational goals and objectives based on the relative benefits and costs of alternative courses of action.

2. To have better *control*—control that assures efficient and effective action in pursuing the organization's objectives. But plans and controls, in turn, require four generic types of information—*planning and performance information* about

- What services the organization will render and to whom
- What resources the organization will use to provide these services
- How effectively the organization is doing its job
- How efficiently the organization is using its resources.

The evolution of information processing has been enhanced by the development of

- Language and mathematical notation,
- The printing press,
- The emergence of mass media and telecommunication systems,

127

- The development of the digital computer, and
- Computer programming.

When coupled with the pressures of

- Increased size and rapid growth of organizations,
- Increased specialization and complexity of organizations, and
- Accountability and increased regulation,

the role and structure of information systems take on major significance for all types of organizations.

Many human service organizations are just now becoming aware of the potential of information systems in planning and managing their activities. For many human service programs, planning has been almost nonexistent. The exigencies of launching programs, day-to-day program survival, and continuous funding crises have thwarted many efforts to engage in creative long-range planning. Consequently, most service programs have only perfunctory planning and development capacity; those that seriously attempt to plan find that events and programs seldom go as planned—something always goes wrong (although the consequences may be handled better as a result of their planning). Most frequently, planners and administrators fail because they lack the requisite information and corresponding information processing capability. Management information is the key to planning an activity, controlling its development, maintaining it on course, and measuring its impact. Management information systems have emerged as the principal tool for dealing with these crucial activities.

CHAPTER OVERVIEW

The theme of this chapter is simple: Integrated management information systems (MISs) contribute to the survival of human service organizations by producing information that

- Assesses the pattern of service delivery (e.g., Who receives what types and amounts of services?)
- Defines how current resources are required and being consumed (e.g., How are professional staff deployed?)
- Provides monitoring aids for various human service providers and managers (e.g., Were particular admissions or client entries into the program inappropriate?)
- Develops data for multiple reporting requirements (e.g., Reporting to federal or state funding agencies or payment agents such as the Social Security Administration or PSRO review)
- Assesses outcomes of rendered services (e.g., Level of functioning of client, changes in symptoms).

How the planning and control are actually accomplished, however, requires detailed answers to four additional interrelated questions.

1. How do the major *requirements and characteristics* of management information relate to differing levels of human service organizational planning and control, varied but essential human service organizational functions, and conceptual content of information required by human service organization managers?

2. What are the major *operational* components of a management information system?

3. How could an information system be set up or *organized* within a human service organization?

4. What are the *guidelines* for developing a competent management information system for human service organizations?

Each question will now be probed briefly to provide a more detailed overview of the chapter's content.

MANAGEMENT INFORMATION

Successful development of an organizational information system emerges from a clear understanding of the management planning and control activities of managers within the organization. Effort allocated to planning activities generally expands at the top levels of an organization, whereas efforts for controlling activities generally expand at the lower levels of an organization. Varying functions of an organization require differing types of information, depending on the function itself as well as the managerial level of the planning or controlling activity. The varying functions of an organization include service delivery, personnel management and development, accounting and financing, and information processing. The levels of decision making all require information of varying content, such as the goals and objectives of the organization, a statistical description of its activities, a financial description of its resources, and information about the external environment of the human service organization.

What emerges is a multidimensional matrix of information subsystems of varying content for a wide range of varying activities and functions. Application of this concept to human service organizations is one of the major pursuits of this chapter.

OPERATIONAL COMPONENTS OF AN INFORMATION SYSTEM

The actual operations of a human service information system include physical components such as computers, computer programs, files, operating procedures, and personnel; processing functions; and documents used to capture data and reports representing the outputs of the information system. Each operating element is examined in providing an overview of the human service organization information system and how it can be assembled.

ORGANIZATIONAL DESIGN

The arrangement of the information system in a human service organization may be focused around two broad approaches: a hierarchical approach with either centralized or decentralized data processing; or a system approach with either an integrated or distributed system.

This final question examines an approach to the design of information systems and identifies several key guidelines to be followed in developing effective human service information systems.

Two overall cautions are pertinent. First, information systems are not free. The management of information costs precious resources. The balance between enough information to make solid planning and control decisions and the cost of developing and maintaining an information system is a constant cost–benefit struggle. Whenever an organization expands its information system beyond the satisfaction of minimal legal requirements and routine problem solving, the continuing question becomes: Are the benefits worth the investment? Second, not all information that managers receive, need, or use comes from the information system. A phone call from a close friend or a casual comment by a colleague in a group discussion may have a large impact and can change the whole course of organizations. This "informal" information system is acknowledged as important, but this chapter focuses on the formal information system as *planned* for managing the organization.

REQUIREMENTS AND CHARACTERISTICS
OF MANAGEMENT INFORMATION

INFORMATION REQUIREMENTS DEPEND ON
LEVEL OF MANAGEMENT ANALYSIS

The information needs of a human service organization manager vary by levels of managerial activity. Because the *level* of the management activity influences the *characteristics* of the information used, information systems must be designed to provide different types of information at different levels (Weinstein, 1975). Three general managerial levels may be identified within human service organizations:

1. Strategic planning that includes
   a. Setting organizational goals
   b. Outlining policies and objectives
   c. Identifying general range of appropriate organizational activities
   d. Long-range planning
2. Tactical or managerial control functions that include
   a. Short-range activities for acquiring and allocating resources
   b. Identifying new services or locations of services
   c. Deciding on service location layout, personnel requirements
   d. Analysis of budgets and variances from budget
3. Operational control functions that include
   a. Ensuring specific tasks are implemented in an effective and efficient manner

   b. Accepting or rejecting specific clients
   c. Ensuring quality of service at point of delivery
   d. Allocating personnel to predetermined programmatic plans
   e. Determining reasons for variations of expenditures from budgeted amounts.

Strategic planning requires distal time-lines so that long-range major changes in plans for the organization may be constructed. Adding to a service program, for example, requires fairly long lead times for

1. Financing the building(s), equipment, and staff
2. Acquiring professional staff
3. Acquiring new facilities and obtaining zoning approval
4. Examining the impact on types of patients served and types of agencies referring clients.

In decisions like the addition of a day-care program, a great deal of information may be required such as

1. What is the current and prospective political environment? (Will the federal or local government support the program with funds?)
2. What are the prospects for the economy? (Will more plentiful jobs change the need for this type of supportive service?)
3. What is the current and prospective competition? (Will other agencies in the area be adding a similar program?)
4. What are the future financial commitments required if the program is added? (Will we be able to meet future salary requirements for competent staff?)
5. What is the rate of technological obsolescence? (Will new licensing regulations require expensive remodeling or increases in staffing?)

Although other questions could be raised, the example clearly identifies the powerful role of *external* information in *strategic planning*.

Tactical (or management) control for the hypothetical program would be required after the program is established and could include, for example:

1. Short-range planning of the staffing pattern and hiring of new staff
2. Planning the yearly budget, anticipating deviations from the approved goals, determining the reasons for deviations, and finding ways to accommodate needed changes
3. Analyzing utilization of the day-care program by type of referral agency and type of client diagnosis or problem area.

Operational control would focus on the day-to-day operations such as screening new clients, carrying out a skills training program, and assessing client progress and readiness for new interventions. Often, preestablished procedures and decision rules and specific data capture forms are used in order to encourage consistent, efficient, and effective services to clients.

Strategic decision making, therefore, is primarily a planning activity, whereas tactical decision making requires a mix of both planning and controlling activities. Operational decision making is essentially controlling according to plans and assessing deviations from those plans.

In summary, the characteristics of information needed for planning and management vary by level of management activity. Strategic levels—especially planning—require more external information, less accuracy, and greater levels of summarization. Tactical decision making requires more accurate, precise, current, and more repetitive information. Operational decisions, however, require much more detailed information. Specific, accurate, frequent, and current data are required for managers to evaluate the immediate response required for short-range changes in day-to-day operation. Table 6.1 summarizes the interaction of characteristics of information and level of decision making.

TABLE 6.1
Information Characteristics by Decision Category[a]

Characteristics of information	Decision making		
	Operational	Tactical	Strategic
Source	Largely internal		. Largely external
Scope	Well-defined, narrow		. Very wide
Level of aggregation	Detailed		. Aggregate
Time horizon	Historical		. Future
Currency	Highly current		. Older
Required accuracy	Higher		. Lower
Frequency of use	Very frequent		. Infrequent

[a] Adapted by permission from G. A. Gorry and M. S. S. Morton, A framework for management information systems. *Sloan Management Review*, 1971, *13*, 55–70. (Copyright 1971, Sloan Management Review Association, Cambridge, Massachusetts.)

INFORMATION REQUIREMENTS DEPEND
ON ORGANIZATIONAL FUNCTION

Another source of variation in the characteristics of information stems from organizational function. In private-sector firms, major organizational functions would include, for example, marketing, production, logistics, personnel, finance and accounting, and information processing. Human service organizations have similar organizational functions but differ in several major ways. Usually human service organizations do not clearly identify the marketing function ("outreach," "interagency linkage," "case finding," and assuring "continuity of care" are aspects of marketing), and "production" is usually accomplished through several types of service delivery. In the case of a general hospital, for example, these services may be medical, surgical, gynecological, obstetrics and new born, outpatient services, and various ancillary services such as x-ray and pharmacy. In a community mental health center, services may be delivered through organizational units such as inpatient, partial hospitalization, emergency, outpatient, and education/consultation. Logistics—acquiring, receiving, and distributing inventories and services—along with personnel, finance and accounting, and information processing often are directly comparable functions in all types of organizations. In addition, special functions such as research, teaching/education, and evaluation are found in human service organizations.

Often, each functional area of an organization requires specific types of information, which frequently leads to functional information subsystems that merge, ideally, as an integrated management information system. This "federation" of functional subsystems, while processing functionally specific informational needs, may often use a common data base or common computer programs. A matrix of functional subsystems *and* managerial activities is summarized in Figure 6.1. The *size* of the subsystem is usually inverse to the level of the managerial activities and is represented by varying-sized rectangles with more of the subsystem being devoted to lower-level managerial activities and comparatively smaller portions being devoted to higher-level activities.

Characteristics of information change as the managerial function changes. For example, the service delivery function needs data on populations at risk, clients, historic and current utilization of services, and progress on treatment plans. The personnel management function, however, needs data on employees' professional training, experience, years of service, pay grade, and rate of likely advancement. Some data will be associated with only one function, whereas other data will be used by several functions. Years of service may only be used by the personnel department, but hours of rendered service may be used by managers in service delivery function as well as by payroll, cost-finding, and billing in the accounting/finance function. Managers in the service delivery function could use hours of rendered service to evaluate the level of effort by various professional staff, whereas accounting/finance may use the same information for billing a specific client, insurance agency, or reimbursing an agency for services received by the client.

Information characteristics, in general terms, vary by managerial function (5). For example, accuracy or precision (less to more accurate), age of data

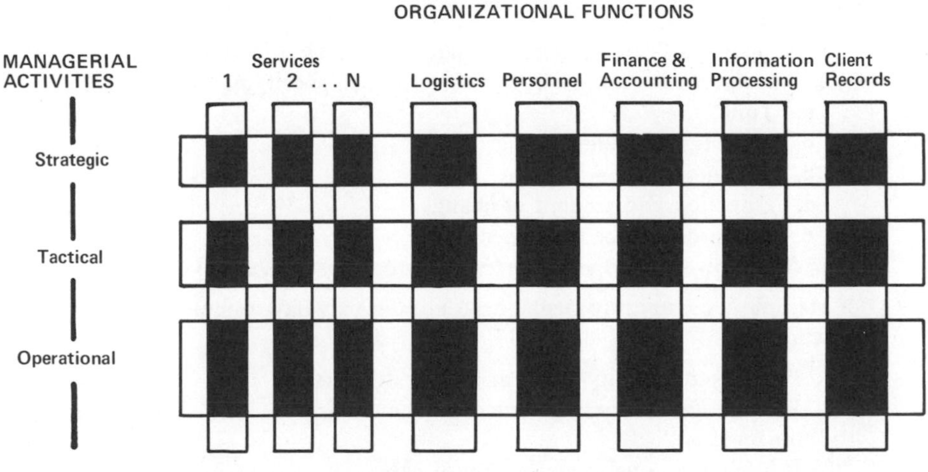

Figure 6.1. A conceptualization of the interaction of the characteristics of organizational information with levels of decision making.

(younger to older), repetitiveness (less to more repetitive), summarization (less to more summarized), descriptive content (less to more descriptive), and source (less to more external) also seem to vary by the particular managerial function. The accounting function, for example, requires precise, linear, older, repetitive, and summarized data at one extreme where the personnel function requires less accurate, configurational, more up-to-date, detailed, descriptive data.

In summary, the characteristics of information vary both by level of decision making and by organizational function. The information system that is created as a human service organization grows must be correspondingly varied and complex. If the MIS is created in an unsystematic, piecemeal fashion, as is often the case, it can be excessively redundant and ineffective. The MIS designer attempts to integrate existing and needed information functions to serve best the organization at its current size and stage of development.

DEFINING ORGANIZATIONAL GOALS

Modern management theories suggest that organizational managers should clarify the goals and objectives they are seeking for their organizational programs (Drucker, 1954; McGregor, 1960). Human service programs presumably are responding to a demand for services and/or assessments of needs (as outlined in Chapters 9 and 10). Although individuals may hold many personal goals and objectives, obtaining consensus on the major ones held by the members of a given organization should lead to clearer organizational structure, more extensive planning, improved management information systems, more control over operations, and better overall organizational performance.

One approach to the study and clarification of goals and objectives distinguishes between goals, objectives, and measures (Drucker, 1954; McGregor, 1960):

1. A *goal* is a "desired state of affairs," whereas
2. An *objective* is an interpretation of a goal, specifying
   a. Time,
   b. Issue (or variable),
   c. Target group,
   d. Direction and amount of change,
   e. Resources (to be consumed), and
3. *Measures* are the operations for assessing the achievement of objectives.

For example, a community mental health center may have (among others) the following goals:

1. Provide community-based mental health services
2. Provide effective case-finding of catchment area residents needing center services
3. Provide high quality continuity of care

4. Provide for diversified financial resources for the center
5. Demonstrate impact/effectiveness with regard to clients and the community.

Each of these goals could be expanded into multiple objectives with multiple measures. The goal of providing community-based care, for example, might be to provide community-based mental health services. This goal may be expanded into several objectives and measures, for example, dealing with the utilization of state hospital inpatient programs by catchment area residents:

1. Objectives
   a. By [date], reduce first admission of catchment area residents from [number] to [number]
   b. By [date], reduce readmission of catchment area residents from [number] to [number]
2. Measures
   a. Admissions by diagnosis and age
   b. Admissions with prior center contact
   c. Admissions with prior center treatment
   d. Admissions with prior inpatient services
   e. Admissions by source of referral
   f. Admissions without prior center contact
   g. Admissions per capita of catchment area
   h. Readmissions per capita of catchment area.

Note, for example, that the first objective has

- Time (by [date] . . .)
- Issue or variable (. . . reduce first admission . . .)
- Target group (. . . catchment area residents . . .)
- Direction/Change (. . . from [number] to [number] . . .)
- Resource (. . . with CMHC programs).

Two other illustrative goals are presented with sample objectives and measures:

Goal: Provide High Quality Care

1. Objective—By [date], the number of treatment plans which specify modality, estimated number of units of service, time table, behavioral objectives for individuals will increase from [number] to [number], with existing staff.
2. Measures
   a. Number of completed treatment plans as a proportion of total number of individual clients
   b. Proportion of treatment plans judged by peer review to be adequately formulated and carried out by each program.

Goal: Provide Efficient Delivery of Services

1. Objective—By [date], the cost per hour (or other unit) of service for outpatients will decrease without a reduction in treatment effectiveness.

2. Measures
   a. Professional cost per hour (or other unit) of service
   b. Total cost per hour of service
   c. Total cost per client treatment episode—cost per unit of change in client functioning from admission to 3-month followup (using a measure such as the Global Assessment Scale [Endicott, Spitzer, Fleiss, & Cohen, 1976]) by type of client, initial level of functioning, and program.

The major yield of this approach for MIS is a clearer specification of what measures the MIS *should* produce. For example, the goal dealing with high quality care requires a periodic inquiry and summary of completed treatment plans and achievement. The goal of efficient delivery would require cost-per-unit calculations, summaries of costs over given periods of time, and a cost–outcome comparison (see Chapter 13).

CONCEPTUAL CONTENT OF HUMAN SERVICE INFORMATION SYSTEMS

Within a human service organization, information is needed for a variety of purposes. Information is required for three general areas: first, clinical or treatment monitoring, including supervision and review of various treatment interventions and communication of background and instructions to those dealing with patients or clients; second, research; and third, management, including planning and controlling acquisition and use of the organization's resources and assessing its efficiency and performance.

OVERLAPPING SYSTEMS

Clinical monitoring, research, and management information requirements overlap. But an intensive examination reveals that the kinds and extent of data needed for each system vary considerably (Weinstein, 1975). The commonalities and differences are conceptualized in Figure 6.2.

1. *Clinical Records*

Clinical records for monitoring a patient's treatment needs and progress must be explicit and as objective as possible. Historically, these files were developed manually and often could not be manipulated statistically because of inconsistencies in recording and difficulties of retrieval from hand-prepared records. With the advent of program evaluation, peer, and utilization review, *specific* elements of the *clinical* record system must be extracted, summarized, and/or compared to specific criteria for operational and managerial control. Length of stay (LOS), type of service, and admitting diagnosis, for example, are elements that serve both the clinical records and management information systems. While a LOS that exceeds established criteria for a given diagnosis may be flagged for possible review by a physician advisor or a peer review committee, a human service administrator may desire profiles of the LOS by diagnosis and service modality to assess the need for modifying the types of

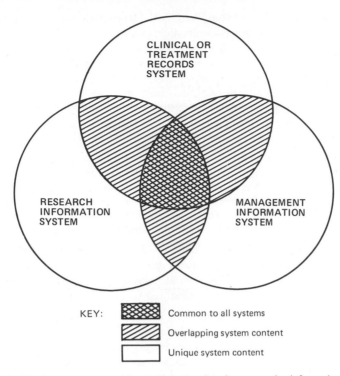

Figure 6.2. Overlapping systems and general content in a human service information system.

services offered or adding additional staff because of changing admission patterns. As program evaluation and quality and utilization review develop, more elements of the clinical record systems will become part of the required elements of the management information system. Initially, the process may be done by manual extractions from manually prepared records. Eventually the overlaps will be automated, and computers (ranging from mini to midi to maxi)will perform routine processing and report preparation for key managers/decision makers within (and outside) the service delivering organization. Service providers may want to be alerted to possible cases of poor quality care, whereas administrators may be interested in the overall incidence and resolution of the same cases. Evaluation teams may press for more detail, whereas administrators are likely to press for greater summarization.

2. Research Data

Research on medical and human service problems requires extensive, often expensive, information on samples of (or, in some cases, on total) patient populations. The distinction between complex research approaches and simpler, management-oriented, program operations evaluation should be drawn clearly. A long-term, prospective, controlled study examining the clinical cost–effectiveness of short-term hospitalization as an alternative to long-term hospitalization for schizophrenic patients (where either type of care is clinically feasible such as in the study by Glick, Hargreaves, and Goldfield, 1974) requires an elaborate design using classical evaluative research procedures. On the other hand, ascertaining if a given community mental health center target group received services that achieved a treatment plan objective and at what cost during the past three months, or which of the two modalities used by a center treating manic–depressives was most effective for the costs incurred, may be accomplished with less complicated approaches. The first type of evaluation is more clearly in the research area and the second type has a greater management flavor. As Levine and Levine (1975) emphasize:

> There should be a clear-cut separation between studies designed to determine relationships between treatment modes and effects, and evaluation studies. The former studies should be undertaken within a pure science context . . . . For evaluation purposes, it is necessary to monitor treatment programs to see that any given approach does not fall below some experientially determined lower limit of production [p. 89].*

Management requires select data on all clientele (usually less detailed) and data on the resources acquired and devoted to providing various services (Cooper, 1973, pp. 10–11). Managers at varying levels usually require report information focused around five broad classes of questions:

1. Questions assessing patterns of patient or client care and services. Illustrative reports would include
   a. Disposition of intakes by organizational service
   b. Ethnic/racial background by sex and type of service received
   c. Residence (e.g., census tract or enumeration district) of service recipients cross-tabulated by service components within the organization
   d. Patients or clients added by major presenting health or human service problem
   e. Patients or clients discharged by major and minor discharge diagnosis or problem area
   f. Number and proportion of admissions (apparently) eligible for third-party reimbursement
   g. Volume of services by type of service and organizational unit
   h. Client or patient load by individual staff or staffing units.
2. Questions defining how various types of resources are acquired and consumed. Typical reports include statistical and financial data.
   a. Statistical data on distribution of staff time by discipline and service
   b. Statistical data on volume of services provided by staff or staffing units
   c. Financial data on cost per unit of service
   d. Financial data on comparison of program costs and fee revenue by type of service

*Reproduced by permission from: A. Levine and M. Levine, Evaluation research in mental health: Lessons from history. In J. Zusman & C. R. Wurster (Eds.), *Program evaluation: Alcohol, drug abuse, and mental health services.* Copyright 1975, D. C. Heath, Lexington, Massachusetts.

    e. Financial data on comparison of budgets and expenses by organizational components.

3. Questions that create monitoring aids for human service case managers and for peer and utilization review. Reports might include

    a. Statistical/medical concurrent review aids, including clients referred to but not admitted by a service; admissions not meeting admissions justification profile criteria by type of admitting diagnosis or problem; listing of admissions exceeding average LOS criteria (local norms); and excessive units of service or extended length of stay by service

    b. Statistical/medical retrospective review aids, including admitting diagnoses not validated; admission justifications not confirmed; case listings of admission not accompanied by treatment plan or therapeutic services; and case listings of diagnoses accompanied by potentially high-risk medical services (e.g., lithium)

    c. Financial concurrent review aids, including admission without determination of third-party payment source and cumulative charges in excess of Medicaid or Medicare allowances

    d. Financial retrospective review aids—Cases where cost per treatment episode exceeds average cost criteria (mean $\pm$ 1 standard deviation).

4. Questions responding to external reporting requirements—Usually, these reports should be completed from existing internally generated reports or by a search of an external source (e.g., census data).

5. Questions identifying client outcomes

    a. Relationship of costs and outcomes for specific target groups

    b. Discharge status by diagnosis and LOS

    c. Specific complications by diagnosis and LOS.

3. *Summary*

Areas of overlap between managerial, clinical, and research information systems should be clearly established. Whether these three kinds of data can be easily and economically integrated into a *single* data system is problematic because of the variations in the depth, nature, and manipulations of their respective system data bases. Information systems for each major system pose challenging but differing design and reporting requirements. Selected clinical information about a client's history of allergic reactions, undesired response to medications, or suicidal tendency, for example, must be immediately accessible for an attending therapist, but the units of service previously received may need to be accessed only periodically. Data on an experimental treatment group may be analyzed long after particular clients have been discharged, but the information may have to meet exacting standards at the time of data collection.

Distinction between these three systems adds clarity to the design (or redesign) of an information system to serve human service managers. To be economical, yet effective, requires an *integrated* approach to information system design—an approach seldom considered in most human service organizations.

CONCEPTUAL CONTENT OF
MANAGEMENT INFORMATION SUBSYSTEMS

INTERRELATIONSHIPS OF MIS CONTENT

The "management information system" is a concept that has emerged only in the last two decades (*1*). It is used to describe the system that generates data on all phases of operations including financial information—both actual and budgetary—and all types of statistical information. The role of the management information system (MIS) in *connecting the organization's structure to the organization's process* is graphed in Figure 6.3. A natural product of

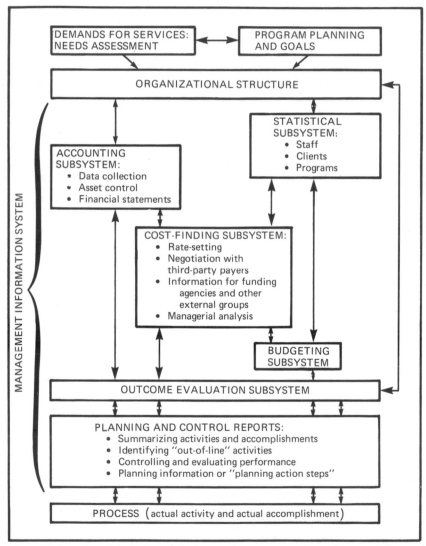

Figure 6.3. Overview of the human service integrated management information system. [Source: Sorensen and Phipps, 1975.]

this formulation is a clear identification of *the vital connective relationships* among the conceptual areas of MIS, especially relationships among the conceptual elements of statistics, accounting, cost-finding, budgeting, and outcome. The elements of MIS are interdependent, mutually interactive, and dynamic over time in their role of connecting an organizational structure to its process. The level of performance of any one content area is highly dependent on other content areas in the MIS. If the accounting, budgeting, statistical, and outcome data are adequately captured, cost-finding and rate-setting tasks or preparing cost–outcome analyses are greatly simplified.

The planning and control reports produced by the MIS are the "eyes and ears" of management in interpreting how the structure of the organization relates to the actual activity (or processes) of a human service organization. The reports are not equated with the process itself because of the abstractions required to create understandable reports. The necessity for abstraction means that some of the complexity of the actual process must be left out and this deletion can (and does) lead to some distortion of actual program activity and accomplishment. Reducing the complexities of a hospital to total patient days and cost per patient day compacts an enormous amount of detail about level of activity and resource consumption. Such computations, while simplified for ease of understanding, can be viewed only as comprising a crude representation of actual processes. Each of the major content areas will now be probed to reveal its individual contribution to the reality simplification provided by the MIS.

ACCOUNTING CONTENT

Traditionally the keystone of most MISs has been the information expressed in dollars provided by the accounting system. An accounting system should provide useful data about expenditures and revenues and becomes the framework for achieving uniform financial reporting throughout an organization. A uniform chart of accounts and standardized procedures for recording entries in those accounts is required for a satisfactory system of recording and reporting financial results (see Cooper, 1973, and Salsbery, 1972, for examples). Costs should be accumulated by cost centers that follow the natural organizational groupings of personnel within the organizational chart. Summaries of both actual and budgeted costs can then be matched to enable individual managers to plan and control the operations of their respective organizational groupings. Costs should be coded so that they may be accumulated from the lowest level of reporting and then collapsed into broader reporting units until the highest level of the organization is reached.

Figure 6.4 outlines an illustrative human service organization with corresponding reporting levels. Cost centers would accumulate actual cost (and revenue) data starting at the subunit level or level five (usually by object of expenditures such as, for example, salary, rent, travel) and would be collapsed into larger and larger reporting units until an aggregate summary for the executive director and board of directors is reached. Note that the cost centers define the structure of the MIS and that the accumulated cost information represents the process of consuming and creating resources in financial terms.

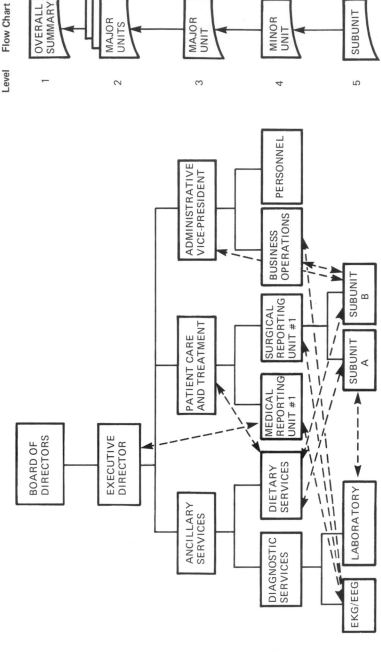

Figure 6.4. Outline of an illustrative human service organization with corresponding reporting levels.

142

STATISTICAL CONTENT

Operating statistics on clients, patients, staff, and programs are vital information for managers of human service organizations. Good statistical information is essential in the allocation of resources to provide the greatest amount of service to the greatest number of clients or patients, and the best utilization of the staff of the organization. Operating statistics can permit the manager to plan for the future with greater certainty because he or she will be able to identify shortages of personnel and resources and, perhaps, even surpluses that might be effectively reallocated. Operating reports also provide the data requested for external reports to funding and various governmental units. Examples of the statistical reports that one human service organization provides for its various managers, staff, and external agencies are summarized in Table 6.2. Table 6.2 highlights the diversity of the recipients receiving various statistical reports:

1. External
   a. State and county
   b. Federal government
2. Internal
   a. Service delivery function for management and staff
   b. Other functions such as the computer section, operations research, patient accounting, research and evaluation, and medical records.

Because the contents of varied statistical reports for managers are illustrated by Elpers and Chapman in Chapter 7, additional examples are not provided at this point.

TABLE 6.2
Examples of Reports Generated by a Computer-Based Information System within a Mental Health/Mental Retardation (MH/MR) Organization[a]

I. REPORTS TO THE STATE AND COUNTY
   A. *Intake and Proposed Service Plan* (MH/MR): Registers center patients with the county office MH/MR (monthly).
   B. *Service Rendered Report and Invoice* (MH/MR): Listing of treatment rendered to each patient, by date, modality, and therapist discipline (monthly).
   C. *Monthly Service Report:* Information on admissions, discharges, and services rendered to catchment area and non-catchment-area residents according to four target groups (children, adult, geriatrics, mental retardation).
   D. *Semiannual Summary Report:*

Frequency distribution of selected demographic variables on four target groups.

II. REPORTS TO THE FEDERAL GOVERNMENT
   A. *NIMH Monthly Patient Load:* Census count on patients in drug programs.
   B. *NIMH Inventory:* Reports yearly statistics on admissions, treatments, movements, costs, etc. (annually).
   C. *Continuation Grant:* Statistics on caseload representativeness and treatment breakdowns (annually).
   D. *Financial Inventory:* An analysis of caseload for potential first and third party sources of revenue (annually).

(Continued)

TABLE 6.2 (Continued)

III. REPORTS TO MANAGEMENT
  A. *Population Report:* Admissions, movements, treatments, and location of treatments by individual clinics and other treatment settings.
  B. *Poverty Report:* Percentage of admissions at or below current definition of poverty (family income by number of dependents), by census tract (periodically).
  C. *Delayed Treatment Report:* Average elapsed time between intake, proposed treatment plan and first treatment rendered, for each treatment team and service (on request).
  D. *Source of Referral Report:* Frequency distribution of sources of referral by treatment teams and services, according to age, diagnosis, etc. (on request).

IV. REPORTS TO LINE STAFF
  A. *90-day No-show:* A listing of patients not seen in the past 90 days.
  B. *Open Case Listing:* A listing of all currently open cases with information tailored for each of the following recipients (weekly).
    1. *To Patient Coordinator:* A listing showing the location of each patient, when, where, and by whom last seen and discharge status (sorted alphabetically within treatment team).
    2. *To Team Administrator:* A listing showing the current census of the team. Listing shows treatment-related information (when, type of treatment, by whom rendered (sorted alphabetically by name, age, race, sex, address, etc.).
    3. *To Emergency Room:* Demographic and treatment-related variables on all patients currently being seen at center; used for referral and treatment decisions (sorted alphabetically).
    4. *To Therapist:* A listing showing

all cases currently under care, used for information about effort and for correcting computer's files (sorted alphabetically by therapist).
    5. *To Data Analyst:* Computer Information Section—a listing showing admission and treatment information; used in the correction of data input.

V. REPORTS OF MANAGEMENT INFORMATION SERVICES DIVISION
  A. *To Computer Information Section*
    1. *Error Report:* Lists all input documents rejected or flagged by computer for possible errors (weekly).
    2. *Error Deck:* A deck containing duplicates of cards rejected by the computer (weekly).
    3. *File Status Report:* Technical data for the Management Analyst on the state of the data base.
    4. *Admissions Report:* A report on all previous admissions for each intake, the census tract, and all other patient matching identification–to detect all non-apparent readmissions (daily).
    5. *History Listing:* Identifying variables on every patient ever seen at the Center, showing present status, admission date, identifying variables, when, where, and by whom last seen, sorted alphabetically and by case number (weekly).
  B. *To Operations Research Section*
    1. *Treatment Activity Records:* a set of cards comprising the previous week's encounter activities (weekly).
    2. *Cohort Data:* Card output containing demographic variables on a cohort of admissions. Also cards for every treatment encounter of members of the cohort (quarterly).
    3. *Other reports:* (as requested).
  C. *To Patient Accounts Section*

Table 6.2 (Continued)

1. *Weekly Transactions:* A listing of treatment records submitted the previous week. Listing contains all information necessary for patient and third party billing. Records listed are those that have passed card edit (weekly).
2. *Late Transactions:* Same as above, except that it contains only those cards that have failed previous edits and have been corrected (weekly).
3. *M. A. Elligibility:* Listing of patients who are not currently eligible for medical assistance, but appear eligible by virtue of income and number of dependents (periodically).
4. *Daily Admissions:* A list of previous day's admissions.
5. *Open Case Listings:* Demographic and treatment information used for billing and monitoring caseload (sorted alphabetically).

D. *Reports to Research and Evaluation Section*
   1. *Drop-outs:* List of patient drop-outs, according to age, race, number of and types of treatments, for each treatment team and for each therapist (on request).
   2. *Missed Appointments:* A listing of patients with missed appointments, containing selected patient characteristics (on request).
   3. *Other Summary Reports:* (on request).

E. *Reports to Medical Records Section*
   1. *Missing Document Report:* A listing of patients missing one or more intake documents (monthly).
   2. *Missing Item Report:* A listing of which intake items are being omitted by which therapist.
   3. *Open Case Listing:* Case listing showing demographic and historical information on each current patient; used to respond to information requests from outside agencies when legal and appropriate (sorted alphabetically by name).

a Adapted by permission from A. R. Goldman (see reference note 6).

COST-FINDING CONTENT

Information as to the amount of money spent on an activity is not particularly useful unless the expense is related to a stated volume of activity. It is not particularly useful to know that Health Organization *A* had a total outpatient expense of $40,000 and that Organization *B* had an outpatient expense of $240,000, unless one also knows the quantity of effort and type of patients the expense represents. The relationship between dollars and units of service gives meaning to the two separate parts. The subsystems designed to capture the statistical data must be using the same organizational unit specification as that used for accounting. If not, statistical data and accounting cannot be matched for assessing the cost for various types of services provided.

The term "cost-finding" may be defined as a system of allocating and reallocating costs from a point of data collection into different sets or subsets of costs. Simply stated, cost-finding is any method that attempts to charge all relevant costs—both direct and indirect—to *final* producing functions or activities, or what accountants have traditionally called "revenue producing functions" (since accountants trace expenses to the cost centers that produce the final product or service, the term "final producing cost center" has been coined for human service organizations). Unlike production organizations that have easily identified products, human service organizations often have difficulty in identifying the appropriate *final* production (or revenue producing) activities. Because of the evolution of the "type of service" concept, one natural way to collect and allocate expenses is by the basic types of service or program. In mental health services, for example, inpatient, outpatient, emergency service, partial hospitalization, and consultation and education represent one possible description of varied services. One could also choose type of patients such as children, adolescents, adults, and geriatrics as being final (or revenue) producing centers. No matter which of the several possible ways is selected, some rational and systematic method of charging all expenses, both direct and indirect, must be utilized to assign those expenses to the final (or revenue producing) activities. Full-cost allocation is appropriate even though some of the defined activities may be subsidized in part or entirely by some level of governmental funding; knowing the total expense of a program can be useful in evaluating cost–efficiency, cost–effectiveness, and cost–benefit ratios or in planning for alternative sources of financial support if government funding ceases.

1. *Determination of Rates for Services*

The degree of emphasis placed on collections for services varies widely among human service organizations. In some organizations, intensive efforts are made to collect a very high percentage of the expenses incurred for client services. In others very little effort is expended to make such collections. As the expense of services increases and the availability of general public funds decreases, the need to recover a higher proportion of the expenses from clients, patients, and third-party payers becomes increasingly important. These developments require the determination of rates for services offered by human service organizations.

Because of the diversity of services rendered in human service organizations, the statistical base for the rate can be problematic; in health care organizations, for example, using frequency of visits, patient contacts, or duration and intensity of treatment for determining patient charges based on averages for most patients (e.g., average cost per patient day) may lead to unsatisfactory rates. Some types of service, such as inpatient and partial hospitalization might rely heavily on average cost for the portion of service cost accruing from the usual hospital facilities including room occupancy, meals, laundry, other housekeeping items, and nursing care because these may be relatively uniform for all patients; on the other hand, because the amount of facilities and support services used in outpatient services are different, this would require a separate accounting and a separate rate. Other expenses such as the direct professional services, pharmacy, x-ray, physical or occupational therapy would probably vary considerably and therefore could be misleading if based on averages tied to "patient day" or "patient visit."

2. *Negotiation with Third-Party Payers*

As the expense of human services has increased, many third-party payers have made revisions in their contracts to increase the coverage of services and, at the same time, have refused to pay for certain client or patient charges not covered by their contracts. They have also increased their auditing procedures to determine which costs are being buried within the overall or average rates being charged patients, especially those expenses that are not—in their judgment—properly charged. Universities, for example, have discovered that federal agencies disallow certain costs in developing overhead rates for contracts. Costs dealing with student health and counseling services are systematically disallowed in determining the reimbursable costs because these costs have little (or no) relevance to the governmental contracts. In a similar way, costs of newborn services are disallowed in hospital rates for geriatric patients covered by Medicare.

As this trend continues, the individual human service organization will need to have accurate records to prove the validity of charges made to each client or patient. Direct services can offer little problem if adequate records are maintained, but the organization must also be able to recover the cost of indirect service as well. A systematic and logical cost-finding methodology becomes imperative if the organization expects to recover charges. The cost-finding system must be designed to eliminate duplications or omissions and to distribute all costs fairly. Although there is no absolutely accurate way to distribute indirect costs, there are methods that do distribute such costs fairly. For example, the costs of administration can be allocated to all of the services (or products) created by a human service organization, using as the ratio the total direct costs of a program to the total direct costs of all programs. While other bases for such calculations could be used, a *consistent* application of an equitable cost allocation method should raise few arguments with third-party payers.

3. *Information for Funding Agencies and Other External Groups*

If a significant portion of a human service organization's total revenue comes from public sources—federal, state, or local sources—there will be a need to provide fiscal reports to the funding agencies about expenses within established accounting methodologies. Such reports frequently focus on the cost and outcome of various service programs and/or service modalities. Funding agencies are usually not unreasonable when they ask for valid information about the costs of various programs; the request, however, often appears unreasonable because the organization has a poor or undeveloped MIS.

Some health care program costs, for example, have been called into question because the information furnished to funding agencies has been based on crude averages. In one mental hospital, for example, as the type of treatment changed from purely custodial care to intensive therapy the expense information furnished led to misleading interpretation; while the daily population had decreased by nearly 80%, the total expense of treatment had more than tripled. The error occurred in the way the treatment population characteristics were related to the type of care, cost of treatment rendered, and outcome. As another example, treatment modalities vary widely from one mental health center to another because some centers favor the use of high-cost intensive therapy with a rapid turnover in the patient population, whereas others use a longer-term approach with lower cost per patient for a given time period and a smaller patient roster. These two examples highlight why comparisions of cost per patient can be a meaningless exercise; only if the costs per episode for comparable problems are accompanied with measures of outcome can meaningful analysis proceed.

Because there is not any unanimity of opinion about the most effective types of programs in human service organizations, programs will differ and so will their costs. Perhaps from the vantage point of several years' experience and good records both as to costs, on the one hand, and the outcomes or benefits obtained by the individuals and communities served on the other, some determination of the most effective programs will be possible. But unless good records are kept about both costs and outcomes the answer may never be clearly identified (*3*).

4. *Information for Managerial Analysis*

Although the need to furnish accurate and meaningful cost information to patients, clients, third-party payers, and funding agencies is becoming increasingly important, usually there is minimal direct opportunity for consumers or funders to change the expenditure patterns of human service organizations. The specifics of this challenge are usually left to the management of the individual organization (although some funding sources may think they can and should influence expenditure patterns). This specific responsibility highlights the information needs of management.

One especially useful managerial application of cost-finding flows from a comparison of the revenue generated by the service or program to the total cost of operating the service or program. Management can identify whether or not the service is producing a net income or requiring a subsidy. From this type of analysis, meaningful adjustments to the rate structure may be achieved as well as evaluating the overall financial desirability of the specific service or program.

Cost-finding is useful in rate-setting, negotiation, and evaluating the overall financial aspects of a specific service but it is *not* a substitute for a budgetary control system that provides financial control over, and administrative evaluation of, specific individuals responsible for these services.

BUDGETING

A budget is a plan expressed in monetary terms (*2*). There are several types of budgets; a *capital* budget, that lists and describes planned capital acquisitions; a *cash* budget, that summarizes planned cash receipts and disbursements; and an *operating* or *expense* budget, that describes planned operating activities for a specified period of time, usually 1 year. This section relates primarily to the operating budget, because the capital budget is derived from decisions made during the programming process and the cash budget is derived from the operating budget.

The foregoing definitions encompass the concepts of planning and control. Horngren (1972) provides a brief explanation of these terms:

> For our purposes we define *planning* as the selection of objectives and their means of attainment. Therefore, planning is a delineation of goals and a choice of a decision model (decision method) for selecting means

PLANNING AND CONTROL

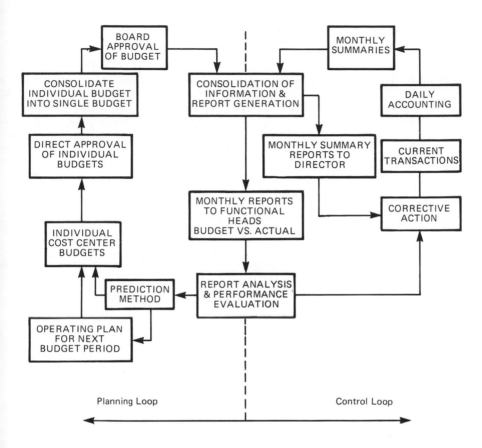

Figure 6.5. A schematic representation of budgetary planning and control loops necessary for management of human service organizations. [Source: Smith and Sorensen, 1974.]

of achieving them. *Control* is the implementation of a decision model and the use of feedback so that objectives are optimally obtained. This definition of control is comprehensive and flexible. It is concerned with the successful *implementation* of a course of action as predetermined by a decision model; but it is also concerned with *feedback* that might (a) change the future plans given the model, and (b) possibly change the decision model itself or change the prediction method that provides input into the decision model [p. 5].*

These concepts can be couched schematically in terms of planning and control loops illustrated in Figure 6.5.

*Reproduced by permission from: C. T. Horngren, *Cost accounting: A managerial emphasis* (3rd ed.). Copyright 1972, Prentice-Hall, Englewood Cliffs, New Jersey.

1. *Relationship to Accounting*

The budget should be constructed to conform with the accounting system. If this is not done, additional work is required to make comparisons between the actual and budget items. The budget acts as a control device to limit spending that has been authorized and to eliminate unauthorized expenditures. A system that employs budgets or goals and makes comparisons of actual results to budgeted results is quite common in most well-managed organizations. In such a system, these comparison reports often highlight only those items that do not conform to the budget. The identification of differences from a plan, and the resulting corrective response, is called "management by exception." Management by exception usually is functional as long as the original estimate (i.e., the budget) was sound when adopted. Budgetary changes may be made when the need to do so becomes apparent, but until such changes are authorized by the governing board or responsible authority, the budget is a control device and should be utilized as such. Table 6.3 shows an example of a human service budget with actual data and variances.

2. *Continuous Budgeting*

It is desirable, whenever possible, to implement a system of continuous budgeting. Traditionally budgets are prepared and adopted on a yearly basis, especially where funds are appropriated to the organization on a yearly basis. But for management purposes it would be preferable to have a planning budget that is always projected for a full year ahead. As the first quarter ends, the first quarter of the following year is budgeted making whatever adjustments seem appropriate from past experience. In this way, planning can be facilitated on a longer range basis. If this approach is followed, the annual budget process will be less troublesome and fewer surprises will crop up. Comparison between the budget and actual results on a frequent basis will aid greatly in spotting undesirable and/or favorable trends that are developing through the year.

The budget can provide the information to determine (in advance) the rates to be used for distributing the indirect costs to the revenue producing activities. In the planning stage, the accountant and staff personnel (clinical and administrative) will have the opportunity to examine the projected events during the coming year and decide on appropriate bases for distribution of support (non-revenue producing) expenses to the final (or revenue) producing centers.

3. *PPB Systems*

An additional perspective on budgeting is the recently developed PPB system viewpoint—the program planning, budgeting system view. The PPB system is well described in the following statement by Charles Schultze (7), who was Director of the Budget at the time PPB was introduced in the federal government:

> As the first step, PPB calls for a careful specification and analysis of basic program objectives in each major area of governmental activity. The key to this part of the operation is forcing federal agencies

TABLE 6.3

Example of a Human Service Program Budget with Actual Data and Variances[a]

A MIDWESTERN COUNTY
ORGANIZATION EXPENDITURE REPORT

Period ending 04-30-73
Run date 05-11-73

Report USA0481
Page 001

ORGANIZATION 3804 ADULT OUTPATIENT
REPORTS TO 3800 MENTAL HEALTH CENTER

| Current month | | Acct | Org description | Year to Date | | | | Annual budget | Remaining budget |
Actual	(over)under			Hours	Actual	(over)under	Encumbered		
24,368	(2,533)	8002	Salaries and wages—regular	10,517	106,752	(8,491)		283,866	177,114
30	(30)	8016	Emergency		240	(240)			−240
29	(29)	8050	Group health		91	(91)			−91
379	28	8052	Group life insurance		113	(113)			−113
1,078	356	8054	Blue cross/MII Insurance		1,517	315		5,293	3,776
674	(674)	8060	F.I.C.A.		5,860	595		18,650	12,790
135	(135)	8062	P.E.R.A.		2,938	(2,938)			−2,938
	1,810	8070	Supplemental Retirement		595	(595)			−595
		8080	Other personal services			8,146		23,533	23,533
26,693	*(1,207)*		Personal services	*10,517*	*118,106*	*(3,412)*		*331,342*	*213,236*
15	10	8102	Office supplies and forms		44	56		300	256
128	(128)	8112	Training and Library		314	(314)			−314
143	*(118)*		Commodities		358	(258)		*300*	*−58*
300	2,063	8212	Consulting		700	8,754		28,363	27,663
	1,881	8248	Rental—buildings			7,525		22,577	22,577
	186	8266	Communication			747		2,241	2,241
300	*4,130*		Services		700	17,026		*53,181*	*52,481*
	93	8420	Conferences and tuition			373		1,120	1,120
10		8470	Publications and periodicals		10	(10)			−10
10	*93*		Other charges		10	363		*1,120*	*1,110*
233	(233)	8625	Office furnish and equip		316	(316)			−316
233	*(233)*		Capital outlay		316	(316)			*−316*
27,369	2,665		Total	10,517	119,490	13,403		385,943	266,453

[a] Adapted from T. S. Smith and J. E. Sorensen (Eds.), *Integrated management information systems for community mental health centers.* (DHEW Publication No. ADM 75-165.) Rockville, Maryland: National Institute of Mental Health, 1974.

to back away from the particular program they are carrying on at the moment and to look at their objectives. What are they really trying to accomplish? The objective of our inter-city highway program, for example, is not to build highways. Highways are useful only as they serve a higher objective, namely transporting people and goods effectively and efficiently and safely. Once this is accepted as an objective, it then becomes possible to analyze aviation, railroads, and highways to determine the most effective network of transportation. But so long as we think of the ultimate objective of the highway program as simply laying concrete, this comparison of different transportation systems is impossible.

At the same time, while we want to view our objectives broadly we are not helped at all by stating them too broadly. Highways or transportation, for example, generally may contribute to the good life and to national unity, but to take these as our sole stated objectives does not tell us much, if anything, useful about the desirable rate of highway building, the character of the highways, their locations, or their relations to other elements of our transportation system. In the case of highways, we want a specification of objectives broader than "laying concrete" but narrower than "improving our national life." As a matter of fact, there is a constant interaction between the decision process and our knowledge of our true objectives. Often, the more we learn about how to reach an objective, the more clearly we begin to understand the objective itself.

The second step, under the PPB system, is to analyze, insofar as possible, the output of a given program in terms of the objectives initially specified in the first step. Again, for example, in the case of highways, we must ask not primarily how many miles of concrete are laid, but more fundamentally what the program produces in terms of swifter, safer, less-congested travel—how many hours of travel time are eliminated, how many accidents are prevented?

The third step is to measure the total costs of the program, not just for one year, but over at least several years ahead. In this year's budget, for example, $10 million in budget funds are requested for the Atomic Energy Commission to design a 200 billion electron volt atom-smasher. But the total cost of constructing this machine will amount to $250 million or more. We have commonly had some estimate of the total capital cost in mind when we have embarked on construction projects. This has not happened systematically, however. And we can't stop here. Once the machine is built, the annual operating costs will run $50 to $100 million per year. This is not to say that because of these costs we should decide to abandon the project. But it does mean that we should be aware of all the costs when we make the initial $10 million decision, not just the capital costs but the follow-on operating costs as well. Or, to cite the highway example again, in deciding to build an expressway through a downtown area we must take into account not only the cost of the expressway, but also the cost of relocating the displaced residents and, in a qualitative sense, the effects of the freeway on the areas through which it is to run.

All of this sounds obvious. Yet, too often large federal investment decisions have been made on the basis of the first-year costs alone—or made without taking into account all of the indirect associated costs.

The fourth and crucial step is to analyze alternatives, seeking those which have the greatest effectiveness in achieving the basic objectives specified in the first step or which achieve those objectives at the least cost. In the highway case, for example, we should be comparing the effectiveness of additions or improvements to highways with that of additions or improvements to aviation and railroads as a means of providing safe and efficient transportation. This does not mean that we pick only one. Of course, we should not. But we do need to decide, at least roughly, which combination of alternatives is the preferred one.

By this process we hope to induce federal agencies to consider particular programs not as ends in themselves—to be perpetuated without challenge or question. Rather, they must be viewed as means to higher objectives and subjected to competition with alternative and perhaps more effective programs. It is this competition among alternatives which is crucial as a means of testing the effectiveness and economy of existing and proposed programs.

The fifth and final element of this approach is establishing this method and these analytic techniques throughout the government in a systematic way, so that, over time, more and more budgetary decisions can be subjected to this kind of rigorous analysis.

Merely writing up academic papers is not enough. The analysis has to be an integral part of the budgetary decisions. The programming concept is the critical link that relates planning to budgeting, converting planning from paper exercise to an important part of the decision process [7].

PPBS was first discussed in the 1950s, first applied in the Defense Department in 1962, spread to other government agencies in 1966, and by 1971 was abandoned by the federal government. The failure of PPB in the federal government was a function of inadequate system implementation, inadequate time to educate preparers and users, discomfort with new methods, and preference for traditional, well-understood methods. Despite this short life in the federal government, many nonprofit organizations have adopted several of the essential features of the PPB approach.

4. A Successful Example

A successful PPB application of a large midwestern county is described in this section with an elaboration focusing on the mental health/mental retardation programs (4).

The county is subdivided into seven major programs: highways, public safety and judiciary, health, education and recreation, social and economic assistance, public records, and general government. Each one of these several "level one" sections are further subdivided into three additional levels. With respect to health, the "level two" (or program level) is divided into physical health, mental health/mental retardation, chemical dependency, environmental health, education and research, and general support.

At "level three" (the subprogram level), mental health/mental retardation is subdivided into prevention, therapy and rehabilitation, inpatient, mental illness and substance abuse commitments, and general support.

At the fourth level (the activity level), the distinct service delivery units of the various agencies come into focus. For example, the following mental health units are located at the activity level under therapy and rehabilitation: day-treatment program, adult outpatient, child outpatient, crisis intervention center, and medical insurance. Under the subprogram of prevention is the activity of consultation and education at the County Mental Health Center. Under the program of education and research, is the mental health training subprogram. A graphic view of four PPBS levels is presented in Figure 6.6.

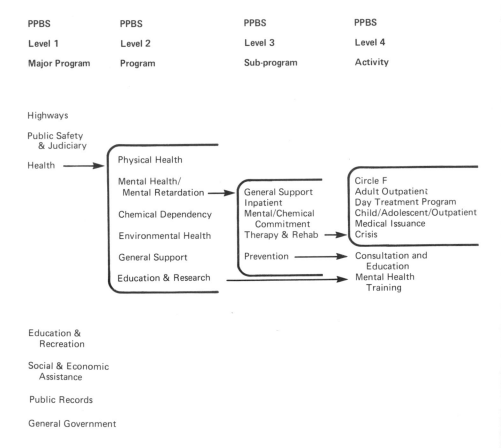

Figure 6.6. A midwestern county mental health program PPBS structure indicating relative placement of service units. [Source: Smith and Sorensen, 1974.]

Approximately 6 months prior to the beginning of a new calendar year, each agency that hopes to contract with the County Area Program must submit a programmatic budget to the Area Program Office. Annually, the County Mental Health Center submits the various programs just listed above in a prescribed budgetary, narrative, and statistical package. The most important items in the package are

1. A general budget message
2. A schedule of personnel positions
3. A performance output data sheet with program evaluation criteria
4. A program activity by line item with justification on each line item.

Other forms included in this total package are new program justifications, justification of additional positions with cost implications and a schedule of conferences.

5. Program Evaluation and Cost–Effectiveness

Of significant value in the budgetary, narrative, and statistical package is its routine attempt to perform program evaluation and analyze cost–effectiveness. Identifying specific criteria to evaluate the attainment of programmatic objectives is crucial. In selecting evaluation criteria, a number of factors must be observed:

1. The selection of evaluation criteria depends upon the objectives formulated for each unit of service
2. Both objectives and criteria should be end-oriented rather than means-oriented (they are to reflect what is ultimately desired to be accomplished and for whom, and not ways to accomplish such objectives)
3. The criteria for evaluation should possess the following characteristics:
   a. Each should be relevant and important to the specific problem
   b. Together, the criteria used should consider all major aspects of the objectives
   c. Each of the criteria should be capable of meaningful quantification.

There are basically two types of data required as measures of performance: *input data,* that indicate the quantity or volume of service activity, and *outcome data,* that relate to the effectiveness criteria. Figure 6.7 is a sample from an annual budget for one of the activity units of the County Mental Health Center. This exhibit indicates the objectives of adult outpatient activity, a brief description of the unit, and some of the program performance data that will be collected. The astute reader will observe that the program/performance data focus on process activities but, unfortunately, not on outcomes (3).

After submission and approval, the budget is implemented. As a logical sequence of its implementation, an accounting subsystem must be operating to report on how the organization is doing with regard to its budget plan.

A MIDWESTERN COUNTY

DEPARTMENT	FUND
General hospital (4000)	Hospital

MAJOR PROGRAM	Health
PROGRAM	Mental health/mental retardation
SUBPROGRAM	Therapy and rehabilitation
ACTIVITY	Adult outpatient

OBJECTIVE

To restore and improve the sociopsychological functioning of adults as individuals and family members.

DESCRIPTION

Adult Outpatient Unit of the Mental Health Center endeavors to assure direct mental health services to a large number of individuals with varying degrees of morbidity who are unable to receive it elsewhere. Nearly half of the patients are self referred while others come from other medical facilities and agencies including County Welfare, Court Services, Public Health Nursing and other social agencies. Services include individual psychiatric, psychological or social evaluations of individuals and families.

PROGRAM/PERFORMANCE DATA

	1971 Actual	1972 Estimated	1973 Estimated
No. of new patients	2,136	2,205	2,000
Referred elsewhere	617	713	700
Retained as patients	1,519	1,492	1,300
No. active patients on 12/31	2,840	2,840	2,700
Total patient visits	16,330	16,304	15,500
Median no. visits/retained patients	9.5	8.3	9.0
Individual therapy visits/year	5,319	5,340	4,500
Group therapy visits/year	3,433	4,056	5,000
Family therapy visits/year	541	456	450
Short term Drug Clinic visits/year	10	440	450
Other chemotherapy visits/year	—	2,772	2,800

Budget	1971 Budget	1972 Budget	1973 Proposed	1973 Approved
8000 Personal Services	346,199	360,997	333,609	331,342
8100 Commodities	41,111	41,111	300	300
8200 Services	30,406	30,406	61,100	53,181
8400 Other charges	36,155	44,080	9,573	1,120
8500 Public aid assistance	0	0	0	0
8600 Capital outlay	1,159	1,159	0	0
Total	455,030	477,753	404,582	385,943

Personnel	1971 Budget	1972 Budget	1973 Proposed	1973 Approved
Administrative	2.0	2.0	2.6	2.6
Professional	14.0	14.0	8.9	8.9
Technical or paraprofessional	—	—	—	—
Semiskilled or skilled	—	—	—	—
Clerical	—	—	6.4	6.4
Total	16.0	16.0	17.9	17.9

Figure 6.7. Sample annual budget for a single program activity in a county mental health center program. [Adapted from: Smith and Sorensen, 1974, p. 6-35.]

EFFECTS OF DEFICIENCIES

Deficiencies in one or more of the conceptual elements of the MIS do not have isolated effects. For example, an ill-defined organizational structure coupled with an inadequate statistical content and weak accounting content will seriously impair the effort to do cost-finding. The consequences, however, do not stop at this point. If the human service organization manager cannot trace costs and delivered services to specific organizational units, the planning and control reports are deficient and, in all likelihood, so is the level of performance by the management team. Certain activities may be impossible; if, for example, the budgeting content is nonexistent, then forward (or planned) rate-setting—based on *expected* activity and *expected* expense—is nearly impossible.

Data reporting systems are often designed more for external reporting purposes than for use by a human service organization's internal management group. Useful information can be furnished to both external and internal user groups. The questions asked by a manager should be greater in number and detail than those asked by external sources. Usually, external questions can be answered with summaries of existing internal reports. Certainly the manager of a human service orgainzation cannot ignore requests for information from those who are called on for financing the organization, but the manager should not design the information system to furnish only that information. Building a system for external groups solely can lead to a patchwork design, with major gaps in information and reports as well as ineffective internal planning and controls.

OPERATING ELEMENTS OF A
HUMAN SERVICE INFORMATION SYSTEM

The elements of an information system may be identified as the physical components, the processing procedures, and the input and output documents (Davis, 1974, pp. 192–197).*

PHYSICAL COMPONENTS

Assuming the system utilizes a computer or some similar processing equipment, the five major *physical* components include (Davis, 1974, p. 192):

1. *Hardware*

Hardware for an information system consists of the computer (central processor, input/output units, file storage units, etc.), data preparation equipment, and input/output terminals.

2. *Software*

Software can be divided into three major types: (*a*) generalized system software, such as operating system and data management system, that makes the computer system operate; (*b*) generalized applications software, such as

*Material from G. B. Davis in this section was adapted by permission from: G. B. Davis, *Management information systems: Conceptual foundations, structure, and development.* Copyright 1974, McGraw-Hill, New York.

analysis and decision models; (c) application software consisting of programs written specifically for individual applications.

3. Files—Data Base

Files containing programs and data are evidenced by the physical storage media (e.g., computer tapes, disk packs) kept in the file library. The files also include printed output and records on paper, microfilm, and other permanent documents.

4. Procedures

Procedures are physical components because they are provided in a physical form such as manuals and instruction booklets. Three major types of procedures are required: (a) user instructions, (b) instructions for preparation of input, and (c) operating instructions for the computer center personnel.

5. Operating Personnel

Operating personnel include computer operators, system analysts, programmers, data preparation personnel (e.g., keypunch operators or key disk operators), and information system management.

Although a computer is not an information system, some type of mechanical equipment and processing routine is required in almost any information system. In less sophisticated systems, the "hardware" may be a bookkeeping machine and the "software" may be a preplanned routine in processing accounts receivable. In any event, files, procedures, and operating personnel are required regardless of the presence or absence of a computer.

A computer can be the basic tool to enhance the operation of an information system—many times doing things that are otherwise impossible. Not all information systems require a computer, and merely adding a computer to an existing system will not necessarily improve its effectiveness. In fact, computerizing a poorly designed system can perpetuate and accentuate flaws and errors. The key is understanding the basics of systems, designing the system, and then adding equipment configurations required to support the system.

PROCESSING FUNCTIONS

A human service information system must carry out four major processing functions (adapted from Davis, 1974, p. 194):

1. Control and Monitor Transactions

A transaction is an activity such as rendering a service. Performance of a transaction by an organization generally requires a document to (a) direct a transaction to take place, (b) record its performance, or (c) report, confirm, or explain its performance.

2. Maintain History Files

Many processing activities require creation and maintenance of history (master) files. For example, payroll processing to prepare an employee's paycheck requires that the employee's rate of pay, deductions, and other pertinent information be known. This type of permanent information is carried in the payroll master files, which are also used to hold accumulated data. The master files must therefore be updated to reflect the most current information.

3. Produce Reports: Regular and ad hoc

Outputs are the usable products of the information system. The major outputs are scheduled reports, but an information system should be able to respond promptly to inquiries and requests for ad hoc reports. A community mental health center, for example, may wish to cross-classify socioeconomic characteristics of clients and type of services received in investigating accessibility to, and utilization of, services by lower socioeconomic status clients. The processing cycle often requires special outputs. For example, a detected error (e.g., a 10 year old reported as being treated in an adult program) results in a message requesting a correction.

4. Interact with Human Users

One must plan how to be able to respond to *unplanned* demands on the system with appropriate flexibility, economy, and promptness. The trend is to applications designed as person–computer systems. The computer does the processing using a planning model, a decision model, for example; the user provides responses to iterate to a satisfactory solution. A superintendent of a hospital may want to assess the length of stay for a particular admitting diagnosis or discharge diagnosis. Other possibilities include assessing the number or percentage of length of stay beyond a norm or expected value.

REPORTS AND DOCUMENTS

Users usually evaluate an information system based on the ease of input and comprehensiveness of output of the system—the types of input documents, reports, or responses to inquiries received. In addition to transaction documents, preplanned reports and preplanned inquiry responses are designed in advance while ad hoc reports and interactive person–computer dialogue usually may be implemented after a system is designed and operating. Transaction documents are the basic input documents containing information, for example, on services rendered, payroll checks, customer billing, purchase orders. Sometimes a single document can serve multiple objectives; for example, a services rendered document could serve personnel, statistical, billing, and cost-finding purposes (or, in terms of the earlier discussion, the functions of personnel and finance/accounting). Preplanned reports are structured as to content and format. These reports summarize activity over a selected *period* of time or describe a status or condition at a *point* in time. Ad hoc reports occur at irregular times in response to specific but unplanned requests for some type of analysis. For example, a special analysis of time of entry, ethnic background, and type of service may be prepared as a special report to respond to inquiries by special interest groups.

SYNTHESIS OF A HUMAN SERVICE
MANAGEMENT INFORMATION SYSTEM

A human service MIS has been portrayed as a *federation of functional subsystems* with each addressing operational, tactical, and strategic *managerial* activities. Each subsystem has physical, processing, and output *operating elements*. Each subsystem may have unique data files used only by that system while other data files will be accessed by more than one subsystem for one or more applications. Files used for general retrieval require special software (e.g., the data base management system) to maintain the common data base. The content of the files may be statistical, financial, or external information.

Software—the computer programs and/or sets of procedures—may be generalized or specific. Common application may emerge from several systems, whereas other programs are specially designed for a given subsystem. Some standardized programs (e.g., cross-tabulation, chi-square, regression analysis, and analysis of variance programs found in the Statistical Package for Social Sciences and Biomedical Computer Programs) may be used as general programs by all subsystems (Dixon, 1973, 1975; Nie, Hull, Jenkins, Steinbrenner, & Bent, 1975). When Figure 6.1 is merged with the operating elements of a MIS, Figure 6.8 emerges. Linkages between files, processing, and type of output are more easily understood.

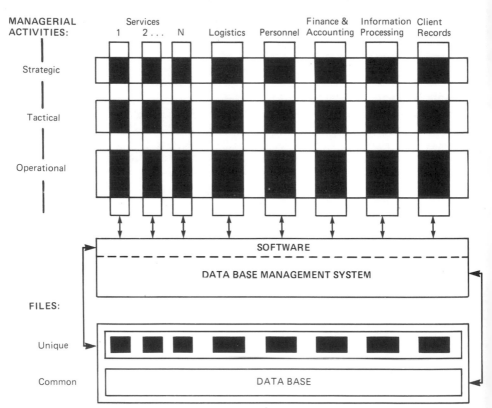

Figure 6.8. A conceptualization of a human service information system linking information processing capacity with differing information characteristics and levels of decision making.

ARRANGEMENT OF THE
INFORMATION SYSTEM
IN THE ORGANIZATION

Two overriding considerations of how an information system is arranged flow from top management's view of how it wants to manage the organization, and the level of diversity within the organization—the level of separateness or interdependencies within the functions and operating units. Management comes in many forms, and so do approaches to information systems. Information systems may be *hierarchically oriented* with either centralized data processing or decentralized data processing, or *systems oriented* with either integrated processing or distributed processing. While these design strategies are not easy to differentiate conceptually, this rough classificatory scheme provides an organizing framework for probing optional approaches to designing organizational information systems. The *hierarchical approach* corresponds to an historical tradition in organizational management, whereas the *systems approach* offers an alternative basis for conceptualizing the logical interrelationship of information flow and, therefore, of MIS subsystems.

HIERARCHICAL APPROACH

Superordinate and subordinate relationships channel the flow and processing of information. Hierarchical organizational units—functional, departmental, or divisional—provide the lines through which information flows upward and downward. Each hierarchical level within a function captures and processes data relevant to its operation and poses summaries up to the next hierarchical level until the top of the organization is reached. Requests for information flow down and reporting information flows up the hierarchy of each function. Data bases are segregated along functional, departmental, or divisional lines. For example, the data base of the service delivery function (e.g., client request) would be maintained separately from the data base of accounting/finance functions (e.g., accounts receivable). Often, communications between the functions are problematic since the data processing activities of each function are handled separately. A classical interface problem has occurred between the service delivery function (delivery of service to clients) and the accounting/finance function (billing clients or third parties).

The actual processing of data may be accomplished with centralized or decentralized data processing facilities. If centralized, the separate data bases of the various functions or departments are processed by a *common* unit such as an electronic data processing department, a service bureau, or time-sharing computer facilities. If decentralized, each function or department has control over its own data processing activities. The essential characteristic of the hierarchical approach is that the data base and processing are geared to specialized interests—functions, departments, divisions—and result in separate data bases for each of the functions, departments, or divisions and are controlled by the unit to which information is reported.

An alternative approach focuses on the systems perspective—one that makes available a broad base of comprehensive information on a timely basis to internal and external users for observation, reaction, and decision making. Strategic, tactical, and operational levels of decision making are incorporated, along with planning and controlling activities, into an interlocking network of subsystems (rather than a vertical organizational hierarchy). Information flows directly to users who need and are supposed to receive it. The superordinate–subordinate "reprocessing" of data is reduced, thus permitting lateral as well as vertical flows of information. Two general systems approaches exist: the *integrated system* (analogous to the centralized data processing used in the hierarchical approach) and the *distributed system* (analogous to the decentralized data processing method in the hierarchical approach).

1. *Integrated System*

The integrated system channels all organizational data into a common data base and services all data processing and information functions for the entire organization. (As a practical matter, this is a theoretical view, since it is not possible, given currently available technology, and is not economically feasible for the vast majority of human service organizations.) Traditional methods of handling data and information are changed since data collection, data processing, production of information (e.g., reports), and communication of information are integrated. Both financial data (e.g., accounting, cost-finding, budgeting) and operational data (e.g., personnel, outpatient services, patient days, intakes) are largely consolidated. For example, when a service is rendered, client and professional staff data are used to update client and professional personnel files for purposes of summarizing services received by a specific client including billing of client or third party; services rendered data, summarized by type of service and specific professional, as well as by classes of varied professionals; and services accumulated data, summarized by delivered units of service by program and geographic location.

Figure 6.9 presents major components of an integrated information system with a common data base. Characteristics of this system are (Burch & Strater, 1974; Murdick & Ross, 1975):

1. Instantaneous and simultaneous updating of files
2. High-speed response to inquiries via remote terminals
3. Massive on-line storage
4. Both centralized batch data processing and on-line processing (although on-line processing is not always necessary as is delineated in Chapter 7).

The advantages of the integrated system include (Burch & Strater, 1974; Murdick & Ross, 1975):

1. Reduction of duplication and redundancy of files and programming
2. Increased standardization

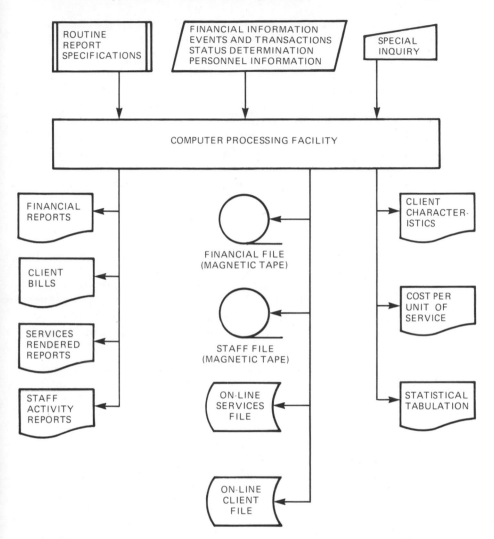

Figure 6.9. Partial outline of an integrated information system with a common data base.

3. Reduction of clerical involvement in input, processing, and output thereby reducing errors
4. Instantaneous and simultaneous updating of files
5. Concurrent processing to allow multiple users to retrieve, update, or delete data from the common base
6. Greater security, controls, and protection of the common data base against unauthorized users
7. Retrieval of data on an economical basis since economics of scale can lead to lower overall costs, fewer errors, and more timely reports.

On the other hand, integrated systems have the following possible disadvantages (Burch & Strater, 1974; Murdick & Ross, 1975):

1. A high level of financial and personnel resources and management commitment are required to make the system successful; cost of development is high
2. Withheld cooperation at any level of management can destroy the potential benefits of the system
3. Downtime can be catastrophic; if the central processing unit (e.g., computer) is down, the system is completely degraded and backup facilities can be costly and redundant
4. Modifications are difficult because of the interdependencies within the programs
5. Threats to client confidentiality may be increased unreasonably.

2. Distributed System

Recognizing the disadvantages of the integrated system, the distributed system uses a group of information systems to provide a "system of subsystems" with relatively independent subsystems that are tied together via varying communication interfaces. Large files are broken down into several files with "need to know" access criteria. An example of a distributed system is presented in Figure 6.10. Advantages from the use of the distributed information system include (Burch & Strater, 1974; Murdick & Ross, 1975):

1. Greater cost–effectiveness of distributed systems and their interaction with individual data bases by using minicomputers and telecommunications
2. Reduced central facility costs (but may be offset by costs of interaction between data bases)
3. Ease of modification to meet user requirements
4. The level of resources (personnel and financial) and level of coordination among levels of management is not as great as in an integrated system
5. Less sophisticated and less expensive technology is required with lower costs
6. Organizational demands for volume, timing, complexity, and processing may be easier to meet
7. Breakdown of one subsystem does not degrade the entire system
8. New subsystems can be added more easily and without upsetting other subsystems.

The distributed system, however, is not without its disadvantages. Some of these are:

1. Difficulty in extracting corresponding data from different files or in making inquiries into different files
2. Increased possibility of inconsistencies in different systems leading to errors (e.g., mismatches of data files on the same client)
3. Duplication of data capture and storage
4. Difficulty in maintaining coordination and communications.

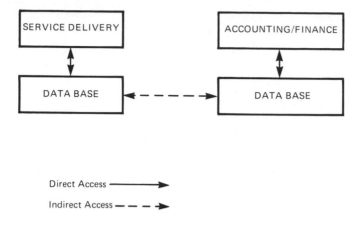

Figure 6.10. Example of a distributed approach to information system design.

SUMMARY

Distributed systems possess some integration, and integrated systems possess some distribution. In brief, the varieties of combinations are endless. *The basic decision is whether to favor a highly integrated system or a distributed system with some integration.* The following conditions may influence the choice:

1. Type of activity of the organization—how diverse are the activities of the organization?
2. Type of management style—does management want to operate as an integrated unit or to decentralize so that each unit makes important decisions about its own activities?
3. Extent of geographic dispersion—are the organizational units geographically dispersed? Commercial airlines, for example, favor integrated systems because of their similarity in operations and the central role of reservations in determining requirements for personnel (e.g., flight crews, maintenance) and other resources (e.g., airplanes). Large manufacturing operations, where the diversity among functional areas is great, lean toward distributed systems. The degree of integration is determined by the extent to which the following holds true:
   a. Data are merged into a common data base (e.g., eliminating diversity of files and providing for planned retrievals), or
   b. Data processing functions are consolidated (e.g., single and general programs process data at common facilities regardless of source), or
   c. Data flows are standardized and merged (e.g., developing flow around a natural mainstream and collecting all information needed downstream at appropriate sources), or
   d. The outputs are planned and standardized (by integrating networks, copying individual files or using general retrieval programs, the report response capability can be similar to an integrated system).

Human service organizations may vary on these aspects of information system integration depending on type of service program activity, organizational structure, and style of management. The examples described by Elpers and Chapman (Chapter 7) and Beigel and Levenson (Chapter 5) are examples of mixed levels of integration. In general, these examples tend to be more distributed than integrated although clear elements of integration are present, especially in Elpers and Chapman (Chapter 7).

INTEGRATION THROUGH SYSTEMS DESIGN

Integration of human service information systems begins with the design process. This stage asks questions about how the system could be designed. Although systems *analysis* focuses on what a system is doing or what it should be doing to meet user needs, system *design* seeks answers to how could the system best meet user requirements. System *implementation* focuses on the installation, development, testing, and evaluation of a detailed system design.

System design involves the following:

1. A specification of the system's goals
2. The formulation of a conceptual model (or approach) to meet user requirements
3. Analysis of the varying organizational constraints/requirements
   a. Cost of acquisition
   b. Cost of maintenance
   c. Reliability
   d. Life expectancy
   e. Level of performance
   f. Flexibility
   g. Potential for growth
   h. Ease of installation
   i. Accuracy.

The relative weights on constraints/requirements vary from one human service organization to another (Weinstein, 1975). Clear examples of alternative weighting of these factors are reflected in the Orange County (Chapter 7) and Southern Arizona (Chapter 5) approaches to the design of their respective information systems. The goals, models, and constraints/requirements (especially cost, ease of installation, growth) vary widely in these two illustrative but operating human service information systems.

THE SYSTEM DESIGN PROCESS

The design process consists of three major phases: preliminary system design, detailed system design, and implementation of the design. Each major segment is elaborated.

1. *Preliminary Design Process*

The sequence of crucial events in the preliminary design are outlined as follows in ten distinct but interrelated steps:

1. Formulation of organizational goals and objectives
2. Determination of questions (or hypotheses) to be addressed by information systems for assessing achievement of organizational goals/objectives
3. Formulation of reports that respond to the questions to be addressed by information systems
4. Determination of data elements to be used in preparing information system reports
5. Creation of data capture instruments to accumulate data for information system reports
6. Identification of most cost–effective approaches to error control
7. Estimation of volumes of data processing and storage requirements
8. Simplification of report requirements, document requirements, and error control mechanisms
9. Derivation of data processing recommendations
10. Review of design by management and staff for decision to move to detailed design, or modify design (e.g., use a manual system by reducing reporting requirements), or abandon the project entirely.

A common fault is to plunge into the creation of data capture instruments (Step 5) with little regard for the crucial role of the first four steps. Inefficient and ineffective systems often result in and create frustrated and disappointed users. "Add-on" or redesigned information requirements to accommodate audit or utilization review and program evaluation are not exempt from the requirement that they be developed using sound systems design methodology. The temptation to pass off the requirements as too time consuming or too rigorous is great. Only good system *design* can produce good clinical and managerial information.

2. *Detailed System Design*

This phase of system design (or redesign) usually involves (Chapman, 1976, pp. 42–73) the following steps:

1. A design of improved record flow that integrates required MIS documents with existing forms. Most systems grow larger and more complex, and, with the addition of new program evaluation requirements, old forms are patched and new ones added. Data gathering becomes inefficient, accuracy drops, and staff resistance grows. An easy way to counteract opposition is to simplify through record-keeping integration —the sequential step of charting current record flow, integrating MIS documents with current flow, and simplifying record flow
2. The design of input documents or forms design. Use of demonstrated techniques on item coding, item format, and form layout reduce the burden of recording data (written document or computer terminal input) and enhance accuracy and completeness
3. The preparation of data processing specifications including
   a. Criteria for editing data inputs from MIS documents and internal procedures (e.g., merge edits)

b. Procedures for undertaking selected computations and statistical summaries (e.g., age, units of service, indices, exception listings)
c. Formats and guidelines for reports
d. Performance criteria for data processing, including programming deadlines, confidentiality, and financial arrangements
4. The determination of firm cost estimates
5. The design review that leads to final approval for implementing the information system.

3. *Implementation of the Design*

Installing the information system requires (Chapman, 1976, pp. 74–85) the following:

1. Preparation of a detailed plan of implementation (using program evaluation and review techniques or PERT)
2. Pretest of forms
3. Preparation of procedure manuals and orientation and training sessions
4. Decisions about inclusions of current caseload and historical data in the data base. (A good way to start is with *current* caseload and to be sure that all of the data loaded into the base have been *thoroughly edited.* This approach ignores most "historical data" captured under different systems, since the accuracy *and* completeness are nearly always seriously deficient.)
5. Develop and test computer programs (if used)
6. Initiate collection of essential data, drawn from the existing caseload, for establishing the data base
7. Initiate collection of current data and develop a process for distribution of reports and other MIS output products.

GUIDELINES FOR DESIGN

The level of integration of conceptual content in managerial decision levels and functions hinges on the approach outlined in the discussion of the systems approach—integrated or distributed. Though strict adherence will vary, human service information systems should observe the key guidelines of good system design (Burch & Strater, 1974; Davis, 1974; Murdick & Ross, 1975):

1. Source data should be collected only once even if used several times by the system (to reduce redundancy and error)
2. The number of steps in data capture should be at a minimum (to increase accuracy)
3. Subsystems should produce data that are compatible with other subsystems; one subsystem should not have to reenter data received from another subsystem
4. Timing of reports should be geared to timing and processing of supporting data; data should not be captured any sooner than required for reports
5. Changes or innovations should be cost–effective from an overall system perspective (e.g., cost of capturing data, correcting errors)

6. Source data should be thoroughly edited so only valid data will be input into the information system

7. Audit trails and record reproduction should be available upon demand

8. Back-up and security procedures should be maintained for all files.

In summarizing a technical approach to system design and the context in which the approach can be used, Chapman (1976) observes that a MIS for any organization:

1. Can be helpful only to the extent that a climate prevails which welcomes the assistance that can be provided by a management tool

2. Must provide information about resource expenditures that can be compared to objectives, intuitive or structured, that can influence decisions about future resource allocations

3. Must determine information collection requirements primarily in terms of the structuring of data for decisions

4. Must be designed by an iterative process in which the broad outlines of organizational structure, as it implies feedback needs, report requirements, data collection needs, and methods of maintaining data integrity are determined in sequence

5. Must determine the details of record-keeping integration, data processing specifications, and input document contents and format only after a total system concept has been conceived so that implications of cost–effectiveness tradeoffs can be traced throughout the system

6. Must be implemented according to the carefully prepared plan that minimizes the consternation of organizational change and gets the system operational without delay and loss of credibility in the eyes of the agency staff.

COSTS OF INFORMATION SYSTEMS

Developing integrated information systems consumes resources, and the outlays should be cost–effective. Another way to state the question is: "What costs (and in what amount) will be different *because* of managerial and program evaluation information requirements?" Many individuals, often well-intended observers, make the mistake of thinking that incremental information requirements can be added to an existing system with little or no inconvenience or expense. Others misguidedly believe that the major cost of a system is the computer configuration. Costs of information systems are extensive and pervasive. A partial list follows:

1. Costs of computer configuration

2. Costs of renovation (e.g., facilities, air conditioning)

3. Costs of training (e.g., including users and preparers of input)

4. Costs of programs and program testing

5. Costs of conversion (e.g., preparing and editing records for completeness and accuracy, setting up file library procedures, preparing and running parallel operations)

6. Costs of operations (e.g., staff, supplies, maintenance, insurance, light and power, computer rental or amortization)

7. Costs of professional staff and support personnel time complying with data capture requirements
8. Costs of error detection and correction process; costs of tracking specific cases emerging in various edit processes
9. Costs of information system changes or modifications elicited by changing external reporting requirements or controls.

The growth of information systems costs start with project planning and increase as the design reaches an operational state. Figure 6.11 is an integrated performance–cost–time (PCT) chart used for controlling the three key variables in a system development process and clearly reveals the pattern of growth of costs over time.

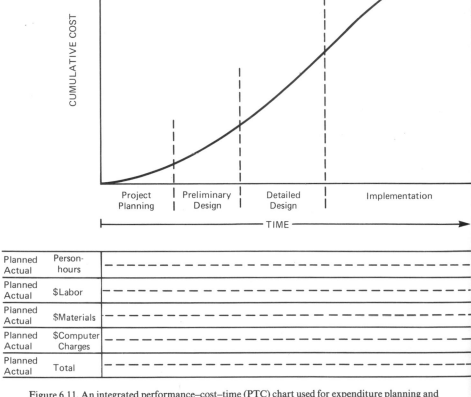

Figure 6.11. An integrated performance–cost–time (PTC) chart used for expenditure planning and control in information system planning, design, and implementation. [Adapted by permission from: R. G. Murdick and J. E. Ross, *Information systems for modern management* (2nd ed.). Copyright 1975, Prentice-Hall, Englewood Cliffs, New Jersey.]

SUMMARY

This chapter has presented a brief overview of

- Levels of decision making
- Essential organizational functions
- Basic conceptual content
- General operating elements
- Optional organizational arrangements
- Basic design processes

relevant for information systems in human service organizations. Armed with this overview, an improved insight and an increased critical analysis is possible when examining Chapters 5 and 7, which outline two dramatically different but successful human service management information systems. While the context happens to be mental health, the experiences are generalizable to nearly any organization where the delivery of human services is the key issue.

REFERENCE NOTES

1. Material in this section and the following sections on MIS accounting content, statistical content, and cost-finding content is adapted from Sorensen and Phipps (1975).
2. Material in this section is adapted from Smith and Sorensen (1974).
3. Material in Chapter 13 on cost–outcome and cost–effectiveness analyses in human service organizations provides a fuller coverage of these issues.
4. The details of this PPB approach were described by Clifford Nelson in Smith and Sorensen (1974).
5. Adams, C., & Schroeder, R. *Current and desired characteristics of information used by middle managers: A survey* (Working Paper No. 72-01.) MIS Research Center, College of Business Administration, University of Minnesota, Minneapolis, Minnesota, 1972.
6. Goldman, A. R. *An integrated management information system.* Paper presented at the National Council of Community Mental Health Centers and HEW Region III Conference, Philadelphia, Pennsylvania, June 1974.
7. Schultze, C. *Statement to the Subcommittee on National Security and International Operations of the Committee on Government Operations.* U. S. Senate, 90th Congress, 1st Session. (Available from the U. S. Government Printing Office in Washington, D. C.)

REFERENCES

Burch, J. G., & Strater, F. R. *Information systems: Theory and practice.* Santa Barbara, California: Hamilton, 1974.

Chapman, R. L. *The design of management information systems for mental health organizations: A primer.* (DHEW Publication No. ADM 76-333.) Washington, D. C.: U. S. Government Printing Office, 1976.

Cooper, E. M. *Guidelines for a minimum statistical and accounting system for community mental health centers: A working handbook with illustrative end-product tables, document forms, and procedures.* (DHEW Publication No. ADM 74-14.) Washington, D. C.: U. S. Government Printing Office, 1973.

Davis, G. B. *Management information systems: Conceptual foundations, structure, and development.* New York: McGraw-Hill, 1974.

Dixon, W. J. (Ed.). *BMD: Biomedical computer programs* (3rd ed.). Berkeley: University of California Press, 1973.

Dixon, W. J. (Ed.). *BMDP: Biomedical computer programs.* Berkeley: University of California Press, 1975.

Drucker, P. F. *The practice of management.* New York: Harper & Row, 1954.

Endicott, J., Spitzer, R. L., Fleiss, J. L., & Cohen, J. The Global Assessment Scale: A procedure for measuring overall severity of psychiatric disturbance. *Archives of General Psychiatry,* 1976, *33,* 766–771.

Glick, I. D., Hargreaves, W. A., & Goldfield, M. D. Short vs. long hospitalization. *Archives of General Psychiatry,* 1974, *30,* 363–369.

Gorry, G. A., & Morton, M. S. S. A framework for management information systems. *Sloan Management Review,* 1971, *13,* 55–70.

Horngren, C. T. *Cost accounting: A managerial emphasis* (3rd ed.). Englewood Cliffs, New Jersey: Prentice-Hall, 1972.

Levine, A., & Levine, M. Evaluation research in mental health: Lessons from history. In J. Zusman & C. R. Wurster (Eds.), *Program evaluation: Alcohol, drug abuse, and mental health services.* Lexington, Massachusetts: Lexington Books, 1975

McGregor, D. *The human side of enterprise.* New York: McGraw-Hill, 1960.

Murdick, R. G., & Ross, J. E. *Information systems for modern management* (2nd ed.). Englewood Cliffs, New Jersey: Prentice-Hall, 1975.

Nie, N. H., Hull, C. H., Jenkins, J. G., Steinbrenner, K., & Bent, D. H. *SPSS: Statistical package for the social sciences* (2nd ed.). New York: McGraw-Hill, 1975.

Salsbery, D. L. *Accounting guidelines for mental health centers and related facilities.* (DHEW Publication No. HSM 73-9068.) Washington, D. C.: U. S. Government Printing Office, 1972.

Smith, T. S., & Sorensen, J. E. (Eds.). *Integrated management information systems for community mental health centers.* (DHEW Publication No. ADM 75-165.) Rockville, Maryland: National Institute of Mental Health, 1974.

Sorensen, J. E., & Phipps, D. W. *Cost-finding and rate-setting for community mental health centers.* (DHEW Publication No. ADM 76-291.) Washington, D. C.: U. S. Government Printing Office, 1975.

Weinstein, A. S. Evaluation through medical records and related information systems. In E. L. Struening & M. Guttentag (Eds.), *Handbook of evaluative research* (Vol. 1). Beverly Hills, California: Sage Publications, 1975.

7

BASIS OF THE INFORMATION SYSTEM DESIGN AND IMPLEMENTATION PROCESS

J. Richard Elpers and Robert L. Chapman

This chapter focuses upon the growing public demand for accountability on the part of human service agency administrators. It also describes emerging complexities in the purviews of human service agencies, and portrays three feedback loops that concern administrators as they monitor program outcomes and relate to community values and needs.

This environmental context makes it imperative for human service administrators to maximize their organizations' capacities to plan, organize, control, and lead—in short, to implement organizational management concepts and skills. The information system as a managerial tool can provide critical program information in the form and with the timeliness that is vital to productive administrative decisions.

In order to give administrators some understanding of information systems as management tools, design criteria are discussed and illustrated by their application in establishing and operating such an information system for the Orange County Department of Mental Health. Examples of cost of a one-time and continuing nature are given, and some problems that typically arise are discussed.

RISING DEMAND FOR ACCOUNTABILITY

The 1960s and early 1970s saw rapid proliferation of community mental health systems. Community organization and social action projects that were never thought to be a part of traditional mental health activities are being undertaken. The acutely and chronically ill are being treated in local programs instead of distant state hospitals. Nonprofessionals and volunteers, as well as professionals, are participating in the treatment of a wider array of people than was formerly thought possible.

Along with these developments there is a rising concern among the public at large, and particularly among those who fund the programs, about program effectiveness and possible goal conflicts with those of welfare, public health, criminal justice, and education. No longer can mental health programs be identified with specific building complexes or with a few prestigious professional groups. The diversity of mental health programs, interrelating with other human services, may seem to have purposes that are vague, obscure, or ill-defined. Regardless of whether conflict does exist between mental health and other human services programs, questions remain about program effectiveness in relation to other human services.

The time has passed when those responsible for delivering human services are provided substantial funds to spend as they deem most appropriate. The demand for accountability goes beyond accounting practices to prevent the embezzlement of public funds; current accountability demands require assurance that services be provided to all who need them, especially the poor, the disadvantaged, and the minorities. Since many of these groups can only be reached with innovative programs, demonstrating that such programs have a restorative effect on people's lives is a difficult problem.

NEEDS FOR MANAGEMENT SKILLS
IN ADMINISTERING HUMAN SERVICES

Beyond the public's demand for accountability lies the personal, professional, and ethical requirement for human service providers to integrate their services with those of others in meeting the variety of social needs that arise. Human service activities are part of a general system with multiple entry points; methods for routing clients to the services most appropriate to their needs have to be established. To do so, agencies must be familiar with each other's clientele, available services, referral patterns, and acceptance criteria.

Figure 7.1 provides a framework for the management processes, and the role of information in them (Chapman, 1970). As will be discussed in Chapters 9 and 10, society at large has some generally held values, determined by many factors, which in turn influence public needs. Public needs are interpreted and translated into public policy through elected and appointed officials. This policy is then transmitted to service providers in the form of legislation, administrative regulations and guidelines, funds with their attendant budgets, and expectations of service. Administrators plan and organize resources into program activities with specific objectives. Program practices evolve as project personnel attempt to achieve definitive program outcomes—effects that should be measurable in terms of changes in the lives of the persons served.

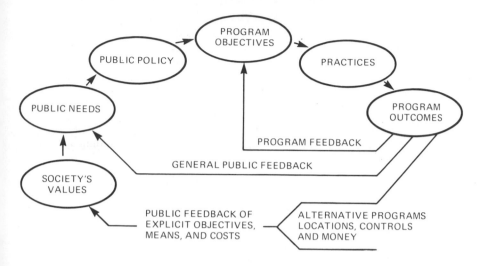

Figure 7.1. Three kinds of feedback.

A management information system (MIS) contributes data for all three feedback loops shown in Figure 7.1. It provides program feedback to permit program managers to compare program outcomes with objectives in order to evaluate their practices. It provides factual information to illuminate the general public feedback about quantity and quality of services. In addition, it provides the basis for analysis and planning that enables the manager to pose cost–effectiveness alternatives to the community so that social values and expressed needs can be clarified (Chapman & Elpers, 1974).

If a manager does not know whether current objectives are being met, he or she cannot tell what to do about existing programs. If the manager does not know what clientele is being served and compare current consumers of service with the community's total needs, he or she does not know what services should be developed. If the manager does not know what services are being delivered, the effectiveness of these services cannot be determined. If the manager does not know the cost of existing services, he or she cannot estimate the cost of different services and make informed judgments about efficient allocation of resources. Therefore, without good information, planning becomes no more than speculation.

Most human service agencies depend on a broad base of funding—federal, state, local, philanthropic, third-party payer, and prepaid contracts—for stable support. Thus, reporting requirements and content variables are multiplied many times. At best, a great deal of clerical and professional time is consumed in meeting multiple reporting requirements; at worst, incomplete data and estimates are submitted.

These then are the problems in delivering human services to which the management information system as an administrative tool is addressed.

DESIGN REQUIREMENTS FOR A
MANAGEMENT INFORMATION SYSTEM

Five major requirements should be considered in designing a MIS. An adequately designed system can

1. Define how current resources are being spent
2. Determine the patterns of service delivery
3. Provide monitoring aids for program managers
4. Provide data for multiple reporting requirements of funding agencies
5. Generate necessary data for planning purposes.

Additional design criteria that all record keeping systems should meet include comprehensive, economical, and accurate data collection; compatibility of data structure with that of other data systems; flexibility of the system to meet changing conditions; and timeliness of reports.

CURRENT RESOURCE ALLOCATION

The first requirement of a MIS is that it show how resources are currently being spent. It must

1. Show how each staff member in each of the agency's units is spending his or her time in direct and indirect services (by subtracting the time spent in these services from total duty time, the time involved in administrative or "overhead" activities can be determined)
2. Determine how many units of service result from a given expenditure of therapist's time (a family or group treatment will reach more people than an individual therapy session)
3. Gather data by the same service units or "cost centers" that are used by the agency's accounting system.

This allows the cost of services to be determined and appropriate rates set. Although there are many ways to determine rates, they all require these particular data in available, usable, and clearly defined form (Sorensen & Phipps, 1975). Without a clear and consensually agreed upon definition of service modalities and types, it is not possible to compare the cost of competing programs.

In addition, the MIS must provide the capability to compare the "at-risk" population against the "receiving-services" population. It must be possible to demonstrate that a program's clientele reflects the community's population that could be expected to need the service if possible distortions in evaluation resulting from initial client selection by a program are to be avoided.

PATTERNS OF SERVICE DELIVERY

The second major requirement of the MIS is the capability to determine patterns of service delivery both within and between agencies. Intraagency concerns should include overlapping responsibilities, differences in professional roles, continuity-of-care, and followup of clients who drop out of treatment. Interagency responsibilities involve overlapping service areas, overlapping responsibilities, and issues of continuity and integration of services. It should be possible to "track" clients throughout the human service delivery system and to be able to cross tabulate "referral-ins" and "referral-outs" against other relevant variables.

MONITORING AIDS FOR PROGRAM MANAGERS

An effective MIS must provide reports to line managers at each echelon of the agency, and agency staff as well, regarding service activities for which they are responsible. Information should be furnished regarding: admissions, discharges, service units delivered (of different types), caseloads, professional hours in direct and indirect service, and tentative treatment outcomes. It should also provide data to permit "management by exception" aids such as rosters of clients missing appointments, dropping out of treatment, not making referrals, and staying in treatment excessive periods of time.

MULTIPLE REPORTING REQUIREMENTS

A fourth requirement of the MIS is that it generate reports required by the several funding sources, such as federal grant providers; state agencies, which frequently contribute the major support; local advisory boards and boards of supervisors, concerned not only with financial matters but also with impact on the community; community chest agencies; third-party payers; and philanthropic sources. Existing requirements, as well as possible future demands, need careful review. Of course, future requirements can only be estimated, so the information system design should be flexible enough to be easily modified at low cost.

DATA FOR PLANNING PURPOSES

The fifth requirement of the MIS is that it provide planning data for short- and long-term decisions. Two short-term decisions are important in this regard: (a) reallocation of staff and other resources, and (b) making services available to those populations identified as underserved. Among the long-range decisions an information system should serve are (a) effectiveness of service elements, treatment methods, and personnel; (b) identification of need for innovative programs to replace ineffective programs; and (c) the design of programs to meet newly recognized needs. The system may not initially provide treatment outcome data of sufficient sophistication for long-range planning, but it should be designed at least to define problem populations for more detailed study. Because changes in treatment outcome need interpretation, the surrounding circumstances must be documented so that explanations can be sought.

Data requirements for planning purposes will change, making it imperative that the design be readily modified, and also, that the MIS contain data from a sufficiently broad base that frequent revisions are not necessary.

OTHER DESIGN CRITERIA

The design of a MIS not only should ensure the collection of comprehensive and accurate data but also ensure that such a process is economical. Input documents should require a minimum of staff time and should be prepared by clerical personnel wherever possible.

Compatibility of information system data with existing external sources of public information is extremely important. As will be discussed in Chapters 9 and 10, there are many external sources of information about communities and the populations that reside within social areas. Perhaps one of the most important sources of external information is data provided by the United States Census Bureau. If MIS data are compatible with census data, a good deal can be learned about populations at risk versus populations treated. Other external sources of information include the criminal justice systems, welfare departments, school systems, government planning agencies (federal, state, and local), health departments, private institutions, private practitioners, and the business, banking, and marketing communities. Obviously, it is not possible to design an internal information system that is compatible with all of these agencies. Therefore, the least common denominator of the census tract is chosen so that it can be aggregated in different ways to match the geographical areas used by other data systems.

THE ORANGE COUNTY DEPARTMENT OF MENTAL HEALTH MANAGEMENT INFORMATION SYSTEM

The Orange County Department of Mental Health developed and implemented its management information system by carefully analyzing five components of the basic design process: (a) the environmental circumstances, (b) the developmental process, (c) the overall design, (d) the input documents, and (e) the report outputs.

ENVIRONMENTAL CIRCUMSTANCES

Orange County is located on the Pacific Ocean, south of Los Angeles and north of San Diego County. The population is in excess of 1,500,000 and continues to grow. It is undergoing rapid urbanization with an attendant influx of a highly diverse group of people. While its mean family income is somewhat above the national average, the county includes the very poor and the very rich and a significant minority population.

The Department of Mental Health is a relatively new organization, its major development having occurred since 1972. Although the department has some centralized services (acute inpatient care, alcoholism, and drug abuse), its major emphasis is on administrative and geographic decentralization— there are now approximately 25 service locations throughout the county. The entire spectrum of mental health services are offered to all age groups, both by county-staffed units and by contract.

THE DEVELOPMENT PROCESS

The MIS had to collect information about this diversified delivery system and provide feedback appropriate to its organizational structure. The system that resulted was the product of close cooperation between the authors, a psychiatrist administrator, and a systems consultant familiar with data processing capabilities and limitations (Elpers & Chapman, 1973). The staff of the entire department participated in determining the kinds of information needed for operating and planning decisions. Staff participation was essential for obtaining acceptance of the management information system and for assuring that data collection procedures were integrated with other record keeping requirements to minimize the burden of filling out forms. The budget for the project limited consideration of such expensive technology as computer terminals in each service location.

The entire system was designed "in-house," with the help of the consultant, including form formats, form flow, and data processing specifications. A data processing contractor, selected by competitive bids, carried out the programming and performs the ongoing keypunching and data processing.

OVERALL DESIGN FOR THE MANAGEMENT
INFORMATION SYSTEM

The overall design of the Orange County MIS, shown in Figure 7.2, consists of: inputs (six basic documents plus some ancilliary forms), the data base (the active and historic), and the outputs (six kinds of reports).

Multicarbon, snap-out forms (with copies for the patient's chart, for the MIS, and other uses) are prepared in each service unit and submitted to the Management Information System Control Unit for manual edit, assembly, and transmission to the data processing contractor. All forms for the current month have to be submitted to the contractor within 2 working days of the end of the month; the contractor, in turn, has 4 working days in which to complete the keypunching, do the data processing, and generate the reports. This meets the requirement for timeliness of reports.

The data base itself is organized by patient name, arranged alphabetically. To avoid the cumbersome clerical burden of assigning patient numbers centrally, the "identifier" used to assemble patient records (selected after considerable study) is that of last name, initials, and birth year.

Control procedures are vital for maintaining the integrity of the data (accuracy, completeness, and logical consistency of the data base). In addition to the manual edit before submitting documents, there are the document edits and merge edits carried out by the computer, which rejects documents that do not pass the specified tests of consistency. Rejected documents are reviewed by the Management Information System Control Unit, corrected, and resubmitted for inclusion in the next month's, and quarterly reports (that are more accurate than the monthly). Available data on Orange County patients in state hospitals are obtained in punched-card form from the State Department of Health and included in the data base.

As indicated in Figure 7.2, the reports are generated from the active data base, with reference to the historical data base for such items as previous history.

Both the input documents and the report outputs will be described in more detail in the material that follows.

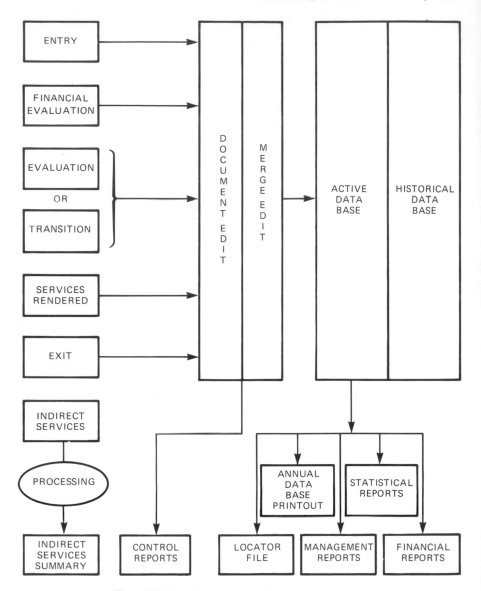

Figure 7.2. Overall management information system design.

THE INPUT DOCUMENTS

Table 7.1 summarizes preparation and general contents of each of the six basic documents that provide the data input to the Orange County MIS.

All the basic documents, except the indirect services document, have the "identifier" information in common, in the upper left-hand corner. Most

TABLE 7.1
Input Document Summary

Type of document	Circumstances of preparation	Content
Entry	35 items completed by clerk at time of entry or status change	Admission conditions, further identification of patient, history of previous mental illness, and background information
Financial	12-plus items completed by financial evaluator at time of entry	Information to establish a patient's account, sources of financial responsibility, ability to pay (can combine accounts for various family members)
Evaluation or transition	18 items by therapist within 3 visits or days of entry 15 items by therapist	*If patient is accepted for treatment*: Diagnosis, treatment plan, evaluating therapist's name *If evaluation is a step in transfer to another service*: Diagnosis, services rendered, status at transition, referral information, evaluating therapist's name
Services rendered	10-plus items by therapist at each outpatient visit (not required for inpatient, partial hospitalization, or medication maintenance)	Treatment date, therapist, type and amount of service rendered, next appointment, and payment received (patient's copy becomes receipt and appointment slip)
Exit	17 items by therapist at time of discharge	Status of discharge, estimate of patient's adjustment and needed support systems in community, evaluating therapist's name
Indirect services	23 items once a month by each professional	Kind and amount of indirect service rendered, to what group, aimed at what target population

181

information needed for coding is printed on the face of the form; some, if too extensive for the space available, is printed on the reverse side of the form. In addition, a coding manual elaborates the code definitions and form preparation procedures. A one-time reading of the coding manual and occasional references, usually suffice to maintain reliable form completion.

Data collection for the MIS is designed to simplify the record keeping burden. Information is recorded once and used for several purposes. Copies of the entry, evaluation, and discharge documents serve as chart inputs (additional space is provided on the chart copies of both the evaluation and discharge forms for written comments not sent to the management information system). The services rendered document provides all the information needed for the computer to compile service delivery units, professional hours in direct service, and charges for financial reports.

THE REPORT OUTPUTS

Table 7.2 shows the purpose and content of each of the reports generated by the MIS; some are furnished monthly (M), some quarterly (Q), some annually (A), and a portion of the statistical reports on special request (S).

The "adjustments" indicated for patient's ability to pay are somewhat involved because California Department of Health regulations are based on a year's liability. Therefore, what a patient can pay monthly is first determined, then the patient must pay that amount for a year, regardless of the duration or cost of treatment until either amounts due are paid or the annual liability has expired.

The monthly reports are available within 6 working days of the end of the month. This timely feedback is vital: Managers are much more interested in current than historical data; bills sent out a month or so late are rarely collectable. Furthermore, this rapid feedback has enhanced staff interest in the MIS, as well as their acceptance of it—a condition that is essential for its optimal functioning.

DEVELOPING AND OPERATING COSTS FOR A MANAGEMENT INFORMATION SYSTEM

Any management information system must provide benefits in excess of cost; thus a system must be tailored to program needs, especially the size of the human service program it supports. Some programs may require data processing by computer, as does Orange County's, but many others may require only a simple card sorter or merely a manual operation. In any case, the volume of data and the required flexibility must be studied before selecting the data processing method. Consultants can prove most valuable in reaching such decisions.

Because a MIS is calculated to influence an agency's activities, and its

TABLE 7.2
Output Report Summary

Type of report	Use	Content
Control report (M)	For control unit to monitor management information system	Number of documents processed and rejected (and reasons why); also identifies gaps and errors not serious enough for outright rejection
Locator file (M)	For central office administrative and control use only	All data concerning each patient currently in the system, alphabetically by name
Annual data base (A)	For central office use only	All data concerning patients that have been in the system during past year
Management reports (M, Q)	For each unit and department as whole for decision and control. Also provides necessary information for multiple reporting requirements	Summaries of admissions and discharges (and salient characteristics), current case load, service units delivered (outpatient and medication maintenance visits, inpatient and partial hospitalization days), professional hours in direct and indirect service, entry times by day and hour. Monitoring aids: patients admitted but not evaluated, patients whose treatment length exceeds plan on evaluation document and those who exceed criterion lengths by diagnosis by unit, patients referred but not admitted, patients who did not keep appointments, patients in open case load
Financial reports 1. Patient ledger (M)	1. For financial evaluation and accounting	1. All financial transactions: charges, payments, adjustments (depending on ability to pay)
2. Patient bills (M)	2. For each account	2. From patient ledger: charges, payments, adjustments, and amounts due and past due
3. Summaries (M, Q, A)	3. For accounting	3. Summary (by unit and department) of charges, revenues by source, adjustments, outstanding claims, amount due and past due (aged)
Statistical reports (M, Q, A)	For planning and evaluation, mainly for central office	General purpose report generator that cross tabs virtually any five variables in data base (30 monthly, 25 quarterly, and 25 on special request)
Indirect service (M)	For each unit and department for planning and control	Summary of professional hours in indirect service devoted to group types, consultation methods, and number of target groups reached

183

associated costs, its expense is hard to isolate completely from other costs, as will be illustrated.

Table 7.3 contains approximate costs for design, start-up, and operations for both Orange County and another county's mental health services. (These latter costs are estimates based on firm bids for a MIS still in the development stage. This other county has a population of 1,500,000.) The contrast shows how somewhat different circumstances affect costs.

TABLE 7.3
Management Information System Costs

Type of cost	Orange County	Another county
Design (consulting fees)	$15,000	$10,000
Start-up		
Programming	31,000	3,000
Staff	3,000	3,000
Operating data processing		
1st Year	42,000	35,000
2nd Year	70,000	
Staff		
1st Year	12,000	12,000
2nd Year	18,000	Current year

Only consulting fees are included in the design cost because the staff time involved is largely devoted to the management functions of planning, organizing, controlling, and leadership. More of the competent consultant's time is spent in gaining staff participation in the process than on the technical design itself. The difference in fees in the two cases does reflect, however, a reduced cost when an existing design is adapted to new conditions.

Programming the system design for computer processing is a one-time cost. A large portion of such a cost can be avoided if the programs for an existing design can be utilized with minor modifications. (In both cases, data processing services are obtained from a private contractor.) Some funds should be budgeted each year for program revisions to meet continuing needs for flexibility.

The annual data processing costs are determined by the volume of processing done, mainly a function of the number of active cases during the year. The jump in Orange County data processing costs from the first year to the second were a result of that increase in volume and system modifications to include handling of indirect services and financial information.

The staff costs for both start-up and operations are for clerks who work in the MIS Control Unit editing input documents and reducing errors discovered in the document and merge edits. Control Unit clerks are primarily responsible for communicating with the entire clerical staff in maintaining the integrity of the MIS.

Other costs associated with MIS operation are less obvious but equally significant. Clerks and therapists in each organizational unit do spend time filling out multiple-copy forms, one of which goes to the system, but if the input documents are appropriately integrated with other record-keeping requirements, the resulting effort will not increase appreciably and may, in fact, be reduced. Although time spent in correcting input errors may seem extra, it only reflects the incompleteness and inaccuracies of previous procedures. Similarly, the expense of snap-out forms may appear to be an additional item, but their costs should be compared to the printing expense of the forms they replace.

Nor are the staff costs of research analysts and statisticians included in the system cost. Research and evaluation is an essential function of every human services agency. Without a MIS, the major effort may have to be spent in data collection; with a MIS the need for additional program evaluation personnel to pursue revealed issues may be exposed.

In considering the cost–effectiveness issue, it should be noted that the annual costs of the operating system is less than 1% of Orange County Department of Mental Health's gross budget (approximately $21 million).

SPECIAL PROBLEMS IN DESIGNING AND OPERATING A MANAGEMENT INFORMATION SYSTEM

Since timely management information is so essential to the functioning of any human service agency, top management's authority is required to establish and maintain a MIS. The implementation and maintenance of the system cannot be relegated to a remote research staff not completely integrated into the day-by-day management decisions of the agency.

As a management tool, a MIS depends for its acceptance and use upon an operating climate that incorporates planning, organizing, and controlling as essential functions. When an agency's personnel are committed to autonomous pursuit of idiosyncratic professional goals with only nominal accountability to the community, installation of a MIS will be resented and resisted. In no event, then, must such a system be arbitrarily imposed on an organization. The key to acceptance is staff participation in determining the kinds of information needed for decision making and how these can be met. When involved in such a process, most staff members recognize the benefits to be realized and may even develop an interest in some of the management concepts that are necessarily associated with a MIS.

Another problem is that of confidentiality. Staff members are appropriately concerned with the handling of patient data they submit, particularly that which identifies the individual by name as having sought treatment for mental illness. Security procedures for handling data and limiting access to it must be developed and explained. The California Lanterman–Petris–Short Act carefully spells out requirements for confidentiality, and written, prior permission from clients must be obtained for any person to have access to the data in any form. But computerizing such data seems to pose special problems. Perhaps because of past abuses in incorporating sensitive information in data bases, or because of the current public distrust of government agencies, establishing a file of mental health information for machine processing can raise anxieties and become an obstacle to acceptance. A special law has been passed in New York (and is being advocated in California) that prohibits subpeonaing of computerized records and requires they be obtained from the facility that originated the information (Curran, Laska, Kaplan, & Bank, 1973; Laska & Bank, 1975). The issue of confidentiality must be regarded as a serious one; the benefits of obtaining the data must be weighed in an unemotional fashion against the possible risks. In no event should the issue be permitted to become the symbol of other, unarticulated anxieties about the influence of a management tool upon individual staff member's prerogatives.

How to meet the challenge of analyzing the volume of data generated by a MIS is also a problem. Although the staff members' interest in the data produced has been remarkable and extremely gratifying, they sometimes get the feeling that they are being inundated with computer printouts. Once the utilization patterns of existing data have been determined, it will be possible to program useful statistical reductions of the output, or perhaps to eliminate some tabulations. It would be premature to eliminate a sizable portion of the outputs until their possible use has been fully explored and exploited. But this has been and will be a problem with a MIS that requires continued concern and attention.

Maintaining the system's flexibility is a problem that requires constant vigilance. On the one hand, compromising the specifications can seriously limit retrievability of data; on the other hand, rigidity in maintaining the specifications detracts from the system's purpose of being responsible to the program's needs.

Another problem is that of drawing the line between serving research needs or those for making management decisions. The decision in Orange County was to design a system to meet management needs. Thus, the primary feedback became the management reports. At the same time, however, it was feasible to obtain the statistical reports for evaluating the process of delivering mental health services in Orange County. These are not routinely distributed to unit staff members, but are made available to answer any questions they have.

It was clear from the outset that the statistical reports could only provide data for identifying and defining research problems; data from the statistical reports alone could not resolve such research problems. Outcome studies, or other forms of clinical research, will draw heavily upon the MIS data but will go far beyond that information in evaluating patients at the beginning, during, at the end of treatment and at various points for followup. Data collection for such research will probably be on the basis of a sample of patients, rather than for the population as a whole as is covered by the MIS.

The administrator of human services may regard computer technology as such alien terrain that he or she hesitates to consider a management information system as a tool for organizational administration. An administrator need not be an expert in systems analysis or design, or in computer programming.

The administrator need only be motivated to add to his or her managerial skill, take a pragmatic approach to problem solving, and find an expert who can effectively assist. A competent consultant will guide the administrator to the key questions, pose alternative ways for meeting informational requirements, raise cost–effectiveness issues, translate management needs into technical specifications, and help the administrator understand what he or she needs to know about the technical side of a MIS and data processing in order to be able to obtain and operate an information system.

SUMMARY

This chapter has discussed the rising demand for accountability on the part of human service programs and agency administrators. These pressures for program accountability make it imperative that human service administrators develop more effective management skills, more useful information systems, and more effective methods of planning, organizing, controlling, and leading. Specific focus of this chapter centered upon the MIS as an administrative tool. Design criteria were discussed and illustrated by their application in implementing such an information system in the Orange County (California) Department of Mental Health. Five major design requirements for a management information system were delineated and exemplified in the Orange County information system. These design requirements stipulate that a human service information system must be able to (a) define how current resources are being spent; (b) determine the patterns of service delivery; (c) provide monitoring aids for program managers; (d) provide data for multiple reporting requirements of funding agencies; and (e) generate necessary data for planning purposes.

Also, special problems in designing and operating a MIS were discussed: (a) involvement of service and support personnel; (b) confidentiality; (c) handling and analyzing the volumes of data collected and stored; (d) maintaining system flexibility and responsivity to information needs; (e) the relationship of information systems to research purposes; and (f) the role of consultative support in system design and implementation.

Finally, tables were presented summarizing (a) the type, preparation, and content of information system input documents; (b) the type, use, and content of output reports useful for management decision making; and (c) the design, development, and operating costs associated with the Orange County information system compared with that of another county system.

REFERENCES

Chapman, R. L. Improving driver licensing programs. *Behavior Research In Highway Safety*, 1970, *1*(3), 172–179.
Chapman, R. L., & Elpers, J. R. Future prediction—Service and transition models. In E. J. Lieberman (Ed.), *Mental health: The public health challenge*. Washington, D. C.: American Public Health Association, 1974.

Curran, W. J., Laska, E. M., Kaplan, H., & Bank, R. Protection of privacy and confidentiality. *Science,* 1973, *182,* 797–802.

Elpers, J. R., & Chapman, R. L. Management information for mental health services. *Administration in Mental Health,* 1973, Fall, 12–25.

Laska, E. M., & Bank, R. (Eds.). *Safeguarding psychiatric privacy: Computer systems and their uses.* New York: Wiley, 1975.

Sorensen, J. E., & Phipps, D. W. *Cost-finding and rate-setting for community mental health centers.* (DHEW Publication No. ADM 76-291.) Washington, D. C.: U. S. Government Printing Office, 1975.

8

A MANAGEMENT INFORMATION AND PLANNING SYSTEM FOR INDIRECT SERVICES

Anthony Broskowski, Jean Driscoll, and Herbert C. Schulberg

It is useful for program evaluation purposes to distinguish "indirect services" provided by human service organizations from direct services provided to individual clients or families. Indirect services such as consultation, education, and certain types of research and planning are directed toward other caregivers or organizations who in turn have *direct* contact with persons or groups needing service. As such, indirect services aim toward primary or secondary prevention, that is, dealing with community sources of human problems, or identifying and intervening in "high-risk" situations before specific services are sought by the potential clients. Since indirect services are frequently organized and managed differently than direct services, evaluation procedures should reflect these differences.

This chapter and Chapter 15 address two aspects of the evaluation of indirect services. Chapter 15 focuses on the evaluation of single indirect service projects, drawing concrete illustration from a common indirect service provided by community mental health centers—consultation to schools. In this chapter we illustrate the application of management information techniques to an organization whose projects are concerned almost exclusively with indirect services—primarily consultation or technical assistance to other caregiver agencies. Here the information system helps to monitor the changing mix of specific projects undertaken by staff. This information system is used by management and staff as a tool (*a*) for ongoing resource allocations, (*b*) for internal integration of separate organizational activities, and (*c*) for planning the future uses of major organizational resources. Although all organizations must face these tasks, an organization providing "indirect" services must be especially capable of flexible resource management while maintaining accountability for its less obvious services.

The system described in this chapter, which we have labeled MIPS (management information and planning system), was designed primarily for human service organizations involved in systemwide planning, research, and development. The specific organization for which MIPS was designed, United Community Planning Corporation (UCPC), conducts long- and short-term planning projects, as well as research and technical assistance projects in a wide variety of human service areas, including social services, public welfare, physical and mental health, recreation, corrections, and training and education. In addition, UCPC provides two direct services to individual citizens and other agencies: information and referral services and volunteer services coordination.

Formerly known as United Community Services of Greater Metropolitan Boston, UCPC was independently incorporated in 1974 when major organizational changes were undertaken in Boston's United Way system. In addition to coping with a new identity and some modifications in its major mission, UCPC in 1974 faced problems similar to those of many other human service agencies—new funds were scarce, pressures for accountability were increasing, and rapid environmental changes were occurring. Management and staff recognized that agency survival would depend upon increased agency efficiency and responsiveness. The chief executive and key staff, therefore, decided to design a data system that would improve information flow, monitor the organization's resource utilization, and provide information relevant to daily operations and future planning. These administrative needs led to the design of MIPS.

In the process of designing MIPS, a new philosophy of organization and management evolved. Beginning with a fresh emphasis on task-oriented, time-limited, and more accountable projects, UCPC also recognized a need to remain responsive to rapidly shifting environmental demands. As indicated in Chapter 3, while task orientation requires stability and continuity, responsiveness requires flexibility and change. These conflicting dimensions were resolved by a radical change in the UCPC organizational model. Significantly, UCPC eliminated the stable but rigid hierarchical table of organization and instituted a project team approach (Chapman, 1973; Kingdon, 1973). Using this approach, major organizational activities have managers responsible for conducting a particular set of tasks and reporting on their progress. Since personnel may shift roles from being manager on one project to staff on another, and thereby manage one another on a day-to-day basis, the organizational structure is more clearly reflected by a matrix of personnel by activities, with authority and control varying from activity to activity. *In essence, MIPS became both a method of collecting and processing information as well as a method of organizing and controlling staff activities.*

MIPS STRUCTURE

Concerned primarily with the utilization of professional staff effort, MIPS differentiates personnel time into two major systemic categories: production activities and maintenance activities. *Production* activities are those generating useful products or services to individuals or organizations in the environment. All production activities, therefore, must have one or more identifiable individual, group, or organizational beneficiaries. *Maintenance* activities are those conducted primarily to support the organization as an adaptive and effective system. In addition to the major distinction between production and maintenance activities, MIPS makes several additional distinctions that relate to the time-frame for activities and how staff are organized to carry them out. That is, MIPS distinguishes whether the activity is time-limited, or routinely conducted on an ongoing basis. Furthermore, whereas some activities are conceptualized as being performed by staff members working as separate individuals, other activities are organized around teams, headed up by a "manager," who is responsible for supervision and coordination. Those activities that are time-limited are classified as *projects;* those activities conducted routinely are called *work centers.* Every project has an assigned manager because various staff must be coordinated in conducting the service. Some work centers have no manager because even though most UCPC staff will engage in a particular ongoing activity, it is not the type of service that requires interstaff coordination. Finally, in reference to projects, the MIPS makes the distinction between (a) UCPC projects and projects primarily sponsored by other organizations to which UCPC lends its staff assistance; and between (b) projects oriented to current client services, contrasted with projects oriented to future undertakings. Feasibility studies and proposal preparation are examples of this latter category, called *developmental* projects.

In brief, MIPS provides management with an overview of staff time expenditures within a framework consistent with a system–environment model of organizational life (see Chapter 3). The major MIPS categories used for staff reporting are briefly outlined in Table 8.1. Detailed definitions are given in a *MIPS operations manual (1),* used to train staff to report time utilization reliably and to document the details of MIPS data processing.

INPUT DOCUMENTS

In the same way that direct service agencies collect initial information on each client, MIPS records initial information to characterize each project and work center. This initial information is collected on three documents: (a) the project activate form, (b) the project/work center identification key (PIK/WIK), and (c) the project operational plan (POP).

The project activate form is completed by the assigned manager who records the names of other staff assigned to the project, the estimated completion date, and a formal project name. Once completed, this form requires the signature of the executive director before it is sent to MIPS staff who assign

TABLE 8.1
Outline of MIPS Activity Categories

I. PRODUCTION ACTIVITIES
    A. Production Work Centers
        1. Work Centers with assigned managers
            a. Information and Referral Services
            b. Voluntary Action Center
            c. Census
            d. Communications
            e. Fiscal Management
            f. Public Policy
            g. Social Action
        2. Work Center without assigned managers
            a. Organizational Services—UWMB[a]
            b. Organizational Services—Other
            c. Environmental Relations
    B. Production Projects (Each with assigned manager)
        1. UCPC—Sponsored Projects
        2. Other—Sponsored Projects
    C. Developmental Projects (Each with assigned manager)
II. MAINTENANCE ACTIVITIES
    A. Maintenance Work Centers
        1. Work Centers with assigned managers
            a. Accounting
            b. Central Office Management
            c. MIPS
            d. Organizational Administration
        2. Work Centers without assigned managers
            a. Environmental Monitoring
            b. Internal Communications
            c. Work Space Management
    B. Maintenance Projects (Each with assigned manager)
    C. Downtime (Holidays, Vacation, Sick Days, Leave, etc.)

[a] UWMB is the United Way of Massachusetts Bay, the primary funding source for UCPC.

a project number and shortened name, both used for later computer storage.

On the PIK/WIK, each project and work center is classified on a number of dimensions: (*a*) source of initiation; (*b*) degree of participation by other organizations; (*c*) funding sources; (*d*) focus of effort (e.g., needs assessment, training, evaluation); (*e*) characteristics of beneficiaries such as age, nature of problem, and other indicators of high-risk (e.g., minority, poverty); (*f*) the geographical area affected; and (*g*) the percentage of the total activity estimated to be of benefit to different types of organizations in the private and public sector. This initial information, collected through the PIK/WIK, is later combined with routinely collected data on the hours spent on each project or work center for a variety of administratively useful analyses.

The project operational plan (POP) is the third major MIPS input document. It is completed by the manager at the outset of each project. The POP stipulates a detailed plan of goals and target dates, and the anticipated re-sources and specific activities necessary to achieve these goals, including specific staff members' time and the costs of supplies and travel. Management subsequently uses the POP as a framework to assess progress in fulfilling the work plan and to identify potential problems.

A fourth major MIPS input document is called the staff activity report. Each professional staff person is required to report on a semimonthly basis the time spent working on each project or work center. Routine MIPS activity categories are already printed on the form. Staff are asked to write in on the form the names or code numbers of the specific projects to which they are assigned. Time spent on each MIPS category is reported in hours or fractions of hours, usually written as decimals. The staff activity report is analogous in function to the logs used by direct service agencies for staff to report on how much of what kind of service they gave to which client(s).

PROCESSING OF MIPS INPUT DOCUMENTS

The staff activity reports are submitted to MIPS staff for addition, editing, and transfer to a keypunch form. These keypunch forms are then processed by a local bank, that also manages UCPC's computerized payroll account. For a small fee, the bank provides time and cost computer printouts based upon the MIPS data. The bank's program sums hours for each MIPS category and translates hours into cost figures, using the hourly rates for each staff person. Data from the PIK/WIKs and POPs are manually combined with the bank's printout to produce a variety of output reports.

OUTPUT REPORTS

Time and cost printouts are the system's major output reports. The printouts display hours spent and cost-equivalency data for each reporting period, as well as the job-to-date and year-to-date totals, for every project, work center, and other MIPS category. Subtotals for major subcategories of production and maintenance are also printed. For each MIPS category, the printout separately lists the amount of effort and costs for each participating staff person. A partial, illustrative printout from a given report period is provided in Table 8.2.

The computer printouts, PIK/WIKs, and POPs are used by MIPS staff to develop additional reports in the variety of formats required by management. These reports include such analyses as a total organizational summary of time and costs for each report period and quarterly analyses on types of projects and work center activities. The MIPS staff also generate a substantial variety of other reports, including quarterly and ad hoc reports on specific projects and work centers by their major purpose, funding source, costs, and characteristics of beneficiaries. Some reports are circulated to all staff, others only to project and work center managers, and still others only to top management or the board of directors. The range of reports and illustrations of how MIPS data is utilized will be presented as the remainder of this chapter discusses the major functions of MIPS.

TABLE 8.2
Sample MIPS Output Report

Employee No.	For Period 2/1/75 to 2/28/75 Name	Hours	Cost
	MIPS Code 1/3/000 Internal Communication		
0/100/10324	J. Able	18	172.20
0/400/30971	T. Cowan	7	62.50
0/100/10473	S. Smith	3	41.10
	Current Totals	28	275.80
	Job-to-date	349	4832.10
	Year-to-date	349	4832.10
	MIPS Code 2/6/004 Cost Accounting Project		
0/300/84721	M. Roe	12	138.40
0/200/01411	A. Zack	6.5	95.00
	Current Totals	18.5	233.40
	Job-to-date	273.5	4078.60
	Year-to-date	183	2743.50
	⋮	⋮	⋮
	MIPS Code Subtotal—all Production Projects		
	Current Totals	198.75	2780.75
	Job-to-date	543.50	7842.77
	Year-to-date	405.30	5827.26

MIPS FUNCTIONS

Routine and ad hoc MIPS reports, when combined with additional information such as cost data on other than personnel expenses, provide management with useful analyses needed for a variety of purposes. In general, the MIPS is useful or essential in the following organizational activities: (a) planning and managing; (b) cost-finding, rate-setting, and budgeting; (c) internal evaluation and external accountability; and (d) personnel development.

To understand fully how the MIPS relates to each of these functions and how these functions relate to one another, it is necessary to spell out the connections between the MIPS activity categories used to report staff time, and the program budget accounts used to record all sources of income and expenditures.

Table 8.3 summarizes how specific MIPS activity categories are reorganized and consolidated to form the organization's chart of accounts, which are the five program budget categories used by the UCPC accountant. All income and expenditures are posted to these five accounts, each of which is further broken down into specific line items, such as salaries, fringe benefits, rent, utilities, supplies, and so forth. This connection between staff reporting and financial accounting provides the necessary foundation for many subsequent functional analyses.

TABLE 8.3

The Organization of MIPS Activity Categories into Five Program Budgets

UCPC Program budget accounts	MIPS Activity categories[a]
I. Planning Activities	Production Projects
	Organizational Services—UWMB
	Organizational Services—Other
II. Direct Services	Information and Referral
	Voluntary Action Center
III. Community Services	Census
	Communications
	Social Action
	Public Policy
	Fiscal Management
	Environmental Relations
IV. Research and Development	Developmental Projects
V. General and Administration	Organizational Administration
	Accounting
	Central Office Management
	MIPS
	Work Space Management
	Environmental Monitoring
	Internal Communications
	Maintenance Projects

[a] The MIPS category, Downtime, is allocated to the five program budget accounts in proportion to their share of the total staff time in all other MIPS categories.

PLANNING AND MANAGING

Managing a multifunctional and highly differentiated organization requires integrated, timely, and relevant information about the nature and efficiency of resource utilization. Since personnel expenses account for almost 80% of the costs of most human service programs, personnel time is often the most critical resource demanding management's attention. MIPS was designed to provide information about the distribution of staff time relative to the various activity categories listed in Table 8.1. With these data, management can make more informed decisions about the appropriateness of time utilization vis-à-vis rapidly emerging or shifting organizational goals. Without such routinized information and feedback, complex organizations can easily drift off course as staff develop defensive and/or nonproductive activities to maintain their own internal priorities and to fill slack time potentially available for new or modified services.

As was noted in Chapter 3, many human services organizations have extremely permeable boundaries and must frequently and quickly respond to a variety of competing demands and pressures from their task environments. How best to reallocate staff time to meet new demands raises difficult issues; making such decisions without information on existing and longer range commitments is hazardous, at best, and may further increase organizational vulnerability.

There are several ways the MIPS can provide information relevant to crucial decisions about allocating organizational resources. The project operational plan (POP) permits forecasting organizational time commitments to projects over a relatively long period. The data-base from the collective POPs can generate summaries of time committed for specific staff members as well, and these data can be used for assigning new tasks as management deems it necessary. The POP also provides for sharpened goal-setting within an individual project. Overall organizational control and integration are similarly supported by the POP inasmuch as project goals can be compared with overall organizational goals to ensure compatibility.

Table 8.4 illustrates the use of data from the POPs and staff activity reports to develop a 1-year plan or budget of staff hours for existing commitments carried over from the previous year, and uncommitted hours available for new activities. The percentage goals for the major categories were based on a knowledge of the previous year's experience and the hopes for the future. It indicates that the organization plans to put 48% of its staff efforts into planning activities, 15% into direct services; 14% into community services; 8% into research and development; and 15% into administration. Commitments to projects and work centers in 1975 that will carry over into 1976 (data available from the POPs), indicate that only 10,921 staff hours will be available for new projects in 1976 and 3029 hours for research and development. By definition, work centers are continuing commitments. If the number of staff working in the organization had shifted up or down from 1975 to 1976, the figures in Table 8.4 would reflect where staff hours were to be added or dropped, respectively.

Table 8.5 illustrates how data from the staff activity reports are combined with all operating expense data to determine the monthly and year-to-date expenses by program budget categories, and compares these actualities against goals. In the illustration presented here, the organization is putting less of its efforts into planning activities than the goal called for and putting more time than it planned into general and administration. These data also indicate that the organization has spent only $244,240 as of April whereas it had expected to spend $265,480. This seasonal savings will be diminished later in the year when large expenses are incurred.

Planning and managing at the level of individual projects is achieved simply by reviewing staff hours actually spent on a project against the plan for the project detailed in the POP. Project managers are also expected to complete each month a 1-page project progress report, which asks them to indicate if the project is on schedule, and if not, to indicate reasons and any requests for changes in the project's plan or budgeted resources. For example, a manager may report a delay due to lack of cooperation by some outside agency or may request additional help from other staff to finish a specific task.

TABLE 8.4

Planned Commitments of Staff Hours from 1975 to 1976 and Uncommitted Hours Available for New Activities[a]

	Total	Planning activities	Direct services	Community services	Research development	General administration
1. Goals for 1976						
a. Hours	37,856	18,171	5,678	5,300	3,029	5,678
b. Goal as percentage of total	100%	48%	15%	14%	8%	15%
2. Commitments to be carried from 1975						
a. Hours	23,906	7,250	5,678	5,300	—	5,678
b. Percentage of goal	63%	40%	100%	100%	0%	100%
3. Available for New Activities/Projects						
a. Hours	13,950	10,921	—	—	3,029	—
b. Percentage of goal	37%	60%	—	—	100%	—

[a] Downtime for vacations, holidays, and estimated sick leave have been allocated proportionately to the program budget categories. Downtime averages 15% of available payroll hours.

TABLE 8.5

Illustrative Values of Monthly and Year-to-Date Operating Expense Figures by Program Budget Categories for April, 1975

	Planning activities	Direct services	Community services	Research and development	General and administration	Total
Monthly						
Goal (%)	48	15	14	8	15	100
Budget ($)	31,858	9,956	9,292	5,310	9,956	66,372
Actual ($)	28,980	12,250	7,740	4,520	10,950	64,440
Variance ($)	2,878	(2,294)	1,552	790	(994)	1,932
Actual in (%)	45	19	12	7	17	100
Year-to-date						
Goal (%)	48	15	14	8	15	100
Budget ($)	127,431	39,822	37,167	21,238	39,822	265,480
Actual ($)	107,790	35,600	33,290	18,720	48,840	244,240
Variance ($)	19,641	4,222	3,877	2,518	(9,018)	21,240
Actual (%)	44.1	14.6	13.6	7.7	20	100

At the level of individual staff activity, the MIPS spells out a procedure whereby each staff person has an individual interview with one of the two top executives on a quarterly basis. At these meetings the staff person and executive review the person's last 3 months of work effort as it is distributed among the productive and maintenance MIPS categories. Project assignments and work progress are also reviewed. At this time, staff may also negotiate for a revised plan for their own future activities. This process also has proven to be valuable in maintaining a closer contact between executives and staff, particularly to the extent that it facilitates staff understanding of the total organization's evolving goals and efforts and each staff's role in achieving them.

When staff resign or retire from the organization, or when staff members are ill or otherwise absent, MIPS reports can provide management with sufficiently detailed information about the uncovered workload to reassign activities as necessary. Thus, project continuity is enhanced and staff transitions made more orderly. MIPS also helps to resolve competing staff demands and conflicts because it improves information flow and communication about present efforts. The MIPS routinely informs all staff of new projects being started, with a brief description of each, staff assignments, and projected time tables. Staff are also informed when projects are closed. Such reports generated by MIPS provide the basis for staff discussions and executive decisions about overall organizational priorities, thus decreasing the probability that competing demands or lack of understanding among staff will remain chronically unresolved and lead to lowered morale.

Finally, long-range organizational planning is enhanced by the routinely collected staff time data and completed PIK/WIKs and POPs. Future goals are established more realistically by using easily retrievable MIPS information about related past activities. Such analysis may consider a project's natural history, levels of staff effort and costs over time, goals and subgoals achieved, and the environmental constituencies that participated and/or benefited from past activities. Services to specific geographic areas, to target population groups, or in the interest of specific fields of service (e.g., recreation, mental health, or corrections) can similarly be plotted over time. These measurements of effort and cost may then be compared with stated organizational priorities, and future resources budgeted differently if desired. For example, in using MIPS data to formulate the 1975–1976 work plan, staff and management became aware of reduced organizational efforts in the area of planning for social services. This trend will be reversed by dropping other activities deemed less significant for the coming year. Further illustrations of such analyses are provided later.

COST-ACCOUNTING, RATE-SETTING, AND BUDGETING

A second major purpose for MIPS information relates to the cost-accounting, rate-setting, and budgeting functions of management. The capacity of a human services organization to identify actual costs and set realistic rates for its services is crucial to its survival.

In terms of cost-accounting, the determination of relative staff time going into production and maintenance categories allows management to calculate the dollar costs of production and maintenance efforts for the entire organization. In systems terms, total cost (TC) equals maintenance costs plus production costs ($TC = MC + PC$). If income is generated only by production activities and the organization is to achieve a *balanced* budget, then it must value an hour of production at a rate such that *production income* (PI) equals *total costs* (TC). This relationship is expressed in Equation (8.1).

$$TC/PI = 1 \qquad (8.1)$$

Substituting the term ($MC + PC$) for TC in the left half of Equation (8.1), we derive Equation (8.2).

$$(MC + PC)/PI = (M + P)C/PI \qquad (8.2)$$

If income (I) must equal costs (C), then the equation reduces to Equation (8.3).

$$(M + P)/P = (M/P) + 1 \qquad (8.3)$$

If the production value index of the organization is defined as $PV = (M/P) + 1$, then PV is a multiplier that may then be applied to the hourly *gross* salary cost (salary plus fringe benefits) of any individual staff member to reflect the cost of a productive hour of that staff person's time. Table 8.6 illustrates such a simplified cost-accounting analysis using illustrative fiscal data. The calculation of the production value index automatically builds in the costs of indirect overhead expenses and the costs of all the organizational maintenance activities necessary to support production efforts. Although subsidized non-profit human service agencies may undertake activities that are not reimbursed at a rate high enough to cover true costs, the ability to determine costs accurately for a productive hour of staff time allows them to differentiate "contributory," from "breakeven" or "profit-making" activities.

TABLE 8.6

Illustration of Simplified Cost Accounting Using Overall Production/Maintenance Ratios to Calculate Production Value Index (PV)

Cost item	Amounts
1. Professional Salaries and Fringe	$520,000
2. Clerical Salaries and Fringe	120,000
3. All Operating Costs	160,000
Total Annual Costs	*$800,000*

If 75% of all professional staff time is spent on productive activities and 25% on maintenance, then allocate above cost items as production or maintenance.

Cost item	Production	Maintenance
1. Professional Salaries and Fringe	$390,000	$130,000
2. Clerical Salaries and Fringe		120,000
3. All Operating Costs		160,000
Total	*$390,000*	*$410,000*

$PV = (M/P) + 1 = (\$410,000/\$390,000) + 1 = 2.051$

The application of this method of cost-accounting to an individual project can be carried out by multiplying the production value (PV) against the hourly salary costs of the staff working on a particular project and further multiplied by the number of hours each staff member worked (2). This procedure is illustrated in Table 8.7, which displays illustrative data from one of the organization's projects and uses the PV index of 2.051 calculated in Table 8.6. The annual salary costs in Column 2 of Part I are the annual salaries paid to the employees plus 20% for fringe benefit costs to the organization. The hourly salary costs in Column 3 are calculated by dividing by 2080, the annual payroll hours for a full-time employee (40 hours × 52 weeks). Production hour costs in Column 4 are calculated by multiplying the values in Column 3 by the PV index of 2.051. Data in Column 5 are obtained from the MIPS printouts based on staff activity reports. Column 6 is the product of Column 4 times corresponding data in Column 5.

Part II of the illustration in Table 8.7 uses the production hour costs, Column 2, and remaining hours to be spent on the project as estimated from the project's operational plan (POP). The projected costs, Column 4, and the costs to date, Column 5, can be added to obtain the estimated total costs. Of course, it is also possible to calculate the actual costs of a project after its completion, including a detailed analysis of direct cost items, such as travel, supplies, consultants, and other items that are otherwise built into the analysis when one does the calculation using only the production value index. In cases when both techniques have been used, the cost estimates of the simplified procedure using PV and the detailed procedures using direct cost accounting have yielded highly similar estimates.

Knowing costs of existing projects and work centers, executives are better able to set billing rates for staff time and are better able to determine budgets for future projects or for the total organization. As the production value index increases or decreases over time, management can monitor its overall cost–efficiency and compare it to estimates in the fiscal budget. For example, since the MIPS was initiated, the production value index decreased from 3.16 to 1.92, indicating a greater shift toward productive activities and accordingly, a reduced cost for such activities. Since the average hourly gross salary costs (salary plus fringe benefit costs) of an employee is presently $13.35 and the PV index is 1.92, the organization must set an average rate for an hour of professional staff time spent on a productive service at $25.63, or approximately $180 for a 7-hour workday.

Finally, long-range fiscal budgeting is facilitated by past MIPS data. In describing a profit-making manufacturing company, Gruber and Niles (1974) point out that as the number of years of actual performance accumulate, the data in information systems becomes increasingly useful and thus makes budgeting more reliable. This principle is equally applicable to human service organizations. Continuous use by management of information based on cost accounting increases the ability to predict accurately and control future income and expenditures.

TABLE 8.7

Estimation of Actual and Projected Project Costs Using the Production Value (PV) Index

Project Name: Access 76-Freedom Trail
Manager: H. Vincent
Staff: S. Song. R. Alexis
Brief Description: This project will review architectural barriers to handicapped persons among the historical sites in Greater Boston and develop a proposal for their removal while maintaining the historical integrity of all sites.

Budget: $5000[a]
Timetable: January 1–June 31, 1975

PART I

Estimated costs as of mid-project point, March 31 , 1975:

(1) Assigned staff	(2) Annual salary costs	(3) Hourly salary costs	(4) Production hour costs	(5) Hours spent	(6) Estimated costs
H. Vincent	$19,200	$9.231	$18.932	47.5	$ 899.27
S. Song	$16,800	$8.077	$16.566	40.0	$ 662.64
R. Alexis	$15,600	$7.500	$15.383	15.5	$ 238.42
Totals				103.0	*$1800.33*

PART II

Projected cost for total project by June 30, 1975:

(1) Assigned Staff	(2) Production hour costs	(3) Projected hours project	(4) Projected costs	(5) Costs to date	(6) Projected total costs
H. Vincent	$18.932	95	$1,798.54	$ 899.27	$2697.81
S. Song	$16.566	115	$1,905.09	$ 662.64	$2567.73
R. Alexis	$15.383	50	$ 769.10	$ 238.42	$1007.52
Totals		260	*$4,472.73*	*$1,800.33*	*$6273.06*

[a] At actual and planned rates of staff time expenditures this project's cost will run approximately $1,273.00 over the budgeted $5000.

201

INTERNAL EVALUATION AND EXTERNAL
ACCOUNTABILITY

Little attention has been given until recently to the need for human service agencies to evaluate their own effectiveness. The importance of this management function has been almost totally ignored in favor of the actual provision of treatment and service activities, even activities that may be of dubious worth relative to the client's or community's needs. However, the limited fiscal resources now available for human services has stimulated increasing demands to evaluate the products from this sector of the economy. Furthermore, in recent years, agency environments have become increasingly diversified, multiply interconnected, at times conflictual, and rapidly changing. If an agency is now to survive and grow, it must remain responsive to the new demands made by environmental constituencies, and it must also provide information about how it is coping with the demands already placed upon it.

Both internal evaluation and external accountability require data about the level of effort being expended, information a MIPS provides routinely and in a way most accessible to the possibility of multiple uses. For example, if the organization is accused of providing insufficient services to certain disadvantaged groups, relevant data from MIPS can easily be generated. Projects directed at high-risk or inner-city populations can be compared with staff activities directed toward low-risk or suburban groups. A MIPS readily provides information about how staff hours and costs are presently allocated among various categories on the PIK/WIK.

Two of the many possible analyses of staff efforts and costs obtained from a combination of staff activity reports, fiscal data, and PIK/WIK data are illustrated in Tables 8.8 and 8.9. The information in Table 8.8 would be used for one type of internal analysis, whereas the information in Table 8.9 is typical of how MIPS data are used in response to external demands for accountability.

Table 8.8 portrays the distribution of all projects active during the first quarter of 1975 by two dimensions: (a) the primary problem or program area, and, (b) the primary focus of the staff's efforts. Such an analysis allows management to review all the recent projects along these two dimensions and compare the array against multiple sets of criteria as to what is most important for the organization to pursue. For example, in 12 of the 34 projects, or 30.1% of all project hours, the staff's efforts were primarily devoted toward the development of new resources for UCPC client agencies. These types of projects were generally geared to helping the client agencies secure new funds or government contracts. This relative emphasis reflects both UCPC's organizational priorities, given the inflationary costs of service delivery, and the pressures from agencies to help them secure additional funds. On the other hand, management may also make note of the fact that none of the active projects in the first quarter were geared to program evaluation. This state of affairs undoubtedly reflects the fact that agencies are more likely to request UCPC to help them get new funds than to evaluate existing programs. Looking at the

TABLE 8.8

UCPC Projects and Staff Hours Expended in First Quarter, 1975, Classified by Primary Focus of Effort and Primary Problem/Program Area

Primary focus of effort		Alcohol-ism	Correc-tions	Drug abuse	Educa-tion	Employ-ment	Health	Mental health	Recrea-tion	Rehabili-tation	Social services	Community settlement	Total	Percent-age of total
								Primary problem/Program area						
Community needs–resource assess.	Number						2				1	1	4	1.8
	Hours						66				139	17	222	8.8
Assessment of agency's programs	Number						1		1		2	1	5	14.8
	Hours						76		205		49	51	381	15.2
Development of new resources	Number					2	1	3	4		1	1	12	35.3
	Hours					51	202	108	122		205	69	757	37.1
Continuing education and training	Number	1							1		2		4	11.8
	Hours	20							37		186		243	9.7
Technical assistance to agencies	Number						1			1	1		3	8.8
	Hours						20			35	110		165	6.6
Public policy and advocacy	Number				1								1	2.9
	Hours				234								234	9.3
Information dissemination	Number						1				2		3	8.8
	Hours						219				84		303	12.1
Program evaluation	Number												—	—
	Hours												—	—
Fiscal management	Number										1		1	2.9
	Hours										70		70	2.8
Allocation studies	Number						1						1	2.9
	Hours						140						140	5.6
Total	Number	1	—	—	1	2	7	3	6	1	10	3	34	100%
	Hours	20	—	—	234	51	723	108	364	35	843	137	2515	100%
Percentage of total	Number	2.9	—	—	2.9	5.9	20.6	8.8	17.6	2.9	29.4	8.8	100%	100%
	Hours	.8	—	—	9.3	2.0	28.8	4.3	14.5	1.4	33.6	5.4	100%	100%

203

TABLE 8.9
Staff Hours and Costs Devoted to the Interest of UWMB and/or Affilitated Agencies
January 1–June 30, 1975

MIPS Category	(1) Staff hours	(2) Average for UWMB (%)	(3) Average costs devoted to UWMB[a]
All projects			
1. Sponsored by UCPC	3585	68	$62,481
2. Sponsored by UWMB	2671	95	65,035
3. Developmental projects	1375	10	3,524
Work Centers			
1. Census	131	25	839
2. Communications	360	10	923
3. Environmental relations	615	—	—
4. Fiscal management	270	10	692
5. Information and referral	1745	100	44,724
6. Organizational services—UWMB	606	100	15,532
7. Organizational services—other	954	—	—
8. Public policy	841	75	16,166
9. Social action	73	75	1,403
10. Voluntary action center	1110	100	28,449
		Total	$239,768

[a] Average costs include all administration and overhead costs and are calculated using the average hourly gross salary costs ($13.35), and a P.V. Index of 1.92 based on an average productivity rate of 81%. ($13.35 $\times$ 1.92) = $25.63 average, costs of an hour of production. Column (3) = (1) $\times$ (2) $\times$ $25.63 rounded to nearest dollar.

primary problem or program areas of the 34 projects, one can see that most project hours were devoted to the categories of *health* (7 projects, 723 hours, and 28.8% of all project hours) and *social services* (10 projects, 843 hours, and 33.6% of all project hours). The reader is reminded that Table 8.8 shows how 2515 hours were spent on projects. Work centers account for another 3152 productive hours for the first quarter, but these are not included in this analysis.

Although there has yet been no formalized and quantifiable goal-setting by top UCPC executives or its board of directors in relation to staff's efforts on various types of projects and work centers, these types of analyses are beginning to stimulate multiple questions as to why the projects and work centers are oriented as they are and whether or not there should be long-range goals in regard to future work. As in all such long-range strategic planning processes, management must examine current commitments as well as assess the direct environmental pressures to provide different patterns of service. Added to this balance, management must judge what it considers to be important tasks based on its own assessment of community problems and issues. The balance between organization reactivity, proactivity, and long-term stability is being sought continually as the management and board of directors review existing projects and work centers against shifting environmental pressures and needs.

The future development of MIPS will attempt to carry the evaluation of projects and work centers one step further by comparing outcomes against explicit and measurable goals. This process will include the collection of "client satisfaction" data by asking representatives of the various beneficiaries of projects and work centers to give their view of our work's utility. The quality of project and work center products and services may also be assessed by a subcommittee of the board of directors, using a variety of information inputs to judge the degree to which we have influenced human services through our influence on governmental statutes or regulations. Some of the methods that may be adopted to evaluate projects and work centers are illustrated in Chapter 15 by the procedures used to evaluate mental health consultation to school systems.

Table 8.9 portrays an analysis conducted in response to a request from the organization's primary funding source, the United Way of Massachusetts Bay (UWMB). In the contract with UWMB it was agreed that UCPC would devote at least 33% of their allocation (less the costs of the information and referral *and* the voluntary action center work centers), to activities of direct interest to United Way or any of the over 200 United Way affiliated agencies. The MIPS aids top management by providing some of the information needed to demonstrate that UCPC is effectively maintaining its agreement. Table 8.9 lists the staff hours and total costs of UCPC projects and work centers carried out for the benefit of UWMB or their affiliate agencies. Estimates as to how much of a project's or work center's efforts are devoted to UWMB or affiliated agencies are based on an analysis by management and staff as to what specific groups of persons or which specific agencies use the service, or benefit from the activity. A judgment in the case of each individual project and work center is made on the PIK/WIK and is sufficiently explicit to allow United Way or other external organizations to challenge the estimate if they disagree. In some cases, for example, a particular project is carried out on the basis of a direct request from the United Way. These projects are classified as "Sponsored by UWMB" and are, in most cases, classified on the PIK/WIK as devoted 100% to the interest of UWMB or an affiliated agency. By prior agreement, all of the activities of two work centers, information and referral center, and the voluntary action center, are considered to be of 100% benefit to UWMB. Some projects are clearly not devoted to UWMB and some work centers, by definition, are devoted entirely to other than UWMB interests.

Table 8.9 shows that the total 6-month costs of all activities devoted to the interests of UWMB or an affiliated agency are $239,768. This represents 60% of the agency's total 6-month operating costs of $399,450, which is well above the minimum agreement of 33%.

PERSONNEL DEVELOPMENT

The design of methods for personnel performance appraisal and incentive systems for staff development are among the most challenging tasks facing government and nonprofit organizations. Staff performance appraisal is necessary for organizational effectiveness as well as staff morale. Government and nonprofit organizations can easily drift toward mediocrity as seniority, civil service, or other tenure systems discourage excellence and productivity. Currently, ineffective workers are frequently protected from penalties and a larger bureaucracy must grow if new ideas and energies are to outweigh the accumulated inertia.

Although not a complete answer to these problems, MIPS has helped to create a *process* in the UCPC organization whereby some standardized measures have become available for the chief executive to use as part of the general staff evaluation procedure. Through the process of quarterly MIPS interviews with management, individual staff member's use of time, quality of performance, and future work goals can be explicitly reviewed. These interviews can recognize unique staff contributions while at the same time develop norms for comparative analyses. Work patterns can also be matched to individual career development goals.

The appraisal of staff performance in turn highlights the importance of staff incentives since effective organizational performance and productivity must build upon the abilities and motivation of staff to carry out assigned tasks. One of the practical difficulties for the nonprofit organization is to develop an incentive method that uses money and other rewards for good performance. At UCPC, a number of incentive systems have been considered, but none are fully satisfactory. Annual merit raises, of course, are always appropriate but with inflationary operating costs and shrinking organizational incomes, these are not always possible. Cash bonuses are difficult to offer in nonprofit agencies since restrictions are placed on the executive's discretionary use of funds. A third approach, tried on a limited basis at UCPC, involves release time for staff to travel or participate in various career development experiences. This option can also serve the purpose of in-service education for staff. Its major disadvantages are that time available for production activities is reduced, and some staff say they do not consider release time for self-education a meaningful reward.

Hospitals have experimented with incentive systems directed at individuals, teams, and large groups (Department of Health, Education, and Welfare, 1972). Incentive plans for individuals supplement a person's earnings in direct proportion to the amount that person's production exceeds a standard level; team plans operate in a similar fashion, with all team members benefiting equally; and large group incentives supplement an individual's earnings in direct relation to *improved* productivity by some large unit or the total organization. Large group incentives used with varying degrees of success include profit-sharing, labor savings, cost savings sharing, and value-added plans.

Each of these incentive systems requires that a standard level of productivity be established and that a mechanism exist to compare actual performance against the standard. The MIPS provides part of the necessary mechanisms in terms of measuring calculable production–maintenance ratios. The project operation plan (POP) further details the planned expenditures of staff effort and project timetables. At present, however, a systematic plan for allocating rewards to staff based on a formal appraisal system is still lacking.

Hopefully, an information system like MIPS can facilitate staff development aside from monetary rewards when used in an organization that is task and goal oriented, has mechanisms for decentralized decision making, and is not hierarchically structured. In such a human services organization, a MIPS can enhance two interrelated organizational functions: (a) stimulate a growth environment for personal development, and (b) allow staff participation in setting the organization's overall direction.

Personal development of staff must be a prime concern to management, if only for organizational self-interest. A highly motivated staff that routinely performs activities deliberately chosen to enhance professional expertise will usually function at a high level of productivity and effectiveness. Such a level of functioning can occur if top executives are comfortable with a project manager–team system whereby staff members can assume multiple roles, ranging from solo work on some activities, to being a team member or team manager on others.

Development of management skills among staff is promoted because project managers are given responsibility for the budgeting and expenditure of staff hours assigned to a project. The MIPS provides feedback on how these resources are being spent. At a project's conclusion, its resource utilization can be compared with the projections in its initial operational plan. When additional indicators of the project's effectiveness are added to the data from MIPS, managers and teams have accurate feedback about their respective performance.

A second MIPS function related to staff development is the distinction that it makes explicit between production and maintenance activities, without negating the value of maintenance. For example, the MIPS maintenance category includes such activities as "environmental monitoring" (e.g., journal reading, conference attendance, or site visits to other facilities) and "internal communication" (e.g., staff meetings and conversations during coffee breaks). While management seeks to maintain an overall production rate of 80–85% throughout the year, individuals can negotiate the use of their time in ways consistent with unique interests, abilities, and career goals. While most staff are involved primarily in production roles, any organization necessarily must (a) have some staff heavily committed to purely maintenance activities, and (b) value the contributions of these staff.

Third, MIPS indirectly functions to aid the personal development of staff by enhancing their understanding of the total organization. Terkel (1972) has vividly documented the alienation of workers who see their jobs as meaningless, repetitive, and disconnected from any whole product or organizational goal. By sharing various MIPS reports with staff, management can clarify the agency's current activities and the role of an individual staff member in carrying them out. Hayes (3) conducted a questionnaire survey of all UCPC staff in regard to their understanding of MIPS and its applicability to management and staff. Her findings indicated that staff strongly supported the system, although they judged the current MIPS reports to be primarily useful for overall organizational decision making and only marginally useful at the level of individual staff. Hayes's findings suggest that additional periodic reports must be designed to reflect each staff member's participation in projects and work centers plotted over time during the year. Presently, such data are available but not routinely reported because of insufficient time and resources among the MIPS staff. These new reports for individual staff might also reflect how their efforts were deployed along the dimensions of project or work center characteristics recorded on the PIK/WIK.

Although the effects of MIPS on job satisfaction at UCPC have not yet been formally determined, we strongly believe that any mechanism allowing staff access to detailed information about their agency's total operation fosters feelings of involvement and participation. Additionally, MIPS can make staff participation in organizational goal setting a reality. Shared information decreases the possibility that only a few staff members privy to data will influence agency policy. Finally, to the degree that MIPS helps the organization monitor itself and turn to the significant problems in its environment, it is less likely to be preoccupied with internal staff conflicts over what or how much each person is contributing. Instead, it can face the issue of how well it is meeting overall responsibilities to deliver human services. Thus, routine measurement of expended effort can help to resolve the continuing question of "How much have we done for whom?" and stimulate the frequently unasked questions of "What should our goals be?" "How can we reach them?" and "How can we do a better job?"

SOME PRINCIPLES OF IMPLEMENTATION

Principles for the development of MISs are discussed elsewhere in this book, and need not be reviewed in great detail here. However, several of the basic principles described in earlier chapters were particularly useful in the development of MIPS and deserve brief review. The basic principles covered in the remainder of this chapter include the importance of (a) understanding managerial decision making, (b) securing management commitment, (c) assuring staff participation, and (d) using an incremental approach.

UNDERSTAND MANAGERIAL DECISION MAKING

Many designers of MISs consistently fail to understand the problems impeding the system's implementation (Gruber & Niles, 1974). Staff resistance to providing data, irrelevant reports to management, and a lack of impact on managerial decision making are all consequences of systems that were designed and implemented without sufficient organizational involvement. A particular prerequisite of MIS design for any organization is a thorough understanding of the multiple decisions that its managers must make for efficient daily operation and in planning future activities (Gorry & Morton, 1971).

To anticipate the multiple types of decisions facing management, it is necessary to understand the organization's environment, the pressures on its boundaries, and what it must produce in order to remain viable. On the basis of such requirements, MIPS was designed only after a thorough analysis of UCPC's organizational environment, internal structure, and management needs. Several methods were used to become sensitive to these characteristics. One designer followed and observed executive staff over time in order to comprehend the environments in which they operate and the types of decisions they must make. In-depth interviews with agency executives, key staff, and important constituents, and minutes of meetings and other records were reviewed to gather information useful for understanding organizational processes and environments.

SECURE MANAGEMENT COMMITMENT

The system designer's understanding of managerial decision making, while crucial, does not necessarily ensure the use of a MIS by the actual work managers. Managers may be unaware of the potential uses of a MIS and unwilling to learn how to use the information it provides, particularly inasmuch as it may be reported to them in unfamiliar ways. Therefore, system designers must carefully design and redesign the format of the information reports until they are comprehensible to managers. Design efforts are enhanced, of course, when managers are willing to work on the report formats so that the MIS meets critical management needs.

ASSURE STAFF PARTICIPATION

In addition to managerial commitment and a design that collects the information needed for management decisions, the system must have the support of all staff required to supply the input data. Therefore, throughout the system's development and implementation, the designers must ensure the participation of the total staff. In addition to involving staff in the early design considerations, it is important to give them continual feedback in the form of reports that help them function at their own levels in the organization.

USE AN INCREMENTAL APPROACH

As the MIS is designed, the question of timing must be considered. Should a MIS be thrust upon an organization fully developed, or can implementation proceed in stages? The United Community Planning Corporation opted for the latter approach for two basic reasons. First, by implementing MIPS incrementally, the designers could work much more closely with UCPC management in determining what essential data should be collected routinely and what could be obtained on an ad hoc basis. Second, during the implementation phase, designers could more fully analyze the nuances of the management decision-making process by observing how the initial MIPS data were being utilized or ignored. As implementation proceeded, inevitably it was found necessary to refine the MIPS categories initially used in describing UCPC activities. To this date, changes are being made while simultaneously trying to maintain the continuity of earlier MIPS data.

SUMMARY

Pressures for accountability are particularly intense for indirect service organizations that find it difficult to identify their products or the beneficiaries of their services. The development of MISs can now assist these types of agencies and programs to determine and evaluate their resources utilization and plan the future deployment of limited resources.

The implementation of the management information and planning system (MIPS) within a nonprofit human services planning and research organization has resulted in several early benefits. Staff have become increasingly aware of overall organizational goal-setting and the importance of efficient utilization of their limited time. The organization is also in a better position to be responsive quickly and flexibly to external sources with regard to the costs and utilization of its resources. Planning for the future and how to shift from the present is enhanced by a better understanding of internal and external commitments.

The theoretical foundation upon which the MIPS was designed (see Chapter 3) does not limit its use to any one particular organizational structure or philosophy of management. While MIPS is consistent with the management styles of organizations with complex and hierarchical tables of organization, it can also act as an integrative mechanism for a more decentralized organization.

MIPS appears to be a tool with several potential uses. As a tool, however, its range of optimal effectiveness and its limitations must still be determined. In any case, the MIS must remain sufficiently flexible if it is to remain responsive and useful to complex organizations functioning within turbulent environments. Thus, there is continuing experimentation and modification of the MIPS in the light of changing organizational structure and shifting informational needs.

REFERENCE NOTES

1. Broskowski, A., Driscoll, J., & Hayes, S. *MIPS operations manual.* Boston: United Community Planning Corporation, 1975. (Available from UCPC, 14 Somerset Street, Boston, Massachusetts 02108.)
2. The use of the *PV* index is based on a number of critical assumptions that may be overlooked by the casual reader. These assumptions, if violated, could lead to misleading applications and interpretations of the suggested method. Specific assumptions are outlined below: a. *All services currently were offered during the time period in which the PV ratio was determined.* b. *No major changes in volume of units of activity are occurring during the current time period.* Major increases or decreases will spread the fixed expenses over a larger or smaller number of activity units thereby increasing or decreasing the actual unit cost for each hour of service. c. *No major changes in productivity or efficiency are occurring during the current time period.* Changes in the approach to consultation, for example, could alter the number of activity units produced by a given staff and thereby shift the actual unit of activity costs. Adding new office locations or shifting the talent mix on a consulting team, for example, may violate this assumption. d. *The levels of "fixed" expenses (expenses that do not vary with volume) and "step" expenses (expenses that increase in a stairstep fashion as volume increases) do not change.* Variable expenses, that in total vary directly with volume, are constant on a per unit of activity basis. Fixed expenses are constant in total, but will vary on a per unit of activity basis, depending on the volume actually achieved. Any increase or decrease in a fixed or step expense will affect unit of activity cost. Starting new services, for example, will add new layers of administrative and support costs that are basically fixed. e. *The proportion*

of the total variable costs to volume of activity remains constant. If new variable costs are added (e.g., an expanded office or team now offers more services and, as a result, increases travel costs), the per unit of activity cost will increase. f. *There are no major time lags between revenues, expenses, and delivery of a service. (Time lags in revenues and expenses are adjusted through accural accounting.)* Substantial lags may exist between the acquisition of resources, development of capacity to deliver services and the actual delivery of services to clients. Unit costs of activity will vary throughout the developmental process, generally decreasing as volume increases until a normal volume is reached, at which time the unit cost tends to stabilize.

3. Hayes, S. *Management information systems: Theoretical concepts and practical applicability.* Unpublished Master Thesis, California State University, Fullerton, 1975. (For availability see Note *1*.)

REFERENCES

Chapman, R. L. *Project management in NASA: The system and the men.* (Stock No. 3300-00514.) Washington, D. C.: National Aeronautics and Space Administration, U. S. Government Printing Office, 1973.

Department of Health, Education, and Welfare. *Employee incentive system for hospitals.* (DHEW Publication No. HSM 72-6705.) Washington, D. C.: U. S. Government Printing Office, 1972.

Gorry, G., & Morton, S. A framework for management information systems. *Sloan Management Review,* 1971, *13,* 55–70.

Gruber, W., & Niles, S. The coming of the new management. *Organizational Dynamics,* 1974, *2,* 67–80.

Kingdon, D. R. *Matrix organizations: Managing information technologies.* London: Tavistock Publications (distributed in U. S. A. by Harper & Row), 1973.

Terkel, S. *Working.* New York: Pantheon Books, 1972.

III

ASSESSMENT OF COMMUNITY SERVICE NEEDS

Information about community needs for services is a vital component of human service program planning and development. Need assessment information provides the contextual framework for evaluating the relevance or adequacy of the available human services within a community or a broader planning area. The chapters in Part III describe need assessment methods that can be used to compile existing information about service needs, develop new information, and integrate existing data with newly developed information. The need assessment methods presented in Part III are organized within three families of methods: (a) social indicator approaches, (b) social area survey approaches, and (c) community group approaches. Basic strategies are described and illustrated within each method family and advantages and disadvantages of each strategy are discussed. An important theme emphasized by the authors is that deployment of a wide range of assessment strategies provides the basis for an integrated perspective on needs—a process that merges the values inherent in each method and produces an overall convergence of information.

9

NEED IDENTIFICATION
AND PROGRAM PLANNING
IN THE COMMUNITY CONTEXT

Larry M. Siegel, C. Clifford Attkisson, and Linda G. Carson

Assessment of service needs is a neglected and misunderstood aspect of human service program planning. Optimally, legislative blueprints for national social and health programs should emerge from systematic, scientific need assessment efforts that are designed to identify the extent and degree of need for specific services in the general population. In practice however, national programs emerge from a political context of confrontation between special and general interests, social service ideologies, demands for service, and the competition for access to resources. As a result, our communities are peppered with uncoordinated and loosely integrated programs that overlap and compete for sparse resources. Without adequate assessment of human service needs, this poorly monitored and uncoordinated situation will persist and worsen.

This chapter describes the central issues of need identification and assessment. Following the initial discussion, several basic need assessment methodologies are described and illustrated. The basic assumptions on which the chapter is based are that identification and assessment of service needs (*a*) must be undertaken at the local community and regional level in a fashion that stimulates coordination and integration of human services at the community level; (*b*) must be a rationalizing force in the regional health and human service planning process; and (*c*) must carefully blend citizen and consumer participation with professional personnel in a planning process designed to stimulate program relevance to human service needs. Need assessment, then, should be a cooperative venture within a human service network—a venture designed to enhance and monitor program integration, relevance, adequacy, and planned change.

A DEFINITION OF NEED
IDENTIFICATION AND ASSESSMENT

Need identification describes health and social service requirements in a geographic or social area, whereas *need assessment* is aimed at estimating the relative importance of these needs. The process of need identification and assessment involves two distinct steps: (a) the application of a measuring tool or an assortment of tools to a defined social area; and, following this attempt at measurement, (b) the application of judgment to assess the significance of the information gathered in order to determine priorities for program planning and service development (Blum, 1974). Assessment is a research and planning activity that is focused on a specific social area. Within social areas, need assessment strategies are designed to provide data that will enable planners to determine the extent and kinds of needs there are in a community; to evaluate existing service resources systematically; and to provide information for planning new service programs in the light of the community's needs and human service patterns.

Basically, the various known assessment techniques produce information that describes or defines social conditions or situations. These conditions are not necessarily predetermined to be positive or negative. The interpretation of social situations depends on the values and expectations of those individuals doing the interpreting. As Blum (1974) states, "The identical situation may be seen as good by those whose value expectations are met, and as bad by those whose values are not; those whose values are unrelated, or who do not connect the condition to values, may not perceive the condition at all, or view it as a natural state of affairs [pp. 219–220]."

The same rationale may be applied when considering the term "need" in situations where assessment activities are characterized as "need identification." Need in this context might usefully be defined as the gap between what is viewed as a necessary level or condition by those responsible for this determination and what actually exists. Need is at best a relative concept and the definition of need depends primarily upon those who undertake the identification and assessment effort.

Nguyen, Attkisson, and Bottino (*3*) have developed a useful definition of *unmet need:*

> An unmet need is said to exist when a problem in living, a dysfunctional somatic or psychological state, or an undesirable social process is recognized, for which a satisfactory solution requires a major mobilization of additional resources and/or a major reallocation of existing resources.

> This definition, stated differently, defines unmet need contingently upon:

> 1. The recognition of a problem, a dysfunctional somatic or psychological state, or an undesirable social process

> 2. The judgment that satisfactory solutions are not accessible, are not currently adequate, or do not exist in the community

3. The necessity to reallocate existing resources or to appropriate new resources.

For Nguyen *et al.* (*3*), this definition of unmet need has several important implications:

1. The concept of *problem* involves (*a*) a perception of what is, (*b*) a comparison level, i.e.,what should be, and (*c*) an evaluation of the extent and saliency of the discrepancy between what is and what should be.

2. The *recognition of a problem* refers to the process of determining the discrepancy between what exists and what is deemed desirable or necessary. This process involves the participation of concerned citizens, interest and political groups, consumers of health and human services, funders, program planners, service providers, as well as health and health-related professionals.

3. A *satisfactory solution* refers to the activity, program, or service which is viewed as capable of reducing the gap between what actually exists and what is deemed desirable or necessary.

4. The processes of *problem identification* and *solution determination* occur within the value and attitudinal frameworks and perspectives of those who participate in them. Furthermore, there is not a necessary isomorphism, i.e., one-to-one relationship, between the problem and its solution regarding either their intrinsic natures or the levels of social organization where they occur.

5. The assessment of *resource* is the key process in arriving at consensus about the relative priorities among unmet needs, since solutions to problems (which may be defined differently depending upon the value and attitudinal perspectives of the participants) require the expenditure or mobilization of resources.

6. Finally, the proper *focus* of need assessment should include all levels of social organization (the individual, the group or family, the organization or social network, the institutional system, the community, and society).

This is necessary since the natures of problems depend on the level of social organization where they are found and the natures of solutions depend on the level of social organization where actions or programs are carried out to meet the problems.*

JUSTIFICATION AND GOALS
FOR NEED STUDIES

The concepts of need identification and assessment are such that there is no set of generally agreed upon steps which, when carefully followed, lead one to a comprehensive assessment of needs. The reality is that planners and program administrators must decide what information will generate the most

*Reproduced by permission of the authors (see reference note *3*).

comprehensive identification and assessment of needs in a specific geographic service area, and what proportion of program resources should reasonably be allocated for this effort. Some of the relevant variables that merit careful consideration when planning an assessment of human service needs include:

1. Information

What assessment data are most relevant for the local program? How easily can the desired data be obtained? What is the potential accuracy and usefulness of the data?

2. Resources Available

What staff and fiscal resources are available to the assessment effort? What is the cost estimate of collecting (purchasing) these data? Will the expected benefits from the data outweigh their cost? Are these resources sufficient to obtain the desired information?

3. State of Program Development

Is the service system new or in early program planning stages? How wide is the range of services currently available? Is there a service system organizational network?

4. Community Attitudes

What is the community tolerance for surveys, community forums, and other approaches to assessment?

Planning human service programs for the future will require an approach to need identification that has clear sanctions and sufficient resources. Collaborative networks must be formed to act as regional information-gathering systems. These regional systems, probably organized at the multicounty level, should perform intensive field surveys and serve as a conduit through which appropriate information will be channeled to the community level. This concept is supported by Demone and Harshbarger's (1974) critical view that the federal government's typical response to pressing or newly emergent human service problems is the addition of new categorical programs. This tendency encourages redundancy, promotes needless expenditure of limited resources, and maintains institutional separatism, which ultimately results in programs that are out of phase with social happenings and problems. Demone and Harshbarger (1974) state: "A comprehensive network that is effective must emerge from within existing organizational relationships . . . the critical issue is the capacity to change, to be responsive to the environment, and not to respond merely in additive ways [pp. 16,19]."

The National Health Planning and Resources Development Act of 1974 (Public Law 93-641) seems a step in the direction of increased systemic integration and collaboration. This legislation dictates that any new health services must be coordinated and integrated with all other existing health services; all applications for new funds must document that the applicant has initiated such arrangements. Specifically, the emphasis of the act is twofold: the assurance of appropriate use of existing services, and the integration of proposed services with those already in existence. Need identification and assessment are critical missing supports for both of these objectives.

The difficulty in conceptualizing need assessment at least partially accounts for the sparse attention this area of planning has received. That there is growing governmental awareness of the necessity for systematic need assessment is, in part, a response to an increasing consumer cry for action. This awareness is reflected in the sections of the Community Mental Health Centers Amendments of 1975 (Public Law 94-63), which, for example, mandate that at least 2% of Community Mental Health Centers (CMHC) operating expenses be allocated for program evaluation (Windle & Ochberg, 1975). Within this framework, the CMHC legislation specifically states that it is encumbent upon program evaluators and administrators to maintain an ongoing dialogue with service-area residents (a) to assure that community needs are being met, and (b) to identify and assess unmet needs. The combined potential impact of Public Laws 93-641 and 94-63 is that program evaluation and need certification must be coordinated within a regional health planning format and auspice. The resulting nationwide data collection network will provide information for the secretary of Health, Education, and Welfare to use in more rational policy analysis, evaluation, and program planning.

SOME IMPORTANT ISSUES RELATED TO NEED IDENTIFICATION

There are several issues that should be considered prior to undertaking an assessment of needs. The first is that even though assessment information may frequently include objective data, planning necessarily remains a human and value-based process. All human service programs have a heterogeneous group of stakeholders. These include elected representatives to local and state governments and Congress; the program funders, including both governmental, private philanthropic, and third party payers; administrative and service personnel; other community service providers; community residents; and service recipients. These stakeholders not only represent diverse vested interests and often disparate values, but *also maintain conflicting expectations* based on their particular interests and values. As a result, the most systematic and objective assessment information must ultimately be filtered through and influenced by the perspectives of those charged with the responsibility of translating that information into priorities and program goals. Consequently the task of translating assessment information about community needs into relevant service programs, is not a simple, orderly process, but rather a political task that entails complex decision making involving skills in negotiation and conciliation. It is essential, then, that the program planning process provide a forum for these different perspectives, and that this forum prevent premature domination by particularly vocal viewpoints to the exclusion of others.

Second, beyond the perspectives of various stakeholders and their influence on the interpretation of data collected, the general characteristics of human service needs add yet another dimension of complexity to need identification. Social and health needs are both diffuse and interrelated. Such needs are rarely identified specifically enough to permit agencies to determine those that are primary and those that are secondary relative to their unique organizational responsibility and resources. As a result, it is difficult to establish priorities rationally and to determine which needs can be met most effectively by which agencies.

Third, the dynamic nature of human service needs further complicates the need identification process. Because the communities in which we live are in a state of almost perpetual transition, the needs that give rise to the original objectives and program structure of an agency may no longer exist or be of the same magnitude when the program is finally implemented. This fact alone is sufficient rationale for an ongoing program of community need identification that is embedded in an ongoing formal planning process.

And, fourth, it is useful to keep in mind that the translation of identified community needs into programs will also be influenced by a number of additional factors not addressed in community-oriented need identification efforts. These factors include such diverse considerations as the capabilities and interests of staff and the availability of both appropriate service technology and adequate financing.

In summary, as one considers the results obtained from the various techniques of need identification, the following must be kept in mind:

1. Needs are relative to the perceiver and are based on values, culture, past history, and experiences of the individual and the community.
2. Human social-service needs are not singular, easily identifiable entities, but are diffuse and interrelated.
3. Communities and their needs are dynamic and in a state of constant flux.
4. The process of translating human service needs into community programs is influenced by characteristics of human resources, availability of adequate technology, and financing considerations.

CONVERGENT ANALYSIS

In a comprehensive need assessment effort *convergent analysis* may be conceptualized as the second of the two operational stages, the first one being need *identification*.

Convergent analysis is a methodological framework in which information relative to human service needs may be identified, defined, evaluated, and given priority in a progressive manner. The tasks to be completed in this final analytical stage are synthesis and integration of all collected information from a variety of data collection methods.

Convergent analysis usually begins with data internal to the service system, such as legal and fundor mandates, historical trends relevant to service delivery, and client utilization information. Other forces feeding into the initial phase of convergent analysis are the orientation, training and interests of administrators and providers, and the perspectives of advisory and policy board members. The process then integrates information assembled about a specified social area or target community via a network of techniques designed to capture a wide range of perceptions about conditions in the community.

Convergent analysis is used here in the sense that the information gathered from a range of need assessment methods, deployed both systematically and sequentially, will yield a reasonably accurate identification of community needs and an assessment of the relative priorities among the needs identified. "Convergent" in this context has several meanings. First, there is a convergence of different information coming from divergent sources (e.g., citizens, consumers, service providers, and political leaders). Second, there is a convergence of different assessment strategies, each with some overlapping, yet unique, bits of information. Third, convergent also describes the cumulative nature of an ideal assessment procedure viewed across time. Information obtained at different (though sequential) points in time (information from a wide range of data collection methods and perspectives) are convergent to the extent that they can be pooled in an ongoing fashion to yield an accurate depiction of human service needs of a particular social area. All three of the above concepts of convergence analysis imply that, with each stepwise increment of information, one more clearly approximates a valid description of the social area under study. In other words, convergent analysis provides a dynamic process for reaching a convergent and discriminant validation of the needs in a social area (Campbell & Fiske, 1959). Finally, the last meaning of convergence in our formulation is to be found in the range of organizational levels through which assessment information must be channeled. Information from both state and national perspectives "converge" on service program networks at the community level. When integrated with regionally and locally generated "need" data, this information allows for more systematic program planning and development.

In summary, a convergent analysis of needs is based on a stepwise, multilevel, multitechnique assessment strategy. Each technique (formal and informal surveys, sociodemographic statistical analyses, and community forums, for example) is targeted at an appropriate informant group (citizens, consumers, professionals in helping professions, educators, police, physicians, clergy, and political leaders). The result of a convergent analysis is an integrated and maximally validated description of the needs in a social area that provides input into a rational planning process.

BASIC PURPOSES OF
NEED IDENTIFICATION AND ASSESSMENT

Assessment provides one important informational input to a much broader *planning process* that leads to (a) the selection of and priority setting among problems and target populations to be addressed; (b) the selection and operationalization of specific community program activities; and (c) the evaluation of these program activities. Assessment information helps to assure that there will be additional inputs to prevent sole reliance on professional formulations of service needs and/or to prevent overriding influence by the most vocal or powerful community groups in program planning.

Assessment also has an important role in established community programs. In such agencies, assessment can provide a continuing examination of the relevance of existing service activities to changing human service needs and priorities.

Assessment strategies are varied, and selection of a particular strategy is dependent upon the type of information sought. Assessment efforts may study the distribution of social problems in a population and the factors that influence the distribution. In the mental health field, for example, some assessment studies attempt to relate certain social or health characteristics of a population to various rates of mental disorder; or, studies may focus upon the relation between ecological characteristics of a social area and the rates of mental disorder (Bloom, 1975). Other studies employ field survey strategies in order to identify mental health problems and service needs more specifically (Warheit, Bell, & Schwab, 1974).

Most field survey efforts are designed to assess the prevalence and incidence of those who already suffer from particular disorders and to identify those subpopulations having the highest risk of experiencing specific mental health problems within a social area. When it is possible to identify populations at risk, such findings are very important in planning for services, especially preventive ones. In addition to collecting information about the range of social and health problems in a community and specification of populations at risk, program planners must also identify cultural and linguistic barriers or other features of the service system that impede effective delivery of services—such as awareness, acceptability, accessibility, and availability of services.

Beyond describing needs, assessment is also useful in identifying those factors within the human service network which aid or impede attempts to meet those needs. First, assessment may be used to specify current and/or potential resources that can be channeled or reallocated to respond to unmet needs. Second, an assessment effort is useful in gaining an understanding of the political and social value system underlying a particular social area. These values often determine what needs are identified and also tend to determine which needs receive priority in the program planning process. Finally, analysis of assessment data may suggest new interventions and may ultimately be helpful in uncovering the etiology of certain conditions. Knowledge about social, environmental, and biologic etiology will eventually lead to more effective preventive programs (Blum, 1974; Broskowski & Baker, 1974).

ASSESSMENT CONTRASTED WITH PROGRAM EVALUATION

Care must be taken not to confuse community need assessment with evaluation. Both program evaluation and need assessment are parts of a larger program planning–implementation–development cycle, but need assessment is an environmental monitoring system. As an environmental monitoring system, it is a conceptually separate and operationally different process when compared to and contrasted with program evaluation.

Nguyen *et al.* (*3*) have summarized the interrelationship between program evaluation and need assessment:

Attkisson and Broskowski [cf. Chapter 1] have defined program evaluation as:

1. The process of making reasonable judgments about program effort, effectiveness, efficiency, and adequacy;

2. Based on systematic data collection and analysis;

3. Designed for use in program management, external accountability, and future planning;

4. With special focus on accessibility, acceptability, awareness, availability, comprehensiveness, continuity, integration, and cost of services.

Need assessment, by contrast, is:

1. An environmental monitoring system that is . . .

2. Designed to measure and make judgments about program relevance, adequacy, and appropriateness;

3. Based on systematic collection and analysis of information . .

4. Regarding the needs for health and human services,

5. As filtered through multiple levels of societal perspectives, and

6. As generated through multiple measurement approaches.

In other words, need assessment studies monitor social area characteristics and population characteristics which influence need, want, and demand for human services. These factors include the value systems and ethno-cultural backgrounds indigenous to the population being served. Especially important in this regard are the analysis of cultural, psychological, physical, environmental, and linguistic barriers to appropriate service utilization. Need assessment analyses therefore must focus on issues related to population characteristics, environmental characteristics, individual citizen need states, as well as *five other critical issues* related to the overall effectiveness and appropriateness of the total service delivery system [cf. Chapter 1]

1. *Availability* of services relative to population characteristics and need states of the social area;

2. *Accessibility* of services relative to population need states, environmental characteristics, and distribution of service resources;

3. *Awareness* of service opportunities among the residents of the social area;

4. *Level of service integration* and *continuity of services* vis-à-vis multi-problem individuals and the availability of service network linkages;

5. *Level of resources and distribution of available resources* vis-à-vis need states in the social area.

Put differently, need assessment data provide a fundamental navigational system for program planning and program modification based on continuous assessment of changing community needs. Without need assessment input, health and human service programs stand little chance to "weather the storms" resulting from the pressures of vested interests, bureaucracy, and professionally defined needs.

Information from program evaluation, on the other hand, is an internal monitoring system that assesses the achievement of the programs in terms of goals and mandates. Without input from program evaluation, health and human service programs will continue to be managed without benefit of critical information about program effort, efficiency, and effectiveness. . . .

Within health and human service programs, there must be a clear and open interface between the need assessment data collection and analysis system and the program evaluation data collection and analysis system. This interface requires specific collaboration and integration of these two program planning systems to avoid redundant activity, particularly in areas where there is a clear overlap in data collection and analysis. The overlapping responsibility is particularly clear in the analyses of:

1. Service acceptability,

2. Service accessibility,

3. Demand for specific services,

4. Continuity of services,

5. Comprehensiveness of services,

6. Pattern of service utilization,

7. Resource availability, and

8. Resource utilization.

Program evaluation and need assessement are, consequently, significantly interdependent processes. Each process consumes information from the other and each provides an information base that is essential for program planning. Planners need both sets of information and the work of planners will be deficient unless information about needs *and* program evaluation data are *simultaneously* available.*

WHEN TO DO A NEED IDENTIFICATION

Considerable attention must be given by human service programs to clarification and specification of the purposes and potential uses of a proposed assessment effort. Since the process requires a substantial expenditure of re-

*Reproduced by permission of the authors (see reference note 3).

sources, it should primarily be considered when there is both an opportunity and a commitment either for planning new services or for restructuring existing ones on the basis of needs that may be identified. If there is no commitment to planning or restructuring programs in accordance with those needs identified, no useful purpose is served by an assessment effort. At best, failure to use need assessment information in planning represents a waste of resources and, at worst, certain assessment procedures (such as the "community forum") may serve to heighten community expectations that needs identified will be addressed in actual service or preventive operations.

AN OVERVIEW OF NEED IDENTIFICATION AND ASSESSMENT METHODOLOGIES

A comprehensive, convergent analysis of human service needs requires utilization of information resources that exist in (or can be obtained from) national, regional, state, and community depositories. At the local level each human service agency has unique informational needs that logically can be identified through local effort. Beyond this, however, there is a large body of information held in common by, and/or is mutually relevant to, a number of agencies comprising the human services network within a given social area. Where informational requirements overlap, a cost–efficient and effective need assessment effort can only be undertaken and/or coordinated at the regional planning level.

As already noted, the framework for this level of planning has been established by the passage of Public Law 93-641, the National Health Planning and Resources Development Act. Within each planning region, a need assessment strategy would allow for consolidation of effort and for economic expenditure of resources aimed at supporting the need assessment plan that has widest relevance for human service agencies in that particular region. This ideal strategy could allow for (a) development of depositories for health and social indicator data as well as a method for the timely dissemination of these data in a form relevant and responsive to the informational requirements of the network of human service agencies and providers; (b) design and implementation of an ongoing series of "time limited" field surveys to measure the extent and degree of particular human service needs in the region; (c) assessment of existing service resources relative to their strengths, weaknesses, and capacities to provide service; (d) establishment of a clearinghouse of information about the human service needs in the area; and (e) coordination and support of community-based need assessment efforts within specific human service programs.

The various approaches to need assessment presented in this chapter may be undertaken at any planning level: community, regional, state, and more rarely, national. The auspices for any particular need assessment will vary accordingly. Nevertheless, mounting effective need assessment programs will require each regional health planning body to develop a master strategy which will coordinate assessment and dissemination of assessment information throughout the region.

A need assessment program that is organized at the regional planning level affords a number of advantages. First, a single regional assessment effort instead of numerous community efforts could guarantee a substantial conservation of financial and human resources. Tremendous duplication of effort and greatly exaggerated cost could ensue if each social agency in a given area were to undertake a unilateral assessment of community needs. Second, an ongoing regional assessment effort could also share successful models that are practical to employ on a smaller scale and that would be more appropriately undertaken at the community agency level. Third, the regional assessment activity could provide readily available, decision-relevant data to community-based programs on a regular, planned basis. And fourth, need assessment conducted under regional auspices would be less influenced by local political pressure, and in that way, could serve as a vehicle for more "objective" data than that which could be obtained at the agency level.

Without the integrative capacity, production capacity, and economic advantages of this regional approach to need assessment, it is doubtful that individual community-based programs will be able to conduct assessment programs that can adequately provide the necessary information. This state of affairs would not only be a serious blow to the development of flexible, responsive human service networks but also would seriously effect the relevance of specific agencies and services.

Several constraints limit the depth and scope of need assessment efforts undertaken by community-based agencies. First, the financial base for program planning and development may be too sparse to support an extensive assessment effort. Second, the time-frame in which an assessment activity is performed may limit the scope of its findings. Many, if not most, need assessments undertaken by community-based agencies are carried out in a relatively short period of time to meet, for example, governmental grant deadlines. These efforts tend to monopolize agency assessment lines. Third, internal pressure from highly vocal consumer groups often requires that immediate action be taken on a human service problem. In such circumstances, a comprehensive, time-consuming assessment effort is neither feasible nor appropriate. In these instances, where accessibility to time and/or money is limited, need assessment plans at the agency level may still be implemented to provide useful information. Excellent examples of such an effort are provided by Beigel, Hunter, Tamerin, Chapin, and Lowery (1974) and Beigel, McCabe, Tamerin, Lowery, Chapin, and Hunter (1974).

Regardless of the level at which need assessment is undertaken (local, regional, or state) there are eight need identification and assessment approaches that can provide the basis for a convergent analysis of human service needs. Each approach can be described as serving one or more information gathering functions: (*a*) *compilation* of information which is available but not yet disseminated within the boundaries of the social system, (b) *development of new information*, and (c) *integration* of all relevant information that is developed from within the system or gathered from outside the system's boundaries. One of the eight approaches performs all three informational functions, three serve two functions, and four represent only one function. The various approaches to need assessment, where the information may be obtained, how the data are formulated, and where "need" information is best utilized in the planning and development process, are summarized in Table 9.1. Table 9.1 is developed from the perspective of the community-based human service program, and assumes that regional health planning bodies will soon join the local community agency in the need assessment data collection, analysis, and dissemination process.

A need assessment approach that collects information from already existing sources and subsequently organizes it in some coherent fashion illustrates a data *compilation* function. Frequently the required information exists outside the boundaries of the community-based program, for example, the National Clearinghouses of Drug Abuse Information, Mental Health Information, and Alcohol Information. Assessment approaches may also *develop* or collect new information. Here, original information bearing on the needs of a particular community is generated. Finally, a technique is classified as an *integrator* of information when data from two or more sources are organized to effect a more valid description of human service needs than is possible when information is drawn from a single source. It is in the combination of all three informational functions (compilation, development, and integration) that a convergent analysis of human service needs is achieved.

There are several important methods that can be employed to obtain information about human service needs. This section provides an outline of the various approaches including (a) a brief definition for each strategy, (b) the time at which utilization of a particular technique is appropriate, and (c) the source(s) from which data can be obtained. Each method provides a different perspective on needs. A more lengthy discussion of each technique follows in the final major sections of this chapter.

SOCIAL AND HEALTH INDICATOR ANALYSIS

The Social and Health Indicator approach to need identification consists of compiling and making inferences of need from descriptive statistics found in public records and reports. It is based on the assumption that particular descriptors such as proximity to the urban core and socioeconomic status, are viable indicators of human service needs (Bloom, 1975; Siegel, Attkisson, & Cohn, 1977). The viability of particular indicators depends upon three factors: (a) the validity and reliability of the descriptive information, (b) the logical and statistical appropriateness of procedures used to derive the social and health indicators for the community (Schulberg & Wechsler, 1967), and (c) the

TABLE 9.1
Need Identification and Assessment Methods

Methods and method families		Perspective being represented	Optimal sponsor	Source of information	Characteristics and technical considerations regarding the use of each method	Measurement expertise needed	Time and resources needed
					Information processing function		
Indicator approaches	1. Social and health indicator analyses	Government and private agencies	Local, state, regional or federal planners	Public archives, planning agencies	Compilation of existing data	Moderate to high	Moderate to extensive
	2. Demands for services	Service agencies and consumers	Community agencies along with above	Information systems	Compilation	Moderate	Moderate
Social area survey approaches	3. Analysis of service providers and resources	Planners	Local and regional planners	Local records and surveys	Compilation and development of new data	Low	Moderate
	4. Citizen surveys	Private citizens	Regional, state or federal planners	Face-to-face, telephone, or mailed surveys	Development of new data	High	Extensive
	5. Community forums	Private citizens and consumers	Community agencies	Public meetings	Integration of existing and new data	Low	Moderate
Community group approaches	6. Nominal group techniques	Planners, service providers, citizens	All levels	Specific projects	Development of new data	Moderate	Minimal
	7. Delphi technique	Planners, service providers, experts	All levels	Specific projects	Development and integration	Moderate	Moderate
	8. Community impressions	Citizens, key informants, consumers, providers	Community agencies, regional planners	Specific projects	Development, compilation, and integration	Moderate	Minimal

228

subjective sense or feel for the given community which is developed through these sources of information about the community.

The Social and Health Indicator approach is invaluable as an initial descriptive approach to understanding a given social area (Sheldon & Parke, 1975). Social indicator approaches range from the very simplistic designs using one or two indicators, such as census data on income, housing or a population density index, to very complex designs that consist of many variables requiring the use of complex statistical procedures such as cluster or factor analysis (Bloom, 1975).

SOCIAL AREA SURVEYS

1. *Demands for Services*

This approach to need identification includes compilation of existing information and integration of those sources of information. Here the aim is to review the various human service providers' (both individual and agency) past and current services rendered patterns and requests for service by citizens in an attempt to understand the number and types of human services demanded in a particular community. These data may be secured through structured interviews with appropriate staff and board members, extrapolations from past and current clinical records and management information systems, or analysis of agency charters, licenses, funding applications, contracts, and grants. Analysis can also identify current commitments, mandates, policies, and goal statements within the human service system. Appropriate target groups include agency management, agency staff and board members, funding organizations, and citizen advocacy groups.

2. *Analysis of Service Resources*

This need assessment device involves a descriptive enumeration of the human service agencies and individual providers within a community. It can best be classified as a compilation and integration of information that exists at the agency level. This integration may take the form of a human services directory for a particular community. Important to the process of identifying existing service resources is the assessment of whether current efforts are efficiently and effectively focused on known needs.

3. *Citizen Surveys*

Here the assessment effort is concerned with eliciting differing perspectives on the nature and magnitude of human service needs from community residents. The main function of this technique is the development of new information through stratified random sampling of the community residents. This technique is most appropriately used to supplement generalized and indirect assessments, such as social and health indicator analyses, with the more personal perspective of community residents. This assessment approach is covered in detail in Chapter 10.

ASCERTAINING COMMUNITY VIEWS
THROUGH COMMUNITY GROUP APPROACHES

1. *Community Forum*

This approach consists of an open meeting to which all members of a community are invited and at which all participants are urged to present their views regarding the human service needs of a particular social area. Although this information is often used to validate previously existing data, the technique itself is concerned with generating new information only; that is, obtaining community residents' input on a particular issue or issues.

2. *Nominal Group Approach*

The nominal group approach is principally a noninteractive workshop designed to maximize creativity and productivity and to minimize the argumentative style of problem-solving and competitive discussion. Within this format, a *selected group of community residents* are invited to share their views regarding community needs or to identify barriers to relevant, effective human service delivery in a social area. The nominal group approach is most appropriately used as a method for obtaining citizen and consumer input into the need assessment and program planning process.

3. *Delphi Approach*

This approach to need identification includes the development of a questionnaire, which is distributed to a panel of resource persons and/or a select group of community residents whose opinions on a particular issue or issues are highly valued. From their responses, a perspective can be derived regarding human service needs. This technique is quite useful and most appropriate when respondents have a minimal amount of time available for an identification effort. The Delphi process of obtaining individual opinions on a particular issue is best classified as development of new information.

4. *Community Impressions Approach*

There are three steps to this assessment procedure. First, a small but representative group of individuals is interviewed about their views of human service needs. Second, this information is then integrated with existing data taken from public records and other assessment efforts to yield, hopefully, a richer understanding of the community needs. Third, the resulting community portrait is then validated and/or revised according to information gained from various groups in the community through the community forum process.

This approach serves as an information integrator and validator. It employs data from three different assessment efforts, and at the same time provides new information in the form of community impressions. The community impressions approach is an economical and necessary step on the path to a creative convergence of need assessment information gained from the various other need assessment approaches.

SOCIAL AND HEALTH INDICATOR ANALYSIS

This approach consumes preexisting, publically available information (census data, public health data, and criminal justice data, for example) and integrates this information in an attempt to gain a clear and parsimonious description of a social area. It does not produce new information. Rather, it analyzes, integrates, and disseminates already existing information. Although the task sounds simple, most social and health indicator analyses are complex, expensive and time-consuming.

Chapter 10 provides a more detailed and systematic approach to social and health indicator analysis. However, before moving on to the approaches to be considered in more detail in this chapter, several primary sources of social and health indicator data are presented:

1. Federations of social and/or health agencies, (such as United Way of Metropolitan Boston or the United Bay Area Crusade in San Francisco) usually have, or have access to, statistical information relevant to need assessment.

2. City planning departments have detailed information on housing characteristics, income, and other economic data by census tracts as well as other descriptive information about communities. Some also undertake population projection studies that may be quite useful for long-range human service planning.

3. State and frequently local health departments have epidemiologic or disease surveillance units and are a resource for a wide range of community health data. Health departments may also have compilations of health indicies such as various mortality rates or incidence or prevalence rates for certain diseases.

4. State and local mental health associations may be of assistance in locating appropriate indicators and in identifying mental health practitioners in the community. They can also provide some sense of state and local human service politics.

5. Comprehensive health planning agencies, funded under Public Law 89-749, have engaged in extensive data collection in order to prepare areawide health plans. They have also been required to identify "medically underserved" populations within their planning areas. Frequently, they combine information from community forums and public hearings with social and health indices in planning reports. The depth and perspective of community information in areas where these agencies exist should not be overlooked by local human service programs. The passage of Public Law 93-641, as noted, has radically changed the administration of health programs in the United States. It basically supercedes comprehensive health planning, Public Law 89-749, regional medical programs, Hill–Burton construction and experimental health service delivery authorities. However, funds for these existing

programs will be authorized until the new health systems agencies, required by Public Law 93-641, can be established. Public Law 93-641 requires health planning, certification of need, review of medical facilities' master plans, and review of institutional services—all through a required state-level administrative program. The program will be established on a state by state basis with intrastate health service areas (and regional health planning agencies—"Health System Agencies") designated by state governors subject to review and revision by the secretary of Health, Education, and Welfare. The governing bodies of health system agencies will have 10–30 members and will consist of a majority of consumers. The health system agencies will (a) develop health services plans and annual implementation plans, (b) review institutional services, and (c) make grants to develop health programs or projects (excluding construction of facilities). Recent articles have described the potential impacts of Public Law 93-641 on specific categorical programs such as mental health services and planning (Milstein, 1976).

6. Universities may be currently involved in, or have knowledge of, relevant community studies. Sociology and political science departments should be most helpful in identifying indices of social and family disorganization. Faculty members with interests in social psychology, human ecology, demography, criminology, public health, social welfare, and other related fields may prove to be valuable resources in locating existing studies and normative data, or as consultants in the design of a local program's assessment strategy. Some potential may exist to interest students in selected aspects of the assessment process.

7. Staff members of both state and federal funding agencies are frequently overlooked as a potential source of help both as consultants to the design of an assessment effort and for suggestions on the location or usefulness of specific indicators.

8. There are a number of publications that are useful in attempting to interpret local indicators since they provide normative data against which comparisons can be made. The Division of Biometry and Epidemiology of the National Institute of Mental Health (NIMH) publishes a "Mental Health Statistical Note" series covering a wide range of topics that may be of interest to local human service programs. Many issues present data gleaned from an analysis of the annual Inventory of Federally Funded Community Mental Health Centers that is conducted by NIMH in cooperation with state mental health authorities. The Department of Health, Education, and Welfare supports three additional clearinghouses, including the National Clearinghouse for Drug Abuse Information, the National Clearinghouse for Mental Health Information, and the National Clearinghouse for Alcohol Information (Human Interaction Research Institute, 1975). All three provide free computer literature searches in their areas of specialization as well as a broad information dissemination program. Also, the NIMH-developed Mental Health Demographic Profile System is an invaluable

resource for data derived primarily from the U. S. Census (Goldsmith, Unger, Rosen, Shambaugh, & Windle, 1975; Windle, Rosen, Goldsmith, & Shambaugh, 1975).

SOCIAL AREA SURVEY APPROACHES TO NEED IDENTIFICATION

One of the first steps in a convergent analysis of human service needs is to survey existing community service resources. Surveys of social and health agencies provide information about major problems existing in a community, about help-seeking behaviors in a community, about service resources and gaps in these resources, and about existing outreach and preventive efforts in a community.

There are three main types of information that a survey of practitioners and agencies can provide. They are (a) the analysis of *demands* for service placed upon agencies and private practitioners; (b) the specification, by type, of the various human services resources in a designated social area and their corresponding capacity to respond to human service problems; and (c) a description of the pattern and the extent of interrelationships among human service resources in the community.

In analyzing demands for service, the objective is to understand the magnitude and types of requests for human services. When assessing human service resources, however, planners are concerned with comprehending the capacity of the service systems to respond to those requests and with the quality of such responses. In delineating the interagency relationships in a particular community, we hope to clarify the extent and kind of collaborative efforts that characterize the human service network.

NEED IDENTIFICATION THROUGH ANALYSIS OF DEMANDS FOR SERVICE

This approach requires a survey of the entire human services network within a community. The typical survey seeks information not only from the primary health service agencies or institutions within a community but also from other community agencies which interface with and provide a range of supporting and interlocking services to the primary health care network. Many agencies can potentially be included: mental health clinics and centers, hospitals (including psychiatric and general hospitals), drug and alcohol treatment and related service programs, private practitioners, family service programs, public health departments, churches, probation and family courts, and other social and health organizations or service providers.

Although analysis of demand for services is an important element of a broader assessment strategy, there are a few caveats related to using this approach exclusively in assessing service needs (Feldstein, 1973; Schaefer, 1975). Even though a service is well utilized, it does not necessarily follow that this service is addressing a high-priority need in the community. A high utilization rate may possibly be due to any of the following: (*a*) the service is well publicized; (*b*) it is inexpensive; (*c*) it is one of the only services available in the community; (*d*) the various professionals in the community are unaware of alternative services; and/or (*e*) more pejoratively, high utilization may reflect professional preferences for particular service modalities. Reciprocally, services addressing high-priority problems may be underutilized because they are unpublicized, because client referral procedures are too cumbersome, or because they have marginal relevance to professional investments. In addition, high service utilization rates may signal the need for development of preventive programs in a particular service area. And, finally, there are likely to be important differences between those who seek or receive care and those who do not. Many "needers" are not utilizers and some utilizers are, relatively speaking, "non-needers." These caveats should be carefully considered as indicators of the hazards involved in extrapolating from populations receiving services to the population at large.

In analyzing demands for services it may be possible to secure satisfactory response from a fairly brief, well-designed, mailed questionnaire. A followup letter or phone call to nonrespondents is usually necessary to increase the response rate. A method for substantially increasing the number of returns from mailed questionnaires has been described by Robin (1965). It involves a minimum of two and a maximum of five contacts with the potential respondent. The first contact is a prequestionnaire letter which, if possible, should be written on letterhead and cosigned by someone who represents broadly recognized authority and who is able to validate the importance of the survey and the appropriateness of the respondent's participation. Optimally, the letter must (*a*) request individual participation; (*b*) explain the assessment methodology, its importance, and possible applications; (*c*) inform the respondent that he or she will soon receive an assessment questionnaire; and finally (*d*) describe procedures for safeguarding confidentiality in handling all information. The second contact consists of a cover letter and the questionnaire. Contacts three to five consist of a series of followup strategies, should these be necessary. The reader is referred to Robin's article for further explanation of this survey strategy (Robin, 1965).

When possible, utilization surveys should be conducted in a systematic site visit format. Personal interviews with through-the-mail followups almost always produce greater reliability and validity of survey results.

ANALYSIS OF EXISTING SERVICE RESOURCES

Beyond assessing demands for human services it is also important for every community to identify and assess its human service resources. A count of resources by type and capacity allows human service program planners to identify gaps and duplications among existing services. This knowledge of existing resources may then be contrasted with information derived from other assessment strategies relative to estimates of met and unmet needs. Usually a single survey can produce information about both (*a*) demands for services in the community, and (*b*) existing service resources.

The specific content and format of social and health agency surveys must vary from community to community to the extent that agencies in a given social area differ in structure and service objectives. Nevertheless there are a number of general interest areas that are applicable to most agencies when conducting this type of survey:

1. Range of human services provided
2. Client entry policies, conditions of eligibility for service, including age, sex, financial criteria, geographic restrictions, and particular focal or target population groups
3. Personnel characteristics and personnel development efforts
   a. Service providers by training and credentials
   b. Provider training and continuing education opportunities
   c. Treatment modalities provided
   d. Number of individuals providing various services
   e. Average client load per staff member
4. Financial characteristics
   a. Charge for services—fee schedule, eligibility for third party reimbursement, sliding scale provisions
   b. Agency support—public or private, fees and other sources of funding categorized as percentage of total support budget
5. Accessibility, availability, and awareness of services
   a. Location of facility—proximity to target populations and proximity to public transportation
   b. Intake procedure—amount of information required, publicity for the available services, hours when services are provided, comfort and acceptability of the facility to clients, and availability of child-care when necessary
6. Referrals (demand)
   a. Number within a standardized time frame
   b. Source categorized by service type or status of referring agent
   c. Reasons (symptoms, problem areas)
   d. Other characteristics such as geographic locale of referring agents, geographic origin of clients who are referred, and temporal patterns of referrals
7. Accepted for service
   a. Number over a specified time period
   b. Diagnosis or other nomenclature for designated problems
   c. Sociodemographic characteristics of clients—age, race, sex, census tract, socioeconomic status
   d. Those refused service and reasons for refusal
8. Waiting list
   a. Number of persons on waiting list
   b. Reasons for waiting list
   c. Symptoms or problem areas of individuals placed on waiting lists
   d. Other characteristics, such as average time on waiting list and proportion of those placed on waiting list who do not eventually receive service

9. Services provided
    a. Human service problem areas thought to be of highest priority as well as services that are in increasing demand
    b. Range of actual services provided categorized by units of service
    c. List of referral resources that interface the agency
10. Referrals initiated
    a. Frequency of referrals made (listed across the range of agencies within the social area)
    b. Problems in making referrals—including such factors as transportation, financial, language, and cultural barriers.

IDENTIFICATION OF NEED THROUGH ANALYSIS OF INTERAGENCY RELATIONSHIPS— SOME FURTHER THOUGHTS

An analysis of the interagency relationships including the extent of collaboration among human service resources in a community is thought to be important in a comprehensive approach to need assessment. Such exploration will (a) uncover underutilized resources; (b) give an indication of how these resources are perceived and utilized by peer agencies; (c) determine the extent to which service continuity exists, the degree of service duplication, and the extent to which there is inadequate integration within the human service network; and (d) identify those agencies or providers who maintain collaborative ties and who might work well in a collective effort. Suggestions for restructuring or in other ways improving services may result. This type of inquiry is probably best accomplished by site visits conducted by skilled interviewers with appropriate credentials.

The main advantages of assessing need through analysis of interagency relationships are the relatively low cost of collecting and analyzing the information and the ready availability of such information. In addition, this type of survey, which tends to increase communication between human service agencies and providers, often leads to a greater sensitivity to the needs of community residents and as a result to a more adequate integration of human services. This strategy also allows for a general inventory of community resources—information that is useful when integrating need assessment information into program planning. One particularly useful subsidiary benefit of human services resource identification is the publication and distribution of a human services information directory complete with referral procedures applicable to the network of human service providers.

The two main disadvantages to this type of need identification involve, first, the difficulty in obtaining reliable data and second, drawing conclusions about a population solely on the basis of service utilization. One must proceed with caution when attempting to estimate the needs of an entire community on the basis of information obtained from an analysis of information about a sample of persons receiving services from the community's public and private care providers. In the mental health field, for example, there is a great deal of research which suggests that there is a wide gulf between the mental health needs of a community as determined by field prevalence surveys and the number of persons receiving mental health care in the same community. Other research has shown that many residents of a community may not require new or additional mental health services, because they are receiving services from agencies or providers outside of the community. A systematic need identification and assessment program must always include data concerning (a) the extent to which identified needs are being met by resources within or outside the social area being studied, and (b) the appropriateness of reliance on external resources to meet social area needs.

CITIZEN SURVEYS: COMMUNITY RESIDENTS' PERSPECTIVES ON HUMAN SERVICE NEEDS

In this section, we describe three survey techniques that allow broader citizen and community participation in the identification of needs and the establishment of service priorities than those discussed to this point. Such surveys provide citizen perspectives on the nature and magnitude of service needs in the community. Either anonymous, through-the-mail, stratified random sampling or direct interview-based methods can be employed to assemble this type of information.

Through-the-mail surveys should include a random sample of people living within a geographically defined service area. The sample may be stratified by such variables as census tract, age, race, or economic status. Almost always, respondents in such surveys are anonymous.

The following types of information that were viewed as particularly relevant to mental health planning were included by Meier (2) in a survey of residents in Contra Costa County, California: (a) community problems in order of perceived importance; (b) sources of help perceived as available for particular problems; (c) mental health problems thought most important; (d) attitudes toward utilization of a public mental health program; (e) mental health services thought most important; (f) mental health problems experienced in their own families; (g) help received for these problems; (h) satisfaction obtained from mental health services received; and (i) nomination of providers from whom one would seek help for problems of drug abuse in children and adolescents.

In some social areas face-to-face interviews with citizens have produced a better response rate and more useful information than anonymous mailed surveys. Since most surveys of this type are not particularly complex, it may be possible, without undue difficulty, to train community volunteers as interviewers (Warheit et al., 1974). This use of community interviewers may have several secondary benefits, which include (a) involving a cadre of community people in the actual planning phase of a program; (b) educating both the interviewers and interviewees about existing or potential services; and (c) conducting the survey in an atmosphere of familiarity, which decreases interviewee's reluctance to provide survey information. Since any survey of community residents requires considerable energy and a significant amount of financial resources, a human service program should carefully contrast the advantages and disadvantages of community surveys with those of community forums as described in this chapter. An approach that combines some survey features with the methodology of a community forum will be described in a later section of this chapter.

Still another option worth consideration when planning a resident survey is the telephone approach, which yields a much higher rate of response than a mailed questionnaire. This may be a more viable technique for programs serving middle-income areas where more people have telephones than in low-income areas, although the bias of an increasing number of unlisted telephone numbers should not be overlooked. One study comparing advantages and disadvantages of mailing or telephoning a followup questionnaire on discharged hospital patients showed that approximately 85% of the patients and relatives completed the telephone interviews as compared with a 35% return of the mailed questionnaires. It was found that certain questions provoked markedly different responses when the type of interview was by mail rather than phone (Schwartz, 1973). We would expect that the differences in response to questions would not be as great when contrasting telephone with personal interviews as they would be when comparing telephone and mail techniques. Nevertheless, design characteristics of any type of survey determine to a great extent the response rate achieved with a survey strategy. Meier (2), for example, employed a mailed questionnaire survey format that was unusually successful—both in terms of response rate and results.

There are three primary advantages in using the survey approach to need identification. According to Warheit *et al.* (1974), carefully designed and conducted surveys provide the most scientifically valid and reliable information obtainable regarding citizen views of their service needs and utilization patterns. It is also the most direct method of obtaining data about the needs of persons in a community. Finally it is very flexible and can be designed in an extremely wide variety of ways to answer questions related to human service needs. The value of selective use of surveys to assess in depth the specific needs of known high-risk populations cannot be overemphasized.

Disadvantages of the survey method of need identification include the following: In comparison to other methods, it tends to be more expensive. Some respondents are reluctant to offer information about themselves or other family members. Finally, the data obtained are based on self-report and are not independently verified in the typical case. A more thorough description of community survey methodology is presented in Chapter 10.

ASCERTAINING COMMUNITY VIEWS
THROUGH GROUP APPROACHES

In addition to surveys, there are many different ways in which citizen and consumer views of human service needs can be ascertained. In this section, we describe four methods that are useful in undertaking a relatively quick and inexpensive assessment from the perspective of the community: (a) community forums, (b) workshops using the nominal group technique, (c) the Delphi technique, and (d) the community impressions approach.

When a human services network must conduct a community assessment rapidly, any one of the community group methods may be used independently; however, they are most usefully employed in conjunction with approaches described in previous sections of this chapter. Once surveys have been undertaken and social and health indicator analyses have been conducted, community group methods can be used to gain an additional perspective on the reliability or the interpretation of the previously collected information. The more formal data collection procedures do not capture all relevant information and the data that are collected by formal data collection approaches may not provide an up-to-date portrait of the human service system in a community.

The community group methods can also be invaluable in determining which need areas among those detected during the formal data gathering have highest priority in the community. Because of disparate values and perspectives, different interest groups in a community will view certain conditions as more important than others; they will also hold varying notions as to the distribution of needs and the most appropriate approaches to interventions.

Linking survey with community group approaches is the only reliable mechanism for achieving a convergent analysis of needs and priorities—an analysis on which planning decisions can be based.

COMMUNITY FORUMS AS A MEANS OF NEEDS ASSESSMENT

Any person living or working in a community is potentially an information resource on the sociological and psychological aspects of that community. Community residents either directly, through personal experience, or indirectly, through observation or study, form impressions about the human service needs in a social area. The perspectives of residents concerning the accessibility, availability, acceptability, and organization of services comprise indispensable clues about the human service needs of the community as a whole. It is unlikely that any one person has a comprehensive view of human service needs or that two people have the same view. Yet, each person's view portrays some potentially important aspect of the existing reality. In the process of integrating these various viewpoints, a useful, although impressionistic, picture of the human service needs in a community begins to emerge. The community forum represents a quick and effective method of eliciting this desired information.

A community forum is an open meeting for all members of a designated community. Its purpose is to provide a setting for members of a community to express their opinions about a particular issue—in this case the human service needs of the community. Forums resemble an old fashioned "town meeting," but can be more open and flexible. Any person attending is considered an important information resource and is encouraged to express his or her views. In general, forums last 3–4 hours and may include a wide range of activities: information exchange, communication of details about new programs or projects, introduction of various community members, and more general social interaction. The major function of the forum, however, is to elicit views from as many people as possible on a single issue. Although it is possible, the forum itself rarely involves decision making on the basis of views presented. At heart it is a means of problem identification and of obtaining citizen reaction to service efforts.

When planning a community forum it is important to keep the following in mind. The better the representation of the diverse elements in the community, the more credible the results. In order to achieve adequate representation, it is necessary to publicize the forum widely and to develop incentives for all invited individuals and groups. Publicity may be done through a number of channels: newspapers, posters in local stores, organizations, short announcements on radio and television stations, leafleting, or mass mailings. The forum organizers should confer with knowledgeable community leaders about the most effective means of communicating with the population of a social area. In general, it is best to use more than one mode of public communication to publicize the forum and, if possible, three or more. If there are other than English speaking groups within the community, publicity must be in *all* relevant languages. The publicity should consist of a concise, clear statement including: place, date, time, purpose, organizers, and leaders. Some publicity about the forum should be conducted several weeks prior to the forum, but the most extensive effort should occur 1 week and then 2 days before the forum.

A community forum should not be implemented without major input from community members. Answers to questions such as how best to publicize the forum, where and when to hold it, as well as how to conduct it can best be answered by those who are well acquainted with the community. For example, some buildings in the community may be regarded as neutral territory, whereas others may be seen as nonneutral. Preferably, the forum should be chaired by a member of the community who is respected by most if not all of the diverse groups within the community. Unless special techniques, such as the nominal group technique (described in the next section) are to be used, the meeting should also be conducted by community members. Those from the group or agency initiating the forum should have an opportunity to describe to the participants the objectives of the forum and the proposed use of the informational products of the forum. They should not, however, feel the need to control the meeting, as efforts to control may inhibit the participation of certain community members.

One of the greatest difficulties with the community forum is providing those who come with an opportunity to speak and otherwise participate. In some cases individuals may have "too much" to say from the perspective of the time allotted for the forum and the number of attendees. One of the most successful ways of avoiding the situation in which a small number of people dominate an open discussion is to develop certain participatory rules for the meeting and to enforce them. For example, no person should be allowed to speak for longer than 3 minutes, and those who have not spoken should have priority over those who have already spoken. A person should be assigned as moderator and the group's permission should be asked at the outset to allow the moderator to enforce the rules. In addition to the difficulty that some individuals may attempt to dominate the discussion, another problem may arise when individuals speak on unrelated topics. Rather than having the moderator or chairperson interrupt participants when they are speaking on seemingly unrelated subjects one should build preventive measures into the forum format. For example, from time to time the moderator could reiterate its purpose and the main questions under discussion in order to emphasize the kinds of topics which are most appropriate for discussion. If some individuals fail to comply, it may be best to simply allow 3 minutes and proceed with the primary discussion.

Finally, success is in part determined by followup steps after the forum. Minimally, a letter should be sent to all attendees thanking them for their participation and informing them of the most immediate outcomes of the forum. Other followup steps are recommended. If the forum is successful, one will have identified specific individuals and groups who can assist in prospective work on the question of human service needs. Meetings with these persons should take place shortly after the forum so as to benefit from the momentum generated by the forum.

There are four advantages in using the community forum approach. First, community forums are, without question, quite economical in relation to other methods of need assessment. Planning for the meeting, including publicity, can be accomplished in a matter of weeks, and the forum itself may only last a few hours. The costs include the publicity, the time of any paid personnel in planning and implementing the forum and in analyzing the forum results, the time of a recording secretary, the provision of necessary transportation and child-care services to facilitate attendance of certain community members, and perhaps the rental of a meeting place. Many of these tasks may be accomplished by community volunteers.

Second, forums allow a wide range of individuals from the community to express their opinions about human service needs. Since the forum is open to all members of the community, a presentation of all important views can potentially be heard. Of particular importance is the fact that the views of those individuals who fall into the underserved or nonserved category in the community can be heard.

Third, the forum may serve as a catalyst for the initiation of plans and actions about the human service needs in the community. During the forum, those who have not previously considered the question of service needs may be stimulated to do so. As a result of interest generated by the forum, one could well expect the initiation of certain activities related to meeting human service needs.

Fourth, the forum provides those responsible for the need assessment with an opportunity not only to hear from many different elements of the community about unmet needs, but also to identify those participants and agencies most interested in doing something about them. These individuals can be invaluable in the convergent analysis phase of assessment and in developing plans to meet the needs identified.

There are also four main disadvantages to community forums. First, given a sizable forum attendance, it is unlikely that everyone who wishes to speak will have a chance to do so. Thus, certain information that could be quite relevant to the assessment of needs may never be presented.

Second, not all members of the community can or will attend a forum. Certain viewpoints about unmet human service needs may not be represented at the forum. The results of the forum provide an impressionistic and probably incomplete picture of needs.

Third, although the forum does provide an opportunity for expressing many valuable perspectives, particularly concerning need identification, it is usually the case that the discussion does not go beyond this point.

Fourth, the forum may mobilize certain elements of the community, or at least heighten the awareness of existing human service needs in the community. As a result, the expectations of community members may be raised in ways that cannot or will not be met. Organizers of the forum have a responsibility to inform attendees of realistic outcomes that may be expected from the forum and to advise participants that the process of problem identification is only the first phase of a problem-solving process.

From the advantages and disadvantages of the community forum approach, it can be concluded that forums are most appropriate if there is interest in (a) uncovering citizen feelings and impressions about human service needs —particularly citizens who represent those groups that are underrepresented in census data and utilization rates; and (b) identifying directly in a public arena the concerns of citizens as well as enlisting stimulating support for planning efforts directed at those needs.

THE NOMINAL GROUP TECHNIQUE

A second community group approach to need identification in human services is the nominal group technique (Delbecq & Van de Ven, 1971) that is used extensively in industrial, governmental, educational, and health organizations. The nominal group technique was developed through a series of experiments over a period of 10 years by Delbecq and his colleagues, and is a model approach to problem identification and program planning (Delbecq, Van de Ven, & Gustafson, 1975). This group process method was designed for the identification of organizational problems and formulation of appropriate and innovative tactics to solve them. Following an initial problem identification and ranking process, the nominal group is a methodology for involving critical reference groups in successive phases of program planning and development: (a) clients (consumers) and first-line staff, in the problem exploration stage; (b) external resource people and internal specialists, in solution and resource exploration; (c) key administrators and resource controllers, in priority development; (d) organizational staff, in program proposal inception and development; and (e) all constituencies, in final approval and designs for evaluation.

The usefulness of the nominal group technique is based on Delbecq and Van de Ven's research, which indicated that a nominal group—one in which individuals work in the presence of one another but initially do not interact —allows production of a greater number of problem dimensions, more high-quality suggestions, and a larger number of more highly differentiated kinds of solutions than groups in which members are encouraged or allowed to interact during the generation of critical problem variables (Delbecq & Van de Ven, 1971).

The nominal group process initially involves silent, individual effort in a group setting, with working groups limited to eight to ten individuals. Basically, the process includes posing a question or a series of questions to a group and inviting each group member to list brief responses or answers to the question during a silent period of 10–15 minutes. These questions may seek possible solutions to a particular problem or may merely seek opinions about a particular human service problem in a community. When used in human service need assessment, participants may be asked to identify their own human service needs, to list the needs they perceive for other groups in the community, or to identify important factors or issues to be considered in a community program planning process. This initial silent time spent in idea generation is followed by an interval in which all ideas generated by individuals are shared with the total group. The group leader, in round-robin fashion, asks each participant to offer one idea from his or her list. Each idea is then recorded on large sheets of paper, which are then displayed for continued review by the total group. Every effort is made to record the ideas exactly as they are offered from the participants. The leader continues the round-robin until all ideas on each participant's list are exhausted. This procedure may take from 1 to 2 hours, depending upon the type of questions posed and the number of ideas generated. During this phase, participants are asked to refrain from making comments or discussing any of the ideas, as the round-robin is for enumeration of ideas only.

Once the round-robin is completed, a discussion period follows in which participants are free to clarify, elaborate, or defend any of the ideas presented. During this discussion, participants may add new ideas to the list; they may eliminate certain ideas; they may combine ideas that seem to overlap substantially; or they may condense ideas that appear similar. One means of facilitating this process is for the leader to read one idea at a time from the list generated, to ask for discussion, comments, or questions in reference to that idea, and then to move on to the next. Participants are not required to defend or otherwise substantiate an idea.

Once the leader feels that sufficient clarification has been achieved, each participant is then asked to select those ideas (from the total list) that are considered most important. Each person selects five or more (as desired) ideas judged personally to be most important, and ranks them accordingly. These "votes" are then tallied, and the result is the group's rank ordering of those ideas generated in order of importance. In a human services need assessment, for example, individuals may be asked to rank those identified needs which are the most critical for program planning and intervention. All selection and ranking is done individually and anonymously.

The nominal group technique allows for group decision making or idea sharing without the typical competitive problems of the interacting group. Also, each participant privately expresses his or her perception of the relative importance of the many different problem areas or need areas generated by the group as a whole. The silent period in the nominal group process is critical to the production of ideas. It allows each member time for reflection and thought. It encourages the generation of minority ideas; it avoids hidden agendas; it imposes a burden on all present to work and contribute and to have a sense of responsibility for the group's success; it facilitates creativity; it allows for the airing of personal concerns; and it is especially useful in a heterogeneous group as it does not allow any one person or point of view to dominate.

By following the silent period with round-robin sharing, all ideas are shared with the group before they are discussed and each member has assurance that all of his or her ideas will be heard. In the discussion that follows, the feedback and information-sharing benefits of the interacting group are gained. The group has a chance to question and to clarify each idea presented. Other advantages accruing to the nominal group technique include social modeling of disclosure by more secure group members, which facilitates disclosure on the part of less secure members; a setting in which the pooling of resources from a heterogeneous, potentially noncollaborative group may occur; and finally, the potential for new perspectives on or cognitive remapping of "old" or existing problems.

The main disadvantage of the nominal group technique is that it lacks precision. Votes or rankings are made without thorough or careful sorting out of all of the ideas generated into appropriate categories. Another disadvantage, and quite an important one in our experience, is that although most participants enjoy the process and feel satisfied with the results, some participants may feel manipulated because they are not used to participating in a highly structured process. These disadvantages are minor and can be handled by careful planning, preparation of participants, and followup feedback to participants.

THE DELPHI TECHNIQUE

An additional community groups approach to human service need identification is the Delphi technique (Dalkey, 1967; Dalkey & Helmer, 1963). The Delphi is a procedure for the systematic solicitation and collation of informed judgments on a particular topic (Delbecq et al., 1975). The Delphi is usually composed of a set of carefully designed sequential questionnaires. With each subsequent questionnaire, summarized information and opinion feedback derived from earlier questionnaires are provided. This summarized information is carefully organized to provide a common reference point against which the Delphi judges base their responses. The sequential questionnaires take the form of a structured dialogue between persons who do not meet, but whose opinions are valuable to the issue at hand.

This method for systematically eliciting and refining group judgments has three defining characteristics (Dalkey, 1969; Delbecq et al., 1975): (a) anonymous response to question or questions, (b) iteration or controlled feedback of various stages of the information collection process, and (c) statistical analysis and formulation of group responses.

First, anonymity may be ensured by the use of questionnaires or, where resources permit, on-line computer communication. Second, the Delphi exercise is conducted in a series of rounds between which a summary of the results of the previous round is distributed to each participant. Third, the form in which this controlled feedback is given is statistical, and usually consists of the group medium (Dalkey, 1967, 1969; Delbecq et al., 1975), although other less directive forms of iteration are being considered (e.g., the quantity of the individual's score).

The Delphi technique consists of five basic steps:

1. A questionnaire is developed relative to a key issue or set of issues
2. Questionnaires are distributed to a panel of experts or key individuals. Since it is not necessary and often not desirable to have these experts meet, the questionnaire can be mailed to the participants serving on the panel
3. When the questionnaires are returned, the results are tallied to determine areas of agreement and disagreement
4. When disagreement occurs, a second questionnaire containing the various reasons given by the experts for their initial judgments is distributed to the panel
5. The above steps are repeated, hopefully until an agreement can be reached.

The Delphi has typically gained widest use in areas of broad- or long-range policy formulation in, for example, the U. S. Air Force and in industry for technological forecasting and evaluation of corporate planning (Helmer, 1967). Various public agencies are beginning to use the Delphi for planning exercises related to education, health, and urban growth. Although the original experiments relating to the Delphi centered around questions having definitive factual answers, the originators believe this method is appropriate in areas of "value judgment" where preset "answers" are not available.

This method of assessment has a number of possible human service applications: to determine or develop a typology of human service needs; to explore or expose underlying assumptions or information leading to different judgments as to human service needs; to correlate informed judgments on a topic spanning a wide range of social roles and/or disciplines; and to educate the respondent group as to the diverse and interrelated aspects of human service needs (Turoff, 1971).

The Delphi involves at least two separate groups of individuals. First, the user body is composed of the individual or individuals expecting some product from the exercise which is useful to their purposes. Next there is a design and monitor team, which constructs the initial questionnaire, summarizes the returns, and designs the followup questionnaires. The final group of individuals involved in a Delphi effort are the respondents. It is important to note that this latter group of persons who are chosen to respond to the questionnaires may in some cases also be the user body.

There are four advantages to the Delphi technique. First, because participation can be anonymous, the inhibiting influences of dominant and more verbal participants are minimized. Second, due to the fact that feedback is controlled in a systematic manner, the negative influences of individual vested interests are reduced to a minimum. Third, because responses are anonymous, group pressure to conform is significantly decreased. Fourth, the Delphi is an efficient user of the respondents' time. Efficiency in the use of time allows the involvement of individuals who cannot otherwise become involved in other more time-consuming procedures.

The main disadvantage of the Delphi technique is the lack of certainty in guidelines on its use or design. For example, there are a number of important questions for which general agreement does not exist among practitioners, users, and critics: (a) Is the respondent group completely anonymous among its own members, to the design team, or to the user body? (b) Should the Delphi be used in conjunction with a committee or ongoing study effort? (c) Should the iterations (controlled feedback) be cycled to the same respondent group, or is there a series of separate respondent groups interacting independently or parallel with one another? (d) How many iterations are needed? and (e) What form should the feedback take? A further disadvantage is that extreme positions may be dropped in order to obtain agreement and consequently many divergent, yet creative ideas may be lost. This latter disadvantage is also shared by the nominal group and other similar approaches.

A use of the Delphi at the national plannning level illustrates this technique (National Institute of Drug Abuse, 1975). The Prevention Branch of the National Institute of Drug Abuse employed the Delphi process as a part of an attempt to develop "a National Strategy for Primary Drug Abuse Prevention." The project involved 420 prevention planners, administrators, and programmers from community programs, state agencies, and federal departments. The main objective was to promote the evolution of a national strategy for primary prevention that would be conceptually sound and capable of implementation. Furthermore, the effort was designed (a) to involve in the strategy development those federal, state and community-based practitioners who would be directly affected by it, and (b) to facilitate collaboration and resource sharing among the scattered advocates of primary prevention.

In order to attain these objectives, the following three tasks were proposed:

1. Development of a sound, supportable definition of primary drug abuse prevention
2. Clarification of what is being done now in prevention, as well as recommendations on the kinds of new strategies that should be implemented
3. Descriptions of the training and technical assistance resources needed at state and local levels.

The project was divided into two phases. In Phase I, a total of 70 participants were convened at three sites to address the objectives. The information generated at these sessions was then refined by 30 of the participants before and during a fourth meeting.

In Phase II, the Phase I recommendations were presented to an additional 340 prevention workers at five regional conferences. The results of the entire process were then tabulated and incorporated into a final report that included:

1. A working definition of primary drug abuse prevention
2. An exhaustive list of those activities that are now being done or should be done by preventors
3. A section devoted to training and technical assistance. This latter section describes the information and program support needs that were identified at all nine conferences.

THE COMMUNITY IMPRESSIONS APPROACH

The community impressions approach was developed by Cohn and her colleagues at the School of Public Health at the University of California, Berkeley (1). It allows for direct focus on those groups in the population that have been identified as having the greatest human service needs and is a procedure for involving those groups in subsequent planning and evaluation activities directed at establishing programs to reduce their needs. A comprehensive view of needs combines hard data with impressions and feelings about need. In this process it is very important to identify and involve those groups with the greatest human service needs in both the assessment and subsequent planning and program development activities.

The community impressions approach integrates existing data about human service needs with community impressions about such needs. First, community impressions are obtained from key individuals living or working in the community. Then, on the basis of all available sources of data (social indicator, survey and community group data) groups identified as having the greatest human service needs are approached in order to verify findings and/or to explore human service needs further. The approach has three major steps:

1. Key Informant Interviews

In this approach, interviews are conducted with 10 or 15 individuals who have extensive first-hand knowledge of the community and who either live or work in the community. Interviewees are selected on the basis of the longevity of their involvement in the community and/or the nature of their involvement with the community. These informants are asked to provide their perspectives on the human service needs of different groups in the community. Thus, a public health nurse, members of any community action agencies, long-time residents, a policeman or fireman, the local health officer, and others are interviewed in order to elicit their impressions. The interviews are conducted from a list of questions about the existing human services in the community and about certain demographic characteristics of the population with the aid of a map of the community under study. Answers to questions such as "Where do the elderly live?" and "What public transportation exists between different parts of the community and the local community mental health center?" are recorded on the map. Slowly, a picture of the community, from service and demographic viewpoints, begins to emerge. Typically, the interview will result in some fairly concrete statements of need. Once 10 to 15 key community members have been interviewed, their impressions are collapsed onto one map. It is highly probable that there will be some discrepancies in both information and impressions. In analyzing the discrepancies in impressions about need, the need assessor should settle the discrepancies by erring "in favor" of identifying groups as having unmet needs (i.e., if one interviewee identified a group as having many human service problems, and another interviewee identified that same group as having few, the group should be recorded at this time as having many—this will be verified with the group under question at a later date).

2. *Integration of Existing Information*

Existing data from the widest possible range of needs assessment methods are then integrated with the community impressions. Emphasis here should be on balancing efforts to integrate as much available, existing data as possible in order to move toward a convergent analysis of needs. Once enough information has been collected to satisfy the assessor's need for factual information about the community, this "hard data" should be added to the map of impressions from interviewees, thus yielding a richer understanding of the needs of the community. This combined picture should not be taken as complete, however. It should ideally be validated with relevant groups in the community.

3. *The Community Forum*

A community forum is planned and held for each group or section of the community identified as having significant unmet human service needs (see the section on community forums). One purpose of the forum is to allow those groups identified as having unmet needs to validate or invalidate those needs. In addition to validation, however, the forum serves as an opportunity to explore in greater depth the nature and perceived etiology of those needs. Moreover, the forum serves as an opportunity to involve those persons with the greatest need in the process of defining and placing priorities on those needs. In this manner, the forum helps to complete the need assessment process while initiating the process of responding to the needs identified.

The community impressions approach has a number of advantages and disadvantages. First, it can be carried out with minimal expenditure of time and resources.

Second, it allows for consideration and convergence of a variety of informational sources, both those that represent what might be regarded as "factual clues" about human service needs and those that might be regarded as "impressionistic clues" about human service needs.

Third, it relies on more than information generated by "outsiders." Those identified as having unmet human service needs have an opportunity to determine whether or not they think and feel that they do in fact have unmet needs. Additionally, these groups have an opportunity to voice opinions about better procedures for meeting their needs and to become involved in activities that may lead to reduction of those needs.

Fourth, through the discussion and interaction that characterizes this approach, channels of communication among different human service agencies in the community may be strengthened or in some cases established. As a result, a more effective, broad-based, community approach to need assessment, to the establishment of priorities, and the allocation of resources may take place.

As fruitful as the community impressions approach may be, the results insofar as possible must be subjected to the same tests of reliability and validity that are applied to the results from the various types of need assessment surveys. Typically it is found that reasonable standards of reliability and validity cannot be confirmed, and the results must be generally considered as impressionistic. Due to this problem, there is no way to ensure that every group with human service needs will be identified or that all of the needs of those identified will have been recorded. Community impressions must be considered as one perspective about needs among many others, and divergencies in perspectives must be resolved in the subsequent program planning process.

The community impressions approach is most useful when one is interested in undertaking quickly and at little cost an assessment of the unmet human service needs in different groups within the community. The approach takes into consideration the content of data from other approaches *and* also the thoughts and feelings of various community members. The approach is particularly useful if one is committed to involving those with greatest needs in processes which will help reduce their needs.

SUMMARY

Need identification and assessment are integral aspects of human service planning and development. *Need identification* is the process of describing the health and social service needs of a geographic area. In the *need assessment* process, planners set priorities on identified needs with reference to relative importance, available resources, and available service technology.

The area of need assessment–identification is in its nascence, and no universally accepted methodology exists that will yield a comprehensive assessment of need. Moreover, the evaluation and interpretation of human service need is influenced by (a) the vested interests and values of those formulating program goals; (b) the diffuse and interrelated nature of social and health needs; (c) the rapidly changing character of human service needs; and (d) the capabilities and interests of staff as well as the availability of appropriate service technology and adequate financing.

Within the limits of current assessment methodologies, information about needs is useful in (a) describing demands for services; (b) assessing service resources; (c) developing detailed community descriptions; (d) delineating groups likely "to be at risk"; (e) examining the relevance of existing services; (f) clarifying those factors that influence the occurence of social and health problems; and (g) enumerating factors that aid or impede effective service delivery.

The most comprehensive picture of human service need can be obtained through a convergent analysis of need. Convergent analysis assumes that useful information about need emerges out of a process that receives input (a) at different, although sequential points in time; (b) from a number of different organizational levels; (c) from a variety of informational sources (community members, public records, service agency data, professional staff); and (d) through a family of assessment strategies. Further assumptions basic to a convergent analysis are that no single stakeholder, no one informational source, no single organizational level, no specific technique, and no single point in time will provide a comprehensive human service need assessment. It is only through the systematic, progressive convergence of multiple perspectives filtered through multiple assessment methods that the most useful information for planning is obtained. A convergent analysis identifies the widest range of need information that is relevant for program planning and service development by assessing need at all community and organizational levels.

The variety of assessment strategies used in a convergent analysis provides three different informational functions: (a) *compiling* existing information; (b) *developing* new information; and (c) *integrating* existing and newly developed information. There are advantages and disadvantages of each need assessment strategy when viewed in isolation. However, when seen as part of a total convergence of information, deployment of a range of methods provides the basis for an integrated perspective on need.

There are three basic orientations to assessing human service need: (a) the social and health indicators approach; (b) social area surveys; and (c) the community groups approaches. The *social and health indicator approach* to need assessment compiles publicly available information, and, on the basis of these data, needs are inferred. *Social area surveys* compile and integrate information about demands for service; provide information about resources that are currently available to meet the needs of the community; and provide citizens' views about needs and need priorities. In addition, new information can be generated on a personal self-report level from community members through direct interview surveys. Finally, the *community group approaches* to assessment are quick and inexpensive methods to use in conjunction with other assessment techniques. The group methods provide perspectives from community members by developing new information, compiling already existing information, and integrating existing information with the perspectives of persons living in the community.

REFERENCE NOTES

1. Cohn, A. H. *Solutions to unique problems encountered in identifying the medically underserved and involving them in the planning process.* Unpublished manuscript, School of Public Health, University of California, Berkeley, 1972.
2. Meier, R. *Contra Costa County mental health needs.* Unpublished manuscript, Contra Costa County Mental Health Services, Martinez, California, 1973.

3. Nguyen, T. D., Attkisson, C. C., & Bottino, M. J. *Definition and identification of human service need in a community context.* A paper presented at the National Conference on Needs Assessment in Health and Human Services, University of Louisville, Louisville, Kentucky, March 1976.

REFERENCES

Beigel, A., Hunter, E. J., Tamerin, J. S., Chapin, E. H., & Lowery, M. J. Planning for the development of comprehensive community alcoholism services: I. The prevalence survey. *American Journal of Psychiatry*, 1974, *131*, 1112–1115.

Beigel, A., McCabe, T. R., Tamerin, J. S., Lowery, M. J., Chapin, E. H., & Hunter, E. J. Planning for the development of comprehensive community alcoholism services: II. Assessing community awareness and attitudes. *American Journal of Psychiatry*, 1974, *131*, 1116–1120.

Bloom, B. L. *Changing patterns of psychiatric care.* New York: Human Sciences Press, 1975.

Blum, H. L. *Planning for health.* New York: Human Sciences Press, 1974.

Broskowski, A., & Baker, F. Professional, organizational, and social barriers to primary prevention. *American Journal of Orthopsychiatry*, 1974, *44*, 707–719.

Campbell, D. T., & Fiske, D. W. Convergent and discriminant validation by the multitrait–multimethod matrix. *Psychological Bulletin*, 1959, *56*, 81–105.

Dalkey, N. C. *Delphi.* Santa Monica, California: Rand Corporation, 1967.

Dalkey, N. C. *The delphi method: An experimental study of group opinion.* Santa Monica, California: Rand Corporation, 1969.

Dalkey, N. C., & Helmer, O. An experimental application of the delphi method to the use of experts. *Management Science*, 1963, *9*, 458–467.

Delbecq, A. L., & Van de Ven, A. H. A group process model for problem identification and program planning. *Journal of Applied Behavioral Science*, 1971, *7*, 466–492.

Delbecq, A. L., Van de Ven, A. H., & Gustafson, D. H. *Group techniques for program planning: A guide to nominal group and delphi processes.* Glenview, Illinois: Scott, Foresman and Company, 1975.

Demone, H. W., & Harshbarger, D. (Eds.). *A handbook of human service organizations.* New York: Behavioral Publications, 1974.

Feldstein, P. J. Research on the demand for health services. In J. B. McKinlay (Ed.), *Economic aspects of health care.* New York: Prodist, Milbank Memorial Fund, 1973.

Goldsmith, H. F., Unger, E. L., Rosen, B. M., Shambaugh, J. P., & Windle, C. D. *A typological approach to doing social area analysis.* (DHEW Publication No. ADM 76-262.) Washington, D. C.: U. S. Government Printing Office, 1975.

Helmer, O. *Analysis of the future: The delphi method.* Santa Monica, California: Rand Corporation, 1967.

Human Interaction Research Institute. *Information sources and how to use them.* Los Angeles: Human Interaction Research Institute, 1975. (also: Rockville, Maryland: National Institute of Mental Health, Mental Health Services Development Branch, 1975.)

Milstein, A. Anticipating the impact of Public Law 93-641 on mental health services. *American Journal of Psychiatry*, 1976, *133*, 710–712.

National Institute of Drug Abuse, Prevention Branch, Division of Resource Development. *Pyramid*, 1975, *1*, 1–2. (Available from: NIDA, 1526 18th Street, N. W., Washington, D. C. 20036.)

Robin, S. A procedure for securing returns to mail questionnaires. *Sociology and Social Research*, 1965, *50*, 24–35.

Schaefer, M. E. Demand versus need for medical services in a general cost–benefit setting. *American Journal of Public Health*, 1975, *65*, 293–295.

Schulberg, H. C., & Wechsler, H. The uses and misuses of data in assessing mental health needs. *Community Mental Health Journal*, 1967, *3*, 389–395.

Schwartz, R. Follow-up by phone or by mail. *Evaluation,* 1973, *1*(2), 25–26.

Sheldon, E. B., & Parke, R. Social indicators. *Science,* 1975, *188,* 693–699.

Siegel, L. M., Attkisson, C. C., & Cohn, A. H. Mental health needs assessment: Strategies and techniques. In W. A. Hargreaves, C. C. Attkisson, & J. E. Sorensen (Eds.), *Resource materials for community mental health program evaluation* (2nd ed.). (DHEW Publication No. ADM 77-328.) Washington, D. C.: U. S. Government Printing Office, 1977.

Turoff, M. Delphi and its potential impact on information systems. *AFIPS Conference Proceedings,* 1971, *39,* 317–326.

Warheit, G. J., Bell, R. A., & Schwab, J. J. *Planning for change: Needs assessment approaches.* Rockville, Maryland: National Institute of Mental Health, 1974.

Windle, C., & Ochberg, F. M. Enhancing program evaluation in the community mental health centers program. *Evaluation,* 1975, *2*(2), 31–36.

Windle, C., Rosen, B. M., Goldsmith, H. F., & Shambaugh, J. P. A demographic system for comparative assessment of "needs" for mental health services. *Evaluation,* 1975, *2*(2), 73–76.

10

SERVICE UTILIZATION, SOCIAL INDICATOR, AND CITIZEN SURVEY APPROACHES TO HUMAN SERVICE NEED ASSESSMENT

Roger A. Bell, Tuan D. Nguyen, George J. Warheit, and Joanne M. Buhl

Since the mid-1960s, observers of health and human service systems have increasingly urged that public programs serving residents of a social area be more directly guided by information about that area's needs. These observers include medical and social scientists, public officials, and administrators who are engaged in policy formulation, planning, and program evaluation at all levels.

As indicated in Chapter 9, our communities typically are served by publicly funded programs that often overlap and frequently compete with one another or with the private sector for the available financial resources. Without better coordination and integration of effort among programs, diversification of effort within organizations, and more accurate identification and assessment of human service needs, this redundancy and competition will persist.

This chapter provides additional information about several of the more technically complicated methods of human service need assessment. Service utilization, social indicator, and citizen survey methodologies are discussed in detail and illustrated by representative data from actual need assessment studies. We begin with a brief overview of issues related to planning a need assessment.

PLANNING NEED ASSESSMENT STUDIES

Care must be taken to plan need assessment studies systematically. Thoughtful planning is necessary to enhance the acceptability of such efforts by the community and service agencies. Careful planning also ensures maximum utilization of the assessment data for planning new services or restructuring existing services to meet the needs that may be identified during the assessment process.

The four most important steps in planning a need assessment study are:

1. Securing a commitment to use assessment data for planning purposes
2. Establishing a steering committee that includes the broadest range of community and professional representatives
3. Locating information sources and fiscal resources
4. Selecting need assessment approaches that are most appropriate for the agency or community that conducts or sponsors the assessment project.

SECURING COMMITMENT TO USE ASSESSMENT DATA

The initiation of a needs assessment study without a prior commitment to use the data for planning purposes is not only a waste of resources, but may also stimulate or intensify conflicts among agencies, citizens, and consumers of services. Furthermore, need assessment studies may increase the expectations for services on the part of community residents. If service programs are not forthcoming to meet the needs identified, alienation from, frustration with, and hostility toward service agencies may develop or be accentuated. Because such consequences are counterproductive for both the agency and the community, it is imperative that need assessment studies be conducted by those who are committed to planning for change.

ESTABLISHING A STEERING COMMITTEE

The next step in planning a need assessment study is the appointment of a steering committee. This committee should include administrative and program staff, research personnel, consumers, citizens, and advisory-board representatives. Representative participation increases the chances of a successful and useful assessment process by permitting the study design to benefit from multiple perspectives before the major objectives are finalized. Without the participation and support of representative vested interest groups, work of the committee will be much more difficult, the assessment will take longer to conduct, it will be more costly to complete, and—most importantly—the findings are less likely to be used. It would probably be better not to assess needs than to proceed without the active assistance of those responsible for the administration and program life of the health and human service system.

The primary tasks of the steering committee are to define the goals, formulate specific operational objectives, and establish the total costs of achieving the objectives of the assessment process. The following list of questions were originally proposed by Warheit, Bell, and Schwab (1974, pp. 17–18) to guide the initial planning and structuring of the assessment of community needs:

1. What do we want/need to know?
2. Why do we want to know it?
3. How will the information be used once it is obtained?
4. Where can we find the data necessary to answer our research questions?
5. How can we obtain these data?
6. What useful data sources already exist at the local, state, and federal levels?
7. How can we most advantageously compile, analyze, and present the data?
8. What agencies in the community must be involved in the program? Why? Why not? How?
9. What will the need study cost?
10. How long will it take to complete?
11. Where can we find the financial and personnel resources necessary to conduct the study?
12. Which of the available need assessment approaches will be most efficient for our purposes?
13. What are the relative advantages and disadvantages of each of these approaches?
14. How much assistance will be necessary from special consultants? Where can we find them?
15. What techniques and processes are available to translate the findings into service programs designed to meet human needs?

By dealing thoroughly with the issues of goal definition, formulating specific operational objectives, and cost analysis, the steering committee will be able to plan the assessment process in such a way as to move it effectively from initiation to implementation.

In addition to the steering committee, a project director should be named. The duties of the director must include clearly specified authority and will normally include direct supervision of the entire project. The director's responsibilities also will likely include the tasks associated with planning the study, formulating the objectives, monitoring the expenditure of funds, supervising the field operations, and ensuring the integration and coordination of assessment tasks. The director should also serve as liaison to administrators and providers in the service system as well as to leaders and residents in the community.

IDENTIFYING COSTS AND RESOURCES

Once the need assessment objectives are established, the planning committee is in a position to identify the sources and accessibility of required information, and the costs of procurement and analysis of the data. Although it may seem premature, this step is logical, since the costs of securing, analyzing, and presenting the data will be important factors in deciding which specific assessment strategies to use. Fortunately, much useful information is available from a wide variety of sources at minimal costs (see Chapter 9 for an extensive list). With such a wide variety of data already available, most health and human service systems can assemble a vast information pool that, without further collection of "new" information, could be compiled and summarized as a background analysis for a more specific assessment effort involving the development of new information.

Fiscal resources to support need assessment studies are often available from federal and state agencies and, at the local level, from health planning agencies and district mental health boards. Community-based agencies may also have limited fiscal resources for research and evaluation purposes. This wide range of potential funding sources underscores the advisability of assessing all available financial resources. Many community agencies are willing to assist in the funding of assessment studies if they have a meaningful opportunity to provide input into the design and content of the assessment effort during its early stages. In addition to enlarging the base of fiscal support, broad-based cooperation by community agencies maximizes future use of need assessment findings, since such involvement increases the number of organizations committed to the process.

SELECTING NEED ASSESSMENT APPROACHES

As indicated in Chapter 9, need assessment approaches vary in comprehensiveness, complexity, and cost; in the length of time required to conduct them; in the amount and reliability of the information obtained; and in their relative effectiveness. The remaining sections of this chapter discuss and illustrate in greater detail three of the more complicated, technically difficult need assessment approaches: (a) service utilization, (b) social indicators, and (c) citizen surveys. These approaches will be reviewed in terms of their designs, costs, and respective advantages and disadvantages.

SERVICE UTILIZATION APPROACH

Moore, Bloom, Gaylin, Pepper, Pettus, Willis, and Bahn (1967) proposed that the analysis of service utilization data is highly relevant to need assessment. They suggest that agencies can secure useful information for program management and planning purposes by analyzing data on referral sources; client characteristics such as age, race, and sex; waiting lists; and types of services being provided to clients. More recently Bloom (1975) has successfully integrated the service utilization approach with the social indicators methodology. Selected features of Bloom's study will be presented later in this chapter.

The service utilization approach to need assessment is based on a descriptive enumeration of persons who have been consumers of the services of health and welfare agencies of a community. Nguyen, Attkisson, and Bottino (7) have offered a useful conceptual framework for delineating need assessment approaches on the basis of underlying assumptions about the needs to be assessed. According to Nguyen *et al.*, ". . . the existing need assessment strategies fall into one of three positions vis-à-vis the conceptualization of a need state: rationalistic, empirical, and relativistic." Within this framework, Nguyen *et al.* viewed the service utilization approach as a representative of the empirical orientation. They stated:

> Adherents to [the empirical] position accept the premise that need for health and human services is best conceived as *deviance from a normative or observed state* of good health and well-being. Advocates of the empirical position assume that deviance from the normative state motivates individuals to seek services. Rarely do they feel that specific procedures for assessing needs are required beyond the study of *demand for services.* The empiricist's assumption is that this deviance will translate into demand for services through the interplay of economic forces and the mechanisms of a free-market economy. Using this economic model, empiricists have recently begun to analyze social-cultural factors that impede or facilitate the translation of wants and desires into demands.*

In essence, the underlying assumption of the service utilization approach is that one can estimate accurately the needs of the community from a sample (or population) of persons who have received care or treatment—especially if the eligibility criteria for care or treatment have been standardized and are universally accepted by professional providers (Lemkau, 1967).

Service utilization analysis has been widely used in research on the epidemiology of physical and mental disorders. Epidemiological research involves the study of the distribution of physical and mental impairments in human populations *and* an analysis of the factors that determine that distribution (MacMahon, 1967). Information about this distribution includes either incidence rates or prevalence rates. Incidence refers to the occurrence of new cases in the population during an observed time period, whereas prevalence refers to the number of existing cases at a given point in time. Such numbers, when expressed in terms of standardized population units such as 1000 or 100,000 persons, give, respectively, incidence rates and prevalence rates. Methodologically, incidence rates are usually estimated by prospective or retrospective longitudinal examination of treatment and admission statistics, whereas prevalence rates are estimated by case-finding surveys.

In the area of psychiatric disorders, epidemiological studies have been carried out using both prevalence and incidence rates. Annual incidence rates for psychiatric disorders have been estimated using treatment and admission statistics for many population centers in the United States. As specific examples, incidence rates have been estimated for Chicago by Faris and Dunham (1939) and by Levy and Rowitz (1973), for Baltimore by Cohen and Fairbanks (1938), for the State of New York by Malzberg (1940), for New Haven, Connecticut by Hollingshead and Redlich (1958), for the State of Texas by Jaco (1957), for Hagerstown, Maryland by Clausen and Kohn (1959), and for Pueblo County, Colorado by Bloom (1975). The treated incidence rates for psychiatric disorders obtained in these studies have been remarkably stable. Admission rates for schizophrenia, for example, have ranged from 28.5 to 47.0 per 100,000 population.

Turning to prevalence studies, Dunham (1965) has identified 10 investigations throughout the world. The two best-known American studies are a

---

*Reproduced by permission of the authors (see reference note 7).

psychiatric case-finding survey of Stirling County, a rural area in eastern Canada (Leighton, 1959; Leighton, Harding, Macklin, MacMillan, & Leighton, 1963) and a similar survey of midtown Manhattan, a subcommunity of New York City (Langner & Michael, 1963; Srole, Langner, Michael, Opler, & Rennie, 1962). These two studies found, respectively, that 17% and 18% of their populations can be classified as *well*, 63% and 59% as *mild-to-moderate* psychiatric cases, and 20% and 24% as having *severe* psychiatric symptoms. This close agreement between the Stirling County and midtown Manhattan studies is rather striking in view of the variations in prevalence rates found in earlier investigations among countries of the world (Dunham, 1965), the differences in rates among different regions of the United States (Lapouse, 1967), and the sociodemographic and cultural differences between the two populations under investigation.

Although both prevalence and incidence rates have been used in epidemiological research, controversy has persisted among epidemiologists concerning which indicator is more appropriate. This controversy is difficult to settle since each measure is obtained by a different methodological approach. In general, because prevalence is a function of both incidence and the duration of the disease or mental disorder (Kramer, 1957), the incidence rate is considered to be a more proper measure in etiological investigations that focus on factors related to the onset and development of disease or disorder (Bloom, 1975; Lapouse, 1967; MacMahon, Pugh, & Ipsen, 1960). Prevalence, on the other hand, is generally recognized as a more useful statistic for service planning and program development (Bloom, 1975; Lapouse, 1967). However, despite this recognition of the utility of prevalence rates, incidence rates established by examining service utilization data still seem to be the preferred measure, even for the purpose of assessing service needs in order to plan or restructure service programs. The preference for relying on incidence rates apparently stems from four reasons. First, rates of treated new cases (*treated* incidence) have exhibited remarkable cross-regional and longitudinal stability, as attested by the investigations we have cited. Second, service utilization data have constituted valuable criteria for establishing the predictive validity of sociodemographic variables to be utilized in the social indicator approach to need assessment. Third, the procedures used to derive incidence rates appear simpler and less open to question than the procedures used to obtain prevalence rates (cf. Lapouse, 1967). Fourth, it may be difficult for many observers to face the programmatic and systemic consequences of acknowledging the size and nature of the problem as indicated by prevalence rates. This apprehension is exemplified in Lapouse's (1967) comment about the findings of the Stirling County and the midtown Manhattan studies: "Does concordance between the two studies confirm the validity of these high rates and the huge estimates of need for psychiatric care implicit in them? An affirmative reply leads to incalculable problems of organization, manpower, and administration. This imposes an obligation to determine whether the reported rates are, indeed, fact or artifact [p. 950]."

In general, when treatment and clinical information is complete, reliable, valid, and readily accessible, service utilization analysis provides one of the simplest ways of estimating health and human service needs in a community.

DESIGN

As with all need assessment approaches, the first task to be completed in a service utilization analysis is to define, conceptualize, and formulate the objectives and methodology of the study. Certain generic questions must be asked first:

- What do we want to know?
- What data do we need to gather?
- Where can we find the data?
- How can we obtain the data?
- How will we analyze the data?
- What are the best methods for presenting the findings?
- How can we use the findings to make judgments and recommendations regarding our human service programs?

1. *Data Sources*

Large bodies of information are routinely collected by public and private service providers about the health status and demographic characteristics of their clients. Such service utilization data can be obtained if the providers are informed and convinced about the need for and usefulness of data collection. Examples of public data sources include records on admissions to state hospitals; numbers of persons receiving public assistance; and the numbers and characteristics of persons being treated at or receiving services from public alcohol treatment facilities, hospitals, clinics, and vocational rehabilitation agencies. It is usually more difficult to obtain information from private practitioners such as physicians, psychiatrists, psychologists, marriage counselors, and clergymen. However, in many instances, these persons will cooperate by providing general kinds of information on the numbers of persons being treated and their presenting problems (Babigian, 1972b; Babigian, Gardner, Miles, & Romano, 1965)

One of the major obstacles to securing information from public and private service agencies and from providers in individual practice is being able to guarantee *total anonymity and confidentiality* of the records. Unless anonymity and confidentiality are assured, agency directors and private caregivers will usually refuse to cooperate or they will provide such limited information that its utility is greatly diminished.

2. *Types of Data*

Data selected as basic input of service utilization analyses can include aggregate information (i.e., rates and averages) about the health status and social well-being of subgroups, or personal information on each client seen in a relevant service setting. Examples of aggregate health-status data include incidence and prevalence rates for infectious disease, hospital admission rates, and rates of admissions to local comprehensive care centers. Linden (1965) listed the following types of aggregate information obtainable from medical and health service records:

1. Numbers of sick persons
2. Numbers of certain physical defects
3. Records of infectious disease
4. Certifications of conditions for special benefits
5. Records of automobile accidents associated with substance abuse
6. Records of treatments for industrial and occupational accidents and disease
7. General hospital inpatient records
8. General hospital outpatient records
9. General records for home-visiting and nursing services
10. Continuous records of health caregivers
11. Voluntary health plans and welfare centers
12. Records of health and welfare centers
13. Medical records of educational institutions.

Most if not all agencies and service providers also collect personal information on persons seeking or utilizing their services. Such data are usually collected for clinical and management information purposes, however its validity depends on the *information capability* of the agencies (see Chapters 4, 6, 7, and 13) and must be independently established. Personal information usually relates to six areas:

1. Sociodemographic characteristics of the client (e.g., age, race, sex, ethnicity, education, place of residence)
2. Presenting problem or problems
3. Characteristics of care/services provided
4. Frequency and duration of the care/treatment process
5. Sources of referral; and, when available
6. Outcomes of treatment or services provided.

3. *Data Gathering and Analysis*

After the data sources are identified and access to them is granted, one should carefully consider how to gather and analyze the necessary information. How information is gathered will depend upon (*a*) the specific goals of the project; (*b*) the kind and amount of data to be gathered; (*c*) the resources available; and (*d*) the adequacy of management information systems within community agencies. When information systems do not exist, the most extensive data retrieval will necessitate coding information from existing service records. This often is a difficult and painstaking task, particularly if the analysis covers an extended period of time or if the records are voluminous. In such instances, a *random sample* from each agency's records can provide representative information about service utilizers and services rendered.

To systematize the data gathering and analysis process, a worksheet is often developed on which the pertinent facts relating to the selected items can be recorded. Worksheets should be designed to facilitate manual tabulations and computations and/or the transfer of information to tape or cards for computer analysis, which is especially useful when the amount of data is large. Examples of data sheets used to code information obtained from interview schedules and questionnaires can be found in Warheit *et al.* (1974).

The choice of computational and statistical procedures used to analyze service utilization data depends on the volume and types of data collected. Simple procedures involving few variables, little data transformation, and simple statistical analyses usually make it easier for a wider range of audiences to understand the results of the study. Discussion of computational and statistical procedures and instructions for using them can be found in many sourcebooks (e.g., Bruning & Kintz, 1968; Isaac & Michael, 1971; Lansing & Morgan, 1971; Linton & Gallo, 1975; Timm, 1975). Although the rigor and appropriateness of statistical analyses must be given careful consideration, special attention must also be given to the presentation of information collected. Tables, figures, and charts must be carefully designed to present information directly relevant to the objectives of the need study. These tables, figures, and charts should also present the data in the clearest manner possible. Tables presenting cross-tabulations, for example, should not involve more than two or three dimensions, or it will become difficult for the audience to interpret the columns and rows. Charts with clearly defined labels are extremely helpful for grasping an overall picture of the information.

ADVANTAGES

There are three major advantages of the service utilization approach. First, service utilization data represent treated cases corroborated by professional caretakers or service providers. This is valuable information from which estimates of need can be made. Second, because of their ready availability, service utilization data can be obtained and analyzed at a relatively low cost. Third, service utilization studies tend to increase communications between the various human service agencies or providers in a community. Improved interagency communication often elevates the agencies' sensitivity to community needs and can facilitate a greater integration among categorical services in the community.

DISADVANTAGES

The overwhelming weakness of the service utilization approach to need assessment is the assumption that *needs* for services are accurately expressed as *demands* for services and that this demand is measurable by admissions to existing health and human service facilities (7). This assumption may not be valid for two important reasons. First, the translation of needs into demand for and utilization of services depends on the extent to which services are available, accessible, and acceptable to clients and on the extent to which potential clients are aware of the existence of services that may satisfy their needs. These four variables—awareness about services, and the availability, acceptability, and accessibility of services—are in turn influenced by administrative, organizational, attitudinal, and economic factors. For example, an unfavorable public attitude toward users of certain services can discourage potential clients from seeking these services. Cultural and linguistic barriers can prevent certain groups of community residents who have legitimate needs for the services from utilizing them. Administrative policies regarding hours of operation, eligibility criteria, and fees charged to clients can create impediments similar to cultural and linguistic barriers. Because of these and other barriers, not all community residents who have legitimate needs for services will use such services. Consequently, service demand and utilization data provide only information on *needs among service utilizers* but cannot, except through questionable inference, identify subgroups whose needs are not met.

Second, data derived from client and service records may not be comparable across agencies that provide the same type of service. Henisz, Tischler, and Myers (1974) have identified three factors that make service utilization data unsuitable for comparison

1. In counting admissions, different agencies may have different definitions of what is to be considered a "case"
2. Admission rates may be misleading because of duplicated counts resulting from a single individual having multiple admissions during a given period
3. The organizational structure of a health and human service facility (e.g., a mental health facility) is defined differently from one geographical area to another.

In addition to the problems with service utilization data identified by Henisz *et al.*, agencies differ in their practices regarding the classification of types of service, diagnostic categories, or problem area designations; and agencies differ in their procedures for collecting other client-related information. For example, income data may not be collected by an agency, may be defined only in terms of employment earnings by another agency, and may be defined in terms of income from all sources in a third agency.

In summary, the consistency, validity, and comparability of client and service information depend to a large extent on the adequacy and comparability of clinical and management information systems within community agencies. This fact, taken together with the difficulty of accurately inferring needs on the basis of utilization data, points to the necessity to corroborate such inferences with information obtained through other approaches.

EXAMPLES OF SERVICE UTILIZATION APPROACHES

We have selected two studies to illustrate how service utilization data can be collected, analyzed, and used to infer and anticipate the needs for psychiatric and mental health services. The first study (Bloom, 1975) demonstrates how special data collection methods can be developed to gather necessary information from clinical records and integrate this information with that obtained by other methods. The second study (Babigian, 1972a) is an example of how information that has been systematically and routinely collected can be utilized to derive estimates of future service needs and to restructure and expand an existing service delivery system on the basis of such need estimates.

1. The Pueblo County, Colorado Study

Bloom (1975) reported a study of all first admissions to private and public psychiatric facilities in Pueblo County, Colorado for two periods separated by 10 years. Bloom began with an analysis of the utilization of psychiatric facilities and then combined this analysis with a social indicators analysis of Pueblo County.

In order to gather the necessary service utilization data for his study, Bloom designed special data collection methods. Information on inpatient psychiatric cases treated in 1959, 1960, and 1961—the 1960 study—was collected from both the private and public facilities through a retrospective record search. Information on persons admitted for treatment between September 1, 1969 and August 31, 1971—the 1970 study—was collected by using (a) the Pueblo Psychiatric Epidemiology Project Inpatient Form for inpatients (see Appendix A in Bloom, 1975) and (b) the Pueblo, Colorado Psychiatric Epidemiology Project Data Collection Form (see Appendix B in Bloom, 1975) and a retrospective record search for outpatients.

Although the data collection methods differed for the two periods under study and for types of patients, the basic data were similiar in many respects. Both the 1960 and 1970 studies included data on diagnostic categories, sex, age, and frequency of individuals having Spanish surnames. Special effort was made in the 1970 study to collect additional sociodemographic information. Bloom's intention was to obtain sociodemographic data that were as comparable as possible to the 1970 census data in order to compare the characteristics of patients treated with those of the resident population of Pueblo County.

The wealth of information in Bloom's research precludes a comprehensive review of his findings. Consequently, we will only present selected data from his study to illustrate the potential relevance of service utilization data for the assessment of mental health needs.

Because data were obtained at two points in time (1960 and 1970), Bloom was able to compare longitudinal changes in the utilization of services by different target groups and changes in diagnosed psychiatric conditions in these groups. For example, distributions of *first inpatient* admissions by age group and diagnostic category were obtained for both study periods. As Bloom noted, the number of first admissions among inpatients remained stable over time for the total population. However, there was a major shift in first inpatient admissions in terms of diagnostic categories within the under-21 age group. In this group, the number of cases with psychoneurotic diagnoses increased from 41% of all admissions in 1960 to 69% in 1970. The greatest increase in inpatient admissions between the two study periods was also found in this under-21 age group. These observed changes are difficult to translate into quantitative measures of needs without further data and information. Nonetheless, they point to the necessity of paying special attention to the under-21 target population, should a restructuring of the service delivery system become desirable or necessary.

Another interesting aspect of Bloom's study is his comparison of the rates of service utilization by Spanish-surnamed and non-Spanish-surnamed populations of Pueblo County over the two time periods. These rates were obtained by dividing the actual number of treated clients by the number of residents in the community and multiplying the results by 1000. Bloom found that the overall utilization rate for non-Spanish-surnamed residents was 1.6 times higher than the rate for Spanish-surnamed residents in 1960. However, by 1970, there was a reversal: The rate of utilization by Spanish-surnamed residents exceeded by 28% the rate of utilization by non-Spanish-surnamed residents. There are undoubtedly many competing explanations for this dramatic reversal in utilization rates by Spanish- versus non-Spanish-surnamed residents. The implication, however, is that the mental health service system of Pueblo County, if it were to be responsive to the needs of Spanish-surnamed clients, could not, in the 1970s, be the same type of service delivery system that had existed in the 1960s.

2. *The Monroe County, New York Experience*

Babigian (1972a) reported the use of data from the Monroe County Psychiatric Case Register for planning and restructuring mental health services in the county. The Monroe County register was established on January 1, 1960, to record the psychiatric experiences and sociodemographic data of Monroe County residents receiving mental health services. For every complete, continuous period of psychiatric treatment, information was forwarded to the register by the provider regarding the client's name, address, birth date, age, sex, race, marital status, psychiatric service received in the past, psychiatric diagnostic impressions, type of service and treatment provided, initial contact and termination dates, frequency of therapy, reason for termination, condition on termination, and the name of the facility and therapist (Babigian, 1972b). All public (i.e., university, state, county, and court) psychiatric facilities and approximately 95% of the private psychiatrists participate in forwarding this information to the register (Babigian, 1972a). Babigian estimates that all but 3% of county residents who contact the psychiatric network are reported to the register (Babigian *et al.,* 1965).

The utility of routine collection and storage of client and service information in the register was demonstrated by studies of diagnostic consistency (Babigian *et al.,* 1965), longitudinal pathology (Babigian, 1972b), movements of patients between different facilities in the community over a period of time (Gardner, 1967; Gardner, Bahn, & Miles, 1964; Miles & Gardner, 1966), longitudinal status of schizophrenic patients (*1*), and other studies of clinical interest.

After 6 years of operation, the usefulness of the register's data for assessing and estimating future levels of need in the county was demonstrated. Following the passage of the Community Mental Health Centers Act, planning was initiated to establish four community mental health centers in Monroe County. After the county was apportioned into four catchment areas, the 1966 register data were used as a basis to estimate the future caseload for each catchment area, anticipate the demand for hospitalization, and to plan for outpatient and emergency services. Babigian (1972a) illustrated how past utilization data were used to estimate future caseload for one of the four planned community mental health centers:

> Twelve thousand nine hundred and forty-five county residents, or approximately 2% of the total county population, were cared for by the psychiatric network of services with each catchment area accounting for a quarter of the total load. One-third of the patients cared for entered psychiatric services for the first time in their lifetime, 8.3% had their first Register contact but this did not represent a first lifetime contact, 20% were already in the Register but returned for care in 1966, and 38.3% continued in care from the previous year. Assuming that a new community mental health center opening its doors on January 1, 1970, would attempt to provide care for its catchment area, they should at least count on serving 80% of both the new contacts and the group that re-enters care from the new catchment area (the other 20% is cared for by private practice). For catchment area B (Rochester Mental Health Center) which started operation on January 1, 1967, this would mean serving a minimum of 1,560 individuals. The average yearly increase since 1960 has been 6%, so the expected number of patients to be served would be 1,654 [pp. 39–40].*

For other illustrative uses of service utilization data to anticipate demand for hospital beds and for outpatient and emergency services, readers are referred to the more complete account by Babigian (1972a).

As a final commentary on the service utilization approach to need assessment, the Pueblo and Monroe County examples demonstrate clearly the implications and potential uses of such data for planning services on the basis of anticipated or identified needs. However, the identification of needs that is based *solely* on past service utilization data will remain incomplete or inaccurate. As Babigian (1972a) noted in his presentation of the process of estimating future caseload: "This figure [of expected number of patients to be served] is an estimate of the minimum number of individuals who would require service. It does not account for new case detection methods or new types of services to populations that have not been adequately cared for in the past [p. 40]." Similarly, Bloom's discussion of the reversal in utilization rates among Spanish- and non-Spanish-surnamed Pueblo County residents revealed that organizational and programmatic changes between 1960 and 1970 produced the observed reversal. Bloom (1975) stated:

> In discussing these findings with groups of mental health professionals and their colleagues in Pueblo (both Chicano and Anglo), the increased utilization of inpatient facilities by Spanish-surnamed persons is generally viewed in very positive terms. First it is their impression that this increased utilization is a consequence of the improved image of the mental health service delivery system, and specifically of the fact that length of hospitalization is now so short . . . Second, it is their impres-

---

*Reproduced by permission from: H. M. Babigian, The role of epidemiology and mental health care statistics in the planning of mental health centers. In A. Beigel & A. I. Levenson (Eds.), *The community mental health center: Strategies and programs.* Copyright 1972, Basic Books, New York.

sion that increased utilization is the result of the employment of larger numbers of Chicano staff throughout the service delivery system and the employment of larger numbers of competent staff regardless of ethnic group. Finally, the availability of a variety of financial assistance programs has had a significant impact throughout the lower socioeconomic groups where . . . Spanish-surnamed persons are over-represented [p. 199].*

Bloom's findings relative to Spanish- versus non-Spanish-surnamed utilization rates and his discussion of the possible causes for the longitudinal changes in these rates illustrate that service utilization data, if they are not corroborated by additional information about the target groups under consideration, can lead to inaccurate estimates of the needs in these target groups. In the Pueblo County case, had the planners relied solely on the 1960 service utilization rates among Spanish-surnamed residents in order to estimate future service needs by this group, Spanish-surnamed residents of Pueblo County would have remained underserved in the 1960s and the observed 1970 rates would not have been obtained. In conclusion, planning future services only on the basis of service utilization data can lead to the maintenance of status quo in health and human services systems.

THE SOCIAL INDICATORS APPROACH

The social indicators approach to need assessment is based primarily on *inferences* of need generally drawn from descriptive social and demographic statistics found in public records and reports. The underlying assumption of the approach is that estimates of the needs and social well-being of those in a community can be made by examining selected social and demographic descriptors that have been found to correlate highly with service utilization. In other words, some social indicators are accepted as empirical predictors of need.

The use of social indicators to assess the relative distribution of service needs in a community stems from two important investigative traditions: epidemiological research and social area analysis. As mentioned earlier, epidemiology is the study of the distribution of physical and mental disorders in human population and an analysis of the factors that determine that distribution. In their attempt to identify as completely as possible the variables that are etiologically related to the incidence and development of physical and mental disorders, many investigators are led to consider social and demographic characteristics of the environments in which such disorders are observed as well as the individual background of persons afflicted by these disorders. Variables such as social class, sex, race, occupation, education, income, and marital status are frequently examined as etiological factors that may underlie the onset and development of physical and mental impairments

---

*Reproduced by permission from: B. L. Bloom, *Changing patterns of psychiatric care.* Copyright 1975, Human Sciences Press, New York.

(e.g., Clark, 1949; Hollingshead & Redlick, 1958; Jaco, 1960; Lemkau, Tietze, & Cooper, 1942; Pasamanick, 1959; Pasamanick, Roberts, Lemkau, & Krueger, 1959, 1966; Srole et al., 1962).

The second investigative tradition behind the use of social indicators analysis as an approach to need assessment is the social area analysis research dating back to the early sociologists at the University of Chicago (cf. Theodorson, 1961). Over the years, many of the basic assumptions originally held by this group of sociologists have been modified in light of subsequent research. Nonetheless, their fundamental orientation—that of describing human habitat and environments and analyzing the interrelationships among the characteristic descriptors of such environments—has remained invariant. Basic to this social area analysis orientation is the notion of a community (e.g., a city) as a constellation of "natural areas." A "natural area" can be defined most simply as a unit within a community, identifiable on the basis of characteristics that set it apart from other units. Some of the variables most commonly used to identify natural areas are topographical features such as rivers, terrain, and land-use patterns; modal sociodemographic attributes of the residents including age, race, sex, ethnicity, income, education, occupation, and family patterns; population factors including distribution, density, mobility, and migration; the spatial arrangements and distribution of institutions; and indicators of health and social well-being such as infant mortality, other age-specific mortality rates, crime and arrest records, suicides, and the prevalence of alcohol and drug abuse.

The work of Farris and Dunham (1939) in Chicago provides a good illustration of the many efforts in the United States to relate the quality of human environments to dysfunctional manifestations. They found that mental disorders were more concentrated in lower-quality environments, that is, urban areas characterized by high rates of "social disorganization" defined in terms of poverty, homelessness, suicide, crime rates, transience, and unemployment. They also found that different natural areas within the city of Chicago manifested different kinds of mental disorders. More recent illustrative social area analyses of mental disorders have been carried out for Baltimore, Maryland by Klee, Spiro, Bahn, and Gorwitz (1967), Chicago by Levy and Rowitz (1973), Los Angeles by Rice and Fowler (8), and Pueblo, Colorado by Bloom (1975). Social area analyses with special focuses have been carried out by Attkisson (1970) concerning suicide, by Keller and Effron (1956) concerning the distribution of alcoholism, and by Galle, Gove, McPherson, and Miller (1972) concerning the relationship between overcrowding and pathology.

The two research orientations—epidemiological research and social area analysis—differ in many respects. The most important difference concerns their analytical focus. Epidemiologists seek to discover the etiology of physical or mental disorders as they affect the individual, in the hope that better diagnosis and treatment of the disorders will ensue from a better understanding of their etiologies. Thus, the primary focus of traditional epidemiological research is the individual or a group of individuals. Environmental factors are considered in so far as they can be theoretically or empirically demonstrated to influence the individual's well-being or propensity for illness. Social area research, on the other hand, focuses specifically on the description and assessment of human habitats and environments, typically in terms of social and economic characteristics. Examples of criteria for evaluating the quality of human environments include indices of social disequilibrium, social disorganization, or anomie; economic affluence; and the quality of air and water. The examination of human environments often leads to the discovery of relationships between the quality of these environments and the extent of physical, mental, and psychosocial dysfunctioning among the residents. However, strictly speaking, empirical relationships between the various forms and levels of human dysfunctioning and the quality of the environment are relevant only to supra-individual levels such as census tracts or natural areas. They therefore have meaningful implications only for intervention strategies at these levels. By contrast, findings from epidemiological research can be meaningful at the individual level both etiologically and in terms of intervention strategies.

Despite the differences in their analytical focus and theoretical relevance, both the epidemiological and social area studies have consistently demonstrated that in the overwhelming majority of our large cities, certain social and personal pathologies become more prevalent as one approaches the urban core areas where social conditions are the worst. This correlation between proximity to the urban core and rates of social and psychological dysfunction is a key relationship in the social indicators approach to need assessment. Without these empirical relationships, it would be difficult to establish the conceptual links between place of residence and needs for service as well as between residence and service utilization patterns (Siegel, Attkisson, & Cohn, 1977). Based on these empirical relationships, one can fruitfully use social indicators analysis as a need assessment tool in any area for which spatial, sociodemographic, health, social welfare, and other relevant data can be gathered.

DESIGN

1. *The Necessary Data*

The first task to undertake in a social indicators study is to outline as specifically as possible its *objectives*. Once this has been done, the next step is to determine what types of data will best serve as "indicators" of need (cf. Bloom, 1975). Typical data in past studies have focused on the following areas:

1. Population characteristics—density, racial and ethnic composition, national origin, marital status, age, sex, and family status
2. Housing characteristics—type of structure, owner- or renter-occupied dwellings, persons per dwelling, and indices of substandard dwellings
3. Sociomedical health indicators—mortality rates, disease prevalence and incidence rates, and health status indices
4. Criminal activity indices—crime patterns and arrest rates for substance or personal abuses (e.g., driving while intoxicated or assaults)
5. Education

6. Income
7. Fertility and fecundity rates.

Data related to each of these informational domains can be gathered from a wide variety of sources. The most common sources of data are public reports, such as those provided by the U. S. Bureau of the Census; reports of national, regional, state, and local health, education, welfare, and law enforcement agencies; bureaus of vital statistics; public service planning agencies; and local community colleges and universities.

The final determination of what data are most important to gather should be based on the use to which the findings will be applied. For example, if one is interested in alcohol use and its consequences for various social groups in the community, data should include such statistics as arrests for driving while intoxicated or arrests for crimes where alcohol was a contributing factor. These data could be obtained from police records and related sources.

2. Units for Analysis

The next step in designing a need study based on social indicators is to identify the geographic unit for analysis. In the past, most studies have utilized existing census subdivisions such as *census tracts* or *block groupings* (block groupings correspond to the census enumeration district). Great care must be given to the choice of the basic geographic unit for analysis, because each type of unit carries different implications for data analysis and the interpretation of results. For example, if census tracts are chosen as units of analysis, the relevance of certain types of data becomes obscure since the social areas covered by the tracts are sometimes quite large and heterogeneous. On the other hand, if smaller geographic units, such as block groupings, are chosen as units of analysis, data may become very thin and the number of units may become so unwieldy that electronic data processing is mandatory.

When using census subdivisions as the unit for analysis, it is usually better to gather data at the block groupings level than at the census tract level, since block groupings are always subdivisions of census tracts and the characteristics of the tract can be obtained by aggregating the block grouping data. On the other hand, data obtained at the tract level cannot be reduced to block groupings without a great amount of additional work. For example, Bell and Mellan (2), employing a social indicators approach within a broader epidemiologic study of mental health needs and services, found that only part of a central Florida county had been subdivided into census tracts. Consequently, comparable census tract data for the entire county was not available. This made comparisons of data at the census tract level impossible. A closer examination of the census subdivisions revealed, however, that census data were available for the enumeration districts for the entire county. The availability of data at the enumeration district level allowed Bell and Mellan to use these districts as geographic units for analyzing and comparing the sociodemographic characteristics, the social behavior of the population, and the general conditions within the county.

The divisions developed by the Bureau of the Census (e.g., census tracts, block groupings, enumeration districts) generally have the greatest utility because they are used extensively by a wide variety of public and private organizations. This permits easy comparison of data gathered by an agency as part of a need assessment program with the research findings of other organizations and agencies. In addition, because these census subdivisions have a considerable degree of permanence, data gathered using a census division as the geographic unit for analysis provide an excellent basis for longitudinal studies. Most importantly, the use of census subdivisions as the units for analysis and census data as social indicators has been greatly enhanced for those in the human services field by the work of a research group at the National Institute of Mental Health (NIMH).

The NIMH group has developed a program for the economical, efficient, and practical use of a vast body of data available through the 1970 census (*3; 4;* Goldsmith, Unger, Rosen, Shambaugh, & Windle, 1975; Rosen, 1974; Rosen, Lawrence, Goldsmith, Windle, & Shambaugh, 1975; Windle, Rosen, & Goldsmith, 1977). Referred to as the *Mental Health Demographic Profile System* (MHDPS), this data resource provides computer-stored demographic profiles on the standard community mental health catchment areas in the United States. These profiles contain data specific to individual catchment areas; they also present comparable data for the United States as a whole and for the state and county (counties) in which the catchment area is located. In addition, it is possible to integrate MHDPS data with other data from the catchment area such as service utilization statistics, public health statistics, vital statistics, and crime statistics. The flexibility of the MHDPS has special value to a need study. The MHDPS output can be expanded or reduced in keeping with the specific interests of individual agencies. The availability of this extensive and useful demographic profile system allows human service agencies to have census data as a core building block for a broader social indicator analysis. The MHDPS tapes are available from state departments or divisions of mental health. The NIMH Division of Biometry and Epidemiology has announced that MHDPS packages are being prepared for distribution to the health service areas created by Public Law 93-641. This package will include the 1970 MHDPS indices for each total health service area and for each county they contain (*6*). Plans are underway to update the MHDPS with 1980 census data.

3. *Analysis and Presentation of the Data*

The methods chosen for analysis will depend in large measure on the complexity of the data, the technical competence of the agency staff, and the availability of outside resources, such as consultants and computer facilities. Where the geographic units for analysis are census tracts, and the quantity of data is limited, one relatively simple and inexpensive technique is the preparation of a series of maps that display, tract by tract, the indicators being analyzed. Another technique that has been used extensively is to prepare a series of transparencies each of which represents, visually, the distribution of a given social indicator (McHarg, 1969; Stewart & Poaster, 1975). A series of such transparencies selectively overlayed offers a very comprehensive portrait of the interaction of indicators across census tracts. A similar method is to use dots, shaded areas or thatchings to represent the occurrences of a given phenomenon. Bloom (1975) provides illustrations of this mapping technique (see Figure 10.1).

Graphic techniques are relatively simple, since maps and transparencies are inexpensive to prepare. However, their usefulness is greatly reduced when there are large numbers of indicators or analytic units. For example, Bloom (1975) used 35 indicators to analyze census tracts in Pueblo, Colorado; and Grey, Warheit, and Schwab (5) examined 22 census tracts and 44 variables in each tract. In view of this quantity of variables and tracts, it becomes difficult to summarize the data in any other way than through analyses that depend on electronic data processing. These examples illustrate that the methods of analysis must be given careful consideration during the formal planning process before any data are collected. The importance of planning for data analysis cannot be overemphasized. Unless early consideration is given to the availability of resources for data analysis, either a great deal of data will be gathered that cannot be used or the quantity of data collected will be insufficient to fulfill the assessment objectives.

ADVANTAGES

There are five major advantages in using the social indicators approach. First, social indicators can be developed from vast data pools already existing in the public domain, e.g., census reports, governmental agency statistics, and social research organizations. Second, most social indicators can be secured at relatively low cost by persons with a limited amount of research training or technical expertise. Third, a social indicators analysis can either include only a selected amount of information about a local community or include comparable data about other communities and the country at large. It is also possible to integrate data from several different sources. These data can relate to sociodemographic characteristics, social behavior and well-being, and community conditions. Multiple sources of data permit agencies with differing levels of resources to select the data analysis procedures that are suited to their objectives and commensurate with their resources. Fourth, the results of a well-executed social indicators analysis can serve as a foundation on which to build or update other need assessment approaches with a minimum of effort and cost. And fifth, because social indicator data are collected uniformly across the United States, it becomes possible to use these data to compare communities or to control for demographic differences when comparing health and human service agencies. Altogether, social indicators approaches have a great deal to commend them.

DISADVANTAGES

Most of the disadvantages in using social indicators to assess needs are theoretical in nature. The first and most serious drawback arises from the fact that many of the social "indicators" are only *indirect* measures of the needs they are supposed to represent. Consequently, there is reason to question the validity of some social indicators. For example, divorce, separation, and illegitimacy rates are often used as indices of family stability and security. However, divorce, separation, and illegitimacy do not represent family instability for all groups in our society. Thus, it can be argued that, in many instances, these indices should not be used to evaluate the ability of persons to perform the necessary instrumental and affiliative functions that make family life stable and secure. Similar criticisms can be made of many other social indicators. Therefore, utilizers of the social indicators approach must be sensitive to their own personal or class biases in their choice of variables to be used as indicators.

Second, users of the social indicators approach have been criticized for their tendency toward *ecological determinism*. Ecological determinism is the conceptual error of viewing the demographic characteristics of a geopolitical unit (such as a census tract or enumeration district) as causing its observed or inferred social conditions. Although the spatial characteristics of an area obviously influence and limit the social conditions and relationships in the area, these characteristics do not totally *determine* or, in an absolute sense, cause the social conditions.

Third, there is the danger of overgeneralization of the findings of a social indicators analysis. Many attempts have been made to equate the *modal* or *average* characteristics of individuals living in social areas (as measured by rates, averages, and the like) with the range of sociodemographic characteristics in these areas. It is inappropriate to impute to an area's residents psychological traits or characteristics that hypothetically correlate with the average or modal descriptors of that area. Generalizations based on summary statistics become somewhat less amenable to this criticism when analyses are done on meaningful sub-populations with demonstrated homogeneity. But, generally, statistical rates and averages should not be used as literal descriptors of "typical" individuals in a community. Taken to the extreme, this practice of drawing inferences at the individual level from data and relationships observed at the social area level is equivalent to stereotyping. It can be misleading, counterproductive, and potentially damaging.

However, these theoretical issues and drawbacks should not dissuade the use of social indicators to assess health and human service needs. The conclusions about needs derived from a social indicators analysis can be valid, reliable, and useful, particularly when such conclusions are corroborated by information obtained from a wide variety of data sources. The goal of social indicators studies is to analyze the relationship of spatial, sociodemographic, and social conditions of an area with the social behavior and well-being of the area's residents. Studies as comprehensive as this would most likely incorporate components of service utilization and citizen survey approaches.

EXAMPLES OF SOCIAL INDICATOR ANALYSES

We have selected two studies to illustrate how sociodemographic information can be integrated with service utilization data in a social indicator analysis. The first study (Bloom, 1975) focused on the relationship of an area's service utilization rate with its sociodemographic characteristics. The second study (Slem, 1975) represents an attempt to identify the smallest set of census variables that can be used to predict mental health service utilization rates.

1. *The Pueblo County, Colorado Study*

After Bloom (1975) collected first mental health admission data for Pueblo County, Colorado, he expanded his analysis to examine the relationship between admission rates and sociodemographic characteristics using the census tract as his unit of analysis.

TABLE 10.1

Census Tract Descriptors and Their Factor Structure in Bloom's (1975) Study[a]

Names of cluster and variable	Definition
Cluster I: Socioeconomic Affluence	
1. Housing Unit Value	Median value of owner-occupied housing unit
2. Family Income	Median family income
3. White Collar Workers	Percentage employed males in professional, technical, and kindred occupations
4. Education	Median school years completed by persons age 25 and above
5. Golf Club Members	Municipal golf club members per 1000 population—age 21 and over
6. Spanish Surname	Percentage Spanish surname (1960); Percentage persons of Spanish language plus other persons of Spanish surname (1970)
7. Central Heating	Percentage all year-round housing units with central heating
8. Families Receiving ADC	Percentage of families receiving Aid to Dependent Children federal assistance
9. Library Card Holders	Public library card holders per 1000 population—age 5 and above
10. Married Women in Labor Force	Percentage nonseparated women in labor force
11. Unemployment	Percentage of male civilian labor force unemployed
12. Household Population Density	Percentage occupied housing units occupied by more than one person per room
Cluster II: Social Disequilibrium	
13. Rooms per Housing Unit	Median number of rooms per housing unit
14. Marital Disruption	Number of divorced and separated males per 1000 married nonseparated males
15. People Living Alone	Percentage occupied housing units occupied by one person
16. Owner-Occupied Housing	Percentage occupied housing units owner-occupied
17. Delinquency	Juvenile delinquents per 100 population—age 18 and under
18. Single Homes	Percentage of all structures containing one housing unit
19. Vacant Housing	Percentage of year-round housing units available and vacant
20. Children Living With Both Parents	Percentage population 18 and under living with both parents
21. Household Fires	First-response household fire runs as percentage of total housing units

(Continued)

Table 10.1 (Continued)

22. School Dropouts	School dropouts per 1000 population—age 18 and under
Cluster III: Young Marrieds	
23. Young Children	Percentage married couples with own children under age 6
24. Household Population	Population per household
25. Median Age	Male median age
26. New Housing	Percentage of all housing units built in ten year period prior to census year
Unclustered Variables	
27. Population	Total population
28. Sex Ratio	Females per 100 males
29. Foreign Born	Percentage foreign born
30. YMCA Members	YMCA members per 1000 population—age 3 and above
31. Public Health Nursing Visits	Public health nursing caseload per 10,000 population
32. Residential Stability	Percentage of population age 5 or above in census year living in same house as 5 years earlier
33. Housing Lacking Plumbing	Percentage all year-round housing units lacking some or all plumbing facilities
34. Suicide Rate	Suicides (accumulated over 6 years) as proportion of total population
35. Fertility Ratio	Number of children under 5 per 100 females age 15–44

[a] Adapted by permission from B. L. Bloom, *Changing patterns of psychiatric care.* Copyright 1975, Human Sciences Press, New York.

As can be seen in Table 10.1, 35 census variables were selected to describe the census tracts. Using the cluster analysis method developed by Tryon and Bailey (1970), Bloom was able to collapse these variables into three major clusters that he designated as "Socioeconomic Affluence," "Social Disequilibrium," and "Young Marrieds." These clusters contained, respectively, 12, 10, and 4 variables, leaving 9 variables that stood alone (see Table 10.1). This data aggregation procedure allowed Bloom to describe Pueblo County using only a few salient social area characteristics. For example, the Pueblo County census tracts can be portrayed, using a shaded graphic technique, along the dimension of Social Disequilibrium as in Figure 10.1. From Figure 10.1, it is clear that Pueblo County, though having only a population of 118,238 in 1970, resembles the ecological arrangement so typical of many large cities in the United States. As mentioned earlier, social disorganization generally becomes more prevalent toward the core of these major cities.

Given the distribution of sociodemographic characteristics and the distribution of utilization rates in the county, the question can be asked: "Does the distribution of first inpatient admissions correspond to the typological description of Pueblo County along the identified social dimensions?" Bloom's analy-

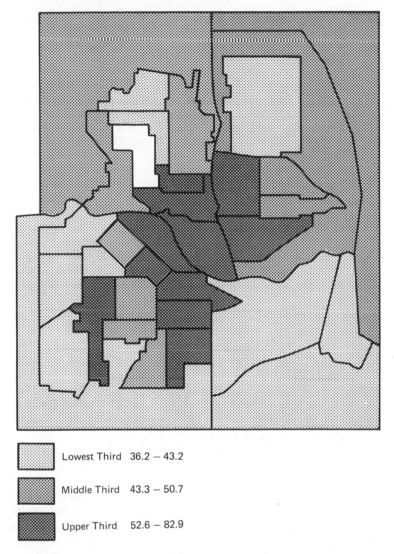

Lowest Third   36.2 − 43.2

Middle Third   43.3 − 50.7

Upper Third   52.6 − 82.9

Figure 10.1. Variation in *Social Disequilibrium* portrayed by Bloom (1975) across census tracts of Pueblo County, Colorado—1970. [Reproduced by permission from: B. L. Bloom, *Changing patterns of psychiatric care.* Copyright 1975, Human Sciences Press, New York.]

ses indicated that the answers were generally positive. As an example, we can examine Bloom's (1975) discussion of the correspondence between admission rates and social disequilibrium:

> Of the 150 correlation coefficients calculated between the social disequilibrium cluster score and the various admission rates, 79 are

significantly different from zero at the 0.05 level. This is ten times the number of significant correlations that would be expected by chance. And what is perhaps more striking is that without exception these significant correlations are all positive, that is, admission rates are highest from those census tracts characterized by high levels of social disorganization. Significant correlations are found not only for total age-adjusted rates but for every age and diagnostic group, although relationships do vary in magnitude. But the great and consistent repository of identified first admission psychiatric inpatients are those census tracts high in measures of social disequilibrium. This measure is most compellingly associated with admission rates for patients with personality disorders, males as well as females, into private as well as public facilities, and for both the 1960 and 1970 study periods. And the index of social disequilibrium is almost as closely related to admission rates for male patients with functional psychoses and for male patients with acute or chronic brain syndromes as it is for patients with personality disorders. Furthermore, the index of social disequilibrium is significantly correlated with age-specific admission rates at all ages except age 65 and above, and is especially highly correlated with admissions in the 35–64 age group [pp. 159–160].*

Bloom's exhaustive documentation of the empirical relationship between social disequilibrium and admission rates provided important corroborative evidence for many other similar past findings (cf. Kohn, 1968, pp. 156–158). Given these empirically documented associations between social conditions and treated incidence rates, epidemiologically oriented investigators would seek to understand the etiological meanings in these relationships. That is, these investigators would want to know, for example: "Whether this association comes about because certain characteristics inherent in the lower socioeconomic groups or environments produce psychopathology (the social causation hypothesis) or because persons already psychiatrically disabled drift or move into lower socioeconomic or more socially disorganized areas (the social selection hypothesis) [Bloom, 1975, p. 318]."

The debate surrounding the etiological meanings of empirical associations between social conditions and pathology is far from being settled. These associations, however, can be viewed in a different light. They can be interpreted as indicating the potential usefulness of social variables and indices as *predictors* of future social and personal disorders that will require intervention or prevention. This latter view prevails in the work of the NIMH group who constructed the MHDPS and in the study by Slem (1975) who attempted to select among the MHDPS variables those that can be used to predict most accurately and consistently the demand for and utilization of services.

2. The Use of MHDPS Variables to Predict Service Utilization Patterns

As we have described, a research group at NIMH has systematically compiled the 1970 census variables for the standard catchment areas in the

---

*Reproduced by permission from: B. L. Bloom, *Changing patterns of psychiatric care.* Copyright 1975, Human Sciences Press, New York.

United States. This compilation—referred to as the MHDPS—contains 131 census variables for each census tract. Most of the census variables were selected for inclusion in MHDPS because they relate theoretically to three social dimensions—social rank, life style, and ethnicity—that are generally used in social area analysis (Redick, Goldsmith, & Unger, 1971). Some of the MHDPS variables, such as "Teenagers not in school," "Aged persons living alone," or "Working mothers with pre-school children," were included because they were perceived as potentially useful in identifying specific high-risk groups (Redick *et al.*, 1971).

The most obvious utility of the MHDPS is to provide information for the description of the catchment area served by a community mental health center. Another potential use is the provision of information for assessing the relative distribution of service needs in the community and for planning services. However, the number of variables is unwieldy and little research has been done to establish the relationship of these variables (or combinations of variables) with specific types of mental health needs. Noting these two deficiencies, Slem (1975) attempted, through factor and correlation analyses, to identify the smallest subset of MHDPS variables that best predicted service utilization rates in Chicago, Detroit, and Baltimore.

TABLE 10.2

MHDPS Variables in Slem's (1975) Study[a]

Name of variable	Definition
Median Income	Median income of census tract
Median School Years	Median school years completed by persons 5 years or older in census tract
Low Occupational Status	Percentage of employed males 16 and older who are operative, service workers, and laborers including farm laborers
Married Persons	Percentage of household with husband-wife families
Divorced/Separated Males	Percentage males 14 and older who are divorced/separated
Single Males	Percentage males 25 and older who have never married
Isolation	Percentage of census tract households with only one person
Sex Ratio	Number of males per 100 females in a census tract
Ethnicity	Percentage of census tract population that is black
Geographic Mobility	Percentage of census tract population who moved there in 1969–70
Vacancy Index	Percentage of year-round housing units that are vacant
Over-Crowding	Percentage of household population in housing units with 1.51 or more persons per room
Single Dwellings	Percentage of all year-round housing units that are single detached, excluding mobile homes and trailers
Standard Housing	Percentage of occupied housing units with direct access, complete plumbing, and kitchen facilities for exclusive use

[a] Adapted by permission from C. M. Slem, *Community mental health need assessment: The prediction of census tract utilization patterns using the Mental Health Demographic Profile System* (Unpublished doctoral dissertation. Wayne State University, 1975).

Slem first identified 14 variables that (*a*) had high correlations with other variables within the same MHDPS social dimension, (*b*) were theoretically and statistically related to service utilization, and (*c*) were similar in definition to variables used in previous research. These 14 variables (see Table 10.2) were then examined for their ability to predict utilization as measured by public and private admissions, inpatient and outpatient admissions, and first and total admission rates. Slem found that, of the 14 variables, three indicators called "income," "divorced or separated males," and "isolation" generally formed the "best" subset of utilization predictors. In discussing his results, Slem (1975) noted:

> Correlational relationships between major MHDPS variables and ad-
> mission rates were consistent with . . . [prediction]. The relationships
> across catchment areas were consistent for the best subset of variables
> [i.e., income, divorced or separated males, and isolation] even though
> Detroit and Baltimore [admission data] were based on a single year of
> admissions. The MHDPS variables proved to be predictive of both
> inpatient and outpatient rates for these brief periods of time in small
> population areas in which rate instability is quite likely. The applica-
> tion of predictions with the MHDPS is not limited to the year sur-
> rounding the Federal Census . . . [since] the Detroit data were collected
> three years after the census, and the Baltimore admission rates were
> based on admissions two years before the census [pp. 150–151].*

Slem's study, therefore, demonstrated that the MHDPS is valuable not only for purposes of describing the community served by a community mental health center but is also a potentially useful tool for anticipating service needs and for identifying high-risk areas or patient subgroups in the community.

The two social indicator analyses discussed in this section, and other similar analyses, have confirmed the potential contribution of social and demographic variables in the identification of higher-risk areas in a community. Although this contribution is extremely valuable, it should be noted that, at present, the social indicator approach to need assessment only provides *qualitative* information about future trends and relative likelihood of needs. That is, one can, on the basis of social and demographic profiles, evaluate only the relative risks that different ecological and social areas in a community may have for social and personal dysfunctioning. However, in order to plan and allocate resources equitably and rationally, planners and administrators must also know the *magnitude* of current and future needs and the extent of potential utilization or demand.

THE CITIZEN SURVEY APPROACH

A citizen survey is a systematic process of gathering information *directly* from a sample or the entire population of persons living in a community. As applied to need assessment, a citizen survey usually consists of structured

*Reproduced by permission from the author.

interview schedules or questionnaires that are designed to elicit information from respondents regarding their health, social well-being, and the patterns of care or services currently received or previously used.

The gathering of information by means of surveys has a very long history. In ancient times, surveys were designed for the enumeration of populations. Their results were often used for purposes of taxation and the procurement of laborers for work projects or military duty. The design and methodologies employed by Caesar's census takers may fare poorly in comparison with the techniques currently employed by the Bureau of the Census. Early Roman censuses were, nonetheless, effective sources of valuable information and, to this day, surveys represent a powerful tool for collecting information about individuals and the social area in which they live.

Surveys to ascertain health and mental health information typically have been employed for the following purposes:

1. To identify psychiatric symptomatology (Langner & Michael, 1963; Leighton et al., 1963; Pasamanick, 1959; Srole et al., 1962)
2. To identify levels of social functioning or resultant disability from mental and physical impairment by considering such factors as employment, interpersonal relationships, levels of aspiration and satisfaction, and human service utilization patterns (2; Hogarty, Katz, & Lowery, 1967; Schwab & Warheit, 1972; Schwab, Warheit, & Holzer, 1972; Warheit et al., 1974)
3. To ascertain service demands placed upon human service agencies and private practitioners and to describe existing human service resources (Moore et al., 1967; 10)
4. To document community residents' views of human service problems and service needs
5. To ascertain the extent of unmet needs, using both self-report data and professional evaluation of the respondent's social and health status (Carr & Wolfe, 1976).

Many types of information are obtainable through the citizen survey approach, but the extent of information to be gathered in a survey must be determined by the objectives of the study and by cost considerations. In the mental health field, Dohrenwend and Dohrenwend (1969) have systematically summarized the major findings of 44 survey studies of psychological disorder that have been conducted throughout the world. A careful reading of their work is recommended for readers interested in the substantive findings and the theoretical and methodological issues that exist in the survey approach to psychological disorder research.

DESIGN

There are five sequential stages in designing a survey study. These stages, as summarized in Table 10.3, involve (a) planning, (b) operational preparation, (c) data collection, (d) data preparation and analysis, and (e) presentation of findings. Table 10.3 also presents illustrative activities that typically occur at

TABLE 10.3
Operational Stages and Activities in Survey Studies

Stage	Illustrative activities
I. Planning	Identify potential utility and relevance of information (i.e., potential users, decision-making area)
	Secure commitment by potential users to use survey information
	Establish a steering committee
	Select the assessment study director
	Locate fiscal resources
II. Operational preparation	Select data gathering techniques
	Select sampling procedure and sample
	Determine specific content area(s) of survey
	Prepare items and construct interview schedules or questionnaires
	Hire and train interviewers
	Field test to evaluate
	• Nonresponse–refusal rate
	• Interviewers' skills and performance
	• Clarity of items and format
	Select data processing, data storage, and data analysis procedures
III. Data collection	Contact and interview respondents
	Edit and check-edit completed interviews
	Prepare keypunch instructions
	Prepare code book
	Hire and train coders
	Code and check-code responses
IV. Data preparation and analysis	Keypunch data and verify keypunching
	Merge card files to tape or disk
	Check and correct out-of-range codes
	Determine consistency checks and use consistency checks to detect and correct invalid data
	Document variable names, file location, values, and value labels
	Compute and generate new variables and indices
	Apply data analysis procedures to data
V. Presentation of findings	Identify audience
	Present and interpret results of study
	Formulate conclusions and recommendations
	Submit preliminary report(s) to decision-makers
	Prepare final report for wider audience

each stage. Since the activities that occur at the planning stage have been discussed earlier, we only want to reemphasize the importance of enlisting the cooperation of other organizations and agencies in the community. Broad-based cooperation is especially necessary if surveys are extensive and have implications or relevance to a wide range of human service programs. This cooperation is valuable for three reasons. First, the involvement of community organizations and agencies during the early stages of the study's development broadens the scope of the survey to include questions that are meaningful to a wide variety of agencies in the community. Such questions may deal with the utilization of services, consumer satisfaction, and perceived barriers to the delivery of services.

Second, other community organizations and agencies can provide approval and legitimization for the survey activities. Local medical societies, chambers of commerce, consumer protection groups, religious and charitable organizations can often facilitate entry into respondents' homes and/or encourage the participation of persons selected for interviewing. This is an important factor in survey design and should not be neglected.

And third, many of the community needs that are revealed by the survey will be broader than the mandate of any single categorical agency. Therefore, referrals, consultations, and the development of cooperative service programs designed to meet identified needs will be made easier by enlisting the guidance and support of the community's human service agencies at the beginning of the planning process.

The activities that occur at the stages of operational preparation, data collection, and data preparation and analysis have been widely discussed in the literature. For example, the Survey Research Center of the University of Michigan Institute of Social Research (1976) has provided an excellent review of the survey planning process and useful instructions for activities undertaken in large economic, social, and political surveys. In the subsequent sections, we focus on five important topics from the vast literature on survey design: the choice of a data gathering technique, interview and questionnaire item construction, sampling procedures, data preparation and analysis, and presenting survey findings and recommendations.

1. *Data Gathering Techniques*

The three most common techniques used in surveys to gather information are (*a*) the telephone interview; (*b*) the mailed questionnaire; and (*c*) the person-to-person interview. Although the methodology of each of these is somewhat different, their basic format is the same. Each contains a series of questions for potential respondents. For need assessment surveys, the questions are designed to elicit information regarding an individual's mental and physical health, medical history, use of human service agencies, self-perceptions of health and social needs, family problems, and other related data.

Each of the three survey techniques has characteristics that strongly influence the following:

1. Sampling procedures

2. Length of the questionnaire or interview schedule
3. Format in which the questions can be asked, recorded, and coded
4. Amount of time required for responding
5. Nonreturn or refusal rates
6. Costs in time and dollars
7. Validity of the findings.

Extensive research has been carried out on the relative merits and short-comings of the three techniques (telephone, mail, and individual interview) as used in economic, sociological, and psychological surveys. Lansing and Morgan (1971, pp. 104–117) provide an excellent review of this literature and the reader is referred to them for their interesting commentary.

Compared with the telephone and person-to-person interviews, the mailed questionnaire technique has the following advantages:

1. It has the greatest potential for ensuring respondents' anonymity
2. The collection of survey data through the mail does not require any special training of interviewers—a fact that minimizes human resource expenditure, simplifies operational organization, and results in low total cost
3. The economy of the mailed survey makes it possible, given the same amount of financial resource, to repeat the survey more frequently than would be the case with the telephone or person-to-person interviews
4. Because it is possible to gather information repeatedly on the same population (though not necessarily the same respondents), it becomes possible to establish a normative baseline with which to compare changes that occur over time.

However, these advantages of mailed surveys must be considered in the context of several disadvantages. From a comprehensive analysis of research done on mail surveys, including comparisons with the personal interview, Scott (1961) was able to summarize the following disadvantages of mail surveys:

1. Questionnaires sent through the mail may be answered by persons other than intended respondents
2. Respondents may not report spontaneous, first reactions since they may take time to think things out or to consult with others for appropriate or desirable responses
3. Respondents may not follow the order of the questions—a fact that precludes the sequencing of questions
4. Respondents may find it difficult to follow complex questions or instructions—a fact that reduces the design flexibility of the questionnaire
5. It is not possible to secure observational, corroborative information on the respondent's immediate environment, such as type of neighborhood, household living conditions and arrangement, or family atmosphere.

Furthermore, refusal rates are generally high in mail surveys; nonreturn rates may reach 60–70%. The refusal rates for telephone interviews, which also tend to be higher than for person-to-person interviews, are still much lower than for mail surveys

The choice between telephone and person-to-person interviews is more difficult to make. The overwhelming advantage of a telephone interview is its lower cost. Other advantages of the telephone interview include the possibilities that (a) the respondents feel a greater degree of control over the situation, since they know that they have the option of hanging up; (b) respondents may feel that their anonymity is better protected; and (c) respondents assume the interview will be brief. These psychological factors may enhance the respondent's cooperation on the phone.

On the other hand, the level of social motivation may be higher in the person-to-person interview, since the presence of an interviewer creates a sense of the importance of the need assessment study and allows the respondent to examine the interviewer's credentials. When the survey requires the collection of clinical diagnostic data, the person-to-person interview also allows the interviewer to take into account facial expression, body movements, and eye contact in evaluating the respondent. Furthermore, it has been found that respondents make more noncommittal answers and are less likely to reveal sensitive information on the phone (Schmiedeskamp, 1962). Finally, often, longer and more complicated interviews can be conducted in person than on the telephone.

2. Item Preparation for the Survey Instrument

The items selected for inclusion in the instrument must have a direct relationship to the specific goals of the need assessment study. The tendency to include a great many items simply because they are interesting must be avoided for several reasons: When items have no immediate relationship to the project's goals, the questionnaire/schedule will be fragmented and its structural integrity will be diminished. The cost of gathering and analyzing the data increases in proportion to the number of questions asked. When the respondent is overburdened with questions, the response rate is reduced, a condition that tends to reduce the validity of the findings.

The following criteria should be applied to screen the ethical propriety and structural adequacy of each question to be included in a survey instrument:

1. Is the question directly related to the goals and objectives of the need assessment study?
2. Is the type of question appropriate?
3. Is the item phrased clearly?
4. Does the question prompt the respondent toward a given type or style of response?
5. Does the question demand knowledge and information that the respondent does not have?

6. Does the question demand personal or sensitive information that the respondent may resist?
7. Have the issues related to cultural, linguistic, and value differences within the social area been fully considered in the preparation and selection of each question?

The Social Science Research Council (Van Dusen & Zill, 1975) has recommended a set of carefully worded questions for ascertaining age, sex, marital status, ethnic and religious affiliations, education, employment status, occupation, income, residential characteristics, and political identification. This core set of questions, together with procedures for coding responses, were selected by a group of representatives of academic, commercial, and federal survey agencies. This select panel reviewed items used in their own major survey programs and those of other organizations. The panel reported a set of questions that will provide adequate definition of important background variables with minimal investments of interview time and coding effort. An extremely helpful feature of the Social Science Research Council publication is the inclusion of comments by the representatives concerning the wording, formating, and coding procedures for the questions they proposed. We recommend that these questions be selected and used when surveyors collect basic descriptive information on respondents.

In addition to choosing carefully the type and wording of survey items, the format of the survey must be designed with care because it influences the response rate, affects the cost of gathering, coding, and processing the data and, most importantly, determines the types of statistical methods that can be used to analyze the results. For example, *open-ended questions* take more time to answer than questions with *fixed alternatives*—a fact that tends to increase the nonresponse rate. Open-ended questions also complicate response recording and coding procedures, and limit modes of analysis. A small number of open-ended questions may be asked in a questionnaire, but these must be clearly stated, easily answered and be placed at the end of the instrument.

The issue of what type of question to ask is related to the debate over the use of *structured* as opposed to *unstructured* schedules and questionnaires— a controversy that has endured among social scientists for a long time. In a structured format, questions are arranged sequentially in a logical order with branching and skipping instructions. Usually, answers to questions in a structured questionnaire are also preselected to represent fixed alternatives. Questions listed in Table 10.4 provide an example of a structured format. Generally the structured format is preferred for several reasons. First, it reduces interviewer contamination. Second, it produces standardized sets of response categories from which data can be more effectively coded and analyzed. Third, structured items, because they take less time to answer, permit inclusion of more questions in a given time period. And fourth, the structured formating, with fixed alternative items, greatly expands the range of statistical analyses that are appropriate and possible. Data gathered by unstructured schedules or questionnaires with a great many open-ended items rarely produce information appropriate for statistical analysis.

3. *Selecting the Sample*

The Bureau of the Census (1968), Kish (1965), and Moser (1958) have discussed in detail the different survey sampling methods and their application. Lansing and Morgan (1971, pp. 51–98) also discussed selected but important aspects of sampling problems. Lansing and Morgan's discussion, although it was aimed at economists, provides generally useful information to persons seeking knowledge about sampling problems and issues.

Some of the salient issues related to sampling methods are as follows:

1. What is the social unit for analysis? Will it be the individual, the family, or the household?
2. What type of data gathering technique should be used to collect the largest amount of reliable and useful information?
3. What is the sample size required to represent the population from which the sample is drawn?
4. What sampling technique should be used in order for the sample to be representative of the population?
5. How can a sampling frame be prepared?
6. What is the degree of statistical confidence the investigator wishes to accept?
7. How will the data be analyzed?
8. What are the relative costs associated with each sampling procedure?

In assessing needs for health and human services, the investigator will often have, from other existing information such as service utilization and social indicator data, a good notion about the prevalence of needs among subclasses of the population. These subgroups (or target populations) may be specified on the basis of such characteristics as area of residence, age, sex, ethnocultural background, and socioeconomic classes. In such instances, instead of randomly sampling the total population, quotas of interviews may be designed to produce a total sample that will match the population with regard to the above characteristics. This quota sampling procedure yields more information per dollar spent in data collection (Lansing & Morgan, 1971).

Given the number of respondents to be contacted in each subgroup (i.e., quota), the selection of interviewees (individual, family, or household) may be done in advance or may be left to the discretion of the interviewers. Preselection of interviewees is the more expensive of the two alternatives. It requires knowledge that potential interviewees meet selection criteria. Interviewers may also have to make several trips in order to contact the designated interviewees. On the other hand, when interviewers are free to select interviewees, the results may be biased. Respondents may be selected who are most available physically and ideologically, and who may, therefore, differ systematically from those who are more difficult to locate or contact. Furthermore, interviewers may select people who are similar to each other—a fact that leads to an underestimation of the variability in the population.

4. Coding and Preparing Survey Data for Analysis

After the data are collected, the information must be coded before it can be tabulated manually or placed on electronic data processing cards or tapes. Coding procedures will depend on the format of the questions (i.e., whether they are fixed alternative or open-ended), the structure of the instrument, the amount of information obtained, and the data analysis procedure planned. When the instrument is structured and contains few open-ended questions, the task of coding the responses is relatively simple. Unstructured instruments with large numbers of open-ended questions complicate the data analysis. Responses to open-ended questions must be sorted into categories before they can be coded or tallied. This is one of the basic advantages of structured instruments and one of the key disadvantages of ascertaining responses through open-ended questions.

The least technical way to prepare most data for analysis is through the use of tally sheets, in which each question is listed along with alternative responses. This approach permits some elementary statistical analysis such as averages and standard deviations for the total sample and for its various subgroups. However, when the sample is large, the data collection process lengthy, and the amount of information extensive, the use of tally sheets is so cumbersome and time-consuming that it is usually much more advisable to transfer the data to cards or magnetic tape for computer analysis. With the aid of a computer, many avenues of statistical analysis are opened. It has come as a surprise to many that computer analysis is often less expensive than analysis that depends on manual tabulations.

Electronic data processing also facilitates the integration of survey data with data obtained by other approaches (e.g., census information such as ecological characteristics, median level of education, and income; information about service utilization rates and about the residential area of the survey respondents).

Electronic processing also speeds up data transformation. There are four types of transformed or derived data: (a) class interval or bracket codes or recodes of quantitative information; (b) variables that are formed by combining other variables; (c) aggregate variables such as means of characteristics for subgroups to which a respondent belongs; and (d) indices that are linear combinations of the values of responses to several items or questions. An example of a variable that is a combination of other variables is the stage in the family life-cycle—a variable derived on the basis of information about age of family head, marital status, presence and number of children, and age of youngest child.

Most measurement of psychosocial functioning relies on multiple-item scales where response values to sets of items are aggregated to form indices. Another example is the socioeconomic status (SES) index, which is derived on the basis of education, occupation, and income. In studies where the number and types of derived variables are few, data coders may be able to compute the transformed variables manually using tally sheets. With electronic data processing, however, such computations are accomplished more rapidly and more accurately.

5. Presenting Survey Findings and Recommendations

The final stage of a survey consists of presenting the findings and making recommendations. Some of the most common forms of presenting the findings include summary tables, charts, and diagrams. The most important factor in choosing the exact mode of presentation is the anticipated audience. Statistical analyses have their place but should be used only with audiences that understand the assumptions and implications of such analyses. For most groups, descriptive summaries, charts, diagrams, and other visual aids will probably be far more useful. Of equal importance is the presentation of priorities and recommendations for action as well as time and cost estimates of the recommended options.

ADVANTAGES

Three of the many advantages of the citizen survey approach will be discussed. First, surveys that are carefully designed and conducted provide the most direct, scientifically valid, and reliable information about the needs and utilization patterns of individuals and families. Of all the approaches to need assessment, the citizen survey approach alone is capable of eliciting from *individuals* specific information about their own needs and utilization of services and about the needs and utilization patterns of their families.

A second important advantage is that survey information can be used to clarify the relevance of information obtained through other need assessment approaches. In many instances, the citizen survey approach is the only means for collecting information that can corroborate and integrate the findings of all other need assessment approaches. A citizen survey can also identify needs among residents who have not, for lack of awareness about services and for other reasons, contacted existing health and human service programs in the community.

A third important advantage of the citizen survey approach is its flexibility. Surveys can be designed in an extremely wide variety of ways to answer questions related to need for services. This design flexibility permits a choice of sampling techniques, item and instrument construction, specificity of inquiry, and also permits a multiplicity of data analysis procedures. This degree of flexibility is lacking in the other assessment techniques.

DISADVANTAGES AND COMMENTARY

Although they are often used, citizen surveys pose a number of problems, some of which are difficult to overcome (cf. Blum, 1974; Crandell & Dohrenwend, 1967; Dohrenwend & Dohrenwend, 1969; Kosa, Alpert, & Haggerty, 1967; Lapouse, 1967; Mechanic, 1970; Siegel *et al.*, 1977). First, as with all need assessment approaches, the validity of survey data is a basic problem. In the mental health field, for example, many have argued that prevalence rates documented through surveys have little value as guides to the planning of services because the basic problems related to psychiatric diagnostic nomenclature and to the definition and criteria for identifying and recognizing problems in living or psychiatric impairment have not been solved. However, citizen surveys that incorporate existing "state of the art" knowledge about human problems, illnesses, and social functioning can provide reliable information about (a) the distribution of physical and mental symptomatology; (b) the levels of physical, psychological, and social functioning; (c) the attitudes toward and utilization of service agencies; and (d) the general quality of life in a community. Such information is useful and important for estimating levels of service needs in the community.

Second, it is often difficult to ascertain the validity and reliability of the responses to survey questions about an individual's health needs and practices (Blum, 1974; Kosa *et al.,* 1967; Marquis, 1970). This difficulty, however, is not unique to survey approaches. The responses of individuals must be considered with caution, whether they report information about themselves or about others. There is no guarantee, for example, that information elicited by an intake worker in an agency is any more valid or reliable than information obtained by an interviewer in a nonagency setting. The problems of memory span, accurate recall, and verbal skills are present in both instances, and must be given careful consideration by those who are going to make judgments on the basis of the information received.

Third, surveys—particularly very large ones that are designed to measure prevalence or incidence—are more difficult to define, conceptualize, and operationalize than any of the other need assessment approaches outlined in this volume. However, surveys need not always be large and complex or prohibitively expensive. Once the objectives are defined and the budgetary limits are set for a definitive need assessment study, one can carefully develop and implement a citizen survey that is compatible with the human and financial resources of community-based planners (Beigel, Hunter, Tamerin, Chapin, & Lowery, 1974; Beigel, McCabe, Tamerin, Lowery, Chapin, & Hunter, 1974).

Fourth, some individuals are reluctant to supply information about themselves or other family members. Although the refusal and nonreturn rates vary depending on the survey technique employed, they are often high enough to reduce the effectiveness of a survey, regardless of the technique employed.

The fifth and final problem with surveys is the potential for *decision submergence.* Decision submergence occurs when the surveyor's curiosity and interest take precedence over the primary objectives of the need assessment study (cf. Thompson, 1975, pp. 86–87). This problem is not unique to the survey approach. However, there is a greater likelihood of its occurrence because (a) the operations necessary for a successful survey are very complex; (b) the design of a survey is flexible and often very fluid; and (c) the data can be subjected to almost unlimited manipulation and analysis. The complexity of the operations, the flexibility of the design, and the availability of data analysis procedures can lead to a tendency to take undue time to plan the survey, to polish the research design to its most elegant form, and to milk all possible knowledge out of the data. When this happens, the survey results may be so delayed that they become irrelevant to the policy or decision-making process. The potential for decision submergence in the survey, as well as in other approaches to need assessment, points to the necessity for a steering committee to monitor persistently the progress of the survey. It also points to the advisability of including in this overseer body the broadest range of community, organizational, and professional representatives.

EXAMPLE OF THE CITIZEN SURVEY APPROACH

We will cite one study from the mental health field in order to illustrate how a citizen survey can be developed and implemented to provide need assessment information. The study, a personal-interview-based survey carried out in a central Florida county, was designed to assess the level of mental and physical health needs and service utilization in the county (2; 5; Schwab et al., 1972; 9).

The need assessors began the study by developing a theoretical framework in which mental illness was defined to involve personal distress, behavior disorders, and deviance that had to be interpreted in terms of interpersonal and social contexts (Schwab & Warheit, 1972). The investigators' operational measures of mental illness status, *social psychiatric impairment,* were assessed with four criteria:

1. Traditional psychological and physical symptom nomenclatures
2. Levels of social functioning—at home, at work, and in other social arenas
3. Meaningfulness (quality) and extent (quantity) of interpersonal relationships
4. Levels of social aspiration and general life satisfaction.

Items that were judged capable of providing information relative to these four types of assessment criteria were incorporated into a survey instrument that was administered through person-to-person interviews to randomly selected residents of the county. This interview also included items pertaining to the respondents' demographic characteristics, social history, religious affiliation and practices, perceptions of social change, and attitudes toward and utilization of mental and physical health services.

Table 10.4 presents a subset of the 147 items employed in the survey and illustrates the format used to record responses, code the answers, and keypunch the coded data. (The subset of items presented in Table 10.4 originally appeared in the Health Opinion Survey that was designed to measure psychological disorder among residents of Stirling County, Canada [Leighton et al., 1963].) As illustrated in Table 10.4, items required fixed-alternative responses. The interviewer read each item and its alternative answers to the respondent who chose one answer. The interviewer then circled the answer on a questionnaire booklet. Subsequently, coders transferred the numerical value of responses in the additional spaces provided for that purpose. These numerical codes were next keypunched on computer cards. Instructions about appropriate card and column numbers for numerical codes were also preprinted on the survey instrument (see Columns 2 and 3 of Table 10.4) to minimize keypunching errors. These instructions also informed data analysts about the location of data on the computer tapes that were subsequently produced.

Sample selection for the central Florida county study was done in three stages. First, 37,000 households were enumerated; second, 2333 addresses were randomly selected from among the enumerated households; and third, a person within each selected household was randomly chosen as the respondent to be contacted. The final sample on which survey information was collected consisted of 1645 respondents.

TABLE 10.4
Examples of Items Used in a Citizen Survey[a]

Item no. in survey instrument[b]	Question	Column Card 5		Response choices
73.	In general, how would you say your mental health has been?	58	_____	1 Excellent 2 Good 3 Fair 4 Poor 5 Very bad 7 Don't know 8 Not answered
74.	Do your hands ever tremble enough to bother you? Would you say:	59	_____	3 Often 2 Sometimes 1 Never 7 Don't know 8 Not answered
75.	Are you ever troubled by your hands or feet sweating so that they feel damp and clammy? Would you say:	60	_____	3 Often 2 Sometimes 1 Never 7 Don't know 8 Not answered
76.	Have you ever been bothered by your heart beating hard? Would you say:	61	_____	3 Often 2 Sometimes 1 Never 7 Don't know 8 Not answered

[a] Questionnaire items reproduced by permission from: D. C. Leighton, J. S. Harding, D. B. Macklin, A. MacMillan, and A. H. Leighton, *The character of danger. Vol. III. The Stirling County study of psychiatric disorder and sociocultural environment.* Copyright 1963, Basic Books, New York.

[b] Item number and format are reproduced from the *Florida Health and Family Life Survey Instrument.* Information about this instrument can be obtained from: G. J. Warheit, Department of Psychiatry, School of Medicine, University of Florida, Box J-265, Gainesville, Florida 32610.

Table 10.4 (Continued)

77.	Do you tend to feel tired in the mornings? Would you say:	62	_____	3 Often 2 Sometimes 1 Never 7 Don't know 8 Not answered
78.	Do you have trouble getting to sleep and staying asleep? Would you say:	63	_____	3 Often 2 Sometimes 1 Never 7 Don't know 8 Not answered
79.	How often are you bothered by having an upset stomach? Would you say:	64	_____	3 Often 2 Sometimes 1 Never 7 Don't know 8 Not answered
80.	Are you ever bothered by nightmares (dreams which frighten you)? Would you say:	65	_____	3 Often 2 Sometimes 1 Never 7 Don't know 8 Not answered
81.	Have you ever been troubled by "cold sweats"? Would you say:	66	_____	3 Often 2 Sometimes 1 Never 7 Don't know 8 Not answered
82.	Do you feel that you are bothered by all sorts (different kinds) of ailments in different parts of your body? Would you say:	67	_____	3 Often 2 Sometimes 1 Never 7 Don't know 8 Not answered
83.	Do you smoke? Would you say:	68	_____	3 A lot 2 Sometimes 1 Never 7 Don't know 8 Not answered
84.	Do you ever have loss of appetite? Would you say:	69	_____	3 Often 2 Sometimes 1 Never 7 Don't know 8 Not answered
85.	Has any ill health affected the amount of work (household) you do? Would you say:	70	_____	3 Often 2 Sometimes 1 Never 7 Don't know 8 Not answered
86.	Do you ever feel weak all over? Would you say:	71	_____	3 Often 2 Sometimes 1 Never 7 Don't know 8 Not answered

(Continued)

Table 10.4 (Continued)

87.	Do you ever have spells of dizziness? Would you say:	72	_____	3 Often 2 Sometimes 1 Never 7 Don't know 8 Not answered
88.	Do you tend to lose weight when you worry? Would you say:	73	_____	3 Often 2 Sometimes 1 Never 7 Don't know 8 Not answered
89.	Have you ever been bothered by shortness of breath when you were not exerting yourself? Would you say:	74	_____	3 Often 2 Sometimes 1 Never 7 Don't know 8 Not answered
90.	For the most part, do you feel healthy enough to carry out the things that you would like to do? Would you say:	75	_____	3 Often 2 Sometimes 1 Never 7 Don't know 8 Not answered
91.	Do you feel in good spirits? Would you say:	76	_____	1 Most of the time 2 Sometimes 3 Very few times 7 Don't know 8 Not answered
92.	Do you sometimes wonder if anything is worthwhile anymore? Would you say:	77	_____	3 Often 2 Sometimes 1 Never 7 Don't know 8 Not answered

Among the many interesting sets of information collected in the study, one subset of data describing mental health service needers and utilizers was selected for illustrative purposes (see Table 10.5). A respondent was judged to be in need of mental health services if his or her total score on the 20-item psychological disorder measure (see Table 10.4) exceeded 30. The second column in Table 10.5 presents the numbers and proportions of respondents in the total sample and in the various race, sex, age, and socioeconomic subgroups who were judged to be in need of mental health services. The overall sample percentage of 18.4 is slightly lower than the figure (20%) obtained in the Stirling County study where the same 20-item psychological disorder scale was used. The distribution of needers, however, varied significantly and widely from one subgroup to another. The third column in Table 10.5 presents the numbers and proportions (across the total sample and for each subgroup) of needers who were using mental health services at the time of the survey. Differences between the second and third column proportions give estimates of the numbers and proportions of persons who needed mental health care but were not receiving such care (see Column 4, Table 10.5).

TABLE 10.5
Mental Health Need and Service Utilization of Sociodemographic Groups in a Central Florida County[a]

Sociodemographic group	Sample size[c]	Mental health service needers		Utilizing needers		Nonutilizing needers	
		Number	Percent[b]	Number	Percent[b]	Number	Percent[b]
Total	1645	303	18.4	76	4.6	227	13.8
Race							
Black	366	108	29.5	7	2.0	101	27.6
White	1267	194	15.3	67	5.3	127	10.0
Sex							
Male	736	107	14.5	29	3.9	78	10.6
Female	909	194	21.3	47	5.2	147	16.2
Age							
16–29	585	74	12.6	45	7.7	29	5.0
30–44	411	78	18.9	17	4.1	61	14.8
45–59	332	76	22.9	9	2.7	67	20.2
60+	315	74	23.5	3	1.0	71	22.5
Socioeconomic status							
(Lowest) 1	216	82	37.9	3	1.4	79	36.6
2	382	100	26.1	18	4.7	82	21.5
3	483	69	14.2	24	5.0	45	9.3
4	341	37	10.9	19	5.6	18	5.3
(Highest) 5	223	16	7.2	11	4.9	5	2.2

[a] Adapted from: G. J. Warheit, R. A. Bell, and J. J. Schwab, *Planning for change: Needs assessment approaches*. Rockville, Maryland: National Institute of Mental Health, 1974.

[b] Percentage of sample size column.

[c] Subsample Ns within sociodemographic classification may not sum to the total sample size because of missing data.

Information of the type presented in Table 10.5 has direct relevance for planning services to underserved subgroups in the community. Comparing, for example, the black and white subsamples, one notes that the proportion of needers was almost twice as large in the black subsample (29.5%) as in the white subsample (15.3%). Yet the opposite was true of the proportions of blacks and whites using mental health services. Consequently, the proportion of "nonutilizing needers" was almost three times as large among blacks (27.6%) as among whites (10.0%). These data indicate clearly that effort and resources should be deployed in order to bring more services to the black population in the county and/or to make services more appropriate and accessible to the black population.

Another stark contrast can be observed between the highest and the lowest SES groups: The proportion of nonutilizing needers was almost 16 times as large in the lowest (36.6%) as compared to the highest group (2.2%). This discrepancy between the two SES groups in terms of unmet need existed because the highest SES group, relative to the lowest group, had both a very low level of need (7.2% versus 37.9%) and a high level of utilization (4.9% versus 1.4%). Again, these data indicate clearly the need to deploy resources toward providing more services to the lower SES residents and/or enhancing the appropriateness and accessibility of current services.

One may argue that the 20-item scale that was employed to determine psychological disorder led to higher estimates than would have been obtained by other case detection or case determination methods (cf. Lapouse, 1967). This argument, however, does not mollify the implications of the data in Table 10.5 in terms of subgroup comparisons, unless one can show that the psychological disorder scale discriminated against residents on the basis of sex, age, race, or SES. To illustrate this point, let us suppose that the estimated black and white proportions of needers in Table 10.5 were in fact higher than was actually the case, and that there was no interaction between test bias sensitivity and race. We would then reduce the black and white percentages in Table 10.5 by a uniform correction factor. This procedure would, however, leave the *relative* black-to-white needers ratio intact and we would still find that there was a greater preponderance of unmet need among blacks than among whites.

SUMMARY

Service utilization analysis, social indicator analysis, and citizen surveys are three of the more technical approaches to need assessment. Each of these approaches can provide important information about the level and/or distribution of needs in a community. The validity of need information derived from each approach depends on the assumptions that underlie the approach. Common to all approaches is the basic assumption that the data employed are reliable and valid. In addition, the *service utilization* approach requires the assumptions that needs are translated directly into demand for services and that utilization data document accurately current levels of needs for services. In the *social indicator* approach, it is assumed that needs for services bear a monotonic relationship with indices of the quality of life and social conditions that prevail in the community. For example, a social indicator analysis might assume that populations living in social areas characterized by a higher standard of living or a lower social disorganization will have a lower need level than populations in social areas with a lower standard of living. Finally, the basic assumption underlying the *citizen survey* approach is that information about social, physical, and psychological impairments obtained directly from survey respondents or through interviewers' observations is comparable to the information obtained in service facilities by professional service providers. In the health and mental health field, it is assumed specifically that survey measures of social, physical, or mental disorders provide data comparable to data obtained by other clinically accepted and standardized diagnostic procedures. In general, if the assumptions underlying each need assessment strategy are not fully met, ambiguous or erroneous information about service needs may result.

In addition to differences in their basic underlying assumptions, the three need assessment approaches discussed in this chapter also differ in terms of the nature and sources of data, the procedures for collecting and analyzing the data, and the amount of resources and expertise required to complete the study. These methodological and procedural differences create differences in the strengths, weaknesses, and utility of the approaches. For example, the usefulness of a service utilization analysis depends largely on the adequacy and comparability of human service information systems within the community agencies. A social indicator analysis can, at present, only provide information about the *relative* distribution of needs within a community or among demographic subgroups of residents. This limitation of the social indicator approach arises because methodological procedures have not yet been developed and validated to allow us to derive *quantitative* estimates of service needs on the basis of information about the community's social and economic conditions. For example, there exists no validated procedure for determining the number or proportion of residents who need a given type of service on the basis of data about the poverty level, social organization, or family structure that prevail in a social area. Finally, a citizen survey, although capable of providing both relative and quantitative estimates of needs, often demands excessive resources, expertise, and organizational support from the service delivery system. Additional difficulties with the citizen survey approach include the reluctance of respondents to supply requested information, the greater potential for decision submergence, and the issues of reliability and validity of questionnaires and diagnostic measuring instruments.

As discussed in Chapter 9 of this volume (see Table 9.1), each approach also reflects a different perspective guiding the determination of community needs. In health and human service programs, the decision as to which persons qualify for services, what types of services should be given, and to what service recipient category a service-seeker belongs, rests with professional service providers. Providers' decisions, therefore, determine to a very significant extent the basic information that is incorporated into a service utilization analysis (7). Thus, statements about the nature and distribution of needs based on service utilization data reflect ultimately the viewpoints of professional service providers. By contrast, statements about the nature, extent, and distribution of community needs derived from a citizen survey reflect generally the viewpoints of citizens as interpretatively filtered through the conceptual perspectives of need assessors. Finally, the social indicator approach extracts information relative to community needs from data collected by government agencies, demographers, or academicians. These agencies and persons are guided by their own views of the community or of the society at large when they define the information domains and data collection procedures. Therefore, need statements based on the social indicator approach reflect the viewpoints and perspectives of the original data gatherers, that is, government agencies, demographers, and academicians.

The perspectives reflected in these differing need assessment approaches may, at times, prove incompatible with each other. However, if they are well integrated, the various perspectives can provide the type of need information that enhances the integration of services and promotes the deployment of services more in concert with conditions in the community.

REFERENCE NOTES

1. Babigian, H. M. *Schizophrenia in Monroe County.* Paper read at "Schizophrenia—The Implications of Research Findings for Treatment and Teaching," a conference sponsored by the National Institute of Mental Health and the John E. Fogarty International Center, National Institutes of Health, May 1970.
2. Bell, R. A., & Mellan, W. *Southern health and family life studies: Vol. I. An assessment of needs: An epidemiologic survey.* Florida Mental Health Evaluation Consortium, 1974. (Available from the first author, Health Sciences Center, P. O. Box 1055, School of Medicine, University of Louisville, Kentucky 40201.)
3. Bodian, C., Gardner, E., Willis, E., & Bahn, A. *Socio-economic indicators from census tract data related to rates of mental illness.* (Working Paper No. 17.) Washington, D. C.: U. S. Department of Commerce, Bureau of the Census, September 5, 1965.
4. Gabbay, M., & Windle, C. D. *Demographic data to improve services: A sampler of mental health applications.* (MHDPS Working Paper No. 33.) Rockville, Maryland: National Institute of Mental Health, 1975.
5. Grey, R. J., Warheit, G. J., & Schwab, J. J. *An index of sociomedical well-being. A case study in assessing community health needs and services.* Unpublished manuscript, 1973. (Available from the second author, Department of Psychiatry, School of Medicine, University of Florida, J. Hillis Miller Health Center, Box J-265, Gainesville, Florida 32610.)
6. *Mental Health Statistical News,* October 4, 1976. A publication of the Division of Biometry and Epidemiology, National Institute of Mental Health, 5600 Fishers Lane, Rockville, Maryland 20852.
7. Nguyen, T. D., Attkisson, C. C., & Bottino, M. J. *Definition and identification of human service need in a community context.* Paper presented at the National Conference on Needs Assessment in Health and Human Services, Louisville, Kentucky, March 1976.
8. Rice, R., & Fowler, G. *The relationship of mental health admission rates and other selected characteristics among 25 geographic areas.* Paper presented at the Western Psychological Association Convention, Anaheim, California, April 1973.
9. Schwab, J. J., Warheit, G. J., & Holzer, C. E. *Mental health: Rural–urban comparisons.* Paper presented at the IV International Congress of Social Psychiatry, Jerusalem, May 1972.

10. Weiss, A. E. *Consumer model of assessing community mental health needs.* (California Data: Methodology and Applications, No. 8.) Sacramento, California: Bureau of Biostatistics, Department of Health, State of California, 1971.

REFERENCES

Attkisson, C. C. Suicide in San Francisco's skid row. *Archives of General Psychiatry,* 1970, *23,* 149–157.

Babigian, H. M. The role of epidemiology and mental health care statistics in the planning of mental health centers. In A. Beigel & A. I. Levenson (Eds.), *The community mental health center: Strategies and programs.* New York: Basic Books, 1972. (a)

Babigian, H. M. The role of psychiatric case registers in the longitudinal study of psychopathology. In M. Roff, L. N. Robins, & M. Pollack (Eds.), *Life history research in psychopathology* (Vol. 2). Minneapolis: University of Minnesota Press, 1972. (b)

Babigian, H. M., Gardner, E. A., Miles, H. C., & Romano, J. Diagnostic consistency and change in a followup study of 1215 patients. *The American Journal of Psychiatry,* 1965, *121,* 895–901.

Beigel, A., Hunter, E. J., Tamerin, J. S., Chapin, E. H., & Lowery, M. J. Planning for the development of comprehensive community alcoholism services: I. The prevalence survey. *American Journal of Psychiatry,* 1974, *131,* 1112–1115.

Beigel, A., McCabe, T. R., Tamerin, J. S., Lowery, M. J., Chapin, E. H., & Hunter, E. J. Planning for the development of comprehensive community alcoholism services: II. Assessing community awareness and attitudes. *American Journal of Psychiatry,* 1974, *131,* 1116–1120.

Bloom, B. L. *Changing patterns of psychiatric care.* New York: Human Sciences Press, 1975.

Blum, H. L. *Planning for health: Development and application of social change theory.* New York: Human Science Press, 1974.

Bruning, J. L., & Kintz, B. L. *Computational handbook of statistics.* Glenview, Illinois: Scott, Foresman, 1968.

Bureau of the Census. *Sampling lectures.* (I. S. P., Supplemental Course Series No. 1.) Washington, D. C.: U. S. Department of Commerce, Bureau of the Census, 1968.

Carr, W., & Wolfe, S. Unmet needs as sociomedical indicators. *International Journal of Health Services,* 1976, *6,* 417–430.

Clark, R. Psychoses, income, and occupational prestige. *American Journal of Sociology,* 1949, *53,* 433–440.

Clausen, J. A., & Kohn, M. L. Relation of schizophrenia to the social structure of a small city. In B. Pasamanick (Ed.), *Epidemiology of mental disorder.* Washington, D. C.: American Association for the Advancement of Science, 1959.

Cohen, B. M., & Fairbanks, R. E. Statistical contributions from the mental hygiene study of the Eastern Health District of Baltimore. I. General account of the 1933 mental hygiene survey of the Eastern Health District. *American Journal of Psychiatry,* 1938, *94,* 1153–1161.

Crandell, D. L., & Dohrenwend, B. P. Some relations among psychiatric symptoms, organic illness, and social class. *American Journal of Psychiatry,* 1967, *123,* 1527–1538.

Dohrenwend, B. P., & Dohrenwend, B. S. *Social status and psychological disorder.* New York: Wiley, 1969.

Dunham, H. W. *Community and schizophrenia: An epidemiological analysis.* Detroit: Wayne State University Press, 1965.

Faris, R. E. L., & Dunham, H. W. *Mental disorders in urban areas.* Chicago: University of Chicago Press, 1939.

Galle, O., Gove, W., McPherson, J., & Miller, J. Population density and pathology. *Science,* 1972, *176,* 23–30.

Gardner, E. A. The use of a psychiatric case register in the planning and evaluation of a mental health program. *Psychiatric Research Reports of the American Psychiatric Association,* 1967, *22,* 259–281.

Gardner, E. A., Bahn, A. K., & Miles, H. C. Patient experience in psychiatric units of general and state mental hospitals. *Public Health Reports,* 1964, *79,* 755–767.

Goldsmith, H. F., Unger, E. L., Rosen, B. M., Shambaugh, J. P., & Windle, C. D. *A typological approach to doing social area analysis.* (DHEW Publication No. ADM 76-262.) Rockville, Maryland: National Institute of Mental Health, 1975.

Henisz, J. E., Tischler, G. L., & Myers, J. K. *Epidemiology and ecologic analyses.* In D. C. Riedel, G. T. Tischler, & J. K. Myers (Eds.), *Patient care evaluation in mental health programs.* Cambridge, Massachusetts: Ballinger, 1974.

Hogarty, G. E., Katz, M. M., & Lowery, H. A. Identifying candidates from a normal population for a community mental health program. *Psychiatric Report,* 1967, *22,* 220–234.

Hollingshead, B., & Redlich, F. C. *Social class and mental illness.* New York: John Wiley, 1958.

Isaac, S., & Michael, W. B. *Handbook in research and evaluation.* San Diego, California: EDITS, 1971.

Jaco, E. G. Incidence of psychosis in Texas: 1951–1952. *Texas State Journal of Medicine,* 1957, *53,* 86–91.

Jaco, E. G. *The social epidemiology of mental disorders.* New York: Russel Sage Foundation, 1960.

Keller, M., & Efron, V. Alcoholism in the big cities of the United States. *Quarterly Journal for the Study of Alcohol,* 1956, *17,* 63–72.

Kish, L. *Survey sampling.* New York: John Wiley, 1965.

Klee, G., Spiro, E., Bahn, A., & Gorwitz, K. An ecological analysis of diagnosed mental illness in Baltimore. In R. Monroe, G. Klee, & E. Brody (Eds.), *Psychiatric epidemiology and mental health planning.* (Psychiatric Research Report No. 22.) American Psychiatric Association, 1967.

Kohn, M. L. Social class and schizophrenia: A critical review. In D. Rosenthal & S. S. Kety (Eds.), *The transmission of schizophrenia.* Oxford: Pergamon Press, 1968.

Kosa, J., Alpert, J. J., & Haggerty, R. J. On the reliability of family health information. *Social Science and Medicine,* 1967, *1,* 165–181.

Kramer, M. A discussion of the concepts of incidence and prevalence as related to epidemiologic studies of mental disorders. *American Journal of Public Health,* 1957, *47,* 826–840.

Langner, T. S., & Michael, S. T. *Life stress and mental health: The midtown Manhattan study* (Vol. II). Glencoe, Illinois: Free Press, 1963.

Lansing, J. B., & Morgan, J. N. *Economic survey methods.* Ann Arbor, Michigan: Survey Research Center, Institute for Social Research, University of Michigan, 1971.

Lapouse, R. Problems in studying the prevalence of psychiatric disorder. *American Journal of Public Health,* 1967, *57,* 947–954.

Leighton, A. H. *My name is legion. Vol. I. The Stirling County study of psychiatric disorder and sociocultural environment.* New York: Basic Books, 1959.

Leighton, D. C., Harding, J. S., Macklin, D. B., Macmillan, A., & Leighton, A. H. *The character of danger. Vol. III. The Stirling County study of psychiatric disorder and sociocultural environment.* New York: Basic Books, 1963.

Lemkau, P. V. Assessing a community's need for mental health services. *Hospital and Community Psychiatry,* 1967, *18,* 65–70.

Lemkau, P. V., Tietze, C., & Cooper, M. Mental hygiene problems in an urban district. *Mental Hygiene,* 1942, *26,* 100–119.

Levy, L., & Rowitz, L. *The ecology of mental disorder.* New York: Behavioral Publications, 1973.

Linden, F. E. National health interview surveys. *Public Health Papers* (No. 27, 78–112). Geneva: World Health Organization, 1965.

Linton, M., & Gallo, P. S. *The practical statistician: A simplified handbook of statistics.* Belmont, California: Brooks/Cole, 1975.

MacMahon, B. Epidemiologic methods. In D. W. Clark & B. MacMahon (Eds.), *Preventive medicine.* New York: Little, Brown, 1967.

MacMahon, B., Pugh, T. F., & Ipsen, J. *Epidemiologic methods.* Boston: Little, Brown, 1960.

Malzberg, B. *Social and biological aspects of mental illness.* Utica, New York: State Hospital Press, 1940.

Marquis, K. H. Effect of social reinforcement on health reporting in the household interview. *Sociometry,* 1970, *33,* 203–215.

McHarg, I. L. *Design with nature.* New York: The Natural History Press, 1969.

Mechanic, D. Problems and prospects in psychiatric epidemiology. In E. Hare & J. K. Wing (Eds.), *An international symposium on psychiatric epidemiology.* London: Oxford University Press, 1970.

Miles, H. C., & Gardner, E. A. A psychiatric case register. *Archives of General Psychiatry,* 1966, *14,* 571–580.

Moore, D. N., Bloom, B. L., Gaylin, S., Pepper, M., Pettus, C., Willis, E. M., & Bahn, A. K. Data utilization for local community mental health program development. *Community Mental Health Journal,* 1967, *3,* 30–32.

Moser, C. A. *Survey methods in social investigation.* London: Heinemann, 1958.

Pasamanick, B. *Epidemiology of mental disorder.* Washington, D. C.: American Association for the Advancement of Science, 1959.

Pasamanick, B., Roberts, D., Lemkau, P. V., & Krueger, D. A survey of mental disease in an urban population: Prevalence by race and income. In B. Pasamanick (Ed.), *Epidemiology of mental disorder.* Washington, D. C.: American Association for the Advancement of Science, 1959.

Pasamanick, B., Roberts, D., Lemkau, P. V., & Krueger, D. A survey of mental disease in an urban population. In F. Reissman, J. Cohen, & A. Pearls (Eds.), *Mental health of the poor.* New York: Free Press, 1966.

Redick, R. W., Goldsmith, H. F., & Unger, E. L. *1970 census data used to indicate areas with different potentials for mental health and related problems.* (DHEW Publication No. HSM 72-9051.) Rockville, Maryland: National Institute of Mental Health, 1971.

Rosen, B. M. *A model for estimating mental health needs using 1970 census socioeconomic data.* (DHEW Publication No. HSM 72-9051.) Rockville, Maryland: National Institute of Mental Health, 1974.

Rosen, B. M., Lawrence, L., Goldsmith, H. F., Windle, C. D., & Shambaugh, J. P. *Mental health demographic profile system description: Purpose, contents, and sampler of uses.* (DHEW Publication No. ADM 76-263.) Rockville, Maryland: National Institute of Mental Health, 1975.

Schwab, J. J., & Warheit, G. J. Evaluating Southern mental health needs and services. *Florida Medical Journal,* 1972, *59,* 17–20.

Schwab, J. J., Warheit, G. J., & Holzer, C. E. Suicidal ideation and behavior in a general population. *Diseases of the Nervous System,* 1972, *33,* 745–748.

Schmiedeskamp, J. Reinterviews by telephone. *Journal of Marketing,* 1962, *26,* 28–34.

Scott, C. Research on mail surveys. *Journal of the Royal Statistical Society,* 1961, *124,* 143–195.

Siegel, L. M., Attkisson, C. C., & Cohn, A. H. Mental health needs assessment: Strategies and techniques. In W. A. Hargreaves, C. C. Attkisson, & J. E. Sorensen (Eds.), *Resource materials for community mental health program evaluation* (2nd ed.). (DHEW Publication No. ADM 77-328.) Washington, D. C.: U. S. Government Printing Office, 1977.

Slem, C. M. Community mental health need assessment: The prediction of census tract utilization patterns using the Mental Health Demographic Profile System (Unpublished doctoral dissertation. Wayne State University, 1975). *Dissertation Abstracts International,* 1976, *36,* 5817-B. (University Microfilms No. 76-11002, 214.)

Srole, L., Langner, T. S., Michael, S. T., Opler, M. K., & Rennie, T. A. *Mental health in the metropolis.* New York: McGraw-Hill, 1962.

Stewart, R., & Poaster, L. Methods of assessing mental and physical health needs from social statistics. *Evaluation,* 1975, *2*(2), 67–70.

Survey Research Center. *Interviewer's manual* (rev. ed.). Ann Arbor, Michigan: Institute for Social Research, University of Michigan, 1976.

Theodorson, G. A. *Studies in human ecology.* Evanston, Illinois: Row, Peterson, 1961.

Thompson, M. S. *Evaluation for decision in social programmes.* Lexington, Massachusetts: D. C. Heath, 1975.

Timm, N. H. *Multivariate analysis with applications in education and psychology.* Belmont, California: Brooks/Cole, 1975.

Tryon, R. C., & Bailey, D. E. *Cluster analysis.* New York: McGraw-Hill, 1970.

Van Dusen, R. A., & Zill, N. (Eds.). *Basic background items for U. S. household surveys.* New York: Social Science Research Council, 1975.

Warheit, G. J., Bell, R. A., & Schwab, J. J. *Planning for change: Needs assessment approaches.* Rockville, Maryland: National Institute of Mental Health, 1974.

Windle, C. D., Rosen, B. M., & Goldsmith, H. F. A demographic system for comparative assessment of needs for mental health services. In W. A. Hargreaves, C. C. Attkisson, & J. E. Sorensen (Eds.), *Resource materials for community mental health program evaluation* (2nd ed.). (DHEW Publication No. ADM 77-328.) Washington, D. C.: U. S. Government Printing Office, 1977.

IV

MEASUREMENT AND EVALUATION OF PROGRAM EFFECTIVENESS

If asked to select the single most distinctive contribution of program evaluation, we would nominate the introduction of information about program effects and relative cost–effectiveness into program management decisions. Examining program effectiveness is an advanced level of program evaluation that requires thoughtful preparation, careful instrumentation, and regular access to service recipients. Because adequate assessment of program effectiveness may be expensive, the allocation of these evaluation resources is itself an important management decision. Consequently, not all programs will be significantly involved in studies of effectiveness and only a few will achieve extensive investment in this area of evaluation.

Outcome evaluation involves the capacity to relate program effects to cost, effort, and client characteristics. For outcome and cost–effectiveness information to be useful, it must be applied within an active planning process designed to modify and improve service programs. The following chapters address the conceptual, methodological, and measurement issues related to this program improvement process.

No fully agreed upon methods of evaluating outcomes have been established and so a wide range of approaches must be considered. Part IV presents various approaches to assessing effectiveness that include (a) routine monitoring of client status as clients progress through service experiences, (b) goal-oriented methods involving tailor-made objectives for individual clients, and (c) more structured studies of program effects involving comparative designs and in-depth measurement with highly developed instrumentation. Also, the relationship of costs to outcomes and comparative effectiveness receives extensive coverage. In the concluding chapter of Part IV an approach to assessing the effectiveness of indirect services is presented.

11

EVALUATING PROGRAM OUTCOMES

William A. Hargreaves and C. Clifford Attkisson

Businesses must be profitable or, in general, they are abandoned. In contrast, it is commonly said that human services resist effective management because they cannot be held accountable for their results. While limited accountability is obtained by requiring a program to maintain specified levels of effort and to be accessible to clients, this level of accountability is easily achieved when services are publicly subsidized or prepaid through some form of insurance. Beyond this, how can we determine that a program is worth its cost? How can we learn to increase the value and benefits received for expenditures on human services? These questions are focal issues in this chapter. We present outcome evaluation as an essential tool for assessing the results of human service intervention. We also emphasize the potential role of outcome evaluation in ongoing service program management and program improvement.

Outcome measurement, to be relevant, must address three specific aspects of program management: (a) the continuous monitoring of program quality; (b) the demonstration of program effectiveness; and (c) decisions about program modifications aimed at improving effectiveness. The first section of this chapter will discuss these three uses of outcome evaluation. The second section focuses on the essential steps in designing specific outcome studies.

USES OF OUTCOME EVALUATION

A particular outcome measurement effort may contribute to more than one of the three aspects of program management just listed. Typically, however, each task requires a different allocation of program evaluation effort.

Therefore the material that follows will focus separately on the three tasks. We will also discuss various approaches to integrating these outcome measurement tasks into a balanced outcome evaluation system.

MONITORING PROGRAM QUALITY

The basic purpose of monitoring is to detect problems or conditions requiring closer examination. Monitoring is accomplished by routinely examining selected indicators of the degree to which program objectives are being met. Management information systems can be designed to provide information on the attainment of program process objectives (e.g., the full utilization of the program's service capacity). In addition, one can usefully monitor low-cost indicators of outcome, including global measures of change in client functioning, and measures of client satisfaction.

Cost considerations require that an economical approach to measuring client functioning be chosen whenever ongoing monitoring of every client is contemplated. Many evaluators limit the measures to a global rating of functioning at the beginning and end of a service episode, plus a measure of clients' satisfaction with services received. Alternatively, a more detailed assessment may be carried out with a small sample of clients. Even a sampling of impressionistic followup interviews by staff members (of each other's clients) might be a feedback tool useful for program improvement, although we have not seen a systematic application of this approach. Because financial constraints reduce the number of available methods, the validity of results derived from routine monitoring of client outcomes may be open to serious question. To mention some common caveats: (a) ratings by service staff may be biased; (b) a simple global rating may obscure the specific client changes that are taking place (c) long-range outcomes may be unrelated to short-range changes seen during the service episode; (d) lack of an unserved comparison group may confuse program effects with improvements that would have occurred even if service had not been provided; (e) measuring change at the end of service may confound effectiveness with length of service; and (f) high-quality assessment of a very limited sample of clients may not adequately represent the results with the entire clientele of the program, even if random sampling is used to eliminate bias, because sample sizes may be too small to yield stable estimates of typical client changes. Therefore one needs to guard against inappropriate overinterpretation of outcome monitoring data.

Some would argue that potentially misleading information should not be gathered at all. Because cost considerations limit more careful and controlled outcome assessment to smaller samples of clients or to special studies, it might be argued that no routine monitoring should be attempted. To us, it seems even more risky not to monitor at least one or two of a program's most important outcome objectives. There is always a risk of erroneous use of even valid outcome data. At this stage in the development of human service program evaluation, we suggest that it is better to continue active experimentation with outcome monitoring so that its utility to program management can be determined.

1. *Global Ratings*

Global ratings can be made rapidly and efficiently by service providers at the first and at subsequent face-to-face contacts with all clients (for example, once each month and at termination). Global ratings not only provide information about client change during the service delivery process, but also allow a comparison of the level of functioning of clients entering different programs. This information alone is valuable for planning purposes. Global ratings also provide a background of information useful in planning more detailed outcome studies.

A global scale relevant for mental health programs, the Global Assessment Scale (Endicott, Spitzer, Fleiss, & Cohen, 1976), is displayed in Tables 11.1 and 11.2. This scale provides a single, global index of client functioning, and can be considered a modest step beyond the "improved–unimproved–worse" outcome rating traditionally required in a psychiatric clinical discharge note. Initial testing of the Global Assessment Scale (Endicott *et al.*, 1976) suggests that it will function as well or better than the Health–Sickness Rating Scale developed by Luborsky (1962). The Health–Sickness Rating Scale is a similar instrument that has been used successfully in psychotherapy outcome research (Luborsky & Bachrach, 1974; Spitzer & Endicott, 1975a); however, it is much more cumbersome to use. Ratings on the Global Assessment Scale range from 0 to 100. This offers several advantages over the typical 5- or 7-point global scale, even if raters cannot reliably distinguish more than seven levels of functioning in the target population of clients. The inclusion of a broad spectrum of functioning levels avoids "ceiling" and "floor" effects seen with some scales, when relatively well-functioning or very poorly functioning clients cannot be rated accurately because variance is restricted by limits in scale range and scores thereby become clustered at one extreme or the other on the scale. The broad range of the Global Assessment Scale allows it to be used in organizations with multiple programs serving diverse client populations. Programs can therefore be compared in terms of the level of functioning of their clients at intake, and each program will still have an adequate range of scale levels available to distinguish differences among clients within their own case load. Examination of the definitions of the scale levels in Tables 11.1 and 11.2 will reveal that they include general descriptions of social functioning plus specific examples of problem behaviors commonly seen among adult clients in mental health programs. It would be reasonable to develop alternate versions of the scale with specific problem examples tailored to other client groups such as children, adolescents, substance abusers, developmentally disabled, and so forth. Other examples of global scales are presented in Chapter 13. Although global scales may seem uncomfortably simplistic, there is some empirical evidence suggesting that they can function adequately (Endicott *et al.*, 1976; McNair, 1974).

Rottenberg, Gordon, and Underhill (5) illustrated the use of continuous outcome monitoring in their report of a county mental health facility that recorded a global rating of each client's level of functioning at admission and at each subsequent contact. Changes in this rating from beginning to end of

TABLE 11.1

Global Assessment Scale[a]

Rate the subject's lowest level of functioning in the last week by selecting the lowest range which describes his/her functioning on a hypothetical continuum of mental health-illness. For example, a subject whose "behavior is considerably influenced by delusions" (range 21–30) should be given a rating in that range even though he/she has "major impairment in several areas" (range 31–40). Use intermediary levels when appropriate (e.g., 35, 58, 62). Rate actual functioning independent of whether or not subject is receiving and may be helped by medication or some other form of treatment.

91–100 No symptoms, superior functioning in a wide range of activities, life's problems never seem to get out of hand, is sought out by others because of his/her warmth and integrity.

81–90 Transient symptoms may occur, but good functioning in all areas, interested and involved in a wide range of activities, socially effective, generally satisfied with life, "everyday" worries that only occasionally get out of hand.

71–80 Minimal symptoms may be present but no more than slight impairment in functioning, varying degrees of "everyday" worries and problems that sometimes get out of hand.

61–70 Some mild symptoms (e.g., depressive mood and mild insomina) OR some difficulty in several areas of functioning, but generally functioning pretty well, has some meaningful interpersonal relationships and most untrained people would not consider him/her "sick."

51–60 Moderate symptoms or generally functioning with some difficulty (e.g., few friends and flat affect, depressed mood and pathological self-doubt, euphoric mood and pressure of speech, moderately severe antisocial behavior).

41–50 Any serious symptomatology or impairment in functioning that most clinicians would think obviously requires treatment or attention (e.g., suicidal preoccupation or gesture, severe obsessional rituals, frequent anxiety attacks, serious anti-social behavior, compulsive drinking).

31–40 Major impairment in several areas, such as work, family relations, judgment, thinking or mood (e.g., depressed woman avoids friends, neglects family, unable to do housework), OR some impairment in reality testing or communication (e.g., speech is at times obscure, illogical or irrelevant), OR single serious suicide attempt.

21–30 Unable to function in almost all areas (e.g., stays in bed all day), OR behavior is considerably influenced by either delusions or hallucinations, OR serious impairment in communication (e.g., sometimes incoherent or unresponsive) or judgment (e.g., acts grossly inappropriately).

11–20 Needs some supervision to prevent hurting self or others or to maintain minimal personal hygiene (e.g., repeated suicide attempts, frequently violent, manic excitement, smears feces), OR gross impairment in communication (e.g., largely incoherent or mute).

1–10 Needs constant supervision for several days to prevent hurting self or others or makes no attempt to maintain minimal personal hygiene (e.g., requires an intensive care unit with special observations by staff).

[a] Reproduced by permission from J. Endicott, R. L. Spitzer, J. L. Fleiss, and J. Cohen, The Global Assessment Scale: A procedure for measuring overall severity of psychiatric disturbance. *Archives of General Psychiatry,* 1976, *33*, 766–771. (Copyright 1976, American Medical Association, Chicago.)

TABLE 11.2
Global Assessment Scale Instructions[a]

The Global Assessment Scale is a single rating scale for evaluating the overall functioning of a patient or subject at a specified time period on a continuum of psychological or psychiatric health-sickness. The time period that is assessed is generally the last week prior to an evaluation, although for special studies a longer time period, such as one month, may be more appropriate.

The range of scale values is from 1, which represents the hypothetically sickest possible individual, to 100, the hypothetically healthiest. The scale is divided into ten equal interval ranges beginning with 1-10, 11-20 and ending with 81-90 and 91-100. The defining characteristics of each 10 point range comprise the scale. The two highest ranges, 81-90 and 91-100, are for those fortunate individuals who not only are without significant symptomatology, but exhibit many traits often referred to as "positive mental health," such as superior functioning, wide range of interests, social effectiveness, warmth and integrity. The next range, 71-80, is for individuals with no or only minimal symptomatology but who do not possess the positive mental health features noted above. Although some individuals rated in the three highest ranges may seek some form of assistance for psychological problems, the vast majority of individuals in psychological or psychiatric treatment will be given ratings in the ranges from 1 to 70. Most outpatients will be in the four ranges from 31 to 70, and most in-patients on admission will be in the four ranges from 1 to 40.

Because the scale covers the entire range of severity it can be used in any situation or study where an overall assessment of severity of illness or degree of health is needed. In most studies only a portion of the scale will be actually used. For example, community studies will rarely have individuals in the lowest ranges, whereas studies involving newly admitted psychiatric patients will rarely have individuals in the highest levels. However, following a course of treatment, many individuals who may have been rated in a very low range on admission may be sufficiently recovered at followup to warrant a rating in one of the highest ranges. This is particularly true of patients with affective disorders whose functioning between episodes may be normal or superior. It is also true that many patients given a diagnosis of schizophrenia during a period of personality disorganization eventually recover and may later function at a relatively high level.

Since the ratings are for overall functioning during a specific time period, it is important that the ratings be based on functioning and symptomatology during that time period and not be influenced by considerations of prognosis, previous diagnosis, or of the presumed nature of the underlying disorder. In a similar fashion, the ratings should not be influenced by whether or not the patient is receiving medication or some other form of help.

The information needed to make the rating can come from any source: direct interview of the patient, a reliable informant, or a case record. Little information may be needed to make a rating at the low end of the scale. For example, knowledge that the individual made a serious suicidal attempt which almost resulted in his/her death is sufficient by itself to warrant rating a patient in the 1-10 range. On the other hand, before an individual can be given a very high rating it is necessary to not only determine the absence of symptomatology and any serious impairment in functioning, but also to ascertain the presence of signs of "positive mental health."

In making a rating, one first selects the lowest range that describes the functioning during the one week time period. For example, a subject whose "behavior is considerably

[a] Reproduced by permission from J. Endicott, R. L. Spitzer, J. L. Fleiss, and J. Cohen, The Global Assessment Scale: A procedure for measuring overall severity of psychiatric disturbance. *Archives of General Psychiatry*, 1976, *33*, 766-771. (Copyright 1976, American Medical Association, Chicago.)

307

Table 11.2 (Continued)

influenced by delusions'' (range 21–30) should be given a rating in that range even though he/she has ''marked impairment in several areas'' (range 31–40). Then the defining characteristics of the two adjacent ranges are examined to determine whether the subject is closer to one or the other. For example, a subject in the range 31–40 who is much closer to the 21–30 range than the 41–50 range would be given a specific rating of 31, 32, or 33. A subject who seemed to be equally distant from the two adjoining ranges would be given a rating of 34, 35, 36, or 37.

---

treatment were tabulated in relation to the type and cost of treatment received. This monitoring process provided a periodic overview of the performance of the facility so that changes from year to year could be documented. Client subgroups that became less functional were identified, and steps were taken to improve the quality and continuity of their care. The tabulation of costs and treatment type according to intake functioning level helped in budgeting for new services, such as an increased load of former state hospital patients. The availability of this very simple and inexpensive outcome measure allows tentative cost–outcome comparisons of different treatment approaches as are described in Chapter 13. Such comparisons may suggest opportunities for program improvement. These suggestions can then be tested more validly in additional experimental studies using more adequate measures of outcome.

2. Client Satisfaction

Client satisfaction ratings are also suitable for routine monitoring. Satisfaction ratings tap a different conceptual domain than other outcome measures, and involve the client directly in evaluating the program (as distinct from the client's self-rating of outcome).

Client satisfaction ratings may be solicited by mail or telephone, used as part of a followup interview, or collected when the client comes in for service. This can be done at a standard time after the client first contacts the program, so as to include both continuing and terminated clients. If service episodes vary greatly in length, or early client dropout is a concern, then it may be useful to collect client satisfaction ratings twice, once shortly after service begins, and again at a later time when most clients will have terminated. Table 11.3 displays a brief client satisfaction inventory suitable for most human service programs. The eight items were selected by Larsen, Attkisson, and Hargreaves (3) after an initial pilot test and statistical analysis of a much larger item pool. A smaller scale—consisting of items 3, 7, and 8 in Table 11.3—also appears to function well as a global measure of client satisfaction. Normative studies of these scales are in progress in various human service programs, with the aim of developing comparative data that will aid in the interpretation of results. Without comparisons to other similar programs or within the same program over time, it is difficult to assess how much the results are influenced by (a) biases to include only satisfied (or unsatisfied) clients, (b) response biases to report what seems to be expected, or (c) systematic differences in satisfaction among initially different client groups. In designing a satisfaction scale for local use it would seem reasonable to include these or other items on which

TABLE 11.3
Client Satisfaction Questionnaire[a]

Please help us improve our program by answering some questions about the services you have received at the _____. We are interested in your honest opinions, whether they are positive or negative. *Please answer all of the questions.* We also welcome your comments and suggestions. Thank you very much, we appreciate your help.

CIRCLE YOUR ANSWER

1. How would you rate the quality of service you received?

4	3	2	1
Excellent	Good	Fair	Poor

2. Did you get the kind of service you wanted?

1	2	3	4
No, definitely not	No, not really	Yes, generally	Yes, definitely

3. To what extent has our program met your needs?

4	3	2	1
Almost all of my needs have been met	Most of my needs have been met	Only a few of my needs have been met	None of my needs have been met

4. If a friend were in need of similar help, would you recommend our program to him/her?

1	2	3	4
No, definitely not	No, I don't think so	Yes, I think so	Yes, definitely

5. How satisfied are you with the amount of help you received?

1	2	3	4
Quite dissatisfied	Indifferent or mildly dissatisfied	Mostly satisfied	Very satisfied

6. Have the services you received helped you to deal more effectively with your problems?

4	3	2	1
Yes, they helped a great deal	Yes, they helped somewhat	No, they really didn't help	No, they seemed to make things worse

7. In an overall, general sense, how satisfied are you with the service you received?

4	3	2	1
Very satisfied	Mostly satisfied	Indifferent or mildly dissatisfied	Quite dissatisfied

8. If you were to seek help again, would you come back to our program?

1	2	3	4
No, definitely not	No, I don't think so	Yes, I think so	Yes, definitely

WRITE COMMENTS BELOW:

[a] Reproduced by permission of the authors (see Reference Note 3).

relevant norms have been gathered, perhaps adding more items focused on specific local issues, and one or two open-ended questions to elicit criticisms or suggestions for improvement.

Ciarlo and Reihman (*1*) provide some reliability, validity, and normative data on a five-item satisfaction scale for use with mental health center clients. McPhee and Zusman (*4*) provide an annotated bibliography of published patient satisfaction studies in health and mental health services. They also report the development of a satisfaction scale for psychiatric inpatients and describe the results obtained during initial use with inpatients in general hospital, state hospital, and community mental health center settings. Zyzanski, Hulka, and Cassel (1974) report initial normative data on a scale for measuring satisfaction with primary medical care. In the published studies they reviewed, McPhee and Zusman (*4*) found that interviews were most frequently used to collect client satisfaction data although mailed questionnaires ran a close second. Self-reports obtained from clients during the service delivery process were used least frequently. For routine monitoring, the mailed questionnaire was most commonly used in a survey of federally funded community mental health centers (McPhee, Zusman, & Joss, 1975). If a satisfaction questionnaire is mailed to clients or former clients, it is common to receive an initial rate of return as low as 25%. A second or even third mailing to nonrespondents, perhaps combined with selected telephone contacts, may be necessary to raise the response rate to 50%. This low return rate may not be a fatal problem if comparative data have been gathered in the same way, especially if the characteristics of nonrespondents can be examined in each case. The percentage of response may be increased by asking the client at intake for permission to be contacted later. If monitoring is carried out by periodic sampling rather than continuous monitoring of every client in each program component, then the expected response rate should be taken into account in deciding how many clients to include in a specific sample of satisfaction ratings. As a rule of thumb, 30 to 50 returned questionnaires is the minimum sample desirable each time a program or program component is assessed.

3. *Additional Outcome Measures*

A simple global status rating plus assessment of client satisfaction represents a minimum level of outcome assessment for routine monitoring. Beyond this minimum level, there is a growing consensus that multiple perspectives on outcome are needed for more valid examination of interventions such as psychotherapy (Waskow, 1975). In striving to increase the quality of outcome assessment within realistic cost limitations, Fiske (1975) suggested that it is more informative to obtain a modest amount of information about a client from each of several respondents than more extensive data from only one respondent. Therefore, in addition to a global rating scale completed by the staff member in closest contact with the client, and a measure of client satisfaction, the evaluator might add a second staff member's rating on a global scale, and/or a client self-rating at intake and discharge. At a level of effort approaching that of funded research, the evaluator might select a sample of clients whom an independent interviewer would assess at intake and followup using a comprehensive rating battery and/or goal attainment scaling (see Chapter 12). Ratings from a client's relative or other appropriate informant might also be sought, if the client gives informed consent. While most evaluators will want to restrict this level of investment to special outcome studies, a monitoring approach using sampled independent interviews has been described by Reihman, Ciarlo, and Hargreaves (1977).

Given the wide array of client outcome indicators available, a sensible approach to monitoring program effectiveness will match the indicators to the functional components of the service delivery process. To illustrate this idea, consider a simplified model of the methadone maintenance treatment of heroin addicts. Four components or stages of this treatment might be called induction, maintenance, growth, and voluntary withdrawal. Each client could be classified at any given time into one of these components or stages. Goals during *induction* might include regular attendance and a steady reduction in the incidence of urine test results indicating use of illicit drugs. The *maintenance* goal might be continued program participation, the absence of positive urine tests, and stable social adjustment. The *growth* stage, by contrast, would be focused on specific improvements in vocational and interpersonal adjustment. Finally, during *withdrawal* program staff would help clients maintain a stable social adjustment and continued abstinence from illicit drugs, while achieving a decreasing dose of the maintenance drug. These outcomes are routinely monitored in most methadone maintenance programs.

In order to provide a rational framework for allocating both treatment and program evaluation resources, it is useful to conceptualize a program as a group of functional components linked to specific treatment interventions with different outcome indicators. In this example, induction and maintenance may require only routine program monitoring procedures, while both an increased treatment effort and a more detailed outcome measurement effort may be focused on the growth and withdrawal components. The key to this approach is to identify the functional components of the service delivery system, whether or not these correspond to existing organizational components.

In summary, monitoring program quality is one use of outcome evaluation, and is a reasonable initial approach to evaluating program effectiveness. For monitoring, one needs an inexpensive measurement procedure for ongoing use in all components of a program. At a minimum, we have suggested global assessment of client status by program staff at intake and periodically thereafter, and measurement of client satisfaction. This monitoring can help to detect program weaknesses or trouble spots, to suggest possible program improvements, and to lay the groundwork for the other uses of outcome evaluation to be discussed in this chapter and in Chapters 12 and 13.

DEMONSTRATING PROGRAM EFFECTIVENESS

Most human service programs today have inadequate evaluation capability. This leaves agency directors with few, if any, straightforward, uniformly accepted ways of portraying the effectiveness of their programs when they deal with advisory boards, county governments, funding agencies, and third-party payers. Demonstrating program effectiveness is becoming increasingly important. Demands for program accountability now extend beyond demonstrations of fiscal responsibility and program activity. The technical problem in demonstrating program effectiveness is the lack of a relevant comparison or norm against which to judge a program's effects. When an ongoing program is not changing and must serve everyone who applies, it is usually impossible to demonstrate rigorously that it has any effect. Nevertheless, there are some practical ways to discuss the effectiveness of one's program. These include the use of existing research results obtained in other programs; citing information from the program's internal management use of outcome monitoring data; and the direct comparison of client outcomes to normative data. Each of these approaches to demonstrating program effectiveness will now be discussed in more detail.

1. *Use of Existing Research Findings*

Program leaders are often called upon to speak to funders or to the public about program effectiveness before they have developed any local outcome evaluation capability. An indirect approach is to present a knowledgeable review of formal research studies that indicate that the particular service strategies adopted by the program are generally effective. Individual community-based programs cannot and should not be expected to demonstrate scientifically the effectiveness of each of their service strategies. This expensive task is best accomplished in selected programs that can attract the skills and resources needed for large-scale service delivery evaluation research. Federal and state agencies concerned with each major type of human service program may have summaries of such research available. Often, of course, there is insufficient research concerning a particular service strategy to take this approach. Nevertheless, a wide spectrum of human services outcome research is being supported, primarily by the federal government, and local program leaders can speak more knowledgeably about their program if they have access to summaries of such research. The program evaluator should be alert for sources of such summaries in books, in review articles in professional journals, and from the national information clearinghouses operated by several federal agencies (see Chapter 9). All programs need to be alert to research findings that can be used to improve the effectiveness of human services, to ensure that funding is maintained or increased for services shown to be effective, and that funding continues to be questioned for services that have not been shown to be effective.

2. *Use of Routinely Monitored Client Change Information*

The second way to argue for the effectiveness of a program is also indirect, namely, by pointing out the extent to which the monitoring of client change is a regular part of program management. Program review approaches to accreditation and quality assurance, that utilize site visits, emphasize this method—since comprehensive, direct assessment of program effectiveness by a group of site visitors is not possible. Program administrators must do more than point with pride to the fact that some minimal client change data are rountinely collected. In addition, administrators should portray the process through which client outcome information is reviewed within the program, and how it does, or is expected to, influence program policy decisions. For example, one may be able to cite an instance when a decrease in client satisfaction alerted program management to a leadership problem which, when corrected, was followed by a return to previous levels of satsifaction. From a scientific perspective, this may be weak evidence of program quality. From an administrative and political perspective it is a realistic and legitimate method of discussing program quality. Funding agency staff and elected officials will rarely have either the time or expertise to review detailed reports of outcome studies from every community-based program they oversee. What they seek is some assurance that programs are skillfully managed, and outcome monitoring will usually be seen as a desirable aspect of management skill.

3. Development and Use of Normative Comparisons

Comparison of client change data to relevant change norms is conceptually the strongest approach to demonstrating program effectiveness. At present, such change norms do not exist for most types of human service programs. In our experience, personnel in regulatory and funding agencies often consider the development of outcome norms to be the obvious next step in human services program evaluation. This creates considerable impetus for the evaluation field to move in this direction. At the same time, personnel in service delivery programs express the fear that simplistic normative comparisons will be misleading and will create harmful political controversy without improving program effectiveness. Indeed, the controversy over standardized achievement tests in elementary and secondary schools is sufficient evidence to suggest rough waters ahead for other human services. While these exigencies are real, our position is that normative comparisons can become a useful aspect of program evaluation. However, a set of rather demanding requirements must be met if normative comparisons are to be meaningful.

The general requirement is for normative methods that are inexpensive, and yet valid enough not to be misleading. A sequence of developmental steps is needed to accomplish this capacity for normative comparison. To begin with, gathering potential normative data requires a data-gathering procedure that incorporates some generally acceptable standard definitions. These include definitions of (a) the target client population, (b) the service modalities, (c) the client sample selection, (d) the timing of assessments, (e) the measuring instruments, and (f) the persons doing the assessments. Obtaining general agreement on these definitions, within the limits of a feasible procedure, will ordinarily require some trial and error. Furthermore, this consensus about definitions probably must be developed separately for each major target group and type of human service program.

Systematic pilot implementation is the next step. This pilot study should be designed to establish the acceptability and reliability of the method during routine use in service settings. The reliability of measuring *programs* rather than individual clients is at issue. To assess this type of reliability one might draw two independent samples of clients in each of a large set of programs to see how closely the mean outcome scores and variances from separate samples in the same program are in agreement.

A validity study of the proposed normative measurement method will also be necessary. For purposes of a validity study, a carefully selected sample of clients in each of several programs can be assessed using the best state-of-the-art assessment procedure, regardless of cost. The average degree of client change seen in each program can then be compared using the state-of-the-art assessment, and separately using the proposed normative data. If similar conclusions about relative program effectiveness are indicated by each method, the validity study results will add credibility to the proposed normative procedure.

If the method passes these hurdles, large-scale collection of preliminary normative data on client change may be justified. Research on the method can then examine program and community characteristics associated with high or low apparent effectiveness. Some of these relationships may lead to the discovery of ways to improve program effectiveness. Other relationships, upon closer study, may reveal problems in the measurement method that, when corrected, will lead to more meaningful norms. At this stage it may also be relevant to gather nonclient community norms using the same method proposed for measuring client status before and after service (1).

These developmental steps for establishing program outcome norms are indeed demanding requirements that may involve years of work for each type of human service program. The actual work is unlikely to follow the orderly sequence described here. However, we see two parallel lines of activity that promise to contribute to the process: (a) extensive but simple monitoring of client change by state and federal funding agencies, and (b) intensive studies of multiple programs by individual investigators. These two approaches can complement each other. Large-scale monitoring of client change by a funding agency brings together data from a wide range of programs. Pooling data from a large number of programs is possible because the funding agency can impose standard measurement definitions and require program participation as a condition of funding. The politics of implementing a mandated outcome evaluation system can engender vigorous discussion of the measurement methods among professionals in that particular service field. Thus these mandated systems can accomplish some of the tasks required to achieve meaningful outcome norms. The limitation of these large systems is that they are unwieldy to manage, and the data produced are of questionable validity. It is expensive and frustrating to design and implement a large-scale client change reporting system, and once implemented, such systems are costly to revise. The extensive cost stems mostly from the need for all of the participating programs to adapt to each change in the data gathering procedure. Even after such a system is installed and operating routinely, it is impossible to ensure the consistent use of the instruments, or to suppress careless data collection or occasional fabrication of data.

Intensive studies of smaller groups of programs offer several advantages that enable them to complement what is learned from mandated reporting systems. In these studies it is possible to measure client change more accurately. Data may be gathered by special research staff rather than service delivery personnel, so that consistent performance can be assured. It is also possible to include a more comprehensive battery of client change measures. Often, in fact, the investigator's aim is to test a new measuring instrument, to compare it to other measures, and to establish preliminary norms in a variety of settings. While such studies are often designed to test specific hypotheses about the effect of certain program characteristics on client outcome, they can also afford an opportunity to validate measures used in a mandated reporting system.

Formal, time-limited outcome studies and mandated outcome data reporting systems can be designed to complement each other more effectively than has been the case in recent practice. Designers of large reporting systems can benefit if relevant measurement methods have been established in smaller research studies. On the other hand, the wide use of a reporting system procedure in turn motivates research on the psychometric properties of the system's measures. Reporting systems generate hypotheses or assertions about the relative effectiveness of different service strategies. These assertions are based on nonexperimental comparisons (i.e., clients are not randomly assigned to services). Such comparisons usually cannot separate the effect of the program from the effects of differences in client selection and community environment. These nonexperimental results, however, can in turn motivate experimental research to demonstrate whether the purported program strategy effects are actually occurring, and to identify the client groups and program settings in which the effects can be obtained.

The cumulative result that we should be seeking from this interplay of reporting system and evaluative research is twofold: (a) identification of the most efficient but valid methods to measure client change, and (b) identification of the client subgroups and program settings for which nonexperimental comparisons can yield valid inferences about program effectiveness. To the extent that these two goals can be reached, we will gain the ability to demonstrate the effectiveness of individual programs.

OUTCOME STUDIES TO AID ADMINISTRATIVE DECISIONS

It is our impression, after reviewing program evaluation efforts in many human service programs, that the best payoff from program evaluation effort is the evaluator's contribution to specific decisions. These decisions may be internal to the program or may involve external decisions, such as a funding agency's decision about whether to fund a new program component. The payoff is possible when the evaluator has both relevant information, or the skill, tools, and staff to gather or review such information rapidly; and a good understanding of the decision process in which the information is to be utilized. The evaluator and other program leaders are then able to respond to emerging decision situations with more relevant information than would otherwise be possible. This means that the evaluator must be ready to respond in a timely way by mounting simple studies or retrieving and effectively delivering existing data. These special studies may consume only a small part (usually less than 20%) of an organization's program evaluation resources. Most of the evaluation effort is devoted to planned ongoing data collection and report generation; but one function of these routine monitoring activities is to provide the resources (data and skills) to respond to emerging decision issues (Attkisson, McIntyre, Hargreaves, Harris, & Ochberg, 1974).

The discussion of the organizational role of the evaluator in Chapter 4 is especially relevant to the issue of evaluator responsivity to policy formulation. These ad hoc studies are not just a matter of the evaluator responding to requests for information. It is our impression that program management rarely uses available information to good advantage unless the evaluator is struggling with the emerging decision issues along with the other program leaders. Unless the management of the organization is structured to foster effective interchange between decision making and program evaluation, these studies will have little utility in program management.

The studies that represent decision-specific evaluative activities will, in most organizations, be initially restricted to brief undertakings. Some studies will include the examination of client outcomes but many will not. An explicit way to propose and negotiate the priorities for special studies must be established in every service setting. As the evaluator and the other program leaders gain skill in maximizing benefit from these brief investigations, they may decide to undertake more substantial assessment of client outcomes in order to focus on anticipated major program decisions.

Two types of program decisions seem most likely to be aided by a comparative outcome study. The first is an administrative policy decision to offer a new or substitute service. The second is the ongoing clinical decision process of assigning each client to the best currently available service. In the former case, when a new procedure is instituted to improve results with a particular problem or client group, one may choose to continue both the new and the old procedure for a time, assigning clients to both procedures and comparing service acceptance and outcome in each group. The second type of question arises when alternate services are available and the choice between them is currently made without any clear or convincing rationale, at least for some portion of the clients. Here a comparison of the overall outcome of the two treatments will not do, since one treatment may be better for some clients and worse for others. Instead, one or more promising "predictor variables" are tested to see whether they can be used in selecting service assignments so that overall client acceptance and outcome are improved.

The evaluator can explore the possible utility of these two types of outcome studies by examining the points in the program at which choices are made about what services to provide each client. These choices may occur at intake, at the termination of specific service components, or when a client shows a major advance, setback, or prolonged failure to benefit from a service. The evaluator can discuss the actual decision process with the personnel involved, attempting to understand what questions are currently most important to these decision makers. Are there types of clients who seem poorly served no matter what service approach is used? Is a new approach being considered for them? If so, what is the readiness of program staff and management to attempt a new approach in a context in which its effectiveness can be compared to the existing approach? One can also ask about the process of matching clients to service modalities. Do staff members say they are unsure about the best approach for certain types of clients? Are any client groups being assigned haphazardly to different services? By exploring these issues the evaluator can judge when a comparative outcome study may help to improve the effectiveness of the program.

An example of a service comparison study emerging from an ongoing program was reported by Donlon, Rada, and Knight (1973). In a large psychiatric daycare program, 250 chronic schizophrenic patients were seen twice weekly in groups of 25 to 30. The staff had identified 24 patients whom they considered "treatment refractory." It was decided to explore two new approaches to these patients. The 24 patients were randomly divided into two groups of 12. Group A was offered a program that featured socialization and refreshments within a group setting. Group B was offered closeness with the therapist through individual supportive psychotherapy but permitted emotional distance from fellow patients. Patient response during an 18-week period was compared by clinic attendance, rated degree of increased socialization, and cost–efficiency—all of which favored Group A. Both groups did somewhat better in the new programs than during a prior 18-week baseline, but attendance progressively fell in Group B. Group A patients were no longer considered "refractory" at the end of the study, and this approach was adopted for future use with such patients. This is an illustration of a brief but clearly designed experiment aimed at program improvement.

If an outcome study is to influence a specific decision, it is essential that the decision makers participate in the design of the study. The decision maker may be a member of the funding agency, the program director, the head of a particular program component, or a group of front-line staff workers. The decision maker must be ready to answer two questions: What service options are possible? What information would be sufficient to justify choosing one alternative over another? In planning the study, one test of its potential usefulness is to consider the possible study results, and ask the decision maker what course of action would be taken in each case. If the actions are the same regardless of the study results, then obviously the study should be redesigned or abandoned (Harper & Babigian, 1971).

The program staff that will directly participate in the study must also be involved in planning the study. Experienced evaluators have noted that successful outcome studies often have a stormy organizational course during their *early* phases (Glaser & Taylor, 1973; Weiss, 1973). It seems that this vigorous interaction is necessary to develop collaboration and avoid later disastrous misunderstandings.

In this section we have asserted that outcome studies can be designed to aid decision-making tasks in program management. Specifically, two types of program decisions—the administrative policy decision to offer a new or substitute service, and the clinical decision process of assigning clients to the best available service—seem most likely to benefit from comparative outcome studies. Nevertheless, although it is possible to identify the contribution of outcome studies to these two types of decision-making tasks, there are as yet no simple rules for specifying the outcome evaluation activities that will yield the most payoff. Choosing occasions to invest outcome evaluation effort requires careful judgment by the evaluator. One purpose of the remainder of this chapter is to prepare the reader to make such judgments successfully.

TEN ISSUES IN PLANNING
AN OUTCOME STUDY

When planning an outcome study that can aid a program decision or serve some other evaluation function, there are 10 issues that must be resolved. The program participants and the administrative users of the study should review and critique these specific details, not just the overall idea of the study. Therefore the evaluator should prepare a written protocol that discusses each of the issues. As the study plan is discussed with the staff, the written protocol is revised until a final working protocol has been agreed upon. These 10 issues are as follows:

1. Selection of the service comparison
2. Assignment of subjects to services
3. Selection of subjects
4. Informed consent
5. Description of the sample
6. Description of services provided
7. Selection of predictor variables
8. Selection of outcome measures
9. Analysis of data
10. Feedback of results into the decision process.

These topics are discussed in a number of texts, such as Fairweather (1967), Guttentag and Struening (1975), Riecken and Boruch (1974), and Struening and Guttentag (1975). Each topic can become complex in a large study, but most of them can be kept manageable in small outcome evaluation studies undertaken by community-based human service programs.

SELECTION OF THE SERVICE COMPARISON

Several issues are important in selecting a service comparison for study. The most obvious is the relevance of the proposed comparison to future management decisions. In addition, there are questions one must raise about the feasibility of the comparison. We will discuss the choice of the sample size, the feasibility of obtaining the needed number of subjects, and the feasibility of limiting subject attrition from the study.

1. Relevance of the Proposed Comparison

The most important issue in the selection of services to compare is the relevance of the proposed comparison to future management decisions. One needs to identify the comparison that will yield the maximum decision relevance for the study cost. This judgment of relevance can best be made in the light of a "policy analysis" of alternative ways to deliver services.

Edwards and his colleagues have described a practical way to apply the decision–theoretic approach to policy analysis (Edwards, 1971; Edwards, Guttentag, & Snapper, 1975). Program directors and evaluators may find it useful to apply this method to important policy decisions for which an outcome study is contemplated. A policy analysis might consist of the following four steps: (a) listing the program policy options under consideration; (b) identifying the set of program objectives against which the policy options are to be judged, and rating the relative importance of these objectives; (c) assessing the probable effect of each policy option upon each program objective; and (d) computing the probable utility of each policy option as a weighted sum of its probable effects on the attainment of program objectives.

Whenever one adopts or persists in a particular policy, one likes to think that one has at least informally made the judgments just listed, and has chosen the policy of maximum probable utility. Some actual policy decisions in organizations are made through a process in which some or all of these steps are recognizable. An evaluator can look for occasions where it appears useful to make this process explicit, such as the review of major long-range policies. The limiting factor in the power of policy analysis is usually in the third step, assessing the probable effect of each policy. Such assessment must usually be a matter of judgment based on experience (and, occasionally, research evidence) about the effects of various service delivery techniques. When a policy analysis makes it clear that the choice hinges on the unknown relative effects of two or more of the options, then an experimental comparison of those options will be relevant to program management. When the key policy-relevant program objectives involve client outcomes, then the experiment will be an outcome study of the sort considered here.

2. Determining the Sample Size

Available sample size is one of the most obvious constraints on study feasibility. A common error is to compare too many different services. More than three usually will be too many to handle in one study. Beyond this it may be difficult to attain a sufficient number of subjects. How many subjects are enough? It is a waste of time to carry out a study that has little ability to detect a difference between service approaches. The size of the sample needed is related to two factors: (a) the size of effect that would be of practical importance, and (b) the variability of outcomes *within* the groups being compared. The smaller the expected difference in outcome between service strategies, and the more variable the outcomes among clients within a given service strategy, the larger the sample size must be. One rule of thumb that has been suggested is a minimum of 20 clients per group (Food and Drug Administration, 1974,

p. 80), but larger groups will often be needed. If the major outcome measure is one that is used routinely to monitor outcomes in the program, existing data can be used to estimate within-group variability in outcomes. The size of effect that is of interest can sometimes be decided a priori. A pilot study with three or four subjects per group is a good way to get a rough estimate of effect size and to try out the study procedures. The size of the effect may also be estimated from a nonexperimental comparison using existing outcome monitoring data. If the pilot or nonexperimental data show an effect that, if true, would motivate a program change, then one has a good reason to do the study, as well as the information needed to calculate the desirable sample sizes. A large sample size will not guarantee that an effect will be found, of course. However, it is possible to compute the probability that an effect will be found by a particular study, given an assumption about the size of the "true" difference in effectiveness between the service strategies being compared, and knowing the variability of individual outcomes. This probability is called the "statistical power" of the study (Cohen, 1977).

An example of sample size estimation will illustrate some of the factors influencing study power in outcome experiments in human service programs. Suppose that a new service strategy is to be compared to the current approach, and that service effects on clients' functioning will be measured by the Global Assessment Scale shown in Table 11.1. Suppose this scale is in current use in the program as a monitoring device, and it is known that the average intake level is 36, while 2 months later clients are typically rated somewhat improved, with an average score of 44. On both occasions the standard deviation of Global Assessment Scale scores (a measure of client-to-client variability) has been found to be 12. Suppose also that it has been found that when two raters independently judge each client's Global Assessment Scale level, the average of the two ratings shows a standard deviation of 9, presumably because the judgment errors of one rater tend to cancel the errors of the other. It is also known that a client's intake score partially predicts his or her score 2 months later (assume a correlation of .53 has been found).

The simplest study design to test whether the new service strategy is better than the standard strategy is to enlist a group of clients as study subjects and randomly assign half of them to receive the new strategy and half to receive the standard approach. One could then use a one-tailed t-test to decide whether the average outcome score is better in the group receiving the new service. Suppose we plan to use the traditional significance level of .05, meaning that we are willing to risk a 5% chance of erroneously concluding that the new service is better when, in fact, it is not.

Given the conditions just outlined, we want to select a sample size that will give us adequate power to detect a meaningful difference in outcome, if the new service is truly more effective. To do this we must define the size of a "meaningful difference" and decide what we mean by "adequate power." Suppose that the service staff in our example felt that an average outcome superiority of 10 Global Assessment Scale points would be a "large" effect that would clearly justify adopting the new strategy, while a "modest" effect of, say,

TABLE 11.4

Sample Sizes Needed in Each Treatment Group to Attain a Statistical Power of .50 or .80
under Various Assumptions about Size of Effect and within-Group Standard Deviation, Using
a One-Tailed t-test or the Corresponding Analysis of Covariance[a]

Number of raters	Type of test	Standard deviation	Size of effect	Sample size needed	
				Power = .50	Power = .80
1	t-test	12.0	10	9	20
1	t-test	12.0	6	22	50
2	t-test	9.0	10	6	11
2	t-test	9.0	6	12	26
2	ANCOVA	7.7	10	5	8
2	ANCOVA	7.7	6	9	20

[a] Adapted by permission from J. Cohen, *Statistical power analysis for the behavioral sciences* (Revised ed.). Copyright 1977, Academic Press, New York.

6 points would still justify careful consideration of the new method. The choice of an "adequate" level of power is a cost–benefit question. If one has less than half a chance of detecting a true meaningful effect, many would question whether it is worth doing the experiment at all. On the other hand, it would take a very large sample size to be 99% sure of detecting a true difference. Cohen (1977, p. 54) has argued that a power of .80 is a reasonable trade-off. This allows a 20% risk of not detecting a true effect, and follows a scientific tradition that an error of this type is not so serious as the error (which we have set at a 5% risk) of incorrectly concluding that there is an effect when, in fact, there is not. Therefore, for this discussion we will consider effect sizes of 10 points and 6 points, and statistical power of .50 and .80, examining the effect of these assumptions on needed sample sizes. The results are shown in Table 11.4.

The simplest outcome measure is the rating of each client by a single rater 2 months after intake. Table 11.4 shows that in this situation one needs 18 clients (9 in each group) to be 50% likely to detect a 10-point effect, and as many as 100 clients for an 80% chance to detect a 6-point effect. But by using two raters we see that we can reduce the needed sample sizes. This will be as efficient if the increased cost in rater time can be repaid by the reduced number of clients to be rated.

The last two lines of Table 11.4 show the additional savings in sample size when we take account of each client's score at study intake. Under our assumption that this score correlates .53 with the outcome score, it will "account for" 28% of the outcome score variance. Therefore we may wish to substitute an analysis of covariance for our t-test. (We will later discuss the other conditions that make analysis of covariance appropriate.) Using the intake score as the covariate, the effective standard deviation of the 2-month outcome score is reduced to 7.7 from its original value of 9. By using two raters and taking account of the baseline score we can now attain a power of .80 to detect a 6-point effect with only 40 subjects (20 per group) whereas without these improvements we needed 100 subjects.

As this example illustrates, the evaluator can use a number of strategies to increase the precision of an outcome experiment. These improvements strive to reduce the effective within-group variability in individual client outcomes. In human services there is often an inherently high variability in client outcome, but large-sample studies are very expensive even when sufficient clients are available to be recruited as study subjects. At the same time, even a modest improvement in service outcome may have a wide-ranging effect. Therefore the evaluator's success in finding the most efficient way to attain adequate study power may determine whether a useful study is feasible.

3. Feasibility of Recruiting the Needed Subjects

With a decision about the needed sample size, the feasibility of a particular service comparison is affected by how many subjects will be available and the length of study intake period needed to recruit them. It is a common error to overestimate subject availability. The screening criteria for the study may reduce the number of eligible clients more than anticipated. When eligible clients are informed of the study and asked to participate voluntarily, many may refuse. Finally, after clients enter the study they may decide to withdraw before the end, or they may need to be removed for their own safety. These factors may reduce the available subject pool so much that the study will fail. As a general rule of thumb it is comfortable to have a potential subject pool three times as large as you think you will need.

4. Feasibility of Preventing High Subject Attrition

Differential subject attrition creates an especially troublesome limit on study feasibility. This is a more serious problem than simply a loss in sample size. If subjects are randomly assigned to achieve comparable groups at the beginning of service, this comparability will be lost if different *types* of subjects refuse or drop out of the different services. In this case the outcome data on the surviving subjects are very hard to interpret, since there is no really satisfactory statistical procedure to correct for this differential attrition. The exception to this rule is when the attrition rate itself is the primary outcome measure (as a measure of service acceptability). But once differential service acceptability is known, a service comparison study is usually relevant only to those clients who will accept all of the services being compared. One should therefore attempt to exclude other clients prior to randomization. For a more extensive discussion of subject attrition, the reader may wish to refer to Riecken and Boruch (1974, pp. 186–192).

ASSIGNMENT OF SUBJECTS TO SERVICES

1. The Random Assignment Design

The basic task is to assign clients to service groups so that differences in outcome can be attributed to the services provided rather than to preexisting differences in the client groups. Random assignment is the most dependable way to achieve this treatment group comparability, and is strongly recommended whenever feasible. However, the idea of random assignment often sparks apprehension among program staff, community groups, and clients. Random assignment should be carried out only with adequate safeguards through careful subject screening and uncoerced informed consent. Some evaluators prefer to avoid randomized trials in favor of nonexperimental designs even in situations where randomization is feasible. However, avoidance of random assignment often means that some basic issues about the value and design of the study are not being faced by the study planners. For example, if it seems unethical to assign a particular group of clients randomly to two alternative services, it may mean that insufficient thought has been given to the criteria for excluding clients for whom the study is inappropriate. If all concerned are in agreement about the proper service assignment for all clients, then there is probably no need for the study. If program staff are not clear about service assignment for some subgroup of clients, then this subgroup may already be assigned haphazardly (randomly?) to the available service options. Program staff may even be "trying out" different assignment strategies or may be offering a new service in the hope that something can be learned about what will work best, but without any clear plan for reaching a conclusion about the results. Gilbert, Light, and Mosteller (1975, pp. 148–150) describe this as "fooling around with people" and argue that a controlled experiment in such circumstances is ethically more defensible. A group of biometrists at the National Institutes of Health have also argued vigorously for random assignment in clinical trials (Byar, Simon, Friedewald, Schlesselman, DeMets, Ellenberg, Gail, & Ware, 1976).

Implementation of randomized designs requires several important steps and attention to several methodological issues. The first step is to obtain a list of eligible subjects. A random number table can then be used to assign subjects to the different services that will be compared. The process of determining eligibility may be done all at once or by "trickle processing" as applicants appear, but in either case determination of eligibility must be kept independent of the randomized subject assignment procedure.

The study intake procedure is also used to help reduce attrition from the study. In the study intake procedure, subjects are told of the possible assignments and of the randomized process and asked if they are willing to participate regardless of the treatment group assignment they receive. This method works well when the assignments all appear to be active services. When one group of subjects feels they have been assigned to a less desirable service (or feels they have been refused service) these subjects may tend to drop out, or seek service elsewhere, or reapply to the same program. Sometimes a "waiting list" group serves as the control, but people on a waiting list may abandon active work on their problem and not attempt to find alternative help. In studies of drug treatment, subject expectation effects are avoided by using a placebo control under "double blind" conditions, where neither subject nor program staff know who is on an active drug or on placebo (Food and Drug Administration, 1974). This method cannot be used with social or interpersonal interventions, but some strategies are available to reduce subjects' reactions to the knowledge that they received the "inactive" intervention. One common method is to select randomly from among the eligible subjects a subset who are offered the experimental service, while the remaining subjects serve as controls without knowing it, or only knowing that they have been asked to participate in a periodic assessment procedure. This method may sometimes raise additional ethical problems and also can entail a high-risk of differential attrition from refusals to participate in the experimental service. Another approach is to provide the control group an intervention that can be viewed as an active service but is hypothesized to be much less effective. The "attention placebo" is a special case of this. If a difference is found between the experimental service and the minimal comparison service, then one may be able to argue that the experimental service will also be better than no service at all. These implementation issues are discussed in greater detail in Riecken and Boruch (1974, pp. 170–192).

There are many situations where randomization is not possible. In these cases, one may attempt a partial control of preexisting subject differences through one of several "quasi-experimental" designs (Campbell & Stanley, 1969; Riecken & Boruch, 1974, pp. 87–116). Although they cannot be interpreted as well as true experiments, they do represent an advance over current practice in which most program innovations are never evaluated at all. Seven of these designs were cited by Riecken and Boruch as being the most useful and the most used for evaluating new programs. We will describe two of the strongest of these designs, the *regression–discontinuity* design and the *interrupted time series with comparison series* design. Our discussion draws heavily on Riecken and Boruch (1974, especially pp. 88–105) and the interested reader is referred to that material for greater detail.

2. The Regression–Discontinuity Design

The regression–discontinuity design (Campbell, 1969; 2, pp. 14–21; Thistlethwaite & Campbell, 1960) is applicable in the common situation in which the services of a program are in short supply and it has been decided that services must be provided to the most needy. Even in this situation a limited randomized experiment may be defensible. The idea of the regression–discontinuity design can be understood most clearly as the extension of this limited randomized design, the "tie-breaking" experiment: Using a quantified need or eligiblity criterion, those most eligible are accepted, those least eligible are refused, but for some middle range of eligibility (within which applicants are considered equally eligible) applicants are randomly assigned to be served or refused service. The results of this "tie-breaking" experiment will not reveal whether the service is effective for persons on the extremes of the eligibility distribution—those most and least eligible—but only for persons near the eligibility cutoff score. Even with this limitation, the results will be quite relevant to decisions to expand or reduce a program. The regression–discontinuity design is a nonrandomized approximation to the "tie-breaking" randomized experiment. Applicants are admitted or rejected according to whether they are above or below some quantified eligibility criterion. Outcomes are assessed on all applicants. The results of an hypothetical quasi-experiment of this sort are shown in Figure 11.1 In this example, subjects below a certain Global Assessment Scale score were accepted for service, and all subjects were rated at followup on the same scale. Subjects with higher Global Assessment Scale scores at the time of application also have higher scores at followup. This appears to be true within both the served and unserved groups. Regression lines fitted to the mean within each group therefore slope upward to the right in Figure 11.1. The regression line in each group can be extended to predict the outcome of a subject at the cutting score on the eligibility criterion, as shown by the two dashed lines. If the score predicted from the treated subjects is significantly higher than the score predicted from the control subjects, this "regression–discontinuity" might be considered evidence for the effectivness of the treatment.

There are several problems in implementing regression–discontinuity designs. The program to be evaluated may not have a quantified eligibility

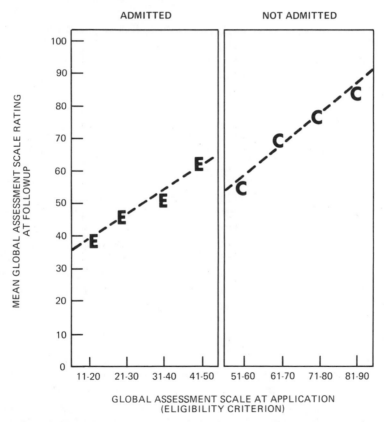

Figure 11.1. Hypothetical outcome of a regression–discontinuity evaluation design in which applicants having a Global Assessment Scale rating of 50 or below were admitted for service. Followup functioning of the admitted applicants and nonadmitted control applicants was rated on the same scale (see Table 11.1).

criterion, or the existing criterion may be used inconsistently. To apply the regression–discontinuity approach, the program must strictly adhere to a sharp cutting point, allowing no exceptions and using the eligibility score as the sole criterion for subject selection or nonselection. Furthermore, full records must be kept of the eligibility criterion scores and identifying data on all applicants, whether accepted or not selected. Whenever program staff feel a particular applicant must be admitted (or not admitted) regardless of his or her eligibility score, this person must be removed from the study. In order to avoid selection bias, this decision to remove an applicant from the study must be made by staff who are unaware of the subject's eligibility score, or else applicants may be more likely to be excluded if their eligibility score would lead to the "wrong" assignment. Bias may also be introduced by falsifying eligibility scores. There is no way to correct for this bias, although one may be able to estimate the direction of its effect. Selection bias can also occur if the cutoff score is publicly known. Potential applicants below the cutoff point may tend not to apply for service, which will tend to exclude the more knowledgeable or aware applicants from the control group. An operational problem will arise if one does not know where to set the cutoff point in order to produce the number of accepted applicants that matches the capacity of the program. This can be solved most easily when a large group of applicants can be considered before any are accepted, but there are methods to cope with a "trickle processing" intake as well. Finally, the regression–discontinuity design is less efficient than a comparable randomized design, so that more subjects will be needed to reach the same level of study power.

In summary, the regression–discontinuity design is less preferable than a randomized design when both are possible. The regression–discontinuity design requires more unverifiable assumptions for its interpretation. For example, one must assume that the eligibility criterion is measured on an equal-interval scale, or at least that one knows the form of the functional relationship between eligibility criterion and outcome on both sides of the cutting point and across the cutting point. The implementation problems outlined in the previous paragraph also show that this design may be more difficult to carry out than a randomized design. Since the "tie-breaking" randomized design will be ethically as justifiable in many circumstances, it should always be given serious consideration before choosing the regression–discontinuity design. However, when randomization is not possible, the regression–discontinuity design is an important alternative methodology.

3. The Interrupted Time Series with Comparison Series Design

A second quasi-experimental design is the interrupted time series with comparison series. In a time series design, a measure is taken repeatedly, so that the "normal" variability of the measure can be observed. Consider, for example, a measure of client satisfaction that is gathered on a sample of new clients each month. Suppose that 70 new clients are admitted to a program each month and all are mailed a questionnaire during the following month, about 4 weeks after admission. About 30 of each month's sample reply to the questionnaire, and an average satisfaction score is computed for them.

Now suppose a major change is introduced in the program, starting abruptly at the beginning of a particular month. (The effects of gradually introduced changes are unlikely to be detected with this design.) One observes that client satisfaction in the next month improves over that in the previous month, as illustrated at the top of Figure 11.2. By itself, this observation reveals very little about the effect of the program change, even if a statistical test of the pre–post change shows that it is a significant difference. The problem is to rule out alternative explanations for the observed change. Some information about this can be obtained by examining a series of monthly scores before and after change. If other factors affect the level of satisfaction, and happened to increase it in the month of the program change, the data might look like the second graph in Figure 11.2. In the third graph, however, the variability before and after the program change is much less, and the scores appear to be consistently higher in the months after the "interruption" in the time series. Yet many other events could have caused this change. For example, when a program change is introduced with the aim of improving client satisfaction, the new interest in this measure may lead to changes in the way it is collected. This alternative explanation can be ruled out if the same satisfac-

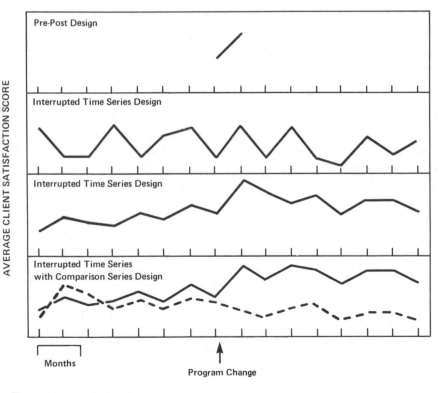

Figure 11.2. Hypothetical client satisfaction data averaged in successive monthly client samples, to illustrate various time series designs.

tion measure is being gathered in the same way for other program components, thereby providing a comparison series. If a comparison series were to show data like the dashed line in the bottom graph of Figure 11.2, it could justify more confidence that the planned program change was the cause of the increased client satisfaction. Each further bit of information that helps to rule out plausible alternative explanations will strengthen the confidence in the primary hypothesis. Thus the more time points in the series the better, and the more ways to make relevant comparisons with parallel time series the better. The key point is that these designs require detailed knowledge of the circumstances surrounding the program change, so that the relevant alternative explanations can be examined.

Data analysis in time series designs consists of common-sense judgments by a group of people who know the situation being examined. Formal statistical analysis generally plays a small role. Ordinary curve-fitting approaches are not appropriate because data at successive time points tend to be correlated, spuriously reducing the error term, which leads to finding "significant" changes in slope or intercept too often. Appropriate tests for this type of autocorrelated time series data have been provided by Box and Tiao (1965) and Glass, Wilson, and Gottman (2).

Application of these nonexperimental time series designs typically occurs in the monitoring of outcome. If outcome monitoring is carried out routinely, and with an eye to providing several parallel comparison series, the evaluator can examine the effects of major program changes even when they are unanticipated or when it is not feasible or economically justifiable to mount a true experiment. If the routine analysis and reporting of outcome monitoring data are designed to facilitate these time series comparisons, it can enable the evaluator to respond to retrospective questions about the effect of particular program changes. However, if prechange data have not been systematically collected on the types of clients affected by the change, the evaluator will have no way to examine the effects of unanticipated changes. This is a further argument for at least some inexpensive, minimal level of outcome and satisfaction monitoring on every program client.

SELECTION OF SUBJECTS

Criteria for inclusion and exclusion of subjects should be agreed upon in advance, and each potential subject screened for appropriateness prior to being invited to participate. Reasons for exclusion should be recorded in each case, to understand the type of clients to which the study results will apply. There are four classes of reasons for client exclusion: (a) the client is not relevant to the study because the services are not designed to deal with the needs presented by the client; (b) there is clear reason to think the client will be endangered unless excluded; (c) the client cannot understand the situation well enough to give an informed, voluntary consent to participate; or (d) the client chooses not to participate.

INFORMED CONSENT

Informed consent is the key component in the adequate protection of the rights and welfare of human subjects. Biomedical and social research practices have recently come under sharp scrutiny by public interest groups. Study planners and program directors should be familiar with *The Institutional Guide to DHEW Policy on Protection of Human Subjects* (Department of Health, Education, and Welfare, 1971). It may also be wise to collaborate with members of the program's community advisory board or other representatives of the larger community in developing specific informed consent procedures.

Any program that regularly engages in research with human subjects should have an established procedure for reviewing the human subjects' safeguards in every study. Informed consent is appropriate whenever research or evaluation alters a client's activities in the program from those that are a routine and necessary part of service delivery—if the client is thereby put at risk with respect to any physical, psychological, or social harm. Random assignment is usually such an occasion, but so are many other research and evaluation activities. For example, it is often considered inappropriate to undertake followup evaluation after a service episode unless clients give their consent for later followup while they are receiving services, and also consent at the time the followup is carried out.

Certain features of a consent procedure are now becoming typical, although institutional practices vary considerably. When consent to participate in a study is solicited, the potential subject is informed of the alternative services that would be available if he or she were to choose not to participate, and of the potential risks and benefits from participation in the study. Subjects are told if they are to be randomly assigned, and told of any procedures that will be required of them that are not a routine part of program services. They are told that they may terminate their participation in the study at any time without jeopardizing their access to the usual program services, and are given the name and telephone number of someone they may later contact if they have further questions about the study. The consent form may not contain language releasing the program from any liability in relation to the study. The entire explanation is presented verbally and also given to the subject on a written consent form. The subject is encouraged to retain a copy of the signed consent form.

DESCRIPTION OF THE SAMPLE

It is usually helpful to record some demographic and prognostic characteristics of subjects in an evaluative study, and a limited amount of information about clients who were considered but screened out of the study, clients refusing to participate, and subjects leaving the study before its completion. These data allow the assessment of the similarities or differences among treatment groups. These analyses are important even if clients were randomly assigned to treatments. Such analyses also allow a description of the ways in which study subjects differ from other clients in the program.

The typical demographic data recorded are age, sex, ethnicity, marital status, highest level of education attained (by client, father, and spouse), occupational level, previous human service utilization history, and type of presenting problem or need for service. The education and occupation data may be combined into an index of socioeconomic status. The choice of prognostic variables will depend on the type of client under study and the outcome variables that will be measured. Past levels of functioning on the outcome variables will often be the best prognostic indicators. *Current* (preservice) functioning also will be a useful prognostic variable unless the nature of the program is such that most clients must fall within a narrow range of dysfunction in order to be admitted. Thus a rating of the client's functioning during the week prior to admission may have less prognostic power than a rating of "typical" functioning during the year prior to admission.

DESCRIPTION OF SERVICES PROVIDED

In order to judge the relevance of a study to other service settings, a clear description of the services being compared is essential. If a major investment has been made in a study, it should be published so that other programs have a chance to benefit as well. Even in studies designed only for local consumption, the decision makers who will use the results may not be directly acquainted with types of services being compared. A second reason for documenting services provided is to monitor whether the intended services were consistently provided. This latter analysis may reveal that the outcome comparison is not relevant because one of the services was not feasible to deliver, or was delivered too sparsely for meaningful comparison. A global description of service philosophy is insufficient for either purpose. One needs records of the service activities carried out (e.g., specific type of service, hours of service contact, who provided the service) and the extent to which each client actually accepted and participated in them. One also needs to know the cost of the service procedures devoted to each study subject. These can be estimated using the methods presented in Chapter 13.

SELECTION OF PREDICTOR VARIABLES

Sometimes one wants to measure client characteristics at intake in order to make predictions about optimal choice of service. Predictor variables are not important if one only wishes to know which of several services is *generally* most effective. Predictor variables come into play when one wishes to learn how to match the client to the right type of service. In other words, predictor variables should be used when it is thought that one service may be more effective for one subgroup of clients, whereas a different service may be more effective for a second group of clients. In this case one needs to measure variables at intake that may be able to identify these subgroups. One then undertakes a study to establish that the predictor variables can be used to allocate clients to types of service so that average client outcomes are maximized. A useful way to select potential predictor variables is to ask program staff who make the service assignment decision to nominate client characteristics that they feel may be relevant.

An example of a service assignment study may help to clarify the role of predictor variables. A large urban mental health clinic had proposed a "contact group" to which clients could come without appointment to talk about their problems or simply listen to others. Some therapists saw the contact group as the treatment of choice for certain clients, but most staff saw it as a holding strategy, an "active waiting list" prior to treatment assignment, and a dumping ground for poorly motivated applicants. Intake interviewers also expressed a more general concern that they lacked clear criteria for assigning applicants to individual therapy, group therapy, or contact group. To explore these issues they carried out a service assignment experiment.

Intake workers rated every applicant on a set of characteristics that they thought were relevant to the assignment decision, mostly items related to motivation for psychotherapy, comfort in interpersonal interaction, and emotional symptoms. Applicants who preferred not to participate or for whom random assignment was judged to be unsafe were excluded, and the remaining applicants were randomly assigned to individual therapy, group therapy, or contact group. The acceptance of this referral was judged by whether the applicant kept the first appointment, and if so, by client and therapist ratings of satisfaction following the first appointment. Poorly motivated applicants tended not to accept either type of group therapy. Shy and distressed clients accepted the contact group, while more articulate and outgoing clients accepted the traditional ongoing weekly group. Clients assigned to the "wrong" type of group therapy showed poor acceptance of the referral, while individuals "correctly" referred to group treatment showed initial acceptance as great as comparable clients assigned to individual therapy (Hargreaves, Showstack, Flohr, Brady, & Harris, 1974).

SELECTION OF OUTCOME MEASURES

A wide variety of measures are available for specific human service programs. It is beyond the scope of this chapter to present a detailed discussion of measurement selection. The primary consideration is that one include the dimensions of outcome felt to be important by the decision makers who are the intended consumers of the study findings. It is also important that the measurement approach be adequate to detect an effect that has some practical importance. Whenever possible it is preferable to utilize well-studied standard rating scales that have been shown to be sensitive to differential service effectiveness with a similar client group. Surprisingly, global measures have often been found quite sensitive in comparisons with multiple-item rating instruments (McNair, 1974; Waskow & Parloff, 1975). It may be that multiple-item ratings remind the rater to consider a broad range of factors when making the global rating, but that the detailed items are not equally relevant to each subject. The differential importance of each item can be taken into account by the rater in making a global rating, but this information is hard to include in the statistical summary of multiple items. The observed sensitivity of global scales, whatever its source, is nevertheless ample reason to include a global scale in any battery of measurement procedures.

The reader who wants an excellent introduction to the many conceptual issues in selecting outcome measures for studies of psychological and social interventions should see Waskow (1975). One specific approach, goal attainment scaling (Kiresuk & Sherman, 1968), while requiring more than minimal staff investment, has some unique advantages and is presented in detail in Chapter 12. Examples of ways to organize a sampled followup assessment program are presented by Reihman *et al.* (1977) and by Showstack, Hargreaves, Glick, and O'Brien (6). A more extensive discussion of rating scale selection, with reproduced examples of rating scales especially relevant to mental health programs can be found in Hargreaves, McIntyre, Attkisson, and Siegel (1977). Spitzer and Endicott (1975b) also present an overview of psychiatric rating scales.

ANALYSIS OF DATA

When the study objectives have been clarified and the overall study plan is being developed, it is important to review the plan with a statistical consultant, unless one of the study planners has a strong background in statistics. The major statistical analyses should be planned before the study is begun, since this may lead to changes in the way data are collected.

The timing of data analysis may influence the study's impact on management decisions. If the study utilizes several outcome measuring instruments, we recommend that one of these be a global outcome rating. This global rating can be analyzed first to provide a preliminary overview of results as soon as possible. Prompt feedback will often maximize the impact of the study in the decision process, and may engage decision makers in raising further questions for exploration in more detailed analyses. In planning a study one should anticipate that data analysis may require an effort equal to the effort invested in data collection. Users of the study results, however, may assume that findings will be available as soon as all the data are collected. A complex data analysis may so delay the presentation of results that this factor alone precludes their immediate and perhaps ultimate relevance. During the planning of the study one should be sure that the data analyses will be reasonably straightforward. If the analyses will be difficult, it may be better to simplify the study so that it addresses only the most important aspect of the decision issue at hand. Data analysis procedures should be set up in advance, and if computer processing is involved, the analyses should be given a "dry run" on preliminary data while the remaining data are being collected. Keypunching or terminal input of raw data should be scheduled to keep pace with data collection. These steps will ensure that at least some initial results from the study can be produced shortly after the end of data collection.

There are several approaches to the analysis of a service experiment in which clients are *randomly assigned* to service types, and one or more outcome measures are obtained before the service assignment and again after the service. The choice depends upon the relationship between the preservice and postservice scores on each outcome measure. Therefore, the first step is to examine this relationship, which can be done by obtaining both a scattergram and the correlation coefficient within each service group. If the pre–post relationships are reasonably linear, the correlations are similar in each service group and reasonably high, then analysis of covariance (ANCOVA) is the preferable approach. In this use of ANCOVA, the preservice scores are used as a "covariate" to adjust the postservice scores, and then the usual analysis of variance (ANOVA) or a *t*-test is performed. The removal from the error term of variance associated with the preservice score increases the statistical power of the test, while this gain is balanced against a reduction in the power because 1 degree of freedom is used to estimate the covariate regression slope. Therefore, the pre–post correlation must be fairly large (above .30) for the covariate to yield a useful increase in statistical power (Winer, 1971, p. 780).

If the conditions for ANCOVA are not found, then other analyses are preferable. If there are significant differences in the pre–post correlations between service groups, then this itself may be the main finding. If the scattergrams show that there is a nonlinear pre–post relationship, one may use the preservice score as a blocking variable in an ANOVA of the post scores, or introduce a nonlinear covariate (e.g., include both the preservice score and its square as covariates). The former of these two techniques would be preferred if the blocking can be done without encountering low frequencies in some cells. In fact, if cell frequencies are relatively large, say five or more, Winer (1971, p. 780) recommends this approach over ANCOVA under any circumstances. In an ANOVA where the preservice score is used as a blocking variable, varying pre–post correlations may be revealed as a significant interaction between the preservice score and the effectiveness of the services being compared. The analysis of pre–post difference scores and the use of repeated measures ANOVA are less desirable approaches in randomized experiments than the ones suggested here (Cronbach & Furby, 1970; Huck & McLean, 1975).

The reader should note that pre–post comparison group studies in which subjects are not randomly assigned present more difficult data analysis problems than the randomized experiments just discussed. Nonrandomized designs are in very common use, and are usually erroneously analyzed using matching, ANCOVA, or gain score techniques. No consensus has developed about the best approach to data analysis, except that the evaluator should treat any analyses of such studies with great caution. Errors of measurement in the pretreatment score (or the covariate in ANCOVA) can lead to either undercorrection or overcorrection for preexisting differences between groups, and there are several other threats to the validity of ANCOVA approaches in these studies. Cook and Reichardt (1976) review a number of articles discussing these problems. The technique most commonly recommended is to adjust the ANCOVA based on an estimate of the reliability of the covariate, but different methods of estimating the reliability can lead to different conclusions. Therefore, Cook and Reichardt suggest that the evaluator think carefully about the various threats to validity in the study—one should consider the alternative explanations for the observed results, aside from the effects of the treatment differences themselves. Usually the evaluator only looks to see whether the groups were similar at the beginning of the experiment on those variables used to measure outcome. In addition, however, one needs to think carefully about other preexisting differences in the subject groups that may affect their readiness to change, aside from the effects of treatments under study. Cook and Reichardt suggest that the evaluator carry out additional analyses that attempt to rule out these alternative explanations. To deal with the uncertainty about how best to estimate covariate reliability, they suggest performing the analysis several times with different reliability estimates that "bracket" the plausible range of values. Nunnally (1975) suggests using repeated measures ANOVA in these studies, since the repeated measures analysis does not depend on the same assumptions as ANCOVA. If the evaluator finds that the conclusions are the same regardless of how the analysis is done, then greater confidence in the result is justified. If the results are not so consistent, then the evaluator is obliged to report the findings with proper qualification. Experiences like this help clarify why it is worth the trouble to use a randomized design in the first place!

These statistical analyses can be computed with the aid of a variety of electronic calculators. The simpler ANOVA designs are discussed in most graduate texts in statistics, while Winer (1971) provides comprehensive coverage of more complex designs. Elashoff (1969) discusses the effect of violations of assumptions in ANCOVA. The resources of any university computer center will include a set of standard statistical programs to carry out the analyses just described, and commercial or small college computer facilities will sometimes have them. Two widely available statistical program packages are the *Biomedical computer programs* (Dixon, 1973; 1975) and the *Statistical package for the social sciences* (Nie, Hull, Jenkins, Steinbrenner, & Bent, 1975). The latter is especially well documented and practical to use by someone with no knowledge of computer programing and only a modest competence in statistics and general computer usage. Ease of usage, of course, does not guarantee appropriateness of usage, and the inexperienced should always proceed with caution and expert consultation.

When the analysis of each outcome dimension is complete, it may still be hard to reach a conclusion about which service is better. If a large number of outcome measures have been employed, and only a few show a significant effect, the result may be due to chance. Five percent of a set of independent statistical tests should be erroneously "significant" at the .05 level of confidence, even if there is no true effect. The various outcome measures are probably correlated with each other, so the appropriate way to test for the combined significance of the entire set of measures is multivariate analysis of variance (Overall & Klett, 1972). There is also the possibility that one service will yield better results than another on some outcome dimensions, but poorer results on other dimensions, or short-term outcomes may favor one service and long-term outcomes another. In practice this may be the exception rather than the rule. If most outcome measures either favor one service or show no difference, there may be little ambiguity of interpretation even when different study "audiences" attach different relative values to the various outcome dimensions. This will be true so long as all agree on the *direction* of the outcome dimension that corresponds to increasing value.

The actual degree of superiority of one service outcome over another will be relatively unimportant if the two services are of equal cost. One simply chooses the approach with the better average outcome. (However, if a new service shows only a slight advantage over an existing service of the same operating cost, costs of changing over to the new service, such as retraining staff, may sometimes make the change inadvisable.) When both cost and effectiveness differ, rational choice depends on cost–effectiveness ratios, which are more complex. First, cost and effectiveness must each be expressed as single dimensions, even though both may be quite complicated upon close examination. One approach is to use a single indicator as a proxy for each dimension, anticipating the need to adjust the actual decision by taking into account a variety of special circumstances. If such a simplistic approach seems inadequate, one must attach relative value weights to each component of the dimension in order to obtain the required composite measure, as in the "policy analysis" method mentioned earlier (Edwards *et al.*, 1975). With regard to cost, for example, one may want to consider not only the monetary unit cost for providing the service, and the start-up cost of implementing a new service, but also certain nonmonetary costs, such as the difficulty of recruiting staff with the required skills. With regard to outcome, one needs to develop relative weights for the variety of program objectives that are being considered in evaluating service effectiveness. These weights can be obtained through a judging procedure by the participants in the policy decision, so the process need not be esoteric or expensive. The judgments of the value weights, and the scaling of the component scores to be weighted must be done so that the participants are satisfied that ratio scaling is preserved. In other words, the judges must be ready to estimate whether one dimension is "twice as important" as another, and whether the average outcome of service *A* is "twice as good" as service *B* on a particular outcome dimension. Edwards *et al.* (1975) present judging techniques to accomplish this type of comparison.

These decision processes, and the derivation of appropriate cost figures for cost–effectiveness comparisons, are discussed in greater detail in Chapter 13.

FEEDBACK OF RESULTS INTO THE DECISION PROCESS

This is the step at which program evaluation has often faltered. The groundwork for implementation must have been laid during the initial negotiation of the study design. The evaluator should be aware of the crucial decision points for management, when study results are most likely to have an impact. These crucial occasions include budget preparation, submission of annual plans, development of grant proposals, and reports to the board of directors. Data should be analyzed and displayed in the context of such management choice points. Program staff should also be given frequent feedback about the progress of the study and of the data analysis.

In order for study results to have maximum impact on program decisions, the evaluator must be an ongoing advocate for consideration of the study findings. This crucial aspect of the role of the evaluator has been discussed in Chapter 4. An evaluator may carry out an excellent and publishable piece of outcome research, but be unable to bring about the program changes that study results seem to suggest. This can result from a lack of openness on the part of program leaders to evidence suggesting change, or from the evaluator's failure to understand why the study results are unconvincing. Both of these failures of communication are likely to occur unless the evaluator is an involved and respected ongoing participant in the leadership of the program. Even under the best of conditions, the evaluator must give especially careful thought to the feedback process in outcome evaluation.

SUMMARY

Outcome evaluation can contribute to three management tasks: monitoring the program, assessing program effectiveness, and planning major program changes. Monitoring is used to detect specific program strengths, weaknesses, and trouble spots. Inexpensive outcome indicators—such as global ratings of client status before and after service and measures of client satisfaction—are practical for the quantitative aspects of monitoring and may be supplemented by qualitative followup contact with selected clients. Overall program effectiveness is important to demonstrate, but this is difficult with current technology. Estimating overall effectiveness requires relevant comparative data, or more specifically, normative studies among subsets of similar programs. However, the development of outcome norms is in its infancy.

The third use of outcome evaluation is to aid a major decision about program change. Such studies deal with policy decisions about service delivery methods and are generally time-limited efforts rather than ongoing monitoring systems. The utility of a comparative outcome study is most obvious when it is unclear whether a proposed new service method will be an improvement over existing procedures.

In planning an outcome· study to compare two or more service approaches, 10 issues must be considered in order to arrive at an effective study plan. These issues include the selection of the service comparison, methods for selecting subjects, obtaining subjects' informed consent, and assigning them to a service strategy. Measurement methods may be needed for describing the sample of clients, describing the services actually delivered, predicting response to the service, and measuring client outcome. The analysis of data and the feedback of findings must be designed to meet the practical constraints of the decision process.

There is no doubt that outcome evaluation is an advanced stage of program evaluation. It calls for careful planning by the evaluator and other program leaders if it is to be used wisely. As "standard" methods evolve to deal with common outcome evaluation issues, human service organizations will be able to utilize outcome evaluation routinely. Public human services resist rational management because the effects of programs are usually unknown. Improving human services requires that program outcomes be made more visible, and this is part of the task of all human service program evaluators.

REFERENCE NOTES

1. Ciarlo, J. A., & Reihman, J. *The Denver community mental health questionnaire: Development of a multi-dimensional program evaluation instrument.* Unpublished manuscript, 1974. (Available from James A. Ciarlo, Denver General Hospital, 70 West Sixth Avenue, Denver, Colorado 80204.)

2. Glass, G. V., Wilson, V. L., & Gottman, J. M. *Design and analysis of time series experiments* (Research Report). Boulder, Colorado: Laboratory of Educational Research, University of Colorado, 1972.

3. Larsen, D. L., Attkisson, C. C., & Hargreaves, W. A. *The assessment of client satisfaction in the evaluation of human service programs: Issues, methods, and the development of a general scale.* Unpublished manuscript, 1976. (Available from C. C. Attkisson, Langley Porter Institute, University of California, San Francisco, California 94143.)

4. McPhee, C., & Zusman, J. *Quality evaluation of mental health services.* Buffalo, N. Y.: State University of New York at Buffalo, 1976. (Available from Carol McPhee, Division of Community Psychiatry, SUNY at Buffalo, 462 Grider Street, Buffalo, New York 14215.)

5. Rotenberg, L., Gordon, M., & Underhill, W. *The Client-Oriented Cost–Outcome Project of the Mental Health Treatment Center of the Reading (Pa.) Hospital.* Unpublished manuscript, 1974. (Available from Dr. Frederick L. Newman, Eastern Pennsylvania Psychiatric Institute, Henry Avenue and Abbottsford Road, Philadelphia, Pennsylvania 19129.)

6. Showstack, J. A., Hargreaves, W. A., Glick, I. D., & O'Brien, R. S. *Psychiatric follow-up studies: Practical procedures and ethical concerns.* Unpublished manuscript, 1976. (Available from W. A. Hargreaves, Langley Porter Institute, University of California, San Francisco, California 94143.)

REFERENCES

Attkisson, C. C., McIntyre, M. H., Hargreaves, W. A., Harris, M. R., & Ochberg, F. M. A working model for mental health program evaluation. *American Journal of Orthopsychiatry,* 1974, *44,* 741–753.

Box, G. E. P., & Tiao, G. C. A change in level of a nonstationary time series. *Biometrika,* 1965, *52,* 181–192.

Byar, D. P., Simon, R. M., Friedewald, W. T., Schlesselman, J. J., DeMets, D. L., Ellenberg, J. H., Gail, M. H., & Ware, J. H. Randomized clinical trials: Perspectives on some recent ideas. *New England Journal of Medicine,* 1976, *295,* 74–80.

Campbell, D. T. Reforms as experiments. *American Psychologist,* 1969, *24,* 409–429.

Campbell, D. T., & Stanley, J. C. *Experimental and quasi-experimental designs for research.* Chicago: Rand-McNally, 1969.

Cohen, J. *Statistical power analysis for the behavioral sciences* (Revised ed.). New York: Academic Press, 1977.

Cook, T. D., & Reichardt, C. S. Statistical analysis of non-equivalent control group designs: A guide to some current literature. *Evaluation,* 1976, *3*(1-2), 136–138.

Cronbach, L. J., & Furby, L. How should we measure "change"—or should we? *Psychological Bulletin,* 1970, *74,* 68–80.

Department of Health, Education, and Welfare. *The institutional guide to DHEW policy on protection of human subjects.* (DHEW Publication No. NIH 72-102.) Washington, D. C.: U. S. Government Printing Office, 1971.

Dixon, W. J. (Ed.). *BMD: Biomedical computer programs* (3rd ed.). Berkeley: University of California Press, 1973.

Dixon, W. J. (Ed.). *BMDP: Biomedical computer programs.* Berkeley: University of California Press, 1975.

Donlon, P. T., Rada, R. T., & Knight, S. W. A therapeutic after-care setting for "refractory" chronic schizophrenic patients. *American Journal of Psychiatry,* 1973, *130,* 682–684.

Edwards, W. Social utilities. *The Engineering Economist,* 1971, Summer Symposium Series, *6.*

Edwards, W., Guttentag, M., & Snapper, K. A decision–theoretic approach to evaluation research. In E. L. Struening & M. Guttentag (Eds.), *Handbook of evaluation research* (Vol. 1). Beverly Hills, California: Sage Publications, 1975.

Elashoff, J. D. Analysis of covariance: A delicate instrument. *American Educational Research Journal,* 1969, *6,* 383–401.

Endicott, J., Spitzer, R. L., Fleiss, J. L., & Cohen, J. The Global Assessment Scale: A procedure for measuring overall severity of psychiatric disturbance. *Archives of General Psychiatry,* 1976, *33,* 766–771.

Fairweather, G. W. *Methods for experimental social innovation.* New York: Wiley & Sons, 1967.

Fiske, D. W. The use of significant others in assessing the outcome of psychotherapy. In I. E. Waskow & M. B. Parloff (Eds.), *Psychotherapy change measures.* (DHEW Publication No. ADM 74-120.) Washington, D. C.: U. S. Government Printing Office, 1975.

Food and Drug Administration. Guidelines for the conduct of clinical trials. *Psychopharmacology Bulletin,* 1974, *10,* 70–91.

Gilbert, J. P., Light, R. J., & Mosteller, F. Assessing social innovations: An empirical base for policy. In C. A. Bennett & A. A. Lumsdaine (Eds.), *Evaluation and experiment.* New York: Academic Press, 1975.

Glaser, E. M., & Taylor, S. H. Factors influencing the success of applied research. *American Psychologist,* 1973, *28,* 140–146.

Guttentag, M., & Struening, E. L. (Eds.). *Handbook of evaluation research* (Vol. 2). Beverly Hills, California: Sage Publications, 1975.

Hargreaves, W. A., McIntyre, M. H., Attkisson, C. C., & Siegel, L. M. Outcome measurement instruments for use in community mental health program evaluation. In W. A. Hargreaves, C. C. Attkisson, & J. E. Sorensen (Eds.), *Resource materials for community mental health program evaluation* (2nd ed.). (DHEW Publication No. ADM 77-328.) Washington, D. C.: U. S. Government Printing Office, 1977.

Hargreaves, W. A., Showstack, J., Flohr, R., Brady, C., & Harris, S. Treatment acceptance following intake assignment to individual therapy, group therapy, or contact group. *Archives of General Psychiatry,* 1974, *31,* 343–349.

Harper, D., & Babigian, H. Evaluation research: The consequences of program evaluation. *Mental Hygiene,* 1971, *55,* 151–156.

Huck, S. W., & McLean, R. A. Using a repeated measures ANOVA to analyze the data from a pre-test–post-test design: A potentially confusing task. *Psychological Bulletin,* 1975, *82,* 511–518.

Kiresuk, T. J., & Sherman, R. E. Goal attainment scaling: A general method for evaluating community mental health programs. *Community Mental Health Journal,* 1968, *4,* 443–453.

Luborsky, L. Clinicians' judgments of mental health: A proposed scale. *Archives of General Psychiatry,* 1962, *7,* 407–417.

Luborsky, L., & Bachrach, H. Factors influencing clinician's judgments of mental health: Eighteen experiences with the Health–Sickness Rating Scale. *Archives of General Psychiatry,* 1974, *31,* 292–299.

McNair, D. M. Self-evaluations of antidepressants. *Psychopharmacologia,* 1974, *37,* 281–302.

McPhee, C. B., Zusman, J., & Joss, R. H. Measurement of patient satisfaction: A survey of practices in community mental health centers. *Comprehensive Psychiatry,* 1975, *16,* 399–404.

Nie, N. H., Hull, C. H., Jenkins, J. G., Steinbrenner, K., & Bent, D. H. *SPSS: Statistical package for the social sciences* (2nd ed.). New York: McGraw-Hill, 1975.

Nunnally, J. C. The study of change in evaluation research: Principles concerning measurement, experimental design, and analysis. In F. L. Struening & M. Guttentag (Eds.), *Handbook of evaluation research* (Vol. 1). Beverly Hills, California: Sage Publications, 1975.

Overall, J. R., & Klett, C. J. *Applied multivariate analysis.* New York: McGraw-Hill, 1972.

Reihman, J., Ciarlo, J. A., & Hargreaves, W. A. A method for obtaining follow-up outcome data. In W. A. Hargreaves, C. C. Attkisson, & J. E. Sorensen (Eds.), *Resource materials for community mental health program evaluation* (2nd ed.). (DHEW Publication No. ADM 77-328.) Washington, D. C.: U. S. Government Printing Office, 1977.

Riecken, H. W., & Boruch, R. F. (Eds.). *Social experimentation: A method for planning and evaluating social intervention.* New York: Academic Press, 1974.

Spitzer, R. L., & Endicott, J. Assessment of outcome by independent clinical evaluators. In I. E. Waskow & M. B. Parloff (Eds.), *Psychotherapy change measures.* (DHEW Publication No. ADM 74-120.) Washington, D. C.: U. S. Government Printing Office, 1975. (a)

Spitzer, R. L., & Endicott, J. Psychiatric rating scales. In M. Freedman, H. I. Kaplan, & B. J. Sadock (Eds.), *Comprehensive textbook of psychiatry* (2nd ed.). Baltimore: Williams & Wilkins, 1975. (b)

Struening, E. L., & Guttentag, M. (Eds.). *Handbook of evaluation research* (Vol. 1). Beverly Hills, California: Sage Publications, 1975.

Thistlethwaite, D. L., & Campbell, D. T. Regression–discontinuity analysis: An alternative to the ex post facto experiment. *Journal of Educational Psychology,* 1960, *51,* 309–317.

Waskow, I. E. Fantasied dialogue with a researcher. In I. E. Waskow & M. B. Parloff (Eds.), *Psychotherapy change measures.* (DHEW Publication No. ADM 74-120.) Washington, D. C.: U. S. Government Printing Office, 1975.

Waskow, I. E., & Parloff, M. B. (Eds.). *Psychotherapy change measures.* (DHEW Publication No. ADM 74-120.) Washington, D. C.: U. S. Government Printing Office, 1975.

Weiss, C. H. Between the cup and the lip. *Evaluation,* 1973, *1*(2), 49–55.

Winer, B. J. *Statistical principles in experimental design* (2nd ed.). New York: McGraw-Hill, 1971.

Zyzanski, S. J., Hulka, B. S., & Cassel, J. C. Scale for the measurement of "satisfaction" with medical care: Modifications in content, format, and scoring. *Medical Care,* 1974, *12,* 611–620.

12

GOAL ATTAINMENT SCALING

Thomas J. Kiresuk and Sander H. Lund

As the name implies, goal attainment scaling rests in the general tradition of goal-oriented evaluation. At its simplest, goal-oriented evaluation involves setting a goal, implementing a program, determining subsequent goal attainment, and using this information to modify future activities. A general form of goal-oriented evaluation is schematized in Figure 12.1. As can be seen, goal-setting, evaluation, and feedback are interrelated operations, constituents of the larger process by which a program is developed and directed.

The initial step in this process, *value formation,* involves specifying the values upon which the program is founded, and the second step, *inspection of the environment,* involves determining if the specified values are being realized. The third step, *need identification,* is the product of this process. A need is an unrealized value. The fourth step, *goal formulation,* is the statement of a goal, the attainment of which will lead to reduction of the need. The goal should specify the time at which its attainment is to be measured, and the measurement method. The fifth step, *program implementation,* consists of organizing a collection of individuals and resources whose activities will be directed toward attainment of the goal. The sixth step, *program evaluation,* is the point at which attainment of the goal is assessed, and the seventh step, *feedback,*involves using this information (a) to modify the program, if it is ineffective, (b) to reassess the goal, if it is unrealistic, or (c) to reassess the original need, if the inspection of environment was incorrect or there was a value conflict.

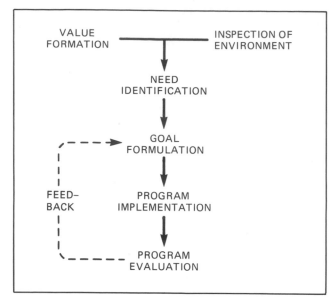

Figure 12.1. A general form of goal evaluation.

GOAL ATTAINMENT SCALING

Goal attainment scaling makes two important additions to the general form of goal-oriented evaluation just described. The first is a 5-point scale of individualized potential outcomes. "Goal attainment" has traditionally been a dichotomous measurement, which means that only two outcomes are possible—attainment or nonattainment. In this traditional model, if a goal is achieved, there is no meaningful standard to determine if expectations were significantly exceeded; and if a goal is not attained, it is difficult to assess the magnitude of the failure. Goal attainment scaling improves this situation by placing the target goal in the center of a range of possible outcomes from "most unfavorable" and "less than expected" on one end, the "expected outcome" in the middle, and the "more than expected" and "best anticipated" on the other end. This is incorporated in the left column of a "goal attainment followup guide" as illustrated in Figure 12.2.

The second modification that makes goal attainment scaling more useful is the summary goal attainment score. Computation of the score is detailed later in this chapter, but it may be thought of as a weighted average of scores on individual goal attainment scales. This provides an appropriate way to recognize that an individual client or a total program may have several goals, yet combines the score for the attainment of each goal into a single overall numerical value. A goal attainment score of 50 indicates that a series of goals have, on the average, been exactly attained; a score of less than 50 indicates

GOAL ATTAINMENT FOLLOW-UP GUIDE

Check whether or not the scale has been mutually negotiated between patient and CIC interviewer. SCALE ATTAINMENT LEVELS	SCALE HEADINGS AND SCALE WEIGHTS				
	SCALE 1: Education Yes X No __ $(w_1=20)$	SCALE 2: Suicide Yes __ No X $(w_2=30)$	SCALE 3: Manipulation Yes __ No X $(w_3=25)$	SCALE 4: Drug Abuse Yes X No __ $(w_4=30)$	SCALE 5: Dependency on CIC Yes X No __ $(w_5=10)$
a. most unfavorable treatment outcome thought likely (-2)	Patient has made no attempt to enroll in high school. ✓	Patient has committed suicide.	Patient makes rounds of community service agencies demanding medication, and refuses other forms of treatment ✓	Patient reports addiction to "hard narcotics" (heroin, morphine).	Patient has contacted CIC by telephone or in person at least seven times since his first visit.
b. less than expected success with treatment (-1)	Patient enrolled in high school, but at time of follow-up has dropped out. ✓	Patient has acted on at least one suicidal impulse since her first contact with the CIC, but has not succeeded. ✓	Patient no longer visits CIC with demands for medication but continues with other community agencies and still refuses other forms of treatment.	Patient has used "hard narcotics," but is not addicted, and/or uses hallucinogens (LSD, Pot) more than four times a month. ✓	Patient has contacted CIC 5-6 times since intake.
c. expected level of treatment success (0)	Patient has enrolled, and is in school at follow-up, but is attending class sporadically (misses an average of more than a third of her classes during a week).	Patient reports she has had at least four suicidal impulses since her first contact with the CIC but has not acted on any of them. *	Patient no longer attempts to manipulate for drugs at community service agencies, but will not accept another form of treatment.	Patient has not used "hard narcotics" during follow-up period, and uses hallucinogens between 1-4 times a month. *	Patient has contacted CIC 3-4 times since intake.
d. more than expected success with treatment (+1)	Patient has enrolled, is in school at follow-up, and is attending classes consistently, but has no vocational goals. *		Patient accepts non-medication treatment at some community agency. *	Patient uses hallucinogens less than once a month.	
e. best anticipated success with treatment (+2)	Patient has enrolled, is in school at follow-up, is attending classes consistently, and has some vocational goal.	Patient reports she has had no suicidal impulses since her first contact with the CIC.	Patient accepts non-medication treatment, and by own report shows signs of improvement.	At time of follow-up, patient is not using any illegal drugs.	Patient has not contacted CIC since intake. *

Figure 12.2. Sample clinical guide: Crisis Intervention Center (CIC).

343

that attainment has tended to fall short of expectations; a score of more than 50 indicates that it has tended to exceed expectations. If the goal attainment of a large number of clients or programs is scored in this way, the resulting distribution of scores has been found to be approximately normal, with a mean around 50 and a standard deviation of about 10. Because goal attainment scores approximate a normal distribution, tables of the normal distribution may be used to convert goal attainment scores to percentile scores. This approximate normality also facilitates the use of parametric statistical tests to assess the significance of differences in scores associated with a variety of variables.

BACKGROUND OF GOAL ATTAINMENT SCALING

Many independently developed goal-based assessment systems were in concurrent use during the 1950s and 1960s (Battle, Imber, Hoehn-Saric, Stone, Nash, & Frank, 1966; Drucker, 1964; Malan, 1963; McClelland & Winter, 1969; Wallerstein & Robbins, 1958; Wallerstein, Robbins, Sargent, & Luborsky, 1956). One of these was goal attainment scaling, developed at the Hennepin County Mental Health Service in Minneapolis, Minnesota (Kiresuk & Sherman, 1968). In the early 1960s, the Hennepin County Mental Health Service was obliged by its funders to adopt some systematic approach to program evaluation. Thomas J. Kiresuk, together with Robert E. Sherman and Byron Brown, reviewed existing evaluation strategies and concluded that none sufficiently solved the problem of how to measure outcomes in mental health. They sought a measuring device that avoided both the relative inflexibility of standardized measures and the diffuseness of unstructured observation, yet would (a) allow individualized problem definition, (b) use each client as his or her own control in the definition of "success," and (c) allow interpretable comparison of diverse treatment modalities (Kiresuk, 1973). Goal attainment scaling was designed to accomplish these aims

THE GOAL ATTAINMENT FOLLOWUP GUIDE

The core of goal attainment scaling is a goal attainment followup guide such as the one illustrated in Figure 12.2. A goal attainment followup guide is a grid-shaped form consisting of a series of discrete 5-point scales. When the followup guide is filled out, each scale represents a separate client or program goal area. The five levels of each scale are defined by concrete behaviors arranged along a hierarchy of possible outcomes. The nature of these outcomes ranges from the "most unfavorable outcome thought likely" to the "most favorable outcome thought likely," with the "expected level of success" at the middle level.

Use of the followup guide involves six steps: (a) selection of goal areas, (b) weighting, (c) selection of a followup time, (d) statement of the "expected outcome," (e) completion of the four ancillary scale levels, and (f) followup using the scale and calculation of a goal attainment score.

1. Goal Area Selection

The first step in the construction of a goal attainment scale involves selecting scale headings that identify high priority goal areas. In terms of an individual client, this most often means identifying areas where an undesirable set of behaviors should be minimized, or where a favorable set of behaviors should be increased. Once a goal area is selected, it is recorded in the title section above the scale. Only those goals considered relevant to the service endeavor are included. Usually between three and five goal areas are identified.

2. Weighting

The second step involves the assignment of a numerical weight to each goal area. A weight may be any number from 1 to 99 (usually 1 to 9 is adequate), and should reflect the relative importance of the goal areas. The higher the weight, in comparison with other weights on the followup guide, the higher the level of importance. Several goal areas may be given the same weight, or all may be weighted equally by assigning no weights at all. This is a subjective judgment by the person constructing the followup guide.

3. Followup Time Selection

The third step entails determining the time period for which the scale will be scored. The followup date may be the same for all goals or it may be adjusted to fit the unique characteristics of each, but in either case the degree of expected attainment specified in the middle level of each scale should be based on the time period for which the goal will be scored. When a group of clients or programs are to be compared, a common time period is ordinarily used.

4. Statement of "Expected Outcome"

The fourth step involves stating the outcome that is expected in each goal area, taking into account the time interval until followup and the type and amount of service that is to be delivered. These can be considered prognoses, in that this middle level is the guide constructor's judgment of the *most probable* level of goal attainment. The goal need not necessarily be quantified, but it must be stated so that two independent observers could agree on whether it has been attained. Although some goals are sufficiently observable in themselves (e.g., "employed full time for the past month" can usually be determined by talking to the client or another informant), the investigation of other goals may require a separate attainment criterion (e.g., "reduced depression" would probably demand a symptom indicator such as "the client is able to sleep eight uninterrupted hours each night"). In stating the "expected outcome," it should be remembered that the criteria of attainment will have to be consistent throughout the balance of the scale. These can include test outcomes (Minnesota Multiphasic Personality Inventory [MMPI] scale scores, Rorschach scores or ratios, for example), or rating scale scores that index social and psychological functioning. Followup is easier, however, if each outcome level is defined by concrete behaviors that can be directly observed or reported.

5. Completion of the Other Scale Levels

Using the "expected outcome" as a benchmark, the next task is to complete the four remaining outcome levels on the scale. In this regard, the "expected outcome" should be the level judged to be the *most* probable result if the client receives effective service (or, in the case of program goals, if the program is competently implemented). The two adjacent cells represent less likely outcomes, whereas the two extreme cells represent unlikely but still plausible outcomes. A completed scale should contain five mutually exclusive levels (cells) and represent an exhaustive and internally consistent continuum of all possible outcomes in relation to a particular goal area. Figure 12.2 presents an illustrative set of goal scales. In practice it is often adequate to define the expected outcome and at least one of the levels above and one below the expected outcome. It is also informative to put a check mark at the level at which the client or program is functioning at the time the goal scales are constructed.

When several goal areas have been identified and scaled in this way, one should review each scale to determine if it contains errors that may render followup scoring problematic. Three kinds of errors in particular should be avoided:

1. *Vagueness*—scales should be specific enough so that two independent followup scorers can agree which level best describes the client or program
2. *Multiple dimensions in one scale*—scales should contain only one criterion variable so that differential change along two or more dimensions will not confuse followup
3. *Incompleteness*—all five outcome levels should be clearly implied by the three or four cells completed.

6. Followup

The last step in the use of goal attainment scaling is followup. Followup scoring simply involves determining which outcome level best describes a client or program at the time of followup, and putting an X or an asterisk in the corresponding cell. Each scale may be scored only at one level, indicating that attainment was at least at that level but not up to the next level. It is permissable to place an X or an asterisk on the line between cells.

THE GOAL ATTAINMENT SCORE

Once goal attainment has been indicated on each scale at followup, it is possible to calculate a goal attainment score. The goal attainment score may be thought of as an average of the outcome scores for various goal dimensions, but an average that has been adjusted for (a) the relative weights assigned to the goals, (b) the varying number of goals, and (c) the typical intercorrelation among goal scales. Conceptually, the goal attainment score is simply a global index of the degree to which outcome expectations have been realized.

The computation formula for the goal attainment score, as derived by Kiresuk and Sherman (1968), is shown in Equation (12.1).

$$\text{Goal Attainment Score} = 50 + \frac{10 \sum (w_i x_i)}{[.7 \sum w_i^2 + .3(\sum w_i)^2]^{1/2}} \quad (12.1)$$

where w_i is the weight assigned to the ith goal scale, x_i is the attainment score (-2 to $+2$) on the ith goal scale, and the summations are across all of the goal scales in the followup guide.

This formula yields a score of 50 if outcomes are at the "expected" level, on the average, and this goal attainment score will have a standard deviation of about 10. If all the scales in a particular goal attainment followup guide are weighted equally, then Table 12.1 can be used to find the goal attainment score. To do this, one must add the raw scale scores, find the row in Table 12.1 corresponding to this sum, and read the goal attainment score from the column corresponding to the number of scales in this followup guide. For example, if there were four scales, and their outcome scores were 2, -1, 0, and 1, their sum is 2 and the goal attainment score is 57.

TABLE 12.1
Goal Attainment Score Conversion Table for Equally Weighted Scales

Total raw score (Sum of scale scores)	Number of scales in followup guide					
	1	2	3	4	5	6
−12						19
−11						22
−10					20	24
− 9					23	27
− 8				21	26	29
− 7				25	29	32
− 6			23	28	32	35
− 5			27	32	35	37
− 4		25	32	35	38	40
− 3		31	36	39	41	42
− 2	30	38	41	43	44	45
− 1	40	44	45	46	47	47
0	50	50	50	50	50	50
1	60	56	55	54	53	53
2	70	62	59	57	56	55
3		69	64	61	59	58
4		75	68	65	62	60
5			73	68	65	63
6			77	72	68	65
7				75	71	68
8				79	74	71
9					77	73
10					80	76
11						78
12						81

   The goal attainment score gains part of its meaning from an assumption that human service workers can, with reasonable accuracy, predict how the client's problems or needs will be affected by the services to be provided. One way to test this assumption is to examine the observed distribution of goal attainment scores to see if the anticipated mean of 50 and standard deviation of 10 obtain. In the early experience with goal attainment scaling the theoretically predicted distributions were empirically verified. For example, in a crisis intervention study of 109 clients the mean goal attainment score was 51.4 with a standard deviation of 12.8. For 402 cases from a mental health service outpatient study the corresponding values were 51.9 and 10.1. For 173 cases treated by psychotherapists, these values were 52.5 and 11.9. Goal attainment scaling has also been used in a wide variety of other human service programs. Generally, it would appear that mental health professionals, some mental health care recipients, and professionals in a wide variety of human services (e.g., vocational rehabilitation, treatment of drug abuse, mental retardation services, child services) can establish accurate treatment outcome forecasts or prognoses.

RELIABILITY

   Reliability is the stability or "repeatability" of a measurement method, and is an important consideration in any rating or judgment procedure to be used in program evaluation. Unreliability in guide construction and unreliability in followup interviewer scoring can both limit the reliability of the goal attainment score. These two sources of unreliability were examined in an initial reliability study (15), in which each of 44 Hennepin County Mental Health Service clients had two followup guides constructed, one by their intake worker and one by their therapist. These two guides were then combined and scored in two separate followup interviews by two separate followup workers who were not involved in the treatment. In this study the resulting intraclass reliability was estimated to fall between $r = .50$ and $r = .65$, which takes into account all major sources of variance including test–retest reliability (.83) and scorer reliabilities ranging from .66 to .81. An extended review of this problem is partially covered in two unpublished reports (5; 15).

   This level of reliability can probably be exceeded when goal attainment guides are constructed and scored by a small group of evaluation interviewers specifically trained for the task. On the other hand, careless or inexperienced users could easily have difficulty reaching the reliability ranges indicated above. On the average, goal attainment scaling may pay a price in reliability by requiring the construction of new items for each client. If this cost is repaid in greater relevance, flexibility, and sensitivity to treatment effects, then we need not be concerned about a modest reduction in reliability. Improved relevance and flexibility are obvious in many applications of goal attainment scaling, but further research is needed to establish whether goal attainment scaling offers greater sensitivity to treatment effects.

We and our colleagues have conducted a number of studies to answer some basic questions about goal attainment scaling reliability: What degree of education is required to perform adequate followup? Can the followup guide be scored on the basis of a telephone contact with results comparable to in-person followup? What is the agreement between patients and staff in guide scoring? One study, for example, compared the scores obtained by two types of interviewers (nurses and social workers) within two types of contact (telephone and in-person interviews). Sixty clients were interviewed twice, using the various combinations of staff discipline and type of contact. The reliability coefficients ranged from .59 to .80 for the various combinations. For the combined group of 60 subjects, the correlation was .65 between goal attainment scale scores from the two interviews, which were typically about 4 weeks apart. Mean goal attainment scores among the two types of followup workers and two modes of interview were similar (1).

VALIDITY

Validity, the extent to which an instrument measures what it purports to measure, is also a crucial consideration in assessing the usefulness of an evaluation device. Although many kinds of validity are discussed in the literature, four are considered here in relation to goal attainment scaling: face validity, content validity, concurrent validity, and construct validity.

1. *Face Validity*

Mauger, Audette, Simonini, and Stolberg (1975) define face validity as ". . . the intuitive appeal of a measuring device . . . [the extent to which it] looks like it should measure what its developers claim." Mauger *et al.* assert that goal attainment scaling has appealing face validity to practitioners and evaluators because it allows treatment goals to be tailored to the specific needs and potentials of each client. This argument is based upon the assumption that human service workers and clients are able both to select problems and predict outcomes accurately.

2. *Content Validity*

Content validity is the representativeness of the behaviors sampled by a measuring device, the extent to which an instrument samples ". . . all relevant aspects of the domain of behaviors which [are] to be assessed [Mauger *et al.*, 1975]." The content validity of goal attainment scaling as a measure of client outcome in a mental health outpatient setting has been illustrated by Garwick and Lampman (1972), who studied the content of goal attainment guides for 113 patients at Hennepin County Mental Health Center. They determined that most goal scales could be classified within the 10 global categories shown in Table 12.2. A similar tabulation of the content areas actually used in one's own human service setting will provide a straightforward illustration of the content validity of goal attainment scaling.

TABLE 12.2

Problem Categories Mentioned at Least Four Times on Goal Attainment Followup Guides of 113 Randomly Selected Outpatients[a,b]

Problem category	Examples of content	Number	Percentage
Family/marital	Children, siblings, separation, divorce, in-laws, marriage.	28	10
Work	Employment, job, performance, work satisfaction, ambition.	49	18
Education	School, grades, vocational goals, attendance at classes.	8	3
Treatment	Hospitalization, medication, group therapy, counseling.	22	8
Sexuality	Dates, intercourse, relations with opposite sex, homosexuality.	17	6
Suicide	Self-destructive acts, suicidal thoughts, self-mutilation.	12	4
Physical complaint	Sleep, weight loss, headaches, aches, physical appearance.	4	2
Anxiety/depression	Nervousness, tension, anxiety, fear, crying, sadness, apathy.	30	11
Relationships	Involvement, communication, social life, friendships, talking.	47	18
Self-definition	Insight, self-awareness, knowledge of self, decisions.	27	10
Miscellaneous	Comfortable, material rewards, defensiveness.	26	10
Totals		270	100%

[a] Adapted by permission from G. Garwick and S. Lampman, Typical problems bringing patients to a community mental health center. *Community Mental Health Journal*, 1972, *8*, 271–280. (Copyright 1972, Human Sciences Press, New York.)

[b] The 270 phrases represent 37% of 730 phrases on the 173 goal attainment followup guides.

3. Concurrent Validity

Neither face nor content validity are sufficient to demonstrate the actual usefulness of a measuring device. Concurrent validity is an important additional indicator—the extent to which the instrument in question correlates with accepted independent measures of a variable. But, are fixed-item measures of symptomatic improvement (or improved social functioning) conceptually similar to individualized goal attainment scales? Not necessarily. A conceptual difference in the two measurement approaches would be consistent with the general finding of low to moderate correlations between goal attainment scores and scores on such instruments as the Brief Psychiatric Rating Scale, the Self Rating Symptom Scale, and the MMPI (4). Nevertheless, the relationship of goal attainment scaling to other methods of measuring outcome has not yet been adequately evaluated.

A special case of concurrent validity is relevant here. If one could compare a known effective treatment to a known ineffective treatment, and could show that some outcome measurement method was sensitive to this difference, this would provide vigorous support for the concurrent validity of the method as a measure of "treatment effectiveness." Of course in practice one rarely, if ever, has criterion treatments of known effectiveness. Yet there are ways to approach this problem, such as when a particular measure has been used along with other measures in several treatment comparison studies. All of the measures will have some face validity or content validity, or they would not be used in the study. If the studies are adequately designed, it will be reasonable to conclude that the treatments being compared differ in effectiveness if one or more of the outcome measures show a statistically significant difference. If none of the measures show a difference, either the treatments are equally effective (or ineffective) or the measures are all insensitive. For the studies that do show some effect, one can then observe whether a particular measure, such as goal attainment scaling, was usually among the measures that showed a difference, or usually failed to show a difference even when one was detected by other measures. In this way it will eventually be possible to identify outcome measures that are more or less sensitive to treatment effects. This approach is exemplified by a review of self-rating scales by McNair (1974), and a direct experimental comparison of various rating approaches by Raskin and Crook (1976).

The criterion of sensitivity to differential treatment effects will ultimately determine whether goal attainment scaling will have a permanent place in research and program evaluation methodology. So far, goal attainment scaling has not been used in enough multiple-criteria treatment experiments to have developed this type of track record. In a major study carried out in Hennepin County, clients randomly assigned to treatment (possible treatments included individual psychotherapy, group psychotherapy, drug treatment, and day hospital treatment) did not differ on any of several outcome measures (4). Other studies by the authors and their colleagues have shown that specific therapists do differ in their effectiveness in individual therapy (16), although this difference is probably not attributable to their discipline (psychiatry, social work, psychiatric nursing, clinical psychology). A study by Austin, Liberman, King, and DeRisi (1976) used goal attainment scaling to compare two psychiatric day-care programs, but the differences found were of borderline statistical significance with samples of 23 and 27 subjects in the two programs. In another study of 14 day-care clients, half were randomly assigned to prepare their own goal attainment followup guides, whereas the remainder did not. A clinician constructed standard goal attainment followup guides for all clients, and these were used to assess outcome. In this study goal attainment scores were significantly higher for the clients involved in their own goal-setting (mean goal attainment score of 71 compared to 59, $p < .015$), and consumer satisfaction measures showed similar trends (9). Similar findings using differing methods have been found by Houts and Scott (8), LaFerreire and Calsyn (11), and Smith (1975). In a well-known study by May (1971) of different treatments of schizophrenic patients, the second most sensitive measure of differential treatment effect was an individual target symptom rating scale that was similar in some respects to goal attainment scaling. Various forms of individualized goal scaling are being used in treatment experiments, and we hope that it will soon be possible to learn more about the validity of goal attainment scaling from this perspective.

4. Construct Validity

Sometimes a measure is designed to assess a new concept, or construct, for which no "outside" criterion is readily available. In this case information about face, content, and concurrent validity cannot provide a complete picture of the potential value of a measure. The ultimate value of a construct, and of a procedure designed to measure that construct, depends on its success in furthering our understanding of some phenomenon. This success, its "construct validity," can be judged by the variety and richness of empirical and theoretical relationships that are established through the use of the construct (Cronbach & Meehl, 1955).

Goal attainment scaling attempts to measure a construct that has not until recently been widely used in evaluating individual client outcomes in human services. This construct, the "attainment of expected service outcome," is not necessarily the same as "improved personal functioning," "reduced level of symptoms," "satisfaction with service," or "service effectiveness." All of these other constructs may be useful in the evaluation of human service programs, but individualized measurement approaches like goal attainment scaling add a new dimension to outcome evaluation. The ultimate validity of goal attainment scaling will not be judged solely by its plausibility or its correlation with more traditional measures, but by its success in adding a meaningful new way to examine and understand the effects of human service interventions. The studies reported in this chapter are encouraging, but the ultimate judgment of the construct validity of goal attainment scaling is for the future.

CHANGE SCORE

One technical issue also needing attention is the differing meaning of the goal attainment score and the goal attainment *change* score. Both of these measures use the same individually developed goal scales and average across several scales to get a total score. However, the goal attainment score uses only the followup score. Thus it gauges outcomes against the *expectations* of the person who constructed the goal scales. The change score includes the scale constructor's expectations only as they are represented in the definitions of the intervals between the five score-levels. From one point of view the change score is undesirable in that the entire goal attainment scaling method was designed to avoid the conceptual and methodological drawbacks of change scores generally (Cronbach & Furby, 1970). Nevertheless, many professionals use goal attainment scaling in a heuristic manner, or for program demonstration or defense, and not for formal treatment comparisons. If the change score seems useful in this context, use it, but use it fully aware of the limitations of change scores generally and of the goal attainment change score in particular.

A goal attainment change score is determined by subtracting the summary goal attainment score calculated on the basis of the client's status before the intervention from the summary score based on the followup after the intervention. A negative score indicates retrogression; a score near zero indicates little or no change; a positive score indicates progress. In most applications of goal attainment scaling, the average change score has been approximately +15 points (a 10-point change indicates movement of about one full goal attainment level), and the standard goal attainment score and the change score have been highly correlated. In general, however, we do not recommend use of the change score.

VARIETIES AND USES OF GOAL ATTAINMENT SCALING

The hallmark of goal attainment scaling is its flexibility. The technique allows individualized problem definition, and consequently can be adapted so that it fits profitably in any situation wherein evaluation consists of setting standards and determining how well they were subsequently satisfied. Goal attainment scaling has been employed throughout the human services, in both formative and summative evaluations and focused both on total programs and individual clients. The purpose of this section is to overview the clinical, organizational, and educational uses to which the technique has been applied.

CLINICAL USES OF GOAL ATTAINMENT SCALING

Goal attainment scaling was originally conceived as a measure of service outcome for individual clients, and has been used most often in that capacity. At the level of the individual client, its role is the creation of a client-specific evaluation criterion. In addition to providing this evaluation criterion, however, a goal attainment followup guide can (a) be used as part of a formal treatment plan, (b) serve as a record of the typical problems and expectations encountered in clients of a particular organization, and (c) help clarify each client's problems and improve the client's motivation to use the available services effectively. The explicit participation of the client in the process of formulating goals is not a necessary part of goal attainment scaling as a measurement method, but can contribute significantly to the quality of services provided.

The initial application of goal attainment scaling occurred at Hennepin County Mental Health Service in Minneapolis, Minnesota. The objective of this effort, called the "Four Mode Study," was to determine the comparative effectiveness of four primary treatment modalities: (a) individual psychotherapy, (b) group therapy, (c) day hospital treatment, and (d) medication treatment. Since this was the first attempt to assess the feasibility of goal attainment scaling, certain controls were necessary. For example, to eliminate the possibility that therapists might set "easy" goals, the goal attainment followup guides were constructed by separate intake workers (rather than by therapists). Also, to mitigate distortion due to preexisting client differences, clients were randomly assigned to treatment whenever more than one type of treatment was judged appropriate by the staff and was acceptable to the client. Furthermore, to prevent service recipients from using followup as a means of inappropriately rewarding or punishing their therapist, clients were not informed as to the existence of the followup guide. Last, as an additional measure to prevent biased results, followup scoring was done by independent interviewers. To maximize the clinical sensitivity of followup scoring, all followup assessments were conducted in face-to-face interviews by experienced therapists with advanced degrees in social work.

During the course of the Four Mode Study, goal attainment followup guides were scored for 248 randomly assigned clients. As indicated, the distribution of these scores conformed to the theoretical expectation of a mean goal attainment score near 50 and a standard deviation near 10. Nevertheless, there were no differences in mean goal attainment score that could be attributed to treatment assignment. As can be seen in Table 12.3, the study data were analyzed as four separate experiments, since one of four different assignment patterns was selected for each client before randomization. This resulted in small sample sizes except in pattern IV. Furthermore, this analysis included only clients who stayed in their assigned treatment mode for at least half of their total treatment sessions. A separate analysis, taking into account attrition and modality-change rates, also failed to differentiate among the treatments.

A further analysis of data from the Four Mode Study suggested that feedback to therapists of goal attainment scores could improve therapist effectiveness (*16*). After the study had been in progress long enough for most therapists to have completed several treatment episodes, they were given a

TABLE 12.3

**Goal Attainment Scores and Consumer Appraisal Scores for Clients Selectively Allocated to
Assignment Pattern but Randomly Assigned to Treatment Who Stayed in Assigned
Treatment Mode at Least Half their Treatment Sessions**

Treatment assignment and outcome categories		Individual therapy	Group therapy	Day treatment	Medication therapy
Assignment Pattern I	Mean goal attainment score	46.4 $N = 3$	53.0 $N = 3$	43.4 $N = 3$	48.1 $N = 4$
	Mean consumer appraisal score	57.1 $N = 3$	67.8 $N = 3$	55.6 $N = 3$	81.6 $N = 4$
Assignment Pattern II	Mean goal attainment score	47.9 $N = 6$	41.4 $N = 7$	49.7 $N = 9$	—
	Mean consumer appraisal score	63.1 $N = 6$	69.0 $N = 7$	67.5 $N = 9$	—
Assignment Pattern III	Mean goal attainment score	52.8 $N = 10$	49.4 $N = 9$	—	55.8 $N = 13$
	Mean consumer appraisal score	77.8 $N = 10$	76.2 $N = 9$	—	78.9 $N = 13$
Assignment Pattern IV	Mean goal attainment score	52.5 $N = 119$	52.7 $N = 62$	—	—
	Mean consumer appraisal score	80.3 $N = 118$	73.0 $N = 61$	—	—

summary chart comparing the goal attainment scores of their own clients to the distribution of scores for the clinic as a whole. After the therapists had received this feedback, the mean goal attainment score of their clients increased. Prior to feedback the mean goal attainment score was 51.6, and it rose to 54.2 for the clients seen after feedback was started ($t = 2.15$, $p < .02$, one-tailed test). These results are only suggestive, since there were no control therapists who did not receive feedback. Thus it is possible that the general followup scoring level of clients had changed for other reasons than a feedback effect on improved therapist effectiveness. Yet this suggests that feedback of outcome data to therapists deserves further study as a potential in-service training technique.

After the early returns from the Four Mode Study confirmed the feasibility of goal attainment scaling, a second study was undertaken, this time at the Hennepin County Crisis Intervention Center. Because the Crisis Center had a relatively small staff and a very large treatment population, it was impossible to separate intake from therapy or to assign clients randomly to treatment. However, in an attempt to improve the face validity of the procedure, Sherman's modification of goal attainment scaling called "contract fulfillment analysis" was utilized (14). In this approach, treatment goals are selected and scaled through a client–clinician negotiation (14; Lombillo, Kiresuk, & Sherman, 1973).

The Crisis Intervention Center study was terminated after 109 clients had been evaluated. The overall impression was that goal attainment scaling was feasible in a crisis center setting; however, most clients in this setting were too disturbed or uncooperative to be successfully engaged in a goal-setting negotiation. Of the 109 clients, 89 had goal attainment guides constructed by the staff alone. Blind judgments of these goals showed that staff-chosen goals did not differ from negotiated goals in rated "difficulty." Thus these clinicians did not seem to set "biased" goals. Twenty-five of the 109 goal attainment guides were constructed by paraprofessional staff members. The paraprofessionals were generally found to be as proficient as professional personnel in the construction of goal attainment followup guides, as well as in the achievement of these goals through their work with the clients. College undergraduates did many of the followup interviews, and we saw no indication that the use of nonprofessional followup workers biased followup scoring appreciably. Contract fulfillment analysis has been applied more successfully in other clinical settings. The experience in a small, rural mental health clinic has been described by Lombillo et al. (1973).

When the grant-supported Four Mode Study was terminated, Hennepin County Mental Health Service was faced with the task of developing a viable evaluation system of its own. The requirement that the system fit within the modest means of a typical mental health service meant that modifications were required in the evaluation procedures. This constraint was in itself an opportunity to demonstrate the viability of goal attainment scaling in a setting where the desirable but expensive controls of a fully developed research study were not possible.

The demonstration task was undertaken by Beaulieu and Baxter (3). While retaining the separation between intake and treatment and the limited randomized allocation of clients to treatment, they encouraged negotiation of the goal attainment followup guides between client and intake worker. In addition, a procedure was established whereby the client's eventual therapist also reviewed the followup guide, with an opportunity to critique its content and add (but not delete) individual scales. For economy, followup scoring was done by the client's therapist, either by phone or in person, but every tenth randomly selected client was also interviewed by an independent followup worker as a reliability check.

The distribution of client goal attainment scaling scores derived from this effort were again consistent with theoretical expectations, with mean and standard deviation near 50 and 10, respectively. There was substantial agreement between intake workers and therapists on the content and expectations incorporated in the clients' followup guides, as shown by the therapist ratings summarized in Table 12.4. The sampled independent followup interviews also supported the contention that therapists can accurately score the goal attainment followup guides for their clients. The sensitivity of the goal attainment score when gathered in this way is illustrated by the results of an intake experiment conducted in the program (13). Clients were seen in either group or individual intake sessions. The study clients were subsequently randomly assigned to either individual or group therapy. Goal attainment scores were significantly higher for clients whose treatment mode matched their intake mode. Since clients were not randomly assigned to intake mode, the results may simply mean that clients do better in a treatment mode that they choose, or that was chosen for them at intake. The point here is simply that goal attainment scores by therapists were sensitive to some type of systematic group differences.

The evolution of goal attainment scaling has been paralleled in the human services by a persistent tendency for expanded client input in decision making. It is a logical step in this progression that a variant of goal attainment scaling should appear in which goals are selected and scaled by the client alone, without significant clinician input. Such a device has been developed by Garwick (6), and is called the *Guide to goals*. The device was initially applied at Hennepin County Day Treatment Program to determine if clients could select and scale personal treatment goals and whether their goals were congruent with clinical expectations. Initial experience suggested that this was the case, and this impression was confirmed in a systematic study of the feasibility of the *Guide to goals* format. Twenty successive admissions to the Day Treatment Center were randomly assigned to two treatment groups. In both groups, the clients had followup guides constructed for them by a staff member, but in one group clients also constructed guides for themselves, using the *Guide to goals* format. The two types of followup guides were then subjected to a content analysis, and the results indicated there were no significant differences between the two categories in type of problems selected. For the 14 clients who completed the study, it was especially interesting to note that the mean goal

TABLE 12.4

Assessment by Therapists of Goal Attainment Guides Constructed by Intake Workers for a Sample of 179 Patient Episodes and a Total of 490 Specific Goal Scales

Rating item	Response option		Number	Percentage
Are the scales relevant?	Yes		541	94
	No		34	6
	Blank		3	—[a]
		Total	578	100
Are the scales realistic?	Very pessimistic		2	—[a]
	Pessimistic		34	7
	Right on		380	78
	Optimistic		47	9
	Very optimistic		14	3
	Blank		13	3
		Total	490	100
Would you modify scale weights?	Yes		13	3
	No		437	89
	Blank		40	8
		Total	490	100
Would you modify the scale levels?	Yes		35	7
	No		437	89
	Blank		18	4
		Total	490	100
Would you add any scales?	Yes		35	20
	No		139	78
	Blank		4	2
		Total	178	100

[a]Less than 1%.

attainment scores on the followup guides constructed by the clinicians were significantly different between the two groups, with the scores being higher for clients who had constructed their own guides (71.2 compared to 59.2, $p < .015$). This suggests that goal-setting may have clinical benefits as well as being a useful research tool (9;10). Further studies of the clinical effects of client participation in goal scaling in various day-care settings has been reported by Houts and Scott (8). In their studies client participation was also shown to have a beneficial effect on outcome, although not in every day-care setting that they studied. As Sherman et al. (15) have cautioned, in some clinical situations ". . . the client may lack the skill or insight to determine realistic goals and attainment levels." In these situations, negotiation of the goals with the client or relative, or construction of scales by a clinician, may be more appropriate (2).

In an attempt to demonstrate that goal attainment scaling possesses the precision necessary for a controlled study, a double-blind experiment was undertaken at Hennepin County Mental Health Service by Greenwald, Kiresuk, Lund, and Jones (7) to determine the comparative efficacy of individual psychotherapy and one type of minor psychotropic medication. Forty mildly anxious or mildly depressed outpatients were selected from the Center's pa-

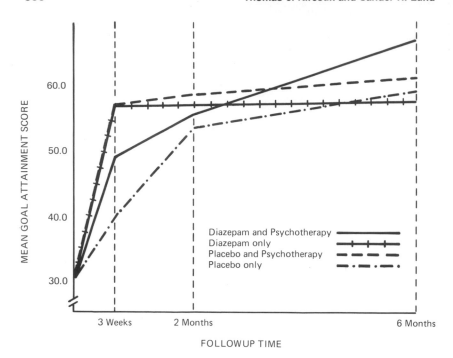

Figure 12.3. Interim results from the psychotherapy–Diazepam comparative treatment study.

tient population and randomly assigned to one of four treatment groups: (*a*) antianxiety medication (diazepam) and psychotherapy, (*b*) medication only, (*c*) psychotherapy and placebo, and (*d*) placebo only. All clients were seen weekly by a psychiatrist to monitor their medication. Some preliminary results of the study are presented in Figure 12.3. As can be seen, all of the treatment groups demonstrated improvement, and there was a trend for progress to be most rapid for those who received some form of active treatment. The differences at the 3-week followup with this first half of the subjects, however, did not quite reach statistical significance ($F = 2.78$; $p < .09$). More interpretable conclusions should be possible when the study is completed, when we will also compare goal attainment scaling results to similar data from the Brief Psychiatric Rating Scale and the Self Rating Symptom Scale.

ORGANIZATIONAL USES OF GOAL ATTAINMENT SCALING

Goal attainment scaling was conceived originally as a device for the evaluation of direct treatment. However, exposure to traditional goal-oriented management procedures made it clear that the technique was applicable in any situation wherein evaluation consisted of setting goals and determining how well they were subsequently attained. At an organizational level, the establishment and followup of goals is thought to optimize effectiveness in the following ways: (a) it can facilitate planning by compelling the organization to anticipate its long-term effects; (b) it can provide a natural vehicle for the allocation of staff time and other resources since the organization "knows" what it will be doing in the future; (c) it can improve vertical and horizontal communication about organizational tasks and products; (d) it provides a series of foci to help keep the organization's attention on the future rather than on day-to-day crises; and (e) it provides criteria for evaluation of performance. To these benefits, goal attainment scaling adds a hierarchy of outcomes, so that "effectiveness" is no longer a dichotomous measurement and it provides a valid and reliable goal-based numerical index of performance.

Organizational goals can be evaluated either in a summative process or a formative process. *Summative* evaluations are those in which goal attainment is assessed only once in order to determine the overall value of a program. *Formative* evaluations are those in which goal attainment is assessed at regular intervals in order to shape and influence the direction and growth of the program. The initial application of organizational goal attainment scaling occurred at Hennepin County Crisis Intervention Center and involved evaluation of the summative variety. Prior to beginning operations, 18 goals were selected and scaled for the center by its director and by the Crisis Intervention Center planning committee. Three of these initial goals are shown in Table 12.5. The goals were then followed up 1 year after the Center was in operation and the results reported to its funding board and to the community at large.

Although the results of the 1-year evaluation were quite favorable, the director of the Crisis Center attributes the greatest benefits of the process to the actual procedure of establishing and publicizing the goals, rather than the subsequent feedback of goal attainment. Specifically, the center's director concluded that the system (a) helped management by objectives by reminding the director of things planned but not accomplished, (b) improved morale by indicating the administration's interest in a smoothly functioning organization, (c) served to motivate staff to achieve along the lines indicated by the goals, and (d) provided corrective feedback (Stelmachers, Lund, & Meade, 1972).

Subsequent to the first followup, irrelevant goals were deleted and new goals were added to the followup guide, and the remaining goals were adjusted to reflect the elevated expectations produced by the first year's successes. Goal attainment scaling is now used throughout the Hennepin County Mental Health Service within a comprehensive evaluation/information system.

The second administrative adoption of goal attainment scaling followed a formative goal-setting and evaluation model. In a comprehensive reorganization of Hennepin County Mental Health Service's evaluation system, Beaulieu and Baxter (3) saw a need for an organizational goal structure that would monitor effectiveness and provide feedback, but that would not have to be restructured at every followup. The Beaulieu–Baxter model consists of (a) developing an overall organizational "mission statement," (b) deriving subcomponent goal statements from the overall "mission statement," and (c)

TABLE 12.5
Sample Goal Scales Applied to a Total Program, in This Case a Crisis Intervention Center[a]

Scale attainment levels	Scale 1: Assumption of suicide telephone responsibilities	Scale 2: Implementation of clinical evaluation of services	Scale 3: Patient satisfaction with the crisis intervention center
A. Most unfavorable outcome thought likely (−2)	Crisis unit is unable to handle all incoming suicide calls.		Patient satisfaction is not systematically sampled by the crisis intervention center, or a format for doing so has been devised but not implemented.
B. Less than expected programmatic success (−1)	Crisis unit is able to handle all incoming suicide calls but is unable to implement improvements, such as the use of multiple phones.	Planning phase is completed to assess alternative research designs for clinical evaluation of the crisis intervention center's services (i.e., various forms of goal attainment scaling are assessed).	Questionnaire format for assessing patient satisfaction is formulated or implemented on a sampling basis. Less than 40% of the patients sampled indicate satisfaction.
C. Expected programmatic success (0)	Crisis unit assumes total responsibility for the suicide service, and improves service by implementing multiple phones, integrating contacts into uniform crisis records, etc.	Planning phase is completed and a decision has been made on most appropriate method of evaluation; implementation has begun.	Patient satisfaction questionnaire is implemented and 40 to 60% indicate satisfaction.
D. More than expected programmatic success (+1)	In addition to the "Expected Level of Success," the Crisis unit routinely followsup on suicide contacts (followups may be defined as contacting the caller or his "significant others," checking with referral agency if a referral has been made, etc.) *	Evaluation methodology has been chosen and has been in operation for at least 6 months.	Patient satisfaction questionnaire is implemented and 61 to 80% indicate satisfaction. *
E. Best anticipated programmatic success (+2)		In addition to "More Than Expected Level of Success," data is used by Unit Director for policymaking and/or feedback of results to staff has begun. *	Patient satisfaction questionnaire is implemented and more than 80% indicate satisfaction.

[a] Three of a set of 18. Asterisks indicate level of functioning at a 1 year followup.

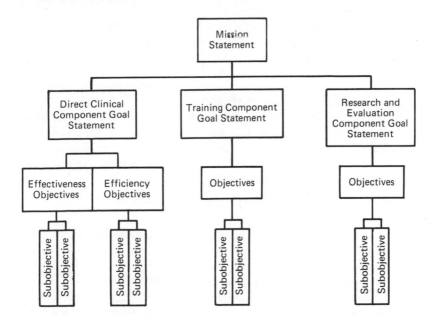

Figure 12.4. Hierarchical relationship among mission, goal, objective, and subobjective statements which is the logical framework of the Beaulieu–Baxter model. [Reproduced by permission from: T. J. Kiresuk and S. H. Lund, Process and outcome measurement using goal attainment scaling. In J. Zusman & C. R. Wurster (Eds.), *Program evaluation: Alcohol, drug abuse, and mental health services.* Copyright 1975, D. C. Heath, Lexington, Massachusetts.]

developing objectives and subobjectives from the subcomponent goal statements. This goal-setting structure is shown in Figure 12.4.

Because of the manner in which they are stated, it is possible to monitor the attainment of each objective and subobjective on a monthly basis. This means that a goal attainment score can be calculated for each program component and subcomponent, and that an overall program performance index can be generated by aggregating the individual goal attainment scores. More details on this method are available in an article by Bolin and Kivens (1975). Although Beaulieu and Baxter feel it is premature to make definitive judgments on the merits of their system, they report being particularly impressed by the flexibility of goal attainment scaling and the ease with which the technique incorporates a manager's value system in determining performance criterion levels that are relevant and realistic. They also feel that the program performance index score is valuable, in that it permits comparison of actual program performance with desired performance. However, they caution that realistic scaling is necessary to minimize random fluctuation of the score, and suggest that more experience is necessary before it can be utilized for major management decisions (3).

The goal attainment scaling methodology has been utilized to set organi-

zational goals in several other agencies as well. For example, the staff of the
Behavior Analysis and Modification Project in Ventura and Oxnard, California, has established objectives for their project using goal attainment scaling, and displays them prominently with changes in attainment marked each
month. Also, a modification of the technique has been made by Spano and
Lund (1976) at the University of Minnesota Hospital Social Service Department. Finding that staff were reluctant to develop 5-point scales, Spano and
Lund allowed them to merely state the "present level" of functioning and
"expected outcome." This afforded them an opportunity to develop their skills
and confidence in goal-setting before they shifted to a more systematic and
continuous use of goal attainment scaling.

EDUCATIONAL USES OF GOAL ATTAINMENT SCALING

Education was one of the first of the human services to evaluate program
success through establishment of specific objectives. Nevertheless, education
goal-setting tends to utilize only dichotomous outcomes and it has been difficult to compare goal attainment between program components. Much of the
early work with educational applications of goal attainment scaling was carried out at the Consultation and Education Unit of Hennepin County Mental
Health Service. The unit has used the technique in two ways: as a contract
negotiated between the unit and a community agency to render a consultation
program, and as a measure of any particular program's ability to meet student
goals. Student goals have been established in many different ways: (a) by
outsiders, without student consultation, (b) by a negotiation between student
and service provider, and (c) by the student alone. An example of negotiated
contract goals is shown in Table 12.6, and an example of student goals in a
training program is shown in Table 12.7. A detailed manual for the use of goal
attainment scaling for the evaluation of training workshops has also been
developed by Canfield and Kliewer (1977).

SUMMARY

Goal attainment scaling has been shown to be feasible and useful in a wide
range of evaluation tasks. It has clear value as a communication aid, as a
vehicle for negotiation between separate viewpoints, and as a method to increase explicit accountability. Some research has also suggested that goals can
function as motivators, and that goal-setting itself can lead to greater accomplishment. Although much work remains, preliminary findings have established goal attainment scaling as an important program evaluation technique.

At this writing we know of about 150 users of goal attainment scaling,
and we assume there are many more unreported users and former users. The
study of goal attainment scaling in this regard is part of a larger enterprise—
the study of the discovery, adoption, evolution and success of innovations
generally. It would be a mistake to evaluate the relative success or failure of
goal attainment scaling solely on the basis of the technical characteristics of
the method, ignoring the extensive literature on the adoption of innovations
cited in a recent National Institute of Mental Health publication (Department
of Health, Education, and Welfare, 1972). It is still early to make a final

TABLE 12.6
Sample Goal Attainment Followup Guide as a Consultation Contract

	Goal attainment followup guide			
Levels of predicted attainment	Scale 1: Consultation to line counselors	Scale 2: Education of line counselors	Scale 3: Consultation to supervisors	Scale 4: Establishment of permanent case conference system
A. Most unfavorable outcome thought likely (−2)	Consultation program is canceled.	None of the activities mentioned in (0) are used to enhance the skills of program staff.	Consultation experience has no impact at all on the supervisors' roles or functions.	No mechanism exists for program staff to get consultation on difficult cases.
B. Less than expected success (−1)	More than half of the scheduled meetings are canceled by either party.	One-to-one consultations include only one or two of the activities mentioned in (0).	Consultation experience has not effected supervisory time spent in troubleshooting for line counselors.	Staff receive case consultation only on informal or inhouse basis.
C. Expected level of success (0)	Provide regular weekly or biweekly consultation time to program staff for a period of 90 days.	Within regular consultations, audio-visual aids, selected readings, and general problem discussions are used.	Provide training and consultation to supervisors on management problems, principles of supervision and organizational problems.	Continuing case conferences made available to staff on one-to-one basis as problem cases come up.
D. More than expected success (+1)	As in (0), plus discussions about other kinds of consultation occurring (e.g., group consultation).	As in (0), plus interest expressed in developing topical staff seminars.	As in (0), plus supervisors spend more time in actual staff supervision and management.	Case conferences established on regular, one-to-one basis.
E. Most favorable outcome thought likely (+2)	As in (0), plus plans developed through group consensus for other kinds of consultation services.	As above, plus topical seminars begun.	As above, plus supervisors begin to function as consultants to line counseling staff.	As above, plus regular group case conferences scheduled.

363

TABLE 12.7
Sample Student Followup Guide for a Clergy Training Program[a]

Scale attainment levels	Scale 1: Degree in pastoral theology (STB) (W =)	Scale 2: Counseling for parish ministers (W =)	Scale 3: Parish involvement in group work (W =)	Scale 4: Use of community resources (W =)
A. Most unfavorable treatment outcome thought likely (−2)	No credit for training program and no plans to pursue a degree.	Reports he doesn't have any of the skills necessary to operate as a counselor for other clergymen.	No groups of any sort.	Reports no knowledge of places to make referrals in south Minneapolis.
B. Less than expected success with treatment (−1)	No seminary credit for program, but still plans to pursue a degree.	Reports uncertainty regarding his ability to function as counselor for other clergymen.	Training program group has terminated but plans for another exist. *	Has knowledge of one referral resource in south Minneapolis. *
C. Expected level of treatment success (0)	Received seminary credit for program.	Reports confidence regarding his ability to function as counselor for other clergymen, but has made no plans to start a group. *	Training program group functioning with new members—an ongoing group.	Has discovered and knows something about at least two referral resources in south Minneapolis.
D. More than expected success with treatment (+1)	As above, with additional work being planned, expected to begin soon*	As above, and plans to begin a group.	As above, and one other group functioning.	As above, and has made at least one referral to one of the agencies he has become familiar with.
E. Best anticipated success with treatment (+2)	As above, with additional work in progress.	At least one clergymen group functioning with himself as leader.	As above, with more than one other group functioning.	As above, plus reports expansion of knowledge to include resources in the larger Metro area.

[a] Asterisks indicate level at followup.

judgment about the value of the existing applications and adaptations of goal attainment scaling. Entirely new areas are also beginning to be explored, such as the coordination of goal attainment scaling with the problem oriented record, and with professional standards review organization (PSRO) approaches to quality assurance.

QUESTIONS CONCERNING
GOAL ATTAINMENT SCALING

The relative popularity of goal attainment scaling is sometimes attributed to the "intrinsic reasonableness" of goal-oriented evaluation. As human service workers focus on individual clients, evaluation based upon attainment of client-specific goals has a certain "natural" appeal. Nonetheless, face validity must eventually be supplanted by concrete evidence of an innovation's worth. The purpose of this section is to present, and attempt to answer, the most frequent questions regarding goal attainment scaling. This will focus the reader's attention on areas of controversy regarding goal attainment scaling, and the future work that will be needed to further refine and evaluate these methods.

QUESTION 1

Because the technique allows open-ended goal selection, don't the evaluation criteria tend to be arbitrary and irrelevant to a client's real need?

Goal attainment scaling is founded in the belief that there are no adequate universal definitions of ultimate human service goals, but rather that service needs are best defined according to the unique problems of each client at a given time. While this places great responsibility on the persons who identify the problems and scale the corresponding goals, there is substantial evidence that goal selectors agree reasonably well with each other and with their clients. For example, Baxter and Dreyer (2) have demonstrated that when service providers review goal attainment followup guides constructed for their clients by independent intake workers, they agree that the goals are appropriate and realistic more than 90% of the time. This finding was confirmed by Lampman and Garwick (12) who compared the content of followup guides constructed by client and service provider and found general agreement. In a related study, Lampman and Garwick (12) have also shown that if goal attainment followup guides are constructed separately for the same client by service provider and intake worker, they agree on the content of the scales about 57% of the time. Taken together, these findings suggest that goal-setters do select reasonably appropriate goals for their clients. Furthermore, greater reliability and relevancy of goals can probably be obtained if two or more people participate in the goal-setting task.

QUESTION 2

Because goal attainment scaling allows the level of goal attainment to be adjusted for each client, is it possible to know whether the outcome was due to treatment or to the goal-setting style of the followup guide constructor?

There are two background concerns in this question: (a) the issue of whether human service workers can predict the probable impact of services on their clients, and (b) even if they can predict accurately, whether they are likely to adjust the levels of attainment to ensure favorable outcomes for themselves or their program. In response to the first concern, the regular appearance of a mean goal attainment score of 50 is retrospective validation of the typical human service worker's ability to realistically gauge the probable impact of providing service. The possibility that service providers might "cheat" the system by scaling easy goals has been the source of concern to some, but has never been validated to our knowledge by actual experience. Various controls commonly used in applications of goal attainment scaling are designed to mitigate this source of potential bias. These include: (a) the separation of intake from therapy (on the assumption that intake workers have less reason to make service providers look good); (b) inclusion of the client in goal selection and scaling (since the client may tend to correct goal statements that seem unrealistically easy or hard); and (c) peer review of followup guides (since easy goals tend to be obvious, and making them public reflects negatively on the service provider's professional image). As reported earlier in this chapter, when clients participated in the construction of their followup guides, the goals were similar in difficulty to goals constructed without client participation.

Whether the service is *producing* the rated goal attainment can be convincingly demonstrated only by comparing the service with some alternate service strategy. This is a more general issue in the design of outcome studies that applies regardless of the method selected to rate treatment outcome. The safeguards that usually prevent rater bias can be applied to goal attainment scaling as well: (a) intake workers can construct goal scales before the client is randomly (or otherwise) assigned to service mode; and (b) a followup interviewer can be used who remains blind to the service assignment. There are often practical difficulties in using such safeguards, but no more so with goal attainment scaling than with any other outcome measurement method.

QUESTION 3

Since goal attainment scores are based upon expectations, how can differences in "true" effectiveness be determined? Isn't it true that a program with good services and high expectations will receive the same score as a program with poor services and correspondingly low expectations?

That is correct. Goal attainment scores cannot be compared between programs without some additional safeguard to be sure that equally difficult goals are set within each program. The most convincing comparison results from using the traditional experimental safeguards—when clients are randomly assigned to programs and the goal-setters do not know the program assignment of their clients. In this case the randomization equalizes the probability that each program component will receive clients with biased followup guides. It is also possible to make nonexperimental comparisons between programs or program components by using other methods to equalize goal difficulty. For example, raters who are blind to service assignments can rate the relative difficulty of the goals set for all the clients being studied. One can then examine the average difficulty of goals in various service mode groups to be sure they are comparable, or select subsets of clients from different service modes who have been matched on rated goal difficulty. These nonexperimental methods will be less convincing to some evaluation "audiences," but may be the most feasible approach in some circumstances.

The question of why a program with marginally effective service and correspondingly low expectations should get a satisfactory score is at first glance rather perplexing. The answer is that one of the fundamental purposes of goal attainment scaling is to allow the tailoring of outcomes according to what is known about the potential of each client to benefit and the potential of each service to help. As Rivlin (1971) has pointed out, one of the problems with evaluation to date has been an almost implicit assumption that all clients enter human service agencies with an equal probability of benefiting from services. The effect of this assumption has been that programs and individuals who deal with difficult clients rarely receive appropriate credit for their efforts, and that some programs actually compete for "attractive" potential recipients of their service. If a client is known to represent a genuinely difficult type of case, and if in addition the service modalities available are known to be only modestly effective, low expectations are reasonable and appropriate as an indicator of effectiveness.

There are two ways to facilitate the selection and scaling of appropriately challenging goals: (a) to allow the client (or client advocate) to participate in the goal-setting process, and (b) to ensure that the goal attainment followup guides produced by a program are subject to peer review or other appropriate quality assurance procedures. One significant additional benefit of goal attainment scaling is that the followup guides produced by a program form a cumulative record of both the kinds of goals selected for clients and the typical outcomes expected. If this record is available, either to clients or significant outsiders, it will be embarrassingly clear if an agency really does not expect much from its services. Such records might also be useful in the formulation of program treatment standards, after the fashion of the Professional Standards Review Organizations.

QUESTION 4

Its reliability, validity, therapeutic benefits and "intrinsic worth" aside, is there any evidence that goal attainment scaling is actually sensitive to variations in service effectiveness?

It has been a source of some chagrin to those in the human services that relatively few systematic evaluations have detected significant differences in service outcome. Consequently, an important characteristic of a useful evaluation technique is a demonstrated sensitivity to variations in service effectiveness. As reported earlier, the first application of goal attainment scaling at Hennepin County Mental Health Service's Outpatient Diagnosis–Treatment Unit failed to find significant differences in goal attainment scores for clients randomly assigned to either individual psychotherapy, group psychotherapy, day hospital treatment or medication treatment. Since that time, at least five investigations have been completed that employed goal attainment scaling and several of these studies have found statistically significant differences in service outcome (8; 9; 11; 13; Smith, 1975).

Also to be determined is the relative sensitivity of goal attainment scaling when compared with other common measures of the outcome of human services. While goal attainment scaling was designed, in part, on the hypothesis that it would be more relevant, and therefore more sensitive to differential service outcomes, the resolution of this question awaits further research and the test of time.

SUMMARY

The advantage of goal attainment scaling is its flexible structure—its ability to accommodate a wide variety of specific goals and measuring scales. A presumed advantage is that the method requires each client to be measured only on dimensions that are believed to be individually relevant. Another presumed advantage is that only the meaningful range of outcomes within a dimension are chosen, while individually unlikely extremes are not retained. The concrete, objectively determinable outcomes that one selects in advance also permit an audit of goal-setting in an agency. Finally, goal attainment scaling lends itself to measuring program goals as well as individual client outcomes.

The difficulties in using the method relate to its novel aspects. It takes a while for some service providers to begin thinking in terms of objective outcomes. Also, because of the intentionally relativistic framework, comparisons across patient populations and repeated measures over time require appraisal of the goals and their outcomes according to the particular value system and standards of a given local frame of reference.

What place does the measure have in total program evaluation systems? In human services one must sooner or later deal with ultimate values of living —those of the client, the staff, and the organization. To be sure, the goal attainment scaling method is only one way to attempt to accommodate these values. Yet in constructing the goal attainment model we and our colleagues have sought to make room for both life strategies: (a) the pragmatic strategy typical of program management, seeking to devise sensible, usable systems; and (b) the strategy of the individual, problem-laden or not, searching for what Lionel Trilling (1972) called the "expression of authentic self."

REFERENCE NOTES

1. Audette, D. M. *Activities of the followup unit.* Unpublished manuscript, 1974. (Available from the Program Evaluation Resource Center, 501 Park Avenue South, Minneapolis, Minnesota 55415.)
2. Baxter, J., & Dreyer, J. *Intake goal attainment guide assessment rating report.* Unpublished manuscript, 1973. (Available from the Program Evaluation Resource Center [see Note *1*].)
3. Beaulieu, D., & Baxter, J. *Evaluation of the adult outpatient program, Hennepin County Mental Health Service.* P. E. P. Report, 1969–1973, Chapter 9, 1974. (Available from the Program Evaluation Resource Center [see Note *1*].)
4. Garwick, G. *A construct validity overview to goal attainment scaling.* Unpublished manuscript, 1974. (Available from the Program Evaluation Resource Center [see Note *1*].)
5. Garwick, G. *An introduction to reliability and the goal attainment score.* Unpublished manuscript, 1974. (Available from the Program Evaluation Resource Center [see Note *1*].)
6. Garwick, G. *Guide to goals I.* Unpublished manuscript, 1973. (Available from the Program Evaluation Resource Center [see Note *1*].)
7. Greenwald, S., Kiresuk, T. J., Lund, S., & Jones, S. Y. *Drug effectiveness study: Interim report.* Unpublished manuscript, 1974. (Available from the Program Evaluation Resource Center [see Note *1*].)
8. Houts, P. S., & Scott, R. A. *To evaluate the effectiveness of achievement motivation training for mental patients being rehabilitated to the community.* Unpublished manuscript, College of Medicine, Pennsylvania State University, Hershey, Pennsylvania, 1973.
9. Jones, S. Y., & Garwick, G. *Guide to goals results in the day treatment center.* Unpublished manuscript, 1973. (Available from the Program Evaluation Resource Center [see Note *1*].)
10. Klinger, D., & Miller, D. *Evaluation of an on-line computer-assisted unit for assessment of mental health patients: Preliminary results.* Paper presented at the Convention of the Society for Personality Assessment, New York, 1976.
11. LaFerriere, L., & Calsyn, R. *Goal attainment scaling: An effective treatment technique in short term therapy.* Unpublished manuscript, Michigan State University, 1975.
12. Lampman, S., & Garwick, G. *Content analysis.* Unpublished manuscript, 1972. (Available from the Program Evaluation Resource Center [see Note *1*].)
13. Schreier, C., Wahlstrom, G., & Baxter, J. *Group intake: An alternative mode of clinical assessment.* Unpublished manuscript, 1972. (Available from the Program Evaluation Resource Center [see Note *1*].)
14. Sherman, R. E. *Contract fulfillment analysis.* Unpublished manuscript, 1969. (Available from the Program Evaluation Resource Center [see Note *1*].)
15. Sherman, R. E., Baxter, J. W., & Audette, D. M. *An examination of the reliability of the Kiresuk–Sherman goal attainment score by means of components of variance.* Unpublished manuscript, 1974. (Available from the Program Evaluation Resource Center [see Note *1*].)
16. Walker, R., & Baxter, J. *Effects of clinical feedback.* Unpublished manuscript, 1972. (Available from the Program Evaluation Resource Center [see Note *1*].)

REFERENCES

Austin, N. K., Liberman, R. P., King, L. W., & DeRisi, W. J. A comparative evaluation of two day hospitals: Goal attainment scaling of behavior vs. milieu therapy. *Journal of Nervous and Mental Disease,* 1976, *163,* 253–262.
Battle, C. C., Imber, S. D., Hoehn-Saric, R., Stone, A. R., Nash, E. R., & Frank, J. D. Target complaints as criteria of improvement. *American Journal of Psychotherapy,* 1966, *20,* 184–192.
Bolin, D. A., & Kivens, L. Evaluation in a community mental health center: Hennepin County Mental Health Service. *Evaluation,* 1975, *2*(2), 60–63.

Canfield, M., & Kliewer, D. Conference evaluation manual. In W. A. Hargreaves, C. C. Attkisson, & J. E. Sorensen (Eds.), *Resource materials for community mental health program evaluation* (2nd ed.). (DHEW Publication No. ADM 77-328.) Washington, D. C.: U. S. Government Printing Office, 1977.

Cronbach, L. J., & Furby, L. How should we measure "change"—or should we? *Psychological Bulletin,* 1970, *74,* 68–80.

Cronbach, L. J., & Meehl, P. E. Construct validity in psychological tests. *Psychological Bulletin,* 1955, *52,* 281–303.

Department of Health, Education, and Welfare. *Planning for creative change in mental health services: A manual on research utilization.* (DHEW Publication No. HSM 71-9059.) Washington, D. C.: U. S. Government Printing Office, 1972.

Drucker, P. F. *Managing for results.* New York: Harper and Row, 1964.

Garwick, G., & Lampman, S. Typical problems bringing patients to a community mental health center. *Community Mental Health Journal,* 1972, *8,* 271–280.

Kiresuk, T. J. Goal attainment scaling at a county mental health service. *Evaluation,* 1973, *1,* Special Monograph, 12–18.

Kiresuk, T. J., & Lund, S. H. Process and outcome measurement using goal attainment scaling. In J. Zusman & C. R. Wurster (Eds.), *Program evaluation: Alcohol, drug abuse, and mental health services.* Lexington, Massachusetts: Lexington Books, 1975.

Kiresuk, T. J., & Sherman, R. E. Goal attainment scaling: A general method for evaluating comprehensive community mental health programs. *Community Mental Health Journal,* 1968, *4,* 443–453.

Lombillo, J. R., Kiresuk, T. J., & Sherman, R. E. Evaluating a community mental health program: Contract fulfillment analysis. *Hospital and Community Psychiatry,* 1973, *24,* 760–762.

Malan, D. H. *A study of brief psychotherapy.* London: Tavistock Clinic, 1963.

Mauger, P., Audette, D., Simonini, C., & Stolberg, A. A study of the construct validity of goal attainment scaling. *Goal Attainment Review,* 1975, *1,* 13–19.

May, P. R. A. Psychotherapy and ataraxic drugs. In A. E. Bergin & S. L. Canfield (Eds.), *Handbook of psychotherapy and behavior change.* New York: Wiley and Sons, 1971.

McClelland, D., & Winter, D. *Motivating economic achievement.* New York: Free Press, 1969.

McNair, D. M. Self-evaluation of antidepressants. *Psychopharmacologia,* 1974, *37,* 281–302.

Raskin, A., & Crook, T. H. Sensitivity of rating scales completed by psychiatrists, nurses, and patients to antidepressant drug effects. *Journal of Psychiatric Research,* 1976, *13,* 31–41.

Rivlin, A. M. *Systematic thinking for social action.* Washington, D. C.: The Brookings Institute, 1971.

Smith, D. L. Effects of goal attainment scaling as an adjunct to counseling (Unpublished doctoral dissertation. The University of Oklahoma, 1974). *Dissertation Abstracts International,* 1975, *35,* 4664-B. (University Microfilms No. 75-6556, 68.)

Spano, R., & Lund, S. Management by objectives in a hospital social service department. *Social Work in Health Care,* 1976, *1,* 267–276.

Stelmachers, Z. T., Lund, S., & Meade, C. Hennepin County crisis center: Evaluation of its effectiveness. *Evaluation,* 1972, *1*(1), 61–65.

Trilling, L. *Sincerity and authenticity.* Cambridge, Massachusetts: Harvard University Press, 1972.

Wallerstein, R. S., & Robbins, L. L. Further notes on design and concepts. *Bulletin of the Menninger Clinic,* 1958, *22,* 117–125.

Wallerstein, R. S., Robbins, L. L. Sargent, H. D., & Luborsky, L. The psychotherapy research project of the Menninger Foundation: Rationale, method, and sample use. *Bulletin of the Menninger Clinic,* 1956, *20,* 221–278.

13

USING COST–OUTCOME AND COST–EFFECTIVENESS ANALYSES FOR IMPROVED PROGRAM MANAGEMENT AND ACCOUNTABILITY

James E. Sorensen and Hugh D. Grove

This chapter reviews several contemporary approaches to cost–effectiveness analysis, an evaluation tool used to achieve increased accountability and improved program management in human service organizations. An analysis of the deficiencies of social indicators, "program planning and budgeting systems" (PPBS), and cost–benefit analysis are presented as a preface to prospective solutions focusing upon costs and outcomes of programs. Cost–outcome assessment is proposed as the key to building viable cost–effectiveness analyses for program evaluation and accountability. Conceptual discussions of costs and outcomes are illustrated by detailed examples and followed by illustrative decision making.

The cost–effectiveness approach to be presented is developed through separate explorations of the difficulties inherent to both cost-accounting and outcome measurement, followed by a merger of costs and outcomes in the overall cost–effectiveness model. Figure 13.1 summarizes the major financial, statistical, and evaluation tasks required for cost–outcome and cost–effectiveness analysis. Starting with total costs of a human service organization, costs are refined to ascertain the per unit cost of service. Statistical data on professional staff activities are required to allocate personnel costs, while information about services rendered (e.g., units of service) is necessary to unitize program and service costs. Armed with unitized costs of service and an accumulation of services received by specific clients, total costs for an episode of care may be computed. Evaluation tasks then involve selection of a target group, preint-

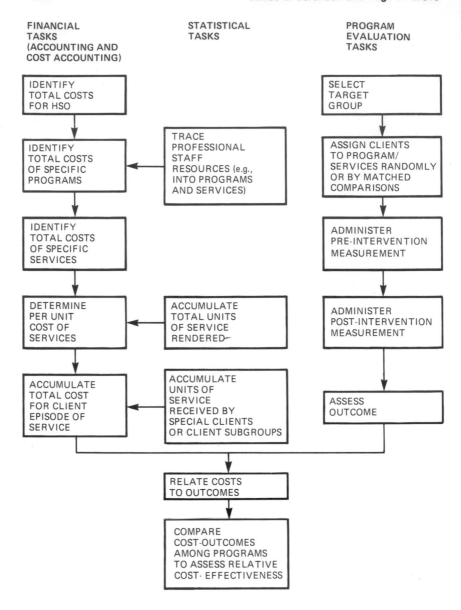

FINANCIAL TASKS (ACCOUNTING AND COST ACCOUNTING)

IDENTIFY TOTAL COSTS FOR HSO

IDENTIFY TOTAL COSTS OF SPECIFIC PROGRAMS

IDENTIFY TOTAL COSTS OF SPECIFIC SERVICES

DETERMINE PER UNIT COST OF SERVICES

ACCUMULATE TOTAL COST FOR CLIENT EPISODE OF SERVICE

STATISTICAL TASKS

TRACE PROFESSIONAL STAFF RESOURCES (e.g., INTO PROGRAMS AND SERVICES)

ACCUMULATE TOTAL UNITS OF SERVICE RENDERED

ACCUMULATE UNITS OF SERVICE RECEIVED BY SPECIAL CLIENTS OR CLIENT SUBGROUPS

PROGRAM EVALUATION TASKS

SELECT TARGET GROUP

ASSIGN CLIENTS TO PROGRAM/ SERVICES RANDOMLY OR BY MATCHED COMPARISONS

ADMINISTER PRE-INTERVENTION MEASUREMENT

ADMINISTER POST-INTERVENTION MEASUREMENT

ASSESS OUTCOME

RELATE COSTS TO OUTCOMES

COMPARE COST-OUTCOMES AMONG PROGRAMS TO ASSESS RELATIVE COST- EFFECTIVENESS

Figure 13.1. Overview of major tasks in cost–outcome and cost–effectiveness studies within human service organizations.

ervention assessment (generally), and random assignment of clients to varied treatment services (or modalities). After postintervention measurements, outcomes may be assessed. At this juncture, costs can be related to outcomes and, if calculated on more than one service, can be comparatively analyzed for assessing the cost–effectiveness of optional approaches for specific target groups. Summary sections emphasizing benefits created for decision making and accountability complete the chapter.

PRESSURES FOR ACCOUNTABILITY

Several emerging external and internal forces are compelling most human service organizations to become more accountable for the services they provide to society. As a starting point, the emerging external forces of social accountability may be traced to dissatisfaction with macroeconomic statistics. Olson (1969) makes this point clearly, when he states:

> For all their virtues, the national income statistics don't tell us what we really need to know about the condition of American society. They leave out most of the things that make life worth living. They leave out the learning of our children, the quality of our culture, the advance of science, the compatibility of our families, the liberties and democratic processes we cherish. They neglect the pollution of the environment, the deprivations of crime, and the toll of illness [p. 86].*

Because many significant aspects of the services needed and received by citizens are ignored in national income data, new and different indicators of service performance are emerging to provide better information for decision making.

Another indication of pressure for service accountability can be detected in the activities of the auditors who serve legislative bodies. For example, the General Accounting Office (GAO), which is the primary auditing force of the Congress of the United States, recently established performance or operational auditing standards (Granof, 1973): "The key feature of the standards is the pronouncement that an audit of a governmental entity should encompass not only an examination of financial transactions, but also a review of efficiency and economy in the use of resources and, most significantly, an evaluation as to whether desired results are being effectively achieved [p. 1079]." To meet these goals of accountability, the GAO standards specify that the performance audit shall include the following (Comptroller General of the United States, 1972): "The relevance and validity of the criteria used by the audited entity to judge effectiveness in achieving program results; The appropriateness of the methods followed by the entity to judge effectiveness in achieving program results and reliability; The accuracy of the results obtained [p. 4]."

Accountability is now being required by federal legislation. Renewal legislation for funding of services to be delivered by Community Mental Health Centers (Public Law 94-63), for example, poses two major accountability objectives: (a) evaluation of the effectiveness of the center's programs in serving the needs of the residents of its area; and (b) monitoring of the quality of the center's services.

With greater frequency, external agencies are asking for evidence of pro-

*Reproduced by permission from: M. Olson, The plan and purpose of a social report. *The Public Interest,* 1969, Spring, 86–97. (Copyright 1969, National Affairs, Inc., New York.)

gram outcome or impact and the relationship of the benefits to expenditures, especially when public monies are involved (Zusman & Wurster, 1975). But the forces are not all external. Internally, the program manager is often faced with limited or decreasing resources to meet varied needs and requires evaluation to aid the planning and controlling of program operations. Managerial decisions, for instance, about levels of funding (or relative levels of support between specific programs) require performance information that is often remarkably similar to the information sought by external agencies.

The emerging forces of accountability, as exemplified by external GAO evaluation standards and internal program evaluation needs, pose problems for human service management information and decision systems. The management information system (MIS), as delineated in Chapters 6, 7, and 8, is now necessary to provide information concerning service accountability.

The challenging problem of how an organization's information system can assemble, process, and report service performance information for internal and external uses has, of course, been ignored in the broad-based GAO and Congressional directives. This challenging and important problem is the focus of this chapter.

ACCOUNTABILITY AND PROGRAM MANAGEMENT: CURRENT APPROACHES

The information system of a human service organization should attempt to provide service or performance measurements. This section focuses upon several approaches to measuring service efforts and outcomes, through brief reviews of (a) the social indicators approach, (b) the program planning and budgeting system approach, and (c) cost–benefit analysis. Problems with these methods are discussed, and the section concludes with a presentation of cost–effectiveness methodology as a recommended solution.

SOCIAL INDICATORS

Social indicators have been utilized for assessing service outcomes in the evaluation of organizational performance (1; Biderman, 1966). A formal definition of a social indicator was given by the Department of Health, Education, and Welfare (Raymond & Richards, 1971):

> A statistic of direct, normative interest which facilitates concise, comprehensive, and balanced judgments about the condition of major aspects of a society. It is in all cases a direct measure of welfare and is subject to the interpretation that, if it changes in the "right" direction, while other things remain equal, things have gotten better, or people are "better off" [p. 43].*

*Reproduced by permission from: R. S. Raymond and E. Richards, Social indicators and business decisions. *MSU Business Topics,* 1971, Autumn, 40–46. (Copyright 1971, Division of Research, Graduate School of Business Administration, Michigan State University, East Lansing, Michigan.)

As this definition implies, a social indicator may be the same variable as a service outcome variable, but it is measured for a total community or society as the last event in a presumed *causal* network which links effort or activity to reward or output. In Chapters 9 and 10, social indicators are described as aspects of the need assessment process, whereas here we discuss their additional potential as indices of the impact of program interventions.

Some social indicators are directly attributable to the effects of human services and some are not. For example, some social indicators may be directly related to human service interventions (e.g., average life expectancy, percentage of an age group completing a 4-year educational program, number of basic scientists, number of individuals living in poverty, number of families in substandard housing). Other social indicators, however, are affected strongly by factors that are extraneous to specific service programs, and a society may be better off without certain misleading social indicators (Siegmann, 1976). For example, property crimes of burglary, larceny, and automobile theft comprise 88% of the Federal Crime Index. With the increased level of affluence in the United States, and with inflation, the average value of stolen property has increased above the $50 cutoff point for reporting these property crimes. Because the Federal Crime Index is highly sensitive to developments such as increased affluence or inflation, yearly increases in crime rates may not be indicative of social decay (Biderman, 1966). To measure the impact of law enforcement or criminal rehabilitation programs by using such an index may be quite misleading.

Educational social indicators, as another example, have also failed to make a useful linkage between input and output measures. Educational indicators normally show number of students, pupil–teacher ratios, pupils per classroom, average salaries, expenditures per pupil and per capita, expenditures on adult education, and education expenditures-in-total or as a percentage of Gross National Product (Gross & Springer, 1969). Separate from this, there have been large scale attempts to obtain standardized measures of the resulting student skills. However, community differences in average student scholastic aptitude and attitudinal readiness for education are confounded with differences in the input variables, so that it is again not possible to estimate the outcome gains that have been produced by specific expenditures.

Social indicators of mental health, like education, suffer from similar difficulties. Measures such as expenditures per capita, staff–patient ratios, and numbers treated specify input rather than output aspects of the causal networks. Surrogate measures for levels of mental health such as census data on percentage in poverty, percentage employed, or national surveys of self-reported "general well-being" may be used in identifying areas of need and perhaps in suggesting desired programs. But mental health programs are only part of the range of human service interventions and therefore changes in these indices cannot be attributed solely to mental health expenditures. Again, therefore, the linkage of cost to impact is lost.

Because none of the current social indicators attempt to link cost or effort to outcome, social indicators do not directly address the problem of input–

output accountability for human services. However, social indicators may be useful as measures of generalized, undifferentiated long-term impacts of health and human services.

THE PROGRAM PLANNING AND BUDGETING SYSTEM APPROACH

Another method of measuring and evaluating services is the program planning and budgeting system (PPBS) approach. This approach relates planning and budgeting considerations to specific program objectives. As suggested in Chapter 6, one view of this technique incorporates the following four steps (Hinricks, 1969):

1. Specify operational objectives
2. Assess outcomes in meeting the objectives
3. Consider all costs in meeting the objectives
4. Evaluate alternatives in meeting the objectives.

These steps will now be briefly elaborated. The first PPBS step is to specify objectives. Program objectives should be sufficiently broad-based to be meaningful, yet narrow enough to define the intent in operational terms. For example, the objective of a highway program is convenience for people through more efficient transportation networks, not merely to build highways. This "convenience for people" objective can be operationally defined in the second PPBS step, which is to evaluate and match outcomes with corresponding program objectives. The output of a highway program should be reduced travel time for the users, not miles of pavement. The third PPBS step is to consider all costs involved in a systems perspective. For the highway program, all costs would include removal costs for houses in the path of freeway construction and corresponding inconvenience to the owners. The fourth PPBS step is to evaluate alternative methods for meeting the original objective. In the highway program the obvious alternative is mass transit, which may increase social convenience of people movement, subject to cost considerations. The crucial aspect in the PPBS approach is the operational definition of objectives. This initial activity influences all other PPBS steps.

1. Pitfalls in PPBS

Although PPB systems are still actively pursued by many human service organizations, many organizations have abandoned or avoided the PPB system (e.g., the federal government). Several of the pitfalls of each step will now be outlined and then discussed.

1. Step 1—Pitfalls in specification of operational objectives
   a. Failure to specify operational objectives
   b. Tenuous relationships between means and ends
   c. Confusion of means with ends
   d. Measurement for the sake of measurement
2. Step 2—Pitfall in assessing outcomes and objectives: Causal models are often too complex in relating costs to outcomes
3. Step 3—Pitfall in consideration of costs: Reliance on incompletely specified causal models and the "externality" cost problem

4. Step 4—Pitfall in evaluating alternatives: Lack of operational techniques for analyzing alternatives to meet objectives.

The first problem relating to the initial PPBS step is the difficulty in specification of an objective at the general decision-making level which can be translated into operational measurement and evaluation terms at a specific measurement level. For example, an adequate highway system contributes to a good life by enhancing personal safety, mobility, and flexibility; but the operational objective is to increase efficiency of transporting people and goods through measurement of reduced travel time. Mental health programs may be expected to help people live their lives according to their own plans; but the operational objective is to improve social functioning in work or family settings.

The second pitfall involves the use of means as ends. In an agricultural fertilizer program, consumers do not eat fertilizer, they eat food. And in health programs, building inpatient beds is not the same as improving the health of a community.

The third pitfall is the converse problem: not regarding means as ends. Effective law does not fill jails or maximize convictions per dollar; effective law guarantees a due process wherein both individual rights and public safety are preserved. In a similar view, an effective social service program does not exist to merely give away its resources; an effective social service program assures a citizen access to basic necessities under conditions of adversity. The process (or the means) of achieving the ends may be the output objective, not the ends themselves.

A fourth major pitfall concerning the first PPBS step is fascination with measurement, that is, to measure is to know, *but not necessarily to know the right thing* (Hinricks, 1969). Meaningful measurement requires a relevant specification of objectives matched with valid operationalization.

In the second PPBS step, the crux of the measurement problem is measuring service outputs and their corresponding relationship to the cost inputs. From a measurement perspective, a causal model or network must be constructed which measures and preserves the relationship of the costs and the benefits (or inputs and outputs). For example, in the highway program, the relationship of costs to increased efficiency in people and goods movement must be determined and measured for both highway and mass transit alternatives before comparative evaluations can be analyzed. Most causal models are enormously complex, and efforts to develop service measures for PPB systems have been overly ambitious and complex in terms of available measurement expertise or procedures.

In the third PPBS step of cost measurement, a systems perspective is needed to obtain the total costs of the specific service program including external costs. In deciding upon an urban freeway project, for example, the total systems cost should include not only the direct cost of building the highway but also costs of relocating displaced residents and property value changes. The Aswan Dam is a poignant example of an incomplete cost analysis. The dam's objectives were to generate electricity and to provide irrigation. The sole cost-projection study that was undertaken considered only the cost of building a concrete dam, but the consequences (or externalities) of the Aswan Dam as summarized by Hardin (1970) were as follows:

> First, the replacement of periodic flooding by controlled irrigation is depriving the flood plains of the annual fertilization it has depended on for 5000 years. (The fertile silt is now deposited behind the dam, which will eventually have to be abandoned.) Consequently, artificial fertilizers will soon have to be imported into the Nile valley.
>
> Second, controlled irrigation without periodic flushing salinates the soil, bit by bit. There are methods for correcting this, but they cost money. This problem has not yet been faced in Egypt.
>
> Third, the sardine catch in the eastern Mediterranean has diminished from 18,000 tons a year to 500 tons, a 97% loss, because the sea is now deprived of flood-borne nutrients. No one has reimbursed the fishermen for their losses.
>
> Fourth, schistosomiasis (a fearsomely debilitating disease) has greatly increased among Egyptians. The disease organism depends on snails, which depend on a steady supply of water, which constant irrigation furnishes but annual flooding does not. Of course, medical control of the disease is possible—but that, too, costs money.
>
> Is this all? By no means. The first (and perhaps only a temporary) effect of the Aswan Dam has been to bring into being a larger population of Egyptians, of whom a greater proportion than before are chronically ill. What will be the political effects of this demographic fact? This is a most difficult question—but would anyone doubt that there will be many political consequences, for a long time to come, of trying to do "just one thing," like building a dam on the Nile? The effects of any sizable intervention in an ecosystem are like ripples spreading out on a pond from a dropped pebble; they go on and on [pp. 17–18].*

Missing from the Aswan Dam planning was an ecologic or systems perspective on the long-range impact of electric generation and irrigation at Aswan. The environmental perspective and ecosystem considerations would have allowed the discovery and prediction of the total costs related to agricultural, fishing, and medical problems. Solving human service problems also demands a systems perspective. Recent federal legislation (Public Law 93-641), for example, created Health Service Areas and Agencies (HSA's) to enforce geographic area planning and integrating of health services. This legislation recognizes the system perspective for coordinating independent health care agencies in order to manage the total costs of health care.

The last major PPBS step analyzes alternatives and attempts either to maximize output benefits or to minimize input costs in achieving the objective stipulated in the first PPBS step. The problem related to this latter step is the lack of operational tools for evaluating alternatives in meeting specific objectives. The cost–effectiveness approach subsequently developed in this chapter

---

*Reproduced by permission from: G. Hardin, To trouble a star: The cost of intervention in nature. *Science and Public Affairs,* 1970, January, 17–20. (Copyright 1970, Educational Foundation for Nuclear Science, Chicago.)

is advocated as one operational method for assessing how well various programs satisfy organizational objectives.

2. *Summary of PPBS Pitfalls*

The PPBS approach suffers from the major problems involved in assessing the effectiveness of human service organizations. These problems can be summarized in the language of the four PPBS steps:

1. Lack of operational objectives,
2. Lack of outcome measures,
3. Lack of external cost measures, and
4. Lack of cost–outcome assessment techniques.

Following a brief discussion of cost–benefit analysis, we will further delineate the cost–effectiveness approach by elaborating the issues of cost measurement, outcome measurement, and cost–outcome assessment.

COST–BENEFIT ANALYSIS

Cost–benefit analysis is a complementary technique to the final PPBS step of evaluating alternatives (2). It emphasizes a systems approach by considering all relevant monetary costs and benefits for alternative methods and attempts to develop cost–benefit causal relationships or linkages. Outcomes may be quantified in either nonmonetary or monetary terms with emphasis on the latter as a means to develop and refine the cost–benefit approach (Hinricks, 1969). Since cost–benefit analysis has traditionally attempted to quantify benefits in monetary terms, the usefulness of cost–benefit analysis has been limited by the problems of measuring outcomes in monetary terms similar to the pitfalls in the second PPBS step. For example, in health care service, what are the monetary benefits associated with saving one life? The present value of an individual's future earnings is not a compelling outcome measure.

The total cost measurement limitations of the third PPBS step are also the problems of cost–benefit analysis. Cost–benefit analysis, like PPBS, faces the service measurement hurdles of defining appropriate cost–outcome relationships and of accumulating accurate total system costs. In saving an individual's life, direct health service costs and indirect costs (e.g., lost wages and sick pay) would have to be included. Accordingly, a systems perspective is advocated in ascertaining those networks where externalities (external social costs) are incorporated or internalized within the cost–benefit network: "Cost–benefit analyses must be carried out with an intellectual framework that comes closer to incorporating the total system . . . . The myth of externalities must be abandoned [Hardin, 1970, p. 20]."

In summary, the problems of cost–benefit analysis are the problems of PPBS: outcome measurement, cost measurement, and the monetary expression of cost–outcome assessment of alternatives.

One promising cost–benefit approach chooses a position that is somewhat less than a thoroughgoing cost–benefit analysis. Identified as "output value analysis," this method was developed within the mental health field and is described by Halpern and Binner (1972) as:

An evaluative framework that relates specifically to the program and fiscal concerns of the . . . administrator. Applicable to any program or components, the framework focuses on estimating the economic value of a program's output and relating this value to the costs of achieving the output. It is simpler than a full cost–benefit analysis, which would require a much more comprehensive picture of all the costs and benefits involved. It focuses on just two of the basic, direct benefits of any mental health program and relates these to immediate program costs [p. 41].

A key concept in the output value analysis approach is the output value index defined in Equation (13.1)

$$\text{Output value index} = \frac{\text{Estimated output value}}{\text{Estimated resource investment}} \quad (13.1)$$

where *estimated output value* consists of estimated economic productivity (viz., income reported during the year prior to admission) plus an estimated value for improved functioning and lessened misery enjoyed by the individual. The second element of the output value ". . . was to redress the neglect of subjective improvement and give it relatively equal status with the traditional economic productivity component [*12*, p. 4]." The mind would appear to have some dollar value if insurance companies are willing to pay $25,000 to $50,000 for physical injuries such as the loss of a leg or an eye. Restoring a client to the average economic productivity of his or her group in treatment is a possible approach for a "valuation" of the mind.

The second part of the estimated output value is called the *estimated response value* and is calculated by multiplying a treatment response percentage times the average twelve month economic productivity (or some other subjectively determined value) of the group of patients studied. The response percentage is a subjective distribution that cross-classifies level of impairment at admission (namely, slight to severe) and level of response at discharge (namely, regressed to marked improvement). The subjective weightings permit the decision maker to ". . . give differential credit for working with patients of different degrees of impairment [Halpern & Binner, 1972, p. 43]." A client entering at a "slight" level of impairment and exiting at "moderate improvement" might be given a 40% response percentage, while a client entering at a "severe" level impairment would be given a 70% response percentage for "moderate improvement." In brief, movement to higher levels of improvement by more severely impaired clients are given more credit in the output achieved. The estimated resource investment accumulates only program costs that are a function of the various kinds of treatment given to a patient.

The output value analysis approach developed by Halpern, Binner and colleagues is an effort at a simplified cost–benefit analysis for mental health. Their method is both promising and encouraging. Improved management flows from improved measures of program performance. In a larger sense, performance measures are subjective, but to the extent that measures can be linked directly with the phenomena they represent, the role of subjectivity is diminished. The output value approach, like cost–benefit in general, incorporates a subjective value, namely the *response value* (which uses a subjective response rate multiplied times a somewhat subjective estimate of average economic productivity). While the intellectual rationale for including *response values* is compelling, the designers admit that ". . . these additional benefits have been regarded [by economists] as too intangible to include in the formal quantitative analysis [*12*, p. 3]." Authors of other, more complicated cost–benefit analyses [e.g., Murphy and Datel (1976, pp. 100–101) on the net savings of community over institutional living] caution their readers about (*a*) the smallness of sample size for data inputs,(*b*)tentativeness of 10 year cost projections, (*c*) sensitivity to altered assumptions, (*d*) confounding of costs for maintenance and support services, and (*e*) the unmeasured psychosocial benefits (or costs).

Although an appealing idea, cost–benefit analyses are fraught with multiple operational problems including the especially difficult task of assigning dollar values to benefits.

COST–EFFECTIVENESS

Newer types of effort–accomplishment measurement methodologies have recognized the lack of monetary output and total cost measurement procedures and have applied a systems perspective linking monetary input measurements to *nonmonetary* output measurements for the effectiveness assessment of a particular service. Levin (1975) has summarized these new developments:

> A crucial assumption for performing benefit–cost analyses of alternatives is that the benefits or outcomes can be valued by their market prices or those of similar alternatives. Yet, the objectives of many, if not most social programs, often have no market counterpart . . . . In such situations the effectiveness of a strategy is expressed in terms of its actual physical or psychological outcome rather than its monetary value. That is, the monetary measures of resource costs are related to the effectiveness of a program in producing a particular impact. When the effectiveness of programs in achieving a particular goal (rather than their monetary values) is linked to costs, the approach is considered to be a cost–effectiveness rather than a cost–benefit analysis . . . . In this context, cost–effectiveness analysis enables us to examine the costs of alternative programs for achieving particular types of outcomes, but prevents us from comparing the costs directly with benefits. That is, the cost–effectiveness approach enables us to rank potential program choices according to the magnitudes of their effects relative to their costs, but we cannot ascertain whether a particular program is "worth it" in the sense that benefits exceed costs, because the latter are generally expressed in monetary units while the former are rendered in units of effectiveness for achieving a particular impact [pp. 92–93].*

Cost–effectiveness should be viewed as a subset of cost–benefit analysis. If the measured effects required for cost–effectiveness can be translated into monetary values, a cost–benefit analysis can be developed. Whenever physical

*Reproduced by permission from: H. M. Levin, Cost–effectiveness analysis in evaluation research. In M. Guttentag & E. L. Struening (Eds.), *Handbook of evaluation research* (Vol. 2). Copyright 1975, Sage Publications, Beverly Hills, California.

or psychological outcomes are converted into monetary measures, both cost–effectiveness and cost–benefit analyses are possible.

1. *Accountability and Program Management*

When examining various ways to provide measures of accountability and to perform evaluation in human service programs, three general types of evaluation emerge (Tripodi, Fellin, & Epstein, 1971) from the literature: (*a*) monitoring techniques; (*b*) social research techniques; and (*c*) cost-analytic techniques. *Monitoring* techniques include accountability or administrative audits and time and motion studies. Heavy emphasis is usually given to re-source input and process activities. Measures of process—statistics on the process of service delivery including measures of efficiency—currently exist and can be and have been applied (Smith & Sorensen, 1974). Process measures deal with an examination of the service process and whether the applied process is appropriate (Decker & Bonner, 1973; Riedel, Tischler, & Myers, 1974). Historically, this has meant:

1. Audit of records (e.g., case-by-case evaluation)
2. Direct observation of staff/program activities
3. Examination of client/patient conditions
4. Testing of professional staff (with hypothetical cases)
5. Comparisons of actual and desired (or normative) profiles or ratios.

Social research techniques include experiments or quasi-experiments, sur-veys (including client satisfaction), and case studies (Campbell & Stanley, 1969; Davis, Weiss, Louis, & Weiss, 1973; Tripodi *et al.,* 1971).

Cost-analytic techniques include approaches where resource consump-tion is a common element of the analysis. These techniques range from cost-accounting and cost-finding for programs, units of services, and episodes (or spells of illness) to techniques that link resource consumption to outcome or benefit such as cost–outcome and cost–benefit analysis. When trying to pick optimal choices among competing optional programmatic choices, cost–effec-tiveness emerges because this method attempts to link cost inputs with benefit outputs in causal models or networks. Figure 13.2 attempts to differentiate between the various levels of cost-analytic analysis (Wilkinson, 1972). Wilkin-son's sequential analysis begins with the budgeted cost reports and proceeds through a sophisticated cost–benefit analysis. To achieve cost–effectiveness requires an intermediate step of *cost–outcome* (a step that is not expressly identified in Figure 13.2). As measures of human service accountability and program management, cost–outcome and cost–effectiveness analyses are quite interrelated: Cost–outcome analysis ascertains the programmatic resources consumed to achieve a change in a relative measure of client functioning (e.g., symptoms, social performance). Cost–effectiveness analysis relies upon the comparison of cost–outcomes to identify the most effective programs in terms of beneficial outcome to the cost of programs, modalities, or treatment tech-niques. This service accountability measurement endeavor must be broken

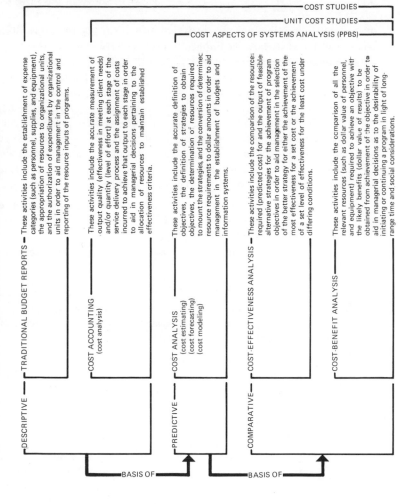

Figure 13.2. A preliminary classification system for costing techniques. [Adapted by permission from: G. L. Wilkinson, *Educational Technology*, 1972, *12*, 33–38. Copyright 1972, Educational Technology Publications, Inc., Englewood Cliffs, New Jersey.]

down into manageable measurement problems: (a) identification of specific service attributes such as mental health care; and (b) identification and measurement of specific causal networks such as the relation of mental health care costs (or input efforts) to mental health improvement (or outcome rewards). These two cost-analytic techniques form a cost–effectiveness approach that links monetary cost inputs to nonmonetary outputs, but does not pursue the nearly hopeless task of expressing more remote and frequently nontangible *outputs* in monetary terms. This approach is advocated as a viable solution to problems of service accountability and program management because it properly attempts to break down complex service measurement and causal networks into manageable portions. The balance of the chapter will focus on:

1. A pragmatic conceptualization of cost–effectiveness for human services
2. Dual measurement problems of cost inputs and service outcomes within a cost–effectiveness approach
3. An integrative illustration of the cost–outcome—cost–effectiveness model in a mental health setting.

2. Linkage of Cost–Outcome to Cost–Effectiveness

Effective program management requires program evaluation. Program evaluation as an important part of any systematic approach to program management (Wholey, Scanlon, Duffy, Fukumoto, & Vogt, 1970):

1. Assesses the effectiveness of an ongoing program in achieving its objectives
2. Relies on the principles of research design to distinguish a program's effects from those of other forces working in a situation
3. Aims at program improvement through modification of current operations.

Measuring program outcomes is a key linkage in assessing program effectiveness (cf. Chapters 11 and 12). Hargreaves, Attkisson, and Ochberg (1977) suggest three reasons why program outcomes are important in program management:

> One of the most useful occasions for an outcome study is when it can aid management and clinical staff in making a specific decision about program change. These are generally time-limited special projects. . . . A second reason to examine outcomes is to routinely detect relative strengths and weaknesses in a system of delivering services. Finally, program managers often need to demonstrate their program's overall effectiveness to funders and other groups who have a stake in the. . . [organization]. For these latter purposes, routine monitoring and public accountability, some simple outcome assessment can be a useful part of an integrated management information system [p. 8-1].

Using cost–outcomes information as building blocks, cost–effectiveness (Fishman, 1975; Goldman, 1967; Quade, 1967; 17) emerges as the last of five sequential steps that occur within three time frames as presented in Table 13.1.

TABLE 13.1
Sequential Steps in Cost–Outcome Cost–Effectiveness Analysis

Time frame	Tasks to be performed
One	• Identifying the objective to be achieved (or treatment goals to be achieved) for specific target groups (e.g., social functioning of neurotic depressives in a catchment area admitted to a community mental health center). • Specifying optional (or alternative) treatment programs to be used (e.g., random assignment to individual versus group therapy).
Two	• Determining the costs of each program, cost per unit of service, and amounts of service rendered (e.g., use of accrual accounting, operating statistics, cost-finding, and rate-setting).
Three	• Assessing the effect or outcome of the program intervention on the target group (e.g., preintervention versus postintervention assessment). • Combining cost and outcome information to present cost–outcome and cost–effectiveness analyses (e.g., use of matrices and statistical analyses).

Cost–effectiveness indices may also be created by relating costs of treating specific subjects to varying forms of outcome (e.g., actual or planned change in level of social functioning where the indices become cost per unit of actual or planned change). Detailed examples are presented later in this chapter.

ASSESSING COSTS IN COST–EFFECTIVENESS STUDIES

In this section problematic aspects of the cost–effectiveness approach are explored including multiple meanings of cost, nonuniformity in cost-accounting, and the use of costs. A suggested model (with an example) of the cost concepts is constructed where primary emphasis is given to costs per hour of service in an ambulatory setting, changing statistical definitions, and cost-based rates. The following cost measurement problems are common to cost–outcome, cost–effectiveness, and cost–benefit studies.

1. Multiple Meanings of Cost

Accounting for cost sounds deceptively simple. However, the meaning of cost differs when viewed from different perspectives. *Operational costs* accumulated from the organization's accounting system may provide a measure of internal resources consumed. *Social costs* may well be different if viewed by a social perspective that incorporates donated goods and services and the impacts on other organizations or the environment. For example, the cost of treating a heroin addict may not be fully assessed by the accounting records because lost work productivity and welfare payments are not included. Operational costs are often different from social costs but are more easily computed.

Opportunity costs, or costs of foregone opportunities such as lost wages or bypassed optional program choices are intriguing but often elusive computations. Costs could be (but are typically not) accumulated from a client perspective. Involvement in different human service programs may have different costs to the client, but most often these variations are not known. Take, for example, the issue of service accessibility; the hours for outpatient services may be extended to evenings and weekends to serve a lower economic group because they cannot afford to miss work to utilize services offered during regular weektime and daytime hours. Time of service availability affects whether or not the client can *afford* to use the service, that is, its cost to the client.

Costs can behave differently depending on the type of cost and the time frame. In Chapter 6, *fixed* costs were shown to be constant in total but to decrease on a unit basis when service activity increases. *Variable* costs increase in total when service activity increases but remain constant on a per unit basis (in the short-run). *Average* and *incremental* costs serve different decision objectives. A full cost is appropriate for rate-setting so all operational costs are uniformly spread among all users. Incremental costs, on the other hand, may be useful in assessing which program changes will produce the least extra costs.

Costs are not static over time. Costs incurred or saved 1 year, 2 years, or 10 years in the future are not the same as today's costs. The time value of money requires *discounting* to equate future expenditures with today's dollars. And not all costs over time are the same in purchasing power; inflation or deflation can change the economic "size" of a dollar so combinations of costs over extended periods of time can be misleading or meaningless (Sorensen & Phipps, 1975).

2. Nonuniformity in Cost Accounting

Even if the analysis is restricted to conventional cost-accounting for human services, the analysis is complex (Sorensen, 1976). The level of cost aggregation desired has an effect on the level of complexity encountered. For example, a legislative decision maker may be trying to evaluate the amount of the personnel costs devoted to vocational training in partial care programs offered by mental health organizations within a total health care budget. Figure 13.3 reveals the number of layers that have to be penetrated to respond to the inquiry about vocational training costs. Similar complex inquiries could be raised about any type of cost at any of the five levels suggested in Figure 13.3.

Besides the task of deciding on the desired level of aggregation, nonuniformity arises because of:

1. Varied definitions of services and programs
2. Varied organizational configurations of services and programs
3. Varied, but acceptable, cost-accounting practices (e.g., allocation and valuation techniques)
4. Varied amounts and types of operating statistics.

The traditional mechanisms for coping with this variety of nonuniformities have been to:

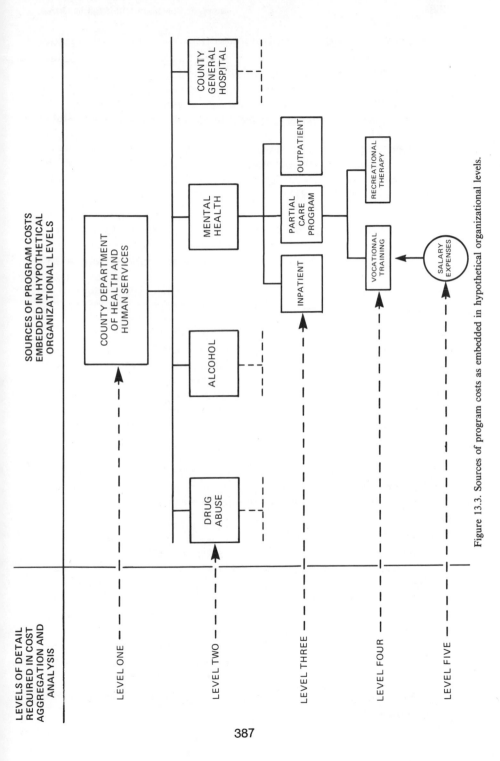

Figure 13.3. Sources of program costs as embedded in hypothetical organizational levels.

387

1. Specify general reporting requirements with the individual organizations handling the detail as they wish (e.g., many federal and state reporting requirements follow this practice);
2. Specify the reporting requirements accompanied by specific definitions of terms, and specific procedures for accumulating/collapsing data (e.g., *Hospital administrative services reports,* American Hospital Association, 1967); and
3. Specify the system to be used in collecting and reporting information (e.g., *Accounting and cost reporting systems* [15]; or *Institutions of the department of mental health, State of Michigan,* Michigan Department of Mental Health, 1971).

Although each of these approaches progressively enhances uniformity, their difficulty and cost of implementation increase exponentially. As the level of aggregation increases, the level of precision decreases. On balance, nonuniform cost-accounting is bound to result. But is the situation hopeless? Only moderately so. The general approach to cost-accounting and its content can be made more uniform, but specific cost-accounting techniques will continue to be nonuniform.

3. *Role of Costs*

Cost aspects of service measurement are important in integrating accounting information and operating statistical information into the calculation of cost per unit of service and cost per program. These cost calculations are useful for rate-setting, negotiations with third-party payers, presentations to funding agencies and other external groups, and managerial and advisory board analyses. Properly formulated, such costing procedures would provide useful data for cost–outcome studies (namely, cost per unit of change in a behavioral index) and cost–effectiveness analyses (namely, cost comparisons between different treatment outcomes). Cost-accounting, then, becomes a vital element of the information system and management decision process beginning with the simple costing of programs up through sophisticated cost–effectiveness studies.

A SUGGESTED MODEL

Minimum information requirements to measure cost elements in a cost–effectiveness analysis would require direct (traceable) cost sorted by program (e.g., mental health), organizational unit (e.g., hospital), service (e.g., outpatient), and object of expenditures (e.g., salary). This cost information requirement implies that a fairly sophisticated accounting system is operational. Also, the sorting process implies that a set of procedures for allocating secondary overhead costs to primary or final producing cost centers exists. The cost-accounting system must have access to operating statistics comparable to the level of service used in the above cost sorting. Examples include:

1. Inpatient care: Days received (which enables cost per episode or month computations)

2. Intermediate or partial care: Hours of *received* service (or some standard number of hours such as 4 hours = 1 unit of partial day; this permits a cost per episode or month computation)
3. Outpatient and ambulatory services, such as
   a. Hours of *rendered* service
   b. Clients enrolled/attending
   c. Visits
   d. Treatments (e.g., relative value units)
   e. Ancillary services (e.g., x-ray, dentistry) associated with primary services received (e.g., counts, relative value units).

At this level of sophistication, the cost-accounting system can provide total costs of programs, cost per unit of service, cost per time period, and cost per treatment episode for subsequent cost–efficiency analysis.

1. *Detailed Example*

To illustrate how one may establish a cost-accounting system for human service care, we will present an example of cost-accounting for ambulatory services. This example assumes that traceable and allocatable costs and operating information have been accumulated for each type of ambulatory service. The next step is to establish unit costs by services which relate each major cost accumulation to operating statistics using the "accounted-for hours" model (*3*) based on information collected by a management information system (MIS). The following four cost components are added to obtain the total cost per hour of a service:

1. *Salary budgeted rate,* which equals total cost of purchased hours divided by total hours of purchased time.
2. *Salary overhead rate,* which equals total cost of *unaccounted-for* purchased time (unabsorbed) divided by total hours accounted-for by MIS.
3. *Other direct cost rate,* which equals all nonpersonnel costs clearly or reasonably identified with a program divided by total hours accounted-for by MIS.
4. *Indirect (allocated) cost rate,* which equals allocated indirect overhead divided by total hours accounted-for by MIS.

To unitize allocated costs, program support unit costs (e.g., indirect costs such as allocated overhead, centerwide administration, research and evaluation, training and development) should be allocated to various service delivery programs to enable total program evaluation and full-cost rate-setting. Program support costs are related to an appropriate statistical basis (e.g., hours of delivered service by program, visits, number enrolled, patient days) to unitize the indirect cost per unit of service. An example of indirect cost rates would be to divide allocated indirect overhead by the same statistical basis (e.g., delivered hours) used in unitizing program delivery costs.

In combining traceable and allocated costs for the accounted-for hours model, managerial indices of actual costs related to hours of service actually rendered are constructed. Figure 13.4 presents a sample of the cost indices that result from this approach (*4*). The cost components of each team are summarized for an outpatient adult program within a selected period of time. The salary overhead rate is a dynamic measure which monitors the utilization of administrative effort (i.e., amount of unaccounted-for time) as well as the cost of the effort (i.e., how expensive).

2. *Cost per Hour*

The hypothetical data presented in Figure 13.4 indicate that Team 1 is able to deliver an hour of direct service in the adult outpatient program for $34.45. The details of the cost in Figure 13.4 include:

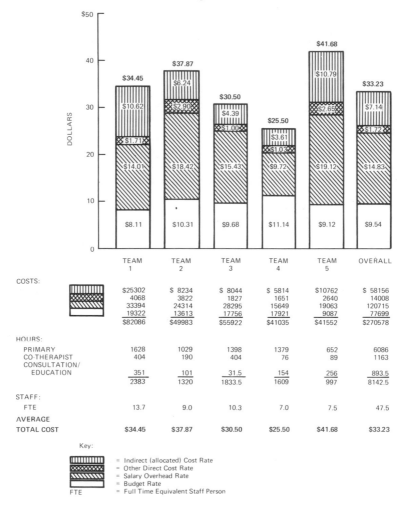

Figure 13.4. Comparison by teams of hypothetical costs per delivered hours of service in a mental health adult outpatient program using "accounted-for" hours (of primary therapists, co-therapists, and consultation–education time).

1. $8.11 for the professional's time to deliver the service
2. $14.01 for the administration of the program
3. $1.71 for other direct expenses
4. $10.62 for facilities and allocated indirect expenses.

The average cost per hour of delivered service in the outpatient adult program across all teams in the center (or county, state) is illustrated at $33.23 with each of the four cost components easily identified.

3. *Changing Statistical Definitions*

Different ways of counting units of service can result in very different conclusions about unit costs (*5*). Figure 13.5 presents cost-finding data from

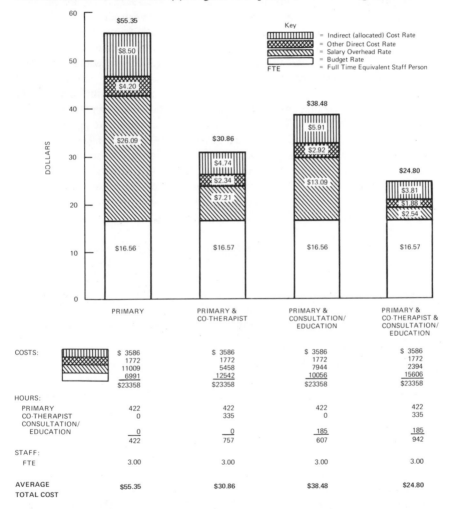

Figure 13.5. Comparison of costs per delivered hour within a mental health outpatient and evaluation unit for children.

a centralized children's outpatient and evaluation program. Four approaches to accumulating total delivered hours of service lead to four different calculations of cost per hour:

1. Cost per delivered primary therapist hour
2. Cost per delivered primary *and* co-therapist hours
3. Cost per delivered primary *and* consultation–education hours
4. Cost per delivered primary, co-therapist, and consultation–education hours.

In the case of cost per delivered primary therapist hour ($55.35) all costs of the program are expressed in terms of the accounted-for time of the primary therapist. The second computation ($30.86) deals with the same total program costs divided by all of the accounted-for time of both primary and co-therapists. (An individual therapist may provide service as either a primary or co-therapist.) The decrease in unit cost ($55.35 to $30.86) reflects a great deal of teamwork rather than individuals working separately. In contrast, if co-therapist accounted-for time is not included in the analysis, but consultation and education hours are combined with primary therapist hours, the cost per delivered hour is $38.48. The difference between primary and primary combined with consultation–education ($55.35 to $38.48) reflects that the program is providing a considerable amount of service time to the community in working with schools, judges, the police, and others. The fourth cost per hour computation in Figure 13.5 combines all accounted-for hours—as primary therapist, as co-therapist, and as consultant to the community—and relates the total hours to the cost of the program; in this case, the cost is $24.80 for an hour of delivered service.

Costs per delivered hour using varying statistical accumulations are useful in describing how resources are consumed in a program. In addition, such costs per hour can be used in establishing fees or billing rates. Such rates may be based upon either: unit costs within specific programs (including reasonable allocations of indirect costs to delivery units) or centerwide average program costs obtained by summing program costs across various service units.

4. Cost Summary

While the procedures of cost-accounting may not become completely uniform, the role of and conceptual approach to human service cost-accounting can become more uniform. The detailed cost example just presented developed the concept of cost aggregation by delivered hours of professional care as a strategy for making human service organization cost-accounting more uniform. However, the more elaborate types of cost-accounting methods are elusive because of their complexity. To develop cost-accounting experience for human service organizations, the more conventional cost-accounting techniques, such as direct and indirect costs, should first be developed. Once a cost framework is developed on a more elementary level, then the more esoteric cost computations, such as delivered hours of professional care, can be undertaken to refine the cost–effectiveness approach and to provide additional cost-accounting information for administrative decision makers. Currently program and per unit costs are of the greatest interest and use. However, there is an emergent need for these new approaches to costs, especially in attempting to meet cost–effectiveness demands imposed by new levels of accountability and need for improved program management.

ASSESSING OUTCOMES IN COST–EFFECTIVENESS STUDIES

In profit-oriented organizations, the amount of profit may be used as a measure of both efficiency and effectiveness. But this profit index approach to effectiveness is not applicable or appropriate for most human service organizations. In profit organizations, decision making is focused on *the impact on profits*. This single, all encompassing, widely understood measure organizes the consideration of multiple resource factors and facilitates comparisons among varying organizational units. No such comprehensive measure exists for nonprofit organizations; to date, there are few good ways of estimating whether additional inputs (or resources) will produce commensurate outputs. The central problem is the *inadequacy of output measures,* and assessing outcomes more accurately is a first step in remedying this deficiency (Nunnally & Durham, 1975). The inadequacy stems from two issues: (a) general expense and lack of precision of outcome measures and (b) difficulty in reaching consensus about the amount of outcome effect that is commensurate with dollar input.

The foregoing analysis of cost suggests that cost measures can be varied because of differential approaches as well as measurement error. Chapter 11 suggests that outcome measures can also vary for similar reasons. Several issues relevant to outcomes are common to cost-accounting. Both costs and outcomes, for example, are sensitive to

1. Time patterns
2. Multiple determinations
3. Varying effects depending on beneficiary
4. Choice of measure
5. Research design within which data are accumulated
6. Issues of reliability and validity.

These factors also have potential impact on cost–effectiveness analyses.

SPECIAL ISSUES IN ASSESSING OUTCOME

1. *Time Patterns of Outcomes*

The effectiveness and costs of human service organizations should be measured at multiple points in time. A specific treatment program may be evaluated at several points in time with each time frame revealing varying levels of effectiveness and costs. In an analogous way, the earnings per share of stock of a major corporation may vary from quarter to quarter or year to year, thus suggesting varying levels of performance of the firm. Choosing the time frame becomes a nontrivial question. Should it be three months? Six months? Five years? If the time period is too short, changes may not be observable, but if the period is too long, important dynamics may be masked, missed, or identified too late for administrative intervention. Experimental research is likely to require highly varied time frames because of the nature of research. But what time frame is appropriate for ongoing or continuous program evaluation? For the latter, periodic assessment (e.g., quarterly) with cumulative restatements (e.g., year-to-date) may be a workable compromise.

2. Multiple Outcomes

All human service programs have multiple outcomes. A drug abuse program may decrease the use of heroin and increase the use of alcohol. An adolescent program may decrease juvenile crime and increase the educational and employment levels. The multiplicity of types and levels of cost aggregation was illustrated earlier. So which outcome or cost or aggregation of outcomes and costs should be used? Any approach is fraught with conceptual and methodological pitfalls, but progress appears possible. In mental health, for example, output criteria in the form of social functioning appear usable for developing measures (Carter & Newman, 1976; Fishman, 1975; Spitzer & Endicott, 1975; Waskow & Parloff, 1975) to be matched with costs for services received to frame a minimal approach toward efficiency and effectiveness.

3. Effects of Costs and Outcomes among Different Populations

Who receives the benefits of a program? The benefits of a program to develop early reading skills may not be uniform across all socioeconomic levels. In fact, the intent may be to have differential impact on lower socioeconomic groups so as to produce greater homogeneity in the reading skills of youngsters entering elementary schools. In this example, the program effects are expected at two levels: (a) improved levels and lower variance in reading skills in the target group of children from lower socioeconomic status, and (b) improved levels and lower variance in reading skills among all children entering primary schools. Tracking the incurred operational costs to specific target groups may be difficult and can become even more difficult if estimated social costs are added (e.g., underemployment because of poor reading skills).

4. Choice of Measures

The results of the program should be observable (Gruenberg, 1966; Mac-Mahon, Pugh, & Hutchinson, 1961). This quickly directs the front-line evaluator to measures of social functioning or problem manifestation. Data capture instruments should be simple to use and understand, economical, and yet clinically meaningful (Davis et al., 1973). In a similar vein, cost accumulations and allocations should adhere to similar criteria and produce cost summaries that relate to observable program structures.

5. Random Assignment to Treatment Groups

In any cost comparison, the results are heavily influenced by the setting in which the accumulation occurs. Similarly, comparisons of human service program outcomes are affected by how subjects are assigned to various treatments. In any comparison of service strategies, comparison samples should be created whenever possible by random assignment of individuals to the services to be compared (Fishman, 1975; MacMahon *et al.*, 1961). While nonequivalent groups are often compared by program evaluators, such comparisons are often hard to interpret, for the reasons discussed in Chapter 11. Randomized controlled field trials are currently the best device for appraising new programs. Randomization avoids self-selection or biased selection, increases objectivity, and neutralizes many variables beyond the control of the experimenter. Conducting such studies is much preferred to just "fooling around with people" [as Gilbert, Light, & Mosteller (1974) described it] in service delivery systems that gather little reliable data on effectiveness, since unreliable or uninterpretable data have no lasting benefits and may often be misleading. Ideal experiments are often not possible, but analysis of improvements of a specific target group must at least be supported by comparison with similar groups which have received different interventions. In this way, changes that are simply concurrent with natural growth or recovery phenomena are less likely to be mistaken for service effects.

6. *Reliability and Validity Must Be Reviewed*

In evaluating financial or cost information produced by an information system, accountants (and auditors even more so) are concerned about the quality of the information produced within the system. Auditors make extensive investigations to evaluate the internal controls of a system to see if errors of omission and comission are adequately controlled. Financial information about the existence and valuation of assets, liabilities, and services rendered or received must be reliable and valid. Evaluation instruments must be assessed for reliability, especially for interrater agreement and for validity (Cronbach, Gleser, Nanda, & Rajaratnam, 1972). A compelling case can be developed for performing reliability tests *at the local service delivery level* of a human service organization. If the interrater agreement among the actual service delivery staff is poor, for example, the meaningfulness of the resulting information is bound to suffer. Similarly, validity should be examined at the level of local service delivery to assure that measures are reflecting what was intended to be measured.

AN EXAMPLE OF OUTCOME EVALUATION IN A MENTAL HEALTH SETTING

Scales that are global in nature [e.g., the Global Assessment Scale (Endicott, Spitzer, Fleiss, & Cohen, 1976) discussed in Chapter 11], or which have subscales that can be combined into global scores, are attractive forms of assessment instruments (6). Generic-dimension assessment techniques [in contrast to individualized goal assessment techniques such as goal attainment scaling described in Chapter 12] may be preferred because of the ability to measure both patient outcome and unmet community mental health needs (Fishman, 1975).

1. *The Carter–Newman Approach*

Carter and Newman (1976) report a high reliability among clinicians using global instruments. They found a high correlation among ratings of selected common case studies by mental health personnel at several centers who used different rating instruments (e.g., 5- versus 7-level global ratings).

To illustrate outcome data needed in applying the cost–outcome method, we now present an illustration of one approach to basic mental health care output scaling. The output "measures" are generated by the mental health professionals who determine the degree of client (patient) impairment or level of functioning at successive points in time. In one such rating procedure, the patients are rated according to the four criteria presented in Table 13.2. These four criteria are used to make a single rating on a 9-point scale indicating overall level of functioning. Table 13.3 presents the definitions of the 9 scale points.

In the Carter and Newman (1976) approach, the final determination of these ratings is based upon consensus among the professional evaluators. The reliability and validity of the ratings are checked with special emphasis on consensus. Several professionals are asked to rate a number of cases. Analysis of variance is performed on the results. The amount of variance due to the cases alone is isolated and determined as a percentage of total variance. This percentage is the reliability coefficient for the professional raters (7). Validity is investigated through reference to external behavioral criteria from other rating procedures, that is, a concurrent validity approach (8).

This particular functional rating procedure was presented to *exemplify* the type of scaling analysis (including reliability and validity verifications) needed for determination of output aspects in the cost–effectiveness approach. Clearly, other kinds of global or aggregated scales dealing with symptoms, problems, or goals could have been used (*13;* Waskow & Parloff, 1975); the social functioning scale will be used here to complete the formulation of the cost–outcome—cost–effectiveness model.

The meaningfulness of scale readings depends on how well the equal interval assumption is satisfied. An analysis of clients who range widely over the scale may be distorted by violations of this assumption. For example, upward movement from extremely low levels of functioning may be less likely (and more costly) than movements (and costs) at the upper end of the scale. In brief, movement on the scale may not be in intervals of equal inherent "difficulty." If the comparison groups are similar in their distributions of preservice levels, however, this measurement problem is less troublesome.

2. *Variations of Service Delivery*

While systematic variations in a program's primary services may be useful for assessing relative costs and outcomes, other imaginative comparisons can be done. For example, alternative procedures such as centralized versus decentralized (e.g., "storefront") intake, or experimental mixtures of professional and paraprofessional personnel may be the focus of the comparisons.

3. *Outcome Summary*

Similar to the nonuniformity problem of cost-accounting, there can be numerous outcome determinations. However, the conceptual approach and role of outcome assessment can become more focused and result in improvements in the quality of the output side of the cost–effectiveness approach to meet vital external and internal accountability demands. We will now combine cost and outcome aspects for the complete development of the cost–effectiveness approach.

TABLE 13.2
Major Criteria for Functioning Level Rating[a]

1. Personal Self-care (for children, adjusted to age level).
   a. Personal maintenance of washing, dressing, eating, elimination chores.
   b. Ability to recognize and avoid common dangers.
   c. Taking responsibility for own maintenance; e.g., caring for own room, personal belongings, daily schedule, personal finance, selecting own clothing and accessories.

2. Social Functioning (adjusted by age, living conditions, and possibly, by community).
   a. *Familiar*—the degree to which those familiar with the person, particularly those in the ordinary social unit (family, roommate, other boarding house residents) can tolerate and interact with the person; i.e., jointly socialize and/or participate in recreational activities with the person.
   b. *Impersonal*—the degree to which relative strangers can interact with the person and vice versa; e.g., store clerks, policemen, or others encountered in ordinary pedestrian, vocational, or recreational activities.

3. Vocational and/or Educational Functioning.
   a. *Working Adults*
      1. The ability to support one's self and one's dependents.
      2. The ability to meet the demands and pressures of one's chosen (or present) vocation, be it lawyer or janitor.
   b. *Homemakers and/or Parents and/or Elderly Persons*
      1. The ability to organize and/or monitor the daily routines of the household; e.g., meals, child care, washing.
      2. The ability to organize, maintain and/or monitor family budgeting, shopping, social and/or recreational activities.
   c. *Children*
      1. Should be considered by general age categories of 0–5, 6–11, 12–14, 15–18.
      2. Play and social activities such that constructive and productive social learning can occur.
      3. Educational activities and performance such as would be expected of that age.

4. Evidence of Emotional Stability and Stress Tolerance.
   a. The degree to which the symptom(s) reflects personality disorganization such that the symptoms and the accompanying disorganization causes discomfort to those with whom the person ordinarily interacts.
   b. The degree to which the person can tolerate the amount of expected daily variation in their *present* social, vocational and/or educational realms.

   NOTE: There is often an interaction among the social, vocational/educational and emotional factors such that the strength in one area is often compensatory for weakness in another. For example, vocational success may come as a result of a person avoiding or minimizing familiar social encounters at home.

---

[a] Adapted from the Central Montgomery MH/MR program scale cited in D. E. Carter and F. L. Newman. *A client-oriented system of mental health service delivery and program management: A workbook and guide.* (DHEW Publication No. ADM 76-307.) Washington, D. C.: U. S. Government Printing Office, 1976.

TABLE 13.3
Nine-Point Scale for Rating by Level of Functioning[a]

Definitions of the Nine-Scale Levels of Functioning

With regard to the balance of the four criteria[b] (personal self-care, social, vocational/ educational, and emotional symptoms/stress tolerance), the person's ability to function autonomously in the community is at "Level X," where X can assume one of the following nine levels:

Level I: Dysfunctional in all four areas and is almost totally dependent upon others to provide a supportive protective environment.

Level II: Not working; ordinary social unit cannot or will not tolerate the person; can perform minimal self-care functions but cannot assume most responsibilities or tolerate social encounters beyond restrictive settings (e.g., in group, play, or occupational therapy).

Level III: Not working; probably living in ordinary social unit but not without considerable strain on the person and/or on others in the household. Symptoms are such that movement in the community should be restricted or supervised.

Level IV: Probably not working, although may be capable of working in a very protective setting; able to live in ordinary social unit and contributes to the daily routine of the household; can assume responsibility for all personal self-care matters; stressful social encounters ought to be avoided or carefully supervised.

Levels V through VIII describe persons who are usually functioning satisfactorily in the community, but for whom problems in one or more of the criteria areas force some degree of dependency on a form of therapeutic intervention.

Level V: Emotional stability and stress tolerance is sufficiently low that successful functioning in the social and/or vocational/educational realms is marginal. The person is barely able to hold on to either job or social unit, or both, without direct therapeutic intervention and a diminution of conflicts in either or both realms.

Level VI: The person's vocational and/or social areas of functioning are stabilized, but only because of direct therapeutic intervention. Symptom presence and severity is probably sufficient to be both noticeable and somewhat disconcerting to the client and/or to those around the client in daily contact.

Level VII: The person is functioning and coping well socially and vocationally (educationally); however, symptom reoccurrences are sufficiently frequent to maintain a reliance on some sort of regular therapeutic intervention.

Level VIII: Functioning well in all areas with little evidence of distress present. However, a history of symptom reoccurrence suggests periodic correspondence with the center; e.g., a client may receive a medication check from a family physician who then contacts the center monthly, or the client returns for bi-monthly social activities.

Level IX: The person is functioning well in all areas and no contact with the Mental Health/Mental Retardation services is recommended.

[a] Adapted from the Central Montgomery MH/MR program scale cited in: D. E. Carter and F. L. Newman. *A client-oriented system of mental health service delivery and program management: A workbook and guide.* (DHEW Publication No. ADM 76-307.) Washington, D. C.: U.S. Government Printing Office, 1976.
[b] See Table 13.2.

COMBINING COSTS AND OUTCOMES:
A MENTAL HEALTH EXAMPLE

Through a mental health example, this section combines costs and outcomes to develop a cost–outcome model in human service program evaluation. The combination of costs and outcomes is a prerequisite to the cost–effectiveness approach to decision making that is developed in the final sections of this chapter.

The combination of service costs and client outcomes may be understandably distasteful to professionals concerned about the well-being of clients, good programs, and quality services. The marriage of costs and outcomes can result, however, in insights that improve the evaluation and allocation of personnel and service efforts. To view outcome or cost as separate elements can create misleading analyses and misdirected management. Higher or lower unit costs by themselves are not fully meaningful for purposes of program evaluation unless objectives are specified; nor is a statement about how successful a program performs especially helpful unless one knows something about the resources required to achieve the successful outcome.

When an estimate is made of a client's global level of functioning at each clinical encounter, summaries can describe the changes that may have occurred to a specific group of clients over a given period of time (*14*). The cost-finding procedures described earlier enable accumulation of the service costs for the same group of clients during the period of time associated with the changes in level of functioning.

1. *Cost–Outcome Matrix*

Consider the matrix of costs and outcomes in Figure 13.6 drawn from an adult mental health program using the 9-point level of functioning scale discussed earlier. Clients grouped by initial level of functioning may be traced over time (*9*). Remaining in a diagonal cell means maintenance or no change over time, whereas horizontal movement to cells on the right of the diagonal implies improvement and horizontal movement to the left implies regression. Total and average costs are accumulated by cell and by column and row (namely, marginals).

2. *Answers to Key Questions*

Observe the kinds of questions that can be answered from the cost–outcome matrix (Carter & Newman, 1976):

1. How many individuals are in the target group (age 45–64) and what was the average cost of service during the quarter ($N = 100$; average cost $= \$850$)?
2. How many individuals were dysfunctional at the end of the time period ($N = 70$)? How many were functional ($N = 30$)? Did these two groups

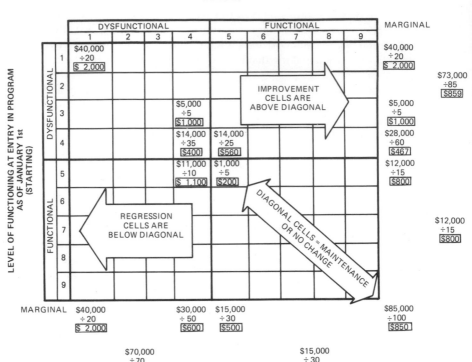

Figure 13.6. A sample cost–outcome matrix for a target group of adult mental health outpatients —ages 45–64.

consume the same amount of resources? (No, the dysfunctional individuals consumed twice as much as the functional: $1000 versus $500 on the average and $70,000 versus $15,000 total.)

3. How many individuals were dysfunctional at the beginning of the quarter ($N = 85$)? How many were functional ($N = 15$)? How much in total was spent on each group ($73,000 and $12,000, respectively)?

4. How many individuals were simply maintained over the quarter ($N = 20 + 35 + 5 = 60$)? At what average cost ($40,000 + $14,000 + $1,000 / 60 = 916.67)?

5. Where are the high cost services being used? (Especially for individuals at level 1)

6. Did the services delivered have the expected or planned impact? (This requires some prior expectations about impact.)
7. Are certain cost values out-of-line? (This also requires some prior expectation or other comparison regarding cost variability.)

In this example—by combining the target populations, level of functioning scale, and the clinician's assessment of client movement from one level to another, and merging them with costs into a cost–outcome matrix—we have structured a basic decision-making system for client and resource management, cost–outcome analysis, and accountability. The usefulness of these cost and outcome data in decision making is subject, of course, to the reliability and validity limitations of the measurement procedures. Accordingly, the efficacy of the cost–outcome approach should improve as more reliable and valid data collection procedures evolve through staff training programs designed to increase common understandings of measurement procedures as indexed through reliability coefficients and criterion validations.

COST–EFFECTIVENESS STUDIES:
ANALYSIS OF COMPARATIVE COSTS
AND OUTCOMES

Cost–effectiveness builds on the same measurement procedures of the cost–outcome approach and strengthens the procedure by attending to the research design issues necessary to make meaningful comparisons between alternative service delivery approaches. At the level of cost–outcome analysis there is no way to document scientifically whether change during service is actually caused by the intervention or is simply concurrent with it (16). Drawing on the research design techniques discussed in Chapter 11, the evaluator gathers comparative outcome and cost data so that the effects of service strategy and cost differences can be separated from preexisting client group differences in expected outcome. Potential intervening variables, such as history, selection bias, practice effects, maturation, and other influences on outcome that are unrelated to the service can be controlled through random assignment to services or by employing the generally less desirable quasi-experimental approaches. Ideally, the service or "treatment" variable is isolated as the only difference between the two groups:

> At the level of cost–effectiveness analysis, the causal relationship between intervention and change over time can be investigated. For example, if two groups of comparable patients each receive different interventions and then are assessed with standard procedures at follow-up, any differences between the two groups at follow-up can be ascribed to the difference between the treatments [16, p. 7].*

*Reproduced by permission of the author (see reference note 16).

The prototypical research design is similar to one of Campbell and Stanley's (1969) "true experimental designs," the pretest–posttest control group design. The sequence of research operations in each subject group is as follows:

Group 1: $R\ O\ X\ O$

Group 2: $R\ O\ \ \ \ O$

Where R = randomization of clients or patients into the two groups; O = process of observation or measurement, for example the functioning level rating at the beginning of the period and again after the service intervention; and X = exposure of the group to the experimental variable or event, for example an altered method of mental health service.

In most service situations a standard and accepted intervention is the most relevant comparison to a new service, rather than a comparison with no service at all (as in Group 2 of the pretest–posttest control group design just described). Therefore, the pretest–posttest control group design is modified to reflect two different sets of treatments:

Group 1: $R\ O\ X\ O$

Group 2: $R\ O\ Y\ O$

Where X = exposure of first group to a specific type of intervention, such as a special token–economy day-care program; and Y = exposure of second group to a different type of intervention, such as the standard therapeutic day-care program. These designs would ordinarily be analyzed using analysis of covariance (*10*).

If randomization is not feasible, then a nonrandom comparison group design may be better than no comparison at all. In this case the evaluator must be appropriately cautious in analyzing, interpreting, and reporting the results.

		Cost of A relative to B		
		A is less costly	A is as costly	A is more costly
Effectiveness of A relative to B	A is less effective	11 ?	12 Choose B	13 Choose B
	A is as effective	21 Choose A	22 No difference	23 Choose B
	A is more effective	31 Choose A	32 Choose A	33 ?

Figure 13.7. Cost–effectiveness matrix. [Reproduced by permission from: D. B. Fishman, Development of a generic cost–effectiveness methodology for evaluating the patient services of a community mental health center. In J. Zusman & C. R. Wurster (Eds.), *Program evaluation: Alcohol, drug abuse, and mental health services.* Copyright 1975, D. C. Heath, Lexington, Massachusetts.]

Reliability-adjusted analysis of covariance and repeated measures analysis of variance are recommended in analyzing such nonrandomized pre–post comparison group studies. For a more extended discussion refer to Chapter 11.

In either an experimental or a nonexperimental comparison, the purpose of the statistical analysis is to reach conclusions about the relative cost of the services, and their relative effectiveness. Having reached these conclusions about a pair of programs, say programs *A* and *B,* one then reviews these conclusions in light of the logical relationships and choice points shown in Figure 13.7. The decision criterion, based upon this cost–effectiveness information, is to maximize output in relation to cost. Seven of the nine choices are self-explanatory. The choice in Cells 11 and 33 is not obvious, since it depends on a judgment of whether the degree of superiority in the outcome is worth the higher cost. This type of judgment must ordinarily be made directly, taking into account all of the available information. More detailed procedures to aid these judgments are being explored (*11*).

A COST–EFFECTIVENESS EXAMPLE

Cost–effectiveness analysis leads to an assertion about the best choice among program options: an assertion of the form, "Program *A* is more cost–effective than Program *B."* The following example illustrates the application of cost–effectiveness analysis to decision making, as well as some of the difficulties in performing cost–effectiveness analyses.

Table 13.4 shows effectiveness (global ratings) and cost data for 30 clients in each of two programs. These data were gathered in a randomized comparison experiment. However, it can be seen that the two groups were very different before receiving the program services, and we have reason to doubt whether a true random assignment to the programs actually occurred.

Under these circumstances, a relatively conservative statistical analysis of the effectiveness measure is analysis of variance (ANOVA) with repeated measures. Results of this analysis are shown in Table 13.5. Analysis of variance assesses the systematic variability due to differences between groups in relation to the "random" variability among individuals. Several "sources of variation" are shown in Table 13.5, which in repeated measures ANOVA are divided into "between subjects" sources and "within subjects" sources. We are interested in three sources of systematic variation:

1. *Programs*—This refers to differences in mean functioning scores in each program, averaged across both time periods
2. *Pre–post change*—This refers to differences between preservice and postservice measures, averaged across the two programs
3. *Programs by pre–post change*—This refers to the "interaction" of the first two sources, or the degree to which the pre–post changes were *different* in the two programs. Therefore this source of variation is the one that can be interpreted as the test of whether the programs differ in effectiveness.

TABLE 13.4

Cost and Effectiveness Data for Two Programs

Score	Program A (N = 30)		Program B (N = 30)	
	Mean	Standard deviation	Mean	Standard deviation
Social functioning at time 1 (preservice)	4.9	1.06	6.1	1.16
Social functioning at time 2 (postservice)	6.0	.91	7.4	.81
Social functioning pre–post Change	+1.1	.84	+1.3	.79
Episode cost[a]	$500	50.86	$550	25.43

[a] Costs are significantly greater in Program B than in Program A ($t = 4.82$; $df = 58$; $p < .001$), although the variance differences suggest caution in interpreting the results. Tests of significance on the social functioning data are discussed in the text and in Table 13.5.

TABLE 13.5

Repeated Measures Analysis of Variance of Social Functioning for Clients in Two Programs

Source of variation	Sum of squares	Degrees of freedom	Mean squares	F
Between subjects				
Programs	1.69	1	1.69	30.73[a]
Subjects within programs	3.17	58	.055	
Within subjects				
Pre–post change	1.44	1	1.44	130.91[a]
Programs by pre–post change	.01	1	.010	.91
Pre–post change by subjects within programs	.65	58	.011	

[a] $p < .01$

The two remaining sources of variation—subjects within programs and pre–post change by subjects within programs—are internal measures of the inherent random variability of the data. These two sources of random variation are used to assess the statistical significance of the "effects" associated with the three systematic sources of variation. More specifically, a large value of the F statistic—the ratio of systematic to random variation—indicates that the effect is larger than would be expected by chance. In Table 13.5, the large F values associated with the first two effects and the small F value associated with the third suggest the following conclusions:

1. *Programs*—Social functioning scores of clients in Program A are significantly lower than in Program B.
2. *Pre–post change*—Clients in both programs tend to have higher functioning scores after receiving service than before.
3. *Programs by pre–post change*—There is no evidence that functioning scores increase more in one program than in the other.

Therefore, this statistical analysis does *not* suggest that Programs A and B differ in effectiveness.

There are other types of statistical analysis that are defensible in this situation. The conclusions they suggest are rather different, and we present them as a sobering note of caution to the reader. For example, we might have assumed that the process of randomly assigning the 60 clients to the two programs had been successfully carried out, and that it had produced two groups with similar mean preservice scores (as would ordinarily have been the case). If we had felt that it was therefore not essential to obtain the preservice scores, and if we had only computed a *t*-test on the postservice scores, then we would have found a statistically significant difference favoring Program B. Consequently we might have concluded that Program B was more effective.

Another alternative analysis in a randomized experiment is analysis of covariance. This is a variant of ANOVA in which the postservice scores are adjusted to take into account differences between subjects in their preservice scores. Analysis of covariance applied to these data yields a significant adjusted effect for programs ($F = 16.57$, $p < .05$) and suggests that Program B is superior. In this instance it appears that certain assumptions important to analysis of covariance were not met, leading to what is probably an erroneous conclusion.

If, in fact, the subjects were not assigned randomly to the two programs, then there are other risks of erroneous conclusions. An example will make clear how this could occur. Suppose Programs A and B are mental health continuing care services. In Table 13.4 we saw that preservice functioning scores were lower for clients in Program A. Suppose this reflected the fact that, compared to Program B, the Program A sample included a higher proportion of patients with chronic schizophrenia (who have a poor prognosis) and a lower proportion of patients with affective disorders (who have a better prognosis). Were this the case, the relatively small pre–post increase in functioning scores in Program A could reflect dazzling program performance, while the larger average change in Program B could reflect nothing more than the degree of improvement one would expect were no services provided. Note that even if the groups being compared have similar preservice scores they may still differ in prognosis. That is one reason why matching the subjects in two comparison groups on their preservice scores is less dependable than random assignment in avoiding biased results.

Costs are the other side of a cost–effectiveness comparison. Referring again to Table 13.4, we see that the mean cost per episode was $50 higher in Program B. A simple *t*-test shows that this difference in treatment cost is statistically reliable ($p < .001$); that is, it was not likely to be due to chance variation. This suggests that Program B is more expensive.

Just as with the functioning scores, one needs to be alert to irrelevant effects on costs. For example, if subjects are not randomly assigned, one program may receive a greater proportion of subjects who lack insurance coverage or other ability to pay for services. These subjects may tend to receive less extensive services, producing an apparent difference in mean cost, even though the cost per unit of service and cost per episode may be the same in both programs when equivalent client groups are compared. Sharfstein, Taube, and Goldberg (1977) have reviewed the problems one encounters in nonexperimental comparisons of program costs.

Having analyzed the relative effectiveness and cost of Programs A and B, we now return to the cost–effectiveness decision matrix in Figure 13.7 to review the possible decision implications of our conclusions. It would appear that, in our example, A costs less than B, which would put us in Column 1 of the matrix. The repeated measures ANOVA failed to detect any difference in outcome between the two programs, which puts us in Row 2 of the matrix. The intersection of Row 2 and Column 1 is Cell 21, which designates the choice of Program A. Program A is chosen as the least expensive of two programs that are not known to differ in effectiveness.

Other analyses suggested that Program B may be more effective. Were this conclusion accepted, it would place us in Cell 11 of the decision matrix, which indicates indecision. To reach a decision, one needs to judge whether the greater cost of Program B is justified by its greater effectiveness.

Given the actual data presented, along with the questions about the study design and execution, the cautious evaluator may decide that the study should be carried out a second time to provide a firmer basis for decision. This example also illustrates the common situation in which it is easier to have confidence in conclusions about relative cost than conclusions about relative effectiveness. This means one is often operating in Row 2 of the cost–effectiveness decision matrix, where the choice is determined entirely by the cost comparison. One goal of program evaluation should be to strengthen the interpretability and statistical power of effectiveness comparisons, so that cost–effectiveness analysis can truly balance the impact of cost and effectiveness information on management decision making.

SUMMARY

The cost–effectiveness method emerges as a summary evaluation technique that incorporates several fundamental types of service accountability information. By comparing the costs and outcomes for two or more service interventions, the more cost–effective program, modality, or technique can be determined. The following steps were discussed in this chapter and make up the information requirements for cost–effectiveness analysis:

1. Identification of the service goals to be achieved for specific target groups
2. Random assignment or other approaches to comparing equivalent groups of clients who are provided alternative service strategies designed to achieve these same service goals
3. Use of accrual accounting, operating statistics, and cost-finding to determine the cost per episode for each client
4. Preintervention versus postintervention assessment of clients to determine the service outcomes within the groups of clients provided each service strategy

5. Statistical analysis to determine the average cost per episode and average outcome in each service strategy, and to determine whether cost and outcome differences can be detected with confidence
6. Presentation of cost and outcome summaries in cost–outcome and cost–effectiveness matricies for decision-making consideration
7. In ambiguous situations, it may be necessary to make further judgments about the relative utilities of observed outcomes in relation to observed costs.

In summary, the cost–effectiveness approach relies upon the cost–outcome measurement procedures. However, the approach further specifies the treatment–outcome linkage by attempting to rule out the possibility that observed cost and outcome differences were caused by nonservice factors occurring concurrently in the treatment period. This advancement in service measurement is achieved by identifying specific types of service or treatment costs with specific results or outcomes. The identification results from implementation of a research design that restricts the effect of other intervening variables in the service cost–outcome relationship. Decision makers are provided with service performance information for program decision making. The cost–effectiveness model was recommended as a more practical general service performance evaluation approach than cost–benefit analysis. The absence of a requirement to convert outcomes to monetary measurements permits a wider range of understandable applications in human service organizations. The method is especially applicable when a choice has already been made to strive for particular goals with a particular target population (e.g., children, elderly), and the important managerial task is to select the most cost–effective program to achieve the goals identified for that group.

While additional illustrations using varied measures and statistical analyses could be offered, the variety, complexity, and difficulties of interpretation of cost–effectiveness measures should not be underestimated. The approach offered in this chapter is neither easy nor obvious when extended in realistic program decision making and accountability. In Levin's (1975) words: "The conceptualization and measurement of both costs and outcomes have not been and probably cannot be routinized [p. 118]."

REFERENCE NOTES

1. A taxonomy with related discussion of social indicators is provided by Biderman (1966, pp. 68–153). An extensive strategy for improving social indicators is provided by Gross (1966, pp. 154–271).
2. Extensive coverage of PPBS and cost–benefit approaches is provided in Hinricks and Taylor (1969).
3. Services using statistical measures other than hours could be used in developing rates. For example, in partial hospital programs, the costs of the program would be more reasonably related to partial hospital days (namely, multiples of 4-hour treatment units). Costs of inpatient operations are easily related to inpatient days while some programs (e.g., methadone maintenance) are more easily understood using rates based on the number of actual or standard (planned) number of medication visits. In some cases, programs containing classroom type instructions may be usefully viewed with rates based on cost per enrolled or

attending person. When possible, however, the costs should be expressed in relationship to the accounted time of the professionals delivering the service. Since direct costs (e.g., salary, benefits, and other direct costs) can be easily related to statistical bases, such as inpatient days, partial days, visits, and enrollment, such per unit computations are not illustrated.

4. The source for this figure is the centerwide rate schedule worksheet using hypothetical data for the third quarter (January, February, March). Fiscal year 197x (Sorensen, 1976).

5. The same source used is the centerwide rate schedule worksheet using hypothetical data for the third quarter (January, February, March). Fiscal year 197x (Sorensen, 1976).

6. Weissman (1975) has a useful review of the optional global scales currently available.

7. Refer to Carter and Newman (1976) for a detailed 17-step procedure for computing this reliability coefficient (the intraclass correlation) based upon Cronbach et al. (1972).

8. Refer to the 9-step validity procedure in Carter and Newman (1976).

9. This example uses the 9-point level of functioning scale presented in Table 13.3 and criteria described in Table 13.2.

10. See Chapter 11 for a more extensive discussion, and Winer (1971) for procedures. Glick, Hargreaves, and Goldfield (1974) provide an example of an application in mental health.

11. Sorensen, J. E., & Grove, H. D. *Cost–outcome and cost–effectiveness analysis: Emerging nonprofit performance evaluation techniques.* Unpublished manuscript, 1976. (Available from the School of Accountancy, College of Business Administration, University of Denver, Denver, Colorado 80208.)

12. Binner, P. R. Output value analysis: An overview. In: *Information and feedback for evaluation* (Vol. 2). Proceedings of the Information and Feedback Conference, York University, Toronto, Canada, November 1974.

13. Edwards, D. W., & Yarvis, R. M. *Illustrative data on the Davis outcome assessment system* (Version 3). Unpublished manuscript, 1976. (Available from the Sacramento Medical Center, University of California, Davis, 2315 Stockton Boulevard, Sacramento, California 95817.)

14. Burwell, B., Reiber, S., & Newman, F. *The client-oriented cost–outcome system of the Fayette County Mental Health–Mental Retardation Program.* Paper presented at the Statewide Conference on Cost Analysis Systems in MR/MH Programs, Hershey, Pennsylvania, June 1975.

15. Comprehensive Health Service Programs, Community Health Service, Public Health Service. *Accounting and cost reporting systems.* Rockville, Maryland: Health Service and Mental Health Administration, 1971.

16. Fishman, D. B. *Suggested guidelines for utilizing 2% evaluation funds in the emergent community mental health center legislation: A cost–effectiveness approach.* Paper presented at the National Council of Community Mental Health Centers Meeting, Washington, D. C., February 1975.

17. Yates, B. *Towards cost–effectiveness analysis in applied psychology: Compiling cost–effectiveness indices for behavioral treatment.* Paper presented at the Western Psychological Association Meeting, Sacramento, California, April 1975.

REFERENCES

American Hospital Association. *Hospital administrative service reports.* Chicago: American Hospital Association, 1967.

Biderman, A. D. Social indicators and goals. In R. A. Bauer (Ed.), *Social indicators.* Cambridge, Massachusetts: M. I. T. Press, 1966.

Campbell, D. T., & Stanley, J. C. *Experimental and quasi-experimental designs for research.* Chicago: Rand-McNally, 1969.

Carter, D. E., & Newman, F. L. *A client-oriented system of mental health service delivery and program management: A workbook and guide.* (DHEW Publication No. ADM 76-307.) Washington, D. C.: U. S. Government Printing Office, 1976.

Comptroller General of the United States. *Standards for audit of governmental organizations, programs, activities, and functions.* Washington, D. C.: United States General Accounting Office, 1972.

Cronbach, L. J., Gleser, G. C., Nanda, H., & Rajaratnam, N. (Eds.). *The dependability of behavioral measurements: Theory of generalizability for scores and profiles.* New York: Wiley, 1972.

Davis, H. R., Weiss, C., Louis, K., & Weiss, J. *Planning for creative change in mental health services: Use of program evaluation.* (DHEW Publication No. HSM 71-9057.) Rockville, Maryland: National Institute of Mental Health, 1973.

Decker, B., & Bonner, P. (Eds.). *PSRO: Organization for regional peer review.* Cambridge, Massachusetts: Ballinger, 1973.

Endicott, J., Spitzer, R. L., Fleiss, J. L., & Cohen, J. The Global Assessment Scale: A procedure for measuring overall severity of psychiatric disturbance. *Archives of General Psychiatry,* 1976, *33,* 766–771.

Fishman, D. B. Development of a generic cost–effectiveness methodology for evaluating the patient services of a community mental health center. In J. Zusman & C. R. Wurster (Eds.), *Program evaluation: Alcohol, drug abuse, and mental health services.* Lexington, Massachusetts: Lexington Books, 1975.

Gilbert, J. P., Light, R. J., & Mosteller, F. Assessing social innovations: An empirical base for policy. In R. Zeckhauser *et al.* (Eds.), *Benefit–cost and policy analysis.* Chicago: Aldine, 1974.

Glick, I. D., Hargreaves, W. A., & Goldfield, M. D. Short vs. long hospitalization. *Archives of General Psychiatry,* 1974, *30,* 363–369.

Goldman, T. A. (Ed.). *Cost–effectiveness analysis.* New York: Praeger, 1967.

Granof, M. H. Operational auditing standards for audits of government services. *The CPA Journal,* 1973, December, 1070–1081.

Gross, B. The state of the nation: Social systems accounting. In R. A. Bauer (Ed.), *Social indicators.* Cambridge, Massachusetts: M. I. T. Press, 1966.

Gross, B., & Springer, M. (Eds.). *Social intelligence for America's future.* Boston: Allyn and Bacon, 1969.

Gruenburg, E. M. (Ed.). Evaluating the effectiveness of mental health services. *Milbank Memorial Fund Quarterly,* 1966, *44* (1), Part 2.

Halpern, J., & Binner, P. R. A model for an output value analysis of mental health programs. *Administration in Mental Health,* 1972, *1*(1), 40–51.

Hardin, G. To trouble a star: The cost of intervention in nature. *Science and Public Affairs,* 1970, January, 17–20.

Hargreaves, W. A., Attkisson, C. C., & Ochberg, F. M. Outcome studies in mental health program evaluation. In W. A. Hargreaves, C. C. Attkisson, & J. E. Sorensen (Eds.), *Resource materials for community mental health program evaluation* (2nd ed.). (DHEW Publication No. ADM 77-328.) Washington, D. C.: U. S. Government Printing Office, 1977.

Hinricks, H. H. Government decision making and the theory of benefit–cost analysis: A primer. In H. H. Hinricks & G. M. Taylor (Eds.), *Program budgeting and benefit–cost analysis.* Pacific Palisades, California: Goodyear, 1969.

Hinricks, H. H., & Taylor, G. M. (Eds.). *Program budgeting and benefit–cost analysis.* Pacific Palisades, California: Goodyear, 1969.

Levin, H. M. Cost–effectiveness analysis in evaluation research. In M. Guttentag & E. L. Struening (Eds.), *Handbook of evaluation research* (Vol. 2). Beverly Hills, California: Sage Publications, 1975.

MacMahon, B., Pugh, T. F., & Hutchinson, G. B. Principles in the evaluation of community mental health programs. *American Journal of Public Health,* 1961, *51,* 963–968.

Michigan Department of Mental Health. *Institutions of the department of mental health, State of Michigan.* Lansing, Michigan: Michigan Department of Mental Health, 1971.

Murphy, J. G., & Datel, W. E. A cost–benefit analysis of community versus institutional living. *Hospital and Community Psychiatry,* 1976, *27,* 265–270.

Nunnally, J. C., & Durham, R. Validity, reliability and special problems in evaluation research. In E. L. Struening & M. Guttentag (Eds.), *Handbook of evaluation research* (Vol. 1). Beverly Hills, California: Sage Publications, 1975.

Olson, M. The plan and purpose of a social report. *The Public Interest,* 1969, Spring, 86–97.

Quade, E. S. Introduction and overview. In T. A. Goldman (Ed.), *Cost–effectiveness analysis.* New York: Praeger, 1967.

Raymond, R. S., & Richards, E. Social indicators and business decisions. *MSU Business Topics,* 1971, Autumn, 40–46.

Riedel, D. C., Tischler, G. T., & Myers, J. K. *Patient Care Evaluation in Mental Health Programs.* Cambridge, Massachusetts: Ballinger, 1974.

Sharfstein, S. S., Taube, C. A., & Goldberg, I. D. Problems in analyzing the comparative costs of private versus public psychiatric care. *American Journal of Psychiatry,* 1977, *134,* 29–32.

Siegmann, A. E. A classification of sociomedical health indicators: Perspectives for health administrators and health planners. *Journal of Health Services,* 1976, *6,* 521–538.

Smith, T. S., & Sorensen, J. E. (Eds.). *Integrated management information systems for community mental health centers.* (DHEW Publication No. ADM 75-165.) Rockville, Maryland: National Institute of Mental Health, 1974.

Sorensen, J. E. Uniform cost-accounting in long-term care. In J. H. Murnaghan & K. L. White (Eds.), *Long-term care data. Medical Care,* 1976, *13,* Supplement.

Sorensen, J. E., & Phipps, D. W. *Cost-finding and rate-setting for community mental health centers.* (DHEW Publication No. ADM 76-291.) Washington, D. C.: U. S. Government Printing Office, 1975.

Spitzer, R. L., & Endicott, J. Assessment of outcome by independent clinical evaluators. In I. E. Waskow & M. B. Parloff (Eds.), *Psychotherapy change measures.* (DHEW Publication No. ADM 74-120.) Washington, D. C.: U. S. Government Printing Office, 1975.

Tripodi, T., Fellin, P., & Epstein, I. *Social program evaluation: Guidelines for health, education, and welfare administrators.* Itaska, Illinois: F. E. Peacock, 1971.

Waskow, I. E., & Parloff, M. B. (Eds.). *Psychotherapy change measures.* (DHEW Publication No. ADM 74-120.) Washington, D. C.: U. S. Government Printing Office, 1975.

Weissman, M. M. The assessment of social adjustment. *Archives of General Psychiatry,* 1975, *32,* 357–365.

Wholey, J. S., Scanlon, J. W., Duffy, H. S., Fukumoto, J. S., & Vogt, L. M. *Federal evaluation policy: Analysis of effects of public programs.* Washington, D. C.: The Urban Institute, 1970.

Wilkinson, G. L. Needed: Information for cost analysis. *Educational Technology,* 1972, *12,* 33–38.

Winer, B. J. *Statistical principles in experimental design* (2nd ed.). New York: McGraw-Hill, 1971.

Zusman, J., & Wurster, C. R. (Eds.). *Program evaluation: Alcohol, drug abuse, and mental health programs.* Lexington, Massachusetts: Lexington, 1975.

14

QUALITY ASSURANCE IN HUMAN SERVICE PROGRAM EVALUATION

J. Richard Woy, Donald A. Lund, and C. Clifford Attkisson

The purposes of this chapter are to alert program administrators and evaluators to an increasingly important and perhaps unfamiliar approach to self-evaluation—that of quality assurance—and to highlight implications of this new development for program evaluation. The discussion will (a) compare and contrast quality assurance and program evaluation, with special attention to their differing goals and legislative histories; (b) describe major concepts and current activities in quality assurance; (c) summarize important trends and issues in quality assurance; and (d) comment on the complementary relationship between quality assurance and program evaluation.

Inclusion of a chapter about quality assurance in this book is important for two reasons. First, both quality assurance and program evaluation are activities required by recent federal health legislation. They are the two primary mechanisms by which health programs must evaluate their own activities to ensure accountability to regulatory agencies, funding sources, and consumers of service. This recent legislative emphasis upon dual approaches to self-evaluation signals the need for clarification of the *differences* between quality assurance and program evaluation. Second, in practice, the activities carried out under the rubric of quality assurance overlap considerably with those activities others consider to be program evaluation. Therefore, to avoid confusion and redundancy in service programs, it is important to understand the *similarities* between the two approaches.

Similarities and differences between program evaluation and quality assurance can be best portrayed along several key dimensions: (a) legislative sanctions, (b) degree of reliance on peer review, (c) level of analysis, (d) basic

411

objectives, and (e) principal methods. These dimensions and the contrasting characteristics of quality assurance and program evaluation are summarized in Table 14.1. In contrast to program evaluation, *quality assurance activities* have more extensive legislative mandates; rely more extensively on peer review and substantially less on administrative review; are client- and service-provider-specific; are organized to assure adequacy and appropriateness of care and to control costs by preventing overutilization; and rely on methods that focus on specific service plans and service transactions—methods that involve minimal data aggregation, focus on service records, and typically do not rely on computer applications for data processing. However, these differences tend to reflect separate historical developments and currently there is a definite trend toward convergence in objectives and methodology. Program evaluation and quality assurance activities share many common information needs and this commonality of interest seems to be stimulating cooperative, nonredundant efforts. The concluding sections of this chapter review this trend toward convergence and coordination.

Because of the relatively limited application of quality assurance methods outside of medicine, this chapter is oriented toward the health care fields and has particular relevance to mental health programs. Application of quality assurance methods, especially the peer review process, to other human services is certain to be prevalent in the near future (*10;11*).

HISTORY AND GOALS

Although quality assurance and program evaluation activities differ in emphasis and methodology, both clearly result from the recently expanding emphasis upon accountability. As S. H. Nelson (1976) indicates:

> Accountability is a word that is increasingly used in today's world, particularly in the health field. Essentially, it means being able to justify what we do, how we do it, and what it costs. Accountability is not a new concept to the field of business, for without it, a business could not succeed. However, the application of systems of accountability, which are being asked of us today, is relatively new to the practice of medicine [p. 57].*

Until quite recently, quality assurance and program evaluation were rarely discussed in the same context. These approaches to self-evaluation have similarities and do overlap in practice, but their interrelationship has not been critically examined because they have separate histories and have evolved out of different substantive concerns. Quality assurance and program evaluation have been linked conceptually (Lorei & Schroeder, 1975) and concurrent implementation was mandated in federal health legislation.

---

*Reproduced by permission from: S. H. Nelson, Accountability in psychiatric practice: PSRO and utilization review. In R. Westlake (Ed.), *Shaping the future of mental health care.* Copyright 1976, Ballinger, Cambridge, Massachusetts.

TABLE 14.1

Program Evaluation and Quality Assurance: Contrasting Characteristics Across Key Dimensions

Key variables	Contrasting characteristics	
	Program evaluation	Quality assurance
Legislative sanctions	Minimal but increasing	Extensive—but only in the past 10 years
Reliance on peer review	Minimal	Extensive
Reliance on administrative review	Extensive	Minimal
Level of analysis	Generalized and program-specific, focused on data-based judgments about program (or service modality) effort, efficiency, effectiveness, and relevance	Client- and service provider-specific and focused on quality of specific service delivery transactions through reliance on service/client records
Basic objectives	• Maintain high levels of effort relative to program capacity for effort • Assess outcome and select most effective/efficient programs • Assess relevance and impact of total program effort with regard to service needs in a specified community	• Assure that individual clients receive appropriate care • Detect deficiencies and errors in service provider capacity • Control costs by preventing overutilization and ensuring that needed services are provided in a timely, efficient manner
Principal methods	• Analysis of resource utilization, capacity for effort, and level of effort • Assessment of outcomes and the effectiveness of program effort • Assessment of program efficiency relative to effort and outcomes • Analysis of comparative cost-effectiveness • Analysis of program adequacy relative to needs for services	• Concurrent review —Admissions certification —Continued stay review —Utilization review and "length of stay" analysis • Retrospective review —Medical (clinical) care evaluation —profile monitoring

413

QUALITY ASSURANCE

Like program evaluation, quality assurance is a relatively old concept that has been implemented in various ways for many years. The oldest and perhaps prototypic form of quality assurance is the common practice of joint staffing of clinical cases. In such case discussions, the responsible clinician presents diagnostic findings and a proposed treatment approach to a group of clinical peers. This mutual or peer review is intended to assure adequate and appropriate care. In addition, third party reimbursers of health care services have required providers to assert that care provided to eligible recipients is essential, adequate, and appropriate.

Quality assurance activities have become prerequisites for receipt of funding under requirements of federal health legislation, and quality assurance requirements are being incorporated into accreditation standards for hospitals and mental health programs—as promulgated by the Joint Commission on Accreditation of Hospitals (JCAH). Previously, quality assurance activities had been voluntary and entirely the province of the professional associations and local health service providers. The trend toward closer scrutiny of services by peers began in the mid-1960s when internal utilization review activities were first required of health care providers in order to receive reimbursement for inpatient care provided to Medicare and Medicaid beneficiaries. Mandated quality assurance activities were further extended in 1972 with the passage of Public Law 92-603, which authorized creation of professional standards review organizations (PSROs) across the United States (Decker & Bonner, 1973). These PSROs were authorized to review the quality and appropriateness of services rendered to beneficiaries of Medicare, Medicaid, and Maternal and Child Health Services (3; Goran, Roberts, Kellogg, Fielding, & Jessee, 1975; Nelson, 1975). Despite the fact that the American Medical Association was largely responsible for the initial thinking on PSRO, the PSRO program has been embroiled in controversy since its inception (Morehead, 1976):

> The law was passed over the bitter objection of organized medicine and state medical societies, some of which are still committed to having it rescinded. However, as in most of the legislative efforts in this country, compromises have been made to the extent that the expressed fears of the profession will in all probability prove unwarranted. The initial requirements and guidelines of federal regulatory agencies give major control to the practicing physicians within each institution, and emphasis is much more on cost control than on quality of patient care. Even had these compromises not occurred, the state of the art of quality assessment is such that "control of the practice of medicine" by non-physicians, the main argument raised by the opposition, probably would not have become a reality [p. 113].*

In passing the PSRO law, the Congress responded to two relatively distinct concerns. First, Congress acted to ensure that inpatient services reimbursed through Medicare and Medicaid mechanisms are appropriate and of

*Reproduced by permission from: M. A. Morehead, P.S.R.O.—Problems and possibilities. *Man and Medicine,* 1976, *1*(2), 113–132. (Copyright 1976, Man and Medicine, Inc., New York.)

high quality. A second and equally important factor in the law's passage was congressional concern that Medicare and Medicaid costs were excessive. The resulting legislation sought to reduce costs through implementation of quality assurance activities designed to reduce unnecessary hospital admissions and to control length of hospital stays. As stated in the introduction to proposed Federal regulations for Public Law 92-603:

> Unnecessary hospitalization not only involves a waste of our available hospital resources and an undesirable drain on our Federal Medicaid funds, but it constitutes a significant health hazard for those who are administered unneeded services. Recent evidence has confirmed that there is much unnecessary hospitalization of Medicare and Medicaid patients. (See Hearings Before the Subcommittee on Oversight and Investigations of the Committee on Interstate and Foreign Commerce, House of Representatives, 94th Congress, 1st Session, on Quality and Care and Utilization of Services in the Surgical Area, Implementation of the Federally Mandated Utilization Review Program and the Effectiveness of these Programs in Achieving Cost Control, 94-37, July 15, 17, 18, 1975, September 3, 1975.) Accordingly, these proposed regulations are intended to establish a system for review of the medical necessity of hospital admissions and continued hospital stays while the services are actually being provided. This "concurrent" review avoids the problems attendant upon later, retrospective review after the patient has already undergone the medical procedures and the expenses for those procedures have been fully incurred [Department of Health, Education, and Welfare, 1976, p. 13452].

Thus, both cost containment and excellence of care have been goals of legislated quality assurance activities.

In July of 1976, inclusion of requirements for implementation of patient care audit procedures within JCAH principles for accreditation of mental health programs reinforced this trend and, significantly, made quality assurance requirements applicable to all patients within the program seeking accreditation regardless of the source of reimbursement for services rendered.

In addition, in July of 1975, Congress passed the Community Mental Health Center amendments (Title III of Public Law 94-63) that also, independent of the PSRO movement, require that Federally funded Community Mental Health Centers (CMHCs) "should have established in accordance with regulations prescribed by the Secretary . . . an ongoing quality assurance program (including utilization and peer review systems) respecting the Center's services . . . [Public Law 94-63, Section 201d]." This provision had never appeared before in any of the previous CMHC legislation or regulations, and it serves to emphasize further the trend toward extensive reliance on quality assurance mechanisms (Windle & Ochberg, 1975).

PROGRAM EVALUATION

The history and goals of program evaluation have been somewhat different. Although the level of analysis in quality assurance activities is typically *client-specific,* the level of analysis in program evaluation is typically more general or *program-specific*—focusing on effectiveness of a type of service, level of effort of staff, cost by modality or unit of service, or comparative cost–effectiveness of service modalities. Consequently, program evaluation emphasizes data aggregation and statistical reduction methods to draw conclusions and make judgments about program effort, efficiency, and effectiveness. Evaluative activities have also begun to focus on program adequacy measures including measures of service accessibility, acceptability, availability, and community awareness of service programs.

As described in preceding chapters, program evaluation has been encouraged and/or required in various ways across the entire human service spectrum; requirements for evaluation have not been limited to the field of medicine. The application of program evaluation methods has been largely independent of the development of quality assurance methods and stems from somewhat different concerns. For example, from their inception in the mid-1960s, federally funded CMHCs were given the option to use a portion of their resources for research and evaluation and were encouraged by the National Institute of Mental Health to do so. Despite this option, the development of program evaluation in CMHCs has not been impressive (Attkisson, McIntyre, Hargreaves, Harris, & Ochberg, 1974; Comptroller General of the United States, 1974; McCullough, 1975; Windle & Volkman, 1973). An analysis of management within the community mental health program conducted by the Comptroller General of the United States (1974) revealed that "program evaluation at most of the 12 centers reviewed was minimal or nonexistant [p. 35]." As a result, the new CMHC amendments now *require* that every CMHC continuously evaluate its program and services, rather than leaving this activity optional as in the past. While concern with the quality of clinical care and the costs of service were a part of the impetus behind legislated requirements for program evaluation, the emphasis upon program evaluation also results from a desire to assess the actual effects of a new mode of mental health service delivery, and a desire to improve the management and administration of CMHC programs by basing decisions upon systematic and reliable information (Windle & Ochberg, 1975).

The CMHC amendments (Public Law 94-63) represent the first instance in which both program evaluation and quality assurance activities are required concurrently. The degree to which the two traditions and their specific techniques and methodologies can serve to complement each other in the service of improved mental health programs remains to be seen. No doubt the results will be of interest to other health and human service programs.

QUALITY ASSURANCE:
CONCEPTS AND ACTIVITIES

Quality assurance of clinical care is a process designed to identify and correct deficiencies in services provided to patients. Quality review is typically accomplished by comparing care provided with professionally developed criteria that specify appropriate treatment for particular illnesses or behavioral problem areas. Clinical care that does not conform to professionally developed criteria are referred to a committee of peers for review and intervention through appropriate educational and/or corrective action.

Analogous to quality assurance is the concept of quality control in manufacturing where acceptable tolerances are set and items exceeding those tolerance limits are rejected. However, quality assurance in the health field differs somewhat from that of quality control practices in manufacturing. In patient care assessment, more emphasis is placed on the practice of "peer review"— the notion that only clinical peers have the capacity and expertise to develop criteria and associated standards pertaining to the quality of clinical care and to exercise sanctions when these standards are not maintained (10).

DONABEDIAN'S CONCEPTS

The definition of "quality" of clinical services is complex and elusive. Donabedian's (1966) classical tripartite framework for quality of care measurement remains very influential. He argues that quality can be assessed from three perspectives—structure, process, and outcome—each of which is necessary but not sufficient for a definition of quality.

1. *Structure*

Structural approaches emphasize aspects of the service organization that have an impact upon patient care, including adequacy of the physical plant, information and record systems, experience and training of professional personnel, ratio of those personnel to patients, equipment, and the like. This approach assumes that high quality care can be provided and quality control maintained only when appropriate structural requirements are met. However, although it is assumed that an adequate structure is necessary for good quality, it is not assumed to be sufficient. Two current structural approaches to assurance of quality care are the accreditation standards of the Joint Commission on Accreditation of Hospitals (JCAH) and the *conditions of participation* under Titles XVIII and XIX of the Social Security Act (Public Law 92-603).

2. *Process*

Process approaches involve specification of those clinical procedures that constitute high quality care for various groups of patients and comparison of actual care rendered with those process criteria. Most of the procedures required in the PSRO Law, in the JCAH standards, and in the quality assurance provisions of the CMHC amendments of 1975, involve process approaches to quality assurance. Process approaches have intuitive appeal as measures of quality because process is under the control of the clinician. However, process measures are insufficient as sole indicators of quality because in some cases "good quality care" can be followed by both desirable and undesirable outcomes. In addition, criteria defining high quality process cannot always be agreed upon by clinicians, and the relationship between standards of practice and desirable outcomes is not well established in many clinical areas. Generally, in the human services, scientific knowledge concerning the relationship of processes to outcomes is not sufficiently established to allow accurate prediction of outcome from knowledge of process.

3. *Outcome*

Assessment of the outcome of clinical interventions constitutes the third approach to quality assurance. Measurement of outcome is discussed in other chapters of this book (see especially Chapters 11, 12, and 13) and is currently a very active area throughout the human service field. Without procedures for evaluating treatment effectiveness, the actual quality of services cannot be known. However, as a single measure of quality, outcome has distinct short-comings because many of the factors affecting a client's outcome are outside the control of the clinician. As Morehead (1976) has stated:

> Measurement of outcome . . . presents difficulties. The time of assess-ment varies with different investigators. For P.S.R.O.'s outcome will probably be assessed at the time of discharge from the hospital. This is clearly an artificial designation, one that is not too useful in an age when chronic disease and disability are the major health problems. However, the academic desire for instant publication and funding agen-cies' desire for immediate definitive answers have pushed the determi-nation of efficacy and patient outcome closer and closer to the point of illness. The resources, time, and commitment to mount and sustain studies over 5- or 10-year periods do not now seem to be on the horizon. Yet only by such long-term studies will definitive answers be obtained to our current major health problems [p. 119].*

4. *Integration of Structure, Process, and Outcome Approaches*

As will become evident in our conclusions, we share with Donabedian the perspective that a multicomponent approach—one that integrates periodic review of structure, continuous monitoring of process, and systematic exami-nation of outcome—is vital if clinical and program managers are to have a more complete view of the effectiveness and efficiency of service delivery. In addition, as will be discussed in the final sections of this chapter, we also advocate close coordination of quality assurance practices with program evalu-ation activities as the optimal approach to accountability.

LEGISLATIVE BENCHMARKS, GOVERNMENTAL REGULATIONS, AND ACCREDITATION STANDARDS

Of particular interest to local health and mental health programs are the specific activities required under the PSRO legislation (Public Law 92-603) and the CMHC amendments within Public Law 94-63. The PSRO law and its implementation quidelines give each PSRO the option of reviewing the clinical care of facilities under its jurisdiction or, if those facilities demonstrate compe-tence, of delegating responsibility for review to the facilities themselves (De-partment of Health, Education, and Welfare, 1974). PSRO review, or review sanctioned by a PSRO, must be carried out on all inpatient services rendered to beneficiaries of Medicare, Medicaid, and Maternal and Child Health pro-grams. PSRO review for outpatient services to the same patient group is

---

*Reproduced by permission from: M. A. Morehead, P.S.R.O.—Problems and possibilites. *Man and Medicine,* 1976, *1*(2), 113–132. (Copyright 1976, Man and Medicine, Inc., New York.)

currently optional. Two kinds of review are required: (a) *concurrent* review of all patients, and (b) *retrospective* review of samples of patients (Goran *et al.,* 1975). The purpose, scope, method, timing, personnel required, and projected results of PSRO review activities as required by Public Law 92-603 are summarized in Table 14.2.

Two types of concurrent review are mandated: (a) *admissions certification* —a process to ensure that each hospitalization is necessary; and (b) *continued stay review*—a process to monitor length of stay and, optionally, quality of services. This form of review focuses upon the "level" of care being provided and upon an assessment of where "continued" care can be most appropriately and economically provided.

Also, two types of retrospective review are mandated:(a)*medical (clinical) care evaluation studies*—retrospective studies of quality variables; other topics left to the discretion of PSROs and participating facilities; and (b) *profile monitoring*—analysis of grouped or aggregated data for institutions, departments, individual clinicians, or individual clients, directed at patterns of care.

Prior to the assumption of these review responsibilities by the local PSRO, hospital staffs must carry out these functions internally. Under Public Law 92-603 each psychiatric hospital seeking reimbursement as a provider under Medicaid and/or Medicare must form a utilization review committee that has responsibility for conduct of admission and continued stay reviews and for medical care evaluation studies.

Federal guidelines require that at least one medical care evaluation study be in progress at all times (Goran *et al.,* 1975). The purpose of these studies is to assure that health care services are appropriate given patient needs and to assure that hospital administrators maintain timely provision of needed services. A computerized information system, the *Professional Activity Study– Medical Audit Program* (PAS–MAP), is available nationally as a support system for medical care evaluation studies. PAS–MAP has been succinctly described by Holloway, Wiczai, and Carlson (1975):

> PAS–MAP provides for abstracting (1) results of admission investigations; (2) whether laboratory tests, x-rays, and other diagnostic tests were performed; (3) categories of drugs administered; and (4) whether other therapeutic services were provided. These data are routinely collected for every patient. Some regional hospital-discharge abstract systems, such as the Hospital Utilization Project (HUP) of Pennsylvania, also provide for the collection of these data but not on a routine basis for every patient. Other regional systems, such as Health Service Data of Wisconsin (HSD-W), California Health Data Corporation (CHDC) and pre-PAS (a nationally available, scaled-down version of PAS–MAP that is also sponsored by CPHA), concentrate on the collection of face sheet data. Since face sheet data alone are insufficient for conducting medical care evaluation studies, hospitals subscribing to these systems must also rely on a manual system . . . .
>
> PAS–MAP is the most popular hospital-discharge abstract system with more than 1,500 (21%) of the 7,000 hospitals in the United States as subscribers. Although PAS–MAP routinely provides more data and

TABLE 14.2
Types of PSRO Review Activities[a]

	Purpose	Scope	Method	Timing	Personnel	Results
Concurrent admission certification	• Certify necessity of admission	All Title XVIII, XIX, & V patients	a. Diagnosis or problem specific criteria & standards b. Hospital level of care criteria & standards	Within 1st working day of admission	Review coordinator/ physician advisor	Admission certified or denied (authorizes or denies payment)
	• Assign checkpoint for continued stay review	All Title XVIII, XIX, & V patients	a. Diagnosis or problem specific norms, criteria and standards b. Hospital level of care norms, criteria and standards	Within 1st. working day of admission Usually performed in conjunction with certification of necessity of admission.	Review coordinator/ physician advisor	Certifies payment up to checkpoint
Continued stay review	• Review the need for continued hospital care	All Title XVIII, XIX, & V patients still in hospital at checkpoint	a. Diagnosis or problem specific norms, criteria and standards b. Hospital level of care norms, criteria and standards	On or before day of checkpoint	Review coordinator/ physician advisor	Extension granted, new checkpoint assigned, and payment certified up to new checkpoint or extension denied
	• Assure that essential elements of care are being provided (concurrent quality assurance)	Sample of Title XVIII, XIX, & V patients	Critical criteria and standards	Usually on or before checkpoint day in conjunction with review of need for continued hospital care	Review coordinator/ physician advisor	Improved compliance with PSRO quality criteria and standards

420

Medical care evaluation studies	• Assure quality of care and effective administration of health care services	1. Conducted on study basis 2. Sample size selected in relation to study topic 3. Study may be restricted to hospital or involve entire PSRO area depending on topic and hospital review delegation 4. Usually conducted on a retrospective basis	a. Classical feedback involving following steps: 1. Determine study objective 2. Establish criteria & standards 3. Design study 4. Data collection 5. Develop reports 6. Analyze results and identify deficiencies 7. Develop corrective plan-linkage with CME 8. Restudy Usually of short duration (a week to a few months) At least one study under way at all times and four conducted per year	• PSRO/Hospital Criteria Committee • PSRO/Hospital MCE or Medical Audit Committee • Health Record Analysts • Review Coordinators	• CME programs and administrative changes recommended to correct identified deficiencies • Criteria established for MCE's may be used in concurrent review or profile analysis • Findings can help focus concurrent review activity • Restudy determines whether deficiencies have been corrected
Profile analysis	1. Identify areas where utilization practices may be inappropriate; focus concurrent review; and assist in topic selection for MCE studies 2. Monitor effectiveness of hospital review activities 3. Display local, regional and national norms of utilization	Aggregate statistical data on all hospital episodes of patients subject to PSRO review	Statistical trend analysis and comparative evaluation using data on hospitals in PSRO area and data from peer PSRO's Periodic review (quarterly to annually, depending on nature of report and number of observations)	Health Data Analysts (in PSRO and hospitals) PSRO Hospital Review Committees	• Priority subjects for MCE studies identified • Priority conditions for in-depth admission certification and continued stay review identified • Impact of concurrent review on health services utilization

[a] Reproduced by permission from: M. J. Goran, J. S. Roberts, M. Kellogg, J. Fielding, and W. Jessee. The PSRO hospital review system. *Medical Care*, 1975, *13*(4), Supplement, 1–33. (Copyright 1975, J. B. Lippincott, Philadelphia.)

is more popular than other systems, no computerized system currently
in use is providing maximum benefit to hospitals [pp. 329–330].*

A recent evaluation of the PAS–MAP system indicated that, in comparison with a manual system, PAS–MAP was ". . . less costly if more than 41
per cent of hospitalized patients were included in medical care evaluation
studies; was as timely as the manual system for data it could provide but
provided fewer clinical data elements than physicians requested; and was less
protective against human error [Holloway *et al.,* 1975, p. 329]."

The adequacy of a hospital's performance of the various quality assurance
activities is assessed (*a*) through audits undertaken by the Department of
Health, Education, and Welfare; and (*b*) through utilization control functions
delegated to the "single state agency." Audits and utilization control procedures essentially attempt to replicate internal utilization review processes by
employing each facility's criteria to determine the reliability of the internal
process. These auditors attempt to determine whether the hospital's internal
review process can be replicated and whether the second, outside review would
result in the same conlusions concerning the "medical" necessity for admission
and/or continued stay.

Audits of medical care evaluation studies include assessment of methodology and, especially, the impact of findings upon clinical and administrative
practice within the facility. In brief, auditors attempt to determine whether the
educational or other corrective actions directed by study findings were implemented and whether the consequences of that implementation were adequately
documented.

As they become operational, PSROs may exercise a prerogative to dele-
gate responsibility for both utilization review and medical care evaluation
studies to a facility based upon an assessment of the adequacy of the quality
review process implemented by an individual facility. The PSRO may, conversely, retain these review responsibilities. However, even when utilization
review responsibilities are retained by the PSRO, hospitals accredited by or
seeking accreditation through the Joint Commission on Accreditation of Hospitals are not relieved of responsibility for the conduct of internal quality
assurance activities. In addition, recent principles pertaining to patient care
audit established by the JCAH Accreditation Council for Psychiatric Facilities
extend requirements for conduct of patient care (previously known as medical
or psychiatric) audits to psychiatric facilities and mental health programs.

These Accreditation Council principles, currently developmental in nature, are proposed for review as beginning steps toward a complete quality
assurance program to be required of facilities or programs seeking accreditation. They are stated as follows (*9*):

Principle I

*Every psychiatric facility or mental health program shall demonstrate
that the quality of care provided is consistently optimal by continuous evalua-*

*Reproduced by permission from: D. C. Holloway, L. J. Wiczai, and E. T. Carlson, Evaluat-
ing an information system for medical care evaluation studies. *Medical Care,* 1975, *13,* 329–340.
(Copyright 1975, J. B. Lippincott, Philadelphia.)

tion *through reliable and valid patient care audit methods.* We interpret this principle as meaning that the quality of patient care should be monitored by audit techniques focusing on analysis of the components of input (structure), process, and outcome. The patient care audit system should include efforts to evaluate all program components, be continuous, and include the analysis of patient characteristics, problems treated, and the status of patients in respect to these problems at the termination of treatment.

Principle II

In order to accomplish the goals and objectives of patient care audit, the psychiatric facility or mental health program shall maintain a written plan describing the organization and functioning of its patient care audit system and systematic utilization of its results. We interpret this principle as meaning that the responsibility for developing, maintaining, and accomplishing the patient care audit system—including delineation of audit criteria, variations, and exceptions—shall rest with the psychiatric facility or mental health program.

Surveyors from the JCAH, during the course of accreditation visits, will examine results of patient care audits with particular emphasis on the impact of findings upon clinical and program operations. These JCAH requirements are particularly significant since they extend the population subject to mandatory quality assurance process beyond Title XVIII and XIX (Public Law 92-603) recipients to include the facility's or program's total patient population. The JCAH requirements also assume capacity for internal quality assurance activity regardless of the status of the local PSRO.

The quality assurance requirements of the recent CMHC amendments (Public Law 94-63) are similar to the PSRO requirements, but are not identical to them. Currently available draft guidelines for Section 201d of Public Law 94-63 (Department of Health, Education, and Welfare, 1976) indicate that each CMHC will be required to prepare a quality assurance plan, to be updated annually, including (a) the establishment of a multidisciplinary quality assurance committee in the CMHC which meets regularly, (b) utilization review procedures, and (c) procedures to ensure educational or administrative action on results of utilization review. Each CMHC will be required to do "case reviews," the concurrent review of services to individual clients, both at the onset of service and at subsequent times thereafter, to determine the necessity and appropriateness of care, and "care evaluation studies," retrospective in-depth studies of the quality and/or utilization of services—usually involving groups of patients or clinicians, at least one of which must be in progress at all times and two of which must be completed each year. Unlike the PSRO law, the provisions of Public Law 94-63 require that *all* of the CMHC's services are subject to review, not just inpatient services and not just services to Medicare and Medicaid beneficiaries.

QUALITY ASSURANCE IN
PSYCHIATRIC INPATIENT SETTINGS

To date, the quality assurance literature in the mental health field remains limited. Under contracts from the National Institute of Mental Health, three state mental health authorities (Colorado, Ohio, and Texas) have received funding to develop model peer review systems (Hagedorn, Beck, Neubert, & Werlin, 1976; *8;* Miller, Black, Ertel, & Ogram, 1974; Ozarin, 1975). Each project was designed to demonstrate an effective peer review process within the public mental hospital in order to achieve delegation of review authority from Professional Standards Review Organizations as provided under Public Law 92-603. Each project has made a unique contribution to the state of the peer review art through development of a creative approach to mandated quality assurance processes.

1. *The Colorado Project*

Colorado's project, under the direction of Jorge L. Paras, extended quality assurance criteria—for review of appropriateness of admission and continued hospital stay—to include social criteria as well as the more traditional clinical criteria (*4*). The decision to include social criteria was based upon the contention that psychopathology alone does not dictate admission or release from programs offered by a public mental hospital. Rather, Paras and his colleagues maintain that the patient's behavior and the characteristics of his or her community in combination with manifestations of psychopathology contribute to presentation for admission to and continued utilization of the public mental hospital. "A social systems approach to psychiatry acknowledges that the social phenomena which occur in the family and community are variables which precipitate actual presentation for psychiatric hospitalization [*4*, p. 27]." Both clinical and social criteria "were designed to be non-diagnostic specific and broad and general enough to serve most circumstances that precipitate application for admission [*4*, p. 18]."

Social criteria adopted for the Colorado project included the following: (*a*) need to interrupt deleterious psychosocial interactions; (*b*) behavior intolerable to patient, family or community; (*c*) interpersonal crisis (e.g., family disruption, loss, addition); (*d*) economic constraints (e.g., patient cannot afford private care any longer); and (*e*) availability of suitable community service. These criteria became the basis for a process of concurrent review in inpatient settings when linked to clinical criteria such as medical emergency (e.g., physiologic decline, toxicity); need for controlled environment (e.g., suicidal, assaultive, disoriented or disabled behavior); need for clarification of diagnosis by 24-hour behavioral observation; need for specialized treatments under 24-hour supervision (e.g., medication regulation or changes, specific treatment programs); and drug/alcohol dependency requiring supervised withdrawal and treatment (*4*, p. 19).

The Colorado demonstration project designed its concurrent review of "necessity for continued stay" to ensure that each patient had an adequately documented data base (in accordance with their adaptation of the problem oriented medical record), appropriate medical and psychological consultation, specific definition of problem areas requiring intervention, appropriate interventions, and discharge goals and plans. In the Colorado system, concurrent reviews were proposed to be conducted at specified time intervals during the course of the patient's treatment "regardless of anticipated length of stay or diagnosis. The process is not specifically tied to pre-determined length of stay criteria developed for general hospitals. It is our view that length of stay is not necessarily a function of psychiatric diagnosis, but is more often a function of symptom manifestation, social disabilities, and adequacy of community resources [4, p. ii]."

While the demonstration project in Colorado included computer resources to determine patterns and trends of patient care, its developers maintain that the system does not require the availability of a computer, and recommend that both admission and continued stay review be undertaken by clinicians.

2. The Ohio Project

The system designed under contract with the Ohio Department of Mental Health and Mental Retardation, on the other hand, proposed extensive use of the computer as the cornerstone of their quality assurance procedures (1; Miller et al., 1974). This decision was not surprising, since a computer-based screening system for general medical care had already been developed by Ohio's Medical Advances Institute. Like Colorado, the Ohio proposal included within the purview of its review process all public mental hospital patients, regardless of source of reimbursement for services. A computer-based system was proposed as the primary data processing vehicle for the review process because of its efficiency in storage and retrieval of information, its projected conservation of professional time, and its facility for comparison of ". . . components of actual care to Quality Criteria stored in the computer, making possible a concurrent review of the quality of care [1, p. 2-3]."

The Ohio system, therefore, was designed to include considerable reliance on computer technology. The proposed quality assurance system requires computer capability to perform concurrent, systematic comparisons of services delivered with specified criteria of appropriateness. This automated process is designed to signal discrepancies between services provided and ". . . generic and discrete problem-based or disease-specific quality criteria [Miller et al., 1974, p. 1368]."

This strong emphasis on continuous, concurrent review in the Ohio system was based upon Black's (1) assessment of the Donabedian (1966) typology and its implication for the peer review process. In searching for a design model for evaluating the quality of care in public mental hospitals, Black began with an assessment of the applicability of structural, process, and outcome approaches to quality assurance. He reported that outcome evaluation, for all its logical appeal, proved to be impractical. The academic question of whether outcome evaluation is "difficult because it isn't done" or "isn't done because it is difficult" was stimulating to debate but Black could not identify an outcome measurement strategy that could be applied routinely and efficiently for purposes of quality assurance. Outcome methods are very expensive, require significant expertise to maintain, and relevant data frequently are not available for extended periods of time following delivery of services. In addition, reliability and validity of measures that could be routinely applied are far from definitively established.*

Structural evaluation was also seriously considered and finally rejected by Black for a number of reasons. Perhaps the most troublesome aspect of structural evaluation was the recognition that there is a fundamental difference between measuring the institutional source of care, and the actual delivery of care. Black concluded that structural models are equivalent to a preconditional assessment only. The validity of such structural assessment depends on the empirical demonstration of a correlation between structural variables affecting the source of care and the quality of care delivered—an hypothesis that is difficult to prove at best. Therefore Black (1) argued in favor of process measures of quality of care:

> Process evaluation also proved to have some shortcomings, yet possessed significant advantages which outweighed the problems. It is client-centered, dynamic, flexible, can be prospective, concurrent, and retrospective and it can (and should) be based on peer judgment only . . . . Process criteria are "purer" care measurement expressions by virtue of their implicit (if not explicit) valid relationship to performance [pp. 1-9, 1-10].

As designed, the Ohio Peer Review System proposed, simultaneously, to perform utilization review functions, medical audit, and assurance of patients' rights documentation. An abstract of the patient's medical record is the primary source document for the review process:

> The computer does all the detailed bookkeeping required for each case and performs an analysis of actual care given as compared to generic and discrete problem-based or disease-specific quality criteria. When the care provided is inconsistent with the appropriate criteria, the computer generates an exception report which defines the discrepancy and where applicable, identifies additional data requirements needed to fulfill the peer review quality criteria [1, p. 1-2].

Exception reports will be referred to physician advisors for further review and for identification of appropriate corrective action. That corrective action may take the form of remedial education or other intervention. Where the required corrective actions exceed the physician advisor's authority (i.e., disciplinary or punitive actions), the exception will be referred to a higher review level. "Utilization exceptions are referred to Utilization Review Subcommittee, clinical exceptions to Medical Audit Subcommittee, and administrative and social (external) deficiencies to administration. In all cases, the concept of review by true peers is the single determinant for channeling deficiency reports for remedial action [1, p. 1-5]."

The Ohio Peer Review System's developers cite several unique features of their proposal including elaborate physical and technical safeguards devel-

*Material from G. C. Black in this section was reproduced by permission of the author (see reference note 1).

oped to maintain confidentiality of patient records and systematic necessity for documentation of appropriate action at each stage of the review process:

> Responsibility is fixed for each inconsistency through which author-
> ized sequence-integrity checks have been designed throughout the in-
> formation system from input through peer judgment and final action.
> The computer maintains an audit check until the deficiency has been
> corrected. This assures that necessary actions can neither be delayed
> nor the responsibility for them diffused [1, p. 1-8].

3. The Texas Project*

In contrast to the Ohio system, the Texas peer review project did not include proposals for automation (2). Rather, its significant contribution to peer review experience within public mental hospitals was the development and testing of three team approaches to the utilization review process: (a) a traveling team from the Texas Research Institute of Mental Sciences (part of the state system but not previously involved with the study of hospitals), (b) a local consultant team not affiliated with any of the study hospitals, and (c) an in-house team composed of staff of the study hospital to serve as its own review agency. Results of the evaluation of performance of each team revealed that the outside consultant team and traveling team brought greater objectivity to the review process:

> Because team members did not owe allegiance to the particular hospital
> in which they conducted their reviews, they were better able to make
> assessments based on what they perceived to be clinically sound and
> did not have their judgments confounded by preconceived ideas about
> what was or was not possible within the system. On the other hand,
> it is possible that the in-house review team, although less objective, was
> more realistic because of their past experience in trying to change their
> system [2, p. 75].

In their conclusions, Texas investigators cited little conclusive data to support adaptation of any one review team configuration. Rather, they suggest that each team was able to review competently:

> Because the in-house team was already a functional part of the hospital
> system which it reviewed, it appears this team achieved the greatest
> amount of improvement in medical records through informal feedback.
> The traveling team's most valuable contribution seemed to be its role
> as facilitator and change agent in each of the test hospitals. Team
> members were well accepted by the staff and were thus successful in
> gaining administrative support during the review process. The local
> consultant team provided objectivity because of the intended disas-
> sociation with the hospital and with the character of reviewed patients
> [2, p. 87].

As a result of their findings, the Texas project's investigators recommended an adaptation of the "in-house review team model" within Texas

*Material from C. Brown, J. R. Hays, J. C. Schoolar, and M. Q. Thorne in this section was
reproduced by permission of the authors (see reference note 2).

public mental hospitals. They also recommended that the in-house team should be supported by a "traveling team" charged with the responsibility of orienting and training in-house review team members. The traveling team would also conduct test reviews to replicate the in-house processes in order to judge their reliability.

QUALITY ASSURANCE IN THE COMMUNITY MENTAL HEALTH CENTER

Two community mental health centers have been highly visible in the quality assurance area, the Connecticut Mental Health Center in New Haven, Connecticut (Riedel, Tischler, & Myers, 1974; Tischler & Riedel, 1973) and the Peninsula Hospital Community Mental Health Center in Burlingame, California (5; Luft, Sampson, & Newman, 1976; Newman, 1974; Newman & Luft, 1974), although various other CMHCs have been active (Block, 1975; Thompson & Cheng, 1976; Weiner & Levine, 1975). In addition, peer review activities have also been undertaken in general hospital psychiatric inpatient units (Richman & Pinsker, 1973; 1974).

1. The Peninsula Hospital Model

The Peninsula Hospital Community Mental Health Center serves a catchment area within San Mateo County, south of San Francisco, and provides its services primarily through a private practice model, in which private practitioners in the area accept referrals and provide treatment to CMHC patients on a fee for service basis. In 1971, the center's administration and professional staff became concerned that financial expenditures were exceeding limited funds from local and state sources, and at that time a peer review system was established to allocate the limited resources in a more judicious manner. The center has three quality assurance committees: (a) an Inpatient and Partial Hospitalization Committee, (b) a Child Outpatient Committee, and (c) an Adult Outpatient Committee.

The review committees meet weekly, and the therapists and the review committees jointly work out treatment plans with explicit goals and time frames. The quality assurance committees' tasks are complex and challenging. As Luft et al. (1976) indicate: "While the committees exercise full control in authorizing the use of services and, therefore, the allocation of the budgeted community funds, the atmosphere of the meetings is more akin to that of a clinical case conference than an administrative review. The overriding goal is to maintain the delicate balance between clinical needs and fiscal realities [p. 891]."

In the Peninsula Hospital Community Mental Health Center, an *outpatient* therapist who wishes to see a patient more than six times must present the case before the appropriate review committee. A recent evaluation of the Peninsula Hospital Community Mental Health Center quality assurance approach to *outpatient* services indicated that, despite the original concern with controlling overutilization, less than three-forths of authorized treatment time was utilized by patients. Furthermore, the peer review committee frequently determined that resources allotted were often minimal for client needs (Luft et al., 1976). This evaluation also revealed that the peer review process was not as disruptive to the treatment process as anticipated, helped therapists formulate specific treatment goals, and had beneficial value to the quality of professional practice for therapists who participated. In addition, Luft et al. reported that patients and therapists had a very high rate of agreement about whether the amount of therapy provided was adequate and whether more treatment was needed.

Several problems were also noted by Luft et al.: (a) third-party peer review influences sometimes created ambiguity about therapeutic commitment and, in these cases, treatment contracts could not be established with the patients until after the peer review; (b) one-third of the patients felt that third-party peer review was an intrusion and also expressed concerns about confidentiality; and (c) a small percentage of therapists and patients felt that the review process interfered with the establishment of therapeutic alliance and with therapeutic progress.

The Peninsula Hospital Community Mental Health Center peer review model for outpatient services is a highly functional approach and is an important landmark in the shift toward comprehensive quality assurance requirements now mandated by Public Law 94-63 for all federally funded CMHC programs. The Peninsula outpatient review model is best characterized as a consultative and educative process aimed at closely monitoring outpatient services, and was designed quite explicitly as a fiscal control mechanism. However, the Peninsula model falls short of a comprehensive strategy since a significant portion of patients, who do not require or who do not participate in outpatient services beyond six visits, are not reviewed. Consequently, *underutilization* and the quality and appropriateness of services for patients in brief treatment are not reviewed within the peer review system as now structured. This limitation does not pertain to inpatient and partial hospitalization services where previously mandated quality assurance procedures for psychiatric patients have been implemented.

2. The Connecticut Mental Health Center Model

An interdisciplinary team at Yale University and the Connecticut Mental Health Center has implemented a mental health care evaluation strategy to ensure program effectiveness and high quality patient care while concurrently meeting the "peer review" requirements of governmental and third-party payers (Riedel, Tischler, & Myers, 1974). In the Connecticut Mental Health Center system the patient record provides source data for quality assurance by detailing explicitly what is being done for the patient and why. A first step in patient care evaluation is an audit of the adequacy and completeness of record content. The audit stage is followed by peer review of data abstracted from the patient's record in comparison with locally established criteria and standards of excellence. If the abstracted data reveal conformity with such standards and criteria, no further action is taken. When deviations from such "standards of excellence" are noted, the patient's record is referred to a peer review process during which the record and care prescribed and delivered are examined.

Patterns of deviation are defined and an intervention through education and training is initiated.

This review process attempts to answer the following questions: Does care rendered meet currently accepted standards? Has the individual received care in accordance with explicit standards given demographic characteristics, manifest symptomatology, and levels of functioning? Does the program do what it claims (in its statement of clinical goals and objectives) to do?

Two types of criteria are in use at the Connecticut Mental Health Center: diagnosis-specific criteria that address adequacy of service provided based upon the patient's psychopathology, and criteria developed around clinical decision points which address appropriateness of treatment choices (e.g., criteria for prescription of group therapy, electroconvulsive therapy, or prescription of medication).

Other elements of patient care evaluation at the Connecticut Mental Health Center include process analysis and review of treatment outcome. Developers of patient care evaluation at the Connecticut Mental Health Center, then, have integrated methodologies that are more traditionally found within the sphere of program evaluation into their quality assurance design. Their work has been an important contribution to both processes.

TRENDS AND ISSUES IN QUALITY ASSURANCE

The emergence of quality assurance as an important method for self-evaluation in the mental health field has raised a number of procedural, programmatic, and conceptual issues. As previously delineated by Hagedorn *et al.* (1976), these issues represent the "cutting edges" of the quality assurance field.

USE OF EXPLICIT CRITERIA

Professional peer review can be based upon implicit or explicit (written down, consensually agreed upon) criteria or a combination of both. *Implicit criteria* are typically used when a peer review committee simply reads the formal record and makes a judgment regarding quality. Implicit criteria have the advantage of flexibility by taking into account the client's unique problems and the many possible contingencies of his or her situation, but do not lend themselves to accountability by creating specific standards of practice against which care can be reviewed and exceptions noted. Use of *explicit criteria* involves applying sets of agreed upon formal criteria to groups of clients, typically on the basis of diagnostic, level of functioning, or problem area categories. Use of explicit criteria offers the advantages of avoiding potential arbitrariness or capriciousness by review groups—a state of affairs that results from continuously shifting, unarticulated rules that characterize the review process when explicit criteria are not employed. Use of explicit criteria is based upon the assumption that clinicians should be able to agree upon and write down the services and therapies appropriate for categories of problems, functioning levels and/or diagnoses. However, not all knowledgeable observers agree with this assumption and rigid insistence on explicit criteria can lead to inflexibility and lack of innovation. However, when feasible, use of explicit criteria allows more clear-cut replication of the review process and examination of its reliability. Yet, "there is the temptation to create an all-inclusive 'laundry list' which may escalate the cost of care without correspondingly improving the quality [Morehead, 1976, p. 118]."

The PSRO law, where applicable, mandates the use of explicit criteria in the quality review process. To avoid inflexibility, explicit criteria are used only as a screening device in concurrent review to identify exceptions to the explicit criteria of acceptable practice, leaving the final judgment (concerning necessity of continued treatment or the configuration of appropriate care) for review by clinical peers. In addition, flexible and dynamic use of explicit criteria can be assured by development of a timetable for periodic revision and renegotiation of these criteria by clinical staff.

In the mental health field, development of explicit, behaviorally oriented criteria will not be an easy task. Because of their ambiguity, current concepts of mental health and mental illness virtually preclude adequate operational definitions. Adaptation of social criteria, similar to those developed in Colorado, or criteria emphasizing behaviorally defined levels of functioning may allow more explicit operational definitions and reliability of measurement.

RELIANCE ON CLINICAL RECORDS FOR DATA

Clinical practice criteria, whether explicit or implicit, must be applied to data documenting the process of patient care. These data are usually contained within the medical record or an abstract of that record. The validity of the peer reviewer's judgment is established only to the extent that the clinical record is accurate or complete, and so, adequate clinical records are necessary for effective quality assurance review. Consequently, peer review procedures require adequate documentation of service activities and an effective information system to monitor those services.

Some observers fear that the necessary emphasis upon precise documentation in quality assurance systems will lead to a bureaucratic and trivial system that produces "records for records' sake" without utility for assuring high quality care. These issues require sensitive handling and clarity about goals (Liptzin, 1974). Acknowledging—from another perspective—the limitations of written records, Luft (5) cautions against neglecting direct observation of clinical care as a source of quality assurance data.

CONFIDENTIALITY

Care must be taken to assure that the confidentiality of client-identified data is guaranteed without exception. The quality review process, of necessity, involves some controlled abridgement of absolute confidentiality since third-party clinical peers must review documentation of services provided and be privy to descriptions of transactions between clients and service providers. Therefore, the planners of quality assurance systems must be sensitive to confidentiality issues in the communication of patient-identified data and build in appropriate safeguards (*1;* Liptzin, 1974; *5*). Legal implications concerning the evidentiary use of quality assurance findings in malpractice litigation must also be clarified.

In essence, a critical aspect of the quality of care that must be assured is that the service recipient will not be harmed either by the treatment, the program evaluation process, the quality assurance process, or any communication of client-identified information.

With the emerging collaborative arrangements between quality assurance reviewers, program evaluators, and directors of information systems, it is most important that each agency or institution have a written, formal policy about the use and protection of client-identified and other confidential information. Though writing primarily for social science researchers and program evaluators, Riecken and Boruch (1974, pp. 255–269) present a very helpful overview of the various issues related to protecting privacy and confidentiality. They also describe five technical procedures that, when employed, allow "outsiders" access to data without compromising confidentiality: (*a*) deletion of identifiers; (*b*) crude report categories for, and restriction of, public variables; (*c*) microaggregation; (*d*) error inoculation; and (*e*) in-file capacity to run outsiders' statistical analyses (pp. 262–266). Detailed descriptions of these strategies and their vulnerabilities can be reviewed in Boruch (1972a;1972b).

USE OF NONCLINICAL PERSONNEL

In many of the recently developed peer review systems, nonclinicians (e.g., record analysts, abstractors, and clerks) have participated in aspects of the review process. This practice has caused some concern among clinicians, who are alarmed by the notion of review by nonclinical staff. One may wish to have nonclinical staff involved in the review process as coordinators, abstractors of information, and the reviewers of case records as guided by explicit, operationalized criteria. To minimize concern among service providers, the literal significance of the concept of *peer review* must be preserved in actual practice and authority for decision making about reimbursement and corrective intervention must remain in the hands of clinical peers. In many respects, quality assurance systems are a mechanism for clinicians to keep their own house in order, and so acceptance of these systems by clinical staff and their active participation in them are necessary (*5*).

COST CONTROL AND QUALITY ASSURANCE

Mandated quality assurance activities have two purposes: to control costs by eliminating unnecessary services, and to assure high quality care by assuring that criteria defining appropriate care are met (Cohen, Conwell, Ozarin, & Ochberg, 1974). Clearly, one can anticipate instances in which improvements in quality of care to meet acceptable standards will cost more rather than less, and perhaps a lot more. *Quality assurance activities also can be expected to add significantly to overhead expenses and to add indirectly to the cost of delivering services.* Who pays the costs of such increases? There is an inherent conflict between cost control and enhancement of service quality. Though better services do not *necessarily* cost more, high quality services—

if they are to be achieved—will require extraordinary efficiency in the service delivery system.

EDUCATION VERSUS ENFORCEMENT

When deficiencies in clinical care are detected by a peer review committee, then what? In general, the policy has been to emphasize an educational approach as the principal response to amelioration of deficiences in care that are detected through peer review. Quality assurance systems have considerable potential as feedback mechanisms to alert clinicians to gaps in knowledge and to stimulate ongoing study and improvement of diagnostic and treatment skills, and it is hoped that this potential will be realized (Dorsey & Sullivan, 1975; 5; Newman & Luft, 1974). While punitive sanctions within the context of peer review mechanisms are possible, in the long run, they will undermine the desired self-enhancement and learning potential of constructive feedback and may not lead to the desired ends of enhanced quality of care.

CLINICIAN RESPONSIBILITIES
AND THE QUALITY ASSURANCE SYSTEM

Some health care professionals are concerned that PSROs and other peer review mechanisms will dictate clinical practice. While peer review systems will affect the provision of health care by subjecting existing practice to comparison against *ideal* criteria, it is important to understand the nature of a peer review system's legitimate and official sanctions. As S. H. Nelson (1976) states:

> . . . it should be made clear that the PSRO will not be able to tell physicians how they must practice. It cannot say that a hospitalized patient must be discharged, for example. It *can* tell a practitioner that it will no longer pay for a patient's care while that patient stays in the hospital. The physician then has to consult with the patient and make the judgment as to whether or not the patient need remain in the hospital at his or her own expense or whether the patient is psychiatrically well enough to be discharged [p. 67].*

While PSROs have direct control over expenditures of Medicare, Medicaid, and Maternal and Child Health funds for services, the specific sanctions of a quality assurance committee in a CMHC under Public Law 94-63 will be decided by each local CMHC, leading to adoption of sanctions that will vary from one center to another. Experimentation with various "sanctions" will be necessary until community mental health practitioners can target those which are most effective.

The issue of ambiguity about sanctions and the expense of quality assurance activities make it difficult to predict the future impact of PSRO and the quality assurance procedures required by Public Law 94-63. Morehead (1976) has proposed a future scenario that merits careful reflection:

> What, then, will be the future impact of the P.S.R.O.? One can assume that quality assurance activities will proceed with marked

---

*Reproduced by permission from: S. H. Nelson, Accountability in psychiatric practice: PSRO and utilization review. In R. Westlake (Ed.), *Shaping the future of mental health care.* Copyright 1976, Ballinger, Cambridge, Massachusetts.

variation in the degree of expertise, commitment, and effectiveness. The utilization reviews that were mandated by the Medicare legislation in 1966 are generally believed to have been of limited usefulness in reducing the numbers of hospital admissions. One reason for this is the economic pressure on given institutions. A prestigious hospital with high occupancy rates which is under considerable pressure to admit patients has a built-in utilization review mechanism. The institution that depends on a given level of occupancy for economic solvency and that transmits these concerns to its staff is not apt to be overly rigorous in reducing the number of admissions or the length of hospital stays, but instead will concentrate on justifying admissions. These same factors will operate in the arena of quality control, with additional complications. The strong teaching institutions will view the proposed assessment activities as just another bureaucratic imposition that escalates cost and demands on physician time without improving quality. They feel, probably with some justification, that the concept of a nurse or health technician initiating censorship of a physician for inappropriate admission or procedures is completely unrealistic. The various techniques that have been proposed to examine care are considered simplistic, substandard, and of little value. One reputable teaching institution has adopted the Joint Commission's recent advised approach emphasizing outcome, which states that if the length of stay is within expectations and the patient is discharged alive, then the outcome is satisfactory and there is no need to look further. Dr. Samuel Standard's frequent comment as a reviewer that "folly that succeeds is still folly" could well be applicable under such circumstances. There can be little optimism that smaller institutions—many staffed by physicians whose performance is most apt to be questioned—will identify problems in staff performance in any meaningful fashion. Nor are P.S.R.O.'s likely to engage in conflict with such institutions in the near future, both because of the nature of their control and the difficulties relating to methodology.

Yet, with all the debate over methodology and all the concerns over the vested interest of those conducting the reviews, there is a glimmer of hope that P.S.R.O.'s can effect change. If nothing else, there will be systematic review of the practice of care by a considerably larger number of physicians and others who have not previously engaged in such activites. These will likely be highly intelligent individuals who will learn from the experience, contribute to methodology, and, in many ways that will probably not come to public attention, effect change in the practice of medicine. Both the physician's education and mode of practice focus, to a large extent, on the individual patient. Few practicing physicians have ongoing access to information regarding care and outcome of large numbers of similar cases. This mandated opportunity to closely examine such experiences may well raise and answer questions which will lead to improvement in the provision of health care.

Such activities clearly are needed. Unnecessary surgery is performed in this country; medical and surgical patients do fail to receive minimally adequate diagnostic workups; mistakes in judgment are made and medication is used inappropriately. There are great gaps in the body of professional knowledge, but there are even greater gaps between what is known and what is applied.

There were "liberals" who opposed Medicare because the bill was not adequate. There are "liberals" who now oppose national health insurance, again because the provisions are not perfect. There will be those in the quality field in favor of physician accountability who will say that P.S.R.O.'s will be expensive and not cost–effective; that they will not improve patient outcome; and, therefore, that they will do little for either medical knowledge or patient care. The "conservatives" will echo these complaints and add others: intrusion into the practice of medicine, violation of the doctor–patient relationship, interference with reimbursement which, while not loudly touted, is key to many of the arguments. It will be a difficult road to pursue between antagonists on the "right" and defeatists on the "left." As in most legislation directed toward social policy, change will come slowly.

It will be important for the public and for other disciplines to become involved and knowledgeable about this process so that physicians and legislators of both persuasions do not prematurely come to the conclusion that the effort to improve the quality of health care is not possible at the present time [pp. 121–122].*

OUTPATIENT AND PARTIAL CARE REVIEW

Requirements for PSROs currently apply only to inpatient services, and quality assurance technology is most highly developed for those services. However, as emphasis on cost containment becomes more acute, PSRO review is likely to extend to outpatient and partial care services where, as Morehead (1976) argues, the greatest payoff from quality assurance efforts is likely to occur. In the medical field, for example, "only one of 10 patients is hospitalized, whereas the average American consults a physician in his office or clinic four times a year [Morehead, 1976, p. 120]." Under Public Law 92-603, however, review of ambulatory services by a PSRO requires the special approval of the secretary of the Department of Health, Education, and Welfare.

The quality assurance provisions of the new CMHC Law apply to *all* CMHC services, including but not limited to inpatient services. Depending upon the regulations and guidelines developed for Public Law 94-63, the development of quality assurance systems for outpatient and intermediate care services may be a major challenge for CMHCs in the near future, and it is virtually certain that such systems will be necessary. Hence, the development of quality assurance systems and technologies for outpatient and partial care services must be accomplished rapidly because there is a gap in technology (Cohen et al., 1974; Thorne, 1975) and also a gap in the readiness of CMHC staffs to implement established technology. Of particular relevance to these issues is the work of the Connecticut Mental Health Center and the Peninsula Hospital CMHC discussed earlier.

*Reproduced by permission from: M. A. Morehead, P.S.R.O.—Problems and possibilities. *Man and Medicine,* 1976, *1*(2), 113–132. (Copyright 1976, Man and Medicine, Inc., New York.)

MULTIDISCIPLINARY REVIEW

To date, quality assurance activities have focused primarily upon the performance of individual physicians, whose work has been reviewed by other physicians. Mental health programs (including psychiatric hospitals and CMHCs) tend to emphasize multidisciplinary and "team" approaches to care with shared authority and responsibility, and so some of the existing quality assurance systems will require modification to fit the mental health context (Cohen et al., 1974; Thorne, 1975).

As indicated, the quality assurance regulations of Public Law 94-63 probably will require a multidisciplinary quality assurance committee within each CMHC. This multidisciplinary review requirement will likely stimulate collaboration among the various mental health disciplines to facilitate development of approaches to quality of care which cut across professional lines. We may also find that functional and/or problem-oriented criteria, that are only partially related to professional affiliation, are most appropriate as review criteria within community mental health programs (2).

REVIEW BY PROFESSIONAL STANDARDS REVIEW
ORGANIZATIONS
VERSUS DELEGATION TO MENTAL HEALTH PROGRAMS

The local PSRO has the option of undertaking quality assurance review or of delegating responsibility for that review to a local program if that program can demonstrate an acceptable quality assurance system for internal review. Given the requirement in Public Law 94-63 that every CMHC develop a quality assurance system and requirements for implementation of quality assurance procedures by the Accreditation Council for Psychiatric Facilities of the JCAH, the advantages of PSRO delegation of review authority to mental health programs are clear-cut. Delegation would avoid redundancy, assure attention to the special issues of mental health services, enhance the educational potential of the system, retain local control of program assessment, and enhance a sense of local responsiblity for the quality of services to the mentally ill.

QUALITY ASSURANCE AND PROGRAM
EVALUATION: COMPLEMENTARY
RELATIONSHIPS

The relationship of quality assurance to program evaluation remains unclear. Therefore, we will attempt to (a) point out key differences in emphasis and operation between these two approaches, and (b) indicate potential synergistic consequences stemming from their coordinated implementation. The differences to be highlighted are more traditional than current, since we perceive gradual convergence and integration of these self-evaluation approaches into a coherent whole. The basic themes of this discussion are summarized in Table 14.3.

TABLE 14.3
Program Evaluation and Quality Assurance: Traditional Differences in Emphasis

| Key variables | Contrasting emphases | |
	Program evaluation	Quality assurance
Focus of analysis	Performance of programs in relation to their objectives concerning level of effort, efficiency, effectiveness, and adequacy	Patient/client-specific and practice of individual clinicians and clinical teams in relation to criteria of quality
Uses in decision making	Programmatic decisions by administrative staff	Clinical care decisions by clinical staff
Technology	Automated data processing and statistical analyses	Manual review of clinical record with an emerging selective use of automated applications (especially in utilization review)
Practitioner role and skills	Evaluation specialist functioning as decision maker and planner	Clinical peers
Derivation of criteria or indicators	Empirical and normative	Consensual—based on professional judgment, clinically derived norms, clinical research, and mandated standards
Level of aggregation	Extensive aggregation by administrative unit, e.g., facility, program institution	Minimal aggregation by patient cluster, e.g., demographic and clinical similarity among patients

FOCUS OF ANALYSIS

Program evaluation in a human service program focuses upon broad issues affecting that program as a whole or elements within it. Programmatic, administrative, fiscal, and clinical issues have been examined by program evaluators, but almost always with reference to a program, service, administrative entity, or mode of treatment intervention. Emphasis in program evaluation has been upon providing information relevant to management decision making. On the other hand, quality assurance systems have been limited, for the most part, to review of individual clinicians' (primarily physicians) services provided to specific patients with emphasis upon monitoring and influencing the process of service delivery rather than upon systemic or program change dictated through policy or administrative action. However, more recent developments in quality assurance, exemplified by the systems implemented at the Connecticut Mental Health Center and proposed for the State of Ohio, place considerable emphasis upon aggregation of patient specific data to review patterns of practice yielding information of considerable utility for program planning and decision making.

USES IN DECISION MAKING

With regard to the uses of the information generated by the two approaches in decision making, data from program evaluation are intended for many uses relative to human service program operation, including planning, management, and resource allocation. The results of quality assurance review are used primarily by service staff in decision making and education regarding the clinical care aspects of a program's operation, particularly in concurrent monitoring of the quality and appropriateness of individual client care. This traditional distinction is blurred in the case of the Peninsula Hospital Community Mental Health Center where peer review committees are given considerable responsibility for decisions concerning internal resource allocation.

Based upon the Colorado, Ohio, and Texas projects, the New York State Department of Mental Hygiene adopted a similar strategy of developing in-house committees for the conduct of utilization review and clinical care evaluation studies. These in-house committees are supported by New York State Central Office staff who provide training and periodic visits for purposes of encouragement, dissemination of new developments, training, and examination of review process reliability. Supplementing these activities are concurrent efforts to develop instrumentation designed to measure patient "level of functioning" for use in determining appropriateness of continued stay at the psychiatric hospital level of care. Within New York State, peer review processes —informed by assessment of patient care needs through automated analysis of level of function, somatic and psychiatric condition, behavioral manifestation, and prognosis—are mobilized to serve a statewide effort toward deinstitutionalization (6). These efforts have resulted in the development of criteria for "levels of care" and programs to serve patient groups for whom appropriate services were not previously available (7). Patient assessments, completed by a trained surveyor, are examined in comparison to clinician developed criteria for appropriateness of service at different levels of care. This utilization review process results in an ongoing analysis of placement appropriateness and location of services for individual patients and assessment of alternatives to current level of care assignments.

TECHNOLOGY AND STAFFING REQUIREMENTS

Traditionally, the skills and roles of staff engaged in the evaluative process have differed from those employed in quality assurance activity. Organizationally, program evaluation staff are a part of the management or administrative component of the human service program rather than a part of the clinical care or direct service component. The skills of the program evaluator can range from research design to computer programming to accounting and budgeting skills. Quality assurance reviewers are always clinical staff (or their delegates) involved in direct patient care who review the work of their peers. Their skills, of course, involve assessment, diagnosis, and treatment. This trend has changed dramatically with the increased application of technology, particularly computer technology, to quality assurance processes. An extreme example of such an application is the highly automated system proposed by the Ohio Department of Mental Health and Mental Retardation. Although this system is designed to serve the *peer review* process, it will require systems analysis and data processing skills for its development and ongoing operation and will also require close cooperation between the clinician and computer systems analyst.

DERIVATION OF CRITERIA

Criteria and indices used in program evaluation are, traditionally, developed through quantitative analysis of a program's information system data base. These evaluation criteria or indices are used *longitudinally,* to compare present program performance against past trends, or *cross-sectionally* for formal comparisons between treatment groups, between service modalities, or between a particular program's performance and a normatively derived threshold.

Quality assurance practitioners, on the other hand, have relied upon professional or clinical judgment for the derivation of quality criteria for use in clinical decision making. Consensual criteria developed through negotiation among clinicians within a discipline or program have been adopted as *standards of excellence* against which to measure current patterns of clinical practice. Such criteria have been stated in vague and ambiguous terms requiring the exercise of *clinical* judgment during the course of utilization review to determine compliance or noncompliance with their stipulations. With increasing concern about the reliability of review processes, we anticipate increased interest in development of operational definitions and explicit criteria in order to make empirical study and measurement possible. This gradual shift is in evidence within the systems proposed in Ohio (*1*) and New York (*7*).

TREND TOWARD CONVERGENCE

A gradual trend toward convergence of quality assurance and program evaluation approaches is evident. While program evaluation and quality assurance have traditionally been associated with different areas of concern and have had differing emphases, recent developments in both areas highlight a trend toward convergence in (*a*) focus of analysis, (*b*) uses in decision making, (*c*) methodology and technology, (*d*) skills brought to bear on the process, and (*e*) the process of criteria development.

In our view, this trend is positive because both approaches are forms of evaluation and both are attempts to gather systematic data for purposes of making decisions that are in turn designed to improve programs and services. Several integrative steps may, if adopted, speed this trend toward convergence.

1. *Data Sharing*

Data and findings available as a result of implementation of both procedures have synergistic consequences when applied in combination. Program evaluation data bases provide a context for utilization review, whereas utilization review findings may enhance program evaluation activity and help target evaluative efforts. We advocate open sharing of data and findings among those responsible for each process. Program evaluation data have implications for clinical decision making just as utilization review and patient care audit results have implications for decisions concerning programs.

2. *Clinical Staff Participation*

Program evaluation can benefit from more extensive involvement by clinical staff. This involvement may have the consequence of making the evaluative findings more relevant and useful. Simultaneously, involvement will ensure greater attention to evaluation results.

3. *Evaluator Contributions to Peer Review*

Program evaluation skills, methodology, and technology can lend sophistication and efficiency to the utilization review process. We advocate including program evaluators on utilization or peer review committees and recommend active collaboration between evaluators and quality assurance personnel in the conduct of medical care evaluation studies.

4. *The Peer Review Model*

Involvement and participation are hallmarks of the quality assurance processes. The program evaluator can learn much from the peer review model and should be encouraged to share evaluative information in a forum of service providers and administrative peers. Those *peers* can help to develop appropriate corrective action and can do much to ensure that evaluative results are used —not shelved and forgotten.

5. *Common Planning Base*

We recommend that program evaluators and quality assurance practitioners explore areas of mutuality, shared interest, and complementary capability. Program evaluation technology can facilitate movement of quality assurance processes from exclusive reliance on the service record as the *sole* data source toward the use of data aggregation methods that may highlight patterns of practice, service, and care. On the other hand, if both share a common informational data base, quality assurance can do much to move program evaluation beyond its current preoccupation with development of information systems toward a focus on process and outcome assessment and their implications for patient care. However, integrated information system capacity is essential to every level of quality assurance or program evaluation activity. In the quality assurance area, without such information system capability, higher levels of analysis beyond manual reviews of client/patient records are not likely to occur. In our view, a flexible information system is the underlying data processing tool that allows quality assurance, quality control, and program evaluation to be done concurrently.

SUMMARY

We have compared and contrasted quality assurance and program evaluation, with special attention to their respective goals and legislative histories; described salient concepts and current activities in the quality assurance field; summarized important issues and trends in quality assurance; described several innovative applications of quality assurance methods within health and mental health programs; and discussed the complementary relationship between quality assurance and program evaluation.

Similarities and differences between program evaluation and quality assurance were portrayed along several key dimensions: legislative sanctions, degree of reliance on peer review, level of analysis, basic objectives, and principal methods. In contrast to program evaluation, *quality assurance activities* have a more extensive legislative mandate; rely more extensively on clinical peer review and substantively less on administrative review; are client- and service provider-specific; are organized to assure adequacy and appropriateness of care and to control costs by preventing overutilization; and rely on methods that focus on specific service plans and service transactions. Also, quality assurance methods usually involve minimal data aggregation, focus on service records, and typically do not rely on computer applications for data processing. However, these differences tend to reflect separate historical developments, and there is now a definite trend toward convergence in objectives and methodology. Program evaluation and quality assurance specialists share many common information needs and this commonality of interests seems to be stimulating cooperative, nonredundant efforts.

In conclusion, we anticipate that distinctions will become less sharp and that program evaluation and quality assurance approaches will blend together as an internal human service facility self-evaluation process with potential consequences ranging from improvement in delivery of clinical care and enhanced decision making about program management, to rationalization of program-wide planning, resource allocation, and the budgeting process. This trend toward convergence appears to have such momentum that the logical blending of quality assurance and program evaluation in a continuing effort to achieve more effective and efficient delivery of services seems inevitable.

REFERENCE NOTES

1. Black, G. C. *Implementation manual: Peer review system for public mental hospital.* Columbus: Ohio Department of Mental Health and Mental Retardation, 1974. (Available from 30 East Broad Street, Columbus, Ohio 43229.)
2. Brown, C., Hays, J. R., Schoolar, J. C., & Thorne, M. Q. *Utilization review and medical care assessment plan for public mental hospitals: Final report.* Houston, Texas: Texas Research Institute of Mental Sciences, Texas Medical Center, 1974. (Available from 1300 Moursund Avenue, Houston, Texas 77030.)
3. Goran, M. J., & Crystal, R. A. *Review of long-term care utilization and quality: Relationship to PSRO.* Paper presented at the Conference on Long Term Care Data, Tucson, Arizona, May 1975. (Available from the Bureau of Quality Assurance, Health Services Administration, DHEW, Parklawn Building, 5600 Fishers Lane, Rockville, Maryland 20852.)
4. Koppin, M., Mayo, A., Paros, J., Seley, L., & Shure, H. *A report of a model assessment program for public mental health hospitals.* Pueblo, Colorado: Colorado State Hospital, 1974.
5. Luft, L. L. *The technology of peer review.* Paper presented at the Annual Convention of the American Psychological Association, Chicago, September 1975. (Available from the Director of Program Evaluation, Community Mental Health Center, Peninsula Hospital and Medical Center, 1783 El Camino Real, Burlingame, California 94010.)
6. Lund, D. A. *Evaluation of the appropriateness of inpatient care: The Pilgrim Project.* Paper presented at the Eastern Psychiatric Research Association Meeting, New York City, April 1976. (Available from the Bureau of Program Evaluation, Department of Mental Hygiene, 44 Holland Avenue, Albany, New York 12229.)

7. Lund, D. A., & Weinstein, A. *Profiling patient needs: The rationalization of a plan for deinstitutionalization.* Paper presented at the National Conference on Mental Health Statistics, New Orleans, June 1976. (Available from the Bureau of Program Evaluation, Department of Mental Hygiene, State of New York [see Note 6].)

8. Meredith, C. *The development and implementation of a model utilization review and medical care assessment program in a public psychiatric hospital.* Paper presented at the Annual Meeting of the Association of Mental Health Administrators, Washington, D. C., September 1975.

9. Sharenberg, C. Personal Communication, May 7, 1976. (From a statement to members of the Ad Hoc Advisory Committee on Patient Care Audit of the Joint Commission on Accreditation of Hospitals re *Revised Principles of Patient Care Audit for Mental Health.*)

10. The application of peer review to assure adherance to standards and quality in professional practice has only a few formal analogues in the human service field outside of health care. One obvious example is the practice in certain government agencies to rely on professional peers to review basic and applied extramural research proposals. There has been considerable discussion of the efficacy of this practice as a mechanism to assure the methodological adequacy and social relevance of government-funded research (Carey, 1975; Nobel, 1974). Other examples are the standard setting activities of professional peer groups to control admission to professional associations and to review applicants for state licensure or certification of service providers (e.g., physicians, nurses, psychologists, social workers). Within most higher educational systems, employment, promotion, and tenure are frequently contingent upon the results of a peer review process.

11. Vogt, L. M., Silverman, W., White, T. W., & Scanlon, J. W. *Field test results of peer review quality assessment of legal services. ALI–ABA CLE Review,* 1976, *7*(38), 1–4. (This report is available in the September 17, 1976 edition of the *ALI–ABA CLE Review* published by the American Law Institute–American Bar Association Committee on Continuing Professional Education, 4025 Chestnut Street, Philadelphia, Pennsylvania 19104.) The application of peer review/quality assessment methods to legal services described in this report is based on work undertaken by Vogt *et al.* who are staff or former staff of the Urban Institute, 2100 M Street, N.W., Washington, D. C. 20037. The methodology developed by the Urban Institute is designed for use in evaluation of alternative legal services delivery methods for the poor.

REFERENCES

Attkisson, C. C., McIntyre, M. H., Hargreaves, W. A., Harris, M. R., & Ochberg, F. M. A working model for mental health program evaluation. *American Journal of Orthopsychiatry,* 1974, *44,* 741–753.

Block, W. E. Applying utilization review procedures in a community mental health center. *Hospital and Community Psychiatry,* 1975, *26,* 358–361.

Boruch, R. F. Relations among statistical methods for assuring confidentiality of data. *Social Science Research,* 1972, *1,* 403–414. (a)

Boruch, R. F. Strategies for eliciting and merging confidential social research data. *Policy Sciences,* 1972, *3,* 275–297. (b)

Carey, W. D. Peer review revisited. *Science,* 1975, *189,* 3.

Cohen, G. D., Conwell, M., Ozarin, L. A., & Ochberg, F. M. PSRO's: Problems and potentials for psychiatry. *American Journal of Psychiatry,* 1974, *131,* 1378–1381.

Comptroller General of the United States. *Need for more effective management of the community mental health centers program.* (Report to the Congress, B-164031-5.) Washington, D. C.: United States General Accounting Office, 1974.

Decker, B., & Bonner, P. (Eds.). *PSRO: Organization for regional peer review.* Cambridge, Massachusetts: Ballinger, 1973.

Department of Health, Education, and Welfare. Social Security Administration. Conditions of participation—Hospitals and nursing facilities, utilization review. *Federal Register,* 1974, *39,* 41604.

Department of Health, Education, and Welfare. Utilization review. *Federal Register*, 1976, *41*, 13452–13463.

Donabedian, A. Evaluating the quality of medical care. *Milbank Memorial Fund Quarterly*, 1966, *44*, 166–206.

Dorsey, R., & Sullivan, F. PSRO: Advantages, risks, and potential pitfalls. *American Journal of Psychiatry*, 1975, *132*, 832–836.

Goran, M. J., Roberts, J. S., Kellogg, M., Fielding, J., & Jessee, W. The PSRO hospital review system. *Medical Care*, 1975, *13*(4), Supplement, 1–33.

Hagedorn, H. J., Beck, K. J., Neubert, S. F., & Werlin, S. H. *A working manual of simple program evaluation techniques for community mental health centers*. (DHEW Publication No. ADM 76-404.) Washington, D. C.: U. S. Government Printing Office, 1976.

Holloway, D. C., Wiczai, L. J., & Carlson, E. T. Evaluating an information system for medical care evaluation studies. *Medical Care*, 1975, *13*, 329–340.

Liptzin, B. Quality assurance and psychiatric practice: A review. *American Journal of Psychiatry*, 1974, *131*, 1374–1377.

Lorei, T. W., & Schroeder, N. H. Integrating program evaluation and medical audit. *Hospital and Community Psychiatry*, 1975, *26*, 733–735.

Luft, L. L., Sampson, L. M., & Newman, D. E. Effects of peer review on outpatient psychotherapy: Therapist and patient followup survey. *American Journal of Psychiatry*, 1976, *133*, 891–895.

McCullough, P. Training for evaluators. In J. Zusman & C. R. Wurster (Eds.), *Program evaluation: Alcohol, drug abuse, and mental health services*. Lexington, Massachusetts: Lexington Books, 1975.

Miller, R. R., Black, G. C., Ertel, P. Y., & Ogram, G. F. Psychiatric peer review: The Ohio system. *American Journal of Psychiatry*, 1974, *131*, 1367–1370.

Morehead, M. A. P.S.R.O.—Problems and possibilities. *Man and Medicine*, 1976, *1*(2), 113–132.

Nelson, A. R. Relation between quality assessment and utilization review in a functioning PSRO. *New England Journal of Medicine*, 1975, *292*, 671–675.

Nelson, S. H. Accountability in psychiatric practice: PSRO and utilization review. In R. Westlake (Ed.), *Shaping the future of mental health care*. Cambridge, Massachusetts: Ballinger, 1976.

Newman, D. E. Peer review: A California model. *Psychiatric Annals*, 1974, *4*(1), 75–85.

Newman, D. E., & Luft, L. L. The peer review process: Education versus control. *American Journal of Psychiatry*, 1974, *131*, 1363–1366.

Nobel, J. H. Peer review: Quality control of applied social research. *Science*, 1974, *185*, 916–921.

Ozarin, L. D. PSROs and mental hospitals: A report. *Administration in Mental Health*, 1975, Spring, 19–22.

Richman, A., & Pinsker, H. Medical audit by clinical rounds. *American Journal of Psychiatry*, 1974, *131*, 1370–1374.

Richman, A., & Pinsker, H. Utilization review of psychiatric inpatient care. *American Journal of Psychiatry*, 1973, *130*, 900–903.

Riecken, H. W., & Boruch, R. F. (Eds.). *Social experimentation: A method for planning and evaluating social intervention*. New York: Academic Press, 1974.

Riedel, D. C., Tischler, G. L., & Myers, J. K. *Patient care evaluation in mental health programs*. Cambridge, Massachusetts: Ballinger, 1974.

Thompson, K. S., & Cheng, E. H. A computer package to facilitate compliance with utilization review requirements. *Hospital and Community Psychiatry*, 1976, *27*, 653–656.

Thorne, M. Q. PSRO—Future impact on community mental health centers. *Community Mental Health Journal*, 1975, *11*, 389–393.

Tischler, G. L., & Riedel, D. C. A criterion approach to patient care evaluation. *American Journal of Psychiatry*, 1973, *130*, 913–916.

Weiner, O. D., & Levine, M. S. A process of establishing norms for inpatient length of stay in a community mental health center. *American Journal of Psychiatry*, 1975, *132*, 842–846.

Windle, C., & Ochberg, F. M. Enhancing program evaluation in the community mental health centers program. *Evaluation*, 1975, *2*(2), 31–36.

Windle, C., & Volkman, E. Evaluation in the centers program. *Evaluation*, 1973, *1*(2), 69–70.

15

EVALUATION OF
INDIRECT SERVICES TO SCHOOLS

Elaine N. Taylor and Robert Vineberg

A distinctive feature of "indirect" human services is that they consist of interagency projects that are usually time-limited and goal-oriented. In this chapter, we discuss the process of developing and evaluating indirect service projects in a specific area—mental health consultation to schools. The administrative accountability process requires identifiable projects that have clearly specified objectives. Such projects usually are proposed only after some exploratory or developmental effort. This developmental work is an essential preliminary to initiating indirect services on a systematic basis.

In some settings, one finds that most of the staff time is spent in exploratory or developmental work with a consultee organization without a clear contract about the goals or stages of the consultation. If exploratory work persists as the sole characteristic of indirect service activity, the indirect services program may become vulnerable from an administrative or accountability point of view. Indirect services that do not become goal-oriented and specific will be viewed as an administrator might view an outpatient clinic where the staff members never see any clients, but spend most of their time talking to referral sources about potential clients.

GOAL SPECIFICATION IN INDIRECT SERVICES

The goal specification process becomes the language through which the consultants, clients, and funders can discuss what the indirect service program plans to accomplish, and why it is worth the resources to be expended. The goal specification process also becomes the language among indirect service providers for talking about how service time is being spent and can become the basis for allocating indirect service effort in ways that seem most useful. For purposes of program evaluation, a goal attainment project model is essential if the impact of indirect services is to be assessed.

Responsibility for negotiating project contracts with service recipients falls to the professional providing indirect services. When this proves impossible for a particular client organization, we must be ready to ask whether effective work can be done with that client or if the effort should be redirected. If the client organization is paying for the consultation or other indirect services, it is usually obvious to all concerned that a clear understanding about objectives, tasks, and measurement of results is needed. However, public or other third-party funds often pay for indirect services. In this latter case an inadequate planning and accountability system may go unrecognized until funding for the program is discontinued.

INDIRECT SERVICES IN MENTAL HEALTH

In the mental health field, the rationale for indirect services has been stated in federal legislation (Public Law 94-63). Indirect services are specified as an essential program component in order for a community mental health center to be eligible for federal funding. Indirect services are defined to include both consultation and education, and involve actions directed toward "other" caregivers (e.g., teachers, clergy, youth authority officers) who have *direct* contact with persons or groups needing mental health assistance or being potentially in need of such assistance because of particular circumstances in their lives. The intention is for these services to provide a major thrust toward primary prevention, first by ameliorating environmental conditions commonly associated with the development of mental health problems, and second, by providing access to treatment when symptoms of such disturbance are first detected.

Most mental health facilities have placed a major emphasis upon schools as recipients of their indirect services. This reflects the common viewpoint that the educational system is second only to the family in its potential influence on the emotional development of children (*3*). In the schools the mental health professional may consult with teachers regarding behavioral or mental health problems of specific students, or work with school staff on program-oriented issues or projects. There seems to be increasing emphasis on the latter type of consultation whenever it is feasible.

MOVING BEYOND EXPLORATORY/DEVELOPMENTAL STAGES

Let us assume that the need for clear project definition is understood and the problem is how to perform the task. The groundwork for project selection and definition is a review of school system indirect service needs. Such methodical planning of indirect services has been rare (McClung & Stunden, 1970). Frequently, consultants are viewed with suspicion and lack credibility with school personnel. The credibility of consultants often depends on the consultees first experiencing the value of consultative services through very specific interventions. Most consultants find that they must spend at least several months responding to interests of specific school staff, usually providing case consultation or crisis intervention. Such interventions are usually isolated and nonprogrammatic in nature. After a consultant has effectively built his or her credentials by assisting in the solution of issues about which school personnel are initially willing to seek consultation, the more systematic approach discussed in this chapter can be considered.

PLANNING AND DEVELOPING INDIRECT SERVICES

Planning an indirect service project should ideally proceed through the following seven stages:

1. Survey school needs
2. Identify problems for potential intervention
3. Specify objectives in relation to each problem
4. Identify the focus of intervention and select intervention procedures
5. Assign priorities; select one or two initial projects
6. Develop evaluation methods for interventions having highest priorities
7. Establish a working agreement about each project to be undertaken and the consultant's role in it.

Each of these steps is necessary and each one contributes to the relevance of the services, with the weight of their contribution to relevance typically being directly related to their order on the list. If the survey of needs is inadequate, the relevance of any intervention will be unclear. If problems have not been adequately identified, objectives may be vague and interventions unfocused. If objectives have not been clearly specified, or if the most suitable intervention procedures have not been selected, assignment of priorities may shift away from important problems that are poorly articulated and toward lesser problems that seem more possible to tackle. Evaluation will be irrelevant if objectives are poorly formulated, or will not produce useful information if the interventions chosen are not feasible or not relevant to the objectives. In addition to avoiding a post-hoc evaluation, an added advantage of developing the evaluation procedures during planning is that early consideration of the evaluative process may lead to a rethinking and clearer formulation of some of the earlier steps. Specific evaluation procedures also may help maintain the focus of the subsequent intervention process on the relevant objectives. Finally, the project agreement assures that the project participants share a common view of the work to be undertaken.

This phased approach to planning and evaluating indirect services has been tested recently in 20 schools across the United States (2; 5). The results have been positive and have frequently stimulated requests from nearby schools for similar consultation services.

SURVEY OF SCHOOL NEEDS

The consultant, working with a planning group composed of the principal and the principal's representatives, should conduct a systematic and comprehensive analysis of the school by reviewing strengths, weaknesses, and systemic constraints upon solutions to problems. This analysis may be undertaken by informal interviews with staff and students in small schools (e.g., staff of less than 15 or 20). In larger schools, the analysis will probably require the use of questionnaires designed for a more formal gathering of information from staff and students. In either case, it is critical that the analysis of the school be comprehensive enough to provide the consultant with a general understanding of the school. Information needed includes (a) *general characteristics,* such as grades served, enrollment, school setting, income levels in the community, ethnic composition of student body; (b) *extrinsic factors,* such as community support for schools, community attitude toward new programs; (c) *specific school characteristics,* such as curriculum, special programs, pressure for student achievement, levels of student achievement on standardized tests, costs of vandalism, groups at risk, policies on discipline; (d) *staff characteristics,* such as size and adequacy of staff, ethnic composition of professional staff, provisions for inservice training, turnover of professional staff, problems of current concern to staff; and (e) *the principal's appraisal* of the major needs, problems and special strengths of the school.

All the preceding information can be obtained from the principal. In a pilot study and field trials of an interview guide developed to obtain this information from principals, 68 of the 70 participating principals cooperated and most registered great satisfaction in having the opportunity to appraise their schools systematically (2; 6).

The entire planning group (staff members, principal, and consultant) should have access to additional data gathered from a larger group of staff and students. These data should convey staff and student perceptions of the special problems and needs of the school and any current special issues in the student–student, student–teacher, teacher–teacher, student–principal, teacher–principal, and school–community relationships. Information about perceptions of problems in these areas has been obtained by questionnaires in some field trials, and taken together with the other planning data, has led to fruitful indirect service projects (2).

IDENTIFICATION OF PROBLEMS

At this stage of overall planning, a list of candidate problems for possible interventions is developed by a planning committee (the consultant, the principal and school representatives). If the assessment of needs has been conducted by interviewing the staff and a sample of students, the most important problems will have been mentioned repeatedly and will be easily identified. Where questionnaires are used to survey needs, descriptive statistics (e.g., frequencies or percentages) will provide the basis for identifying the most commonly perceived problems.

SPECIFICATION OF OBJECTIVES

In general, problems will fall into several classes. Among these are problems involving interactions among various elements of the school (students, teachers, administrators, specialized personnel); student characteristics (low motivation, drug abuse, absenteeism, language barriers); teacher characteristics (low motivation, rigidity, lack of standards); principal characteristics (lack of leadership, authoritarian behavior); program and policy problems (inadequate counseling services, inadequate remedial services, dress code), and community problems (changing neighborhood characteristics, divisive community influences, ethnic tensions).

For the most important problems that have been identified, objectives of intervention should be defined. Each objective should specify the nature of the change that needs to be accomplished and the criteria that are felt to be acceptable evidence of goal attainment. Criteria may be "all-or-none" statements, outcome dimensions as described in the example at the end of this chapter, or scaled steps organized according to the goal attainment scaling format presented in Chapter 12.

SELECTION OF PROCEDURE

When objectives have been stated, alternative methods for obtaining these objectives should be considered and the most appropriate procedure selected. The suitability of different interventions will vary depending upon the focus of the problem and the objective sought. Consider the following examples. To deal with potential drug abuse problems among the general student body, the consultant might assist school staff in developing a series of lectures on drug abuse. On the other hand, such a didactic approach would usually be considered ineffective for interventions relevant to an identified group who are already drug abusers. If authoritarianism among staff members is to be addressed, a discussion of the origins and manifestations of authoritarian behavior is probably less effective than "role playing" or some other form of intervention in which persons can directly experience the consequences of authoritarian behavior and also rehearse new ways of behaving.

The general relationship between problem focus and type of intervention is suggested in Table 15.1. The focus or objective may be to impart information or technical competence to school staff or to develop a specific service project for a well-defined "high-risk" group. Such objectives may require the communication of new information and not be complicated by divergent staff attitudes or potential conflict. A second class of problems are those that can be resolved only by changing the attitudes or improving the interpersonal skills of some of the participants—circumstances that are sometimes called "human factors" problems. Finally, there are "system" problems that call for some new decision, or for consensus, or for personal commitment from a diverse group of participants.

Three general intervention strategies are often thought to be differentially useful in relation to the types of problems just described: (a) formal didactic techniques to communicate information; (b) development of ideas and understandings through group discussions and other participative activities led by the consultant; and (c) problem-solving in which the consultant helps the consultees to define the problem, identify contributing factors, note additional information that is needed, generate candidate solutions, and obtain a consensus about the most promising or optimal solution.

TABLE 15.1

Relative Usefulness of Didactic, Participative, and Problem-Solving Intervention Strategies in Relation to the Focus or Goal of Intervention

Intervention procedures	Goals of intervention							
	Education and imparting information	Introducing formalized techniques	Project development for groups	Influencing understanding and attitudes	Enhancing interpersonal skills	Identifying program goals	Designing a new program	Reviewing program policies
Didactic methods including lectures and demonstrations	Usually	Usually	Possibly	Possibly	Possibly	Possibly	Possibly	Possibly
Participative development including discussion, seminar, role-playing, and sensitivity training	Possibly	Possibly	Usually	Usually	Usually	Possibly	Possibly	Possibly
Problem solving	Possibly	Possibly	Possibly	Rarely	Rarely	Usually	Usually	Usually

ASSIGNMENT OF PRIORITIES FOR INTERVENTION

Priority assignment is appropriately delayed until after the objectives and techniques have been identified for several possible projects. Priorities are not judged solely by the importance of problems, but are also based upon the probable cost and benefit of proposed interventions. The importance of a problem is gauged by the extent to which it may disrupt attainment of educational goals. One might use the following guidelines for making such judgments:

1. Problems ranking highest in impact are those that have the potential to render the school inoperable. Racial conflict and student unrest are, under some conditions, such problems.
2. Generally, next in order of disruptiveness are those problems that preclude effective learning by sizable numbers of students. Linguistic barriers between students and teachers (in the form of a foreign language or "nonstandard" English) and drug abuse are good examples of such problems. Problems of this type virtually preclude communication between teachers and students and generally interfere with learning.
3. Problems that might be judged moderately disruptive are systemic problems of the school that interfere with the successful accomplishment of its mission. Difficulties in interpersonal communication among the school staff, or of role definition, intergroup conflicts over school goals and policies, inequities or uncertainties in decision making are examples.
4. Finally, problems at the lower end of the disruptiveness hierarchy are those that interfere with the learning and/or socialization of individual students; for example, the underachieving student or the habitual absentee (6).

Usually a school and mental health facility can undertake only one intervention at a time. The assignment of priorities should be based upon the sequence or combination of interventions that will maximize the total benefit of the consultation services to the school. The combination chosen will need to be based not only on considerations of problem impact, but also on the estimates of the cost in time, personnel, and money for each intervention, and the probable success of each intervention. Fine discriminations of cost–benefit will not be needed in order to reach the objective of this step, namely that the consultant and consultees reach an agreement, based on a considered judgment, about the problems that are the best focus for immediate action in the continuing collaborative work.

DEVELOPMENT OF METHODS FOR EVALUATION

The last step *before* agreeing on a work plan is the development of methods for evaluating the intervention. Feedback and evaluation have been described as the most neglected areas in school consultation programs (7). As with any evaluation, one may attempt to assess ultimate outcomes or have to be content with information on intermediate outcomes. The evaluation must also monitor the process of the intervention.

Final outcomes (products) of intervention in a school setting will be changes in students. These may focus on attitudes or self-concepts; classroom behaviors such as attending, following directions, and persistence; patterns of rebellious, disruptive, bizarre, withdrawn, or overdependent behaviors; academic performance; and plans for future development in both vocational and avocational areas.

Intermediate outcomes might include changes in teachers, counselors, administrators, supporting staff, or parents that are believed to be a necessary prerequisite or correlate to a final desired change in students. Examples of intermediate outcomes are increased information about children at different stages of development; knowledge and skill in the use of different techniques for interacting with children; and understanding and acceptance of teachers who have different ways of doing things. Intermediate outcomes may also be the addition or alteration of specific programs such as career education, leadership development, driver education, drug education, and sex education; or changes in school policies regarding promotion, dress code, suspension and expulsion practices, and so forth.

Process measures are data about the occurrence of intervention activities of the consultant and consultees. These are typically such things as continuing attendance of consultees at a series of lectures; increase in level and uniformity of participation among consultees over a series of discussions; emergence of new concepts or ideas during role playing; progression through various phases in a problem-solving process, or decreasing occurrence of subjective, emotional remarks and increasing occurrence of task-oriented statements that indicate acceptance or compromise during problem solving. Examples of instruments that have been developed as prototypes for such measurement can be found in Montague and Taylor (4).

These different kinds of measurement serve different functions. Measures of product or ultimate outcome provide the clearest indication of program success. However, it is not always feasible to measure final outcomes. In such cases the measurement of intermediate outcomes may provide indirect indications of program success. Intermediate outcomes can also be available early enough to provide corrective feedback during the project. Finally, intermediate outcomes may suggest where the program failed, if ultimate goals are not attained.

Process measurement also serves diagnostic functions. It is used during the intervention to monitor whether planned actions are being carried out and can also help determine why an unsuccessful project failed to attain its objectives.

It may take considerable ingenuity to work out practical outcome measures that are relevant to project goals. The examples at the end of this chapter, and in Chapter 12, on goal attainment scaling, may be helpful. Mannino and Shore (1975) have reviewed 35 studies of the outcome of mental health consultation. Some of the studies they cite will also provide suggestive examples.

AGREEMENT ON THE PROJECT

Under ideal circumstances the agreement to implement a consultation project will be based on a thoughtful execution of the entire planning sequence. In a large or complex organization, the planning steps may need to proceed fairly formally within a planning committee. In a small organization, the consultant may carry out most of the process informally.

The need for an explicit *agreement* with the agency (e.g., a school) is quite separate from the mental health center's need for a well-formulated project plan by the consultant. A working agreement with the school functions to acknowledge the school's desire for the project and its ability to provide the occasion, setting, and resources to carry it out. The organization that is administratively and financially responsible for the consultant needs the project plan for different reasons. The plan is the mechanism by which the administration knows that the school is willing to use the consultant, that the problems addressed are not trivial, and that the consultant will be responsible for obtaining the information necessary to evaluate the project. This latter responsibility rests logically with the consultant, since the program evaluation techniques must be designed as an integral part of the specific project (and because the funding of the consultant's position may depend on the quality of the evaluation even more than is the case with direct services). Each consultant should be able to draw upon the program evaluation resources of his or her own organization for help. Nevertheless, it is doubtful that this type of accountability is feasible unless the consultant responsible for a project is also responsible to see that the project has a design that allows evaluation, and that the project is, in fact, evaluated.

AN EXAMPLE OF EVALUATION PLANS FOR A PROJECT

A few illustrations of the relationship between objectives, interventions, and evaluation measures may assist the reader in seeing where to begin in designing the evaluation of a school project. Tables 15.2–15.5 present examples drawn from a coordinated series of projects undertaken in a large urban school district by Weeks, Yen, Krenkel, Lathan, Gin, and Noronha (8). The projects arose from concerns associated with a desegregation program in the elementary grades. Four overall goals were identified as follows:

1. Increased multicultural understanding
2. Reduced tension and conflict related to desegregation
3. Increased community support and involvement
4. Reduced disparity between minority and nonminority students on oral and written academic achievement.

Many specific objectives and projects were identified in relation to these goals. Tables 15.2–15.5 list a few of these objectives and the corresponding interventions and measures. The measures are labeled as process measures,

TABLE 15.2

Objectives, Interventions, and Measures Related to the Goal of "Increased Multicultural Understanding"

Objectives	Interventions	Measures
Objective 1: 40% of the students in the schools will show an increase in multicultural understanding and appreciation.	1. Work in study groups in each class will be multi-ethnic. 2. Multi-ethnic materials will be used in general education (e.g., reading, social studies, art, music). 3. Ethnic materials and ethnic resources (speakers and programs) will be used to show contributions of all ethnic groups. 4. Students will plan and carry out ethnic and multicultural lunches, holidays, celebrations. 5. At least one field trip per semester will explore the culture and life style of this metropolitan area.	*Process:* Records of observation, activities and attendance used to verify that 1. Work groups in classrooms are racially mixed. 2. Each classroom has used multi-ethnic materials in social studies, art, music, reading, etc. 3. Materials and speakers indicate contributions of all ethnic groups. 4. Events are student planned and carried out. 5. At least one field trip per semester was conducted involving each pupil. *Ultimate outcome* 1. Preprogram survey. Grades 2 and 5 take multiple choice items sampling knowledge of facts and understandings extracted from multicultural materials to be used in intervention. 2. Postprogram survey data from postprogram survey will be compiled by grade, schools, and racial/ethnic group and compared with preprogram survey findings.
Objective 2: 30% of the students in the schools will demonstrate a decrease in voluntary self-imposed racial isolation.	The interventions are the same as carried out for Objective 1.	*Process:* Same as for Objective 1. *Intermediate outcome:* Third and sixth grade teachers identify pupils who tend to interact exclusively with pupils of same racial or ethnic group in various situations (e.g., playground, classroom working groups, changing classes). Periodic observations are made to determine whether downward trend in such voluntary, self-imposed racial isolation occurs.

454

Objective 3: 70% of the teachers in the schools will demonstrate an increase in the use of multicultural materials and ethnic programs.

1. The resource center will provide a list of ethnic and multi-cultural resources, including materials, programs, ethnic consultants and speakers.
2. Three teachers from each school will participate in a 4-day workshop on the development and use of student and staff multicultural materials.
3. Resource center staff will go to schools on request for followup help in use of materials.
4. The resource center will develop multi-ethnic materials that are lacking in social studies, art, music, etc.
5. Principals will encourage the use of the multicultural resources in their schools.

Process

1. The workshop participants complete a report form describing similar workshops conducted by them in their schools (number of meetings, number attending, list of materials developed subsequently).
2. Resource center staff will complete logs on followup visitations.

Intermediate Outcome: A random sample of 25% of K–6 teachers will complete a questionnaire indicating their level of usage of the listed materials. The questionnaire will be completed three times: at the end of the 2nd, 4th, and 6th months of the program.

Objective 4: 70% of the teachers will demonstrate an increase in knowledge and application of techniques for working with diverse ethnic groups and techniques for handling the special learning problems of minorities.

1. The teachers from each school will participate in a four-day workshop (simultaneously with Objective 3) on techniques for working with diverse ethnic groups of children and special learning problems of minorities.
2. Resource center staff will visit schools on request for followup help in application of techniques learned in workshop.

Process

1. External evaluator attends workshop and gathers data on attendance, activities, and teacher and workshop staff critique of the activities.
2. Principal of each school, assisted by an external evaluator will visit the classroom of each teacher at least once during the year to observe a multicultural activity.

Intermediate outcome: Principal rated instructional activities as "excellent," "satisfactory," or "needs improvement" must be expressed by external evaluator.

Objective 5: 50% of the parents who attend two Saturday workshops will have used multicultural materials in their homes and taken their child on at least two multicultural field experiences by the end of the school year.

Staff of resource center will conduct two all day Saturday workshops for parents in ways that parents can reinforce multicultural understanding at home.

Intermediate Outcome: External evaluator will mail to parents attending both Saturday workshops a questionnaire requesting report on subsequent use of multicultural materials in the home and on type and number of field experiences they have provided for their children.

TABLE 15.3

Objectives, Interventions, and Measures Related to the Goal of "Reduced Tension and Conflict Related to Desegregation"

Objectives	Interventions	Measures
Objective 1: Selected school counselors will be prepared to provide counseling for minority students who exhibit isolation and racial tension.	Selected counselors participate in in-service training program in techniques and methods of reducing Minority pupils' isolation and racial tension.	*Process* 1. Data on attendance and activities of in-service training sessions will be gathered by external evaluator who attends sessions. 2. Data on the number of students who have received this specialized counseling, gathered by external evaluator who will interview each selected counselor at least three times during the year to monitor their activities and their record keeping.

Objective 2: By the end of the school year, isolation and racial tension will be reduced by 50% as demonstrated by a decrease in pupil acting-out behaviors, poor classroom performance, referrals to special placement classes, suspensions, fighting and vandalism.

1. Pupils will participate in a specially designed and supervised school bus program that will enhance pupil interaction in route to and from school.

2. A crisis room with counseling services will be established. The supportive counseling will assist pupils to fit back into the mainstream of the school when short-term problems have been dealt with.

3. Counselors will train teachers in positive intervention techniques such as role-playing among pupils to encourage them to perceive themselves and others differently.

4. Counselors will assist faculty in planning interracial/ethnic programs in cooperation with the P.E., Art, and Music teachers for yard and noon-time activities.

5. Counselors will assist teachers, administrators, pupils and parents in developing flexible coping skills to deal with unexpected and/or frustrating situations.

6. Pupils identified as "high risk" learners will receive direct counseling for negative behavior patterns in learning and citizenship situations.

Ultimate outcome: Principals will maintain a daily record of conflict incidents between pupils and teachers or other adults in the school and among pupils which, in his judgment, stem primarily from desegregation/integration activities. Records made early in the school year will be compared to those made late in the school year.

457

TABLE 15.4

Objectives, Interventions and Measures in Relation to the Goal of "Increased Community Support and Involvement"

Objectives	Interventions	Measures
Objective 1: There will be an increase in parental involvement with the school as measured by at least a 30% increase in attendance by parents at school functions.	Specially trained coordinators will encourage previously noninvolved parents (especially low-income and parents whose language is other than English) to attend and participate in school functions by 1. Telephoning parents. 2. Multilingual announcements. 3. Personal contacts. 4. Information bulletins and newsletters. 5. Arranging for child care and transportation.	*Intermediate outcome:* Principals will keep records of parental attendance at school site functions during the year. Records from October–November will be compared with records from April–May.
Objective 2: There will be a 30% increase in the use of community resources.	Parents will be provided with information about various community resources (such as tutorial centers, health clinics, community recreational programs, field trip sites, guest speakers, etc.) at school functions. (See Objective 1 above.)	*Intermediate outcome:* Parents will indicate on a checklist their frequency of usage of community resources during personal contacts (see Objective 1 Intervention 3). Near the end of the school year they will be mailed a second checklist to complete. Data collected early and late will be compared.
Objective 3: There will be an increase in parental knowledge of policies and programs within the school district.	Specially trained coordinators will: 1. Develop and distribute multilingual news bulletins covering topics of special concern to parents. 2. Inform parents by personal contact or phone of the discussion topics at various meetings which might be of concern to them or to their child's school regarding: (a) school assignments, (b) transportation, (c) school operations, etc. (d) board of educational policies. 3. Conduct informal multi-lingual workshops to raise parental skills and knowledge of educational techniques, programs and policies.	*Process:* A questionnaire will be mailed to parents to see if they have received the news bulletins, been contacted by phone or in personal visits, etc. *Intermediate outcome:* The same questionnaire will be designed to assess parental knowledge of policies and programs of the school. The questionnaire will be mailed to parents near the beginning and again at the end of the school year.

458

TABLE 15.5

Objectives, Interventions, and Measures in Relation to the Goal of "Reduced Disparity between Minority and Nonminority Students in Oral and Written Academic Achievement"

Objectives	Interventions	Measures
Objective 1: Teachers who have completed a workshop on instructional techniques for improving oral and written expression will screen minority pupils in their classrooms on a diagnostic checklist designed by the district.	Remedial teachers, working with these classroom teachers, will use the diagnostic instruments to measure proficiency of pupils in oral/written communication skills.	*Process:* The principal will forward a copy of the individual diagnostic screening checklist for each minority pupil to the district office. These data will be compiled district-wide by school, grade, racial/ethnic group, skill and rating.
Objective 2: After participation in the workshop, teachers will receive monthly inservice training. Seventy percent of teachers will demonstrate skills in individualization of instruction, use of media in language instruction, and preparation of instructional materials that are sensitive to cultural differences.	Remedial teachers will assist classroom teachers in developing a repertoire of prescriptive teaching techniques and instructional materials. Teachers will utilize the techniques and materials, assess their relevance and effectiveness in the classroom, and revise unworkable materials and techniques.	*Intermediate outcome:* The workshop and inservice training staff will visit each classroom at least twice during the year to observe language instruction. The teacher's instructional activity will be rated "excellent," "satisfactory," or "needs further improvement." Opinion by teacher and observer as to what will contribute to "further improvement" must be recorded.
Objective 3: Minority pupils who receive a rating of "unsatisfactory" in the screening will participate, in their regular classrooms, in special learning activities. Upon re-evaluation at the end of the year, 50% of the targeted pupils will be rated "satisfactory."	1. Remedial teachers will assist classroom teachers in developing activities for children involving dramatic play, taping, cassettes. 2. Children will participate in dramatization, choral readings, video taping, film making, and other sequential learnings to bring about feelings of success and security in oral/written communication. 3. Children will gather, organize and present information and materials of a cultural-social and experiential nature using above media. They will review and critique each others presentations.	*Process:* Teachers will complete a questionnaire reporting the degree of utilization of these materials and techniques and offer their opinions on their appropriateness and effectiveness. *Ultimate outcome:* The diagnostic checklist will be complete again at the end of the year. Pre- and post- ratings of targeted pupils will be compared.

459

intermediate outcomes, and ultimate outcomes. A similar classification might be applied to the objectives. Therefore an "ultimate objective" could have process, intermediate, and ultimate outcome measures. While a "process objective" is logically subordinate to outcome objectives, process measures are the only indicators relevant to the attainment of a process objective as such.

The project leader and project evaluators report that an early step after project funding was to review the objectives and measures to be sure that they were still appropriate (1). This resulted in some adjustments in the levels of attainment expected, and some changes in format. In this large project, specific evaluation staff were assigned to work with operating staff in an ongoing way during the implementation. The cost of such evaluation staff are ordinarily budgeted as part of the total project cost in large grant-funded projects such as this. In smaller projects that arise in the context of a mental health consultation relationship, the evaluation work may best be carried out by the consultant as an ongoing part of the work, and the consultant must budget the necessary time for the evaluation effort.

The experienced evaluators who participated in this school project reported that the evaluation activities seemed to serve several useful functions. The evaluation approach that was employed demanded clear thinking about project objectives when the initial funding proposal was written and again when implementation began. The discipline of formulating a realistic measurement plan inhibited the tendency to make grandiose, unattainable claims of potential project impact and reduced the resulting eventual disappointment that follows the inevitable failure to reach unattainable aspirations.

The ongoing presence of the evaluator during implementation also stimulated questions about project management problems that might otherwise have been ignored. Operating staff were often uncomfortable about this aspect of the evaluator's role, but a tactful evaluator sometimes became a valued consultant after a time. The clarity of the evaluation plan, which informed operating staff how their program would be evaluated, was important in enabling them to work more comfortably with the evaluator.

The evaluation report served as a public record of the activities and results of the project. This protected the school from the criticism that "all that tax money" was spent without knowing what came of it. The evaluation staff told us that one concrete effect of evaluation has been that when critics attacked a particular project, school officials could ask the critics if they had read the evaluation report. This would sometimes raise the level of discussion of the project. Nevertheless, the evaluators reported ruefully that sometimes the discussion had risen only to the level at which the critic, having now read the report, dismissed the document as "totally useless."

Program staff often hope that when an evaluation report clearly documents the success of their program, this will lead to extended funding. In the real world, carefully evaluated projects are probably the least likely to survive. This is not the paradox it might seem. New undertakings, especially those supported by temporary extramural funding, are in a poor position to compete for stable funding from local sources, yet are also the most likely to be evaluated. Traditional functions that are not under public attack are the most likely to continue and the least likely to be vigorously evaluated. Mental health consultation is in an intermediate position, as a required function in federally funded community mental health centers. As federal support is withdrawn and replaced by local support, indirect services are often seen as having a lower service priority. A collection of evaluation reports will not change this fact. Yet if the indirect service program has attracted a constituency that is ready to fight for its survival, these reports can be useful tools both for the advocates and for the decision makers.

SUMMARY

This chapter presented a project goal attainment model for evaluating mental health consultation services to schools. This model supplements the management information techniques outlined in Chapter 8. After the consultant accomplishes initial entry tasks and is ready to negotiate a specific new project with the consultee organization, the consultant must establish a project contract that can be evaluated, with identified objectives and outcome indicators. While this is not an easy task, without a viable project contract, a meaningful evaluation of the impact of mental health consultation is not possible.

REFERENCE NOTES

1. We appreciate the helpfulness of Mr. Harold L. Weeks, Director of Research, Ms. Katherine Yen, ESAA Evaluator, and Mr. Paul Cheng, ESAA Program Coordinator, all of the San Francisco Unified School District, in sharing with us their experiences in educational evaluation.
2. Goffard, S. J., Taylor, E. N., & Vineberg, R. *Field trials of instruments designed to survey problems in schools.* (Tech. Rep. No. WD-CA-75-18.) Alexandria, Virginia: Human Resources Research Organization, 1975. (Available from HumRRO, 300 North Washington Street, Alexandria, Virginia 23314.)
3. MacLennan, B., Quinn, R., & Windle, C. Foreword in E. K. Montague & E. N. Taylor, *Preliminary handbook on procedures for evaluating mental health indirect service programs in schools.* (Tech. Rep. No. 71-18.) Alexandria, Virginia: Human Resources Research Organization, 1971. (For availability see Note 2.)
4. Montague, E. K., & Taylor, E. N. *Preliminary handbook on procedures for evaluating mental health indirect service programs in schools.* (Tech. Rep. No. 71-18.) Alexandria, Virginia: Human Resources Research Organization, 1971. (For availability see Note 2.)
5. Taylor, E. N., & Vineberg, R. (Eds.). *Mental health consultant reports of the field trials of instruments for surveying problems in schools.* (Tech. Rep. No. FR-WD-CA-75-28.) Alexandria, Virginia: Human Resources Research Organization, 1975. (For availability see Note 2.)
6. Taylor, E. N., Vineberg, R., & Goffard, S. J. *Surveying school problems: Some individual, group, and system indicators.* (Tech. Rep. No. 74-22.) Alexandria, Virginia: Human Resources Research Organization, 1974. (For availability see Note 2.)
7. Behavior Science Corporation. *Evaluation of the impact of community mental health center consultation services on school systems.* (BASICO Tech. Rep. No. 645-01.) Los Angeles: Behavior Science Corporation, 1973.

8. Weeks, H. L., Yen, K., Krenkel, N., Lathan, D., Gin, S., & Noronha, F. *Final evaluation report, elementary, Emergency School Aid Act, school year 1974-75.* San Francisco: San Francisco Unified School District, 1975. (Available from H. L. Weeks, San Francisco Unified School District, 170 Fell Street, San Francisco, California 94102.)

REFERENCES

Mannino, F. V., & Shore, M. F. Effecting change through consultation. In F. V. Mannino, B. W. MacLennan, & M. F. Shore (Eds.), *The practice of mental health consultation.* (DHEW Publication No. ADM 74-112.) Washington, D. C.: U. S. Government Printing Office, 1975.

McClung, R. B., & Stunden, A. H. *Mental health consultation programs for children.* (PHS Publication No. 2006.) Rockville, Maryland: National Institute of Mental Health, 1970.

V

RETROSPECT AND PROSPECT

The final section of this volume assesses major strengths, areas needing development, and future directions within the program evaluation field. In this context we also discuss the areas of training most relevant to the preparation of program evaluators and evaluation-oriented professionals and administrators.

16

EVALUATION: CURRENT STRENGTHS
AND FUTURE DIRECTIONS

C. Clifford Attkisson, William A. Hargreaves,
Mardi J. Horowitz, and James E. Sorensen

In this chapter we present an overview of the current state of the art in human service program evaluation. Since each of the preceding chapters represents a specific summary, our emphasis at this point will be to review the current status of four general domains of program evaluation (structural, process, outcome, and community impact) and to review the status of major evaluation methods that are now available for general use (information systems, need assessment, and outcome assessment). In addition we assess what is now known about optimal organizational role functions for evaluators and venture some thoughts about evaluator roles of the future. Our comments are organized to respond to four important questions that must be raised about contemporary program evaluation: What kinds of evaluation activities can now be expected to make a useful contribution to program management? Is there consensus about how evaluation activities should be organized and implemented? What role expectations will the future evaluator face? What methodologies and guidelines will be available in the future? In a concluding section we will suggest several goals on which we might focus our attention so that future program evaluation will be more effective and useful.

THE STATE OF THE ART

We know that useful evaluation cannot proceed without consensus on program goals. When program goals are so controversial or so vague that no workable measures of their accomplishment can be defined, then evaluation is not possible. Legislators and administrators are slowly beginning to understand this crucial step in the evaluation process. Because realistic statements of goals and objectives occur so rarely in human service systems, much evaluation must be "goal free" by default. Fortunately, even goal free evaluation seems to stimulate more appropriate attention to goal setting and the specification of intended program results in objective, measurable language. Program and client goals can range across many different content areas. These content areas tend to define what type of evaluation is undertaken and the evaluation methods that are employed. Therefore, as the evaluator undertakes to assess the attainment of program objectives, choices must be made as to the main focus of evaluation. Evaluative attention is ordinarily distributed across structural, process, outcome, and community impact objectives.

Structural objectives are often identified in regulations affecting the program (e.g., requirements and standards related to availability of various types of services, adequacy of facilities, staffing patterns, personnel systems, accounting systems, case records), but the monitoring of compliance with these structural requirements is usually handled by a business manager or program administrator. Recently, however, program evaluators have become increasingly involved in evaluating structural compliance. These activities are best conceived as extensions of traditional accounting and administrative approaches to accountability and often can have a powerful impact on organizational structure and service capacity. Evaluation studies of program process and effectiveness often suggest innovations or problem solutions that require changes in program structure. To ensure effective implementation of program decisions that have grown out of evaluation activities, the evaluator may work closely with other program staff to install needed changes and to monitor their effects.

Evaluative effort is frequently devoted primarily to *process* monitoring. For example, the evaluator may examine demographic characteristics of clients served in order to assess the attainment of accessibility goals, may monitor service activity levels to contribute to cost-finding by linking costs to effort and other resources (the goal of efficiency), may monitor the referral of clients from one level of care to another (the goal of continuity of care), and may contribute to utilization review and other quality assurance activities (the goals of appropriateness and quality of services in relation to existing process standards). These activities are all examples of process evaluation. In process monitoring the evaluator carries out at least two distinct roles: (a) improving the information procedures used by the program to assemble process data, and (b) examining these data in relation to current management issues and objectives so that program leaders can make more informed decisions. These two roles are distinct from routine data gathering, storage, and report generation processes. The latter may also fall under the direction of the evaluator, but in larger organizations one increasingly sees this statistical work closely coordinated with accounting, budgeting, and cost-finding in an integrated management information system using the methods described in Chapters 6, 7, and 8.

Outcome information is also being introduced into human service management and planning. Outcome evaluation tends initially to focus on routine monitoring using very simple (many would say simplistic) global outcome measures, often in response to reporting requirements imposed by state or federal agencies. The evaluator may then supplement this basic outcome monitoring with time-limited outcome studies involving more intensive assessment of selected samples of clients. These outcome studies usually do not consume a large share of the evaluation effort, especially when pressure to develop routine process and outcome monitoring procedures is competing for evaluative resources. Even in established evaluation units one may see few outcome studies. This is partly because outcome study results are available only after several months or longer, and therefore it is difficult to plan outcome evaluation studies that can be kept relevant to changing management issues. However, lack of attention to outcome also reflects the lack of experience and skill on the part of evaluators and program managers in formulating useful outcome studies. Both of these limiting factors probably account for the tendency toward specific, decision-oriented outcome studies being undertaken only in relatively large programs with well developed program evaluation resources. We expect this pattern to continue; outcome studies will be undertaken mostly in larger programs, but almost all programs will learn to make effective use of routine outcome monitoring.

Evaluation of the *community impact* of programs is still almost nonexistant. This deficiency is significant when viewed in the context of one of the major crises in contemporary service planning and management. This crisis stems from our failure to integrate the human services at the community level, and our failure to present to funders, and to the public, an understandable rationale for the present pattern and cost of the total human service system. A first step would be to develop a workable framework of objectives for regional services systems, in terms that would allow direct monitoring of service adequacy. We also need a widely acceptable method of measuring the degree of human services integration in a community. Such measurement seems possible in principle, although even if we succeed in measuring the degree of service integration it would still be a further research challenge to study the relationship of service integration to service effectiveness and community impact. As we move toward the time when effective regional planning and evaluation will be possible, evaluators can contribute to service integration by laying the groundwork in their own organization. This can be accomplished by developing methods of evaluating service integration, as well as developing linkages between functional elements or components within their organization. We also encourage evaluators to support the process of regional planning, and thereby attend to the linkage of their own agency with the rest of what some have called the current "nonsystem" of human services.

Community planning and service integration can be conceptualized as essentially process measures and methods within the community impact focus of program evaluation. Beyond the process measurement issue are the problems of determining the community impact effects of a specific program or a configuration of programs. The interdependency of variables within communities and current methodological limitations preclude meaningful analysis of actual community impact at this time. The needed developmental work will most likely include comparisons among sets of care systems in several different communities, with multiple measures of the characteristics of communities, of care systems, of populations at risk, and of clients before and after various service episodes.

MAJOR EVALUATION TOOLS

Many new evaluation methods are being developed to make evaluation tasks easier, and as a result to make useful evaluation available to an ever widening group of programs. In this volume we presented three important methodological areas: information systems, need assessment, and outcome evaluation.

INFORMATION SYSTEMS

If one had to pick the most important technical development in the evaluation field in recent years, it would probably be the concept of the integrated management information system. At this point within the text the reader should realize that one cannot install some ready-made computer package from a mail-order catalog and expect to have a useful tool. An integrated information system within an organization must be achieved, not simply installed.

Furthermore, information procedures drift into misalignment and obsolescence if not actively maintained. This is true of every organization's information system, and every organization has one, regardless of the organization's size or whether the organization uses a computer. The important tools now available are the concepts and design procedures that can be employed by the evaluator to review an organization's management information practices to determine whether the attained level of information capability meets internal and external information requirements as cost–effectively as possible. Evaluators sometimes feel they are distracted from "real" program evaluation by the organization's urgent needs for improved information procedures, but, as Lund (*1*) has reported, such "diversions" can lead to valuable improvements in the organization's management capability while also providing valuable lessons for the evaluator.

NEED ASSESSMENT

Need assessment is the effort to determine the appropriate mix of human services for a community and to detect important gaps in those services. The program evaluator often is called upon to help with need assessment, and indeed there are some relatively simple approaches that have been found useful in program planning and in strengthening requests for funding. Chapters 9 and 10 discussed available methods such as social and health indicator analyses, social area surveys, and community group approaches. No one of these approaches can provide definitive conclusions about needs, but taken together they blend available methods for gathering data with essential political processes to converge on informed decisions about service priorities. Many of the approaches are useful across the entire range of human services planning. There is an emerging consensus that need assessment and planning should be coordinated within geographic regions for all health and other human services, rather than expecting narrowly defined categorical programs with their vested interests to plan to fill gaps or avoid excessive duplication. New legislation and organizational efforts are attempting to strengthen regional planning, and the evaluator can sometimes gain useful help on need assessment from such agencies.

OUTCOME EVALUATION

Outcome assessment tools have also seen major development in recent years. This reflects a growing consensus about the service objectives in many types of human service programs. Earlier arguments about which outcome dimensions represent the "real" primary objectives have been replaced with the recognition that programs have multiple objectives and the evaluator must attend to them all. For example, mental health programs providing services to patients who display irrational acts are concerned with reducing symptoms, maintaining the social functioning of the person, treating the patient in the least restrictive environment possible, and protecting the community from destructive behavior. There may be conflict about the relative importance of various goals, but multiple perspectives are no longer seen as an insuperable barrier to evaluation—these are facts of life with which the evaluator must cope. Only the total lack of objectives leads to disaster. The competent evaluator strives to examine the range of service outcomes that are important to all groups that have a vested interest in the program.

We do not mean to imply that the major outcome measurement problems have already been solved. One needs to be especially cautious when interpeting any outcome data that do not comprehensively sample the relevant dimensions of outcome and the relevant followup time periods. Clients, especially those treated for psychological problems, may become more aware of problems during the course of treatment. Therapies often include techniques that promote self-recognition, stimulate awareness of conflicting feelings, and encourage problem-solving thought. Such therapies, if successful, may temporarily increase the level of subjective distress in self-reports by clients, or influence ratings by an observer listening to a client's more insightful posttreatment descriptions. For example, some clients defensively avoid recognition of difficult issues before treatment, face issues and even levels of feeling more squarely during treatment, and on rating scales or symptom checklists report more anxiety and depression *after* rather than *before* service delivery. On the basis of individualized treatment goals or data on other aspects of the client's functioning, evaluators may be able to distinguish such instances from cases where increased distress is an undesirable outcome. Similarly, a client may attain a treatment goal of becoming more assertive and less compliant with previously dominant relatives or friends. Ratings from these significant others may then give a false negative impression, or seemingly positive reports from relatives may sometimes reflect the failure to attain such a treatment goal. Client satisfaction can also be misleading. Ratings of satisfaction often seem unrealistically high. Nevertheless, a tough service provider who really confronts a client may cause the client some anguish, yet be very helpful in the long run. In the meantime such clients may be angered and rate themselves less satisfied compared to clients who are comforted but helped less in other ways. Finally, both positive changes and relapse may take place only later, after ratings and reports are accumulated, unless long range followup is undertaken. These measurement issues require careful attention when major program decisions are to be based on an outcome study.

As agreement evolves regarding the major outcome dimensions and how to measure them, evaluators are moving toward an even more difficult issue —how to combine ongoing outcome monitoring and time-limited outcome studies to obtain the most cost–effective improvement in program management. We see no consensus on this evaluation strategy question as yet, and we encourage evaluators to report their successes and failures in utilizing outcome information.

THE ROLE OF THE EVALUATOR

The organizational role of the evaluator has received much attention in the preceding chapters. There seems to be a growing consensus that evaluators make their most effective contribution when they are ongoing members of the decision-making team. The need for evaluator participation at all important administrative levels implies that program evaluation resources are needed at each major administrative level, rather than expecting managers to rely solely on evaluation carried out at other administrative levels. The need for ongoing, direct evaluator participation in administration also implies that managers usually will want to develop an internal evaluation staff oriented to the specific evaluative needs of their program level rather than contract exclusively with outside evaluators. Much current evaluation effort is still focused on one-time summative evaluations of temporary grant-funded service projects, while the ongoing bulk of human services goes unevaluated. This distribution of effort does not match our current understanding of how to maximize the impact of evaluation. Evaluators must be close enough to the decision-making process to grasp clearly the needs and problems of management. If evaluative results are not used under these circumstances, then the evaluator is not doing the job effectively.

Evaluators at federal, state, and community levels of program management are making some headway in sorting out their roles in relation to each other. The major clarification is coming from a growing acknowledgement of a single organizing principle—evaluators at each level must identify the most cost–effective way to aid management decisions within *their own level* of program organization. This principle follows from our conviction that an evaluator is most effective when he or she functions as a part of the decision-making group for which the evaluation work is done. While these assertions may seem obvious, if taken seriously they can help prevent common false starts in designing program evaluation strategies. For example, in a statewide reporting system only relatively simple aggregate information is necessary or usable at the state level for such tasks as portraying to the legislature what the budgetary appropriations are buying for the taxpayer. Yet groups that design such systems easily get caught up in their enthusiasm and curiosity and add additional details "that might be nice to know." The result can be a reporting system that is more elaborate, and therefore more expensive, than is justified.

State or federal evaluators often suggest that broad scale outcome monitoring can be used to compare programs and identify those that are below standard in effectiveness. There are problems in the utilization of such nonexperimental comparisons, and this area needs further development. Nevertheless, states and the federal government do have the responsibility to evaluate major funding programs and regulatory policies. For this latter purpose a routine reporting system will rarely, if ever, be adequate. Instead, planners must formulate the potential policy alternatives, estimate their relative cost–effectiveness on the basis of existing information (here some data from reporting systems may be useful), and then design specific studies to compare the most promising alternatives.

Program evaluation efforts in state level human service agencies can also be directed toward enhancing program evaluation capability at the community facility level. Typical activities include developing evaluation methods and materials, adopting evaluation staffing standards and job descriptions for state institutions, providing consultation and technical assistance, promoting statewide exchange among evaluators, and evaluating local evaluation activities. We have observed several states carrying out this secondary role quite skillfully, but this remains the exception rather than the rule.

AN EVALUATOR OF THE FUTURE

In a more whimsical mood, what can we anticipate about the life of the evaluator of the future? We claim no special gifts as writers of utopian science fiction, but we do have a view of the future that is based partly on current trends in the field, and partly on our own hopes and trepidations. Our purpose is to encourage the reader to envision other possible futures, and choose a potential future that is worth working toward.

Our evaluator of the future will function in an organizational environment where managers and staff are well informed about the role of the evaluator and, based on this knowledge, have well-formed expectations of the program evaluator. Administrators will have experienced the value and the impact of timely management information on their decision tasks, and will expect the management information and evaluation staff to anticipate correctly the occasions and tasks for which these data will be needed.

Creative managers will imagine many kinds of information that could be relevant to emerging problems and anticipated decisions. The evaluator can expect to be deluged with information demands that are unpredictable, unorganized, but put forth with great urgency. The evaluator will be expected to quickly evaluate the feasibility and cost of meeting each request, to help the organization leaders prioritize competing information needs, to be able to allocate evaluation effort in a flexible manner, and to meet most of these information needs quickly and with very little expense to the program. The evaluator will be expected to manage this rapidly changing environment without ever losing perspective on the organization's overall operating constraints and its long range objectives. The evaluator will be expected to maintain a core evaluation function that will independently and systematically examine the performance of each program component. From these core activities the evaluator will be expected to come forth with evaluative reviews that are seen by a majority of the staff as thoughtful and fair-minded and yet also seen as directly relevant to key operating difficulties of the organization. The evaluator will be expected to disseminate these reviews so skillfully through participation in organizational management that creative, constructive changes usually follow.

The front line staff of the agency of the future will also present different expectations to the evaluator. They will be more accustomed to their unit's productivity and effectiveness being open to public view. They will understand some of the value of this increased visibility, and in a supportive organization they will enjoy the friendly rivalry among work units engendered by the inevitable intra-organizational comparisons. In a nonsupportive organization they may also learn how a poor unit performance record can be used to remove an unpopular supervisor or invoke the wrath of client advocates.

The staff will also be accustomed to the routine information needs of the organization because standard data collection procedures will have been in operation for a long time, and will be fairly similar from one organization to another. They will also have experienced competent management information systems in which clerical staff handle every data gathering task that does not require professional judgment, using methods by which data can be recorded simply and quickly, and when once recorded can be retrieved, corrected, or supplemented without wasteful redundancy. They will have come to depend on a variety of information system products to provide handy support and assistance in their work. These products will include client rosters, scheduling assistance, accurate historical records on clients, and summaries of staff effort and productivity. Having experienced this level of information capability, service providers and managers will be impatient with evaluators who allow information systems to drift into cumbersome redundancy and useless irrelevance.

We therefore expect evaluators of the future to be more productive, even if no less frustrated or immersed in organizational struggles than they are today. The evaluator's initial education and beginning work experience will have fostered the necessary skill required for rapid recognition of common decision-making situations that call for various types of evaluation activities. The evaluator will have gained carefully supervised experience in working with program managers to negotiate and execute specific evaluation tasks. These skills will be aided by powerful new tools to allow greater evaluator productivity and impact.

In larger organizations, computer-based management information systems will have been established and will be taken for granted, but their maintenance and revision will be a persistent problem. The great depth of management information system experience in similar organizations will aid the evaluator, and it should be as easy to call in a consulting systems analyst as it now is to call in an accountant to set up or revise an accounting system. Often the same consultant will do both, in fact. New developments in computer systems will make computer methods cost–effective even in smaller organizations. Information processing hardware will be an integral part of every office, a byproduct of the telephone on the desk, the appointment book, the dictating machine, and the typewriter. Statistical and cost information will be solicited and checked as a continuous byproduct of the ongoing flow of activities. Special attention will be required only when routinely expected information is inconsistent or missing. Computerized editing routines will call for clarification at the time the data are being gathered from the client or other source, so that omissions and errors can be corrected efficiently, and staff will be continuously trained to execute these routine tasks accurately.

The highly integrated nature of future management information systems will also enable the evaluator to modify the way information is organized and reported without affecting the activities of the staff who initially record the data. When statistical and cost data are gathered interactively by information hardware, fewer paper forms will be used, so that the addition or deletion of a specific data item will involve reprogramming the system rather than reprinting the form. Reprogramming may not be a simple task, but it will be a task that many future evaluators will be trained to carry out. Simplified management information system programming languages will require a relatively unsophisticated level of programming skill that will be attainable by most evaluators. The same complex negotiation will be needed in order to determine the need for new data collection, and to orient staff to the change, but the interactive system will simplify the task of training the staff for reliable performance. Flexible data retrieval and analysis for unanticipated needs will be at the evaluator's fingertips. This increased flexibility of the information system will enable the evaluator to respond almost as quickly and economically as decision makers will have come to expect

More difficult professional judgments will still be no easier, of course, but quality assurance procedures will provide valuable inservice training. When service activities take advantage of improved information technology for routine record keeping, it will be easier to help professional staff avoid careless oversights and inadvertent misjudgments. As service decisions enter the information system (or fail to enter when expected) they will be compared with well developed utilization review standards. This will allow the professional staff of the organization to monitor service decisions, and to ask for explanations of unusual actions by their colleagues and trainees. Statistical summaries of service practices will be readily available from the automated portion of the client's clinical record, so that a utilization review committee, through its clinical care evaluation studies, can provide vigorous leadership in shaping the system of services delivered by the organization.

A highly developed "language of accountability" will change the relationship of future community programs to funding and regulatory agencies. Organizations will define the services they offer not primarily by their service process, as at present, but by reference to a standard lexicon of problem definitions and service objectives. Even very unusual programs will be defined by the degree to which these standard terms fit the program, and where they differ. Since entire regional human service systems of the future will be planned as an integrated mosaic of problem definitions and service objectives, this language will describe how each organization's services contribute to attaining the overall objectives of the system. These objectives will focus not just on the outcome, productivity, and cost of individual services—they will also include impact objectives that are defined in relation to overall estimated community needs.

This regional "language of accountability" will be possible because evaluators already will have developed and tested its components within many community-based human service organizations. Since evaluators typically work in conjunction with managers of multicomponent organizations, rather than single-purpose service providers, they already face a small scale version of the regional planning task. Every human service organization will have become accustomed to defining itself in terms of target problems, outcome objectives, and productivity objectives. Each organizational component will be evaluated against its expected contribution to these organizational service objectives. Managers and professionals at every level will support this accountability structure because they will have experienced the way in which it protects them from the external imposition of inappropriately rigid structure and process constraints. The structure will facilitate planned change because it will provide a common language for the proponents of new approaches, the defenders of established services, and those who must allocate program resources. This language will allow more open and informed discussion of the promise and the performance of both innovative and traditional service components.

The evaluator will have a wealth of technical assistance available as choices are made about the methods to be used in measuring the attainment of program objectives. Vigorous psychometric research will have been attracted by the established lexicon of standard objectives, and will shape its continuing revision. We speculate that the Human Services Division of the National Bureau of Standards (formally the National PSRO Network), the Joint Commission on the Accreditation of Human Services (formerly JCAH), and several university-based research groups will have accumulated massive data banks of program and community characteristics in relation to attainment of various subsets of the standard objectives. By following a standard measurement protocol, an evaluator will be able to generate a data set that provides a comparison with hundreds of similar programs in similar communities, and allows an assessment of the areas of comparative strength and weakness in his or her own program. We can also imagine the Evaluation Research Society (ERS) periodically voting to reaffirm its stand against the use of these comparisons in decisions about program funding, pointing out the importance of community need and equity of care issues in allocating service funds.

[*News Item:* "In a press conference ERS President Dr. Eve Alooator warned that the proliferation of so-called 'evaluation planning' firms was symptomatic of the possible decay of the whole standards comparison system that has fostered so many improvements in the human services in the last decade. These firms offer, for a tidy sum, to select the standards comparison strategy that will make your program look best. Dr. Alooator's assertions prompted a vigorous rejoiner from the chief of one of the university-based systems. He pointed out that the method used by these new firms was published by their research group more than five years ago, and is incorporated in their standard analysis and report system to identify submitted data sets that probably show the source organization in an unusually good or poor light. This reporter suspects that the controversy will continue, however, since . . ."].

["In that same press conference, President Alooator expressed concern about the weakened professionalism of working evaluators. She cited as evidence for this trend the fact that only 27,000 ERS members dialed in to any of the closed-circuit sessions of the continuous ERS national convention during November, down from a 43,000 monthly peak in that same month four years ago. While acknowledging that more innovative symposia and more intimate conversation hours with nationally known figures might bring up the ratings, Alooator cited a number of other surveys to support her concern about decreased professionalism. It seems that many program directors no longer feel that the six-year DPE degree preparation is really essential. She cited one program chief, Dr. Adam Inistrator, as asserting that any capable program staff member can pick up the necessary skills from the programmed instruction that comes with a good management information package, and use the consulting network as a backup. To use the consulting network an authorized staff member can dial 800-PEV-*xxxx* (where *xxxx* is a problem code) and talk to a relevant consultant. Even with one or two calls each week the consulting fees only come to a fraction of the cost of hiring a doctoral level evaluator. President Alooator predicted dourly that the recent antitrust decision in favor of the consulting network will spell the end of professional program evaluation as we know it today."]

Actually, the future will probably be sufficiently troublesome without additional help from us. For the present, program evaluation remains a challenging task that cannot be learned from a recipe book or a computer terminal. There is yet to emerge a pattern of program evaluation that one can say with confidence will return its investment in improved program performance. Evaluators have a few years to demonstrate their value. Some of the tools and concepts now being developed show promise when they are used by unusually creative program evaluators and managers. The challenge is to develop routine competence in program management, rather than occasional bursts of light (or heat).

CONCLUSION

This overview of the present and the possible future of the art of program evaluation suggests six goals to be addressed in the current decade.

- Employ competent program evaluators routinely at all major federal, state, and community levels of management in the human services
- Coordinate needs assessment regionally and clarify system objectives for human services as a whole in each geographic region
- Clarify the outcome and process objectives of every component of a regional human service system, including the relation of these objectives to overall system objectives
- Maintain vigorous ongoing monitoring, within each major system component, of that component's attainment of outcome and process objectives, and carry out this monitoring in ways that contribute directly to the internal management capability of that component of the human service system
- Develop better methods for informative comparisons of program goal attainment across relevant reference groups of similar programs
- Develop methods to monitor regional human services integration, as well as other system process and impact objectives, and methods for making relevant comparisons among sets of regions

The first goal is being approached as every component of the human services system develops requirements for evaluation tasks and personnel, and as colleges and universities begin to train individuals to fill these new positions. Our final chapter examines several issues faced by these educational programs. The next three goals must continue to be pursued by evaluators working in each community-based program, although technical support provided by state and federal evaluators and their grantees and contractors can be helpful. In contrast, the primary responsibility for developing inter-program and interregional comparison methods may fall to state, federal, and quasi-private regulatory, accreditation, and quality assurance agencies, with the collaboration of independent research groups. While evaluators in community-based programs are in a poor position to develop inter-program comparison methods, they must contribute to the planning of beginning comparison attempts, if such methods are to be broadly useful.

REFERENCE NOTE

1. Lund, D. A. *Mental health program evaluation: Where you start?* Unpublished manuscript, 1976. Paper presented to the Florida Mental Health Program Evaluation Training Workshop, Tampa, Florida, July 1976. (Available from the Bureau of Program Evaluation, New York State Department of Mental Hygiene, 44 Holland Avenue, Albany, New York 12229.)

17

THE EDUCATION OF EVALUATORS

William A. Hargreaves, C. Clifford Attkisson, Mardi J. Horowitz,
and James E. Sorensen

The demand for skilled program evaluators in health and human services
has stimulated an increasing need for relevant educational opportunities. In
addition to teaching the core program evaluation concepts and skills, training
programs must also help students with the many practical problems that are
encountered by evaluators in the field. Several universities now offer educational opportunities designed to meet these needs. In this chapter, our purpose
is neither to survey the many types of educational programs that have developed, nor to design a general purpose educational program that will suit
everyone. Our aim is simply to call attention to the specific areas of knowledge
and skill that, we feel, will result in productive evaluative activities.

Only part of the necessary preparation can be provided in a formal
educational program. A further step that is essential to the education of an
evaluator is a year or more of closely supervised practical experience. A
specialized masters degree in program evaluation might therefore be structured as a year of course work followed by a year of field placement. In
doctoral programs a more extensively supervised practicum experience would
be desirable.

AN ILLUSTRATIVE EDUCATIONAL PROGRAM

While we do not wish to present a curriculum plan, it seems convenient
to discuss desirable areas of knowledge and skill using course titles and descriptions. Table 17.1 shows 16 course titles divided into a set of seven core courses

TABLE 17.1
Suggested Course Titles in a Program Evaluation
Curriculum

Core courses
  1. Principles of program evaluation
  2. Program planning and need assessment
  3. Process and outcome monitoring
  4. Information system design
  5. Information system implementation
  6. Organizational behavior
  7. Practicum I, II, III
Elective and Advanced Courses
  8. Program administration
  9. Community psychology
  10. Human service systems
  11. Group dynamics
  12. Basic computer methods
  13. Basic statistics
  14. Measurement
  15. Advanced study design
  16. Systems programming

and another nine elective and advanced courses. These courses could become the basis of a specialized masters program, or a specialization track within a doctoral program.

In a specialized masters degree program, the first year could include the six *core* courses shown in Table 17.1, and the practicum sequence, leaving room for three *electives.* The suggested electives and advanced courses would allow one of three areas of secondary emphasis for a masters student: (*a*) the courses "program administration," "community psychology," and "group dynamics" would emphasize development of psychological and organizational knowledge and skills; (*b*) "basic statistics," "measurement," and "advanced study design" would emphasize research skills; and (*c*) "basic computer methods," "basic statistics," and "systems programming" would provide further preparation for developing and maintaining computer-based management information systems. The second year of a specialized masters degree program would ordinarily be a full time field placement year.

Doctoral programs in the social sciences and human service fields increasingly provide opportunities for training in program evaluation. The courses described here could provide a flexible framework for accomplishing this task. The first course in Table 17.1 could be used as a survey of the field by students who wish no further preparation in program evaluation. The remaining six core courses and the practicum could be taught as a "program evaluation track" for doctoral students in the human service professions who are considering program administration as a possible career option. Finally, students who wish to prepare for specialized leadership roles in program evaluation would cover the entire curriculum. Social science doctoral programs usually include most of the material in the elective and advanced courses shown in

Table 17.1, so it should be possible to cover the material unique to a program evaluation track within one year of a doctoral program.

A description of the 16 course topics follows. As we discuss these course topics, we have in mind three hour, one quarter courses, so that a full time student would take twelve courses during a three quarter academic year.

CORE COURSES

1. *Principles of Program Evaluation*

This course provides an overview for specialty students and can also serve as a brief introduction for students in the service professions who will not go on to be program evaluators. The organization of the present textbook embodies our suggestions about the scope and organization of the course material. Topics would include the role of evaluation in human services, management information systems, need assessment, and outcome evaluation. In addition to discussions of the text chapters, class time can include presentations by program managers about their expectations for and utilization of program evaluation. Students may also be assigned an exercise in which they interview a program evaluator and write a description of that evaluator's function in a specific organization, or write a "case history" of a specific evaluation project and its utilization in an organization.

2. *Need Assessment and Program Planning*

Regional need assessment and planning should be discussed, followed by instruction in specific need assessment techniques. Each major need assessment approach would be examined. An exercise might illustrate a social and health indicator analysis of the type often requested in program funding proposals. Program planning, and particularly the process of planned organizational change would be examined as the locus of the utilization of need assessment results. This could lead to instruction in the formulation of program goals and objectives. Actual need assessment and planning case studies may be examined to integrate the topics and to emphasize the political participation processes that are involved in need assessment and program planning.

3. *Process and Outcome Monitoring*

Topics here include service utilization, quality assurance, cost-finding, and outcome monitoring. Each can be organized around a prepared exercise in which the student is given a data set and a series of questions to explore. The unit on *service utilization* would teach the student to compare client characteristics with community characteristics that are documented by census and social indicator data, in order to discuss such issues as accessibility and equity of care. The *quality assurance* unit could examine a case example of the procedures of a utilization review committee and the practice standards used to screen cases for review. As an exercise the students may be asked to carry out a statistical analysis of data abstracted from case records, establish new review criteria on the basis of these data, and perform a retrospective service and care audit. Class discussion could focus on current PSRO or other regulatory and quality assurance requirements. The *cost-finding* topic should expose the student to the fundamentals of cost accounting in a human service setting. A specific exercise would include a step-down cost-allocation and a cost-finding procedure utilizing summary accounting data, staff time allocation data, and service productivity data. While emphasizing an understanding of the basic concepts of cost-finding, the exercise should also concentrate upon the application of the resulting unit costs to various management issues. A final unit on *outcome monitoring* can focus on the selection of monitoring indicators to assess a program's achievement of its objectives, and on cross sectional and time-series analysis techniques used in the interpretation of monitoring data.

4. *Information Systems Design*

Management information systems design includes the assessment of existing information systems, issues in organizational implementation and ongoing revision, preliminary documentation of report needs, design of each report's information content, design of input forms and report formats, estimation of system volume, choice of computerization procedures, design of error control procedures, and writing bid specifications for contracted programming.

5. *Information Systems Implementation*

While the preceding course will have provided an overview of the principles and major steps in the design of management information systems, the evaluator will need careful preparation for the organizational planning process necessary to install new information collection and processing methods. For many evaluators, this design and implementation process will be their first experience with the actual details of planned organizational change. This course will focus on case studies and simulation exercises in identifying system content requirements, designing and testing user acceptance of intake forms and report formats, orienting and training staff to new procedures, and dealing with error control and data reliability problems following installation.

6. *Organizational Behavior*

This course is designed as an integrative course to be taken as late in the curriculum as practical. Topics are selected from fields such as organizational behavior, organizational design, program administration, group dynamics, planned organizational change, and from previous courses in program evaluation. This material could then be integrated with a focus on maximizing the practical utility of evaluation activities in program management. Written management problems and simulation exercises in class can be used to give the student practice in thinking about program evaluation activities within specific organizational contexts, in assessing the priorities for various program evaluation activities, and in planning and maintaining the linkages necessary for maximum utilization of evaluation results.

7. *Practica I, II, III*

A practicum is less easily structured into topics since it requires the student to cope with tasks and situations that are close to actual field conditions. Suitable practica sites would be small service programs or program components where the student could be placed for an entire academic year. In each quarter of the practica we suggest that each student be assigned a single major task. Careful recruitment of practica sites and delineation of students' tasks by the faculty will be needed to limit the scope of work and allow students to integrate all phases of the task. A weekly practicum seminar at which students present their progress should help trainees to gain perspective on their work, but individual supervision and consultation will also be essential.

In the first quarter of the practica the student might assess the stage of development of program evaluation and information capability in an organization or organizational component. This assessment could include such tasks as a systematic inventory of management information and fiscal control procedures, the review and/or reformulation of program objectives, review of management issues of greatest concern to program staff, and formulation of a work plan for the following quarter.

The second quarter of the practica can focus on the execution of the work plan developed in the previous quarter. It is probably wise to have students plan data collection or other technical activities such that all data will have been gathered and analyzed by the end of this quarter. The availability of these results then allows work in the third quarter to focus on feedback and decision processes, and additional data analyses engendered by the feedback process.

The suggested lock-step timing of the practica work will keep it somewhat removed from the realities of program evaluation practice. In this and other respects a practicum is intermediate between contrived course exercises and program evaluation experience during a field placement or a predoctoral internship year. If, in addition, students can have a brief experience of responding rapidly to at least one emergent management issue during a practicum assignment, we believe that field placements will have an important educational impact.

ELECTIVE AND ADVANCED COURSES

8. *Program Administration*

Basic aspects of program administration would be surveyed in this course. Topics can include theories of organizational design and organizational behavior, and introduction to the basic procedures in policy formulation, budgeting, expenditure control, and personnel supervision.

9. *Community Psychology*

Selected topics from community psychology can include methods of community organization, citizen participation in the planning and the evaluation of human service programs, the consultation process, and primary prevention. It may also be appropriate here to focus on other aspects of the *environments* of human service programs, such as governmental structures, regulatory processes, human services legislation, and regional planning.

10. *Human Service Systems*

Evaluators need familiarity with the specific service systems in which they will be working. Doctoral students in the human service professions will have received this training elsewhere. Students in specialized masters programs may need an introduction to the tasks and methods of specific human services as part of their preparation for supervised evaluation field work experiences.

11. *Group Dynamics*

The basic interpersonal processes in groups will form much of the working environment of the program evaluator. This course would aim to sensitize the student to major group processes, and teach the student how to be more effective in task group settings. In addition, nominal group and Delphi techniques (cf. Chapter 9) can be presented, along with other structured group interaction processes useful for accomplishing specific types of tasks.

12. *Basic Computer Methods*

This course would begin by introducing students to batch processing and library programs with a cross-tabulation exercise. The remainder of the course would then be spent developing basic competence in one of the standard programming languages. The goal is not to create systems programmers, but to enable students to write simple programs, make simple modifications in existing programs, and to understand the programming tasks that they may later supervise.

13. *Basic Statistics*

This course assumes an undergraduate background in statistics and focuses on enhancing students' proficiency in the choice and execution of appropriate statistical analysis procedures. It also aims to develop skills in using standard library computer programs. About half of the course should be devoted to developing competence in efficient and error-free use of programs to obtain histograms, cross-tabulations, scatterplots, and simple descriptive statistics. The remainder of the course can briefly review the major classes of inferential statistics, with laboratory exercises in t-tests, simple analysis of variance, and multiple regression.

14. *Measurement*

Several aspects of the data gathering process are brought together in this course. These include advanced forms design, data coding, review of typical funder data reporting requirements, rating scale development, and measurement of the psychometric properties of scales. The course then can review the major established methods for measuring client social functioning or symptoms (as appropriate), client satisfaction, and individualized client target problems and response to services. Exercises can include practice in the interviewing skills needed in data collection, construction of a multiple-item rating scale, and the examination of the internal consistency, interrater reliability, factor structure, correlational validity, and discriminatory power of such a scale. These exercises could also be expanded to provide experience with the various procedures for preparation of data for computer processing, such as keypunch, optical scanner sheets, preperforated data processing cards, and interactive remote entry.

15. *Advanced Study Design*

The design of controlled outcome experiments and quasi-experiments, their implementation, statistical analysis, and the utilization of experimental data in decision processes would be the main topics of this course. Design exercises can pose problems to which the students respond with an experimental design. Data analysis exercises can utilize data and hypotheses that call for repeated measures analysis of variance, analysis of covariance, and covariate blocks analysis.

16. *Systems Programming*

This course builds on the basic computer methods course and provides additional supervised practice in formal programming techniques. Exercises would introduce the student to a user-oriented system for file creation, update, and retrieval, and to techniques for integrating various data sets and program modules into working systems.

DISCUSSION

As we said at the outset, this listing of course topics is intended to stimulate discussion, not to provide a blueprint for educational practice. We have taught a few of its component courses, but the entire curriculum has not been tested in practice. Many will disagree with the scope and emphasis of the curriculum. The authors invite comments and would appreciate receiving descriptions of other curriculum plans. In presenting our suggestions, we have outlined a curriculum that can be very full and demanding for both students and faculty. The emphasis on course exercises requires considerable faculty effort when each course is first offered, ongoing effort in providing adequate individual feedback on performance, and adequate budget for student and faculty computer use. The practica will be limited by the availability of suitable sites and of faculty time for individual supervision.

We do feel that several levels of preparation and education for program evaluation are necessary. The job classifications adopted by the State of New York Department of Mental Hygiene illustrate this need (*1*). This classification system recognizes a "Program Evaluation Trainee" category and four levels of "Program Evaluation Specialist." Entry to the higher levels can be direct or through prior experience at the next lower level. A trainee is required to possess a bachelors degree in a relevant field. Specialist I requires a year of postgraduate experience or a masters degree in a relevant field, while level II requires a second year of experience or a "specialized masters degree in program evaluation." Level III requires further experience or a doctorate. Specialist IV, typically the head of an evaluation unit with about ten staff in a large facility, must have some postdoctoral experience. These are all *minimum* qualifications to be considered for hiring. Consequently, the actual education and experience of personnel hired tend to be higher. Such a classification system seems to be a sensible approach to staffing program evaluation units in health organizations in which doctoral level training is typical for program leadership and for key service delivery personnel. Human service fields in which the masters degree is the usual terminal degree should probably also apply that standard to the staffing patterns for program evaluation units.

The field of human services program evaluation is developing rapidly. The education of evaluators must track this development if program evaluation is to fulfill its promise as a major tool for enhancing management and the quality of services. The authors hope that these suggestions, as well as this textbook as a whole, can contribute to the strengthening of educational programs for evaluators in human services.

REFERENCE NOTE

1. Lund, D. A. Personal communication, January 1977. (Bureau of Program Evaluation, New York Department of Mental Hygiene, 44 Holland Avenue, Albany, New York 12229.) The job descriptions are contained in Memorandum #76-28 from Charles J. Murphy, Director of Personnel, December 8, 1976, titled: *Approved staffing plan for program evaluation units.*

SUBJECT INDEX